Frommer's

Florence, Tuscany & Umbria

4th Edition

by Reid Bramblett

Here's what the critics say about Frommer's:

"Author Reid Bramblett really knows his subject. . . . He does an excellent job."
—*Times-Picayune*

"Amazingly easy to use. Very portable, very complete."
—*Booklist*

"Detailed, accurate, and easy-to-read information for all price ranges."
—*Glamour Magazine*

"Hotel information is close to encyclopedic."
—*Des Moines Sunday Register*

WILEY

Wiley Publishing, Inc.

9-FDI-865

Published by:

Wiley Publishing, Inc.

111 River St.
Hoboken, NJ 07030-5744

ISBN 0-7645-4219-2

Editor: Myka Carroll
Production Editor: Heather Wilcox
Cartographer: John Decamillis
Photo Editor: Richard Fox
Production by Wiley Indianapolis Composition Services

Front cover photo: San Miniato, Tuscany
Back cover photo: Florence's Ponte Vecchio at night

For information on our other products and services or to obtain technical support, please contact our Customer Care Department within the U.S. at 800/762-2974, outside the U.S. at 317/572-3993 or fax 317/572-4002.

Wiley also publishes its books in a variety of electronic formats. Some content that appears in print may not be available in electronic formats.

Manufactured in the United States of America

5   4   3   2   1

Contents

List of Maps

About the Author

Reid Bramblett learned Italian on the playground of a Roman parochial school when he was 12, explored Italy with his parents for 2 years in a hippie-orange VW camper, and spent a year studying there during a break from the anthropology department at Cornell. After a stint in Frommer's editorial offices, Reid vaulted over the desk to write Frommer's first guide to Tuscany and Umbria and hasn't stopped exploring, learning, interviewing, taking notes, and reporting it all in guidebooks since. He has also written *Frommer's Northern Italy, Frommer's Portable Florence, Frommer's Memorable Walks in New York*, is a coauthor of *Frommer's Italy from $70 a Day*, and contributes to *Frommer's Europe* and *Frommer's Europe from $70 a Day*. When not on the road, he lives in Maspeth, Queens, New York.

Acknowledgments

First and foremost, no thanks will ever be enough for **Frances C. Sayers,** without whose diligence, research skills, willingness to put up with my long hours and longer absences, sharp editorial eye, and, um, let's call it "constant gentle prodding," this book would never have gotten finished on time. I promise next time we visit the Chianti, it won't be during a blizzard.

Thanks are also in order for all the folks who have helped do some of the grunt work in researching this book over the past four editions, especially my ex-assistants extraordinaire (and good buds) **Jay Sayers** and **Matt Finley.** I also tip my hat to **Myka Carroll,** the able editor who turned this mess of a manuscript into a sleek, useable book.

And, of course, no amount of gratitude will ever be enough for my parents, **Frank and Karen Bramblett,** who in addition to the usual stuff (giving me life, bankrolling the first 20 or so years of my existence), instilled in me from an early age a deep love of the world and its cultures. They taught me to enjoy everything that travel has to offer, on all levels, from camping under the stars to sipping fine wines, admiring the esoterica of fine art and getting good and rowdy with the locals during a festival. They also dragged me off to live in Italy for 2 years when I was 11, which may have had some effect on my later career. Most importantly, they gave me a gift not all kids are lucky enough to receive: They traveled wide, traveled often, and always, but always, took me with them.

An Invitation to the Reader

In researching this book, we discovered many wonderful places—hotels, restaurants, shops, and more. We're sure you'll find others. Please tell us about them, so we can share the information with your fellow travelers in upcoming editions. If you were disappointed with a recommendation, we'd love to know that, too. Please write to:

Frommer's Florence, Tuscany & Umbria, 4th Edition
Wiley Publishing, Inc. • 111 River St. • Hoboken, NJ 07030-5744

An Additional Note

Please be advised that travel information is subject to change at any time—and this is especially true of prices. We therefore suggest that you write or call ahead for confirmation when making your travel plans. The authors, editors, and publisher cannot be held responsible for the experiences of readers while traveling. Your safety is important to us, however, so we encourage you to stay alert and be aware of your surroundings. Keep a close eye on cameras, purses, and wallets, all favorite targets of thieves and pickpockets.

Other Great Guides for Your Trip:

Frommer's Europe by Rail

Frommer's Irreverent Guide to Rome

Frommer's Italy from $70 a Day

Frommer's Northern Italy

Frommer's Tuscany & Umbria's Best-Loved Driving Tours

Hanging Out in Italy

Suzy Gershman's Born to Shop: Italy

Frommer's Star Ratings, Icons & Abbreviations

Every hotel, restaurant, and attraction listing in this guide has been ranked for quality, value, service, amenities, and special features using a **star-rating system.** In country, state, and regional guides, we also rate towns and regions to help you narrow down your choices and budget your time accordingly. Hotels and restaurants are rated on a scale of zero (recommended) to three stars (exceptional). Attractions, shopping, nightlife, towns, and regions are rated according to the following scale: zero stars (recommended), one star (highly recommended), two stars (very highly recommended), and three stars (must-see).

In addition to the star-rating system, we also use **seven feature icons** that point you to the great deals, in-the-know advice, and unique experiences that separate travelers from tourists. Throughout the book, look for:

Finds	Special finds—those places only insiders know about
Fun Fact	Fun facts—details that make travelers more informed and their trips more fun
Kids	Best bets for kids, and advice for the whole family
Moments	Special moments—those experiences that memories are made of
Overrated	Places or experiences not worth your time or money
Tips	Insider tips—great ways to save time and money
Value	Great values—where to get the best deals

The following **abbreviations** are used for credit cards:

AE	American Express	DISC	Discover	V	Visa
DC	Diners Club	MC	MasterCard		

Frommers.com

Now that you have the guidebook to a great trip, visit our website at **www.frommers.com** for travel information on more than 3,000 destinations. With features updated regularly, we give you instant access to the most current trip-planning information available. At Frommers.com, you'll also find the best prices on airfares, accommodations, and car rentals—and you can even book travel online through our travel booking partners. At Frommers.com, you'll also find the following:

- Online updates to our most popular guidebooks
- Vacation sweepstakes and contest giveaways
- Newsletter highlighting the hottest travel trends
- Online travel message boards with featured travel discussions

What's New in Florence, Tuscany & Umbria

The biggest news in Tuscany is that, finally, after more than a decade, the Leaning Tower of Pisa has reopened to visitors.

The only slightly smaller piece of news is not so good: When Italy replaced the lira with the euro, the currency changeover brought a staggering degree of instant inflation. Tuscany, never all that cheap to begin with, has, along with the rest of Italy, seen a dramatic rise in prices since the euro debuted on January 1, 2002—we're talking anywhere from 15% to 100% on everything from groceries and bus tickets to hotel rooms, restaurants, and museum tickets. When coupled with the price hikes that came with the Jubilee celebrations in 2000, prices across the board have largely doubled, and in some cases tripled, in just 3 years. I kid you not.

One other sad note: The *International Herald Tribune,* the single best source of English-language news for the traveler and expat, has gone from being a *New York Times* and *Washington Post* co-venture into just a mini-*Times,* and it has dropped the *Italy Weekly* insert (which had been failing for a while; it was *Italy Daily* until a year ago).

Remember, other changes will occur throughout Tuscany and Umbria during the lifetime of this edition, so if you're dead set on staying in a particular hotel, dining in a certain restaurant, or visiting a site, call ahead to be sure you can enjoy the experience. *Buon viaggio!*

FLORENCE They've finally finished rearranging all the rooms at the end of the **Uffizi Galleries,** Piazzale degli Uffizi 6 (② **055-294-883** or www.firenzemusei.it to reserve tickets), meaning that the 16th to 18th century collections are once again on permanent display, including works by Il Parmigianino, Tintoretto, Caravaggio, Artemisia Gentileschi, Tiepolo, Rubens, and Rembrandt.

For lack of staff, the **Orsanmichele,** Via Arte della Lana 1/Via de' Calzaiuoli (② **055-284-944**), no longer keeps regular hours—odd, since it sits smack dab on the main tourist thoroughfare of the city, halfway between the Duomo and the Uffizi, so you'd figure it would get tons and tons of visitors.

In an awful turn of events, two major churches—**Santa Croce** (② **055-244-619**) and **San Lorenzo** (② **055-216-634**)—have followed the lead of **Santa Maria Novella** (② **055-215-918**) and have begun charging an admission fee to visitors; San Lorenzo and Santa Maria Novella now cost about 2.60€ ($3) each, Santa Croce nearly 4.35€ ($5). While we're on the subject of admission charges, the **Casa di Dante** (② **055-219-416**) now seems to think someone would be willing to pay nearly 7€ ($8) to stare at three rooms filled with secondhand documents about the great medieval writer. (*Note:* Despite the name, this wasn't even Dante's actual house, just a home of the same era in the same neighborhood.) Also, the **tourist information office,** Via Cavour 1r (© **055-290-832**), has begun charging (0.50€/60¢) for most of its informational pamphlets. Shame on them.

In hotel news, the **Burchianti,** Via del Giglio 8 (© **055-212-796**), has moved up the block and gone from being a cheap *pensione* to a reasonably priced (and rather elegant) boutique hotel.

On the nightlife front, most of the major discos and clubs have either closed down or changed style, but a new one called **Universale,** Via Pisana 77r (© **055-221-122**), has opened in the Oltrarno and become vastly popular.

This has nothing to do with changes in Florence per se, but since the last edition of this guide several **bestselling books** have made their way onto just about every American book club's reading list—*Brunelleschi's Dome, Galileo's Daughter,* and *Artemesia*—piquing the interest of thousands more Americans in Florence's Renaissance period. See chapters 3 and 4 for complete information on Florence.

THE CHIANTI Just about every castle and vineyard and most country homes seem to have jumped on the *agriturismo* wagon, offering tours and tastings and renting out a handful of rooms to folks eager to spend a few days in the fabled heart of Italy's wine country. Oddly enough, one of the early properties to adopt an agriturismo venture, **Castello da Uzzano,** has now opted out, shuttering its rental apartments and refusing to let people tour its cellar and gardens. See chapter 2 for more information about agriturismo and chapter 5 for details about the Chianti region.

SIENA The **Santa Maria della Scala** complex, Piazza del Duomo 2 (© **0577-49-153**), has continued to increase its presence on the tourism scene, sponsoring ever more intriguing temporary exhibitions and incorporating into its structure the modest **Museo Archeologico** (which was already next door; they just opened up a doorway to add its rooms on to the rambling ones of the main museum). See "Siena: A Taste of the Tuscan Middle Ages" in chapter 5.

SAN GIMIGNANO The cumulative ticket to most of the town's sights no longer includes admission to the **Collegiata** (main church), which itself only started charging for entry 2 years ago. *(Sigh!)* The old Museo Etrusco has become a **Museo Archeologico,** Via Folgore 11 (© **0577-940-384**), by expanding and moving across town into an historic medieval/Renaissance pharmacy, also adding to its attractions a modern art gallery (okay, so that doesn't seem to fit thematically, but what the heck). See "San Gimignano: The Medieval Manhattan" in chapter 5.

PRATO They've closed off traffic to the busiest corner of Piazza del Duomo, making just that much more of the city blessedly **pedestrians only** (though local drivers are probably incensed). The great post-theater restaurant Osvaldo Baroncelli has new owners and a new name, **Il Borbottino,** Via Fra' Bartolomeo 13 (© **0574-23-810**), but the cuisine and decor have remained largely unchanged. See "Prato & the Virgin Mary's Girdle" in chapter 6.

LUCCA The old hostel Il Serchio has closed, but a new one has opened up: **Ostello S. Frediano,** Via della Cavallerizza (© **0583-469-957**). It's much closer to town, too—just outside the north walls. See "Lucca & Its Mighty Medieval Walls" in chapter 6.

PISA Yes folks, in December 2002, the **Leaning Tower of Pisa,** Piazza del Duomo (© **050-560-547**), reopened its door to the public after 11 years and .45 extremely expensive and laborious meters (1.5 ft.)—that's how much of the lean they finally managed to reign in using weights and cables and a new foundation, all to keep the tower from toppling over and to make it safe to climb again. Of course, you must reserve a visit weeks in advance, and pay a hefty 17€ ($20) or so for the privilege, but you know what? It's probably worth it.

The **Tenuta di San Rossore** coastal nature park and wildlife preserve (✆ **050-530-101**) just outside town has begun keeping regular weekend hours for public access. Also it and other **parks all down the Tuscan coast** (included in chapter 7) have become much more aware of the benefits of tourism and all have begun instituting regular guided tours by foot, horseback, bike, and sometimes even canoe. See "Pisa & Its Tipsy Tower" in chapter 7.

ASCIANO   The town has combined all its best collections, of art and archaeology, into a single new museum inside the 14th-century **Palazzo Corboli,** Corso Matteotti 122. See "En Route to Montalcino" in chapter 8.

MONTALCINO   The **Enoteca La Fortezza** (✆ **0577-849-211**), a fantastic wine shop installed inside the tall stone chambers of the town's glowering fortress, has new owners and management. They have wisely decided not to change a thing about running the place, which remains one of the best, and most atmospheric, spots to get familiar with Tuscany's mightiest red wine. See "Montalcino: Home of the Mighty Brunello" in chapter 8.

MONTEPULCIANO   The Consorzio del Vino Nobile di Montepulciano wine consortium (www.vinonobiledi montepulciano.it) has installed a **showroom and tasting center** in the Palazzo del Capitano on Piazza Grande where you can sample the wares of every single member—which means most Vino

Nobile vineyards. I'll toast that! See "Montepulciano & Its Noble Wine" in chapter 8.

AREZZO   The famous *Crucifix* by Giotto's teacher Cimabue has been fully restored and returned to its rightful place above the High Altar of **San Domenico** (✆ **0575-22-906**). What's shocking, given the trends elsewhere in Tuscany, is that they have since dropped the admission fee that had been charged to peek at the work during the restoration process (it was to help fund that restoration). Kudos, Arezzo. See "Arezzo: Where Life Is Beautiful" in chapter 9.

PERUGIA   The **Osteria del Gambero,** Via Baldeschi 8/a (✆ **075-573-5461**), my favorite fine dining experience for moderate prices in town, has moved up the block to a more prominent location on the ground floor. They've kept the cuisine and surprisingly low prices, though, which is nice. See "Perugia: Capital of Umbria & Quaint Hill Town" in chapter 10.

ASSISI   I'm happy to report that, at least so far as tourist sights are concerned, Assisi has recovered enough from the 1997 earthquakes to throw open the doors once again to all its churches, museums, and monuments (albeit a few museums have had to relocate).

The only real change is that the museum attached to the Duomo has changed its name to the **Museo della Cattedrale** (✆ **075-812-712** or 347-874-0224) and will, during the lifetime of this edition, expand to display even more liturgical, artistic, and archaeological artifacts. Also, half of the **Rocca Maggiore** fortress above town remains closed while workers complete renovations. See "Assisi: An Artistic Pilgrimage" in chapter 10.

GUBBIO   The restored Palazzo dei Canonici next door to the Duomo now contains a small **Museo Diocesano** (www.museogubbio.it), with paintings by Sassoferrato and Il Pomarancio—and an inflated admission price. See "Gubbio: Town of Festivals" in chapter 10.

SPOLETO The town's cumulative admission ticket has been done away with, which also means that the pretty little church of **SS. Giovanni e Paolo,** which was part of it, no longer keeps set hours (you can call ℂ **0743-232-511** to have someone unlock it for you, though). See "Spoleto & the Spoleto Festival" in chapter 11.

ORVIETO There's a new ticket in town, called the *Carta Unica,* a cumulative ticket that gets you into the most popular sights: Duomo's Cappella San Brizio, the Musei Archeologici Faina e Civico, the Torre del Moro, and onto the Orvieto Underground tour—plus either one funicular plus one bus ride *or* five hours in the ex-Campo della Fiera parking lot. Sweet deal. See "Orvieto: Etruscan Ruins & Fine White Wine" in chapter 11.

The Best of Florence, Tuscany & Umbria

This book will provide you with countless insider tips, show you places as yet undiscovered by most tourists, and tell you where to find a comfortable room and a great meal in an out-of-the-way town. Get ready to discover some of the best of both known and hidden Tuscany and Umbria.

1 The Best Tuscan & Umbrian Experiences

- **Exploring the Back Roads:** Rural Tuscany and Umbria just beg to be explored by car, and your own set of wheels really is the only way to discover the hidden side of these often overtourited regions. Just picture yourself winding your way among olive groves and forests on back roads, cruising past vineyards and waving fields of emerald grass dotted with sheep. You'll find tiny medieval villages that don't appear in any guidebook, and you'll turn off at every VENDITA DIRETTA (direct sales) sign to meet the vintner or farmer and sample his wine, herb-scented honey, or home-pressed olive oil. Buy the best regional map you can find, fill the tank, and get ready to put your rental car to the test on dirt roads, steep mountain switchbacks, and the occasional manic Italian highway.

- **Enjoying a 3-Hour Dinner:** A simple pleasure, but one that can make for a most memorable evening. Good friends, good conversation, and good wine can easily extend a meal for hours, and the Italian dinner is a perfect excuse and vehicle, what with four or five major courses, big pauses in between, and cheese, dessert, coffee, and *digestivo* liqueur all lined up at the end.

- **Catching Festival Fever:** Italians will throw a *festa* at any excuse—the local saint's day, the harvest, boar-hunting season, or sometimes just because it's the second Tuesday in May. Flower-strewn streets, fountains spewing wine, solemn religious processions, people in Renaissance garb shooting crossbows, horse and footraces through medieval streets, big roasting spits of wild birds, mass blessings of sheep and Fiats, violent Renaissance soccer, jousting matches, High Masses, and vats bubbling with polenta—you never know what you'll be in for, but it's bound to be memorable. See "Tuscany & Umbria Calendar of Events" in chapter 2 and each town's "Essentials" section.

- **Haggling in Florence's Leather Market:** Every day, the streets around the Mercato Centrale and San Lorenzo are filled with proprietors hawking marbleized paper, knockoff Gucci silk scarves, T-shirts emblazoned with Michelangelo's *David,* and wallets, purses, jackets, and other leather products galore. All the stall keepers promise "the lowest prices in Florence." That so-called lowest price is usually far from it, and the best part of shopping here is using every bargaining trick in the book to drive the "lowest price" even lower. See "Shopping" in chapter 4.

- **Hiking the Hills of Florence:** The walk from Florence up to Fiesole is famous enough to earn a scene in the movie adaptation of E. M. Forster's *A Room with a View* (even if they cheated and took carriages). But don't neglect the hills of San Miniato and Bellosguardo that rise south of the Arno; the views over the city here are closer at hand, and the land is less developed. See chapter 4.

- **Biking Lucca's City Walls:** The elegant republic of Lucca is still snuggled comfortably behind its 16th-century walls, ramparts so thick they were able to be converted into a narrow city park—a tree-lined promenade running a 4.9km (2⅔-mile) loop around the city rooftops. The bicycle is the preferred mode of transportation in Lucca, and you'll be in good company as you tool under the shade past parents pushing strollers, businessmen walking their dogs, and old men at picnic tables in their 40th year of a never-ending card game. See "Walking the Walls" on p. 276.

- **Picnicking Under the Leaning Tower:** Pisa is home to the most felicitously gorgeous piazza in all Italy, the Campo dei Miracoli. Even if you're in town for just half a day, grab a sandwich or a slice of pizza and picnic on the small triangle of grass in front of the famous leaning tower—the campanile with the world's worst posture. Afterward, saunter down to the patch of green surrounding the baptistery and take a nap on the grass with the sun warming your face. And, oh yeah: You can climb the tower, too. See "Pisa & Its Tipsy Tower" in chapter 7.

- **Taking an Evening Stroll in Perugia:** Perugia's wide Corso Vannucci is perfect for the early-evening stroll Italians everywhere turn out for—the *passeggiata*. It's the time to see and be seen, to promenade arm in arm with your best friend dressed in your best duds. The crowd flows up the street to one piazza, and then turns around and saunters back down to the other end. When you tire of meandering, take a break to sip cappuccino and nibble Perugia's fine chocolates in one of the classy cafes lining the street. See "Perugia: Capital of Umbria & Quaint Hill Town" in chapter 10.

- **Going Off the Beaten Path in Assisi:** Who would've thought you could find a primal Tuscan country experience in over-touristed Assisi? Save the basilica's frescoes for the afternoon and get up early to hike into the wooded mountains of Monte Subasio to St. Francis's old hermitage. After a morning spent in contemplation with the monks and wandering the state parkland, head back to Assisi, but be sure to stop a mile outside town for a big lunch at **La Stalla,** one of the last die-hard countryside trattorie in central Italy (see "The Best Countryside Trattorie," later in this chapter). See "Assisi: An Artistic Pilgrimage" in chapter 10.

2 The Best Hill Towns

- **San Gimignano:** The "Medieval Manhattan" bristles with more than a dozen tall stone towers, all slightly askew. It wins the Most

Densely Decorated Church award for its old Duomo, whose interior walls are slathered with 15th-century frescoes. San Gimignano's skyline and back alleys, especially when moonlit, make it one of Italy's most romantic hill towns. Stay until all the tour buses have left, when you'll have the gardens and small piazze all to yourself. See "San Gimignano: The Medieval Manhattan" in chapter 5.

- **Volterra:** Proud Volterra has been important in western Tuscany since the Etruscan Age. From its magnificent rocky promontory, the city surveys the sometimes wild, vast countryside surrounding it. Volterra is full of workshops where artisans craft the native alabaster into translucent souvenirs. And from a windswept terrace road you can look over some of Tuscany's best-preserved Roman ruins. See "Volterra: City of Alabaster" in chapter 5.

- **Montalcino:** Impressive from a distance with its broken-toothed fortress on a high hill, Montalcino turns out to be surprisingly tiny when you get close. It has a few sights and churches and a good small museum, but what you really come for is to sip the town's beefy Brunello wine, take a *passeggiata* with the locals in the evening, and watch the shadows fill the valley far below your hotel window as the sun goes down. See "Montalcino: Home of the Mighty Brunello" in chapter 8.

- **Montepulciano:** Although Montepulciano has medieval side streets galore, its main attractions are the deep red Vino Nobile wine and one of Italy's finest centrally planned Renaissance temples, a church set in its own little green park below the ancient walls of the town. See "Montepulciano & Its Noble Wine" in chapter 8.

- **Cortona:** This stony hill town is no longer big enough to fill its medieval walls, but it still has its museums of paintings by Fra' Angelico and local boys Luca Signorelli and Pietro da Cortona. The restaurants serve steak from the famed Chiana cattle, raised in the valley below, where Etruscan tombs hint at the city's importance in a pre-Caesar Tuscany. See "Cortona: 'City of Art'" in chapter 9.

- **Gubbio:** This ancient Umbrian stronghold and renowned ceramics center is like the last outpost of civilization before the wilderness of the high Apennines. The central piazza cantilevers over the lower town like a huge terrace. The square is bounded on one end by a mighty palace, all sharp stone lines and squared-off battlements. Inside is a cluttered archaeological museum and the same echoey medieval atmosphere that pervades the whole town. Gubbio is unique among hill towns—an antique center unto itself, to which surprisingly few visitors venture. See "Gubbio: Town of Festivals" in chapter 10.

- **Todi:** When they were handing out quaintness to Italian hill towns, Todi took far more than its share. Many of its streets are so steep they've been chipped with shallow staircases down the middle. Vistas across the valley open up unexpectedly, and on the perfectly medieval main piazza is a town hall sprouting a staircase perfect for an Errol Flynn swordfight scene. The church on the outskirts of town is perhaps Italy's most beautiful High Renaissance construction. See "Todi: A Taste of the Middle Ages" in chapter 11.

3 The Best Festivals

- **Florence's Gioco di Calcio:** First, divide the city into its traditional neighborhoods, cover Piazza Santa Croce with dirt, and don Renaissance costumes. Next, combine two parts soccer, one part rugby, one part football, and a heaping helping of ice-hockey attitude. This game, in which a few dozen men forget all the rules as they do anything they can to score goals, makes regular soccer look like croquet on Quaaludes. Give the winners a whole calf to roast in the streets and write it all off in honor of St. John the Baptist. See "Tuscany & Umbria Calendar of Events" in chapter 2.

- **Siena's Palio:** Anything goes at this bareback, breakneck horse race around the dirt-packed Il Campo, and the competitive *contrade* (traditional neighborhood wards) usually make sure everything does. The square is filled with costumed pageantry before the race, and massive feasts are set up on long outdoor tables that can stretch for blocks on the medieval side streets. See "Siena: A Taste of the Tuscan Middle Ages" in chapter 5.

- **Prato's Display of the Virgin's Girdle:** Prato keeps the Madonna's girdle under heavy lock and key year-round, but takes it out occasionally, amid much religious pomp and some medieval drum rolling, to show it to the crowds massed on the piazza. See "Prato & the Virgin Mary's Girdle" in chapter 6.

- **Arezzo's Giostra del Saracino:** Arezzo really comes alive for this Renaissance titling tournament where the target at which the mounted jousters aim their lances swivels around and can actually hit back. See "Arezzo: Where Life Is Beautiful" in chapter 9.

- **Perugia's Umbria Jazz:** Umbria's capital gets mellow and funky every summer in one of Europe's biggest jazz fests. Headliner acts and little-known maestros fill the squares, streets, and bars with some of the smoothest music around. See "Perugia: Capital of Umbria & Quaint Hill Town" in chapter 10.

- **Assisi's Calendimaggio:** This pagan rite of spring fest is held in Italy's holiest hill town. The town's almost-forgotten factions revive to wage medieval competitions and display feats of strength, and the whole town spends the week in courtly Renaissance dress. After a singing competition on the main square, the winner gets to crown his own fair damsel Lady Spring. The town returns to Christianity the next day. See "Assisi: An Artistic Pilgrimage" in chapter 10.

- **Gubbio's Corso dei Ceri:** In one of Italy's most ancient festivals, teams of burly, costumed men trot about town all day carrying three huge towers topped with statues of saints. After a wild invocation ceremony in the piazza, they shoulder the towers and tear up the mountainside as fast as they can. The town's patron saint invariably wins. See "Gubbio: Town of Festivals" in chapter 10.

- **Spoleto & the Spoleto Festival:** Gian Carlo Menotti's annual bash brings some of the biggest names in orchestral music, dance, and theater to this ancient hill town. Many of the events are staged outside in the Piazza del Duomo or the remains of a Roman theater. See "Spoleto & the Spoleto Festival" in chapter 11.

4 The Greatest Artistic Masterpieces

- **Michelangelo's** *David* (Galleria dell'Accademia, Florence): The Big Guy himself, the perfect Renaissance nude, masterpiece of sculpture, icon of homosexual camp, and symbol of Italy itself. See p. 163.

- **Sandro Botticelli's** *Birth of Venus* (Gallerie degli Uffizi, Florence): Venus on the half shell. The goddess of love is born from the sea; a beauty drawn in the flowing lines and limpid grace of one of the most elegant masters of the early Renaissance. See p. 149.

- **Leonardo da Vinci's** *Annunciation* (Gallerie degli Uffizi, Florence): A young Leonardo had already figured it all out in this painting, with classical details, graceful figures, and his patented *sfumato* technique of blurring all edges and fuzzing the background to achieve a remarkably realistic illusion of depth and perspective. See p. 148.

- **Lorenzo Ghiberti's** *Gates of Paradise* (Battistero, Florence): In 1401, young Ghiberti won a sculpture competition to craft the doors of Florence's Baptistery. Fifty-one years later, he completed his second and final set, boosting the Gothic language of three dimensions into a Renaissance reality of invented space and narrative line. Art historians consider that 1401 competition to be the founding point of the Renaissance. Michelangelo looked at the doors and simply declared them "so beautiful they would grace the entrance to Paradise." See p. 139.

- **Filippo Brunelleschi's Dome** (Duomo, Florence): Florence's noble orangey-russet cupola reigns over the town in perfectly engineered immensity. When the cathedral was built, all the learned architects in town agreed the space was far too large to support a dome. Brunelleschi revived the secrets of Rome's ancient Pantheon to prove everyone wrong. See p. 138.

- **Masaccio's** *Trinità* **and the Cappella Brancacci** (Santa Maria Novella and Santa Maria della Carmine, Florence): The greatest thing since Giotto. Masaccio not only redefined figure painting with his strongly modeled characters of intense emotion and vital energy but also managed to be the first painter to pinpoint precise mathematical perspective and create the illusion of depth on a flat surface. The world's first perfecter of virtual reality. See p. 160 and p. 175.

- **Fra' Angelico's** *Annunciation* (San Marco, Florence): This is the summation of the devout friar's exacting early Renaissance style—a graceful Mary, a deep cloistered space, and a carpet of wildflowers behind the rainbow wings of the angel Gabriel, communing intensely with the Madonna. See p. 164.

- **Pisano Pulpits** (Duomo, Siena; Sant'Andrea, Pistoia; Baptistery and Duomo, Pisa): Between father Nicola and son Giovanni, Gothic sculpture was first invented and then refined, bringing a new emotional language and volume to sculpture and turning hard stone into fluid grace. See p. 214 in chapter 5, p. 265 in chapter 6, and p. 293 and p. 295 in chapter 7.

- **Ambrogio Lorenzetti's** *Allegory of Good and Bad Government* (Museo Civico, Siena): This is the single greatest piece of secular art to survive from the Middle Ages. Ambrogio's depiction of the effects of good government on the town is a detailed encyclopedia of a medieval urban utopia. See p. 235.

- **Duccio's *Maestà*** (Museo dell'-Opera Metropolitana, Siena): This is the painting on which the Sienese school was founded—ranks of angels on glittering gold and a masterful Gothic comic book on the life of Christ in square-foot panels. See p. 216.

- **Rossellino's Pienza:** Many Renaissance artists painted their idea of the perfect city; however, Rossellino was the only architect who actually got the funding to build one. Pope Pius II used his money and power to remake the central square of his home village in the image of Renaissance order, proportion, and grace. A papal bull has ensured that not a whit has changed over the centuries. See "Pienza: The Ideal Renaissance City" in chapter 8.

- **Piero della Francesca's *Resurrection of Christ*** (Museo Civico, Sansepolcro): Piero's dead-on geometric perspective and exquisitely modeled figures helped make this haunting work the model for all later depictions of the Risen Christ. This is quite possibly the only fresco whose reputation as the "best painting in the world"

actually saved it from Nazi bombs during World War II. See p. 357.

- **Giotto's *Life of St. Francis*** (Basilica di San Francesco, Assisi): This fresco cycle shocked the painting world out of its Byzantine stupor and thrust it full tilt on the road to the Renaissance. Giotto perhaps did more groundbreaking work in this one church than any other single painter in history, bringing a realism, classicism, concept of space and bulk, and pure human emotion that parlayed humanist philosophy into paint. These frescos were damaged in the 1997 earthquakes that destroyed other works in the church, but restoration was completed in November 1999. See p. 388.

- **Luca Signorelli's *Last Judgment*** (Duomo, Orvieto): Having recently emerged from years of restoration, Signorelli's signature piece uses the separation of the blessed from the damned as an excuse to display his mastery of the human nude. Michelangelo studied this seminal work before having his own go at the subject in the Sistine Chapel. See p. 432.

5 The Best Offbeat Sights & Experiences

- **Ballooning over Tuscany:** What better way to see Europe's most famous countryside than floating lazily over the olive- and vine-covered hillsides in a hot-air balloon with a champagne breakfast? Many outfits offer this indulgent pastime. Rates start around 200€ ($240) for a sunrise 1½-hour flight (champagne included). Contact **Ballooning in Tuscany** at © **0577-725-517** (fax 0577-725-519; www.ballooningintuscany.com).

- **Museo Zoologico la Specola** (Florence): As if a 19th-century natural history museum full of glass cases displaying stuffed specimens from

all species around the world weren't enough, you've also got room after room of well-crafted late-18th-century wax models of human beings in just about every stage of dissection imaginable. These models are medical study aids from the days before genuine corpses for gross anatomy were available in every med school. See p. 176.

- **Museo Stibbert** (Florence): This former private museum of an eccentric Scottish-Italian is made up of the general clutter of more than 50,000 random items and a huge collection of armor from all eras and world cultures, including an entire regiment of armored mannequins. See p. 177.

- **Prehistoric Lunigiana Statue-Stele** (Pontrémoli): These mysterious tombstone-shaped statues were carved over a 3,000-year period starting about 3000 B.C. by an extraordinarily long-lived cult isolated in the Lunigiana. Some of the abstracted figures bear a suggestive resemblance to how ancient Roman historians described Celtic warriors from Gaul. See "North of Lucca: The Garfagnana & the Lunigiana" in chapter 6.

- **Etruscan "Sunken Roads"** (Maremma): No one is quite sure why the Etruscans of the Maremma carved a network of passages, some more than 20m (65 ft.) deep, into the tufa surrounding Pitigliano, Sorano, and Sovana.

Many stretches of the Via Cave have survived the millennia, and you can follow them sometimes up to a kilometer (a half-mile) in what are kind of open-air cave tunnels. See "The Maremma: Tuscany's Deep South" in chapter 7.

- **Saturnia's Outdoor Sulfur Springs** (Maremma): Bright azure pools of steaming sulfur springs spill down the hillside like steppingstones. They're open-air Jacuzzis, with mineral mud on the bottom for free facials and general aqueous relaxation for everyone. The best part is that the springs are out in the countryside, with no spas built up around them and nothing but trees, birds, and a few cognoscenti here for a dip. See "The Maremma: Tuscany's Deep South" in chapter 7.

6 The Best Wines & Vineyards

See "A Taste of Tuscany & Umbria" in Appendix A for a primer on Italian wines.

- **Chianti Classico:** This is Italy's most famous product of Bacchus. Chianti is as variable as it is versatile, and while there's plenty of mass-produced cheap wine out there, the vintners of the Chianti Classico zone in the hills between Florence and Siena craft excellent wines of the highest quality. Premier estates abound, and the top, most accessible ones are highlighted in chapter 5.

- **Vernaccia di San Gimignano:** In his *Divine Comedy,* Dante wrote of this dry, peppery, straw-colored white that deepens to gold with age. Tuscany's best white is available all over the Town of Towers. It was the first DOC wine in Italy and is one of the few DOCG whites in Italy. The consortium of Vernaccia producers dates back at least to 1276; you can contact

them in town at the **Villa della Rocca** (🕾 **0577-940-108**). See "San Gimignano: The Medieval Manhattan" in chapter 5.

- **Morellino di Scansano:** This is a popular Maremman riff on the chianti formula smoothed out and juiced up with Spanish Alicante (Grenache). The top producers are **Le Pupille** (🕾 0564-505-129), **Mantellassi** (🕾 0564-592-037), and **Erik Banti** (🕾 0564-602-956).

- **Brunello di Montalcino:** Brunello is the smell of mossy, damp earth and musky berries. It tastes of dark, jamlike fruits and dry vanilla. This is Tuscany's most powerful red, perhaps the top wine in all Italy. Break out this complex elixir to accompany the mighty *bistecca alla fiorentina* (Florentine-style steak). Visit American-owned **Banfi** (🕾 **0577-840-111**) for the wine museum in its medieval castle or **Poggio Antico** (🕾 **0577-848-044**) for the direct sales of its award-winning Brunello. See "Sampling the Vino" on p. 320.

- **Vino Nobile di Montepulciano:** This purple-garnet wine smells of violets and tastes of juicy red berries, dark fruits, and a hint of musty, mossy earth. Of the traditional wines (no French grape intrusions), it plays second banana to Brunello, but many people find this Noble Wine a far more forgiving *vino,* and much more versatile. Although it's powerful and complex, you can drink it with just about anything but fish. The best producers are all represented by **Maddalena Mazzeschi** (𝄐 **0578-758-465**), and if you must choose just one bottle, make it an **Avignonesi** (𝄐 **0578-757-872**). See "Underground Tunnels & Noble Wine" on p. 334.

- **Rubesco Riserva:** This unique and elegant Umbrian wine made by a single estate was so deliciously demanding of attention the authorities had to create a tiny DOCG zone just to incorporate the vineyard. The vintner responsible was Giorgio Lungarotti, experimenting with his grapes in Torgiano south of Perugia. Although all the **Cantine Lungarotti** (𝄐 **075-988-0294**) wines are excellent, the best is the Rubesco Riserva label. The estate also runs a fascinating wine museum in Torgiano itself. See "Perugia: Capital of Umbria and Quaint Hill Town" in chapter 10.

- **Orvieto Classico:** Orvieto's white is an ancient wine, made at least since the days of the Etruscans. In Orvieto itself, you can get the traditional *abboccato* variety, a juicy, semisweet version hard to find elsewhere in this age that demands gallons of dry white table wines. Although Ruffino is a perfectly fine vineyard, you can usually pick up a bottle of its Orvieto Classico

secco at your local U.S. wine shop. As long as you're in the actual neighborhood, try smaller producers like **Decugnano dei Barbi** (𝄐 **0763-308-255**) and **Barberani** (𝄐 **0744-950-113**). See "Orvieto's Liquid Gold" on p. 433.

- **Sagrantino di Montefalco:** This dark wine with a rounded mouth feel and tannic bite—about the biggest and most complex wine you'll get in Umbria—has finally been recognized by the new DOCG classifications. You can get a taste at top producers **Antonelli** (𝄐 0742-791-5852) and **Cantina A. Fongoli** (𝄐 0742-350-359) in San Marco di Montefalco, **Il Girasole** in Montefalco (𝄐 0742-379-280), **Rocca di Fabbri** in Fraz, and **Fabbri** (𝄐 0742-399-379) and **Cantina Paolo Bea** (𝄐 0742-379-668) in Cerrete di Montefalco.

- **Tignanello:** One of the most successful blends of native Sangiovese and cabernet grapes, this complex "table wine" is made by the **Antinori** vineyards near San Casciano, just southwest of Florence (𝄐 **055-23-595**).

- **Sassicaia di Bolgheri:** This is a huge and complex cabernet sauvignon; the vines originally came from Château Lafite. The estates around Bolgheri on Livorno's coast all make wine from a mix of cabernet, merlot, and/or Cab Franc varietals—no Sangiovese in these parts. The actual Sassicaia wine with the DOCG label is astronomically priced, and the lone estate that produces it **(Tenuta San Guido)** is unapproachable, as is the neighboring and similar **Tenuta dell'Ornellaia.** But the nearby **Grattamacco** vineyards at Podere Santa Maria, near Castagneto Carducci (𝄐 **0565-763-933**), will welcome you, and their drinkable

Frenchified wines are much more affordable.

- **Vin Santo:** Grapes that have begun to turn to raisins on the vine and then been sun-dried are fermented in oak *barriques* to produce Tuscany's powerful sweet dessert "holy wine." The amber drink is fine on its own, but the real way to enjoy it is to use *cantucci* (twice-baked hard almond cookies) as sponges. Every winemaker sets aside a few barrels of vin santo, but some of the best is made by the chianti-inventing **Cantina di Brolio** (© **0577-73-01** or 0577-749-066). Umbria's resounding answer to Tuscany's vin santo is **Sagrantino Passito,** from the Montefalco region, a red dessert wine of high refinement. For more information on it, contact the **Centro Nazionale di Studi sui Vini Passiti** in Montefalco on weekday mornings (© **074-79-122**).

7 The Best Museums

- **Gallerie degli Uffizi** (Florence): One of the world's top museums, the Uffizi houses some of the seminal works of the Renaissance, including Giotto's *Maestà,* Botticelli's *Birth of Venus* and *Allegory of Spring,* Leonardo da Vinci's *Annunciation,* and Michelangelo's only panel painting, the *Holy Family.* Few rooms go by without three or four masterpieces. Thoroughly brain-draining . . . but worth it. See p. 145.

- **Museo Nazionale del Bargello** (Florence): Past early Michelangelo marbles and Giambologna bronzes, the main attraction at the primary sculpture museum of the Renaissance is a room full of famous works that survey the entire career of Donatello, the greatest sculptor since antiquity. See p. 155.

- **Palazzo Pitti** (Florence): The Pitti, with thousands of paintings hung thickly in the dozens of rooms of the Medici's old palace, all sumptuously frescoed and decorated, makes the Uffizi look like a preamble. Not only is room after room full of works by Raphael, Rubens, Titian, Caravaggio, Andrea del Sarto, and countless others, but once you get through the paintings, you've got the lavish Medici apartments, a costume gallery, a decorative arts collection, a modern art museum, and the baroque Boboli Gardens to see. You could spend a week here and still not be done. See p. 171.

- **Galleria dell'Accademia** (Florence): The line stretches for blocks from the door, everyone waiting to get in and see Michelangelo's *David,* easily the most famous sculpture in the world. Once inside, you're also treated to his unfinished and powerful *Slaves,* along with works by Perugino, Giambologna, and Botticelli. See p. 161.

- **Palazzo Pubblico** (Siena): The Museo Civico portion of Siena's medieval town hall preserves the masterpieces of the late Gothic Sienese school. See p. 212.

- **Museo Etrusco Guarnacci** (Volterra): A staggering 600 Etruscan cinerary urns—playing out in stony relief the Etruscans' views on death, art, and life—fill dozens of rooms here. The tiny sarcophagi are topped with the enduring image of the Etruscan: barechested and comfortably pot-bellied, half reclining at a feast laid out in his or her honor. See p. 246.

- **Museo Civico** (Sansepolcro): The hometown of Piero della Francesca, one of the geniuses of the early Renaissance, retains four of the master's works, including the *Madonna della Misericordia* and his masterpiece *Resurrection of Christ* (see earlier in this chapter). The rest of the collections are padded with works by his student Luca Signorelli, and mannerist and Baroque paintings by the likes of Il Passignano and Santi di Tito, the latter also a native of the city. See p. 356.

- **Galleria Nazionale** (Perugia): Umbria's National Gallery boasts more Peruginos than it knows what to do with. It also has one of the masterpieces of his teacher, Piero della Francesca, the *Polyptych of Sant'Antonio,* with its Annunciation scene of remarkable depth. Duccio, Arnolfo di Cambio, Fra' Angelico, and Gentile da Fabriano add to the collections. See p. 378.

8 The Best Etruscan Sights

- **Volterra:** One of Dodecapolis's ancient centers, Volterra has a medieval core still surrounded in places by the old Etruscan city walls. The best section encompasses the 4th-century B.C. Porta all'Arco gate, from which worn basalt gods' heads gaze mutely but protectively over the valley. The Museo Etrusco Guarnacci here houses hundreds of funerary caskets and the *Shade of the Evening,* a tiny bronze youth of elongated grace (also above under "The Best Museums"). See chapter 5.
- **Populónia** (Tuscany's Coast): Once an important Etruscan center, the seaside town of Populónia today retains little more than bits of its predecessor's walls. Outside the walls, however, are some excellent *tumuli* and other tombs in several necropoli dotting either side of the road leading to Populónia's promontory. Though most of the best portable pieces were carried off to Florence, the town was able to scrape together enough to fill a small museum. See "Livorno: A Busy Port City with Great Seafood" in chapter 7.
- **Grosseto:** The modern capital of the Maremma has the region's best museum of Etruscan artifacts, collected from many sites across Tuscany's deep south. See "The Maremma: Tuscany's Deep South" in chapter 7.

- **Chiusi:** The small but well-regarded archaeological museum here contains just some of the many finds from the dozens of tombs littering the valley floor between the town and small Lake Chiusi. Although the best tombs, including one with frescoes, have been indefinitely closed for restorations, you can arrange through the museum to visit a few, and there are others just lying open to you and your trusty flashlight. A few hundred yards of the old underground aqueduct systems carved into the rocky hillside by the Etruscans has recently been opened. Tours through it lead to a wide and deep cistern, atop which now sits the cathedral bell tower. See "Chiusi: In the Footsteps of the Etruscans" in chapter 8.
- **Arezzo:** Though little remains of the Etruscan city *Arretium*—the town's best artifact, the bronze chimera, got shipped to Florence long ago—some of the Roman city it became peeks out at its museum. The collection of Etruscan ceramics sets you up for the *corallino* pottery display, which showcases the vast Arretium industry that eventually opened branches and workshops all across Roman Italy and France to mass produce the famous waxy red earthenware. See "Arezzo: Where Life Is Beautiful" in chapter 9.

- **Cortona:** Three significant tombs lie along the slope and valley of Cortona's mount, including the one where the biggest find in Etruria of the past century was only recently discovered: a sophisticated altar with a sphinx-flaked stairway jutting out of the "Melone II" tumulus. Up in town, a museum houses a bronze Etruscan oil-lamp chandelier, as well as documented findings and displays about the ongoing excavations of "Melone II." See "Cortona: 'City of Art'" in chapter 9.
- **Perugia:** Umbria's capital still preserves its 3rd-century B.C. Porta Marzia (Mars Gate), the only structure that compares to Volterra's mighty city gate. An Etruscan well still supported by its massive travertine trusses was discovered in the heart of town, and just outside of town is a tomb where the funerary urns have been left in place just as they were discovered. See "Perugia: Capital of Umbria & Quaint Hill Town" in chapter 10.
- **Orvieto:** Orvieto, Etruria's ancient religious center, contains three archaeological museums that taken together make up one of the best collections of Etruscan artifacts outside Florence and include Umbria's only accessible tomb paintings, now detached, and works from the Etrusco-Roman period. The town has also started running tours of some of the tunnels and caverns under the city, parts of which, including wells and a possible temple, were carved by the Etruscans. On the edge of town are the grassy remains of an Etruscan temple, and around the edge of the city's walls is a tidy suburban-like necropolis of tombs, some still with inscriptions on the door lintels. See "Orvieto: Etruscan Ruins & Fine White Wine" in chapter 11.

9 The Best Luxury Hotels

Not all the hotels below are officially rated as luxury hotels, but all offer luxurious accommodations and amenities. See also **Il Falconiere,** the **Locanda dell'Amorosa,** and **La Badia** under "The Best Countryside Retreats," below.

- **Hotel Helvetia & Bristol** (Florence; ℂ **800/346-5358** in the U.S.): This most central of Florence's luxury addresses was the city's leading hotel in the 19th century, and an award-winning restoration a decade ago returned the guest rooms and lounges to their opulent turn-of-the-20th-century look. The bright and refreshing small Winter Garden bar, with trailing ivy and a splashing fountain, doubles as the breakfast room. See p. 106.
- **Hotel Regency** (Florence; ℂ **055-245-247**): The cozy wood reading rooms crowded with antique furnishings feel like a bit of old England. The service is some of the best and most discreet in the city, and the restaurant is the justifiably famous Relais le Jardin—Tuscan food from the kitchen of a master chef. Guest rooms are somewhat modernized, but marble-clad bathrooms and daily fresh fruit and newspapers in your room add to the prevailing quiet comfort. See p. 111.
- **Villa Vignamaggio** (Chianti; ℂ **055-854-661**): Leonardo da Vinci might have approved of the saturated color schemes in the minisuites of this *agriturismo* (working farm) high in the hills of the Chianti. In fact, the Mona Lisa who sat for his famous portrait grew up in the villa. Most suites are in the peasant stone outbuildings

scattered across the property and come outfitted with minibars, satellite TVs, and complimentary bottles of the estate's award-winning vintage. It's the best base for a wine-buying trip. See p. 198.

- **Grand Hotel & La Pace** (Montecatini Terme; © **0572-9241** or 0572-75-801): The most elegant old-world hotel in a town full of 19th-century bastions of grandeur, the Grand has coffee lounges as big as ballrooms and dripping with stuccoes and chandeliers. In the 2-hectare (5-acre) private park are clay tennis courts, several pools, and jogging paths. It offers the full array of services, amenities, and facilities you'd expect from the leading inn of a famed spa town. See p. 269.

- **Hotel Il Chiostro di Pienza** (Pienza; © **0577-748-400**): This former 15th-century Franciscan convent in the middle of tiny Pienza has been the best hotel in southern Tuscany since it opened in 1993. Some rooms have 19th-century frescoes; in another wing rooms feature exposed stonework and big ol' peasant wood

furnishings. The restaurant, which moved onto a panoramic gravel terrace in summer, is highly recommendable as well. See p. 330.

- **Hotel Gattapone** (Spoleto; © **0743-223-447**): This hotel is comprised of a cluster of tiny 17th-century buildings huddled on the brink of a sheer ilex-covered slope. The secluded Gattapone is just a short stroll from Spoleto's Duomo but is completely surrounded by nature. The stone-silled picture windows of the spacious guest rooms open onto the monumental green of a wooded mountain that's been sacred since Roman times. See p. 422.

- **Fonte Cesia** (Todi; © **075-894-3737**): This meld of 13th-century palazzo and modern lines opened in 1994 as the first hotel in Todi's historic center. The public rooms are filled with brick vaulting, and the huge terrace planted with palms is for taking breakfast. The suites are each themed and decorated with fine antique pieces or modern design, such as Empire-style desks and dressers or Wassily chairs. See p. 428.

10 The Best Moderately Priced Hotels

- **Pensione Maria Luisa de' Medici** (Florence; © **055-280-048**): This hotel's owner collects both baroque art and modern design, so the halls are hung with museum-quality Vignale and Van Dyck and the rooms are furnished with classics of 1950s design. You also get a full breakfast served in bed. Did I mention it's as central as you can get in Florence? See p. 103.

- **Hotel Torre Guelfa** (Florence; © **055-239-6338**): The name is very apt for a hotel that incorporates the tallest privately owned tower in the city and is set in the medieval streets near the Ponte Vecchio. When you tire of sipping

aperitivi on top of the 13th-century tower with its 360-degree panorama of the city, you can retire to your canopied bed or follow the wafting classical music to the long Renaissance-style lounge. See p. 107.

- **Morandi alla Crocetta** (Florence; © **055-234-4747**): One of the most genteel and hospitable of Florence's hotels, the Morandi is set in a 1511 convent. You feel as if you're guests in the palazzo of some absentee well-off Florentine family from the 1800s. Each room is decorated with a shrewd eye to keeping the late Renaissance alive, with exposed brickwork and the occasional 16th-century fresco. Most hotels like this charge up to three times as much. Book early. See p. 111.

- **Antica Torre** (Siena; ✆ **0577-222-255**): The rooms here are small but soothing, with light gray stone accents and hand-hewn wood ceilings that hearken back to the building's history as a towerhouse in the 1500s. The tiny brick breakfast room is actually a potter's workshop from the 14th century. The friendly family that runs the hotel only adds to the atmosphere. See p. 226.
- **L'Antico Pozzo** (San Gimignano; ✆ **0577-942-014**): The Medieval Manhattan's newest hotel is also its best, set in a restored 15th-century palace built into the palazzo where Dante stayed during his diplomatic visit to town. Inquisition trials are no longer held here, but you can get an enormous junior suite with a canopied bed or 17th-century-frescoed ceilings, or a top-floor double with views of the city's towers. See p. 238.
- **Hotel Royal Victoria** (Pisa; ✆ **050-940-111**): Pisa's first hotel is still run by the same family that founded it in 1839—now in its sixth generation. The rooms of this rambling palazzo are romantically worn, but many have 19th-century frescoes or look out over the Arno. See p. 300.

11 Florence's Best Rooms with a View

"Camera con vista, per piacere." That's what you need to ask to guarantee a vista out your window, whether it's a view of the Arno, the Duomo, or the hills you crave.

- **Hotel Chiari Bigallo** (✆ **055-216-086**): If you get a room along the front, you can practically lean out your window and poke Giotto's campanile with a stick. The view from these rooms is a living postcard—a foreshortened shot with the Duomo facade and campanile 50 feet away and Brunelleschi's dome rising above them. See p. 101.
- **Hotel Hermitage** (✆ **055-287-216**): Several good vistas await you at this old favorite. Room 602 has a balcony and view of the Palazzo Vecchio, while other rooms look down on the tiny Romanesque facade of Santo Stefano. Several overlook the Corridorio Vasariano to the Arno and the Ponte Vecchio. See p. 104.
- **Hotel Bellettini** (✆ **055-213-561**): Ask the friendliest sisters in Florence to give you either room 28, with its view of the Duomo, or room 45, featuring one of the most unique panoramas in Florence: a close-up sweep from the Medici Chapel dome of San Lorenzo over to a full view of the Duomo, facade and all. See p. 105.
- **Westin Excelsior** (formerly the Hotel Excelsior; ✆ **800/WESTIN-1** in the U.S., or 055-264-201): The penthouses, and especially the presidential suite, at Florence's premier luxury hotel have drop-dead panoramas from their terraces. You get everything: starting with the Arno at your feet and San Miniato's hill beyond it, panning past the Palazzo Vecchio, the Badia and Bargello Towers, the Duomo's cupola, and Fiesole. If you've got upward of $1,000 to drop on a room, check in here and spend your vacation on the balcony. See p. 108.
- **Hotel Loggiato dei Serviti** (✆ **055-289-592**): It isn't often you can wake up and throw open your shutters to a view of the most beautiful square in Florence and get an art-history lesson in the

bargain. Below your window in Piazza Santissima Annunziata are bronze statues by Giambologna and Pietro Tacca, and across the square is a Brunelleschi-designed loggia studded with Andrea della Robbia terra cottas. See p. 111.

- **Torre di Bellosguardo** (℃ 055-229-8145): Set on the hill where Hawthorne wrote *The Marble Faun*, the Bellosguardo's gardens and most of its guest rooms offer the closest-range vista of the Florentine skyline available. This 14th-century castle is the most Renaissance-feeling hotel in the city, with echoey vaulted chambers, beautiful antique beds, intricately carved and inlaid wood pieces, and ponderous stone staircases. The most spectacular view is from the tower suite. See p. 114.

- **Pensione Benescistà** (℃ 055-59-163): The small lounges and smoking rooms scattered throughout this early Renaissance mansion located halfway up the hill to Fiesole have picture windows opening onto Brunelleschi's dome and the whole of the Florentine skyline. Breakfast in summer is on a panoramic terrace. See p. 114.

12 The Best Countryside Retreats

Though there are plenty of regular hotels in the countryside, don't overlook *agriturismo* options (see "Tips on Accommodations, Villa Rentals & Farm Stays" in chapter 2), which offer travelers the opportunity to stay on a working farm. Besides the following best bets, a mix of both countryside hotels and *agriturismo* establishments, don't forget the **Torre del Bellosguardo** and **Pensione Benescistà,** both just outside Florence and listed above under "Florence's Best Rooms with a View."

- **Villa Vignamaggio** (near Greve in Chianti; ℃ 055-854-4840): Your home here is a luxurious suite in one of the peasant houses dotting the vine-covered property of a 15th-century villa. Take a dip in the pool or wander the manicured gardens. Kenneth Branagh's 1993 film adaptation of *Much Ado About Nothing* was filmed at the villa. (See also "The Best Luxury Hotels," above.) See p. 198.

- **Hotel Castagneto** (outside Siena; ℃ 0577-45-103): This simple brick farmhouse from the 1780s contentedly watches over its olive groves on a ridge outside Siena. The guest rooms are large and plain, filled with country air and Tuscan sun. Some have terraces and all enjoy views over farmland, even though just a few feet from the gate you can catch a city bus into Siena. See p. 226.

- **Fattoria Maionchi** (near Lucca; ℃ 0583-978-194): This *agriturismo* estate, lost in a tangle of olive-lined country roads in the foothills 13km (8 miles) east of Lucca, produces some of the province's finest red Colline Lucchese wine. The apartments are pretty standard but very large, and there's an outdoor pool where you can refresh yourself just yards from the vineyards. Signora Maionchi and her husband are two of the friendliest hosts around; they'll be glad to show you the gardens in back of their 17th-century villa. See p. 281.

- **Relais Il Falconiere** (near Cortona; ℃ 0575-612-679): At the end of a long winding dirt road in the foothills behind Cortona lies this early-17th-century farm, an oasis of fine dining and countryside quiet. The main villa has country-simple doubles, some with frescoes. But the best rooms are the suites flanking the tiny chapel, with big beds on ancient terra-cotta floors, wood-beam ceilings, and windows opening onto the olive trees and stone structures of the property. In the old building where lemon trees were once kept in winter is Cortona's best restaurant and some of the finest dining in Tuscany. See p. 366.

- **Castello di Gargonza** (Valdichiana; ℂ **0575-847-021**): The 13th-century walled village of Gargonza offers one of the most unique hotel experiences in Italy—the chance to live in a real medieval *borgo*. The ancient central piazza with its well is your open-air living room and an old olive press your den. Each of the stone peasant houses has been converted into an efficiency apartment, and the hamlet is isolated on all sides by wooded mountains. See p. 370.
- **Locanda dell'Amorosa** (Valdichiana; ℂ **0577-679-497**): The

central buildings of this 14th-century farming estate are situated around a triangular gravel courtyard like a Spanish hacienda. The guest rooms behind the second-story brick loggia either look onto this piazza or out over vineyards and fields. The spacious country-style loft accommodations have large beds and are very quiet. The restaurant, though mind-bogglingly expensive, is one of Tuscany's best. See p. 370.

- **Hotel La Badia** (outside Orvieto; ℂ **0763-301-959**): A disused abbey built between the 8th and 14th centuries, La Badia is just far enough away from it all to offer an oasis of peace and quiet. You can relax in the richly appointed and medievally atmospheric rooms or just wander around the property. The city glows across the valley, and in just minutes you can be in town enjoying frescoes, dinner, and Orvieto's perfect white wine. See p. 438.

13 The Best Restaurants in Town

- **Cibrèo** (Florence; ℂ **055-234-1100**): The amalgamated country-style decor of this restaurant belies its status as one of the city's finest kitchens. The dishes are Tuscan at heart—though they buck the standard by serving no pasta and little grilled meat—with innovative touches and plenty of peperoncino for spice. You may have to wait for an hour even with a reservation, but the wait is invariably worth it. See p. 128.
- **La Giostra** (Florence; ℂ **055-241-341**): A closet prince and double Ph.D. decided in retirement to indulge his love of cooking and open this little-known fine restaurant a few blocks east of the Duomo. He doesn't stick strictly to Tuscan dishes, but rather lets his

culinary imagination and half-Hapsburg heritage marry Italian and Austrian cooking, with occasionally spectacular results. He also makes the best *Sacher torte* this side of Vienna. See p. 129.

- **Osteria le Logge** (Siena; ℂ **0577-48-013**): In a room that looks a bit like an 18th-century apothecary shop, Siena's most accommodating staff serves some of the city's finest food. They take pride in their die-hard Tuscan dishes and urge you to try their traditional specialties. There's a reason the Sienese come here when they want to celebrate—taste for yourself. See p. 229.
- **Il Piraña** (Prato; ℂ **0574-25-746**): One of the best seafood restaurants in Italy is stuck in the

modern outskirts of landlocked Prato. The atmosphere is refined but thoroughly modern, and the chef really knows what he's doing with any kind of fresh fish (flown in daily from both of Italy's seas), crustacean, or mollusk. A meal will set you back, but for any lover of *frutti di mare* (fruits of the sea), it's worth the side trip from nearby Florence. See p. 260.

- **La Buca di Sant'Antonio** (Lucca; ✆ **0583-55-881**): This maze of a restaurant hidden in the maze of Lucca's central alleys has been pleasing palates since 1782. The decor is hodgepodge trattoria style, but the service is professional and the food is high-toned Tuscan. The stuffed pastas are excellent and the sauces light and delicate. The spit-roasted kid is the knockdown second course. See p. 284.

- **La Chiave** (Livorno; ✆ **0586-888-609**): La Chiave is the finest seafood restaurant in a port city renowned for its seafood. In a refined atmosphere reminiscent of a private dinner club, you can enjoy a masterfully prepared fresh catch of the day or meat dish. They don't stick to tradition when a nouvelle touch would do better, and the soft R&B music and pleasant service make for the most enjoyable meal in town. See p. 306.

- **Ristorante Zaira** (Chiusi; ✆ **0578-20-260**): Chiusi has several fine dining spots, but this one just edges out the others for its *pasta del lucumone*—ziti, ham, and three cheeses baked in a ceramic bowl until a crunchy brown crust forms—and for the moldy ancient wine cellars you can tour after your meal. See p. 343.

- **Il Falchetto** (Perugia; ✆ **075-573-1775**): Years of success and a location on the edge of the town's main square haven't encouraged Perugia's most popular restaurant to lower its standards or to stop making some of the best Umbrian food in town. The homemade pastas are great, but the specialty is a melt-in-your-mouth casserole of spinach-and-ricotta gnocchi. See p. 385.

- **Osteria del Gambero (Ubu Re;** Perugia; ✆ **075-573-5461**): You could make a meal here just out of the delicious and seemingly bottomless assortment of fresh breads and rolls. Of course, that would entail ignoring the incredible pasta and meat courses. The intimate candlelit restaurant is up on the second floor on a side street, so few people even know it exists. Get here before Michelin starts strewing stars about the place. See p. 386.

- **Il Tartufo** (Spoleto; ✆ **0743-40-236**): The floor of the lower dining room actually dates to the Roman Imperial era, but it's open only during the festival season. People really come here to taste some of the most refined and successful culinary uses of truffles in Italy. They work all seasons of the truffle here, and the chef is a master at coaxing out the tuber's delicate flavor in both Umbrian and international dishes. See p. 423.

14 The Best Trattorie in Town

When you're not in the mood for a formal restaurant, head instead to a homey trattoria, where locals and families go for filling and tasty simple fare at great prices.

- **I' Cche' c'è c'è** (Florence; ✆ **055-216-589**): Tuscan standbys like tagliatelle with wild mushrooms and beef cooked in Chianti wine get a refined touch here. This place is far from undiscovered, but being crowded at the long central table (much more fun than the private reservable ones ringing the room) with diners from across the globe has its own charm. See p. 122.

- **Il Latini** (Florence; ✆ **055-210-916**): Squadrons of prosciutto ham hocks hang from the ceiling, and the waiters scamper around cracking jokes as they fit new arrivals into spaces at long communal tables like a jigsaw puzzle and lay huge platters of grilled meats and bowls of steaming *ribollita* (vegetable soup) in front of hungry diners. Although tourists have known about this place for decades, it remains a fun-loving local's-style trattoria, concerned above all with showing you a noisy good time and stuffing you with hearty Florentine fare. See p. 126.

- **Il Pizzaiuolo** (Florence; ✆ **055-241-171**): Florentines can't make a decent pizza. But owner Carmine emigrated from Naples and brought with him that city's ancient trade secrets and the plans for a huge brick oven. This place is like a bit of old Napoli, with long tables, loud conversations, historic Naples photos lining the walls, incredible bubbling pizzas being passed to and fro, and basil leaves as table centerpieces. Come early, stay late, eat hearty. See p. 130.

- **Il Cantinone** (Florence; ✆ **055-218-898**): Under the brick barrel vault of an old Chianti cellar stretch long wooden tables where students, intellectuals, and extended families crowd nightly. The wine list is outstanding, as are the piping hot *crostoni* (pizzalike slabs of peasant bread slathered with toppings like prosciutto,

gooey mozzarella, spinach, and tomatoes). This is the perfect place to head for a noisy, cheap but tasty meal. See p. 132.

- **Trattoria S. Omobono** (Pisa; ✆ **050-540-847**): This tiny, no-nonsense room behind Pisa's daily food market serves real Pisan food the way *Mamma* used to make it. The place fills up early at every meal. See p. 302.

- **Cittino** (Montepulciano; ✆ **0577-757-335**): Marcella will bustle you upstairs to her expanded den cum dining room and serve you heaping portions of pasta—she spends the morning whipping up batches of homemade gnocchi and *pici*—smothered in ragout or spicy tomato sauce. It's a no-frills place with excellent food, ridiculously low prices, and the biggest smiles in town. See p. 338.

- **Ristorante Fiorentino** (Sansepolcro; ✆ **0575-742-033**): In Sansepolcro's old inn for visiting Piero fans, you'll get the best fundamental Tuscan food in the city. If you're lucky, the burly owner may pull over a chair to explain the finer points of Piero della Francesca's art or jab his thumb at tables and rattle off lists of famous people who've eaten his humble but tasty cooking in that chair right over there. See p. 358.

- **Umbria** (Todi; ✆ **075-894-2390**): The traditional dishes of southern Umbria are at their best here, with fresh ingredients like wild asparagus tips, wood mushrooms, wild duck and boar, fresh river trout, truffles, and handmade pastas. In summer, the vine-shaded back terrace offers sweeping views across hilly farmscape. In winter, you can warm by the open fire where they grill your second course. See p. 428.

15 The Best Countryside Trattorie

- **Trattoria le Cave di Maiano** (near Florence; ✆ **055-59-133**): This is many a Florentine's not-so-secret culinary escape in the cool hills above the city. You can dine inside the rustic farmhouse or out on the famous tree-shaded terrace with its distant view of Florence. The food is classic, well-prepared Florentine. See p. 133.

- **La Cantinetta di Rignana** (Chianti; ✆ **055-852-601**): After an eternity of potholes and twisting dirt roads, you'll come upon a group of houses lost in the hills between Greve and Badia a Passignano. Curing meats hang in the doorway, and the cloth-covered tables are amusingly lit by end-table lamps. The homemade pasta is first rate, as are the grilled meats. Settle back after a hearty lunch on the glassed-in porch with some hard biscotti and a glass of vin santo to soften them and drink in the vista spilling across the vine-covered hills of the Rignana estate. See p. 199.

- **Rafanelli** (outside Pistoia; ✆ **0573-532-046**): Though Pistoia's miniature tree nursery industrial zone has grown up around this one-time countryside trattoria over the past 60 years or so, the Rafanelli family hasn't changed its commitment to the fundamentals of Tuscan cooking: wide homemade noodles in hare sauce, wild boar cooked in red wine, and risotto with porcini mushrooms, all served in abundant portions. See p. 267.

- **Ristorante di Poggio Antico** (near Montalcino; ✆ **0577-849-200**): The cheap, old trattoria on this famous wine estate shocked many when it reopened with a new minimalist interior and a talented *nuova cucina* chef spearheading the kitchen. Surrounded by vines that produce some of the silkiest Brunello wines in the region, you can dine on the most refined food in this part of Tuscany, where everything from the breadsticks to the dessert is homemade. See p. 325.

- **Fattoria Pulcino** (outside Montepulciano; ✆ **0578-758-711**): If you're hankering for a country lunch on a working farm, come to this huge, sun-filled dining hall. You get the kind of rib-sticking food once dished out to the farm hands—plates of homemade *pici* pasta, platters of grilled meats—along with the owner's famous honeyed fruitcake for dessert. See p. 338.

- **Relais Il Falconiere** (outside Cortona; ✆ **0575-612-679**): The food and service are impeccable, and the atmosphere sophisticated. Classical music floats across your table; when it's warm and the tables are set on the lawn, crickets take over for Vivaldi. The chefs marry the best fresh ingredients, many cultivated by the owners themselves, with Tuscan recipes to make this one of the most popular restaurants in Tuscany. Follow the foodies who know which turnoff leads to this culinary hideaway. See p. 367.

- **La Stalla** (outside Assisi; ✆ **075-812-317**): This is the quintessential countryside trattoria, the sort of place where scattered Italian families get together for monthly reunions. The low ceilings are black with centuries of wood smoke pouring from the open fire over which grilled meats sizzle. At the long wooden communal tables you can wash down a platter of homemade pasta and another of grilled lamb with copious quantities of the house red. See p. 402.

2

Planning Your Trip to Tuscany & Umbria

Planning a trip doesn't have to be hard work. This chapter will help you smooth out most of your preparations for a trip to Tuscany and Umbria.

1 The Regions in Brief

Tuscany and Umbria are divided into administrative provinces centered around major cities. These official designations aren't perfect for organizing a travel guide, so the following "regions" into which this book is divided group towns and sights based on similarities, with most chapters focused on a major city. Keep in mind that none of these "regions" is very large—Tuscany is, at 23,728 sq. km (9,197 sq. miles), a bit smaller than New Hampshire, and Umbria, at 8,725 sq. km (3,382 sq. miles), makes about two Rhode Islands.

FLORENCE

The capital of Tuscany is **Florence,** one of Italy's most famous cities. It was once the home of the colorful Medici dynasty, which actively encouraged the development of the Renaissance by sponsoring masters such as Donatello, Leonardo, and Michelangelo. Art treasures like those found at the Accademia (Michelangelo's *David*), the Uffizi Galleries (Botticelli's *Birth of Venus*), and the Pitti Palace (Raphael's *La Velata*) draw millions of visitors every year. Throw into the mix fabulous architecture (the Duomo with Brunelleschi's dome, Giotto's campanile, Santa Croce), fine restaurants and earthy trattorie, and leading designer boutiques and bustling outdoor markets, and the city of the Renaissance becomes quite simply one of the world's must-see sights.

THE CHIANTI, SIENA & THE WESTERN HILL TOWNS

The land of high hills stretching from Florence south to Siena is among the most famous countrysides on earth, the vine-covered Arcadia of **Chianti.** Here you can drive along the Chiantigiana roadway, stopping to soak up the scenery and sample the vino. **Siena** is Tuscany's medieval foil to the Renaissance of Florence. It's a city built of brick, with Gothic palaces, excellent pastries, and its own stylized school of Gothic painting. With steep back streets and a mammoth art-packed cathedral, it's the region's second most popular city. The hill towns west of it—medieval tangles of roads perched atop small mountains—are almost as famous: **San Gimignano,** with its medieval stone skyscrapers; Etruscan **Volterra,** with its alabaster workshops; and the undervisited **Massa Marittima,** a medieval mining town with a gorgeous cathedral.

LUCCA & NORTHWESTERN TUSCANY

The Apuan Alps along the shore of the Tyrrhenian Sea kick off a series of mountain chains that rides across the northern edge of Tuscany, separating it

Tuscany & Umbria

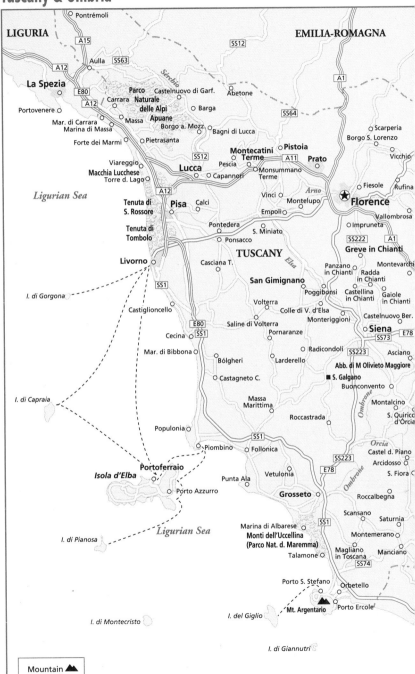

LIGURIA

EMILIA-ROMAGNA

Pontrémoli

A15

SS12

Aulla

SS63

A12

La Spezia

E80

Parco

Castelnuovo di Garf.

Abetone

Carrara

Naturale

A12

delle Alpi

A1

Portovenere

Mar. di Carrara

Massa

Apuane

Barga

SS64

Marina di Massa

Borgo a. Mozz.

Scarperia

Forte dei Marmi

Pietrasanta

Bagni di Lucca

Borgo S. Lorenzo

Viareggio

SS12

Montecatini

Pistoia

Vicchio

Macchia Lucchese

Terme

A11

Prato

Torre d. Lago

Lucca

Pescia

Monsummano

Fiesole

Rufina

A12

Capannori

Terme

Arno

Vinci

Montelupo

Florence

Ligurian Sea

Tenuta di

Pisa

Calci

Empoli

Vallombrosa

S. Rossore

Imbruneta

Pontedera

S. Miniato

SS222

A1

Tenuta di

Ponsacco

Greve in Chianti

Tombolo

TUSCANY

Casciana T.

Panzano

Montevarchi

Livorno

in Chianti

Radda

San Gimignano

in Chianti

I. di Gorgona

SS1

Poggibonsi

Castellina

Gaiole

in Chianti

in Chianti

Volterra

Castelnuovo Ber.

Castiglioncello

Colle di V. d'Elsa

Monteriggioni

Siena

E80

Saline di Volterra

SS73

E78

Cecina

SS1

Pornaranze

Asciano

Mar. di Bibbona

Radicondoli

SS223

Bólgheri

Larderello

Abb. di M Olivieto Maggiore

Castagneto C.

S. Galgano

Buonconvento

I. di Capraia

Massa

Montalcino

Marittima

S. Quirico

Roccastrada

d'Órcia

Populonia

Orcia

SS1

Castel d. Piano

Piombino

Follonica

SS223

Arcidosso

Portoferraio

Vetulonia

E78

S. Fiora

Isola d'Elba

Punta Ala

Roccalbegna

Porto Azzurro

Grosseto

Scansano

Saturnia

Ligurian Sea

Marina di Albarese

SS1

Montemerano

Manciano

I. di Pianosa

Monti dell'Uccellina

(Parco Nat. d. Maremma)

Magliano

Talamone

in Toscana

SS74

Porto S. Stefano

Orbetello

I. di Montecristo

I. del Giglio

Mt. Argentario

Porto Ercole

I. di Giannutri

Mountain ▲▲

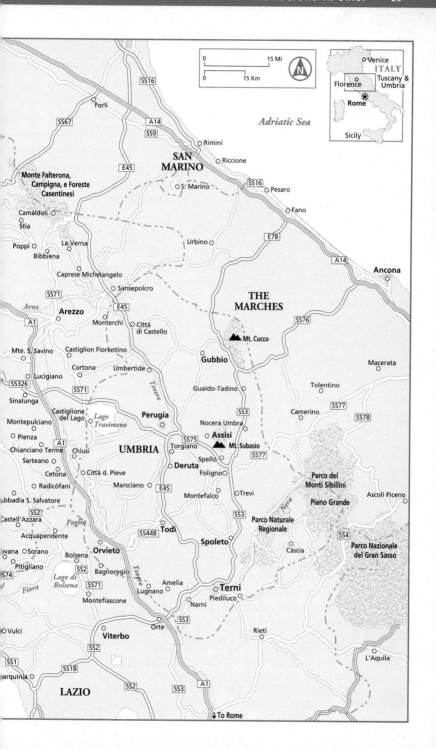

from Emilia-Romagna to the north. In the valley below this string of mountains sit several worthy towns little visited by most travelers rushing from Florence to Lucca or Pisa. The medieval textile center of **Prato** is Italy's fastest-growing city and about the friendliest town in Tuscany. Its historic core is filled with Renaissance art treasures overlooked by many who don't realize a city just 16km (10 miles) from Florence can be so different and rewarding. Its neighbor **Pistoia,** an old Roman town, is more firmly stamped with the art stylings of the Romanesque Middle Ages. Farther along in the *Valdinievole* (Valley of Mists) you'll find relaxation at **Montecatini Terme,** Italy's most famous spa, and **Monsummano Terme,** a Dantean underworld of natural "steam room" caverns hidden beneath a luxury hotel.

The elegant old republican city of **Lucca** is packed with Romanesque churches, livened by the music of native sons Puccini and Boccherini, and teeming with grandmothers on bicycles going shopping. Along the coast north of Lucca are Tuscany's most developed resort beaches, **Viareggio** and **Forte di Marmi.** Farther inland are the old mining towns of **Massa** and **Carrara,** from whose mountainside comes the world's most brilliant white marble, favored by Michelangelo and Henry Moore.

PISA, TUSCANY'S COAST & THE MAREMMA

This region consists of much of Tuscany's coast, from the ancient maritime republic of **Pisa** and its tilting tower to **Livorno,** a Medici-built port city and seafood mecca, and, farther down the coastline, the **Maremma,** Tuscany's deep south. Once a stronghold of the Etruscans, the Maremma was a swamp from the Dark Ages to the 1600s and is still a highly undeveloped region. Also covered is the old iron-mining island of **Elba,** once Napoléon's reign in exile and now one of Italy's more proletarian resorts.

SOUTHERN TUSCANY

"Southern Tuscany" is a bit of a misnomer here, because the Maremma is technically the most southerly region. But the province of Siena stretches south to abut Umbria in a landscape of soft green hills, lone farmhouses, stands of cypress, patches of cultivated fields, and the occasional weird erosion formations known as the *crete senesi* and *biancane.* This area is postcard-perfect Tuscany. The medieval hill towns of **Montalcino** and **Montepulciano** craft some of Italy's finest red wines, and **Pienza,** prodigious producer of pecorino sheep's cheese, is the only perfectly designed town center of the Renaissance. If the spa waters of **Chianciano Terme** don't catch your fancy, perhaps you'll enjoy the ancient Etruscan center of **Chiusi,** with its tombs, archaeological museum, and excellent restaurants.

AREZZO & NORTHEASTERN TUSCANY

Arezzo may once have been an important Etruscan city, but it's not much more than a hill town today, with some Piero della Francesca frescoes and a world-class monthly antiques market. East of Arezzo, near the Umbrian border, is Piero's hometown of **Sansepolcro,** a modest industrial city with an old core devoted to preserving Piero's great works. South of Arezzo stretches the **Chiana Valley,** where the cattle for Florence's famous steaks are raised, and the thriving art city of **Cortona,** which contains some of Tuscany's finest small museums.

PERUGIA, ASSISI & NORTHERN UMBRIA

Perugia, the capital of Umbria, is a refined city of soft jazz, velvety

Integrated City Codes

In 1998, Italy incorporated what were once separate **city codes** (for example, Florence's was 055) into the numbers themselves. Therefore, you must dial the entire number, *including the initial zero,* when calling from *anywhere* outside or inside Italy and even within the same town. For those of you familiar with the old system, this means that now, to call Florence from the States, you must dial **011-39-055-XXX-XXXX.** Increasingly, you'll notice Florence numbers beginning with prefixes other than 055; these are usually cellphone numbers. Fixed-line phone numbers in Italy can range anywhere from 6 to 12 digits in length.

chocolates, medieval alleys, and one of Italy's top painting galleries, featuring the works Perugino, master of the modeled figure and teacher of Raphael. Just east is one of Italy's spiritual centers, the hill town of **Assisi,** birthplace of St. Francis. The basilica raised in his honor is the nerve center of the vast Franciscan monastic movement and home to some of the greatest fresco cycles of the early Renaissance. Umbria gets even wilder to the north, where the rocky border city of **Gubbio** is home to one of Italy's wildest pagan festivals and its own quirky early Renaissance school of art.

SPOLETO & SOUTHERN UMBRIA

Spoleto was once seat of the Lombard duchy that controlled most of Umbria in the Dark Ages, but it's most famous these days for its world-class music and dance Spoleto Festival. Spoleto's beautiful Duomo and the odd reliefs on its early Romanesque churches draw a small but select crowd of admirers. Moving west we hit **Todi,** a quintessential Italian hill town that just oozes medieval charm, and **Orvieto,** an implacable city of tufa rising above the valley on its volcanic outcropping, with a giant gem of a cathedral and the best white wine in Italy.

2 Visitor Information

TOURIST OFFICES

For general information in your home country, try your local branch of the **Italian Government Tourist Board (ENIT)** or www.italiantourism.com. Some Frommer's readers have reported that the office isn't really that helpful.

In the United States: 630 Fifth Ave., Suite 1565, New York, NY 10111 (✆ **212/245-4822** or 212/245-5618; fax 212/586-9249); 500 N. Michigan Ave., Suite 2240, Chicago, IL 60611 (✆ **312/644-0996** or 312/644-0990; fax 312/644-3019); and 12400 Wilshire Blvd., Suite 550, Los Angeles, CA 90025 (✆ **310/820-1898** or 310/820-9807; fax 310/820-6357).

In Canada: 175 Bloor St. E., Suite 907, South Tower, Toronto, Ontario M4W 3R8 (✆ **416/925-4882;** fax 416/925-4799; enit.canada@on.aibn.com).

In the United Kingdom: 1 Princes St., London W1B 2AY England (✆ **020/7399-3562;** italy@italiantouristboard.co.uk).

For more specific details on **Tuscany,** contact the regional tourist office in Florence: APT, Via Manzoni 16, 50121 Firenze (✆ **055-23-320;** fax 055-234-6286; www.firenzeturismo.it). For **Umbria,** contact the Ufficio Promozione Turistica, Corso Vannucci 30, 06100 Perugia (✆ **075-50-41;** fax 075-504-2483). To get even more details, put yourself in contact with the regional and city tourism offices, listed in each chapter section (or you can get a list from the ENIT).

USEFUL WEBSITES

Websites and e-mail addresses are included throughout this guide for everything from tourist offices, hotels, and restaurants to museums and festivals.

The official site for Tuscany is **www.turismo.toscana.it**, with links to every provincial tourist office site. The official Florence information site, **www.firenze turismo.it**, contains a wealth of up-to-date information (events, museums, practical details) on Florence and its province. Included is a searchable "hotels" form allowing you to specify amenities, categories, and the like; it responds by spitting out a list of comparable hotels, and it lists contact info and current room rates. The official site for Umbria is **www.umbria-turismo.it**.

Firenze by Net (www.mega.it/florence), **Firenze.Net** (http://english.firenze.net), and **FlorenceOnLine** (www.fol.it) are all Italy-based websites with English translations and good general information on Florence. Also check out **The Heart of Tuscany** (www.nautilus-mp.com/tuscany), and **Chianti Doc Marketplace** (www.chianti-doc.com). And of course there's **Frommer's** (www.frommers.com), where you'll find excerpts from this guide, occasional updated information, and links to travel packages from Gate 1 Travel.

3 Entry Requirements & Customs

ENTRY REQUIREMENTS

U.S., Canadian, U.K., Irish, Australian, and New Zealand citizens with a **valid passport** don't need a visa to enter Italy if they don't expect to stay more than 90 days and don't expect to work there. If after entering Italy you find you want to stay more than 90 days, you can apply for a permit for an extra 90 days, which as a rule is granted immediately. Go to the nearest *questura* (police headquarters) or your home country's consulate.

For passport information and applications in the **U.S.,** call © **202/647-0518** or check http://travel.state.gov; in **Canada,** call © **800/567-6868** or check www.dfait-maeci.gc.ca/passport; in the **U.K.,** call © **0870/521-0410** or visit www.passports.gov.uk; in **Ireland,** call © **01/671-1633** or check www.irl-gov.ie/iveagh; in **Australia,** call © **131-232** or visit www.passports.gov.au; and in **New Zealand,** call © **0800/225-050** or check www.passports.govt.nz. Allow plenty of time before your trip to apply for a passport; processing usually takes 3 weeks but can take longer during busy periods (especially spring).

When traveling, safeguard your passport and keep a copy of the critical pages with your passport number in a separate place. If you lose your passport, visit the nearest consulate of your native country as soon as possible for a replacement.

CUSTOMS

WHAT YOU CAN BRING INTO ITALY

Foreign visitors can bring along most items for personal use duty-free, including fishing tackle; a sporting gun and 200 cartridges; a pair of skis; two tennis racquets; a baby carriage; two hand cameras with 10 rolls of film; and 200 cigarettes or 50 cigars or pipe tobacco not exceeding 250 grams. There are strict limits on importing alcoholic beverages. However, limits are much more liberal for alcohol bought tax-paid in other countries of the European Union. For more information regarding customs, visit the Italian-language website www.agenziadogane.it and follow links to "carta dogonale del viaggiatore," the travelers' custom charter.

WHAT YOU CAN TAKE HOME

FOR U.S. CITIZENS A recent change in the personal exemption rule allows returning U.S. citizens who have been away for at least 48 hours to bring back into the States up to $800 worth of goods (per person) without paying a duty once every 30 days. On the first $1,000 worth of goods over $800 you pay a flat 3% duty. Beyond that, it works on an item-by-item basis. There are a few restrictions on amount: 1 liter of alcohol (you must be over 21), 200 cigarettes, and 100 cigars. Antiques more than 100 years old and works of fine art are exempt from the $800 limit, as is anything you mail home. Once per day, you can mail yourself $200 worth of goods duty-free; mark the package FOR PERSONAL USE. You can also mail gifts to other people without paying duty as long as the recipient doesn't receive more than $100 worth of gifts in a single day; label each gift package UNSOLICITED GIFT. Any package must state on the exterior a description of the contents and their values. You can't mail alcohol, perfume (it contains alcohol), or tobacco products worth more than $5.

For more information on regulations, check out the **U.S. Customs and Border Protection** website at www.cbp.gov or write to them at 1300 Pennsylvania Ave., NW, Washington, DC 20229, to request the free *Know Before You Go* pamphlet.

To prevent the spread of diseases, you cannot bring into the States any plants, fruits, vegetables, meats, or most other foodstuffs. This includes even cured meats like salami (no matter what the shopkeeper in Europe says). You may bring in the following: bakery goods, all but the softest cheeses (the rule is vague, but if the cheese is at all spreadable, don't risk confiscation), candies, roasted coffee beans and dried tea, fish, seeds for veggies and flowers (but not for trees), and mushrooms. Check out the **USDA**'s website at www.aphis.usda.gov/oa/travel for more details.

FOR U.K. CITIZENS You can bring home almost as much as you like of any goods from any EU country as long as the goods are for your own use. You're likely to be questioned by Customs if you bring back more than 90 liters of wine, 3,200 cigarettes, or 200 cigars. If you're returning home from a non-EU country or if you buy your goods in a duty-free shop, you're allowed to bring home 200 cigarettes or 50 cigars, 2 liters of table wine, plus 1 liter of spirits or 2 liters of fortified wine. Get in touch with **Her Majesty's Customs and Excise Office,** New King's Beam House, 22 Upper Ground, London SE1 9PJ (✆ **020/7620-1313;** www. hmce.gov.uk), or call their Advice Service at ✆ **0845/010-9000** for more information.

FOR CANADIAN CITIZENS For a clear summary of Canadian rules, write for the booklet *I Declare,* issued by **Revenue Canada,** 2265 St. Laurent Blvd., Ottawa K1G 4KE (✆ **613/993-0534** or 800/959-2221; www.ccra-adrc.gc.ca). Canada allows citizens a C$750 exemption if you've been out of the country for at least 7 days. You're allowed to bring back duty-free 200 cigarettes, 2.2 pounds of tobacco, 40 imperial ounces of liquor, 50 cigars, and 1.5 liters of wine. In addition, you're allowed to mail gifts to Canada from abroad at the rate of C$60 a day, provided they're unsolicited and aren't alcohol or tobacco (write on the package "Unsolicited gift, under C$60 value"). All valuables should be declared on the Y-38 form before departure from Canada, including serial numbers of, for example, expensive foreign cameras that you already own. For more information, call the **Automated Customs Service** at ✆ **800/461-9999** toll-free within Canada or ℂ 204/983-3500 outside Canada.

FOR AUSTRALIAN CITIZENS

The duty-free allowance in Australia is A$400 or, for those under 18, A$200. Personal property mailed back from Italy should be marked AUSTRALIAN GOODS RETURNED to avoid payment of duty. On returning to Australia, citizens can bring in 250 cigarettes or 250 grams of loose tobacco, and 1,125ml of alcohol. If you're returning with valuable goods you already own, such as foreign-made cameras, you should file form B263. A helpful brochure, available from Australian consulates or Customs offices, is *Know Before You Go.* For more information, contact **Australian Customs Services,** GPO Box 8, Sydney NSW 2001 (ℂ **1300-363-263** within Australia, or 02-6275-6666 from overseas; www.customs.gov.au).

FOR NEW ZEALAND CITIZENS

The duty-free allowance for New Zealand is NZ$700. Citizens over 17 years can bring in 200 cigarettes, or 50 cigars, or 250 grams of tobacco (or a mixture of all three if their combined weight doesn't exceed 250g); plus 4.5 liters of wine or beer, or 1.125 liters of liquor. New Zealand currency doesn't carry import or export restrictions. Fill out a certificate of export, listing the valuables you are taking out of the country; that way, you can bring them back without paying duty. Most questions are answered in a free pamphlet available at New Zealand consulates and Customs offices: *New Zealand Customs Guide for Travellers, Notice no. 4.* For more information, contact **New Zealand Customshouse,** 50 Anzac Ave., Box 29, Auckland, NZ (ℂ **0800/ 428-786** within New Zealand; 09-359-6655 from overseas; www.customs. govt.nz).

4 Money

Italy falls somewhere in the middle of pricing in Europe—not as expensive as, say, London, Switzerland, or Scandinavia, but not as cheap as Spain and Greece. Popular central Italy, especially Tuscany, comes just behind Venice in terms of costliest bit of Italy to travel through, but the advice in this book should help guide you to the best options to fit any budget.

Luckily, ATMs (automated teller machines) are now to be found just about everywhere, even in the smallest towns, so cash is readily available, and as luck would have it, banks in Italy do not (as of yet) charge you a fee for using their bank—though your home bank probably will for using an out-of-network ATM, and these days often a premium for withdrawing foreign currency.

It's a good idea to exchange at least some money—just enough to cover airport incidentals and transportation

to your hotel—before you leave home, so you can avoid lines at airport ATMs. You can exchange money at your local American Express or Thomas Cook office or your bank (often, though, only at the major branches). If you're far away from a bank with currency-exchange services, American Express offers travelers checks and foreign currency—though with a $15 order fee and additional shipping costs—at www.american express.com or ℂ **800/807-6233.**

CURRENCY

In January 2002, Italy retired the lira and joined most of Western Europe in switching to the euro. Coins are issued in denominations of .01€, .02€, .05€, .10€, .20€, and .50€ as well as 1€ and 2€; bills come in denominations of 5€, 10€, 20€, 50€, 100€, 200€, and 500€.

Exchange rates are established daily and listed in most international

The Euro, the U.S. Dollar & the British Pound

At this writing, 1€ equaled approximately $1.15—a historic high, as the euro and dollar were usually on a par since the euro's inception. The rate fluctuates from day to day and might not be the same when you travel to Italy. For the latest rate, check www.xe.com.

Likewise, the ratio of the British pound to the euro fluctuates constantly; at press time, £1 equaled approximately 1.39€.

Euro	US$	UK£	Euro	US$	UK£
0.50	0.60	0.35	30	35.40	21.60
1	1.15	0.70	40	46	28.80
2	2.30	1.45	50	57.50	36
3	3.45	2.15	60	69	43.20
4	4.60	2.90	70	80.50	50.40
5	5.75	3.60	80	92	57.60
6	6.90	4.30	90	103.50	64.80
7	8.05	5.05	100	115	72
8	9.20	5.75	125	143.75	90
9	10.35	6.48	150	172.50	108
10	11.50	7.20	200	230	144
15	17.25	10.80	300	345	216
20	23	14.40	400	460	288
25	28.75	18	500	575	360

newspapers. To get a transaction as close to this rate as possible, pay for as much as possible with credit cards and get cash out of ATMs.

Traveler's checks, while still the safest way to carry money, are going the way of the dinosaur. The aggressive evolution of international computerized banking and consolidated ATM networks has led to the triumph of plastic throughout the Italian peninsula—even if cold cash is still the most trusted currency, especially in smaller towns or cheaper mom-and-pop joints, where credit cards may not be accepted.

You'll get the best rate if you **exchange money** at a bank or one of its ATMs. The rates at "Cambio/change/wechsel" exchange booths are invariably less favorable but still a good deal better than what you'd get exchanging money at a hotel or shop (a last-resort tactic only). The bill-to-bill changers you'll see in some touristy places exist solely to rip you off.

ATMS

The ability to access your personal checking account through the **Cirrus** (℃ 800/424-7787; www.mastercard.com) or **PLUS** (℃ 800/843-7587; www.visa.com) network of ATMs—or get a cash advance on an enabled Visa or MasterCard—has grown by leaps and bounds in Italy in the last few years. It works just like at home. All you need do is search out a machine that has your network's symbol displayed, pop in your card, and punch in your PIN (make sure it's four digits; six-digit PINs won't work). It'll spit out local currency drawn directly from your home checking account (and at a more favorable rate than converting traveler's checks or cash). Also keep in mind that many banks impose a fee every time a card is used at a different bank's ATM, and that fee can be higher for international transactions (up to $5 or more) than for domestic ones (where they're rarely more than $1.50). However, as I mentioned above, banks in Italy do not (at least yet) charge you a second fee to use their ATMs. To compare banks' ATM fees within the U.S., use www.bankrate.com. For international withdrawal fees, ask your bank.

An ATM in Italian is a *Bancomat* (though Bancomat is a private company, its name has become the generic word for ATMs). Increased internationalism has been slowly doing away with the old worry that your card's PIN, be it on a bank card or credit card, need be specially enabled to work abroad, but it always pays to check with the issuing bank to be sure. If at the ATM you get a message saying your card isn't valid for international transactions, it's likely the bank just can't make the phone connection to check it (occasionally this can be a citywide epidemic); try another ATM or another town.

When you withdraw money with your bank card, you technically get the interbank exchange rate—about 4% better than the "street rate" you'd get exchanging cash or traveler's checks. Note, however, that some U.S. banks are now charging a 1% to 3% "exchange fee" to convert the currency. (Ask your bank before you leave.)

Similarly, **Visa** has begun charging a standard 1% conversion fee for cash advances, and many credit card–issuing banks have begun tacking on an additional 1% to 3% (though as we go to press, Visa is currently being taken to court over this practice in a class-action lawsuit, so stay tuned to the news to see what the future holds). Basically, they've gotten into the "commission" game, too. And, unlike with purchases, interest on a credit card cash advance

starts accruing *immediately*, not when your statement cycles. Both methods are still a slightly better deal than converting traveler's checks or cash and considerably more convenient (no waiting in bank lines and pulling out your passport as ID). I use credit card advances only as an emergency option and get most of my euros with my bank card.

ATM withdrawals are often limited to 200€ ($230), or sometimes 300€ ($345), per transaction regardless of your cash advance allowance. **American Express** card cash advances are usually available only from the American Express offices in Florence (see "Fast Facts: Florence" in chapter 3 for more information).

CREDIT CARDS

Visa and **MasterCard** are now almost universally accepted at most hotels, restaurants, and shops; the majority also accepts **American Express. Diners Club** is gaining some ground, especially in Florence and in more expensive establishments throughout the region. If you arrange with your card issuer to enable the card's cash advance option (and get a PIN as well), you can also use them at ATMs.

Some credit-card companies recommend that you notify them of any impending trip abroad so that they don't become suspicious when the card is used numerous times in a foreign destination and block your charges. Even if you don't call your credit-card company in advance, you can call always the card's toll-free emergency number if a charge is refused—a good reason to carry the phone number with you. For emergency numbers, see "Lost & Found" in "Fast Facts: Tuscany & Umbria," later in this chapter.

TRAVELER'S CHECKS

Traveler's checks are something of an anachronism from the days before the

What Things Cost in Florence	U.S.$	U.K.£
Taxi (from the train station to Ponte Vecchio)	6	3.75
Public bus (to any destination)	1.20	.85
Local telephone call	.12	.07
Double room at Hotel Helvetia and Bristol (very expensive)	388–553	243–346
Double room at Hotel Mario's (moderate)	94–194	59–121
Double room at Pensione Maria Luisa de' Medici (inexpensive)	79–94	49–59
Continental breakfast (cappuccino and croissant standing at a bar)	2.50	1.55
Lunch for one at Nerbone (inexpensive)	7	4.40
Dinner for one, with table wine, at La Giostra (expensive)	56	35
Dinner for one, with table wine, at Il Latini (moderate)	35–41	22–26
Dinner for one, with table wine, at Le Mossacce (inexpensive)	17	11
Glass of wine	1–6	.65–3.75
Coca-Cola (standing/sitting in a bar)	1.60/4.15	1/2.60
Cup of espresso (standing/sitting in a bar)	.75/2.35	.45/1.45
Roll of color film, 36 exposures	11.20	7
Admission to the Uffizi Galleries	9.45	5.90
Movie ticket	9.45	5.90

ATM made cash accessible at any time. Traveler's checks used to be the only sound alternative to traveling with dangerously large amounts of cash. They were as reliable as currency, but, unlike cash, could be replaced if lost or stolen.

These days, traveler's checks are less necessary because most cities have 24-hour ATMs that allow you to withdraw small amounts of cash as needed. However, keep in mind that you will likely be charged an ATM withdrawal fee if the bank is not your own, so if you're withdrawing money every day, you might be better off with traveler's checks—provided that you don't mind showing identification every time you want to cash one.

Most banks issue checks under the names of **American Express** (© **800/721-9768** in the U.S. and Canada; www.americanexpress.com) and **Thomas Cook** (© **800/223-7373** in the U.S. and Canada, or 44-1733-318-950 collect from anywhere in the world; www.thomascook.com)—both offer versions that can be countersigned by you or your companion—**Visa** (© **800/227-6811** in the U.S. and Canada, or 44-020-7937-8091 collect from anywhere in the world; www.visa.com), or **Citicorp** (© **800/645-6556** in the U.S. and Canada, or 813/623-1709 collect from anywhere in the world). AAA members can obtain Visa checks without a commission fee at most AAA offices or by calling © **866/339-3378.** Note that you'll get the worst possible exchange rate if you pay for a purchase or hotel room directly with a traveler's check; it's better to trade in the traveler's checks for euros at a bank or the American Express office.

To report lost or stolen traveler's checks in Italy, call toll-free: **American**

Express (© 800-872-000), **Thomas Cook** (© 800-872-050), **Visa** (© 800-874-155), or **Citicorp** (© 813/623-1709 collect from anywhere).

WIRE SERVICES

If you find yourself out of money, a wire service can help you tap willing friends and family for funds. Through **TravelersExpress/MoneyGram** (© **800/666-3947;** www.moneygram. com), you can get money sent around the world in less than 10 minutes. Cash is the only acceptable form of payment. MoneyGram's fees vary based on the cities the money is wired from and to,

but a good estimate is $20 for the first $200 and $30 for up to $400, with a sliding scale for larger sums. A similar service is offered by **Western Union** (© **800/CALL-CASH**), which accepts Visa, MasterCard credit or debit cards, or Discover. You can arrange for the service over the phone, at a Western Union office, or online at www.western union.com. A sliding scale begins at $15 for the first $100. A currency exchange rate will also apply. Additionally, your credit card company may charge a fee for the cash advance as well as a higher interest rate.

5 When to Go

The best times to visit Tuscany and Umbria are in the **spring** and **fall.** Starting in late May, the **summer** tourist rush really picks up, and from July to mid-September the country is teeming with visitors. August is the worst month to visit. Not only does it get uncomfortably hot, muggy, and crowded (the lines for the Uffizi and the Accademia can stretch for blocks), but the entire country goes on vacation at least from August 15 until the end of the month, and many Italians take off the entire month. Many hotels, restaurants, and shops are closed—except at the spas, beaches, and islands, which are where 70% of the Italians are headed. In **winter** (late Oct to Easter), most sights go on shorter winter hours or are closed for restoration and rearrangement, many hotels and restaurants take a month or two off between November and February, spa and beach destinations become padlocked ghost towns, and it can get much colder than most people expect—it may even snow on occasion.

WEATHER

Tuscany and Umbria cover some pretty diverse terrain and climate areas. Tuscany has lowlands along the coast with the most moderate of climes, but there are also snow-capped

Apennine mountains in the north of Tuscany and eastern Umbria that stay cooler throughout the year and can get downright frigid in winter. Both regions are made up primarily of hills, however, and the climate varies with the seasons and the landscape. It can get uncomfortably hot at the height of August in valley cities such as Florence, but the breeze-cooled hill towns are usually eminently livable in summer. The long spring is temperate and very comfortable, with occasional showers. Fall is also fairly mild, with lots of rainfall being the only drawback. Winter, though mild for most months, can get quite cold in late December or January; it can drizzle a great deal, and snowfall isn't impossible.

HOLIDAYS

Official state holidays include January 1, January 6 (Epiphany), Easter Sunday and Monday, April 25 (Liberation Day), May 1 (Labor Day), August 15 (Ferragosto and Assumption Day), November 1 (All Saints Day), December 8 (Day of the Immaculate Conception), December 25, and December 26 (Santo Stefano). Florence also shuts down to honor its patron, St. John the Baptist, on June 24.

Hot Tickets

For major events where tickets should be procured well before arriving on the spot, check out **Box Office** at ☎ **055-210-804** or www.boxoffice.it. They will only deliver tickets to an Italian address, but you can buy ahead of time and have tickets held for you.

TUSCANY & UMBRIA CALENDAR OF EVENTS

No Italian village can let the year run its course without a handful of celebrations of church, history, local talent, or just good food and wine. And no visit to Italy is complete without taking part in at least one of them. Those listed below represent merely the biggest and most spectacular Tuscany and Umbria have to offer. Under the introduction to each city throughout this book, you'll find these events described in greater detail along with dates for smaller *feste* and weekly markets.

January

Regatta on the Arno, Florence. The city of the Renaissance kicks off the new year with a boat race. Call ☎ **055-23-320** for details. January 1.

Befana (the Christmas Witch) Caroling, Maremma, Tuscany. In the countryside of Tuscany's deep south, carolers costumed as the Christmas witch go from farm to farm and house to house, singing both traditional tunes and modern melodies in honor of the Epiphany. After dark on January 5.

February

Olive and Bruschetta Festival, Spello, Umbria. The town celebrates the olive harvest by drizzling the new oil over toast in a bruschetta fest accompanied by traditional music. Call the tourist office at ☎ **0742-354-459** for more. February 5.

Carnevale, throughout Italy. Carnival was originally a pagan festival that looked forward to the bounty of spring, but in modern times it has been conveniently grafted onto the last 5 to 10 days before Ash Wednesday, which on the Christian calendar signals the start of the sober Lenten period. Every Italian town celebrates in some way—Venice is famous for it. *Martedi Grasso* is Fat Tuesday, the final day of Carnevale before Lent, and the best of the fest is saved for this time, with parades, fireworks, and the like. The most outstanding Tuscan Rite of Spring occurs in the coastal town of **Viareggio** ★★ (for details, contact the **Cotitaio Carnevale,** Palazzo dell Muse, Piazza Mazzini, Viareggio; ☎ **0584-47-503** or 0584-962-568), with a colorful and sophisticated parade of mechanized floats subtly lampooning political figures and celebrities. (If you take the train from Florence, your rail ticket will get you a discount on admission to the event.) Other Carnevale festivities worth dropping in on are the costumed parade in **San Gimignano** (call ☎ **0577-940-008** for details) and a similar masked procession at **Vinci** (call ☎ **0571-568-012** for details). The week before Ash Wednesday (Feb/early Mar).

March

Torchlit Procession and Pagan Feast, Pitigliano, Tuscany. After the locals set fire to a giant human-shaped straw effigy of Winter, they break out the sweets, song, and dance, and party all night on the piazza. For details, call ☎ **0564-614-433.** March 19.

Easter is always a big event. Some of the most colorful yet solemn celebrations are held in St. Francis's Umbrian hometown, **Assisi** (call ☎ **075-812-534** for details), and in **Florence** (see below). Easter Sunday.

Scioppo del Carro (Explosion of the Cart), Florence. Florentines celebrate Easter with Renaissance pyrotechnics. When the bishop inside the cathedral gets to the "Gloria" part of High Mass, a mechanical dove is let loose from high over the altar, and it slides down a wire toward the front doors. Waiting for it on Piazza del Duomo outside is a tall 18th-century cart—pulled there by two snowy white oxen and loaded with fireworks—which the dove ignites (it's hoped). (No one seems at all concerned that this occurs within spitting distance of the Baptistery's *Gates of Paradise.*) Contact the tourist office at ℭ **055-290-832** for details. Easter Sunday.

National Kite-Flying Championship, San Miniato, Tuscany. Italians fly kites in a competitive manner. Call ℭ **0571-42-745** or 0571-42-233 for details. The weekend after Easter.

April

Festival of Sacred Music, Lucca, Tuscany. For 3 months, Lucca's churches put on various concerts and choir recitals. Call ℭ **0583-419-689** or fax 0583-442-505 for details. April through June.

May

Calendimaggio, Assisi, Umbria. This pagan spring festival is held in Umbria's holiest of cities. There are lots of singing, dancing, feats of prowess, and medieval costumes as Assisi's Romeos vie for the right to call their own fair damsel Lady Spring. Call ℭ **075-812-534** for details. First weekend (starting Thurs) after May 1.

Maggio Musicale (Musical May), Florence. Florence's rather chichi concert series, which now stretches May through June, has become one of the finer musical events on Europe's calendar over the past 66 years. The concerts and dance recitals take place in the more atmospheric palazzi and churches about town, and tickets don't come cheap. Contact the **Maggio Musicale Fiorentino** (ℭ **0935-564-767**), or visit the box office at Teatro Comunale, Corso Italia 12, 50123 Firenze (ℭ **055-213-535;** fax 055-277-222; www.maggiofiorentino.com)   for details and tickets. May to late June.

Festa del Grillo (Cricket Festival), Florence. In the Cascine Park, vendors sell crickets in decorated cages, and, after a parade of floats on the Arno, everybody releases the bugs into the grass. Contact the tourist office at Via Cavour 1r (ℭ **055-290-832**) for details. First Sunday after Ascension Day (mid- to late May).

Corso dei Ceri (Candle Race), Gubbio, Umbria. One of Italy's most spectacular and oldest festivals, this one has to be seen to be believed. Color-coded teams of burly men from the city's three districts run about town all day long carrying 30-foot-high wooden "candles" (read: phallic symbols) topped with statues of saints. After a seafood dinner, they carry the things at a dead trot more than 1,000 vertical feet up a mountain. Perhaps the tourist office can explain it: Call ℭ **075-922-0693.** May 15.

Giostro dell'Archiado (Crossbow Competition), Cortona, Tuscany. This crossbow competition is held in late-14th-century costume. Contact the tourist office at ℭ **0575-630-353** or 0575-630-352 for details. May 18.

Balestro del Girifalco (Crossbow Competition), Massa Marittima, Tuscany. Massan crossbow sharpshooters in 13th-century costume fire bolts into impossibly small targets, following all the requisite processions and flag tossing. Contact **Amatur** at ℭ **0566-902-756** for details. May 20 or the following

Sunday and again the second Sunday in August.

Palio della Balestra (Crossbow Competition), Gubbio, Umbria. 'Tis the season to fire crossbows. Eugubians, all dudded up medieval style, test their crossbow skills against teams from historical rival Sansepolcro. In September, Sansepolcro gets to host the annual rematch. Call ✆ **075-922-0693** for details. Last Sunday in May.

Regatta of the Great Maritime Republics, Pisa, Tuscany. Every year, the four medieval maritime republics of Italy celebrate their glorious past with a boat race that rotates among Venice, Amalfi, Genoa, and Pisa. Venice hosted the event in 2003; Amalfi will host in 2004, Genoa in 2005, and Pisa in 2006. Call the tourist office of the host city for details. First Sunday in June.

June

Corpus Cristi Procession, Orvieto, Umbria. In the town where this religious holiday was first proclaimed, the holy liturgical cloth onto which a communion wafer once miraculously dripped blood is carried through town in a procession of hundreds dressed in medieval costume. Contact the tourist office at ✆ **0763-341-772** for details. Corpus Cristi (early June).

Festa di San Ranieri, Pisa, Tuscany. The city celebrates its patron saint by lining the Arno River with flickering torches. Call ✆ **050-42-291** for details. June 16 and 17.

Regatta del Palio (Boat Race), Florence. This is the first and most important of several regattas held on the Arno on this day. Spectators line the quays between the Uffizi and Santa Trinita Bridge as teams from Florence's four traditional neighborhoods compete to win a painted banner. Later in the day, united Florentine teams duke it out with rowers from Pisa and Livorno for titles and trophies. Contact the tourist office at Via Cavour 1r (✆ **055-290-832**) for details. June 23.

Gioco di Calcio (Historic Soccer), Florence. St. John is Florence's patron, and what better way to celebrate his holy day than with a violent Renaissance version of soccer played in 16th-century costume? Two teams of 26 men battle each other tooth and nail on dirt-packed Piazza di Santa Croce (the 1st June match) and Piazza della Signoria. The teams hail from each of Florence's four historic quarters—San Giovanni in green, Santa Maria Novella in red, Santa Croce in blue, and Santo Spirito in white. The season opens on June 16, but the big game is on June 24, after which fireworks explode over the Arno at 10pm. The teams also butt heads on December 24 in the full Christmas Eve spirit. Contact the tourist office at Via Cavour 1r (✆ **055-290-832**) for details. June 24 and 28.

Gioco del Ponte (War on the Bridge), Pisa, Tuscany. Pisan teams from opposite banks of the river get into Renaissance garb, stand on the city's oldest bridge, and have a push-of-war with a 7-ton cart. For details, call ✆ **050-42-291.** Last Sunday in June.

Spoleto Festival, Spoleto, Umbria. This world-renowned festival of music and the performing arts (formerly called the Festival of Two Worlds) was started by Italian-American composer Gian Carlo Menotti in 1958—the "two worlds" were originally Spoleto and Charleston, South Carolina, but Melbourne, Australia, has also joined the family of cities putting on a month-long series of concerts, opera, ballet, film, and theater (see chapter 11 for more information). Tickets usually sell out by March. For details, contact the

Associazione Spoleto Festival, Piazza Duomo 8, 06049 Spoleto (PG; ✆ **800-565-600** in Italy, or 0743-220-032; fax 0743-220-321; www.spoletofestival.it). Also try the **Teatro Nuovo** at ✆ **0743-40-265.** Mid-June to mid-July.

Estate Fiesolana (Fiesolean Summer), Fiesole, near Florence. This summertime festival of music, ballet, film, and theater is held above the oppressive Florentine heat in the ancient hill town of Fiesole. Most of the performances are staged in the remains of the 1st-century A.D. Roman theater. You can get information and tickets in advance through the **Agenzia Box Office,** Via Alamanni 39 Firenze (✆ **055-210-804;** www.estatefiesolana.it), or at the Roman Theater on the day of performance after 4:30pm. Late June to August.

July

Palio delle Contrade (Horse Race), Siena, Tuscany. The Palio between Siena's traditional neighborhoods vies with Venice's Carnevale as Italy's premier festival. It's a breakneck bareback horse race around the dirt-packed main square prefaced by three days of parades, trial runs, and heavy partying. The night before the race is a regular bacchanal to which visitors are often welcome. The best 80€ to 200€ ($92–$230) grandstand seats sell out years in advance, but some are always available a few months before. Standing in the center of the piazza is free. Afterward, winners and losers alike celebrate with the aid of much chianti. Hotel rooms in the whole city are booked more than a year in advance of the July 2 event. And they do it all over again on August 16. For more information, see chapter 5, or contact Siena's **Ufficio Informazione Turistico,** Piazza del Campo 56 (✆ **0577-280-551;** fax 0577-270-676). July 2.

Umbria Jazz, Perugia, Umbria. This has been one of Europe's top jazz events for more than 30 years— 2 weeks of performances, concerts, and jams from top names and bands that cool out Umbria's capital during the summer heat. For more information, contact the **Associazione Umbria Jazz-Perugia,** Piazza Danti 28 (✆ **075-573-2432;** www.umbria jazz.com). Mid-July.

Wine Festival, Portoferraio, Elba. This *festa* to toast the island's excellent but seldom exported white and red wines takes place at Le Ghiaie beach behind Elba's main town. Call ✆ **0565-914-671** for details. Last week of July.

Giostra del Orso (Joust of the Bear), Pistoia, Tuscany. This medieval-costumed jousting match pits mounted knights against targets shaped like bears. Not nearly as death-defying as the olden days when they used real bears, but still a rousing good time. Call ✆ **0573-34-326** for details. July 25.

Sangimignanese Summer, San Gimignano, Tuscany. This nearly 80-year-old cultural festival of moderate note offers open-air concerts, opera, and film in the Town of Towers. For details, contact the tourist office at Piazza del Duomo, San Gimignano (SI; ✆ **0577-940-008;** fax 0577-940-903; www.sangimignano.com). Last weekend in July.

Settimana Musicale Senese (Sienese Music Week), Siena, Tuscany. This festival brings a week of the best concerts and opera Siena's prestigious music center can muster. Contact the **Accademia Musicale Chigiana,** Via di Città 89 (✆ **0577-46-152**). One week in July or August.

Classical Concerts in the Roman Theater, Gubbio, Umbria. In the valley below town, you get the Roman experience by attending concerts in the overgrown ruins of a 1st-century A.D. theater. Meanwhile, up in town, the **Gubbio Festival** brings in international performers for more of the same in less scenic settings. The tourist office (✆ **075-575-951**) can fill you in on both. Late July to early August.

Todi Festival, Todi, Umbria. This annual bash started in the 1980s brings theater, music, ballet, and opera to the medieval hill town for 10 days in late summer. Contact www.todiartefestival.it or ✆ **075-894-2526** for details. Late July (some years in Aug).

August

La Palombella (The Unlucky Dove), Orvieto, Umbria. A live white dove surrounded by flares ignites a pile of fireworks outside the Duomo. Great fun, unless you're the bird. Call ✆ **0763-341-772** for details. Pentecost Sunday.

Ferragosto, throughout Italy. This isn't an event; it's an exodus. The feast of the Assumption marks the beginning of the August holiday, when everything in Italy closes, hotels and restaurants included. Everyone goes on vacation. Unless you're at the beach, you might not see more than 10 Italians all day. Some things will reopen on the 16th, but most of Italy takes the rest of the month off. August 15.

Cowboy Parade and Rodeo, Albarese, Tuscany. The gateway town to the Maremma's best natural park hosts a rodeo of the top *butteri* stars of Tuscany's deep south. *Butteri* are the old-fashioned Italian cowboys who've watched over the white Maremma cattle herds for generations. The **Monti dell'Uccellina** park information office may have details at ✆ **0564-407-098.** August 15.

Feast of the Hams, Sorano, Tuscany. Local pig population plummets. Prosciutto and sausage consumption rises dramatically. Butchers prosper. Pork enthusiasts can call ✆ **0564-633-023** for details. Mid-August.

Palio delle Contrade (Horse Race), Siena, Tuscany. An encore of Siena's famous horse race. This edition is more popular and even more crowded. August 16.

Palio Marinaro (Boat Race), Livorno, Tuscany. This annual neighborhood boat race is held at Tuscany's major port. For details, call ✆ **0586-899-111** or fax 0586-896-173. August 17.

Bravio delle Botti (Barrel Race), Montepulciano, Tuscany. This is something akin to a medieval fraternity stunt. Teams of *poliziani* (police officers) dress like their 14th-century ancestors in order to pull various important muscles trying to be the first to roll a 175-pound barrel uphill to the top of town. Come for the pageantry and feasting afterward. Contact the tourist office at ✆ **0578-758-687** for details. Late August.

September

Giostro del Saracino (Saracen Joust), Arezzo, Tuscany. This jousting tournament is between mounted knights in 13th-century armor and the effigy of a Saracen warrior. It's held on Arezzo's main square and is one of the few versions of this sport in which the target, which swivels and is armed with a whip, actually hits back. Contact the tourist office at ✆ **0575-377-678** (fax 0575-20-839) for details. First Sunday in September.

Flag Tossing, Volterra, Tuscany. Townies in 14th-century get-ups practice the ancient art of juggling silken banners on one of Tuscany's most medieval of piazze. The tourist office (✆ **0588-86-150**) can tell you more. First Sunday of September.

Festa della Rificolona (Candlelit Procession), Florence. Children carry paper lanterns around town, especially up to Piazza Santissima Annunziata. It's a dim memory of the sheerly practical lanterns peasants from the surrounding countryside carried as they filed into town on this night, the eve of the birth of the Virgin, to pay their respects at the church. The farmers usually stuck around the next day to throw a produce market, which is now held the weekend before the event. Contact the tourist office at Via Cavour 1r (✆ **055-290-832**) for details. September 7.

Palio dei Balestrieri (Crossbow Competition), Sansepolcro, Tuscany. Sansepolcro gets the home-turf advantage in part two of the medieval crossbow competition with Umbrian rival Gubbio. Call ✆ **0575-75-827** for details. Second Sunday in September.

Rassegna del Chianti Classico (Wine Festival), Greve in Chianti, Tuscany. Greve's annual wine fair showcases the newest vintages from both the top and the smaller vineyards in the Chianti Classico zone. Call ✆ **055-854-5243** for details. September 12 to 15.

Candlelit Procession, Lucca, Tuscany. In honor of their highly revered Volto Santo statue of Christ, an image blackened with age (they hold that Nicodemus himself, present at the crucifixion, carved it from a Lebanon cedar), the Lucchesi hold a solemn parade through the streets at 8pm. Call ✆ **0583-419-689** or fax 0583-442-505 for details. September 13.

Sagra Musicale Umbra (Festival of Sacred Music), Perugia, Umbria. This over-60-year-old festival of sacred music draws important composers and groups from around the world. Contact the **Associazione**

Sagra Musical Umbra-Perugia, Via Podianai 11 (✆ **075-572-1374;** fax 075-572-7614; www.sagramusicale umbra.com). Second and third weeks of September.

Perugia Classico (Festival of Classical Music), Perugia, Umbria. As the sacred musicians are packing up, the secular ones ride into town to finish off Perugia's music-filled summer with a week of classical and chamber music. Details are available from the **Comitatio Promotore Perugia Classico,** c/o Comune di Perugia, Ripartizione XVI Economia e Lavoro, Via Eburnea 9 (✆ **075-577-2253;** fax 075-572-4252; www. perugiaclassico.it). Last week in September.

International Festival of Choral Singing, Volterra, Tuscany. Saintly music fills the air in this Etruscan city. Contact the tourist office at ✆ and fax **0588-86-150.** Last Saturday of September.

Biennale di Firenze (Fashion Exhibits), Florence. This new biannual (held in even years) fashion exhibit is installed all around town in museums, galleries, and public buildings to juxtapose fashion with art. Prato gets its share as well. Call ✆ **055-234-0742** or fax 055-244-145 for details. Late September to mid-December.

October

Sagra del Tordo (Feast of the Thrush), Montalcino, Tuscany. Montalcini wander around all weekend in medieval costume throwing archery tournaments and parades, mainly for an excuse to roast hundreds of tiny thrushes, whose passing they toast with plenty of Brunello wine. Call ✆ or fax **0577-849-331** for details. Last weekend in October.

White Truffle Fair, Gubbio, Umbria. The world's most expensive form of edible fungus, highly prized by food connoisseurs, is the center-piece of Gubbio's annual agricultural fair. Call ✆ **075-922-0693** for details. October 29 to November 2.

November

Concert and Theater Season Begins, Prato, Tuscany. The season begins at Prato's premiere **Teatro Metastasio.** November through March.

Opera, Concert, and Ballet Seasons Open, Florence. The season at the **Teatro Comunale** (✆ **055-211-158**) and the **Teatro Verdi** (✆ **055-212-320**) runs November through April.

Vino Novello (New Wine) Festivals, various towns. By law, New Wine can't be released before November 4, and several towns have become centers for small street festivals celebrating the coming-out weekend of these light, short-lived red wines. The main event is a weekend of tastings, along with the usual stands lining the streets during any festival (offering everything from traditional candy to underwear). A big dinner night is arranged in the better restaurants in town, where you sample *vini novelli* with your meal. Two of the larger and more easily accessible from Florence are the festival in **Montespertoli** (✆ **0571-609-412** for details), for which you can take a SITA bus, and the festival in **Pontassieve** (✆ **055-83-601** for details), for which you can take a train. First weekend after November 4.

December

World's Largest Christmas Tree, Gubbio, Umbria. According to the *Guinness Book of World Records,* said "tree" is what disfigures the slope of Gubbio's mountain every Christmas in all its illuminated-bulb glory. December 7 to January 10.

Olive Oil and Wine Festival, Pitigliano, Tuscany. You can enjoy heaps of bruschetta garlic toast and gallons of wine. Call ✆ **0564-616-039** for details. December 15.

Live Nativity Procession, Barga (in the Garfagnana north of Lucca), Tuscany. Just before Christmas, a live procession of locals dressed as the Holy Family passes through town, where other inhabitants are costumed as traditional tradespeople. The procession starts sometime after 7pm and arrives at the Duomo around 11pm. For details, call ✆ **0583-723-499.** Usually held December 23.

Display of the Virgin's Girdle, Prato, Tuscany. This is the final and most sumptuous of the five yearly occasions on which the bishop releases Mary's Sacred Girdle—the belt she handed to Thomas upon her Assumption—from its jewel-encrusted treasure chest and shows it to the people massed inside the Duomo and crowding the piazza outside. Plenty of Renaissance-styled drummers and fifers are in attendance. The pomp is repeated at Easter, May 1, August 15, and September 8. Call ✆ or fax **0574-24-112** for details. December 25.

Umbria Jazz Winter, Orvieto, Umbria. Wine tasting and internationally renowned jazz artists come to Orvieto for part two of Umbria's premier jazz festival. Call ✆ **075-572-1653** or check www.umbria jazz.com for details. December 27 to January 1.

6 Travel Insurance

Check your existing insurance policies and credit-card coverage before you buy travel insurance. You may already be covered for lost luggage, cancelled tickets or medical expenses. The cost of travel insurance varies widely, depending on the cost and length of your trip, your age, health, and the type of trip you're taking.

TRIP-CANCELLATION INSURANCE Trip-cancellation insurance helps you get your money back if you have to back out of a trip, if you have to go home early, or if your travel supplier goes bankrupt. Allowed reasons for cancellation can range from sickness to natural disasters to the State Department declaring your destination unsafe for travel. (Insurers usually won't cover vague fears, though, as many travelers discovered who tried to cancel their trips in Oct 2001 because they were wary of flying.) In this unstable world, trip-cancellation insurance is a good buy if you're getting tickets well in advance—who knows what the state of the world, or of your airline, will be in 9 months? Insurance policy details vary, so read the fine print—and especially make sure that your airline or cruise line is on the list of carriers covered in case of bankruptcy. For information, contact one of the following insurers: **Access America** (© 800/807-3982; www. accessamerica.com); **Travel Guard International** (© 800/826-4919; www.travelguard.com); **Travel Insured International** (© 800/243-3174; www.travelinsured.com); and **Travelex Insurance Services** (© 888/457-4602; www.travelex-insurance.com).

MEDICAL INSURANCE Most health insurance policies cover you if you get sick away from home—but check, particularly if you're insured by an HMO.

With the exception of certain HMOs and Medicare/Medicaid, your medical insurance should cover medical treatment—even hospital care—overseas. However, most out-of-country hospitals make you pay your bills up front, and send you a refund after you've returned home and filed the necessary paperwork. And in a worst-case scenario, there's the high cost of emergency evacuation. If you require additional medical insurance, try **MEDEX International** (© 800/527-0218 or 410/453-6300; www.medexassist.com) or **Travel Assistance International** (© **800/821-2828;** www.travelassistance.com; for general information on services, call the company's Worldwide Assistance Services, Inc., at © **800/777-8710**).

Again, most health insurance plans covering out-of-country illnesses and hospital stays require you to pay your local bills up front (your coverage takes the form of a refund after you've returned and filed the paperwork). However, **Blue Cross/Blue Shield members** (© 800/810-BLUE or www.bluecares.com for a list of participating hospitals) can now use their plans and cards at select hospitals abroad as they would at home, which means much lower out-of-pocket costs. In Florence, the card is honored at the **Villa Donatello,** Piazza Donatello 14 (© **055-323-3373**); in Pisa at **Casa di Cura San Rossore,** Viale delle Cascine 152f (© **050-586-111**); and in Siena at **Casa de Cura Rugani** at Piazza Matteotti 45 (© **0577-261-611**).

LOST-LUGGAGE INSURANCE On international flights (including U.S. portions of international trips), checked baggage is automatically covered at approximately $9.07 per pound, up to approximately $635 per checked bag. If you plan to check items more valuable than the standard liability, see if your valuables are covered by your homeowner's policy, get baggage insurance as part of your comprehensive travel-insurance package or buy Travel Guard's "BagTrak" product. Don't buy insurance at the airport, as it's usually overpriced. Be sure to take any valuables or irreplaceable items with you in your carry-on luggage, as many valuables (including books, money and electronics) aren't covered by airline policies.

If your luggage is lost, immediately file a lost-luggage claim at the airport, detailing the luggage contents. For most airlines, you must report delayed, damaged, or lost baggage within 4 hours of arrival. The airlines are required to deliver luggage, once found, directly to your house or destination free of charge.

7 Health & Safety

STAYING HEALTHY

There are no special health risks you'll encounter in Italy. The tap water is safe, and medical resources are of a high quality. In fact, with Italy's partially socialized medicine, you can usual stop by any hospital emergency room with an ailment, get swift and courteous service, given a diagnosis and a prescription, and sent on your way with a wave and a smile—and not even a sheet of paperwork to fill out.

BEFORE YOU GO

In most cases, your existing health plan will provide the coverage you need. But double-check; you may want to buy **travel medical insurance** instead. (See the section on insurance, above.) Bring your insurance ID card with you when you travel.

If you suffer from a chronic illness, consult your doctor before your departure. For conditions like epilepsy, diabetes, or heart problems, wear a **Medic Alert Identification Tag** (© 800/825-3785; www.medicalert.org), which will immediately alert doctors to your condition and give them access to your records through Medic Alert's 24-hour hot line.

Pack **prescription medications** in your carry-on luggage, and carry prescription medications in their original containers, with pharmacy labels—otherwise they won't make it through airport security. Also bring along copies of your prescriptions in case you lose your pills or run out. Don't forget an extra pair of contact lenses or prescription glasses. Again, carry the generic name of prescription medicines, in case a local pharmacist is unfamiliar with the brand name.

Contact the **International Association for Medical Assistance to Travelers** (**IAMAT;** © 716/754-4883 or 416/652-0137; www.iamat.org) for tips on travel and health concerns in the countries you're visiting, and lists of local, English-speaking doctors. In **Canada,** contact them at 40 Regal Road, Guelph, Ont., N1K 1B5 (© **519/836-0102;** fax 519/836-3412); and in **New Zealand** at P.O. Box 5049, Christchurch 5 (fax 643/352-4630).

The United States **Centers for Disease Control and Prevention** (© 800/311-3435; www.cdc.gov) provides up-to-date information on necessary vaccines and health hazards by region or country. Any foreign consulate can provide a list of area doctors who speak English. If you get sick, consider asking your hotel concierge to recommend a local doctor—even his or her own. You can also try the emergency room at a local hospital; many have walk-in clinics for emergency cases that are not life threatening. You may not get immediate attention, but you won't pay the high price of an emergency room visit.

STAYING SAFE

Italy is a remarkably safe country. The worst threats you'll likely face are the pickpockets that sometimes frequent touristy areas and public buses; just keep your valuables in an under-the-clothes money belt and you should be fine. There are, of course, thieves in Italy as there are everywhere, so be smart; don't leave anything in your rental car overnight, and leave nothing visible in it at any time to avoid the temptation to a passing would-be thief.

8 Specialized Travel Resources

FOR TRAVELERS WITH DISABILITIES

Italy certainly doesn't win any medals for being overly accessible, though a few of the top museums and churches are beginning at least to install ramps at the entrances, and a few hotels are converting first-floor rooms into accessible units by widening the doors and baths.

Other than that, don't expect to find much of Tuscany and Umbria easy to tackle. Builders in the Middle Ages and the Renaissance didn't have wheelchairs or mobility impairments in mind when they built narrow doorways and spiral staircases, and preservation laws keep modern Italians from being able to do much about this. Buses and trains can cause problems as well, with high, narrow doors and steep steps at entrances. There are, however, seats reserved on public transportation for travelers with disabilities.

Luckily, there's an endless list of organizations to help you plan your trip and offer specific advice before you go. Many travel agencies offer customized tours and itineraries for travelers with disabilities. **Flying Wheels Travel** (© 507/451-5005; www.flyingwheelstravel.com) offers escorted tours and cruises that emphasize sports and private tours in minivans with lifts. **Accessible Journeys** (© 800/846-4537 or 610/521-0339; www.disabilitytravel.com) caters specifically to slow walkers and wheelchair travelers and their families and friends.

Organizations that offer assistance to disabled travelers include the **MossRehab Hospital** (www.mossresourcenet.org), which provides a library of accessible-travel resources online; the **Society for Accessible Travel and Hospitality** (© 212/447-7284; www.sath.org; annual membership fees $45 adults, $30 seniors and students), which offers a wealth of travel resources for all types of disabilities and informed recommendations on destinations, access guides, travel agents, tour operators, vehicle rentals, and companion services; and the **American Foundation for the Blind** (© 800/232-5463; www.afb.org), which provides information on traveling with Seeing Eye dogs.

For more information specifically targeted to travelers with disabilities, the community website **iCan** (www.icanonline.net/channels/travel/index.cfm) has destination guides and several regular columns on accessible travel. Also, check out the quarterly magazine *Emerging Horizons* ($15 per year, $20 outside the U.S.; www.emerginghorizons.com); **Twin Peaks Press** (© 360/694-2462; http://disabilitybookshop.virtualave.net/blist84.htm), offering travel-related books for travelers with special needs; and *Open World Magazine,* published by the Society for Accessible Travel and Hospitality (see above; subscription: $18 per year, $35 outside the U.S.).

FOR GAY & LESBIAN TRAVELERS

Italy isn't the most tolerant country regarding same-sex couples, but it has grown to accept homosexuality, especially over the past few decades. Homosexuality is legal, and the age of consent is 16. Luckily, Italians are already more affectionate and physical than Americans in their general friendships, and even straight men regularly walk down the street with their arms around each other—however, kissing anywhere other than on the cheeks at greetings and goodbyes will certainly draw attention. As you might expect, smaller towns tend to be less permissive and accepting than cities. Florence has the largest and most visible homosexual population (not that that's saying much), though university cities like Pisa also take gayness in stride. Elba's beaches are Tuscany's big gay vacation destination.

Italy's national association and support network for gays and lesbians is **ARCI-Gay/ARCI-Lesbica.** The national website is www.arcigay.it, but they've recently launched a Tuscany-specific one at www.gaytoscana.it, and the new head regional office is in **Siena** at Via Massetana Romana 18, 53100 Siena (℃ 0577-288-977; fax 0577-271-538; www.gaysiena.it). There are other offices in **Pisa** (Arcigay Pride!; Via San Lorenzo 38; ℃ 050-555-618; fax 050-831-0605; www.gay.it/pride), in **Pistoia** (no address yet; cellphone contact 333-667-6873; www.gay pistoia.it), and **Grosseto** (Via Ravel 7; ℃ 339-440-9049 or 347-078-8972; www.grossetogay.it). Their cousin association in Florence is called Ireos (www.ireos.org), in the Oltrarno at Via dei Serragli 3, 50124 Firenze (℃ and fax 055-216-907).

The International Gay & Lesbian Travel Association (IGLTA; ℃ **800/ 448-8550** or 954-776-2626; www.iglta.org) is the trade association for the gay and lesbian travel industry, and offers an online directory of gay and lesbian-friendly travel businesses; go to the website and click on "Members."

Many agencies offer tours and travel itineraries specifically for gay and lesbian travelers. **Above and Beyond Tours** (℃ **800/397-2681;** www.above beyondtours.com) is the exclusive gay and lesbian tour operator for United Airlines. **Now, Voyager** (℃ **800/255-6951;** www.nowvoyager.com) is a well-known San Francisco–based gay-owned and operated travel service.

The following travel guides are available at most travel bookstores and gay and lesbian bookstores, or you can order them from **Giovanni's Room** bookstore, 1145 Pine St., Philadelphia, PA 19107 (℃ **215/923-2960;** www.giovannisroom.com): *Frommer's Gay & Lesbian Europe*, an excellent travel resource; *Out and About* (℃ **800/929-2268** or 415/644-8044; www.outand about.com), which offers guidebooks

and a newsletter 10 times a year packed with solid information on the global gay and lesbian scene; *Spartacus International Gay Guide* and *Odysseus,* both good, annual English-language guidebooks focused on gay men; and the *Damron* guides, with separate, annual books for gay men and lesbians.

FOR SENIORS

Italy is a multigenerational culture that doesn't tend to marginalize its seniors, and older people are treated with a great deal of respect and deference throughout Italy. But there are few specific programs, associations, or concessions made for them. The one exception is on admission prices for museums and sights, where those over 60 or 65 will often get in at a reduced rate or even free. There are also special train passes and reductions on bus tickets and the like in various towns (see "Getting Around," later in this chapter). As a senior in Italy, you're *un anciano* (*una anciana* if you're a woman) or "ancient one"—consider it a term of respect and let people know you're one if you think a discount may be in the works.

Members of **AARP,** 601 E St. NW, Washington, DC 20049 (℃ **800/424-3410** or 202/434-2277; www.aarp.org), get discounts on hotels, airfares, and car rentals. AARP offers members a wide range of benefits, including *AARP The Magazine* and a monthly newsletter. Anyone over 50 can join.

Sadly, most major **airlines** have in recent years cancelled their discount programs for seniors, but you can always ask when booking. Of the big **car-rental** agencies, only National currently gives an AARP discount, but the many rental dealers that specialize in Europe—Auto Europe, Kemwel, Europe-by-Car—offer seniors 5% off their already low rates. In most European cities, people over 60 or 65 get reduced admission at theaters, museums, and other attractions, and they

Tips **A Note for Families & Seniors**

At most state-run museums, children under 18 and seniors get in free *but only if* they hail from one of the countries that has signed a reciprocal international cultural agreement to allow children and seniors this privilege. These countries include England, Canada, Ireland, Australia, New Zealand, and indeed much of the world—but *not* the United States. (However, many museum guards either don't ask for citizenship ID or wave kids and seniors on through anyway.) Children and seniors, no matter what their nationality, also get discounts on trains (see "Getting Around," later in this chapter).

can often get discount fares or cards on public transportation and national rail systems. Carrying ID with proof of age can pay off in all these situations.

Grand Circle Travel, 347 Congress St., Boston, MA 02210 (© **800/959-0405** or 800/321-2835; www.gct.com), is one of the literally hundreds of travel agencies specializing in vacations for seniors. But beware: Many packages are of the tour-bus variety. Seniors seeking more independent travel should probably consult a regular travel agent. **SAGA Holidays,** 1161 Boylston St., Boston, MA 02115 (© **800/343-0273;** www.sagaholidays.com), has 40 years of experience running all-inclusive tours and cruises for those 50 and older. They also sponsor the more substantial "Road Scholar Tours" (© **800/621-2151**), fun-loving tours with an educational bent.

Many reliable agencies and organizations target the 50-plus market. **Elderhostel** (© **877/426-8056;** www.elderhostel.org) arranges study programs for those aged 55 and over (and a spouse or companion of any age) in the U.S. and in more than 80 countries around the world. Most courses last 5 to 7 days in the U.S. or 2 to 4 weeks abroad, and many include airfare, accommodations in university dormitories or modest inns, meals, and tuition. **ElderTreks** (© **800/741-7956;** www.eldertreks.com) offers small-group tours to off-the-beaten-path or adventure-travel locations, restricted to travelers 50 and older.

FOR FAMILIES

If you have enough trouble getting your kids out of the house in the morning, dragging them thousands of miles away may seem like an insurmountable challenge. But family travel can be immensely rewarding, giving you new ways of seeing the world through smaller pairs of eyes. As an added plus, little helps mature the kids faster than international travel.

Familyhostel (© **800/733-9753;** www.learn.unh.edu/familyhostel) takes the whole family, including kids ages 8 to 15, on moderately priced domestic and international learning vacations. Lectures, field trips, and sightseeing are guided by a team of academics.

You can find good family-oriented vacation advice on the Internet from sites like the **Family Travel Network** (www.familytravelnetwork.com); **Traveling Internationally with Your Kids** (www.travelwithyourkids.com), a comprehensive site offering sound advice for long-distance and international travel with children; and **Family Travel Files** (www.thefamilytravelfiles.com), which offers an online magazine and a directory of off-the-beaten-path tours and tour operators for families.

How to Take Great Trips with Your Kids (The Harvard Common Press) is full of good general advice that can apply to travel anywhere.

FOR WOMEN

Women will feel remarkably welcome Italy—sometimes a bit too welcome, actually. Yes, it sometimes seems every young Italian male is out to prove himself the most irresistible lover on the planet; remember, this is the land of Romeo and Casanova, so they have a lot to live up to.

From parading and preening like peacocks to wooing each passing female with words, whistles, and, if they can get close enough, the entirely inappropriate butt-pinch, these men and their attentiveness can range from charming and flattering to downright annoying and frustrating. The more exotic you look—statuesque blondes, ebony-skinned beauties, or simply an American accent—the more irresistible you become to these suitors. And, as everyone around the world knows from watching Hollywood movies, American women are all uninhibited and passionate sex kittens. That this isn't actually true doesn't make much of a dent in Italian boys' fantasies.

Flirting back at these would-be Romeos, even mildly, only convinces them that you're ready to jump into bed. Heck, mere eye contact encourages them to redouble their efforts. Unless you want all this attention, take your cue from Italian women, who may wear tight skirts and fishnets but, you'll notice, usually ignore the men around them entirely unless it's someone they're already walking with.

If you find yourself moderately molested on a bus or other crowded place—mostly the infamous bottom-pinching and rather inappropriate rubbing—tell him to "*Smetti la!*" (stop it) and proceed to pinch, scratch, elbow, and so on to further discourage him or enlist the aid of the nearest convenient elderly Italian woman to noisily chastise the offender and perhaps whap him with her purse.

Note that much of the attention is kept to verbal flirtation and that occasional inappropriate touching that deserves a slap in the face. These men

want to conquer you with their charm, not their muscles; rape is near unheard-of in Italy. Most women report feeling far safer wandering the deserted streets of an Italian city back to their hotels at 2am than they do in their own neighborhoods back home, and that feeling is largely justified. You'll probably get tons of ride offers, though, from would-be chivalrous knights atop their Vespa or Fiat steeds.

Women Welcome Women World Wide (5W; ☎ 203/259-7832 in the U.S.; www.womenwelcomewomen. org.uk) works to foster international friendships by enabling women of different countries to visit one another (men can come along on the trips; they just can't join the club). It's a big, active organization, with more than 3,500 members from all walks of life in some 70 countries.

Check out the website **Journeywoman** (www.journeywoman.com), a lively travel resource, with "GirlTalk Guides" to destinations like New York, Hong Kong, and Toronto and a free e-mail newsletter; or the travel guide *Safety and Security for Women Who Travel,* by Sheila Swan Laufer and Peter Laufer (Travelers' Tales, Inc.), offering commonsense advice and tips on safe travel.

FOR STUDENTS

You'd be wise to arm yourself with an **International Student Identity Card (ISIC),** which offers substantial savings on rail passes, plane tickets, and entrance fees; your own school's ID will often suffice to snag you those discount admission at sights and museums across Europe, but the ISIC helps. It also provides you with basic health and life insurance and a 24-hour help line. The card is available for $22 from **STA Travel** (☎ 800/781-4040, and if you're not in North America there's probably a local number in your country; www.statravel.com), the biggest student travel agency in the world.

If you're no longer a student but are still under 26, you can get a **International Youth Travel Card (IYTC)** for the same price from the same people, which entitles you to some discounts (but not on museum admissions). (**Note:** STA Travel bought competitors **Council Travel** and **USIT Campus** after they went bankrupt. It's still operating some offices under the Council name, but they're owned by STA.)

Travel CUTS (© **800/667-2887** or 416/614-2887; www.travelcuts.com) offers similar services for both Canadians and U.S. residents. Irish students should turn to **USIT** (© **01/602-1600;** www.usitnow.ie).

The Hanging Out Guides (www.frommers.com/hangingout), published by Frommer's, is the top student travel series, covering everything from adrenaline sports to the hottest club and music scenes. And, as luck would have it, there's an Italy edition out now.

If you enjoy meeting other travelers on the road—and want to save money—consider staying in **hostels.** There are hostels scattered throughout Tuscany and Umbria, and some are quite nice, but they're usually on the outskirts of town. They charge around $10 to $25 per night for what's generally a bunk in a dormlike room (often sex-segregated) sleeping from 4 to 50 or more. There are lockers for your bags, and you often must bring your own sleep-sack (basically a sheet folded in half and sewn up the side) or buy one on-site. For many, you'll need a Hostelling International membership card; at some, the card is required for you to stay there, at others it'll get you a discount, and at some hostels the card doesn't matter at all. Membership in **Hostelling International/ American Youth Hostels** (**HI-AYH;** © **301/495-1240;** www.hiayh.org), an affiliate of the International Youth Hostel Federation (IYH), is free for those under 18, costs $28 per year for people 18 to 54, and $18 for those 55 and older. Also check out the independently run website **www.hostels. com**. At most hostels, there's usually a lockout from morning to mid-afternoon and a curfew of around 10pm to 1am.

9 Planning Your Trip Online

SURFING FOR AIRFARES

The "big three" online travel agencies, **Expedia.com, Travelocity.com,** and **Orbitz.com** sell most of the air tickets bought on the Internet. (Canadian travelers should try Expedia.ca and Travelocity.ca; U.K. residents can go for Expedia.co.uk and Opodo.co.uk.) Each has different business deals with the airlines and may offer different fares on the same flights, so it's wise to shop around. Expedia and Travelocity will also send you **e-mail notification** when a cheap fare becomes available to your favorite destination. Of the smaller travel agency websites, **Side-Step** (www.sidestep.com) has gotten the best reviews from Frommer's authors. It's a browser add-on (you have to download it) that "searches 140 sites at once," saving you the trouble of doing so independently, but it only works on PCs.

Also remember to check **airline websites,** especially those for low-fare carriers in Europe such as EasyJet (www.easyjet.com) and Ryanair (www.ryanair.com), whose fares are often misreported or simply missing from travel agency websites. Even with major airlines, you can often shave a few bucks from a fare by booking directly through the airline and avoiding a travel agency's transaction fee. But you'll get these discounts only by **booking online:** Most airlines now offer online-only fares that even their phone agents know nothing about. For the websites of airlines that fly to and from your destination, go to "Getting There," later in this chapter.

Great **last-minute deals** are available through free weekly e-mail services provided directly by the airlines. Most of these are announced on Tuesday or Wednesday and must be purchased online. Most are only valid for travel that weekend, but some can be booked weeks or months in advance. Sign up for weekly e-mail alerts at airline websites or check mega-sites that compile comprehensive lists of last-minute specials, such as **Smarter Living** (www.smarterliving.com). For last-minute trips, **site59.com** in the U.S. and **last minute.com** in Europe often have better deals than the major-label sites.

If you're willing to give up some control over your flight details, use an **opaque fare service** like **Priceline** (www.priceline.com; www.priceline.co.uk for Europeans) or **Hotwire** (www.hotwire.com). Both offer rock-bottom prices in exchange for travel on a "mystery airline" at a mysterious time of day, often with a mysterious change of planes en route. The mystery airlines are all major, well-known carriers and the airlines' routing computers have gotten a lot better than they used to be. But your chances of getting a 6am or 11pm flight are pretty high. Hotwire tells you flight prices before you buy; Priceline usually has better deals than Hotwire, but you have to play their "name our price" game. If you're new at this, the helpful folks at **BiddingFor Travel** (www.biddingfortravel.com) do a good job of demystifying Priceline's prices. Priceline and Hotwire are great for flights within North America and between the U.S. and Europe. But for flights to other parts of the world, consolidators will almost always beat their fares.

For much more about airfares and savvy air-travel tips and advice, pick up a copy of *Frommer's Fly Safe, Fly Smart*.

SURFING FOR HOTELS

Shopping online for hotels is much easier in the U.S., Canada, and certain parts of Europe than it is in the rest of the world. If you try to book a Chinese hotel online, for instance, you'll probably overpay, but in Italy, the system is as svelte as is it in the U.S. However, note that most smaller hotels and B&Bs (especially outside the U.S.) don't show up on these booking engine websites at all—a shame since, by and large, those smaller places tend to be the most charming and least expensive.

Of the "big three" sites, **Expedia** may be the best choice, thanks to its long list of special deals. **Travelocity** runs a close second. Hotel specialist sites **hotels.com** and **hoteldiscounts.com** are also reliable. An excellent free program, **TravelAxe** (www.travelaxe.net), can help you search multiple hotel sites at once, even ones you may never have heard of.

Priceline and Hotwire are even better for hotels than for airfares; with both, you're allowed to pick the neighborhood and quality level of your hotel before offering up your money. Priceline's hotel product even covers Europe and Asia, though it's much better at getting luxury lodging for mid-level prices than at finding anything at the bottom of the scale. *Note:* Hotwire overrates its hotels by one star—what Hotwire calls a four-star is a three-star anywhere else.

In Italy, two long-established hotel booking engines—with far more choices than the big international ones listed above—are **www.venere.com** and **www.itwg.com**.

SURFING FOR RENTAL CARS

For booking rental cars online, the best deals are usually found at rental-car company websites, although all the major online travel agencies also offer rental-car reservations services. Priceline and Hotwire work well for rental cars, too; the only "mystery" is which

Frommers.com: The Complete Travel Resource

For an excellent travel-planning resource, we highly recommend Frommers.com (www.frommers.com). We're a little biased, of course, but we guarantee that you'll find the travel tips, reviews, monthly vacation giveaways, and online-booking capabilities indispensable. Among the special features are our popular **Message Boards,** where Frommer's readers post queries and share advice (sometimes we authors even show up to answer questions); **Frommers.com Newsletter,** for the latest travel bargains and insider travel secrets; and **Frommer's Destinations Section,** where you'll get expert travel tips, hotel and dining recommendations, and advice on the sights to see for more than 3,000 destinations around the globe. When your research is done, the **Online Reservations System** (www.frommers.com/book_a_trip) takes you to Frommer's preferred online partners for booking your vacation at affordable prices.

major rental company you get, and for most travelers the difference between Hertz, Avis, and Budget is negligible.

The best prices on rentals in Europe are found at **Auto Europe** (www.auto europe.com), which acts as a sort of consolidator for rentals—you actually pick up your car at, say, the Avis or Hertz office in the destination, but you pay a rate below what those rental agencies charge the public. This company will also work out long-term leases for periods longer than 17 days; it saves you lots over a rental, plus you get a brand-new car and *full* insurance coverage), as with **Europe By Car** (www.europebycar.com).

10 The 21st-Century Traveler

INTERNET ACCESS AWAY FROM HOME

Travelers have any number of ways to check their e-mail and access the Internet on the road. Of course, using your own laptop—or even a PDA or electronic organizer with a modem—gives you the most flexibility. But even if you don't have a computer, you can still access your e-mail and even your office computer from cybercafes.

WITHOUT YOUR OWN COMPUTER

It's hard nowadays to find a city that *doesn't* have a few cybercafes. Although there's no definitive directory for cybercafes—these are independent businesses, after all—three places to start looking are at **www.cybercaptive.com,** www.netcafeguide.com, and **www. cybercafe.com**.

Aside from formal cybercafes, most **public libraries** across the world offer Internet access free or for a small charge. **Hotels** that cater to business travelers often have **in-room dataports** and **business centers,** but the charges can be exorbitant. Also, most **youth hostels** nowadays have at least one computer where you can access the Internet.

Most major airports now have **Internet kiosks** scattered throughout their gates. These kiosks, which you'll also see in shopping malls, hotel lobbies, and tourist information offices around the world, give you basic web access for a per-minute fee that's usually higher than cybercafe prices. The kiosks' clunkiness and high price means they should be avoided whenever possible.

To retrieve your e-mail, ask your **Internet Service Provider (ISP)** if it has a Web-based interface tied to your existing e-mail account. If your ISP doesn't have such an interface, you can use the free **mail2web** service (www.mail2web.com) to view and reply to your home e-mail. For more flexibility, you may want to open a free, Web-based e-mail account with **Yahoo! Mail** (mail.yahoo.com) or **Fastmail** (www.fastmail.fm). (Microsoft's Hotmail is another popular option, but Hotmail has severe spam problems.) Your home ISP may be able to forward your e-mail to the Web-based account automatically.

If you need to access files on your office computer, look into a service called **GoToMyPC** (www.gotomypc.com). The service provides a Web-based interface for you to access and manipulate a distant PC from anywhere—even a cybercafe—provided your "target" PC is on and has an always-on connection to the Internet (such as with a cable modem or DSL). The service offers top-quality security, but if you're worried about hackers, use your own laptop rather than a cybercafe to access the GoToMyPC system.

WITH YOUR OWN COMPUTER

Major ISPs have **local access numbers** around the world, allowing you to go online by simply placing a local call. Check your ISP's website or call its toll-free number and ask how you can use your current account away from home, and how much it will cost (hint: a scandalous amount).

If you're traveling outside the reach of your ISP, the **iPass** network has dial-up numbers in most of the world's countries. You'll have to sign up with an iPass provider, who will then tell you how to set up your computer for your destination(s). For a list of iPass providers, go to www.ipass.com and click on "Individuals." One solid provider is **i2roam** (© **866/811-6209** or 920/235-0475; www.i2roam.com).

Wherever you go, bring a **connection kit** of the right power and phone adapters (Italian phone jacks are often three thick round poles, though they're slowly switching over to the familiar little plastic box with a click-down tab we use in the States), a spare phone cord, and a spare Ethernet network cable. You can get the phone jack adaptor, plus things like line testers (useful to see if you've got a useable signal) and polarity reversers (try this when the tester reports no signal, as often the problem is that the wires are merely reversed inside the system) from **Magellan's** catalog (www.magellans.com).

Most business-class hotels throughout the world offer dataports for laptop modems, and a few thousand hotels in the U.S. and Europe now offer high-speed Internet access using an Ethernet network cable. You'll have to bring your own cables either way, so **call your hotel in advance** to find out what the options are.

If you have an 802.11b/**Wi-fi** card for your computer, several commercial companies have made wireless service available in airports, hotel lobbies and coffee shops, though primarily still in the U.S. Community-minded individuals have also set up free wireless networks in major cities around the U.S., Europe, and Australia. These networks are spotty, but you get what you (don't) pay for. Each network has a home page explaining how to set up your computer for their particular system; start your explorations at www.personaltelco.net/index.cgi/WirelessCommunities.

USING A CELLPHONE

The three letters that define much of the world's **wireless capabilities** are GSM (Global System for Mobiles), a big, seamless network that makes for easy cross-border cellphone use

Online Traveler's Toolbox

Veteran travelers usually carry some essential items to make their trips easier. Following is a selection of online tools to bookmark and use.

- **Visa ATM Locator** (www.visa.com), for locations of PLUS ATMs worldwide, or **MasterCard ATM Locator** (www.mastercard.com), for locations of Cirrus ATMs worldwide.
- **Foreign Languages for Travelers** (www.travlang.com). Learn basic terms in more than 70 languages and click on any underlined phrase to hear what it sounds like.
- **Intellicast** (www.intellicast.com) and **Weather.com** (www.weather.com). Gives weather forecasts for all 50 states and for cities around the world.
- **Mapquest** (www.mapquest.com). This best of the mapping sites lets you choose a specific address or destination, and in seconds, it will return a map and detailed directions.
- **Travel Warnings** (http://travel.state.gov/travel_warnings.html; www.fco.gov.uk/travel; www.voyage.gc.ca; www.dfat.gov.au/consular/advice). These sites report on places where health concerns or unrest might threaten American, British, Canadian, and Australian travelers. Generally, U.S. warnings are the most paranoid; Australian warnings are the most relaxed.

throughout Europe and dozens of other countries worldwide. In the U.S., T-Mobile, AT&T Wireless, and Cingular use this quasi-universal system; in Canada, Microcell and some Rogers customers are GSM, and all Europeans and most Australians use GSM.

If your cellphone is on a GSM system, and you have a world-capable phone—dual- or tri-band—such as many (but not all) Sony Ericsson, Motorola, or Samsung models, you can make and receive calls across civilized areas on much of the globe, from Andorra to Uganda. Just call your wireless operator and ask for "international roaming" to be activated on your account. Unfortunately, per-minute charges can be high—usually $1 to $1.50 in Western Europe and up to $5 in places like Russia and Indonesia.

World-phone owners can bring down their per-minute charges with a bit of trickery. Call your cellular operator and say you'll be going abroad for several months and want to "unlock" your phone to use it with a local provider. Usually, they'll oblige. Then, in your destination country, pick up a cheap, prepaid phone chip at a mobile phone store and slip it into your phone. (Show your phone to the salesperson, as not all phones work on all networks.) You'll get a local phone number in your destination country—and much, much lower calling rates.

Otherwise, **renting** a phone is a good idea. (Even worldphone owners will have to rent new phones if they're traveling to non-GSM regions, such as Japan or Korea.) While you can rent a phone from any number of overseas sites, including kiosks at airports and at car-rental agencies, we suggest renting the phone before you leave home. That way you can give loved ones your new number, make sure the phone works, and take the phone wherever you go—especially helpful when you rent overseas, where phone-rental agencies bill in local currency and may not let you take the phone to another country.

Phone rental isn't cheap. You'll usually pay $40 to $50 per week, plus airtime fees of at least a dollar a minute. If you're traveling to Europe, though, local rental companies often offer free incoming calls within their home country, which can save you big bucks. The bottom line: Shop around.

Two good wireless rental companies are **InTouch USA** (© 800/872-7626; www.intouchglobal.com) and **Road-Post** (© 888/290-1606 or 905/272-5665; www.roadpost.com). Give them your itinerary, and they'll tell you what wireless products you need. InTouch will also, for free, advise you on whether your existing phone will work overseas; simply call © 703/ 222-7161 between 9am and 4pm EST, or go to http://intouchglobal.com/travel.htm. You can also usually lease a cellphone from **major car rental firms;** as with the best rates on the cars themselves, the prices at consolidator Auto Europe (www.autoeurope.com) tend to be better than those at the major firms like Hertz or Avis.

For trips of more than a few weeks spent in one country, **buying a phone** becomes economically attractive, as many nations have cheap, no-questions-asked prepaid phone systems. Stop by a local cellphone shop and get the cheapest package; you'll probably pay less than $100 for a phone and a starter calling card. Local calls may be as low as 10 cents per minute, and in many countries incoming calls are free.

11 Getting There

BY PLANE
FROM NORTH AMERICA
No carrier flies directly from the United States or Canada to any airport in Tuscany; however, with most airlines (and their affiliates) you can connect through a handful of European cities to the small international airports at Pisa or Florence. You may find it most convenient simply to fly to Rome and connect to Florence by plane (a bit over 1 hr.) or by train (close to 3 hr.).

THE MAJOR AIRLINES Italy's national airline, **Alitalia** (© 800/223-5730; www.alitalia.it), offers more flights daily to Italy than any other airline. It flies direct to both Rome and Milan from New York, Newark, Boston, Chicago, Los Angeles, and Miami. You can connect in Rome or Milan to any other Italian destination, including Pisa or Florence. If you're flying from the New York City area and planning to connect directly to Florence, note that itineraries that route you through Milan often have a layover that's 3 hours shorter than one that routes you through Rome's airport.

British Airways (© 800/247-9297; www.ba.com) flies direct from dozens of U.S. and Canadian cities to London, where you can get connecting flights to Pisa, Rome, or Milan. **Air Canada** (© 888/247-2262 or 800/361-8071 [TTY]; www.aircanada.ca) flies daily from Toronto and Vancouver to Rome. **Continental** (© 800/231-0856; www.continental.com) doesn't fly to Italy itself, but it's partnered with Alitalia for the Newark-to-Rome and New York JFK-to-Milan flights, so if you're a Continental Frequent Flyer you can reserve through Continental and rack up the miles.

Delta (© 800/241-4141; www.delta.com) flies daily out of New York JFK (you can connect from most major U.S. cities) to Rome and Milan, where it's possible to change to one of Delta's local partner airlines (Lufthansa, Iberia, and so on) for the last leg to Tuscany. From either city you can take a train to Tuscany, or from Rome you can connect to an Alitalia flight to Florence or Pisa.

Possibly less convenient alternatives are **American Airlines** (𝄢 **800/433-7300;** www.aa.com), whose flights from the United States to Milan all go through Chicago; **United** (𝄢 **800/528-2929;** www.ual.com), which flies once daily to Milan out of New York, Newark, and Washington, D.C. Dulles; or **US Airways** (𝄢 **800/622-1015;** www.usairways.com), which offers one flight daily to Rome out of Philadelphia. (You can connect through Philly from most major U.S. cities.)

FROM GREAT BRITAIN & IRELAND

British Airways (𝄢 **0845/773-3377;** www.ba.com) flies twice daily from London's Gatwick to Pisa. **Alitalia** (**020/8745-8200;** www.alitalia.it) has four daily flights from London to both Rome and Milan and three daily from London Gatwick into Florence. **KLM UK** (formerly Air UK; 𝄢 **08705/074-074;** www.klmuk.com) flies several times per week from London Heathrow to Milan (both airports) and Rome. In each case, there's a layover in Amsterdam. No-frills upstart **Ryanair** (𝄢 **0871/246-0000** in the U.K.; www.ryanair.com) will fly you from London to Pisa (as well as Rome, Milan, Bologna, Ancona, and other Italian destinations); its competitor EasyJet (www.easyjet.com) flies from London to Milan and Bologna. Both usually charge less than £25 each way for such service.

The best and cheapest way to get to Italy from Ireland is to make your way first to London and fly from there to Rome or direct to Pisa (see above; to book through **British Airways** in Ireland, dial 𝄢 **800/626-747**). **Aer Lingus** (𝄢 **0818/365-000** in Ireland; www.aerlingus.com) flies direct from Dublin to both Rome and Milan about 5 days a week. **Alitalia** (𝄢 **01/677-5171**) puts you on a British Midland to get you to London, where you change to an Alitalia plane for the trip to Rome. For **RyanAir,** call 𝄢 **0818/303-030** in Ireland.

FROM AUSTRALIA & NEW ZEALAND

Alitalia (𝄢 **02-9922-1555;** www.alitalia.it) has a flight from Sydney to Rome every Thursday and Saturday. **Qantas** (𝄢 **13-13-13** in Australia or 0649/357-8900 in Auckland, NZ; www.qantas.com) flies three times daily to Rome via Bangkok, leaving Australia from Sydney, Melbourne, Brisbane, or Cairns. Qantas will also book you through one of these Australian cities from Auckland, Wellington, or Christchurch in New Zealand. You can also look into flying first into London and connecting to Italy from there. (There are more flights, and it may work out to be cheaper.)

GETTING TO TUSCANY OR UMBRIA FROM ROME'S AIRPORTS

Most international flights to Rome will arrive at **Fiumicino Airport** (officially named **Leonardo da Vinci International Airport,** but few, including the airlines themselves, call it that). Some inter-European and transatlantic charter flights may land at the less convenient **Ciampino Airport.** You can connect to a plane at either to take you to Pisa's or Florence's airport, but it's often simpler, almost as fast in the long run, and cheaper to take the train.

Fiumicino (𝄢 **06-659-51;** www.adr.it) is 30km (19 miles) from Rome's center. You can take the **express train** (8.80€/$10) from Fiumicino to Rome's central train station, Termini. A taxi to the station costs about 36€ ($41). From Termini, you can grab one of many daily trains to Florence, Pisa, and most other destinations. If you happen to fly into **Ciampino Airport** (𝄢 **06-7934-0297**), 15km (9 miles) south of the city, a none-too-frequent COTRAL bus will take you to the

Anagnina metro station, where you can take the metro to Termini, the whole trip costing around 3€ ($3.45). A taxi to Rome's center from Ciampino should run about 25€ ($29).

Information on getting to most major Tuscan and Umbrian cities and towns from Rome **by train** is included under each destination throughout this book.

GETTING TO TUSCANY OR UMBRIA FROM MILAN'S AIRPORT

Your flight may land at either **Linate Airport** (© 02-7485-2200; www.sea-aeroportimilano.it), about 8km (5 miles) southeast of the city, or **Malpensa Airport** (© 02-2680-0613), 45km (28 miles) from downtown—closer to Como than to Milan itself.

From **Malpensa,** a 40-minute express train heads half-hourly to Cadorna train station in western Milan rather than the larger or more central Stazione Centrale from which most trains onward to Tuscany will leave (you'll have to take the Metro to get there). To grab a bus instead, which will take you directly to that central downtown rail station, your choices are **Malpensa Express** (© 02-9619-2301) which costs 5.05€ ($5.80), or the slightly cheaper **Malpensa Shuttle** (© 02-5858-3185)—same service, different price:

4.50€ ($5.20)—two or three times per hour for the 50-minute ride to the east side of Milan's Stazione Centrale.

From **Linate,** buses, **STAM buses** (© 02-717-100) make the 25-minute trip to Milan's Stazione Centrale, every 20 to 30 minutes daily from 7am to 11pm, and costs 2€ ($2.30; buy on bus). The slightly slower city bus no. 73 leaves hourly for the S. Babila metro stop downtown (1€/ $1.15 for a regular bus ticket bought from any news agent inside the airport, but not on-board).

From Milan's Stazione Centrale, you can get trains to Florence (see "Getting There" in chapter 3).

GETTING THROUGH THE AIRPORT

With the federalization of airport security, security procedures at U.S. airports are more stable and consistent than ever. Generally, you'll be fine if you arrive at the airport **2 hours** before an international flight; if you show up late, tell an airline employee and she'll probably whisk you to the front of the line.

Bring your **passport** as photo ID (you need that to get into Italy anyway!) and if you've got an E-ticket, print out the **official confirmation page;** you might need to show it at the security checkpoint.

Security lines are getting shorter, but some doozies remain. If you have

---

Tips **The Milan Connection**

Note that if you find yourself flying into Milan, the domestic airport (Linate) is separate from the international one (Malpensa), and transferring planes to a connecting flight to Florence or Pisa requires switching airports (an 8€/$9.20 bus connects the two airports), sometimes changing airlines, and an innate trust in the gods of luggage transfer. If you fly into Milan, a train to Tuscany is probably your best bet. This isn't a problem for flights on Alitalia, however, which uses Milan's Malpensa airport for both international arrivals and domestic departures—a blatantly nationalistic protectionist scheme which has all other major airlines, European and American, up in arms.

trouble standing for long periods of time, tell an airline employee; the airline will provide a wheelchair. Speed up security by **not wearing metal objects** such as big belt buckles or clanky earrings. If you've got metallic body parts, a note from your doctor can prevent a long chat with the security screeners. Keep in mind that only **ticketed passengers** are allowed past security, except for folks escorting disabled passengers or children.

Federalization has stabilized **what you can carry on** and **what you can't.** The general rule is that sharp things are out, nail clippers are okay, and food and beverages must be passed through the X-ray machine—but that security screeners can't make you drink from your coffee cup. Bring food in your carry-on rather than checking it, as explosive-detection machines used on checked luggage have been known to mistake food (especially chocolate, for some reason) for bombs. Travelers in the U.S. are allowed one carry-on bag, plus a "personal item" such as a purse, briefcase, or laptop bag. Carry-on hoarders can stuff all sorts of things into a laptop bag; as long as it has a laptop in it, it's still considered a personal item. The Transportation Security Administration (TSA) has issued a list of restricted items; check its website at **www.tsa.gov** for details.

In 2003, the TSA phased out **gate check-in** at all U.S. airports. Passengers with E-tickets and without checked bags can still beat the ticket-counter lines by using **electronic kiosks** or even **online check-in.** Ask your airline which alternatives are available, and if you're using a kiosk, bring the credit card you used to book the ticket. If you're checking bags, you will still be able to use most airlines' kiosks; again call your airline for up-to-date information. **Curbside check-in** is also a good way to avoid lines, although a few airlines still ban curbside check-in entirely; call before you go.

At press time, the TSA is also recommending that you **not lock your checked luggage** so screeners can search it by hand if necessary (and in this author's experience, they often find it necessary), and this often happens after you've abandoned it to the baggage handling system, so you won't be on hand to unlock the thing for them; they'll simply destroy the lock to get to your stuff. The agency says to use plastic "zip ties" instead, which can be bought at hardware stores and can be easily cut off.

FLYING FOR LESS: TIPS FOR GETTING THE BEST AIRFARE

Passengers sharing the same airplane cabin rarely pay the same fare. Travelers who need to purchase tickets at the last minute, change their itinerary at a moment's notice, or fly one-way often

Travel in the Age of Bankruptcy

At press time, two major North American airlines were struggling in bankruptcy court and most of the rest weren't doing very well either. To protect yourself, **buy your tickets with a credit card,** as the Fair Credit Billing Act guarantees that you can get your money back from the credit card company if a travel supplier goes under (and if you request the refund within 60 days of the bankruptcy). **Travel insurance** can also help, but make sure it covers against "carrier default" for your specific travel provider. And be aware that if a U.S. airline goes bust mid-trip, a 2001 federal law requires other carriers to take you to your destination (albeit on a space-available basis) for a fee of no more than $25, provided you rebook within 60 days of the cancellation.

Flying with Film & Video

Never pack film—developed or undeveloped—in checked bags, as the new, more powerful scanners in U.S. airports can fog film. The film you carry with you can be damaged by scanners as well. X-ray damage is cumulative; the faster the film speed, and the more times you put it through a scanner, the more likely the damage. Film under 800 ASA is usually safe for up to five scans. If you're taking your film through additional scans, U.S. regulations permit you to demand hand inspections. In international airports, you're at the mercy of airport officials. On international flights, store your film in transparent baggies, so you can remove it easily before you go through scanners. Keep in mind that airports are not the only places where your camera may be scanned: Highly trafficked attractions abroad are X-raying visitors' bags with increasing frequency.

Most photo supply stores sell protective pouches designed to block damaging X-rays. The pouches fit both film and loaded cameras. They should protect your film in checked baggage, but they also may raise alarms and result in a hand inspection.

An organization called **Film Safety for Traveling on Planes (FSTOP;** ✆ **888/301-2665**; www.f-stop.org) can provide additional tips for traveling with film and equipment.

Carry-on scanners will not damage **videotape** in video cameras, but the magnetic fields emitted by the walk-through security gateways and handheld inspection wands will. Always place your loaded camcorder on the screening conveyor belt or have it hand-inspected. Be sure your batteries are charged, as you will probably be required to turn the device on to ensure that it's what it appears to be.

get stuck paying the premium rate. Here are some ways to keep your airfare costs down.

- Passengers who can book their ticket **long in advance,** who can **stay over Saturday night,** or who **fly midweek** or **at less-trafficked hours** will pay a fraction of the full fare. If your schedule is flexible, say so, and ask if you can secure a cheaper fare by changing your flight plans.
- You can also save on airfares by keeping an eye out in local newspapers for **promotional specials** or **fare wars,** when airlines lower prices on their most popular routes. You rarely see fare wars offered for peak travel times, but if you can travel in the off-months, you may snag a bargain.
- Search **the Internet** for cheap fares (see "Planning Your Trip Online").
- **Consolidators,** also known as bucket shops, are great sources for international tickets. Start by looking in Sunday newspaper travel sections; U.S. travelers should focus on the *New York Times, Los Angeles Times,* and *Miami Herald.* For less-developed destinations, small travel agents who cater to immigrant communities in large cities often have the best deals. *Beware:* Bucket shop tickets are usually nonrefundable or rigged with stiff cancellation penalties, often as high as 50% to 75% of

the ticket price, and some put you on charter airlines with questionable safety records.

Several reliable consolidators are worldwide and available on the Net. **STA Travel** (www.statravel.com) is now the world's leader in student travel, thanks to their purchase of Council Travel. It also offers good fares for travelers of all ages. **Destination Europe,** the airfares branch of car renter Auto Europe (www.autoeurope.com), consistently offers the some of the best transatlantic fares at any time of year. **Flights.com** (© **800/TRAV-800;** www.flights.com) started in Europe and has excellent fares worldwide, but particularly to that continent. It also has "local" websites in 12 countries. **FlyCheap** (© **800/FLY-CHEAP;** www.flycheap.com) is owned by package-holiday megalith MyTravel and so has especially good access to fares for sunny destinations. **Air Tickets Direct** (© **800/778-3447;** www.airticketsdirect.com) is based in Montréal and leverages the currently weak Canadian dollar for low fares; it'll also book trips to places that U.S. travel agents won't touch, such as Cuba.

- Join **frequent-flier clubs.** Accrue enough miles, and you'll be rewarded with free flights and elite status. It's free, and you'll get the best choice of seats, faster response to phone inquiries, and prompter service if your luggage is stolen, your flight is canceled or delayed, or if you want to change your seat.

BY CAR

You'll get the **best rental rate** if you book your car from home instead of renting direct in Italy—in fact, if you decide to rent once you're over there, it's worth it to call home to have someone arrange it all from there. You must be over 25 to rent from most agencies (although some accept 21).

Though it once was smart shopping to see what rates Italian companies were offering, they're all now allied with the big agents in the States: **Avis** (© **800/230-4898;** in Italy toll-free 199-100-133; www.avis.com), **Budget** (© **800/527-0700;** www.budget.com), **Hertz** (© **800/654-3131** or 800/654-3001; www.hertz.com), and **National** (© **800/227-7368;** www.nationalcar.com).

You can usually get a better rate by going through one of the rental companies specializing in Europe: **Auto Europe** (© **888/223-5555;** www.autoeurope.com), **Europe by Car** (© **800/223-1516** or 212/581-3040; www.europebycar.com), **Kemwell** (© **800/678-0678;** www.kemwell.com), and **Maiellano** (© **800/223-1616** or 718/727-0044). With constant price wars and special packages, it always pays to shop around among all the above.

When offered the choice between a compact car and a larger one, always choose the smaller car (unless you have a large group)—you'll need it for maneuvering the winding, steeply graded Italian roads and the impossibly narrow alleyways of towns and cities. Likewise, if you can drive stick shift, order one; it'll help you better navigate the hilly terrain. It's also a good idea to opt for the **Collision Damage Wavier (CDW)** that for only $10 to $20 a day gives you the peace of mind and nerves of steel that driving in Italy requires; you can pay only $7 per day for this service if you buy it through a third party insurer such as Travel Guard (www.travelguard.com). Although the 19% IVA value-added tax is unavoidable, you can do away with the government airport pick-up tax of 10% by picking up your car at an office in town.

For more on driving in Italy, from road rule to maps to gasoline, see the "Getting Around" section later in this chapter.

BY TRAIN

Every day, up to 14 **Eurostar** trains (reservations in London © **0875/186-186;** www.eurostar.com) zip from London to Paris's Gare du Nord via the **Chunnel** (Eurotunnel) in a bit over 4 hours. In Paris, you can transfer to the Paris Gare de Lyon station or Paris Bercy for one of three daily direct trains to **Milan** (from which you can transfer to Florence), two to **Pisa,** or two to **Florence.** Some of the Milan runs are high-speed TGV trains, a 6½-hour ride requiring a seat reservation. At least one will be an overnight Euronight (EN) train, with reservable sleeping couchettes; the Euronight leaves Paris around 10pm and gets into Milan around 8:45am. The two Euronight trains going directly from Paris to Pisa take about 10 hours; to Florence, it takes 12½ hours.

The definitive 500-page book listing all official European train routes and schedules is the *Thomas Cook European Timetable,* available in the United States for $28 (plus $4.50 shipping and handling) from Forsyth Travel Library, P.O. Box 2975, Shawnee Mission, KS 66201 (© **800/ 367-7984**) or at travel specialty stores. You can also order the schedule online at **www.thomascooktimetables.com.**

EUROPE-WIDE RAIL PASSES If Tuscany and Umbria are only part of a larger European tour for you, the famous Eurailpass or new Eurail Selectpass may be useful (see below). The granddaddy of passes is the **Eurailpass,** covering 17 countries (most of Western Europe except England). It has recently been joined by the more modest but flexible Eurail Selectpass (an improvement on the old Europass), which can be customized to cover three to five contiguous countries.

If, however, you're traveling only in the regions covered by this guide or just in Italy, these passes will be a waste of money. Similarly, if you're merely coming straight to Italy by train from another point within Europe, it'll be cheaper to buy just a regular one-way ticket. If this is the case and you're **under 26,** get a BIJ (Billet International de Jeunesse, or youth ticket, known as BIGE in Italy), which gets you a 30% to 50% discount on the second-class one-way fare. It also allows you a full month to get to your destination, during which time you can hop on and off the trains as often as you wish so long as you stay headed in the direction of your final destination. BIJ tickets are sold only in Europe, under the names of Wasteels and Eurotrain, but you can get further information on them at **Wasteels Travel** (www.wasteels.com). In London, you can get the tickets at the Wasteels office at Victoria Station (© **020/7834-7066**).

For the Eurailpass and Eurorail Selectpass described below, you need to scribble the date on the pass as you hop on the train; you don't need to wait in line at the ticket window. However, you will need to go to the ticket window if the train you want to take requires you to reserve a seat (such as the Pendolino, which, as a 1st-class train, doesn't accept the 2nd-class youth passes) or if you want a spot in a sleeping couchette. The Eurailpass gets you only a 33% discount on the TGV train through the Chunnel from London to Paris. The

---

Countries Honoring Eurail Passes

Austria, Belgium, Denmark, Finland, France, Germany, Greece, Hungary, Ireland, Italy, Luxembourg, the Netherlands, Norway, Portugal, Spain, Sweden, and Switzerland. *Note:* Great Britain isn't included in any pass.

passes below are available in the United States through **Rail Europe** (© **877/257-2887**; www.raileurope. com). No matter what everyone tells you, they *can* be bought in Europe as well (at the major train stations) but are more expensive. Rail Europe can also give you information on the rail-and-drive versions of the passes.

Railpasses are available in either **consecutive-day** or **flexipass** versions (you have, say, 2 months in which to use 10 days of train travel of your choosing as you go along). Consecutive-day passes are best for those taking the train very frequently (every few days), covering a lot of ground, and making many short train hops. Flexipasses are for folks who want to range far and wide but plan on taking their time over a long trip and intend to stay in each city for a while.

If you're under age 26, you can opt to buy a regular first-class pass or a second-class youth pass; if you're 26 or over, you're stuck with the first-class pass. Passes for kids 4 to 11 are half price, and kids under 4 travel free.

The rates quoted below were for 2003; they'll rise each year.

- **Eurailpass:** Consecutive-day Eurailpass $588 for 15 days, $762 for 21 days, $946 for 1 month, $1,338 for 2 months, or $1,654 for 3 months.
- **Eurailpass Flexi:** Good for 2 months of travel, within which you can travel by train for 10 days (consecutive or not) for $694 or 15 days for $914.
- **Eurailpass Saver:** Good for two to five people traveling together, costing $498 per person for 15 days, $648 for 21 days, $804 for 1 month, $1138 for 2 months, or $1,408 for 3 months.
- **Eurailpass Saver Flexi:** Good for two to five people traveling together, costing $592 per person for 10 days within 2 months or $778 per person for 15 days within 2 months.
- **Eurailpass Youth:** The second-class railpass for travelers under 26, costing $414 for 15 days, $534 for 21 days, $664 for 1 month, $938 for 2 months, or $1,160 for 3 months.
- **Eurailpass Youth Flexi:** Only for travelers under 26, allowing for 10 days of travel within 2 months for $488 or 15 days within 2 months for $642.
- **Eurail Selectpass:** For the most tightly focused of trips, covering three to five contiguous Eurail countries connected by rail or ship. It's valid for 2 months, and cost varies according to the number of countries you plan to visit. A pass for three countries is $356 for 5 days, $394 for 6 days, $470 for 8 days, and $542 for 10 days. A four-country pass costs $398 for 5 days, $436 for 6 days, $512 for 8 days, and $584 for 10 days. A pass for five countries costs $438 for 5 days, $476 for 6 days, $552 for 8 days, $624 for 10 days, and $794 for 15 days.
- **Eurail Selectpass Saver:** Same as the Eurail Selectpass (and slightly less expensive), but for two to five people traveling together. Per person, the three-country pass is $304 for 5 days, $336 for 6 days, $400 for 8 days, and $460 for 10 days. A pass for four countries is $340 for 5 days. $372 for 6 days, $436 for 8 days, and $496 for 10 days. A five-country pass is $3,744 for 5 days, $406 for 6 days, $470 for 8 days, $530 for 10 days, and $674 for 15 days.
- **Eurail Selectpass Youth:** Good in second class only for travelers under 26. Cost varies according to the number of countries you plan to visit, but all passes are valid for 2 months. For three countries, it's $249 for 5 days, $276 for 6 days,

$329 for 8 days, $379 for 10 days. A four-country pass costs $279 for 5 days, $306 for 6 days, $359 for 8 days, and $409 for 10 days. A five-country pass is $307 for 5 days, $334 for 6 days, $387 for 8 days, $437 for 10 days, and $556 for 15 days.

- **Italy Rail 'n Drive:** Combines train and car travel throughout Italy, allowing you to visit some of the smaller Tuscan and Umbrian towns—or anywhere else in Italy. The pass gives you 4 days of first or second class train travel within Italy and 2 days of car rental. Prices (per person one adult 1st class/one adult 2nd class/two adults 1st class/two adults 2nd class) vary: $329/$279/$249/$209 economy; $365/$319/$269/$229 compact; $379/$335/$275/$235 midsize. You may add as many as 6 rail days to the pass for $25/$21/$21/$17 per person per day. Additional car days are $45 economy, $65 compact, $75 midsize.

- **EurailDrive Pass:** This pass offers the best of both worlds, mixing train travel and rental cars (through Hertz or Avis) for less money than it would cost to do them separately (and one of the only ways to get around the high daily car-rental rates in Europe when you rent for less than a week). You get four first-class rail days and 2 car days within a 2-month period. Prices (per person for one adult/two adults) vary with the class of the car: $452/$409 economy, $481/$423 compact, $496/$431 midsize, small automatic (Hertz only) $531/$447. You can add up to 6 extra car days ($49 each economy, $64 compact, $75 midsize, $95 small automatic [Hertz only]). You have to reserve the first "car day" a week before leaving the States but can make the other reservations as you go (subject to availability). If there are more than two adults, the extra passengers get the car portion free but must buy the 4-day railpass for about $365.

- **Eurail SelectPass Drive:** This pass, like the EurailDrive Pass, offers combined train and rental car travel, but only for very focused trips: within any three to five adjoining Eurail countries. A flexipass, it includes 3 days of unlimited, first-class rail travel and two days of unlimited mileage car rental (through Avis or Hertz) within a 2-month period. Prices (per person for one adult/two adults) are $335/$291 economy, $365/$305 compact, $392/$315 midsize, $429/$331 small automatic. You can add up to 7 additional rail days for $39 each and unlimited extra car days for $49 to $95 each, depending on the class of car.

12 Packages for the Independent Traveler

Before you start your search for the lowest airfare, you may want to consider booking your flight as part of a travel package. Package tours are not the same thing as escorted tours. Package tours are simply a way to buy the airfare, accommodations, and other elements of your trip (such as car rentals, airport transfers, and sometimes even activities) at the same time and often at discounted prices—kind of like one-stop shopping. Packages are sold in bulk to tour operators—who resell them to the public at a cost that usually undercuts standard rates.

One good source of package deals is the airlines themselves. Most major airlines offer air/land packages, including **American Airlines Vacations** (© 800/321-2121; www.aavacations.com), **Delta Vacations** (© 800/221-6666; www.deltavacations.com), **Continental**

Airlines Vacations (© 800/301-3800; www.coolvacations.com), and **United Vacations** (© 888/854-3899; www.unitedvacations.com).

The single best-priced packager to Europe, though, is **Go-Today.com** (www.go-today.com), offering packages throughout Italy and Tuscany. **Italiatours** (© **800/845-3365;** www.italiatourusa.com) is the tour operator branch of Alitalia airlines and offers package and escorted tours at extremely attractive prices. **TourCrafters** (© **800/ITALY-95** or 847/816-6510; www.tourcrafters.com) offers escorted, hosted, and independent tours throughout Italy. They also arrange villa rentals in Tuscany and Umbria.

Several big **online travel agencies**— Expedia, Travelocity, Orbitz, Site59, and Lastminute.com—also do a brisk business in packages. If you're unsure about the pedigree of a smaller packager, check with the Better Business Bureau in the city where the company is based, or go online at www.bbb.org. If a packager won't tell you where it's based, don't fly with them.

Travel packages are also listed in the travel section of your local Sunday newspaper. Or check ads in the national travel magazines such as *Arthur Frommer's Budget Travel Magazine, Travel & Leisure, National Geographic Traveler,* and *Condé Nast Traveler.*

Package tours can vary by leaps and bounds. Some offer a better class of hotels than others. Some offer the same hotels for lower prices. Some offer flights on scheduled airlines, while others book charters. Some limit your choice of accommodations and travel days. You are often required to make a large payment up front. On the plus side, packages can save you money, offering group prices but allowing for independent travel. Some even let you to add on a few guided excursions or escorted day trips (also at prices lower than if you booked them yourself) without booking an entirely escorted tour.

Before you invest in a package tour, get some answers. Ask about the **accommodation choices** and prices for each. Then look up the hotels' reviews in a Frommer's guide (note, however, that most hotels offered with package tours are cookie-cutter chain places very short on atmosphere, hence they might not appear within this book; use the Internet to suss them out and see some pictures) and check their rates for your specific dates of travel online. You'll also want to find out what **type of room** you get. If you need a certain type of room, ask for it; don't take whatever is thrown your way. Request a nonsmoking room, a quiet room, a room with a view, or whatever you fancy.

Finally, look for **hidden expenses.** Ask whether airport departure fees and taxes, for example, are included in the total cost.

Finally, if you plan to travel alone, you'll need to know if a **single supplement** will be charged and if the company can match you up with a roommate.

13 Escorted Tours

Escorted tours are structured group tours, with a group leader. The price usually includes everything from airfare to hotels, meals, tours, admission costs, and local transportation.

Far & Wide/Central Holidays (© 800/935-5000; www.centralholidays.com) is one of the larger tour operators to Italy, offering fully escorted guided tours to completely independent packaged ones. One of the most famous Italy tour specialists, **Perillo Tours** (© **800/431-1515;** www.perillotours.com), offers a fully escorted 15-day, "Off the Beaten Path" tour that, along with some other central and northern

Italian cities, visits many Tuscan and Umbrian towns. You can also get good itineraries from **Italiatours** (© **800/845-3365;** www.italiatourusa.com), the tour branch of Alitalia airlines, and **TourCrafters** (© **800/ITALY95** or 847/816-6510; www.tourcrafters.com).

Many people derive a certain ease and security from escorted trips. Escorted tours—whether by bus, motor coach, train, or boat—let travelers sit back and enjoy their trip without having to spend lots of time behind the wheel. All the little details are taken care of; you know your costs up front; and there are few surprises. Escorted tours can take you to the maximum number of sights in the minimum amount of time with the least amount of hassle—you don't have to sweat over the plotting and planning of a vacation schedule. Escorted tours are particularly convenient for people with limited mobility.

On the downside, an escorted tour often requires a big deposit up front, and lodging and dining choices are predetermined. As part of a cloud of tourists, you'll get little opportunity for serendipitous interactions with locals. The tours can be jam-packed with activities, leaving little room for individual sightseeing, whim, or adventure—plus they also often focus only on the heavily touristed sites, so you miss out on the lesser-known gems.

Before you invest in an escorted tour, ask about the **cancellation policy:** Is a deposit required? Can they cancel the trip if they don't get enough people? Do you get a refund if they cancel? If *you* cancel? How late can you cancel if you are unable to go? When do you pay in full? *Note:* If you choose an escorted tour, think strongly about purchasing trip-cancellation insurance, especially if the tour operator asks you to pay up front. See the section on "Travel Insurance," earlier in this chapter.

You'll also want to get a complete **schedule** of the trip to find out how much sightseeing is planned each day and whether enough time has been allotted for relaxing or wandering solo.

The **size** of the group is also important to know up front. Generally, the smaller the group, the more flexible the itinerary, and the less time you'll spend waiting for people to get on and off the bus. Find out the **demographics** of the group as well. What is the age range? What is the gender breakdown? Is this mostly a trip for couples or singles?

Discuss what is included in the **price.** You may have to pay for transportation to and from the airport. A box lunch may be included in an excursion, but drinks might cost extra. Tips may not be included. Find out if you will be charged if you decide to opt out of certain activities or meals. The sections on accommodations choice, hidden expense, and single supplements discussed above under "Packages for the Independent Traveler" apply here as well.

14 Special-Interest Vacations

COOKING SCHOOLS

One of Italy's most respected cookbook authors, and former TV cooking show star, **Giuliano Bugialli** ★★ shares his secrets in summertime weeklong classes, with lodging in Florence and classes conducted in a kitchen in the Chianti wine zone. One-week courses run $3,800 per person, including first-class accommodations and most meals. For more info, contact 252 Seventh Ave., #7R, New York, NY 10001 (© **646/638-1099;** fax 646/638-0381; www.bugialli.com).

Perhaps the classiest, highest-profile school is the one started by **Lorenza de' Medici** ★, author of 30 kitchen tomes (including the coffee-table favorite *Tuscany: The Beautiful Cookbook*) and star of her own PBS cooking series. Unfortunately, she's now hung up her apron and now leaves the lessons to an acolyte. May through October, her 1-week "The Villa Table"–brand courses take place in the 12th-century abbey and wine estate, Badia a Coltibuono (see chapter 5 for more information). The courses aren't cheap—around $3,900 double occupancy—but room and board in the late medieval abbey complex are included. The courses book up quickly. Another option is the half-day cooking course offered Wednesdays and Fridays from 10am to 3:30pm, which must be booked at least 36 hours in advance at © 0577-744-832 or www.coltibuono. com. For more info, contact Louise Owens, 3128 Purdue, Dallas, TX 75225 (© 214/739-2846; fax 214/ 691-7996).

If a week's time or near $4,000 investment are too rich for your cooking lesson tastes, check out Judy Witts Francini's **La Divina Cucina** ✦✦✦ (© and fax **055-292-578;** www. divinacucina.com) for 1-, 2-, and 3-day courses designed to teach you to cook as the Florentines do. You start off each class by shopping in Florence's large central market at 11am, and by 4pm you've put together a meal based on the freshest ingredients available on that day. Each day costs $250 per person, and classes are offered Tuesday, Wednesday, and Thursdays each week, year-round. (As a bonus, you get a copy of Judy's *From the Market to the Table* cookbook to take home.) She also offers Florence walking tours and daylong Chianti tours. In Florence, she's located at Via Taddea 31, 50123, Firenze; in the States, you can get info by writing to 2130 Comistas Dr., Walnut Creek, CA 94598 (© and fax **925/ 939-6346**).

April through October, **Inland Services,** 708 Third Ave., 13th floor, New York, NY 10017 (© **212/687-9898;**

www.cookeuro.com), offers a weeklong course, "Love of Italian Cooking," with visits to wine estates and cultural day trips. Many of the language schools (below) also offer cooking classes, and for a real treat you can take a culinary class or two or an entire cooking course on some of the Chianti wine estates. The **Castello Vicchiomaggio** (© **055-854-079;** fax 055-853-911; www. vicchiomaggio.it) may be good for dabblers, offering a 1-day course for 155€ ($178) per person (minimum six people).

EDUCATIONAL & STUDY TRAVEL

There are dozens of Italian language schools in Florence and other Tuscan and Umbrian cities. The following is just a sampling in Florence: The **British Institute of Florence,** Piazza Strozzi 2, 50123 Firenze (© **055-2677-8200;** fax 055-2677-8222; www.britishinstitute. it), offers courses from 3 days to 4 weeks in Italian language, cultural and art history, cooking, and drawing. The **Centro Lorenzo de' Medici,** Via Faenza 43, 50122 Firenze (© **055-287-360** or 055-287-143; fax 055-289-514), runs evening courses from 1 to 3 months. The **ABC Centro di Lingua and Cultura Italiana,** Via dei Rustici 7, 50122 Firenze (© **055-212-001;** fax 055-212-112; www.abcschool.com), offers everything from single lessons to 4-week programs in Italian and month-long classes in history, art, literature, and cooking.

According to one school of thought, the Sienese speak the purest form of Italian in the country. So if you want to get your pronunciation perfect, try the **Centro Internazionale Dante Alighieri,** Via Tommaso Pendola 37, 53100 Siena (© **0577-49-533;** fax 0577-270-646; www.dantealighieri. com). It offers 1- to 8-week courses mainly in language, including a series of evening courses in practical Italian, as well as a couple of cooking and painting classes.

For some heavier study, Umbria's capital, Perugia, has a famous **Università per Stranieri (Foreigner's University)** ✸, Palazzo Gallenga, Piazza Fortebraccio 4, 06122 Perugia (✆ **075-57-461;** fax 075-573-2014; www.unistrapg.it), devoted to the study of Italian language, art, history, and culture. It's the top language school for foreigners in the country, and courses run 1 to 6 months. **Siena** has a similar, but not as renowned, Università per Stranieri, Segreteria Studenti, Via Pantaneto 45, 53100, Siena (✆ **0577-240-347** or 0577-345-343; fax 0577-283-163; www.unistrasi.it), that offers the same sorts of courses from 2 weeks to 4 months.

BIKE TOURS

The best way to experience Tuscany and Umbria just may be by bike. Bike-it-yourselfers should arm themselves with a good map (see "Getting Around," below) and make use of the resources of the **Club Alpino Italiano,** 7 Via E. Fonseca Pimental, Milan 20127 (✆ **02-2614-1378;** fax 02-2614-1395; www.cai.it). You can rent a bike by the week or longer at outlets in most cities.

Several operators specialize in setting up itineraries and making some of the arrangements for you or in leading fully guided tours. **Ciclismo Classico** ✸✸ (✆ **800/866-7314** in the U.S. or 781/646-3377; fax 781/641-1512; www.ciclismoclassico.com) is one of the best operators and has more been leading bike and walking tours in Italy since 1988. April through November, the outfit runs several guided tours through Tuscany and Umbria, always van-supported, and will help you arrange a do-it-yourself tour as well. Six- to 15-day trips usually include Italian and cooking lessons along with

wine tasting and cultural itineraries. Groups average 10 to 18 people, with all ages and ability levels welcome.

Experience Plus (✆ **800/685-4565** in the U.S. or 970/484-8489; www.xplus.com) offers both a guided (Sept–Oct) and a self-guided (Apr–Oct) biking and walking tours through Tuscany lasting 8 or 9 days. Florence-based **I Bike Italy** (✆ **561/388-0783** in U.S.; www.ibikeitaly.com) ✸ offers guided 1- and 2-day rides in the Tuscan countryside. The 2-day tour requires a minimum of four participants and ends in Siena. They provide a shuttle service in and out of the city, the bike, and a bilingual guide. The 1-day tour returns to Florence around 5pm. Tours cost around 70€ ($81) per person, lunch included. The same company leads less extensive walking tours in Tuscany.

WALKING TOURS

If you don't feel the need to cover so much territory, you can appreciate even more of the countryside by walking or hiking (called *trekking* in Italian). Italy's resource for everything from country-side ambles to serious mountain trekking is the **Club Alpino Italiano** (see "Bike Tours" above). Many outfits run walking tours in Tuscany and Umbria. Besides Ciclismo Classico (above), you might want to try **Butterfield & Robinson,** 70 Bond St., Suite 300, Toronto, ON M5B 1X3 (✆ **800/678-1147** or 416/864-1354; fax 416/864-0541; www.butterfield.com); or **Country Walkers** ✸ (✆ **800/464-9255** in the U.S. or 802/244-1387; www.countrywalkers.com), which has a rather refined, romantic outlook on Italy and offers several Tuscan tours, one of which divides your time between exploring hill towns on foot and taking cooking and wine appreciation lessons.

15 Getting Around

This book covers a predominantly rural area made up of small towns, so budget plenty of travel time for winding

roads, slow local trains, and long lay-overs. The twisty roads aren't the kindest to **motion sickness** sufferers, but

Tips Prime Sightseeing Hours

One mistake many people make when scheduling their hopping from hill town to hill town is getting up early in the mornings to travel to the next destination. Because many of Tuscany and Umbria's sights are open only in the morning and almost all close for *riposo* (afternoon rest) from noon-ish to 3 or 4pm, this wastes valuable sightseeing time. I do my traveling just after noon, when everything is closing up. There's often a last train before *riposo* to wherever you're going or a country bus run (intended to shuttle schoolchildren home for lunch). If you're driving, you can enjoy great countryside vistas under the noonday sun.

fortunately Italy's pharmacies are blessed with a miraculous chewing-gum medicine called Travelgum that, unlike Dramamine, starts working within a minute or two. Also, be warned that town-to-town coach drivers in particular seem to be trained to drive in such a way as to disturb even the most iron of stomachs.

MAPS A city street plan is a *pianta;* a map of a region or larger area is a *mappa* or *carta.* Before you leave home, you can pick up one of the **Touring Club Italiano's (TCI)** enormous pristine maps of Italy's regions at 1:200,000 scale. You can find both "Tuscany" and "Umbria" at some bookstores and most map and travel specialty stores in the United States, Canada, and the United Kingdom. TCI also publishes some pocket-size street maps of cities, Florence among them, and makes laminated bound map booklets (if you don't like sheets), both regional and collections of city plans. **Edizione Multigraphic** covers all Tuscany and Umbria in varying scales with contour-lined maps so detailed that some actually show individual farms. Their "Carta Turistica Stradale" 1:50,000 maps are perfect for exploring back roads, while the 1:25,000 "Carta dei Sentieri e Rifugi" sheets include hiking trails and alpine shelters for those hoofing it or on bike. The maps are widely available at bookstores, newsstands, and souvenir shops throughout Tuscany and Umbria. **Litografia Artistica Cartografica** makes very complete and large foldout city maps with searchable indices. They also publish 1:150,000 province maps that are less detailed than the Edizione Multigraphic sheets, but because of this are easier to glance at while driving.

BY CAR

Tuscany and Umbria are best explored by car. In fact, one of the most common and convenient ways to take a tour of this area is to fly or take a train into Florence, see the city, then pick up a rental car to wend your way through Tuscany and Umbria toward Rome, where you can drop off the car and fly home.

That said, driving in Italy is also expensive and notoriously nerve-racking—for both the winding roads and the Italian penchant for driving a Fiat like a Ferrari. Both rental and gas prices are as high as they get in all Europe. Before leaving home, apply for an **International Driver's Permit** from the American Automobile Association (AAA; ✆ **800/222-1134** or 407/444-4300; www.aaa.com). In Canada, the permit is available from the Canadian Automobile Association (CAA; ✆ **613/247-0117;** www.caa.ca). Technically, you need this permit, your actual driver's license, and an Italian translation of the latter (also available from AAA and CAA) to drive in Italy, though in practice the license itself often suffices. (Take all three along to be safe.)

Italy's equivalent of AAA is the **Automobile Club d'Italia (ACI),** a branch of the Touring Club Italiano. They're the people who respond when you place an emergency 116 call for road breakdowns, though they do charge for this service if you're not a member. If you wish, you may join at the border as you're driving into Italy or at one of the club's regional offices (in Florence, Viale Amendola 36, ✆ **055-24-861;** in Rome, Via C. Colombo 261, ✆ **06-514-971**). You can also join online at **www.aci.it**.

DRIVING RULES   Italian drivers aren't maniacs; they only appear to be. Actually, they tend to be very safe and alert drivers—if much more aggressive than Americans are used to. If someone races up behind you and flashes her lights, that's the signal for you to slow down so she can pass you quickly and safely. Stay in the right lane on highways; the left is only for passing and for cars with large engines and the pedal to the metal. If you see someone in your rearview mirror speeding up with his hazard lights blinking, get out of the way because it means his Mercedes is opened up full throttle. On a two-lane road, the idiot passing someone in the opposing traffic who has swerved into your lane expects you to veer obligingly over into the shoulder so three lanes of traffic can fit—he would do the same for you.

Autostrade are superhighways, denoted by green signs and a number prefaced with an A, like the A1 from Rome to Florence. A few aren't numbered and are simply called *raccordo,* a connecting road between two cities (such as Florence–Siena and Florence–Pisa). On longer stretches, autostrade often become toll roads. *Strade Statale* are state roads, usually two lanes wide, indicated by blue signs. Their route numbers are prefaced with an SS or an S, as in the SS222 from Florence to Siena. On signs, however, these official route numbers are used infrequently. Usually, you'll just see blue signs listing destinations by name with arrows pointing off in the appropriate directions. Even if it's just a few miles down on the road, often the town you're looking for won't be mentioned on the sign at the appropriate turnoff. It's impossible to predict which of all the towns that lie along a road will be the ones chosen to list on a particular sign. Sometimes, the sign gives only the first miniscule village the lies past the turnoff; at other times it lists the first major town down that road, and some signs mention only the major city the road eventually leads to, even if its hundreds of miles away. It pays to study the map and fix in your mind the names all three possibilities before coming to an intersection.

The **speed limit** on roads in built-up areas around towns and cities is 50kmph (31 mph). On rural roads and the highway it's 110kmph (68 mph), except on weekends when it's upped to 130kmph (81 mph). Italians have an astounding disregard for these limits. However, police can ticket you and collect the fine on the spot. Although there's no official blood alcohol level at which you're "legally drunk," the police will throw you in jail if they pull you over and find you soused.

As far as *parcheggio* (**parking**) is concerned, on **streets** white lines indicate free public spaces and blue lines pay public spaces. Meters don't line the sidewalk; rather, there's one machine on the block where you punch in how long you want to park. The machine spits out a ticket that you leave on your dashboard. Sometimes streets will have an attendant who'll come around and give you your time ticket (pay him or her when you get ready to leave). If you park in an area marked PARCHEGGIO DISCO ORARIO, root around in your rental car's glove compartment for a cardboard parking disc (or buy one at a gas station). With this device, you dial up the hour of your arrival (it's the honor system) and display it on your dashboard. You're allowed *un ora* (1 hr.) or *due ore* (2 hr.), according to the sign. **Parking lots** have ticket dispensers but usually *not* manned booths as you exit. Take your ticket with you when you park; when you return to the lot to get your car and leave, first visit the office or automated payment machine to exchange your ticket for a paid receipt you then use to get through the automated exit.

ROAD SIGNS Here's a brief rundown of the road signs you'll most frequently encounter. A **speed limit** sign is a black number inside a red circle on a white background. The **end of a speed zone** is just black and white, with a black slash through the number. A red circle with a white background, a black arrow pointing down, and a red arrow pointing up means **yield to oncoming traffic,** while a point-down red-and-white triangle means **yield ahead.** In town, a simple white circle with a red border or the words *zona pedonale* or *zona traffico limitato* denotes a **pedestrian zone** (you can drive through only to drop off baggage at your hotel); a white arrow on a blue background is used for Italy's many **one-way streets;** a mostly red circle with a horizontal white slash means **do not enter.** Any image in black on a white background surrounded by a red circle means that image is **not allowed** (for instance, if the image is two cars next to each other: no passing; a motorcycle means no Harleys permitted, and so on). A circular sign in blue with a red circle-slash means **no parking.**

GASOLINE *Benzina* (gas or petrol) is even more expensive in Italy than in the rest of Europe. Even a small rental car guzzles between 30€ and 50€ ($35–$58) for a fill-up. There are many pull-in gas stations along major roads and on the outskirts of town, as well as

24-hour rest stops along the autostrada highways, but in towns most stations are small sidewalk gas stands where you parallel park to fill up. Almost all stations are closed for *riposo* and on Sundays, but the majority now has a pump fitted with a machine that accepts bills so you can self-service your tank at 3am. Unleaded gas is *senza piombo.*

BY TRAIN

Italy has one of the best train systems in Europe, and even traveling on a regional level through Tuscany and Umbria, you'll find many destinations connected. Most lines are administered by the state-run **Ferrovie dello Stato** or **FS** (© **892-021** for national train info, 199-166-177 to buy tickets; or www.trenitalia.com), but servicing the Casentino and western Valdichiana in Tuscany is a private line called **LFI,** and northern Umbria is serviced by the private **FCU.** About the only difference you'll notice is that these private lines don't honor special discount cards or passes (see "Special Passes & Discounts," below).

Italian trains tend to be very clean and comfortable. Though increasingly trains are of the boring straight-through commuter variety, on long-haul runs especially you'll still be blessed with those old-fashioned cars are made up of *couchette* compartments that seat only six or occasionally eight. (Try to find one full of nuns for a fighting chance at a smoke-free trip.) First class *(prima classe)* is usually only a shade better than second class *(seconda classe),* with four to six seats per couchette instead of six to eight. The only real benefit of first class comes if you're traveling overnight, in which case four berths per compartment are a lot more comfortable than six.

Few visitors are prepared for how **crowded** Italian trains can sometimes get, though with the increase in automobile travel, they're not as crowded as they were in decades past. An Italian train is only full when the corridors are packed solid and there are more than eight people sitting on their luggage in the little vestibules by the doors. Overcrowding is usually only a problem on Friday evenings and weekends, especially in and out of big cities, and just after a strike. In summer the crowding escalates, and any train going toward a beach in August all but bulges like an overstuffed sausage.

Italian trains come in six varieties based on how often they stop. The **ETR/Pendolino (P)** is the "pendulum" train that zips back and forth between Rome and Milan, stopping at Florence and Bologna along the way. It's the fastest but most expensive option (first class only, a meal included); it has its own ticket window at the stations and *requires* a seat reservation. **Eurostar/Eurocity (ES/EC, EN** if it runs overnight) trains connect Italian cities with cities outside the country; these are the speediest of the standard trains, offering both first and second class and always requiring a supplement (except for Eurailpass holders, though the conductors won't always believe you on this one); **Intercity (IC)** trains are similar to Eurocity trains in that they offer both first and second class and require a supplement, but they never cross an international border.

Of the regular trains that don't require supplements—often called *Regionale* (R) if they stay within a region (Tuscany) or *Interregionale* (IR) if they don't (Tuscany to Umbria)— the **Espresso** stops at all the major and most of the secondary stations, the **Diretto** stops at virtually every station, and the snail-paced **Locale** (sometimes laughingly called *accelerato*) frequently stops between stations in the middle of the countryside for no apparent reason.

When buying a **regular ticket,** ask for either *andata* (one-way) or *andata e ritorno* (round-trip). If the train you plan to take is an ES/EC or IC, ask for

the ticket *con supplemento rapido* (with speed supplement) to avoid on-train penalty charges. On a trip under 200km (124 miles), your ticket is good to leave within the next 6 hours; over 200km you have a full day. (This code isn't rigorously upheld by conductors, but don't push your luck.) On round-trip journeys of less than 250km (155 miles), the return ticket is valid only for 3 days. This mileage-time correlation continues, with an extra day added to your limit for each 200km above 250 (the maximum is 6 days). If you board a regular train without a ticket (or board an IC/EC without the supplement), you'll have to pay a hefty "tax" on top of the ticket or supplement the conductor will sell you. Most conductors also get extremely crabby if you forget to **stamp your ticket in the little yellow box** on the platform before boarding the train.

Schedules for all lines running through a given station are printed on posters tacked up on the station wall. *Binario (bin.)* means track. Useful schedules for all train lines are printed biannually in booklets (which are broken down into sections of the country—you want *nord e centro Italia,* north and central Italy, or simply *centro*) available at any newsstand. There are official FS-published booklets, but the better buy is the **Pozzorario,** which not only is cheaper but also lists private lines (and it's just as accurate). You can also get official schedules (and more train information, some even in English) on the web at **www.trenitalia.com**.

Stations tend to be well run and clean, with luggage storage facilities at all but the smallest and usually a good *bar* attached with surprisingly palatable food. If you pull into a dinky town with a shed-size or nonexistent station, find the nearest *bar* or *tabacchi,* and the man behind the counter will most likely double as the "station master" to sell you tickets.

SPECIAL PASSES & DISCOUNTS

To buy the **Italy Flexi Railcard,** available only outside Italy, contact **Rail Europe** (www.raileurope.com). It works similarly to the Eurailpass, in that you have one month in which to use the train a set number of days; the base number of days if four, and you can add up to six more. For adults, the first class pass costs 207€ ($239); adults traveling together can get the Saver version for 176€ ($203) each. The second-class version costs 166€ ($191) for adults (142€/$163 on the Saver edition), or for youths under 26, the price is 139€/$160. Extra days cost 21€ ($24; 17€/$20 for Saver passes) in first class, 16€ ($19; 14€/$16 for Saver), and 14€ ($16) for youths.

A 4-day **Trenitalia Pass** is 447€ ($514) in first class, 357€ ($415) in second; a 5-day pass is 492€ ($566) in first class, 393€ ($452) in second; a 6-day pass is 536€ ($616) in first class, 428€ ($492) in second; a 10-day pass is 716€ ($823) for first class and 570€ ($656) for second. The **Youth Pass** version (for ages 16–25) is available for second-class travel only. A 4-day pass is 229€ ($263); a 5-day pass is 329€ ($378). Each additional day (up to 10 days) is an additional 30€ ($35). A **Saver Pass** allows two to five people to ride the rails for 4 to 10 days in either first or second class. A 4-day pass is 379€ $436) in first class, 305€ ($351) in second class; a 5-day pass is 417€ ($480) in first and 335€ ($385) in second; a 10-day pass is 604€ ($695) for first class and 484€ ($557) for second class. Children aged 4 to 11 pay 50% of the adult fare.

There is also a **rail-and-drive** pass, with 1 month during which you can use 4 rail days and 2 car days (and add more car days cheaply), available from Rail Europe. Price ranges depend on the class of car, how many people are traveling, and what class train travel you buy, but start at 182€ ($209) per person for two adults in an economy car and second-class train seats.

When it comes to regular tickets, if you're **under 26,** you can buy at any Italian train station a 26€ ($30) **Carta Verde (Green Card)** that gets you a 15% discount on all FS tickets for 1 year. Present it each time you go to buy a ticket. The same deal is available for anyone **over 60** with the **Carta d'Argento (Silver Card).** Children under 12 always ride half price (and can get the passes mentioned below at half price), and kids under 4 ride free.

BY BUS

Regional intertown buses are called *pullman,* though *autobus,* the term for a city bus, is also sometimes used. When you're getting down to the kind of small-town travel this guide describes, you'll probably need to use regional buses at some point. You can get just about anywhere through a network of dozens of local, provincial, and regional lines (see below), but schedules aren't always easy to come by or to figure out—the local tourist office usually has a photocopy of the schedule, and in cities some companies have offices. Buses exist mainly to shuttle workers and schoolchildren, so the most runs are on weekdays, early in the morning and usually again around lunchtime. All too often, though, the only run of the day will be at 6am.

A town's bus stop is usually either the main piazza or, more often, a large square on the edge of town or the bend in the road just outside a small town's main city gate. You should always try to find the local ticket vendor—if there's no office, it's invariably the nearest newsstand or *tabacchi* (signaled by a sign with a white T), or occasionally a *bar*—but you can usually also buy tickets on the bus. You can also flag a bus down as it passes on a country road, but try to find an official stop (a small sign tacked onto a telephone pole). Tell the driver where you're going and ask him courteously if he'll let you know when you need to get off. When he says *"E la prossima fermata,"* that means yours is the next stop. *"Posso scendere?"* (*poh*-so *shen*-dair-ay?) is "May I please get off?"

TUSCAN & UMBRIAN BUS LINES

The ticketing offices and depots of most Tuscan bus lines based in Florence are very near the main train station, Santa Maria Novella.

Lazzi, Via Mercadante 2, Florence (© **055-363-041;** www.lazzi.it), and **SITA,** Viale dei Cadorna 105, Florence (© **055-478-21** or 800-373-760 in Italy; www.sita-on-line.it), have service to all Italy.

The following companies service northern Tuscany: **CAP,** Largo Alinari 11, Florence (© **055-214-637** or 055-292-268); **CLAP,** Via Luporini 895, Lucca (© **0583-5411;** www.clapspa.it); and **COPIT,** Via XX Settembre 71/Stazione FS in Pistoia (© **0573-363-243;** www.copitspa.it). **CAT,** Via G. Pietro 2, Carrara (© **0585-85-211**), and Via Fiume 5a, Florence (© **055-283-400**), services central and southern Tuscany and some of Arezzo province. **CPT,** Via Nino Bixio, Pisa (© **050-505-511** or 800-012-773 in Italy; www.cpt.pisa.it), services Pisa province. **LFI,** Via Guido Monaco 37, Arezzo (© **0575-324-294** or 0575-39-881; www.lfi.it), services Arezzo province and the Valdichiana. **RAMA,** Via Topazio 12, Grosseto (© **0564-475-111;** www.griforama.it), services the Maremma and southern Tuscany. **Tra-in,** Piazza San Domenico, Siena (© **0577-204-111** or 0577-204-246; www.trainspa.it), services Siena province.

In Umbria, **ATC,** Piazzale della Rivoluzione Francese, Terni (© **0744-492-711;** www.atcterni.it), services southern Umbria and Orvieto. **APM,** Pian de Massiano, Perugia (© **075-506-781;** www.apmperugia.it), services Perugia, Assisi, Todi, and northern Umbria. **SSIT,** Piazza della Vittoria, Spoleto (© **0743-212-208;** www.spoletina.com), services the Spoleto area. And **SULGA/ACAP,** Pian di Massimo, Perugia (© **075-500-9641** or 075-74-641; www.sulga.it), has service to Perugia, Assisi, Todi, and northern Umbria.

16 Tips on Accommodations, Villa Rentals & Farm Stays

Alas, Italy is no longer the country of dirt-cheap *pensione,* with shared baths and swaybacked beds. Most hotels have private bathrooms in the rooms now (if not, my reviews state this), regulations and standardization have become much stricter, and prices have soared. Many **bathrooms** are still dismal affairs—often a closet-size room with a sink, toilet, and bidet and just a shower head on the wall, a drain in the floor, and no curtain (rescue the toilet paper from a drenching before you turn on the water). Towels are often flat, pressed cotton sheets, though terry-cloth towels are coming into style. Soap isn't a given, but the water is safe to drink.

Italy's old *pensione* system no longer exists, and hotels are now **rated** by regional boards on a system of one to five stars. Prices aren't directly tied to the star system, but for the most part, the more stars a hotel has, the more expensive it'll be—but a four-star in a small town may be cheaper than a two-star in Florence. The number of stars awarded a hotel is based strictly on the amenities offered and not how clean, comfortable, or friendly a place is or whether it's a good value for the money overall.

A few of the four- and five-star hotels have their own private **garages,** but most city inns have an accord with a local garage. In many small towns, a garage is unnecessary because public parking, both free and pay, is widely available and never too far from your hotel. Parking costs and procedures are indicated under each hotel, and the rates quoted are per day (overnight).

The **high season** throughout most of Tuscany and Umbria runs from Easter to early September or October—peaking June through August—and from December 24 to January 6. You can almost always bargain for a cheaper rate if you're traveling in the shoulder season (early spring and late fall) or winter off-season (not including Christmas). You can also often get a discount for stays of more than 3 days. Always ask.

Supposedly, Italian hotels must quote the price for **breakfast** separately from the room and can't force it on you if you don't want it. However, most hotels include breakfast automatically in the room rate hoping you won't notice, and many also argue that breakfast is required at their hotel. I've tried to include the separate per-person breakfast price for each hotel. With very few exceptions, Italian hotel breakfasts tend to consist of a roll or *cornetto* (croissant) and coffee, occasionally with juice and fresh fruit as well. It's rarely worth the 3€ to 15€ ($3.45–$17) charged for it, as you can get the same breakfast—and freshly made instead of packaged—for around 2€ ($2.30) at the *bar* down the block. Ask for your room quote with a *prezzo senza colazione* (pretz-zoh *sen*-zah coal-lat-zee-*oh*-nay), or price without breakfast.

VILLA RENTALS
Each summer, thousands of visitors become temporary Tuscans by renting an old farmhouse or "villa," a marketing term used to inspire romantic images of manicured gardens, a Renaissance mansion, and chianti martinis, but in reality guaranteeing no more than four walls and most of a roof.

Actually, finding your countryside Eden isn't that simple, and if you want to ensure a romantic and memorable experience, brace yourself for a lot of research and legwork. Occasionally you can go through the property owners themselves, but the vast majority of villas are rented out via agencies (see below).

Shop around for a trustworthy agent or representative. Often several outfits will list the same property but charge radically different prices. At some you sign away any right to refunds if the place doesn't live up to your expectations. Expect to pay 9€ to 22€ ($10–$25) for a copy of each company's catalog; most refund this expense if you rent through them. Make sure the agency is willing to work with you to find the right property. Try to work with someone who has personally visited the properties you're considering, and always ask to see lots of photos: Get the exterior from several angles to make sure the railroad doesn't pass by the back door, as well as pictures of the bedrooms, kitchen, and baths, and photos of the views out each side of the house.

If you're traveling with several couples, ask to see a floor plan to make sure access to the bathroom isn't through one couple's bedroom. Find out if this is the only villa on the property—some people who rent the villa for the isolation find themselves living in a small enclave of foreigners all sharing the same small pool. Ask whether the villa is purely a rental unit or if, say, the family lives there during winter but lets it out during summer. Renting a lived-in place offers pretty good insurance that the lights, plumbing, heat, and so on will all be working.

One of the best agencies to call is **Renvillas.com** (formerly Rentals in Italy), 700 E. Main St., Ventura, CA 93001 (© **800/726-6702** or 805/641-1650; fax 805/641-1630; www.rentvillas.com). Its agents are very helpful in tracking down the perfect place to suit your needs. A United Kingdom agency—and one of the best all-around agents in Britain—is **International Chapters,** a division of Abercrombie & Kent, Sloane Square House, Holbein Place, London SW1W 8NS (© **08450/700-618;** www.villarentals. com). Marjorie Shaw's **Insider's Italy,** 41 Schermerhorn St., Brooklyn, NY 11201 (© **718/855-3878;** fax 718/855-3687; www.insidersitaly.com), is a small, upscale outfit run by a very personable agent who's thoroughly familiar with all of her properties and Italy in general.

Also in the United States, is **Parker Company Ltd.,** Seaport Landing, 152 Lynnway, Lynn, MA 01902 (© **800/280-2811** or 781/596-8282; fax 781/596-3125; www.theparkercompany.com) handles overseas villa rentals.

For some of the top properties, call the local representative of the **Cottages to Castles** group. In the United Kingdom, contact **Cottages to Castles,** Tuscany House, 10 Tonbridge Rd., Maidstone, Kent ME16 8RP (© **1622/775-217;** fax 1622/775-278). In Australia and New Zealand, call **Italian Villa Holidays,** P.O. Box 2293, Wellington, 6015, New Zealand (© **800/125-555** in Australia, 800/4-TUSCANY in New Zealand; fax 64-4-479-0021). At press time, the organization was searching for a representative in the United States.

One of the most reasonably priced agencies is **Villas and Apartment Abroad, Ltd.,** 370 Lexington Ave., Suite 1401, New York, NY 10017 (© **212/897-5045;** fax 212/897-5039; www.vaanyc.com). **Homeabroad.com,** formerly Vacanze in Italia, 22 Railroad St., Great Barrington, MA 02130 (© **413/528-6610;** www.homeabroad. com), handles hundreds of rather upscale properties. A popular but *very* pricey agency is **Villas International,** 4340 Redwood Hwy., Suite D309, San Rafael, CA 94903 (© **800/221-2260** or 415/499-9490; fax 415/499-9491; www.villasintl.com).

AGRITURISMO (STAYING ON A FARM)

Tuscany and Umbria are at the forefront of the *agriturismo* movement in Italy, whereby a working farm or agricultural estate makes available accommodations for visitors who want to stay out in the countryside. The rural atmosphere is ensured by the fact that an operation can call itself "agriturismo" only if (a) it offers fewer than 30 beds total and (b) the agricultural component of the property brings in a larger economic share of profits than the hospitality part—in other words, the property has to remain a farm and not become a glorified hotel.

Agriturismi are generally a crapshoot. They're only loosely regulated, and the price, quality, and types of accommodation can vary dramatically. Some are sumptuous apartments or suites with hotel-like amenities; others are a straw's width away from sleeping in the barn on a haystack. Most, though, are mini-apartments, often furnished from secondhand dealers and usually rented out with a minimum stay of 3 days or a week. Sometimes you're invited to eat big country dinners at the table with the family; other times you cook for yourself. Rates can vary from 15€ ($17) for two per day all the way up to 250€ ($288)—as much as a board-rated four-star hotel in town. I've reviewed a few choice ones throughout this book, but there are hundreds more.

Probably the best most fantastic resource—because it is both user-friendly and has an English version—is **www.agriturismo.regione.toscana.it**, with databases of hundreds of farmstay searchable both by text or by clickable map down to the locality level, with info about each property, a photo or two, and a direct link to each agriturismo's own website.

Otherwise, if you feel handy enough with Italian, you can avail yourself of the three independent national organizations that together represent all agriturismi (or, at least, all the reputable ones).

Go to the website of **Terranostra** (www.terranostra.it) and click on "La tua vacanza," then "ricerche." This will pop you up a map of Italy. Mouse over Toscana or Umbria, click, and you'll get 524 choices in Tuscany and 127 in Umbria, arranged, unfortunately, alphabetically by name of the actual property (not by, say, town, which would make selecting one so much easier), with price categories of *basso* (low), *medio* (medium), and *alto* (high). Click on the property name, you get a review with pictures and symbols (in Italian, but understandable enough) plus contact info and a link to the place's own website, if available. In Tuscany, you can contact **Terranostra Toscana,** Via Magazzini 2, 50122 Firenze (© **055-280-539** or 055-20-022; fax 055-292-161); in Umbria, contact **Terranostra Umbria,** Via Campo di Marte 10, 06124 Perugia (© **075-500-9559;** fax 075-509-2032).

At the site of **Turismo Verde** (www.turismoverde.it), click on "La guida agrituristica on-line." On the search page that pops up, you can choose to search by Regione (Toscana or Umbria) or by Provincia (Firenze, Siena, Pisa, Lucca, Livorno, Grosseto, Arezzo, Perugia, and so on), and the results pages that come up based on your criteria are pretty much like the ones at Terranostra, only this time it returns all the results on a single page (rather than by pages of 10 each), so it's a bit easier to quickly find, say, all the ones near Lucca. Again, click on a property name

to learn much more about it and find a direct link. In Tuscany, contact the organization directly at **Turismo Verde Toscana,** Via Verdi 5, 50122, Firenze (© **055-200-2216;** fax 055-234-5039); in Umbria, contact **Turismo Verde Umbria,** Via Mario Angeloni 1, 06124 Perugia (© **075-500-2953;** fax 075-500-2956).

The easiest to navigate—since, one you click on a region (Tuscany or Umbria) on the map or text list, the next page gives you the option of continuing in English—is **Agriturist** (www.agriturist.it), but the site fails after that. You can, indeed, find hundreds upon hundreds of individual properties via a search engine. Stupidly, though, they do not then provide each farm's own website (possibly because they want you to book via their own site), so tracking the agriturismi down is that much more difficult; plus the info provided about each is far skimpier than with the other resources. In Tuscany, you can contact them at **Agriturist Toscana,** Piazza San Firenze 3, 50122, Firenze (© **055-287-838**); in Umbria, contact **Agriturist Umbria** c/o Federumbria Agricoltori, Via Savonarola 38, 06121 Perugia (© and fax **075-32-028**).

In the States, a few agencies are popping up to help you track down a perfect agriturismo in Italy, including Ralph Levey's **Italy Farm Holidays,** 547 Martling Ave., Tarrytown, NY 10591 (© **914/631-7880;** fax 914/631-8831; www.italyfarmholidays.com), which represents many of the more upscale agriturismo properties in Tuscany and Umbria.

17 Tips on Dining

For a quick bite, go to a *bar*—though it does serve alcohol, a *bar* in Italy functions mainly as a cafe. Prices at *bars* have a split personality: *al banco* is standing at the bar, while *à tavola*

means sitting at a table where they'll wait on you and charge 2 to 4 times as much for the same cappuccino. In *bars* you can find *panini* sandwiches on various rolls and *tramezzini,* giant

Getting Your VAT Refund

Most purchases have a built-in **value added tax (IVA)** of 17.36%. Non-EU (European Union) citizens are entitled to a refund of this tax if they spend more than 154.94€ (before tax) at any one store. To claim your refund, request an invoice from the cashier at the store and take it to the customs office (dogana) at the airport to have it stamped before you leave. **Note:** If you're going to another EU country before flying home, have it stamped at the airport customs office of the last EU country you'll be visiting (so if flying home via Britain, have your Italian invoices stamped in London).

Once back home, mail the stamped invoice back to the store within 90 days of the purchase, and they'll send you a refund check. Many shops are now part of the "Tax Free for Tourists" network. (Look for the sticker in the window.) Stores participating in this network issue a check along with your invoice at the time of purchase. After you have the invoice stamped at customs, you can redeem the check for cash directly at the tax-free booth in the airport, or mail it back in the envelope provided within 60 days. For more info, check out www.globalrefund.com.

triangles of white-bread sandwiches with the crusts cut off. These run 1.50€ to 5€ ($1.70–$5.75) and are traditionally stuck in a kind of tiny pants press to flatten and toast them so the crust is crispy and the filling hot and gooey; microwaves have unfortunately invaded and are everywhere turning *panini* into something that resembles a very hot, soggy tissue.

Pizza à taglio or **pizza rustica** indicates a place where you can order pizza by the slice, though Florence is infamous for serving some of Italy's worst pizza this way. Florentines fare somewhat better at **pizzerie,** casual sit-down restaurants that cook large, round pizzas with very thin crusts in wood-burning ovens. A *tavola calda* (literally "hot table") serves ready-made hot foods you can take away or eat at one of the few small tables often available. The food is usually very good, and you can get away with a full meal at a *tavola calda* for well under 15€ ($17). A *rosticceria* is the same type of place with some chickens roasting on a spit in the window.

Full-fledged restaurants go by the name *osteria, trattoria,* or *ristorante.* Once upon a time, these terms meant something—**osterie** were basic places where you could get a plate of spaghetti and a glass of wine; **trattorie** were casual places serving simple full meals of filling peasant fare; and **ristoranti** were fancier places, with waiters in bow ties, printed menus, wine lists, and hefty prices. Nowadays, though, fancy restaurants often go by the name of *trattoria* to cash in on the associated charm factor, trendy spots use *osteria* to show they're hip, and simple inexpensive places sometimes tack on *ristorante* to ennoble their establishment.

The **pane e coperto** (bread and cover) is a cover charge of anywhere from .50€ to 10€ (60¢–$12) that you must pay at every Italian restaurant for the mere privilege of sitting at the table. Most Italians eat a full meal—appetizer and first (*primo*) and second (*secondo*) courses—at lunch and dinner and will expect you to do the same, or at least a first and second course. See "A Taste of Tuscany & Umbria" in Appendix A for details of the meal and typical dishes to try. To request the bill, ask *"Il conto, per favore"* (eel *con*-toh pore fah-*vohr*-ay). A tip of 15% is usually included in the bill these days, but if unsure ask *"è incluso il servizio?"* (ay een-*cloo*-soh eel sair-*vee*-tsoh?).

You'll find at many restaurants, especially larger ones and those in cities, a *menù turistico* (tourists' menu) costing from 10€ to 35€ ($12–$40). This set-price menu usually covers all meal incidentals, including table wine, cover charge, and 15% service charge, along with a first and a second course. But it almost invariably offers an abbreviated selection of rather bland dishes: spaghetti in tomato sauce and slices of roast pork. Sometimes better is a *menù a prezzo fisso* (fixed-price menu), which usually doesn't include wine but sometimes covers the service and *coperto* and often has a wider selection of better dishes, occasionally including house specialties and local foods. Ordering a la carte, however, offers you the best chance for a memorable meal. Even better, forego the menu entirely and put yourself in the capable hands of your waiter.

Many restaurants that really care about their food—from *osterie* to classy *ristoranti*—will also offer a *menù degustazione* (tasting menu), allowing you to sample small portions of the kitchen's bounty, usually several antipasti, a few primi, and a secondo or two (and sometimes several local wines to taste by the glass). They're almost always highly recommendable and usually turn out to be a huge feast. Prices can vary wildly, anywhere from 20€ to over 100€ ($23–$115), though about 40€ to 50€ ($46–$58) is most common.

The *enoteca* (wine bar) is a growingly popular marriage of a wine bar and an osteria, where you sit and order from a host of local and regional wines by the glass while snacking on finger foods and simple primi. It's also possible to go into an *alimentari* (general food store) and have sandwiches prepared on the spot, or buy the makings for a picnic.

18 Recommended Books & Films

BOOKS

GENERAL & HISTORY *Florence, Biography of a City* (W. W. Norton, 1993) is popular historian Christopher Hibbert's overview on the City of the Renaissance, written in his extremely accessible storylike prose. Hibbert is also the author of *The House of Medici: Its Rise and Fall* (Morrow Quill Paperbacks, 1980), a group biography of Florence's most famous rulers.

Luigi Barzini wrote his classic *The Italians* (Simon & Schuster, 1996) in 1964, but the insights it gives into what makes modern Italy tick are surprisingly relevant today.

The Stones of Florence (Harcourt Brace, 1959) contains Mary McCarthy's indispensable, often scathing views on contemporary Florence (written in the early 1950s, but later editions are updated slightly).

The only favorable sequel to McCarthy's classic is *The City of Florence* (Henry Holt, 1995) by Yale professor R. W. B. Lewis.

Recently, a few literary histories set in Florence have enjoyed wild success. Ross King's slim tome *Brunelleschi's Dome* (Walker & Company, 2000) tells the fascinating story behind the building of Florence's Duomo.

Dava Sobel's *Galileo's Daughter* (Penguin, 2000) uses the scant documents available (letters and such) to recreate the relationship between the great Pisan scientist and one of his illegitimate daughters, whom he placed in a Florentine convent (only real place for a bastard girl in those times, other than the streets). The book deals largely with the trials and tribulations of Galileo and his fight against the Vatican's blasphemy charges, which nearly got him killed.

ART & ARCHITECTURE The first work of art history ever written was penned in 1550 (with a later, expanded edition published in 1568) by a Tuscan artist. Giorgio Vasari's **Lives of the Artists Vols. I and II** (Penguin Classics, 1987) is a collection of biographies of the great artists from Cimabue up to Vasari's own 16th-century contemporaries.

For a more modern art-history take, the indispensable tome/doorstop is Frederick Hartt's **History of Italian Renaissance Art** (H. N. Abrams, 1994). An easier, more colorful introduction, complete with illustrations, is Michael Levey's **Early Renaissance** (Penguin, 1967) and **High Renaissance** (Penguin, 1975).

Michelangelo, a Biography by George Bull (St. Martin's, 1995) is a scholarly, well-written take on the artist's life. For a livelier look, try Irving Stone's **The Agony and the Ecstasy** (Doubleday, 1961). Written as a work of historical fiction, it takes some liberties with the established record, but it's a good read.

LITERATURE & FICTION No survey of Tuscan literature can start anywhere but with Dante Alghieri, the 14th-century poet whose **Divine Comedy,** also published separately as **Inferno, Purgatorio,** and **Paradiso,** was Italy's first great epic poem since antiquity and the first major work to be written in the local vernacular (in this case, Florentine) instead of Latin. Allen Mandelbaum's edition of **Inferno** (Bantam, 1982) has the Italian and English side-by-side.

The next generation of Tuscan writers produced Giovanni Boccaccio, whose **Decameron** (Penguin Classics, 1995), a story of 100 tales told by young nobles fleeing the Black Death, is Italy's **Canterbury Tales.**

Tuscany also came up with the third great medieval Italian writer, Francesco Petrarca (Petrarch), whose **Selections from the Canzoniere and Other Works** (Oxford University Press, 1986) gives you a taste for lyrical poetry.

Even more real-world practical was Niccolò Machiavelli, whose handbook for the successful Renaissance leader, **The Prince** (Yale University Press, 1997), won him fame and infamy simultaneously.

If you don't have time for all of the above, pick up **The Renaissance Reader** (Penguin Meridian, 1987), edited by Julia Conaway Bondanella and Mark Musa, with selections from the Boccaccio's **Decameron,** Petrarch's **Canzoniere,** Leonardo da Vinci's notebooks, Benvenuto Cellini's **Autobiography,** Machiavelli's **The Prince,** Michelangelo's sonnets, and others.

E. M. Forster's **A Room with a View** (Dover, 1995), half of which takes place in Florence, and **Where Angels Fear to Tread** (Dover, 1993), set in San Gimignano, are perfect tales of uptight middle-class Edwardian society in Britain and how it clashes with the brutal honesty and seductive magic of Italy.

TRAVELOGUE Wolfgang von Goethe was, by many figures, the world's first famous grand tourist, and he recorded his traipse through Italy in **Italian Journey** (Princeton University Press, 1994).

Mark Twain became nationally famous for his report on a package tour of Europe and Palestine called **The Innocents Abroad** (Oxford University Press, 1996), a good quarter of which is about Italy. Henry James's **Italian Hours** (Penguin Classics, 1995) pulls together essays written by the young author.

A Traveller in Italy (Dodd, Mead, 1982/Methuen, 1985) is the informed account H. V. Morton wrote of his trip through the peninsula in the 1930s, with gorgeous, insightful prose by one of the best travelogue writers of this century.

Poet and professor Frances Mayes can make us all jealous with her best-selling *Under the Tuscan Sun* (Chronicle Books, 1996), and its sequel *Bella Tuscany* (Broadway Books, 1999), which chronicle her experience of buying and renovating a Tuscan dream house outside Cortona, exploring her new neighborhood, and cooking in her new kitchen. Note that the history and art history she describes is often just a wee bit incorrect (wrong dates and such), and that the recipes which liberally sprinkle the book are as much California Cuisine as Tuscan home-cooking, but, as she's a poet by profession, it's all beautifully written. It also spawned a huge industry of "I bought a house in Tuscany/Umbria/Sicily/wherever and renovated it and here's the charming story of how I learned to fit into Italian society" books—or, rather, it breathed new life, and a more prominent placement on the bookshelves, into a tiny and largely ignored genre that had already been perfected (and done much better) by the likes of Tim Parks (in the Veneto) and the late Barbara Grizzuti Harrison (in Sicily).

FILMS

Tuscany's countryside and hill towns have served as backdrops for everything from Kenneth Branagh's *Much Ado About Nothing* (you can stay in the villa where it was filmed; see chapter 5 for more information) to 1999's *A Midsummer Night's Dream* and *Tea with Mussolini.* And, in *The English Patient,* Ralph Fiennes convalesces in a monastery outside Siena, and there are cameos by Montepulciano and Pienza.

The Taviani brothers' *Fiorile (Wildflower)* is a story within a story, reviewing the last 100 years of Italian history as a father details the lineage of a family curse.

James Ivory's *A Room with a View* (1986) is based on the E. M. Forster novel (see above). Though only half the film is actually set in Florence, it's the best introduction to the 19th-century British infatuation with Tuscany.

The greatest talent to come out of Tuscany in the past few years is actor, director, writer, and comedian Roberto Begnini, creator of several slapstick mistaken-identity romps (*Johnny Stecchino, Il Mostro*) available with subtitles on the foreign film shelf of your favorite video store. Then, in 1998 this Prato-area native won three Oscars, including Best Foreign Film and Best Actor (only the 2nd non-English-speaking actor to do so)—with *La Vita è Bella (Life Is Beautiful),* an unlikely yet successful tragicomic fable set partly in Arezzo of one Jewish father trying to protect his young son from the horrors of the Holocaust by pretending the concentration camp they've been sent off to is one big game.

FAST FACTS: Tuscany & Umbria

The following list provides general info to cover both regions. You can find more specific information for Florence in its own "Fast Facts" section in chapter 3, including the local American Express office.

Area Codes Italy no longer uses separate city codes. Dial all numbers exactly as written in this book, and you should be fine.

Business Hours General open hours for **stores, offices,** and **churches** are from 9:30am to noon or 1pm and again from 3 or 3:30pm to 7:30pm. That early afternoon shutdown is the *riposo,* the Italian *siesta.* Most stores close all day Sunday and many also on Monday (morning only or all day). Some shops, especially grocery stores, also close Thursday afternoons. Some services and business offices are open to the public only in the morning. Traditionally, **museums** are closed Mondays, and though some of the biggest stay open all day long, many close for *riposo* or are only open in the morning (9am–2pm is popular). Some churches open earlier in the morning, but the largest often stay open all day. **Banks** tend to be open Monday through Friday from 8:30am to 1:30pm and 2:30 to 3:30pm or 3 to 4pm.

Use the *riposo* as the Italians do—take a long lunch, stroll through a city park, cool off in the Duomo, travel to the next town, or simply go back to your hotel to regroup your energies. The *riposo* is an especially welcome custom during the oppressive afternoon heat of August.

Drugstores You'll find **green neon crosses** above the entrances to most *farmacie* (pharmacies). You'll also find many *erborista* (herbalist) shops, which usually offer more traditional herbal remedies (some of which are marvelously effective) along with the standard pharmaceuticals. Most *farmacie* of any stripe keep everything behind the counter, so be prepared to point or pantomime. *Some help:* Most minor ailments start with the phrase *mal di* in Italian, so you can just say "Mahl dee" and point to your head, stomach, throat, or whatever. Pharmacies rotate which will stay open all night and on Sundays, and each store has a poster outside showing the month's rotation.

Electricity Italy operates on a 220 volts AC (50 cycles) system, as opposed to the United States' 110 volts AC (60 cycle) system. You'll need a simple adapter plug (to make our flat pegs fit their round holes) and, unless your appliance is dual-voltage (as some hair dryers and travel irons are), a currency converter.

For more information, call or send and self-addressed stamped envelope to **The Franzus Company,** Customer Service Dept., B50, Murtha Industrial Park, Box 142, Beacons Falls, CT 06403 (© 800/706-7064 or 203/ 723-6664; www.franzus.com). It'll send you a pamphlet called *Foreign Electricity Is No Deep Dark Secret,* with, of course, a convenient order form for adapters and converters on the back. You can also pick up the hardware at electronics, travel specialty stores, luggage shops, airports, and from Magellan's catalog (www.magellans.com).

Embassies/Consulates The **U.S. Embassy** is in Rome at Via Vittorio Veneto 119a (© **06-46-741;** fax 06-488-2672 or 06-4674-2217); www. usembassy.it. The **U.S. consulate in Florence**—for passport and consular services but *not* visas—is at Lungarno Amerigo Vespucci 38 (© **055-266-951;** fax 055-284-088), open to drop-ins Monday through Friday from 9am to 12:30pm. Afternoons 2 to 4:30pm, the consulate is open by appointment only; call ahead. The **U.K. Embassy** is in Rome at Via XX Settembre 80a (© **06-4220-0001;** fax 06-4220-2334; www.UKinitalia.it), open Monday through Friday from 9:15 to 1:30pm. The **U.K. consulate in Florence** is at Lungarno Corsini 2 (© **055-284-133;** fax 055-219-112). It's open Monday to Friday 9:30am to 12:30pm and 2:30 to 4:30pm.

Of English-speaking countries, only the United States and Great Britain have consulates in Florence. Citizens of other countries must go to their consulates in Rome for help: The **Canadian** consulate in Rome is at Via Zara 30, on the fifth floor (℗ **06-445-981** or 06-44598-2905; www.canada.it), open Monday through Friday from 8:30am to 12:30pm and 1:30 to 4pm. **Australia's** Rome consulate is at Via Alessandria 215 (℗ **06-852-721;** fax 06-8527-2300; www.australian-embassy.it). The consular section is open Monday through Thursday from 8:30am to noon and 1:30 to 4pm. The immigration and visa office is open Monday to Thursday 10am to noon; telephone hours are from 10 to 11:30am. **New Zealand's** Rome consulate is at Via Zara 28 (℗ **06-441-7171;** fax 06-440-2984), open Monday through Friday from 8:30am to 12:45pm and 1:45 to 5pm.

Emergencies Dial ℗ **113** for any emergency. You can also call ℗ **112** for the *carabinieri* (police), ℗ **118** for an ambulance, or ℗ **115** for the fire department. If your car breaks down, dial ℗ **116** for roadside aid courtesy of the Automotive Club of Italy.

Hospitals The emergency ambulance number is ℗ **118.** Hospitals in Italy are partially socialized, and the care is efficient, very personalized, and of a high quality. There are also well-run private hospitals. Pharmacy staff also tend to be very competent health-care providers, so for less serious problems their advice will do fine. For non-life-threatening, but still concerning, ailments you can just walk into most hospitals and get taken care of speedily—no questions about insurance policies, no forms to fill out, and no fees to pay. Most hospitals will be able to find someone who speaks English, but there's also a Florence-based **free medical translator service** available by calling ℗ **055-425-0126.** Also see the "Doctors & Dentists" and "Hospitals" listings under "Fast Facts: Florence" in chapter 3.

Internet Access Cybercafes are in healthy supply in most Italian cities. In smaller towns you may have a bit of trouble, but increasingly hotels are setting up Internet points. In a pinch, hostels, local libraries, and, often, pubs will have a terminal for access. For getting online in Florence, see its own "Fast Facts" section in chapter 3.

Language Though Italian is the local language around these parts, English is a close second, especially amongst anyone below about age 40 since they all learned it in school. Anyone in the tourism industry will know the English they need to help smooth transactions with you. Besides, most Italians are delighted to help you learn a bit of their lingo as you go. To help, I've compiled a short list of key phrases and terms in the Appendix B of this book.

Liquor Laws Driving drunk is illegal and not a smart idea on any road—nevermind Italy's twisty, narrow roads. Legal drinking age in Italy is 16, but that's just on paper. Public drunkenness (aside from people getting noisily tipsy and flush at big dinners) is unusual except among some street people—usually among foreign vagabonds, not the Italian homeless.

Lost & Found Be sure to tell all of your credit card companies the minute you discover your wallet has been lost or stolen and file a report at the nearest police precinct. Your credit card company or insurer may require a police report number or record of the loss. Most credit card companies have an emergency toll-free number to call if your card is lost or stolen; they may be able to wire you a cash advance immediately or deliver an emergency credit card in a day or two.

To report a lost or stolen card, call the following Italian toll-free numbers: **Visa** at © **800-819-014, MasterCard** at © **800-870-866,** or **American Express** at © **800-872-000,** or collect © **336-393-1111** from anywhere in the world. As a back up, write down the collect-call number that appears on the back of each of your cards (*not* the toll-free number—you can't dial those from abroad; if one doesn't appear, call the card company and ask).

Identity theft or fraud are potential complications of losing your wallet, especially if you've lost your driver's license along with your cash and credit cards. Notify the major credit-reporting bureaus immediately; placing a fraud alert on your records may protect you against liability for criminal activity. The three major U.S. credit-reporting agencies are **Equifax** (© **800/766-0008;** www.equifax.com), **Experian** (© **888/397-3742;** www.experian.com), and **TransUnion** (© **800/680-7289;** www.transunion.com). Finally, if you've lost all forms of photo ID, call your airline and explain the situation; they might allow you to board the plane if you have a copy of your passport or birth certificate and a copy of the police report you've filed.

Mail The Italian mail system is notoriously slow, and friends back home may not receive your postcards or aerograms for up to 8 weeks (sometimes longer). Postcards, aerograms, and letters, weighing up to 20 grams (.7 oz.), to North America cost .52€, to the United Kingdom and Ireland .41€, and to Australia and New Zealand .52€.

Newspapers & Magazines The *International Herald Tribune* (published by the *New York Times* and with news catering to Americans abroad) and *USA Today* are available at just about every newsstand, even in smaller towns. You can find the *Wall Street Journal Europe,* European editions of *Time* and *Newsweek,* and often the *London Times* at some of the larger kiosks. For events guides in English, see each individual city's "Visitor Information" listing.

Police For emergencies, call © **113.** Italy has several different police forces, but there are only two you'll most likely ever need to deal with. The first is the urban *polizia,* whose city headquarters is called the *questura* and can help with lost and stolen property. The most useful branch—the cops to go to for serious problems and crimes—is the *carabinieri* (© **112**), a national order-keeping, crime-fighting civilian police force.

Restrooms Public toilets are going out of fashion in northern Italy, but most *bars* will let you use their bathrooms without a scowl or forcing you to buy anything. Ask *"Posso usare il bagno?"* (*poh*-soh oo-*zar*-eh eel *ban*-yo). *Donne/signore* are women and *uomini/signori* men. Train stations usually have a bathroom, for a fee, often of the two-bricks-to-stand-on-and-a-hole-in-the-floor Turkish toilet variety. In many of the public toilets that remain, the little old lady with a basket has been replaced by a coin-op turnstile.

Safety Other than the inevitable pickpockets, especially in Florence, random violent crime is practically unheard of in the country. You won't find quite as many **gypsy pickpocketing children** as in Rome, but they have started roving the Santa Maria Novella area of Florence in packs and have even shown up in cities as far off the beaten path as Cortona. If you see a small group or pair of dirty children coming at you, often waving cardboard and jabbering in Ital-English, yell *"Va via!"* (go away) or simply "No!," or invoke the *polizia.* If they get close enough to touch you, push them away forcefully—don't hold back because they're kids—otherwise within a nanosecond you and your wallet will be permanently separated.

There are plenty of locals, of course, who prey on tourists as well, especially around tourist centers like the Uffizi and the Duomo in Florence. In general, just be smart. Keep your passport, traveler's checks, credit and ATM cards (if you feel the need to), and a photocopy of all your important documents under your clothes in a money belt or neck pouch. **For women:** There's occasional drive-by purse snatching in Florence by young moped-mounted thieves. Keep your purse on the wall side of the sidewalk and sling the strap across your chest. If your purse has a flap, keep the clasp side facing your body. **For men:** Keep your wallet in your front pocket and perhaps loop a rubber band around it. (The rubber catches on the fabric of your pocket and makes it harder for a thief to slip the wallet out easily.)

Taxes There's no sales tax added onto the price tag of your purchases, but there is a **value-added tax** (in Italy: IVA) automatically included in just about everything. For major purchases, you can get this refunded (see the box above). Some five-star and four-star hotels don't include the 13% luxury tax in their quoted prices. Ask when making your reservation.

Telephones/Fax **Local calls** in Italy cost .10€. There are three types of public pay phones: those that take coins only, those that take both coins and phone cards, and those that take only **phone cards** (*carta* or *scheda telefonica*). You can buy these prepaid phone cards at any *tabacchi* (tobacconists), most newsstands, and some bars in several denominations from 1€ to 7.50€. Break off the corner before inserting it; a digital display tracks how much money is left on the card as you talk. Don't forget to take the card with you when you leave!

For **operator-assisted international calls** (in English), dial toll-free ☎ 170. Note, however, that you'll get better rates by calling a home operator for collect calls, as detailed here: To make **calling card calls,** insert a phone card or .10€—it'll be refunded at the end of your call—and dial the local number for your service. For **Americans:** AT&T at ☎ **172-1011,** MCI at ☎ **172-1022,** or Sprint at ☎ **172-1877.** These numbers will raise an American operator for you, and you can use any one of them to place a **collect call** even if you don't carry that phone company's card. **Canadians** can reach Teleglobe at ☎ **172-1001.** **Brits** can call BT at ☎ **172-0044** or Mercury at ☎ **172-0544.** The **Irish** can get a home operator at ☎ **172-0353.** **Australians** can use Optus by calling ☎ **172-1161** or Telstra at ☎ **172-1061.** And **New Zealanders** can phone home at ☎ **172-1064.**

To **dial direct internationally from Italy,** dial ☎ **00,** then the country code, the area code, and the number. Country codes are as follows: the United States and Canada 1; the United Kingdom 44; Ireland 353; Australia 61; New Zealand 64. Make international calls from a public phone if possible because hotels charge ridiculously inflated rates for direct dial, but take along plenty of *schede* to feed the phone.

To call free national **telephone information** (in Italian) in Italy, dial ℂ **12.** International information for Europe is available at ℂ **176** but costs .60€ (70¢) a shot. For international information beyond Europe, dial ℂ **1790** for .50€ (60¢).

Your hotel will most likely be able to send or receive **faxes** for you, sometimes at inflated prices, sometimes at cost. Otherwise, most *cartoleria* (stationery stores), *copista* or *fotocopie* (photocopy shops), and some *tabacchi* (tobacconists) offer fax services.

Time Zone Italy is 6 hours ahead of Eastern Standard Time in the United States. When it's noon in New York, it's 6pm in Florence.

Tipping In **hotels,** a service charge is usually included in your bill. In family-run operations, additional tips are unnecessary and sometimes considered rude. In fancier places with a hired staff, however, you may want to leave a .50€ daily tip for the maid, pay the bellhop or porter 1€ per bag, and a helpful concierge 2€ for his or her troubles. In **restaurants,** 10% to 15% is almost always included in the bill—to be sure, ask *"è incluso il servizio?"*—but you can leave up to an additional 10%, especially for good service. At **bars and cafes,** leave a 10€ coin per drink on the counter for the barman; if you sit at a table, leave 10% to 15%. **Taxi** drivers expect 10% to 15%.

Water Although most Italians take mineral water with their meals, tap water is safe everywhere, as are any public drinking fountains you run across. Unsafe sources will be marked *"acqua non potabile."* If tap water comes out cloudy, it's only the calcium or other minerals inherent in a water supply that often comes untreated from fresh springs.

3

Settling into Florence: Birthplace of the Renaissance

ary McCarthy famously described Florence *(Firenze)* as a "City of Stone." This assessment digs deeper than merely the fact that the buildings, streets, doorjambs, sidewalks, windowsills, towers, and bridges are all cobbled together in shades of gray, stern rock hewn by generations of the stonecutters Michelangelo grew up with. Florence's stoniness is evident in both its countenance and its character. Florentines often seem more serious and slower to warm to strangers than the stereotypical Italians. The city's fundamental rhythms are medieval, and it's fiendishly difficult to get beyond the touristy surface and see what really makes Florence tick. Although the historic center is compact, it takes time and effort to get to know it personally, get the hang of its alleys, and understand the deep history of its palace-lined streets.

This chapter will equip you with the basic tools (the hammer and chisel, so to speak) you'll need to get under the stony skin of Florence. It breaks down the city layout and neighborhoods and explains the sorts of facts and services you'll need. It also reviews the best hotels and restaurants the city has to offer; you're sure to find something to fit your tastes and your budget.

1 Essentials

GETTING THERE

BY PLANE   For flights into Florence, see "Getting There" in chapter 2. Several European airlines are now servicing Florence's expanded **Amerigo Vespucci Airport** (✆ **055-30-615** for the switchboard or 055-373-498 for flight updates; 055-306-1700 for national flight info, 055-306-1702 for international flight info; www.safnet.it or www.aeroporto.firenze.it), also called **Peretola,** just 5km (3 miles) northwest of town. There are no direct flights to or from the United States, but you can make easy connections through London, Paris, Amsterdam, Frankfurt, and other major European cities. The regularly scheduled **city bus 62** connects the airport with Piazza della Stazione downtown, taking about 30 minutes and costing 1€ ($1.15). Rather more expensive (4€/$4.60) but without the local stops is the half-hourly **SITA bus** to/from downtown's bus station at Via Santa Caterina 15r (✆ **055-214-721,** 800-424-500, or 800-373-760), behind the train station. Metered **taxis** line up outside the airport's arrival terminal and charge a flat, official rate of 15€ ($17) to the city center.

The closest major international airport is Pisa's **Galileo Galilei Airport** (✆ **050/500-707;** www.pisa-airport.com), 97km (60 miles) west of Florence. Two to three **trains** per hour leave the airport for Florence (70–100 min., 5.40€/$6.20). If your flight leaves from this airport and you'll be going there by train from Florence, you can check in your baggage and receive your boarding

Florence

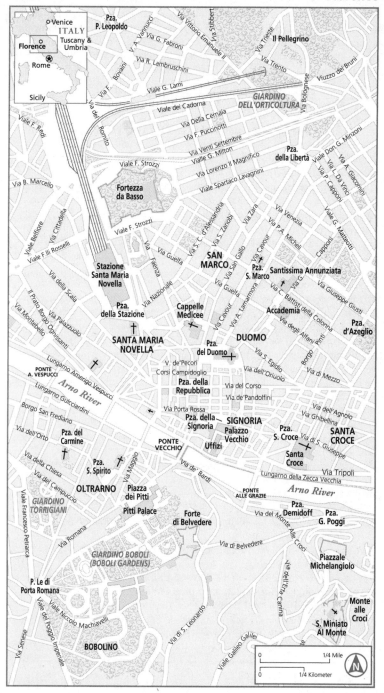

pass at the Air Terminal on Track 5 in Florence's Stazione Santa Maria Novella; show up 30 minutes before your train departure. Early-morning flights might make train connections from Florence to the airport difficult; the solution is the regular train from Florence into downtown Pisa, with a 10-minute taxi 2.60€ ($3) from the Pisa train station to the nearby Pisa airport; the no. 7 bus makes the same hop in twice the time for .77€ (90¢).

BY TRAIN   Florence is Tuscany's rail hub, with connections to all the region's major cities. To get here from Rome, you can take the Pendolino (four daily, 1¾ hr.; make sure it's going to Santa Maria Novella station, not Rifredi; you must reserve tickets ahead), an EC or IC train (24 daily, just under 2 hr.), or an inter-regionale (seven daily, around 3 hr.). There are also about 16 trains daily from Milan (3 hr.) through Bologna (1 hr.).

Most Florence-bound trains roll into the **Stazione Santa Maria Novella,** Piazza della Stazione (ⓒ **800-888-088** toll-free in Italy, or 055-288-765; www. trenitalia.it), which you'll often see abbreviated as **S.M.N.** The station is on the northwestern edge of the city's compact historic center, a 10-minute walk from the Duomo and a 15-minute walk from Piazza della Signoria and the Uffizi. There are loads of budget hotels immediately east of there around Via Faenza and Via Fiume.

With your back to the tracks, toward the station's left exit (across from track 16) and next to a 24-hour pharmacy you'll find a tiny **tourist info office** open daily from 8:30am to 9pm, with a hotel-booking service (charging 2.30€–8€/ $2.65–$9.20). The **train information office** is near the opposite exit to your right, across from Track 5. The yellow posters on the wall inside the anteroom list all train times and routes for this and other major Italian stations. Another copy of the Florence poster is just inside the sliding glass doors of the second, main room. For personalized help, you have to take a number from the color-coded machine (pink is for train information) and wait your turn—often for more than an hour.

Back at the head of the tracks, the **ticketing room** (*Salone Biglietti*) is located through the central doors; at *sportelli* (windows) 9 to 18 you can buy ordinary unreserved train tickets (see the "By Train" section under "Getting Around," in chapter 2, for details on which trains need supplements or reservations). The automatic ticket machines were installed mainly to taunt us and rarely work. Around the corner from this bank of ticket windows is a smaller room where you can buy **international tickets** (window 7), make **reservations** for high-speed and overnight trains (windows 1–4), or pay for a spot on the **Pendolino/ETR express** to Milan, Bologna, or Rome (window 7).

At the head of Track 16 is a 24-hour luggage depot where you can drop your bags (2.60€/$3 per piece for 12 hr.) while you search for a hotel.

Exit out to the left coming off the tracks and you'll find many bus lines as well as stairs down to the underground **pedestrian underpass** which leads directly to Piazza dell'Unità Italiana and saves you from the traffic of the station's piazza.

Note that some trains stop at the outlying **Stazione Campo di Marte** or **Stazione Rifredi,** both of which are worth avoiding. Although there's 24-hour

---

⸨Tips⸩ Stamp Your Ticket

Remember, if you're leaving Florence on the train, stamp your ticket in the yellow box at the start of the track before getting on the train.

> **Tips   Florence's "City Code"**
>
> What used to be Florence's city code of **055** is now an integral part of
> every phone number. You must now always dial it—including the initial
> zero—even when calling to another number from within Florence itself.
> Soon, new numbers in Florence may be issued starting with something
> other than 055.

---

bus service between these satellite stations and S.M.N., departures aren't always
frequent and taxi service is erratic and expensive.

BY BUS   Because Florence is such a well-connected train hub, there's little reason to take the longer, less comfortable intercity coaches. Dozens of companies
make dozens of runs here daily from all of Tuscany, much of Umbria, and the
major cities in Italy (the express bus from Rome's Tiburtina Station takes 4½ hr.).
Most bus stations are near the train station; see "Getting Around" in chapter 2 for
more details.

BY CAR   The **A1 autostrada** runs north from Rome past Arezzo to Florence
and continues to Bologna. The **A11** connects Florence with Lucca, and **unnumbered superhighways** run to Siena and Pisa.

Driving to Florence is easy; the problems begin once you arrive. Almost all
cars are banned from the historic center—only residents or merchants with special permits are allowed in. You'll likely be stopped at some point by the traffic
police, who'll assume from your rental plates that you're a visitor heading to your
hotel. Have the name and address of the hotel ready and they'll wave you
through. You can drop off baggage there (the hotel will give you a sign for your
car advising traffic police you're unloading), then you must relocate to a parking
lot. Ask your hotel which is most convenient: Special rates are available through
most of the hotels and their nearest lot.

Standard rates for parking in private lots near the center are 2€ to 3€
($2.30–$3.45) per hour; many lots offer a daily rate of 15€ to 30€ ($17–$35).
However, it is difficult to find spots, and they often keep weird hours, so your
best bet is one of the city-run garages, which are also less pricey. Although the
finally finished parking lot under Santa Maria Novella (1.55€/$1.80 per hour)
is closer to the city center, the best deal if you're staying the night (better than
most hotels' garage rates) is at the **Parterre parking lot** under Piazza Libertà,
north of Fortezza del Basso. If you're staying at least 1 night in Florence at a
hotel, you can park here, are welcome to a free bike, and (on presentation of
your hotel receipt as you leave or the hotel's stamp on your parking receipt) pay
only 10€ ($12) per night.

Don't park your car overnight on the streets in Florence; if you're towed and
ticketed, it will set you back substantially—and the headaches to retrieve your
car are beyond description.

VISITOR INFORMATION

TOURIST OFFICES   The city's **largest tourist office** is at Via Cavour 1r
(© **055-290-832;** fax 055-276-0383; www.firenzeturismo.it), about 3 blocks
north of the Duomo. Outrageously, they now charge for basic, useful info: .50€
(60¢) for a city map (though there's still a free one that differs only in lacking relatively inane brief descriptions of the museums and sights), 2€ ($2.30) for a little

guide to museums, and 1€ ($1.15) each for pamphlets on the bridges and the piazze of Florence. The monthly *Informacittà* pamphlet on events, exhibits, and concerts is still free. It's open Monday through Saturday from 8:30am to 6:30pm and Sunday from 8:30am to 1:30pm.

At the head of the tracks in Stazione Santa Maria Novella is a **tiny info office** with some maps and a hotel-booking service (see "Where to Stay," later in this chapter), open Monday through Saturday from 9am to 9pm (to 8pm Nov–Mar), but the station's **main tourist office** (© **055-212-245**) is outside at Piazza della Stazione 4. With your back to the tracks, take the left exit, cross onto the concrete median, and turn right; it's about 100 feet ahead. The office is usually open Monday through Saturday from 8:30am to 7pm (often to 1:30pm in winter) and Sunday 8:30am to 1:30pm.

Another office sits on an obscure side street south of Piazza Santa Croce, Borgo Santa Croce 29r (© **055-234-0444**), open Monday through Saturday from 9am to 7pm and Sunday 9am to 2pm.

PUBLICATIONS   At the tourist offices, pick up the free monthly *Informacittà.* The bilingual *Concierge Information* (www.florence-concierge.it) magazine, free from the front desks of top hotels, contains a monthly calendar of events and details on attractions. *Firenze Spettacolo,* a 1.55€ ($1.80) Italian-language monthly sold at most newsstands, is the most detailed and up-to-date listing of nightlife, arts, and entertainment.

WEBSITES   The official Florence information, **www.firenzeturismo.it**, contains a wealth of up-to-date information on Florence and its province, including a searchable hotels form allowing you to specify amenities, categories, and the like.

Firenze By Net (www.mega.it/florence), **Firenze.Net** (http://english.firenze. net), and **FlorenceOnLine** (www.fol.it) are all Italy-based websites with English translations and good general information on Florence. The site for **Concierge Information** (www.florence-concierge.it) is an excellent little guide to this month's events, exhibits, concerts, and theater. Other sites worth checking out are **Your Way to Florence** (www.arca.net/florence.htm), and **Time Out** (www.timeout. com/florence).

CITY LAYOUT

Florence is a smallish city, sitting on the Arno River and petering out to olive-planted hills rather quickly to the north and south but extending farther west and to a lesser extent east along the Arno valley with suburbs and light industry. It is a compact city best negotiated on foot. No two sights are more than a 20- or 25-minute walk apart, and all the hotels and restaurants in this chapter are in the relatively small *centro storico* **(historic center),** a compact tangle of medieval streets and *piazze* (squares) where visitors spend most of their time. The bulk of Florence, and most of the tourist sights, lies north of the river, with the Oltrarno, an old artisans' working-class neighborhood, hemmed in between the Arno and the hills on the south side.

MAIN STREETS & PIAZZE   The center is encircled by a traffic ring of wide boulevards, the Viale, that were created in the late 1800s by tearing down the city's medieval defensive walls. The descriptions below all refer to the *centro storico* as the visitor's city. From Piazza Santa Maria Novella, south of the train station, Via de' Panzani angles into Via de' Cerretani to Piazza del Duomo and the connected Piazza San Giovanni, the city's religious heart around the cathedral. From Piazza del Duomo, Via dei Calzaiuoli, the wide road popular during

The Red & the Black

Florence's address system has a split personality. Private homes, some offices, and hotels are numbered in black (or blue), while businesses, shops, and restaurants are numbered independently in red. This means that 1, 2, 3 (black) addresses march up the block numerically oblivious to their 1r, 2r, 3r (red) neighbors. You might find the doorways on one side of a street numbered: 1r, 2r, 3r, 1, 4r, 2, 3, 5r . . .

Florence keeps proclaiming that it's busily renumbering the whole city without the color system—plain 1, 3, 5 on one side, 2, 4, 6 on the other—and will release the new standard soon, but no one is quite sure when. Conservative Florentines who don't want their addresses to change have been helping to hold up the process. This is all compounded by the fact that the color codes occur only in the *centro storico* and other older sections of town; outlying districts didn't bother with the codes and use the international standard system common in the United States.

the *passeggiata* (evening stroll), leads south to Piazza della Signoria, Florence's civic heart near the river, home to the Palazzo Vecchio and the Uffizi Galleries. Traffic winds its way from the back of the Duomo to behind the Uffizi along Via del Proconsolo.

Another route south from the Duomo takes you down Via Roma, through cafe-lined Piazza della Repubblica, and continues down Via Calimala and Via Por Santa Maria to the Ponte Vecchio, the most popular and oldest bridge over the Arno, lined with overhanging jewelry shops. Via degli Strozzi leads east of Piazza della Repubblica to intersect Florence's main shopping drag, Via de' Tornabuoni, running north toward Piazza Santa Maria Novella and south to Piazza Santa Trínita on the river. Borgo de' Greci connects Piazza della Signoria with Piazza Santa Croce on the city center's western edge.

North from the Duomo, Via dei Servi leads to Florence's prettiest square, Piazza Santissima Annunziata. Via Riscasoli leads from the Duomo past the Accademia Gallery (with Michelangelo's *David*) to Piazza San Marco, where many city buses stop. Via de' Martelli/Via Cavour is a wide traffic-laden road also connecting the Duomo and Piazza San Marco. From the Duomo, Borgo San Lorenzo leads to Piazza San Lorenzo, the old neighborhood of the Medici that's these days filled with the stalls of the outdoor leather market.

On the Oltrarno side of the river, shop-lined Via Guicciardini runs toward Piazza dei Pitti and its museum-filled Pitti Palace. From here, Via Mazzetta/Via Sant'Agostino takes you past Piazza Santo Spirito to Piazza della Carmine; these two squares are the Oltrarno's main centers.

STREET MAPS   The tourist offices hand out two versions of a Florence *pianta* (city plan) free: Ask for the one *con un stradario* (with a street index), which shows all the roads and is better for navigation. The white pamphlet-size version they offer you first is okay for basic orientation and Uffizi-finding, but it leaves out many streets and has giant icons of major sights that cover up Florence's complicated back-alley systems.

If you want to buy a more complete city plan, the best selections are at the newsstand in the ticketing area of the train station and at **Feltrinelli International** and **Libreria Il Viaggio** bookstores (see "Shopping" in chapter 4 for more information). Falk puts out a good pocket-sized version, but my favorite is the palm-sized 1:9,000 **Litografica Artistica Cartografia** map with the yellow and blue cover. It covers the city in three overlapping indexed sections that fold out like a pop-up book. If you need to find a tiny street not on your map, ask your hotel concierge to glance at his or her *TuttoCittà*, a very complete magazine of fully indexed streets that you can't buy but residents (and hotels and bars) get along with their phone books.

THE NEIGHBORHOODS IN BRIEF

I've used the designations below to group hotels, restaurants, and (in chapter 4) sights in Florence. Although the city does contain six "neighborhoods" centered around the major churches (Santa Maria Novella, Il Duomo, Santa Croce, San Lorenzo, and Santo Spirito and San Frediano in the Oltrarno), these are a bit too broad to be useful here. I've divided the city up into more visitor-oriented sections (none much more than a dozen square blocks) focused around major sights and points of reference. The designations and descriptions are drawn to give you a flavor of each area and help you choose a zone in which to base yourself.

The Duomo The area surrounding Florence's gargantuan cathedral is about as central as you can get. The Duomo is halfway between the two great churches of Santa Maria Novella and Santa Croce as well as at the midpoint between the Uffizi Galleries and the Ponte Vecchio to the south and San Marco and the Accademia Gallery with Michelangelo's *David* to the north. The streets north of the Duomo are long and often traffic-ridden, but those to the south make up a wonderful medieval tangle of alleys and tiny squares heading toward Piazza della Signoria.

This is one of the most historic parts of town, and the streets still vaguely follow the grid laid down when the city began as a Roman colony. Via degli Strozzi/Via dei Speziali/Via del Corso was the *decumanus maximus,* the main east-west axis; Via Roma/Via Calimala was the key north-south *cardo maximus.* The site of the Roman city's forum is today's Piazza della Repubblica. The current incarnation of this square, lined with glitzy cafes, was laid out by demolishing the Jewish ghetto in a rash of nationalism during Italian unification in the late 19th century, and (until the majority of neon signs were removed in the early 1990s) it was by and large the ugliest piazza in town. The area surrounding it, though, is one of Florence's main shopping zones. The Duomo neighborhood is, understandably, one of the most hotel-heavy parts of town, offering a range from luxury inns to student dives and everything in between.

Piazza Della Signoria This is the city's civic heart and perhaps the best base for museum hounds, because the Uffizi Galleries, Bargello sculpture collection, and Ponte Vecchio leading toward the Pitti Palace are all nearby. It's a well-polished part of the tourist zone but still retains the narrow medieval streets where Dante grew up—back alleys where tourbus crowds running from the Uffizi to the Accademia rarely set foot. The few blocks just north of the Ponte Vecchio have good shopping, but unappealing modern buildings were planted here to replace the district destroyed during World War II (a Nazi commander with a Romantic soul couldn't bring himself to blow up the Ponte Vecchio during the

German army's retreat, as they had every other bridge over the Arno, so he blew up the buildings at either end of it to impede the progress of Allied tanks pushing north). The whole neighborhood can be stiflingly crowded in summer, but in those moments when you catch it off-guard and empty of tour groups, it remains the most romantic heart of pre-Renaissance Florence.

San Lorenzo and the Mercato Centrale This small wedge of streets between the train station and the Duomo, centered around the Medici's old church of San Lorenzo with its Michelangelo-designed tombs, is market territory. The vast indoor food market is here, and most of the streets are filled daily with hundreds of stalls hawking leather jackets and other wares. It's a colorful neighborhood, though perhaps not the quietest.

Piazza Santa Trinita This piazza sits just off the river at the end of Florence's shopping mecca, Via de' Tornabuoni, home to Gucci, Armani, Ferragamo, Versace, and more. Even the ancient narrow streets running out either side of the square are lined with the biggest names in high fashion. It's a very pleasant, well-to-do, but still medieval neighborhood to stay in even if you don't care about haute couture. But if you're a shopping fiend, there's no better place to be.

Santa Maria Novella This neighborhood, bounding the western edge of the *centro storico,* really has two characters: the rundown unpleasant zone around Santa Maria Novella train station and the much nicer area south of it between the church of Santa Maria Novella and the river.

In general, the train station area is the least attractive part of town in which to base yourself. The streets are mostly outside the pedestrian zone and hence heavily trafficked, noisy, and dirty, and you're removed from the major sights and the action. This area does, however, have more budget options than any other quarter. Some streets, like Via Faenza and its tributaries, contain a glut of budget joints, with dozens of choices every block and often two, three, or even six bottom-scraping dives crammed into a single building. It's the best place to go if you can't seem to find a room anywhere else; just walk up the street and try each place you pass. And while many hotels simply pander uninspiredly to tourists, a few (those recommended later) seem to try twice as hard as central inns to cater to their guests and are among the friendliest hotels in town. Just avoid anything on traffic-clogged Via Nazionale.

The situation improves dramatically as you move into the San Lorenzo area and pass Santa Maria Novella church and head toward the river. Piazza Santa Maria Novella and its tributary streets are attracting something of a bohemian nightlife scene (but parts of it can be seedy). Two of Florence's premier inns, the Excelsior and the Grand, are on the Arno at Piazza Ognissanti—just a bit south of the station but miles away in atmosphere.

San Marco and Santissima Annunziata These two churches are fronted by piazze—Piazza San Marco, now a busy traffic center, and Piazza Santissima Annunziata, the most beautiful in the city—that together define the northern limits of the *centro storico.* The neighborhood is home to the University, Michelangelo's *David* at the Accademia, the San Marco monastery, and long, quiet streets with some real hotel gems. The daily walk back from the heart of town up here may tire some, but others welcome its removal from the worst of the high-season tourist crush.

Santa Croce This eastern edge of the *centro storico* runs along the Arno. The bulky Santa Croce church is full of famous Florentine art and famous dead Florentines. The church is also the focal point of one of the most genuine neighborhoods left in the old center. While the area's western edge abuts the medieval district around Piazza della Signoria— Via Bentacordi/Via Torta actually trace the outline of the old Roman amphitheater—much of the district was rebuilt after World War II in long blocks of creamy yellow plaster buildings with residential shops and homes. Few tourists roam off Piazza Santa Croce, so if you want to feel like a city resident, stay here. This neighborhood also boasts some of the best restaurants in the city.

The Oltrarno "Across the Arno" is the artisans' neighborhood, still packed with workshops where craftspeople hand-carve furniture and hand-stitch leather gloves. It began as a working-class neighborhood to catch the overflow from the expanding medieval city on the Arno's opposite bank, but it also became a rather chic area for aristocrats to build palaces on the edge of the countryside. The largest of these, the Pitti Palace, later became the home of the grand dukes and today houses a set of museums second only to the Uffizi. Behind it spreads the landscaped baroque fantasies of the Boboli Gardens, Florence's best park. Masaccio's frescoes in Santa Maria della Carmine here were some of the most influential of the early Renaissance.

Florence tacitly accepted the Oltrarno when the 14th-century circuit of walls was built to include it, but the alleys and squares across the river continued to retain that edge of distinctness. It has always attracted a slightly bohemian crowd—the Brownings lived here from just after their secret marriage in 1847 until Elizabeth died in 1861. The Oltrarno's lively tree-shaded center, Piazza Santo Spirito, is a world unto itself, lined with bars and trendy salad-oriented restaurants (good nightlife, though young druggies have recently been encroaching on it); and, its Brunelleschi-designed church faces pointedly away from the river and the rest of Florence.

In the Hills From just about any vantage point in the center of Florence, you can see the city ends abruptly to the north and south, replaced by green hills spotted with villas, small farms, and the expensive modern homes of the upper-middle class. To the north rises Monte Ceceri, mined for the soft gray *pietra serena* that accented so much of Renaissance architecture and home to the hamlet of Settingnango, where Michelangelo was wet-nursed by a stonecutter's wife. The high reaches harbor the Etruscan village of Fiesole, which was here long before the Romans built Florence in the valley below.

Across the Arno, the hills hemming in the Oltrarno—with names like Bellosguardo (Beautiful Glimpse) and Monte Uliveto (Olive Grove Hill)—are blanketed in farmland. With panoramic lookouts like Piazzale Michelangiolo and the Romanesque church of San Miniato al Monte, these hills offer some of the best walks around the city, as Elizabeth Browning, Henry James, and Florence Nightingale could tell you. They're crisscrossed by snaking country roads and bordered by high walls over which wave the silvery-green leaves of olive trees.

Because of the lack of public transportation, first-time visitors who plan a strenuous sightseeing agenda probably will not want to choose accommodations in the hills. But for those who don't need to be in town every day and want a cooler, calmer, and altogether more relaxing vacation, they can be heaven.

GETTING AROUND

Florence is a walking city. You can leisurely stroll between the two top sights, the Duomo and the Uffizi, in less than 5 minutes. The hike from the most northerly sights, San Marco with its Fra' Angelico frescoes and the Accademia with Michelangelo's *David,* to the most southerly, the Pitti Palace across the Arno, should take no more than 30 minutes. From Santa Maria Novella across town to Santa Croce is an easy 20- to 30-minute walk.

Most of the streets, however, were designed to handle the moderate pedestrian traffic and occasional horse-drawn cart of a medieval city. Sidewalks, where they exist, are narrow—often less than 2 feet wide. Though much of the *centro storico* is closed to traffic, this doesn't include taxis, residents with parking permits, people without permits who drive there anyway, and the endless swarm of noisy Vespas and *motorini* (scooters).

In high season, especially July and August, the cars and their pollution (catalytic converters aren't yet standard), massive pedestrian and tourist traffic, maniac moped drivers, and stifling heat can wear you down. On some days Florence can feel like a minor circle of Dante's Inferno. Evenings tend to be cool year-round, bringing residents and visitors alike out for the traditional beforedinner *passeggiata* stroll up and down Via Calzaiuoli and down Via Roma and its continuations across the Ponte Vecchio.

BY BUS   You'll rarely need to use Florence's efficient **ATAF bus system** (© **055-565-0222** or 800-424-500; www.ataf.net) since the city is so wonderfully compact. Many visitors accustomed to big cities like Rome step off their arriving train and onto a city bus out of habit, thinking to reach the center; within 5 minutes they find themselves in the suburbs. The cathedral is a mere 5- to 7-minute walk from the train station.

Bus tickets cost a ridiculous 1€ ($1.15) and are good for an hour. A four-pack *(biglietto multiplo)* is 3.90€ ($4.50), a 24-hour pass 4.50€ ($5.20), a 2-day pass 7.60€ ($8.75), a 3-day pass 9.60€ ($11), and a 7-day pass 16€ ($18). Tickets are sold at *tabacchi* (tobacconists), bars, and most newsstands. Once on board, validate your ticket in the box near the rear door to avoid a steep fine. If you intend to use the bus system, you should pick up a bus map at a tourist office. Since most of the historic center is limited as to traffic, buses make runs on principal streets only, save four tiny electric buses that trundle about the *centro storico.*

BY TAXI   Taxis aren't cheap, and with the city so small and the one-way system forcing drivers to take convoluted routes, they aren't an economical way to get

Tips A Walking Warning

Florentine streets are mainly cobbled or flagstone, as are the sidewalks, and thus can be rough on soles, feet, and joints after awhile. Florence may be one of the world's greatest shoe-shopping cities, but a sensible pair of quality walking shoes or sneakers is highly recommended over loafers or pumps. In dress shoes or heels, forget it.

about town. Taxis are most useful to get you and your bags between the train station and your hotel in the virtually busless *centro storico*. The standard rate is .80€ (90¢) per kilometer, with a whopping minimum fare of 2.38€ ($2.75) to start the meter (that rises to 4.03€/$4.65 on Sun; 5.16€/$5.90 10pm–6am), plus .57€ (65¢) per bag. There's a taxi stand outside the train station; otherwise, you have to call **Radio Taxi** at ℂ **055-4242,** 055-4798, 055-4390, or 055-4499.

BY BICYCLE & SCOOTER   Despite the relatively traffic-free historic center, biking has not really caught on here, but local authorities are trying to change that with free bikes (well, in past years there has been a nominal .50€/60¢ fee). **Firenze Parcheggi,** the public garage authority (ℂ **055-500-0453;** www. firenzeparcheggi.it), has set up temporary sites about town (look for stands at the train station, Piazza Strozzi, Via della Nina along the south side of Palazzo Vecchio, and in the large public parking lots) where bikes are furnished free from 8am to 7:30pm; you must return the bike to any of the other sites.

If no bikes are left, you'll have to pay for them at a shop like **Alinari,** Via Guelfa 85r (ℂ **055-280-500;** www.alinarirental.com), renting bikes (2.50€/$2.90 per hour; 12€/$14 per day) and mountain bikes (3€/$3.45 per hour; 18€/$21 per day). It also rents 50cc scooters (8€/$9.20 per hour; 28€/$32 per day) and 100cc mopeds (10€/$12 per hour; 47€/$54 per day). Another renter with the same basic prices is **Florence by Bike,** Via San Zanobi, 120–122r (ℂ **055-488-992;** www.florencebybike.it).

BY CAR   Trying to drive in the *centro storico* is a frustrating, useless exercise. Florence is a maze of one-way streets and pedestrian zones, and it takes an old hand to know which laws to break in order to get where you need to go—plus you need a permit to do anything beyond dropping off and picking up bags at your hotel. Park your vehicle in one of the huge underground lots on the center's periphery and pound the pavement (see "Getting There: By Car," earlier in this chapter). For car rental firms in town, see "By Car" under "Getting Around" in chapter 2.

BY GUIDED TOUR   **American Express** (see "Fast Facts: Florence," below) teams with venerable **CAF Tours,** Via Roma 4 (ℂ **055-283-200;** www.caf tours.com), to offer two half-day bus tours of town (39€/$45), including visits to the Uffizi, the Medici Chapels, and Piazzale Michelangiolo. They also offer several walking tours for 23€ to 33€ ($26–$30); day trips to Pisa, Siena/San Gimignano, the Chianti, Lucca, or Medici villas for 35€ to 69€ ($40–$79); and farther afield to Venice, Rome, or Perugia/Assisi for 82€ to 105€ ($94–$121). You can book similar tours through most other travel agencies around town.

Walking Tours of Florence (ℂ **055-264-5033;** www.artviva.com) offers a basic 3-hour tour daily at 9:45am for 25€ ($29) adults, 20€ ($23) students under 26, or 10€ ($12) children aged 6 to 12. Meet at their office on the mezzanine level of Piazza Santa Stefano 2, a pocket-sized piazza hidden off Via Por Santa Maria between Via Lambertesca and the Ponte Vecchio. They provide many other thematic tours as well as private guides.

Call **I Bike Italy** (ℂ **055-234-2371;** www.ibikeitaly.com) to sign up for 1-day rides in the surrounding countryside: Fiesole year-round for $70, or the Chianti April 15 through October for $85. A shuttle bus picks you up at 9am at the Ponte delle Grazie and drives you to the outskirts of town, and an enjoyable lunch in a local trattoria is included. You're back in town by 5pm. It might stretch your budget, but you should get out of this tourist-trodden stone city for a glimpse of the incomparable Tuscan countryside. They also offer a summertime, 2-day trip (Tues–Wed) to Siena for $280.

FAST FACTS: Florence

American Express Amex, Piazza Cimatori/Via Dante Alghieri 22r, 50122 Firenze (© **055-50-981**), will act as a travel agent (for a commission), accept mail on your behalf (see "Mail," below), and cash traveler's checks at no commission. (They don't have to be Amex checks.) The office is open Monday through Friday from 9am to 5:30pm and Saturday from 9am to 12:30pm (no travel services on Sat).

Business Hours Hours mainly follow the Italian norm (see "Fast Facts: Tuscany & Umbria," in chapter 2). In Florence, however, many of the larger and more central shops stay open through the midday *riposo* (ORARIO NO-STOP).

Consulates See "Embassies/Consulates," under "Fast Facts: Tuscany & Umbria" in chapter 2.

Doctors/Dentists A **walk-in clinic** (© **055-483-363** or 0330-774-731) is run by Dott. Giorgio Scappini Tuesday, and Thursday office hours are brief, 5:30 to 6:30pm or by appointment at Via Bonifacio Lupi 32 (just south of the Tourist Medical Service; see "Hospitals" below); Monday, Wednesday, and Friday, go to Via Guasti 2 from 3 to 4pm (north of the Fortezza del Basso). **Dr. Stephen Kerr** keeps an office at Via Porta Rossa 1 (© **0335-836-1682** or 055-288-055 at home), with office hours Monday through Friday from 3 to 5pm without an appointment (home visits or clinic appointments 24 hr.).

For general dentistry, try **Dr. Camis de Fonseca,** Via Nino Bixio 9, northeast of the city center off Viale dei Mille (© **055-587-632**), open Monday through Friday from 3 to 7pm; he's also available for emergency weekend calls. The U.S. consulate can provide a list of other English-speaking doctors, dentists, and specialists. See also "Hospitals," below, for medical translator service.

Emergencies Dial © **113** for an emergency of any kind. You can also call the **Carabinieri** (the national police force; more useful than local branches) at © **112.** Dial an **ambulance** at © **118,** and report a **fire** at © **115.** All these calls are free from any phone. For **car breakdowns,** call ACI at © **116.**

Hospitals The **ambulance number** is © **118.** There's a special **Tourist Medical Service,** Via Lorenzo il Magnifico 59, north of the city center between the Fortezza del Basso and Piazza della Libertà (© **055-475-411**), open 24 hours; take bus 8 or 80 to Viale Lavagnini or bus 12 or night bus 91 to Via Poliziano.

Thanks to socialized medicine, you can walk into most any Italian hospital when ill but not an emergency and get taken care of speedily with no insurance questions asked, no forms to fill out, and no fee charged. They'll just give you a prescription and send you on your way. The most central are the **Arcispedale di Santa Maria Nuova,** a block northeast of the Duomo on Piazza Santa Maria Nuova (© **055-27-581**), and the **Misericordia Ambulance Service,** on Piazza del Duomo across from Giotto's bell tower (© **055-212-222** for ambulance).

For a **free translator** to help you describe your symptoms, explain the doctor's instructions, and aid in medical issues in general, call the volunteers at the **Associazione Volontari Ospedalieri (AVO;** © **055-425-0126** or 055-234-4567) Monday, Wednesday, and Friday from 4 to 6pm and Tuesday and Thursday from 10am to noon.

Internet Access To check or send e-mail, head to the now massive **Internet Train** (www.internettrain.it), with 15 locations in Florence including their very first shop at Via dell'Oriuolo 25r, 3 blocks from the Duomo (✆ **055-263-8968**); Via Guelfa 24a, near the train station (✆ **055-214-794**); Borgo San Jacopo 30r, in the Oltrarno (✆ **055-265-7935**), and in the underground tunnel from the train station towards town (✆ **055-239-9720**). Actually, there are now 126 offices across Italy (36 in Tuscany, 4 in Umbria—in Perugia and Orvieto), and the magnetic access card you buy is good at all of them, making plugging in throughout your journey that much easier. Access is 4€ ($4.60) per hour, or 1€ ($1.15) for 10 minutes; they also provide printing, scanning, Webcam, and fax services, plus others (bike rental, international shipping, 24-hr. film developing) at some offices. Open hours vary, but run at least daily from 9am to 8:30pm, often later.

The **Netgate,** Via Sant'Egidio 10–20r (✆ **055-658-0207**; www.thenet gate.it), has similar rates but also offers a Saturday "happy hour" of free access from 10:30 to 11am and from 2 to 2:30pm. It's open daily from 10am to 10:30pm (until 8:30pm in winter).

Laundry/Dry Cleaning Though there are several coin-op shops (mostly of the OndaBlu chain), you can get your wash done for you even more cheaply at a pay-by-weight *lavanderia*—and you don't have to waste a morning sitting there watching it go in circles. The cheapest are around the university (east of San Marco), and one of the best is a nameless joint at **Via Alfani 44r** (✆ **055-247-9313**), where they'll do an entire load for 6€ ($6.90), have it ready by afternoon, and even deliver it free to your hotel. It's closed Saturday afternoon. At other, non-self-service shops, check the price *before* leaving your clothes—some places charge by the item. Dry cleaning *(lavasecco)* is much more costly and available at *lavanderie* throughout the city (ask your hotel for the closest).

Mail You can buy *francobolli* (stamps) from any *tabacchi* or from the central post office. Florence's **main post office** (✆ **160** for general info, or 055-211-147) is on Via Pellicceria 3, 50103, Firenze, off the southwest corner of Piazza della Repubblica. You can pick up letters sent *Fermo Posta* (Italian for *poste restante* or held mail) by showing ID; see below. The post office is open Monday through Friday from 8:15am to 7pm and Saturday 8:15am to 12:30pm. All packages heavier than 2kg (4½ lb.) must be properly wrapped and brought around to the parcel office at the back of the building (enter at Via dei Sassetti 4, also known as Piazza Davanzati).

Drop postcards and letters into the boxes outside. To mail larger packages, drop them at *sportello* (window) 9/10, but first head across the room to window 21/22 for stamps. If that window is closed, as it often is, you buy your stamps at the next window, 23/24, which is also the pickup for *Fermo Posta*. You can also send packages via **DHL,** Via della Cupola 243 (✆ **055-308-877** or 800-345-345 for free pick-up) or **UPS,** Via Pratignone 56a in Calenzano (✆ **055-882-5501**).

To receive mail at the central post office, have it sent to [your name], Fermo Posta Centrale, 50103 Firenze, Italia/ITALY. They'll charge you .25€ (15¢) per letter when you come to pick it up at window 23/24; bring your passport for ID. For people without an Amex card, this is a much better deal than American Express's similar service, which charges 1.50€ ($1.75) to receive and hold non-cardholder's mail. For Amex members, however, this service is free, so you can have your mail sent to [your name], Client Mail, American Express, Via Dante Alghieri, 22r, 50123 Firenze, Italia/ITALY.

Newspapers & Magazines You can pick up the *International Herald Tribune* and *USA Today* from almost any newsstand, and you'll find the *Wall Street Journal Europe* and the *London Times,* along with *Time* and *Newsweek* magazines, at most larger kiosks. There's a 24-hour newsstand in the train station. For upcoming events, theater, and shows, see "Visitor Information," earlier in this chapter.

Pharmacies For pharmacy information, dial ☎ **110.** There are 24-hour pharmacies (also open Sun and state holidays) in **Stazione Santa Maria Novella** (☎ **055-216-761;** ring the bell between 1 and 4am); at **Piazza San Giovanni 20r,** just behind the baptistery at the corner of Borgo San Lorenzo (☎ **055-211-343**); and at **Via Cazzaiuoli 7r,** just off Piazza della Signoria (☎ **055-289-490**).

Police For emergencies, dial ☎ **112** for the Carabinieri police. To report lost property or passport problems, call the *questura* (urban police headquarters) at ☎ **055-49-771.**

Post Offices See "Mail," above.

Safety Central Italy is an exceedingly safe area with practically no random violent crime. There are, as in any city, plenty of pickpockets out to ruin your vacation, and Florence has the added joy of light-fingered gypsy children (especially around the train station), but otherwise you're safe. Do steer clear of the Cascine Park after dark, when it becomes somewhat seedy and you may run the risk of being mugged, and you probably won't want to hang out with the late-night heroin addicts shooting up on the Arno mudflats below the Lungarno embankments on the edges of town. See "Fast Facts: Tuscany & Umbria" in chapter 2 for more safety tips.

2 Where to Stay

Throughout the 1990s, through the turn of the millennium, and especially at the introduction of the euro in 2002, inflation ran rampant in Italy, and hotel prices more than tripled in cities like Florence. I'm going to say that again because it is pretty astounding and pretty awful: Prices have nearly tripled. It's now fairly difficult to find a double you'd want to stay in for less than 100€ ($115). Because hotel prices actually outpaced inflation, the hoteliers stockpiled some surplus cash, and in the last few years they've been reinvesting in their properties. In many hotels, the amenity levels are now at or above what Americans expect to find at home, and the days of the bathroom-down-the-hall cheap pensione are fading—or at least those properties are now mostly student dives. Almost everyone seems to have put in new bathrooms. Extras like heated towel racks, whirlpool tubs, satellite TVs with CNN and the BBC, and direct-dial phones that once only the top few inns boasted are now in four-fifths of the properties listed here. I've tried to balance the selections to suit all tastes and budgets.

For help finding a room, visit the Santa Maria Novella train station for the **Consorzio Informazioni Turistiche Alberghiere (ITA)** office, near Track 9 (☎ **055-282-893**), and the tiny tourist office, near Track 16, both of which will find you

Where to Stay in Florence

Albergo Azzi **2**
Albergo Merlini **2**
Burchianti **8**
Campeggio Michelangelo **43**
Grand Hotel Cavour **21**
Hotel Abaco **10**
Hotel Alessandra **15**
Hotel Aprile **6**
Hotel Bellettini **9**
Hotel Brunelleschi **24**
Hotel California **37**
Hotel Calzaiuoli **23**
Hotel Casci **36**
Hotel Chiari Bigallo **26**
Hotel de' Lanzi **25**
Hotel Firenze **22**
Hotel Helvetia & Bristol **12**
Hotel Hermitage **39**
Hotel La Scaletta **16**
Hotel Le Due Fontane **34**
Hotel Loggiato dei Servi **33**
Hotel Mario's **3**
Hotel Medici **27**
Hotel Monna Lisa **38**
Hotel Nuova Italia **4**
Hotel Pensione Pendini **29**
Hotel Regency **31**
Hotel Ritz **41**
Hotel Savoy **28**
Hotel Tornabuoni Beacci **13**
Hotel Torre Guelfa **14**
Il Guelfo Bianco **35**
Instituto Gould **17**
Mia Cara/Archi Rossi Hostel **1**
Morandi alla Crocetta **32**
Palazzo Antellesi **40**
Palazzo Castiglione **7**
Pensione Benescistà **30**
Pensione Maria Luisa de' Medici **20**
Pensione Sorelle Bandini **18**
Silla **42**
Torre di Bellosguardo **19**
Villa Azalee **5**
Villa Camerata (Ostello della Gioventù) **30**
Villa San Michele **30**
Westin Excelsior **11**

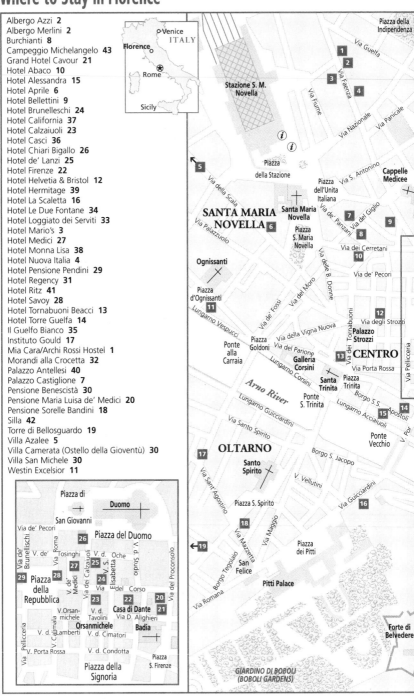

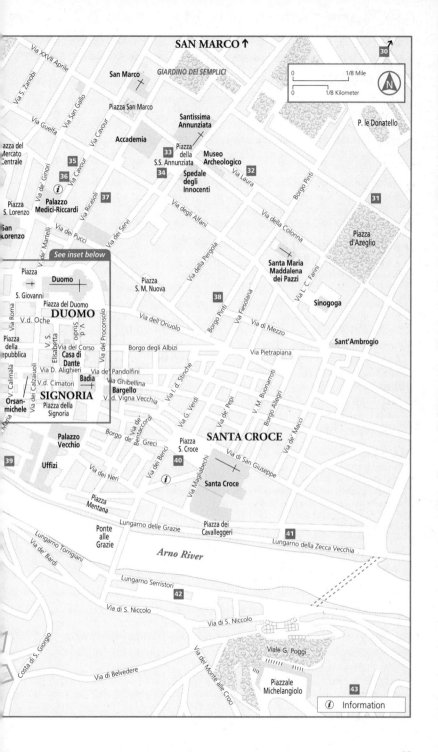

SAN MARCO ↑

GIARDINO DEI SEMPLICI

30

0   1/8 Mile
0   1/8 Kilometer

Via XXVII Aprile

Via S. Zanobi

Via Guelfa

Via San Gallo

Via Cavour

San Marco

Piazza San Marco

Santissima
Annunziata

Accademia

P. le Donatello

Piazza del
Mercato
Centrale

35

36

Via de' Ginori

Via de' Martelli

Via Cavour

ⓘ

Palazzo
Medici-Riccardi

37

Via Ricasoli

Piazza
S. Lorenzo

San
Lorenzo

Via dei Pucci

Via dei Servi

33 Piazza
della
S.S. Annunziata

34

Museo
Archeologico

Spedale
degli
Innocenti

Via Laura

32

31

Via degli Alfani

Via della Colonna

Borgo Pinti

Piazza
d'Azeglio

See inset below

Piazza

Duomo

S. Giovanni

Piazza del Duomo

DUOMO

V.d. Oche

Via Roma

V. S.
Elisabetta

Via dello Studio

Via del Corso

Via del Proconsolo

Casa di
Dante

Piazza
della
Repubblica

Via D. Alighieri

Badia

V.d. Calzaiuoli

V.d. Cimatori

V. Calimala

SIGNORIA

Bargello

Orsan-
michele

V. Maria

Piazza della
Signoria

V.d. Vigna Vecchia

Via de' Pandolfini

Via Ghibellina

Via della Pergola

Piazza
S. M. Nuova

Via dell'Oriuolo

Borgo degli Albizi

Borgo Pinti

Via Fiesolana

38

Santa Maria
Maddalena
dei Pazzi

Via di Mezzo

Sinogoga

Via L. C. Farini

Sant'Ambrogio

Via Pietrapiana

Palazzo
Vecchio

39

Uffizi

Via dei Neri

Borgo de' Greci

Via de' Bentaccordi

Via G. Verdi

Via d. Stinche

Via de' Pepi

V. M. Buonarroti

Borgo Allegri

Via de' Macci

SANTA CROCE

Piazza
S. Croce

40

ⓘ

Santa Croce

Via di San Giuseppe

Via dei Benci

Via Magliabechi

Piazza
Mentana

Ponte
alle
Grazie

Lungarno delle Grazie

Piazza dei
Cavalleggeri

41

Lungarno della Zecca Vecchia

Lungarno Torrigiani

Via de' Bardi

Arno River

Lungarno Serristori

42

Via di S. Niccolo

Via di S. Niccolo

Costa di S. Giorgio

Via di Belvedere

Via del Monte alle Croci

Viale G. Poggi

Piazzale
Michelangiolo

43

ⓘ Information

99

a room in your price range (for a small commission). Or go to the official tourist office's website subsection on accommodations at **www.toscanaeturismo.net/ dovedormire**.

Many budget hotels are concentrated in the area around the Stazione Santa Maria Novella. You'll find most of the hotels in this convenient and relatively safe (if charmless) area on noisy Via Nazionale and its first two side streets, Via Fiume and Via Faenza; an adjunct is the area surrounding the Mercato San Lorenzo. The area between the Duomo and Piazza della Signoria, particularly along and near Via dei Calzaiuoli, is a good though invariably more expensive place to look.

Peak season is mid-March through mid-July, September through early November, and December 23 through January 6. May and September are particularly popular whether in the city or in the outlying Tuscan hills.

To help you decide in which area you'd like to base yourself for exploring the city, consult "The Neighborhoods in Brief," earlier in this chapter.

NEAR THE DUOMO
VERY EXPENSIVE

Hotel Savoy ⭐⭐   This 1893 hotel underwent a complete transformation in 2000 by Sir Rocco Forte and his sister, who designed the warm, stylishly minimalist modern interiors. Rooms are standardized, with walk-in closets, dark brown marble bathrooms, and mosaics over the tubs. The different room "styles"—classic, executive, and deluxe—really just refer to size. Four suites (two rooms, two TVs, leather easy chairs, white marble bathrooms) are on the back, four on the piazza. Rooms on the fifth floor, added in 1958, just peep over the surrounding buildings for spectacular views, especially those on the Duomo (back) side. You're just a few steps in any direction from all the sights and the best shopping. The building actually belongs to Ferragamo (their decor tip o' the hat is to include shoe images in most public area art).

Piazza della Repubblica 7, 50123 Firenze. ✆ **800/223-6800** in the U.S.; 055-27-351 in Italy. Fax 055-273-5888. www.roccofortehotels.com. 107 units. 495€–627€ ($569–$721) double; 770€ ($886) studio; 1,089€–1,375€ ($1,282–$1,581) suite; 1,870€ ($2,151) Repubblica suite. Breakfast 25.30€ ($29). Parking 29€ ($33). AE, DC, MC, V. Bus: A, 22, 6, 11, 36, or 37. **Amenities:** Restaurant; bar; small gym w/view; concierge; tour desk; car-rental desk; courtesy car; secretarial services; 24-hr. room service; in-room massage; babysitting; laundry service; same-day dry cleaning; nonsmoking rooms. In room: A/C, TV w/pay movies, VCR on request, dataport, fax on request, minibar, hair dryer, safe.

EXPENSIVE

Hotel Brunelleschi ⭐   The mishmash of historical structures making up this hotel—including a Roman *calidarium* in the foundations—was so confusing they installed a small museum in the basement to explain it all. The property rambles through the remains of various medieval houses, a deconsecrated church, and a 6th-century Byzantine tower. Most of the interiors mix curving modern lines with the salvaged vestiges of the medieval buildings. The rooms are spacious and very comfortable, with large bathrooms, but are disappointingly modern. A few, especially on the upper floors, share with the panoramic roof terrace a view of the Duomo. The location is prime but the price a bit steep for those who don't get a thrill from sleeping near the fossilized remnants of the Middle Ages.

Piazza Sant'Elisabetta 3 (off Via de' Calzioli), 50122 Firenze. ✆ 055-27-370. Fax 055-219-653. www.hotel brunelleschi.it. 96 units. 340€ ($391) double; 500€ ($575) suite. Rates include breakfast. AE, DC, MC, V. Valet parking in garage 30€ ($35). Bus: B, 14, 23, or 71. **Amenities:** Intimate restaurant; bar (in the tower); concierge; tour desk; car-rental desk; courtesy car; business center and secretarial services; limited room service; in-room massage; babysitting; laundry service; same-day dry cleaning; nonsmoking rooms. In room: A/C, TV, minibar, hair dryer, safe.

MODERATE

Burchianti ★★ *(Finds)*   In 2002, rising rents forced the kindly owner of this venerable inn (established in the 19th c.) to move up the block into the *piano nobile* of a neighboring 15th-century palazzo. She definitely traded up. Incredible frescoes dating from 17th century and later decorate every ceiling but one tiny single, and many of the walls—actually, virtually all the walls are painted, but the yahoos of a previous age whitewashed over them and the hotel could afford to uncover only a few of them for the time being. When I visited, the workers were painting the trim, wiping off the terra-cotta tile floors, and finishing up installing the inlaid marble baths and period-style furnishings. This promises to become one of the most sought-after little hotels in Florence.

Via del Giglio 8 (off Via Panzani), 50123 Firenze. ℂ **055-212-796**. Fax 055-272-9727. www.hotelburchianti. com. 10 units. 120€–200€ double ($138–$230); 160€–230€ ($184–$265) suite. Rates include continental breakfast. No credit cards. Parking in garage next door about 23€ ($26). Bus: A, 1, 6, 14, 17, 22, 23, 36, or 37. **Amenities:** Concierge; tour desk; car-rental desk; limited room service (breakfast); babysitting; laundry service; dry cleaning. *In room:* A/C, TV on request, minibar in suites, hair dryer, safe.

Grand Hotel Cavour ★   The Cavour is an address of some refinement in Dante's old neighborhood, and about as central as you can get. The plush chairs in the large vaulted lobby focus around an antique stone pillar, and the roof terrace has a positively spectacular view of the Duomo, the Palazzo Vecchio, and other Florentine landmarks. The rooms, carpeted and furnished with contemporary good taste, tend to be on the small side, though a few enjoy brick arches and other 10th-century holdovers. The bathrooms are new, and the firm beds are spread with patterned quilts. Accommodations along the front and side get a view of the towers sprouting from the Bargello and the Badia, but be warned: The double-glazed windows are no match for the clamorous buses that grumble down the busy street in front.

Via del Proconsolo 3 (next to the Badia), 50122 Firenze. ℂ **055-282-461**. Fax 055-218-955. www.hotel cavour.com. 108 units. 198€ ($228) double. Rates include breakfast. AE, DC, MC, V. Valet parking in garage 26€ ($30). Bus: 14, 23, or 71. **Amenities:** Elegant and famous Beatrice restaurant; bike rental; concierge; tour desk; car-rental desk; salon; limited room service; babysitting; laundry service; same-day dry cleaning; nonsmoking rooms. *In room:* A/C, TV, dataport, minibar, hair dryer, safe.

Hotel Calzaiuoli ★   As central as you can get, the Calzaiuoli offers comfortable, well-appointed rooms on the main strolling drag halfway between the Uffizi and the Duomo. The halls' rich runners lead up a *pietra serena* staircase to the midsize and largish rooms decorated with painted friezes and framed etchings. Rooms were refurbished in 2001 with the addition of stylish wood furnishings and mirrored armoires. The firm beds rest on patterned carpets, in the older rooms surrounded by functional furniture beginning to show some wear. The bathrooms range from huge to cramped, but all have and fluffy towels (and a few enjoy Jacuzzis). The rooms look over the street, with its pedestrian carnival and some of the associated noise, or out the back—either over the rooftops to the Bargello and Badia towers or up to the Duomo's cupola.

Via Calzaiuoli 6 (near Orsanmichele), 50122 Firenze. ℂ **055-212-456**. Fax 055-268-310. www.calzaiuoli.it. 45 units. 88€–245€ ($102–$282) double. Rates include breakfast. AE, DC, MC, V. Valet parking 23€–26€ ($26–$30) in garage. Bus: 22, 36, or 37. **Amenities:** Concierge; tour desk; car-rental desk; limited room service; babysitting; laundry service; dry cleaning. *In room:* A/C, TV, minibar, hair dryer, safe.

Hotel Chiari Bigallo ★ *(Finds)*   I was quite cross 2 years ago to find that the owners had decided to renovate this formerly super-cheap standby with *the* single best location (across from the Duomo)—and more than double the prices.

Its rooms are modular modern now, but in the location competition, it still wins for being above the Loggia del Bigallo on the corner of Piazza del Duomo. If you get one of the few rooms facing the Duomo, you'll have a view like no other, within poking distance of Giotto's bell tower. The traffic-free zone doesn't mean you won't have significant pedestrian noise that drifts up from the cobbled street below, as this is the city's most tourist-trammeled intersection.

They renovated this place to bring it in line with their other three hotels, including, a few blocks away on Via delle Oche and with side views of this living postcard, the quieter de' Lanzi (below).

Vicolo degli Adimari 2 (off the Via Calzaiuoli near the Piazza Duomo), 50122 Firenze. ☎ and fax **055-216-086.** www.hotelbigallo.it. 17 units. 186€ ($214) double; 251€ ($289) triple. Rates include continental breakfast. AE, DC, MC, V. Valet parking in garage 21€. Bus: A, 1, 6, 11, 14, 17, 22, 23, 36, or 37. **Amenities:** Concierge; tour desk; car-rental desk; limited room service; laundry service; dry cleaning; nonsmoking rooms. *In room:* A/C, TV, minibar, hair dryer, safe.

Hotel de' Lanzi 🏆🏆   A much quieter alternative to the Hotel Chiari Bigallo,
its sister hotel around the corner (see above), the Lanzi is just as centrally located and more comfortable; it just doesn't have those drop-dead views of the Duomo and bell tower. The beds have firm mattresses and spreads embroidered in an antique Florentine pattern. The accommodations, in fact, are all done very tastefully for a hotel of this price. (Ask for a Frommer's discount and it may drop into the "Moderate" category.) The rooms come with shiny new bathrooms sporting heated towel racks (in most). Many rooms on the front get a magnificent window-filling side view of the Duomo, but even if you don't get the vista, you can be assured of cozy, relaxing accommodations just steps from the city's major sights and shopping. Breakfast is a full buffet, with fruit and ham.

Via delle Oche 11 (off Via Calzaiuoli around the corner from the Duomo), 50122 Firenze. ☎ and fax **055-288-043.** www.florence.ala.it/lanzi. 44 units. 186€ ($214) double, 251€ ($289) triple. Prices can drop up to 80–100% in low season (the website has details); also ask for Frommer's discounts. Rates include breakfast. AE, DC, MC, V. Valet parking 18€ ($21). Bus: 22, 36, or 37. **Amenities:** Concierge; tour desk; car-rental desk; limited room service; laundry service; dry cleaning; nonsmoking rooms. *In room:* A/C, TV, hair dryer, safe.

Hotel Pensione Pendini 🏆   Built during the heyday of the 1880s when Florence was briefly the capital of the newly unified Italy, the Pendini rises above the storefronts of Piazza della Repubblica. The Abolaffio brothers, Emmanuele and David, took over this former pensione in 1994 and have since installed double-glazing on all windows so that street noise has virtually disappeared. All bathrooms are also being redone in green tile with large tubs. Many rooms boast an airy country style, with original and reproduction antiques and brass-framed beds. The rather large accommodations on the piazza are best, with views over the bustle of the cafe-lined square. The lounge, offering 24-hour bar service, contains a comfortable mélange of 19th-century furnishings with scattered rugs, plus a computer with free Internet access. The location and price make this hotel a good choice for shoppers who'd rather give their money to Armani and Ferragamo.

Via Strozzi 1 (Piazza della Repubblica), 50123 Firenze. ☎ **055-211-170.** Fax 055-281-807. www.florence italy.net. 42 units, all with bathroom. 110€–150€ ($127–$173) double; 150€–210€ ($173–$242) triple; 170€–250€ ($196–$288) quad; 170€–330€ ($196–$380) family suite. Rates include continental breakfast. AE, DC, MC, V. Valet garage parking 21€–31€ ($24–$36). Bus: A, 6, 11, 22, 36, or 37. **Amenities:** Concierge; tour desk; car-rental desk; 24-hr. room service (breakfast and bar). *In room:* A/C, TV, dataport, hair dryer on request.

INEXPENSIVE

**Hotel Abaco 🏆🏆 🏆*Value*   Bruno is a bit of a Calabrian dynamo, running his clean, efficient little hotel in a prime location with gusto, and he's one of the more helpful, advice-filled hoteliers in town. The hotel has inherited a few nice touches from its 15th century palazzo, including high wood ceilings, stone floors (some are parquet), and in tiny no. 5 a carved *pietra serena* fireplace, and each room is themed after a Renaissance artist, with framed reproductions of the painter's works and a color scheme derived from them. Bruno's slowly replacing the mismatched furnishings with quirky antique-style pieces like gilded frame mirrors and rich half-testers over the beds. It's at a busy intersection, but the double paned windows help. There's a free Internet point, and he'll do a load of laundry for you for just 7€ ($8.05), wash and dry.

Via dei Banchi 1 (halfway between the station and the Duomo, off Via de' Panzani), 50123 Firenze. ℂ 055-238-1919. Fax 055-282-2289. www.abaco-hotel.it. 7 units, 3 with shower and sink, 3 with full bathroom. 67€ ($77) double without bathroom, 70€ ($81) double with shower only, 87€ ($100) double with bathroom. Breakfast 5€ ($5.75), free if you pay for the room with cash. AE, MC, V (they prefer cash). Valet parking 25€ ($29) in garage. Bus: 1, 6, 11, 14, 17, 22, 23, 36, or 37. **Amenities:** Bike rental; concierge; tour desk; car-rental desk; coin-op laundry. *In room:* A/C (costs an extra 5€/$5.75 to turn on), TV, dataport, hair dryer.

Hotel Firenze

A recent renovation has transformed this former student hangout (still partly used as a study-abroad dorm) into a board-rated two-star hotel. Its location is divine, tucked away on its own little piazza at the heart of the *centro storico*'s pedestrian zone, but it's a bit too institutional to justify the midrange rates. The rooms are brightly tiled but bland. This is a large operation without any of the warmth or ambience of a small, family-run hotel, and the concierge and management are efficient but generally uninvolved.

Piazza Donati 4 (on Via del Corso, off Via dei Calzaiuoli), 50122 Firenze. ℂ 055-268-301 or 055-214-203. Fax 055-212-370. 60 units. 88€ ($102) double; 120€ ($138) triple; 154€ ($177) quad. Breakfast 8€ ($9.20). Parking 26€ ($30) in nearby garage. No credit cards. Bus: A, 14, or 23. **Amenities:** Tour desk. *In room:* TV, hair dryer.

Hotel Medici 🍊 *Value*

In the heart of town with killer views, this place is more than worth it for budgeteers who can secure a room on the fifth or (better yet) sixth floor. All rooms are a good size but plain, with functional furniture, tile floors, tiny bathrooms, and firm beds. But who looks at the room when your window is filled with a vista of Florence's Duomo—facade, campanile, dome, and all? Only the top two levels of rooms get the full effect, but the sixth floor has a wraparound terrace everyone can enjoy. If you're lucky, you might happen in at a moment when one of the many regulars haven't booked one of the sixth-floor rooms with French windows opening directly onto the terrace. The price is excellent for this kind of location and panorama.

Via de' Medici 6 (between Piazza della Repubblica and Via de' Calzaiuoli), 50123 Firenze. ℂ 055-284-818. Fax 055-216-202. www.hotelmedici.it. 39 units, 26 with bathroom (shower only). 35€–105€ ($40–$121) double without bathroom; 45€–125€ ($52–$144) double with bathroom. MC, V. Rates include breakfast. Valet parking 20€ ($23) in nearby garage. Bus: A, 22, 36, or 37. **Amenities:** Concierge; tour desk; car-rental desk; limited room service (breakfast). *In room:* TV in some units, minibar in 6 units, hair dryer.

Pensione Maria Luisa de' Medici 🍊🍊🍊 *Kids* *Finds*

In the 1950s and '60s, Angido Sordi was into Italian design, and the rooms of his hotel—each frescoed with a different Medici portrait by his wife—have lamps, chairs, and tables you'd normally have to go to New York's Museum of Modern Art to see. In the 1970s and '80s, Sordi got into baroque art, so the halls are hung with canvases by the likes of Van Dyck, Vignale, and Sustermans. I can't wait to see what he gets into next. The 1645 palazzo setting goes well with the artistic theme, and while Dr. Sordi convalesces in a back room, his Welsh partner Evelyn Morris runs the place, cooking hearty breakfasts served to you in your room. Most rooms are large

---

Kids Family-Friendly Hotels

Hotel Casci (p. 105)   This inexpensive family favorite near the Palazzo Medici-Ricciardi has a series of extra-large rooms set aside especially for families. The hotel is housed in a 15th-century palazzo, and the family that runs it is very friendly and helpful. A great family value!

Hotel Nuova Italia (p. 109)   The Italian-American couple that runs this hotel near the station are just about the most helpful hoteliers I've ever run across. The rooms aren't overly large but are immaculate. And here's an added perk: With this Frommer's guidebook in hand, you and your brood can get a discount off the already reasonable prices.

Instituto Gould (p. 115)   The best bet for families on a tight budget is like a hotel masquerading as a hostel. It draws more families than students to its institutionally clean and large accommodations. Almost all rooms have a private bathroom, and you can get a family of four into your own quad with a private bathroom for around 60€ ($69).

Pensione Maria Luisa de' Medici (p. 103)   An amicable pair of proprietors runs this very central hotel just a few blocks from the Duomo. Most rooms are enormous, with multiple beds and dressers and tabletops on which to spread your family's stuff. The home-cooked Welsh breakfast served in your room is included in the low prices. Just be sure to admonish the more curious youngsters from touching the genuine—and valuable—baroque paintings in the hall.

---

enough to accommodate four to five people comfortably. The firm beds are set on carpeted or tiled floors scattered with thick rugs. There are four shared bathrooms, so you usually don't have to wait in the morning. One drawback: You have to walk up three flights. There is a curfew, which varies with the season.

Via del Corso 1 (2nd floor; between Via dei Calzaiuoli and Via del Proconsolo), 50122 Firenze. ☎ **055-280-048**. 9 units, 2 with bathroom. 67€ ($77) double without bathroom, 80€ ($92) double with bathroom; 93€ ($107) triple without bathroom, 113€ ($130) triple with bathroom; 118€ ($136) quad without bathroom, 140€ ($161) quad with bathroom. Rates include breakfast. No credit cards. Nearby parking about 24€–28€ ($27–$32). Bus: A, 14, or 23. **Amenities:** Concierge; tour desk. *In room:* Hair dryer, no phone.

NEAR PIAZZA DELLA SIGNORIA
EXPENSIVE
Hotel Hermitage ✦   This ever-popular hotel right at the foot of the Ponte Vecchio was renovated in 1998 to give each room wood floors or thick rugs, shiny new bathrooms (most with Jacuzzis), and fresh wallpaper. The rooms are of moderate size, occasionally a bit dark, but they're full of 17th- to 19th-century antiques and boast double-glazed windows to cut down on noise. Those that don't face the Ponte Vecchio are on side alleys and quieter. Their famous roof terrace is covered in bright flowers that frame postcard views of the Arno, Duomo, and Palazzo Vecchio. The charming breakfast room full of picture windows gets the full effect of the morning sun. The owners and staff excel in doing the little things that help make your vacation go smoothly—but prices are a bit inflated.

Vicolo Marzio 1/Piazza del Pesce (to the left of the Ponte Vecchio as you're facing it), 50122 Firenze ☎ **055-287-216**. Fax 055-212-208. www.hermitagehotel.com. 28 units. 245€ ($282) double; 260€ ($299) triple; 299€ ($344) family suite. Rates up to 20% lower in winter. Rates include breakfast. MC, V. Parking 21€–34€

($24–$39) in nearby garage. Bus: 23 or 71. **Amenities:** Concierge; tour desk; limited room service; babysitting; laundry service; dry cleaning. *In room:* A/C, TV, hair dryer, safe.

NEAR SAN LORENZO & THE MERCATO CENTRALE
MODERATE

Hotel Bellettini ★ *Value*   A hotel has existed in this Renaissance palazzo since the 1600s. Gina and Marzia, sisters and third-generation hoteliers, run this gem of terra-cotta tiles, wrought-iron or carved wood beds, antiques, and stained-glass windows. Room 44 offers a tiny balcony that, blooming with jasmine and geraniums by late spring, makes it second best only to room 45 with its view of the Medici chapels and the Duomo's dome. In 2000, they added a lovely six-room annex with frescoes, marble bathrooms, minibars, and coffeemakers (those are the double rooms that cost 160€/$184). The hotel shares management with the 26-room **Le Vigne,** Piazza Santa Maria Novella 24 (© **055-294-449;** fax 055-230-2263), which absorbs some of the overflow into large but simple renovated rooms. The rates are slightly lower than at the Bellettini, and duplex 119 is great for families. Breakfast is an impressive spread.

Via dei Conti 7 (off Via dei Cerretani), 50123 Firenze. © **055-213-561.** Fax 055-283-551. www.hotel bellettini.com. 28 units. 100€ ($115) double without bathroom, 130€–160€ ($150–$184) double with bathroom; 160€ ($184) triple with bathroom; 200€ ($230) quad with bathroom. Rates include buffet breakfast. AE, DC, MC, V. Nearby parking 18€ ($21). Bus: A, 1, 6, 14, 17, 22, 23, 36, or 37. **Amenities:** Concierge; tour desk; limited room service; laundry service; dry cleaning. *In room:* A/C, TV, hair dryer on request, safe.

INEXPENSIVE

Hotel California ★ *Value*   The California is a good budget option on a lightly trafficked street near the Duomo. Rooms were completely overhauled in 2000–01 with stylish modern furnishings, richly colored bedspreads, and spanking new bathrooms—a few with Jacuzzi tubs, and almost all with spacious marble sink counters. There are 18th-century fresco fragments and stuccoes on many of the ceilings, and breakfast is served on a flower-covered terrace in nice weather. A few of the rooms have balconies and views of the Duomo's cupola, and they offer good deals for families.

Via Ricasoli 30 (1½ blocks north of the Duomo), 50122 Firenze. © **055-282-753.** Fax 055-216-268. www. californiaflorence.it. 22 units. 90€–173€ ($104–$199) double; 120€–233€ ($133–$268) triple; 140€–294€ ($161–$338) quad. Ask about special promotions that can lower rates up to 40%. Rates include breakfast. AE, DC, MC, V. Valet parking around 25€ ($29). Bus: 1, 6, 7, 10, 11, 17, 20, 25, 31, 32, 33, 67, 68, or 91. **Amenities:** Concierge; tour desk; limited room service. *In room:* A/C, TV, dataport, minibar in 10 units, hair dryer, safe.

Hotel Casci ★ *Kids*   This clean hotel in a 15th-century palazzo is run by the Lombardis, one of Florence's nicest families. It's patronized by a host of regulars who know a good value when they find it. The Lombardis bicker among themselves Italian style but are amazingly accommodating toward guests—their favorite phrase in English is "No problem!" They even offer a free museum ticket to everyone who stays at least 3 nights (and with admissions running nearly $10 for most major museums, that's saying something). The tiny frescoed bar room was, from 1851 to 1855, part of an apartment inhabited by Giacchino Rossini, legendary composer of *The Barber of Seville* and *The William Tell Overture.* The rooms ramble on toward the back forever, overlooking the gardens and Florentine rooftops, and are mouse-quiet except for the birdsong. A few large family suites in back sleep four to five. The central location means some rooms (with double-paned windows) overlook busy Via Cavour, so for more quiet ask for a room facing the inner courtyard's magnolia tree. They serve an ample breakfast buffet in a frescoed dining room.

Via Cavour 13 (between Via dei Ginori and Via Guelfa), 50129 Firenze. (€ **055-211-686.** Fax 055-239-6461. www.hotelcasci.com. 25 units. 90€–140€ ($104–$161) double; 120€–180€ ($138–$207) triple; 180€–220€ ($207–$252) quad. Rates include buffet breakfast. Off-season rates 20%–30% less; check website for special offers, especially Nov–Feb. AE, DC, MC, V. Valet parking 23€–25€ ($26–$29), or in nearby garage (no valet) for 15€ ($17). Bus: 1, 6, 11, or 17. **Amenities:** Bar; concierge; tour desk; babysitting; laundry service; dry cleaning; nonsmoking rooms; free Internet access. *In room:* A/C, TV, dataport, fridge, hair dryer, safe.

Il Guelfo Bianco 🏛🏛 (*Value*   Once you enter this refined hotel (completely renovated in 1994 and enlarged in 2001), you'll forget it's on busy Via Cavour. Its windows are triple-paned, blocking out nearly all traffic noise, and many rooms overlook quiet courtyards and gardens out back. It gets a value icon for providing excellent service and luxury rooms at some of the lowest prices for a board-rated three-star hotel in all of Florence—and all that just a few blocks from the Duomo. The room decor is very pretty, with marble-topped desks, antique-style furnishings, modern art, and painted tile work in the large new bathrooms. The ceilings faithfully reproduce the beam and terra cotta look this 15th-century palazzo once had. Some rooms have retained such atmospheric 17th-century features as frescoed or painted wood ceilings, carved wooden door-ways, and the occasional parquet floor. Superior rooms are larger than executive ones (and can be made easily into triples), while "de luxe" rooms are larger still with a semi-separate sitting area—think junior suite. The friendly staff is full of advice, and they've installed a new bar and reading room on the ground floor.

Via Cavour 29 (near the corner of Via Guelfa), 50129 Firenze. (€ **055-288-330.** Fax 055-295-203. www. ilguelfobianco.it. 43 units. 105€–135€ ($121–$155) executive double, 144€–180€ ($166–$207) superior double, 170€–210€ ($196–$242) de luxe double; 200€–245€ ($230–$282) superior triple, 225€–265€ ($259–$305) de luxe triple. Rates include breakfast. AE, MC, V. Valet parking 24€–30€ ($27–$35) in garage. Bus: 1, 6, 7, 11, 17, 33, 67, or 68. **Amenities:** Concierge; tour desk; car-rental desk; 24-hr. room service; in-room massage; babysitting; laundry service; same-day dry cleaning. *In room:* A/C, TV, VCR in some units, data-port, minibar, hair dryer, safe.

NEAR PIAZZA SANTA TRÍNITA
VERY EXPENSIVE
Hotel Helvetia & Bristol 🏛🏛   This Belle Epoque hotel is the most central of the top luxury properties in town, host in the past to the Tuscan Macchaioli painters as well as De Chirico, playwright Pirandello, and atom-splitting Enrico Fermi. The attentive staff oversees the rather cushy accommodations outfitted with marble bathrooms; large, firm beds; and heavy curtains. Most rooms have at least one antique work of art on the fabric-covered walls, and all are well insu-lated from the sounds of the outside world. The large 17th-century canvases add an air of dignity to the plush sofas of the lounge, while the Winter Garden bar/breakfast room is tricked out with trailing ivy and a splashing fountain. Prices, though, are starting to get a little exaggerated.

Via dei Pescioni 2 (near the Palazzo Strozzi), 50123 Firenze. (€ **888/770-0447** in the U.S., 800-505-050 toll-free in Italy or 055-287-814. Fax 055-288-353. www.hotelhelvetiabristolfirenze.it. 67 units. 330€–470€ ($380–$541) double; 500€–650€ ($575–$748) suite. Breakfast 30€ ($35). AE, DC, MC, V. Valet parking in garage 35€ ($40). Bus: 6, 11, 36, 37, or 68. **Amenities:** Intimate restaurant; bike rental; concierge; tour desk; car-rental desk; 24-hr. room service; in-room massage; babysitting; laundry service; same-day dry cleaning; Internet terminal. *In room:* A/C, TV, VCR in deluxe rooms, minibar.

EXPENSIVE
Hotel Tornabuoni Beacci 🏛   The 80-year-old Beacci continues a 200-year hostelry tradition in this 16th-century Strozzi family palace. The staff greets

return guests and new friends alike with genuine warmth. Everything is a bit worn, but there's a concerted effort to furnish the rooms with period pieces. The dining room is sunny, and the lunches and dinners are well prepared. In summer, you can take breakfast on a terrace bursting with flowers and a view of the Bellosguardo hills. Off the terrace is a small bar, and there's an atmospheric reading room with a 17th-century tapestry and a large fireplace that roars to life in winter. They're currently expanding into the floor below with a small conference room and 12 more guest rooms, including a suite overlooking Piazza Santa Trínita and a honeymoon suite covered with beautiful 17th-century frescoes.

Via Tornabuoni 3 (off the north corner of Piazza Santa Trínita), 50123 Firenze. ☎ 055-212-645. Fax 055-283-594. www.tornabuonihotels.com. 28 units. 185€–220€ ($213–$253) double; 240€ ($276) jr. suite; 280€–360€ ($322–$414) double. Rates include buffet breakfast. AE, DC, MC, V. Parking 23€–25€ ($26–$29) in garage. Bus: 6, 11, 36, 37, or 68. **Amenities:** Restaurant; concierge; tour desk; 24-hr. room service; babysitting; laundry service; dry cleaning. In room: A/C, TV, minibar, hair dryer.

MODERATE

Hotel Alessandra ⭐ (Value) This old-fashioned pensione in a 1507 palazzo just off the river charges little for its simple comfort and kind hospitality. The rooms differ greatly in size and style, and while they won't win any awards from *Architectural Digest*, there are a few antique pieces and parquet floors to add to the charm. Air-conditioning was recently installed in 23 rooms. The bathrooms are outfitted with fluffy white towels, and the shared bathrooms are ample, clean, and numerous enough that you won't have to wait in line in the morning. They also rent out an apartment in a quiet section of the Oltarno (across the bridge from the Santa Croce neighborhood) for 775€ ($891) per week for two people; check it out at www.florenceflat.com.

Borgo SS. Apostoli 17 (between Via dei Tornabuoni and Via Por Santa Maria), 50123 Firenze. ☎ 055-283-438. Fax 055-210-619. www.hotelalessandra.com. 27 units, 19 with bathroom. 108€ ($124) double without bathroom, 145€ ($167) double with bathroom, 160€ ($184) double overlooking river; 145€ ($167) triple without bathroom, 191€ ($220) triple with bathroom; 160€ ($184) quad without bathroom, 212€ ($244) quad with bathroom; 160€ ($184) jr. suite; 200€ ($230) Baccio suite. Rates include breakfast. Ask about low-season rates. AE, MC, V. Parking in nearby garage 20€ ($23). Bus: B, 6, 11, 36, or 37. **Amenities:** Concierge; tour desk; limited room service (breakfast); massage; babysitting; laundry service; same-day dry cleaning; nonsmoking rooms (doubles overlooking river and suites). In room: A/C in most units, TV (PlayStation on request), hair dryer, safe in most units.

Hotel Torre Guelfa ⭐⭐⭐ Giancarlo and Sabina Avuri run one of the most atmospheric hotels in Florence. The first of many reasons to stay here is to drink in the breathtaking 360-degree view from the 13th-century tower, Florence's tallest privately owned tower. Although you're just steps from the Ponte Vecchio, you'll want to put sightseeing on hold and linger in your canopied iron bed. So many people request room 15, with a huge private terrace and a view similar to the tower's, they've had to tack 10€ ($12) onto the price. Follow the strains of classical music to the salon, whose vaulted ceilings and lofty proportions hark back to the palazzo's 14th-century origins.

The owners' newest hotel endeavor is the 18th-century **Palazzo Castiglione,** Via del Giglio 8 (☎ 055-214-886; fax 055-274-0521; pal.cast@flashnet.it), with four doubles (170€/$196) and two suites (200€/$230). Also ask them about their Tuscan hideaway, the **Villa Rosa di Boscorotondo** outside Panzano (p. 198).

Borgo SS. Apostoli 8 (between Via dei Tornabuoni and Via Por Santa Maria), 50123 Firenze. ☎ 055-239-6338. Fax 055-239-8577. www.hoteltorreguelfa.com. 22 units. 155€–210€ double ($178–$242); 190€–250€ ($219–$288) triple or jr. suite. Rates include continental breakfast. Parking in nearby garage 25€ ($29). AE, DC, MC, V. Bus: B, 6, 11, 36, or 37. **Amenities:** Concierge; tour desk; car-rental desk; courtesy car; limited room service; babysitting; laundry service; dry cleaning. *In room:* A/C, TV (in all but 6 1st-floor doubles), minibar, hair dryer.

SOUTH OF SANTA MARIA NOVELLA
VERY EXPENSIVE

Westin Excelsior ✪   This is Florence's prime luxury address; the sumptuousness will bowl you over, if the staggering price tags don't do it first. The old palazzi that make up the hotel, once partly owned by Napoléon's sister Caroline, were unified and decorated in 1927, the rooms decorated in three styles: Florentine 17th-century, Tuscan 18th-century, and Empire. All are done with a liberal use of colored marbles, walnut furniture, *pietra serena* accents, Oriental rugs, and neoclassical frescoes. Try to book a room overlooking the Arno (junior suites do not). The penthouses have terraces with drop-dead views over the city. Second-floor riverside doubles have balconies, and you can sometimes book half a luxurious suite at the price of a regular room. The staff is renowned for its genial attentiveness, offering a full array of amenities and services.

Piazza Ognissanti 3, 50123 Firenze. ✆ **800/937-8461** in the U.S.; 055-264-201 or toll-free 800-3253-5353 in Italy. Fax 055-26-8008. www.starwood.com. 171 units. 599€–756€ ($689–$869) Classic double (no Arno view), double 658€–832€ ($757–$957) deluxe double (with Arno view); 3,791€ ($4360) penthouse double; 1,209€ ($1,390) junior suite; 2,290€ ($2,634) suite. Breakfast 45€ ($52). AE, DC, MC, V. Valet parking 17€ ($20) in garage. Bus: B, C, or 9. **Amenities:** Faux 18th-century restaurant; 3-story chic Donatello bar; bike rental; children's program; concierge; tour desk; car-rental desk; courtesy car; business center; secretarial services; 24-hr. room service; in-room massage; babysitting; laundry service; same-day dry cleaning; nonsmoking rooms; executive-level rooms (a few outfitted for business work). *In room:* A/C, TV, dataport, fax on request, minibar, hair dryer, safe.

MODERATE

Hotel Aprile   The Aprile fills a semi-restored 15th-century palace on this busy hotel-laden street near the station. The corridors are hung with detached fresco fragments, highly ruinous from centuries of exposure on the palazzo's original facade. Portions of 16th- and 17th-century frescoes in much better shape grace many of the accommodations, and those on the ceiling of the breakfast room are beautifully intact (though in summer you can also breakfast in the garden out back). Aside from antique touches, the simple guest rooms are nothing to write home about. The street noise gets through even the double glazing, so light sleepers will want to request a room off the road—besides, some of the back rooms have a breathtaking view of Santa Maria Novella. The frescoes and relative quiet of no. 16 make it an excellent choice. Historical footnote: Cavernous room no. 3 has had a bathroom attached to it since the 15th century, one of the first "rooms with bathroom" ever!

Via della Scala 6 (1½ blocks from the train station), 50123 Firenze. ✆ **055-216-237.** Fax 055-280-947. www.hotelaprile.it. 30 units. 180€ ($207) double; 230€ ($265) triple; 215€ ($247) suite. Rates include breakfast. AE, DC, MC, V. Parking 18€–26€ ($21–$30) in nearby garage. Bus: 1, 2, 12, 16, 17, 22, 29, or 30. **Amenities:** Concierge; tour desk; car-rental desk; babysitting; laundry service; same-day dry cleaning. *In room:* A/C (in all but 1 unit), TV, minibar, hair dryer.

Villa Azalee ✪ *Finds*   The atmosphere of this 1870 villa on the historic center's edge, with its prizewinning flowers, soundproofed rooms, and comfortable beds, makes you forget the eight lanes of traffic flowing a few dozen feet away along Florence's inner ring road. There's a sunroom in the main villa, tapestries on the walls, and a very friendly staff. The rooms are floral print–oriented—perfect for Laura Ashley buffs, but for others the pink taffeta and gauzy canopies might seem over the top. The old *scuderia* (stables) out back were reconstructed in a hybrid Italian-English style, and many of the rooms in it echo of a cozy Cotswalds cottage. The best accommodations are on the *scuderia*'s ground floor, with heavy beamed ceilings, and on the villa's first (upper) floor, with wood floors, sleigh beds, and Empire bathrooms. I'd give it another star if only it weren't so far from the action.

Viale Fratelli Rosselli 44 (at the end of Via della Scala, between the station and Cascine Park), 50123 Firenze. ✆ **055-214-242.** Fax 055-268-264. www.villa-azalee.it. 25 units. 167€ ($192) double; 224€ ($258) triple. Rates include breakfast. AE, DC, MC, V. Parking 30€ ($35) in nearby garage. Bus: 1, 2, 9, 13, 16, 17, 26, 27, 29, 30, or 35. **Amenities:** Bike rental (3€/$3.45 a day); concierge; tour desk; car-rental desk; 24-hr. room service; laundry service; same-day dry cleaning. *In room:* A/C, TV, minibar, hair dryer.

BETWEEN SANTA MARIA NOVELLA & MERCATO CENTRALE
MODERATE

Hotel Mario's ★★   In a traditional Old Florence atmosphere, Mario Noce and his enthusiastic staff run a first-rate ship. Your room might have a wrought-iron headboard and massive reproduction antique armoire and look out onto a peaceful garden; the amenities include fresh flowers and fruit. The beamed ceilings in the common areas date from the 17th century, although the building became a hotel only in 1872. I'd award Mario's three stars if not for its location—it's a bit far from the Duomo nerve center. Hefty discounts during off-season months (as low as the lowest rates listed below) de-splurge this lovely choice.

Via Faenza 89 (1st floor; near Via Cennini), 50123 Firenze. ✆ **055-216-801.** Fax 055-212-039. www.hotel marios.com. 16 units. 80€–165€ ($92–$190) double; 100€–210€ ($115–$242) triple. Rates include continental breakfast. AE, DC, MC, V. Valet parking 20€–25€ ($23–$29). Bus: 7, 10, 11, 12, 25, 31, 32, or 33. **Amenities:** Concierge; tour desk; limited room service (breakfast); babysitting; laundry service; dry cleaning; nonsmoking rooms. *In room:* A/C, TV, hair dryer, safe.

Hotel Nuova Italia ★★ (Kids)   A Frommer's fairy tale: With her trusty *Frommer's Europe on $5 a Day* in hand, the fair Eileen left the kingdom of Canada on a journey to faraway Florence. At her hotel, Eileen met Luciano, her baggage boy in shining armor. They fell in love, got married, bought a castle (er, hotel) of their own called the Nuova Italia, and their clients live happily ever after. The staff here really puts itself to task for guests, recommending restaurants, shops, day trips— they gave me tips the tourist office didn't know about. The rooms are board-rated two-star standard, medium to small, but the attention to detail makes the Nuova Italia stand out. Every room has a bathroom (with fuzzy towels), orthopedic mattress, and triple-paned windows (though some morning rumble from the San Lorenzo market street carts still gets through). It's also one of a handful of hotels in all Tuscany with mosquito screens in the windows. Expected soon is new furniture custom-designed by Eileen. The family's love of art is manifested in framed posters and paintings, and Eileen is a great source about local exhibits.

Via Faenza 26 (off Via Nazionale), 50123 Firenze. ✆ **055-268-430** or 055-287-508. Fax 055-210-941. www. hotelnuovaitalia.com. 20 units. *For Frommer's readers:* 125€ double ($144); 145€ ($167) triple. Rates include continental breakfast. There are frequent discounts, so ask when booking. AE, DC, MC, V. Valet garage parking about 18€–22€ ($21–$25). Bus: 7, 10, 11, 12, 25, 31, 32, or 33. **Amenities:** Concierge; tour desk; car-rental desk; babysitting; laundry service; dry cleaning. *In room:* A/C, TV, hair dryer on request.

INEXPENSIVE

Albergo Azzi   Musicians Sandro and Valentino, the new young owners of this ex-pensione (aka the Locanda degli Artisti/Artists' Inn), are creating here a haven for artists, artist manqués, and students. It exudes a relaxed bohemian feel—not all the doors hang straight and not all the bedspreads match, though strides are being made (and they've even recently discovered some old frescoes in rooms 3 and 4). You'll love the open terrace with a view where breakfast is served in warm weather, as well as the small library of art books and guidebooks so you can enjoy a deeper understanding of Florence's treasures. Four of the rooms without a full bathroom have a shower and sink (but no toilet). In the same building, under the same management and with similar rates, are the **Anna** (8 units, 4 with bathroom; © **055-239-8322**) and the **Paola** (7 units, 4 with bathroom and some with frescoes; © **055-213-682**).

Via Faenza 56 (1st floor), 50123 Firenze. © and fax **055-213-806** (fax in 2004 may be 055-264-8613). hotel azzi@hotmail.com. 12 units, 7 with bathroom. 56€ ($64) double without bathroom, 60€ ($69) double with shower but no toilet, 75€–80€ ($86–$92) double with bathroom; 25€ ($29) bed in shared room. Breakfast 3€ ($3.45). AE, DC, MC, V. Parking in nearby garage 16€ ($18). Bus: 7, 10, 11, 12, 25, 31, 32, or 33. **Amenities:** Concierge; tour desk. *In room:* Hair dryer on request, no phone.

Albergo Merlini ⭐ *Value*   Run by the Sicilian Gabriella family, this cozy third-floor walk-up boasts rooms appointed with wooden-carved antique headboards and furnishings (and a few modular pieces to fill in the gaps). It's one of only two hotels in all Florence with mosquito screens. The optional breakfast is served on a sunny glassed-in terrace decorated in the 1950s with frescoes by talented American art students and overlooking a leafy large courtyard. Rooms 1, 4 (with a balcony), and 6 to 8 all have views of the domes topping the Duomo and the Medici Chapels across the city's terra-cotta roofscape. A recent renovation tripled the number of private bathrooms and freshened up everything. This is a notch above your average board-rated one-star place, the best in a building full of tiny pensioni. There's a 1am curfew.

Via Faenza 56 (3rd floor), 50123 Firenze. © **055-212-848**. Fax 055-283-939. www.hotelmerlini.it. 10 units, 6 with bathroom. 45€–65€ ($52–$75) double without bathroom, 50€–79€ ($58–$91) double with bathroom; 60€–90€ ($69–$104) triple without bathroom; 80€–100€ ($92–$115) quad without bathroom. Breakfast 6€ ($6.90). MC, V. Bus: 7, 10, 11, 12, 25, 31, 32, or 33. **Amenities:** Concierge; tour desk. *In room:* Hair dryer on request, no phone.

Mia Cara/Archi Rossi Hostel *Value*   The only way you'll pay less than at the Mia Cara is at the Noto family's hostel on the ground floor. At the hotel you'll find double-paned windows, spacious no-frills rooms, renovated plumbing (no shower curtains), and attractive iron headboards. Now if they'd only up the wattage of the light fixtures. The rooms overlooking the small garden out back are more tranquil than those on the street side.

Angela, the English-speaking daughter, can be reached at the numbers below or at © **055-290-804** for information on the downstairs **Archi Rossi Hostel** (www.hostelarchirossi.com), where units sleep four to six, without bathroom for 19€ ($22) per person, and with bathroom for 17€ to 19€ ($20–$22) depending on how many beds in the room (there are also private, bathless singles in the hostel for 29€/$33 including breakfast, and family rooms sleeping three to five for 24€/$27 each including breakfast). The hotel is closed 11am to 2:30pm, with a 1am curfew. Both the hotel and the hostel have their own TV room and public phone. They are planning a renovation that will double to size of both hotel and hostel, and may turn the hotel into a moderate property, but just when this will happen is anybody's guess.

Via Faenza 58 (2nd floor), 50123 Firenze. © **055-216-053**. Fax 055-230-2601. 22 units, 9 with bathroom. 50€ ($58) double without bathroom, 60€ ($69) double with bathroom. Extra bed 35% more. Ask about off-season discounts. No credit cards. No breakfast offered in hotel (only in hostel). 4 parking spots, sometimes free, sometimes up to 8€. Bus: 7, 10, 11, 12, 25, 31, 32, or 33. **Amenities:** Concierge; tour desk; nonsmoking rooms. *In room:* No phone.

NEAR SAN MARCO & SANTISSIMA ANNUNZIATA
VERY EXPENSIVE
Hotel Regency ✦✦   The Regency, converted from two 19th-century mansions, is set on a wooded piazza at the edge of town that looks remarkably like a giant London residential square. The posh old England feel continues into the salon and bar lounge, furnished with worn antiques and darkly patterned carpets and wall fabrics. This decoration scheme dominates in the comfortable rooms as well, with a liberal use of mirrored wall panels in the smaller rooms (though none are tiny by any stretch). The marble-clad bathrooms feature heated towel racks, and the discreet service includes fresh fruit and candies left in your room and a complimentary *Herald Tribune* each morning.

Piazza Massimo d'Azeglio 3, 50121 Firenze. 🕐 055-245-247. Fax 055-234-6735. www.regency-hotel.com. 35 units. 297€–363€ ($342–$417) comfort double, 330€–440€ ($380–$506) superior double, 385€–484€ ($443–$557) deluxe double; 473€–605€ ($544–$696) jr. suite, 671€–880€ ($772–$1,012) suite. Rates include breakfast. AE, DC, MC, V. Valet parking 26€ ($30). Bus: 6, 31, or 32. **Amenities:** Justifiably famous Relais le Jardin restaurant; cozy bar; bike rental; concierge; tour desk; car-rental desk; 24-hr. room service; in-room massage; babysitting; laundry service; dry cleaning; nonsmoking rooms. *In room:* A/C, TV, minibar, hair dryer, safe.

EXPENSIVE
Hotel Loggiato dei Serviti ✦✦   The Loggiato is installed in the building designed by Antonio da Sangallo the Elder in 1527 to mirror the Ospedale degli Innocenti across the piazza, forming part of one of Italy's most beautiful squares. Twelve years ago, this was a student pensione, but the renovation that converted it into a board-rated three-star hotel has restored the Renaissance aura. High vaulted ceilings in soft creams abound throughout and are particularly lovely supported by the gray columns of the bar/lounge. The wood or brick-tiled floors in the rooms are scattered with rugs, and most of the beds have wood frames and fabric canopies for an antique feel. The rooms along the front can be a bit noisy in the evenings because traffic is routed through the edges of the piazza, but I usually reserve one anyway, just for the magical view. They are in the process of adding 10 rooms to the hotel by expanding into the building next-door.

Piazza Santissima Annunziata 3, 50122 Firenze. 🕐 **055-289-592.** Fax 055-289-595. www.loggiatodeiservitihotel.it. 29 units. 205€ ($236) double; 266€ ($306) triple; 230€–380€ ($265–$437) suite. Rates include breakfast. AE, DC, MC, V. Parking 22€ ($25). Bus: 6, 31, or 32. **Amenities:** Concierge; tour desk; car-rental desk; limited room service; babysitting; laundry service; dry cleaning. *In room:* A/C, TV, minibar, hair dryer, safe.

MODERATE
Hotel Le Due Fontane   The only thing this place has over its neighbor the Hotel Loggiato dei Serviti (see above) is that the rooms get a view of all three loggia-blessed sides of the harmonious piazza (in the Loggiato, you look out from one of them). Although installed in a 15th-century palace, both the accommodations and the public areas are done along clean lines of a nondescript modern style. Unless you get a room with the view of the piazza (along with unfortunate traffic noise), it might not be the most memorable place to stay.

Piazza Santissima Annunziata 14, 50122 Firenze. 🕐 **055-210-185.** Fax 055-294-461. www.leduefontane.it. 57 units. 160€–181€ ($184–$208) double; 240€–270€ ($276–$311) suite. Rates include breakfast. AE, DC, MC, V. Parking 15€ ($17) in nearby garage. Bus: 6, 31, or 32. **Amenities:** Concierge; tour desk; car-rental desk; courtesy car; limited room service; babysitting; laundry service; dry cleaning; nonsmoking rooms. *In room:* A/C, TV, dataport, minibar, hair dryer.

Morandi alla Crocetta ✦✦ *Finds*   This subtly elegant pensione belongs to a different era, when travelers stayed in private homes filled with family heirlooms and well-kept antiques. Though the setting is indeed historic (it was a 1511 Dominican nuns' convent), many of the old-fashioned effects, like the wood beam ceilings, 1500s artwork, and antique furnishings, are the result of a recent redecoration. It has all been done in good taste, however, and there are still plenty of echoes of the original structure, from exposed brick arches to one room's 16th-century fresco fragments. An octogenarian Irishwoman, Katherine Doyle, still oversees the hotel business, but daily operations are mainly handled (with great care and hospitality) by her family and friends. They are currently engaged in a long project to open up a few new rooms on the first floor and transfer the reception there alongside a bar and small library.

Via Laura 50 (a block east of Piazza Santissima Annunziata), 50121 Firenze. ℂ **055-234-4747**. Fax 055-248-0954. www.hotelmorandi.it. 10 units. 170€ ($196) double; 220€ ($253) triple; 260€ ($299) quad. Breakfast 11€ ($13). AE, DC, MC, V. Parking 16€ ($18) in garage. Bus: 6, 31, or 32. **Amenities:** Concierge; tour desk; car-rental desk; limited room service; babysitting; laundry service; dry cleaning. *In room:* A/C, TV, dataport, minibar, hair dryer, safe.

NEAR SANTA CROCE
EXPENSIVE
Hotel Monna Lisa ⭐⭐ There's a certain old-world elegance to the richly decorated sitting and breakfast rooms and the gravel-strewn garden of this 14th-century palazzo. Among the potted plants and framed oils, the hotel has Giambologna's original rough competition piece for the Rape of the Sabines, along with many pieces by neoclassical sculptor Giovanni Duprè, whose family's descendants own the hotel. They try their best to keep the whole place looking like a private home, and many rooms have the original painted wood ceilings, as well as antique furniture and richly textured wallpaper or fabrics. In 2002, they restructured 15 additional rooms in another, recently acquired building bordering the courtyard and dubbed it "La Limonaia," with rooms overlooking the garden.

Borgo Pinti 27, 50121 Firenze. ℂ **055-247-9751**. Fax 055-247-9755. www.monnalisa.it. 45 units. 181€–325€ ($208–$374) double; 232€–413€ ($267–$475) triple; 410€–700€ ($472–$805) suite. Rates include breakfast. AE, DC, MC, V. Parking 11€ ($13) in their own garage. Bus: B, 14, 23, or 71. **Amenities:** American bar; small gym; concierge; tour desk; car-rental desk; limited room service; babysitting; massage; laundry service and dry cleaning (not on weekends). *In room:* A/C, TV, minibar, hair dryer, safe.

MODERATE
Hotel Ritz ⭐ One of the more intimate hotels along the Arno, the Ritz was taken over in 1996 and renovated by the Abolaffio brothers—who also own the Hotel Pensione Pendini (p. 102). The walls are hung with reproductions of Italian art from the Renaissance to Modigliani, and the reading room and bar are cozy. The room decor varies—some floors have wood or marble, others are carpeted. The mix-and-match furniture is mostly modern yet tasteful. Two rooms on the front have balconies to better enjoy the Arno view, and two on the back (nos. 37 and 38) have small private terraces, and there's a roof terrace with its view of Fiesole. The rather roomy bathrooms have been completely redone with new tile and heated towel racks.

Lungarno della Zecca Vecchia 24, 50122 Firenze. ℂ **055-234-0650**. Fax 055-240-863. www.florenceitaly.net/ritz. 30 units. 110€–180€ ($127–$207) double; 150€–230€ ($173–$265) triple; 170€–280€ ($196–$322) quad; 170€–330€ ($196–$380) family suite. Rates include breakfast. AE, DC, MC, V. Valet parking in garage 25€ ($29). Bus: B, 13, 14, or 23. **Amenities:** Concierge; tour desk; car-rental desk; 24-hr. room service (breakfast and bar). *In room:* A/C, TV, dataport, minibar, hair dryer, safe.

IN THE OLTRARNO
MODERATE

Hotel La Scaletta ✹ *Kids*   The Barbiere family runs this well-worn old shoe of a place in one of the only remaining palazzi on this block between the Pitti Palace and Ponte Vecchio. The inn's star is the flower-bedecked, sun-kissed terrace offering a 360-degree vista over the Boboli Gardens, the Oltrarno rooftops, and (beyond a sea of antennas) the monumental heart of Florence, plus a shoe-biting turtle they found here when they bought the place 25 years ago. Return visitors book months in advance for the homey rooms that have tiny bathrooms and old tiled floors. Some beds are lumpy to a fault, others fully firm, but street-side accommodations have double-paned windows that really do block the noise, and the worn, dark wood lacquer furniture is pleasantly unassuming. At breakfast, you can ask Manfredo to cook you a superb 11€ ($13) dinner that night.

Via Guicciardini 13 (2nd floor; near Piazza de Pitti), 50125 Firenze. ✆ **055-283-028** or 055-214-255. Fax 055-289-562. www.lascaletta.com. 13 units, 11 with bathroom. 93€ ($107) double without bathroom, 140€ ($161) double with bathroom; 165€ ($190) triple with bathroom; 190€ ($219) quad with bathroom. Rates include continental breakfast. Ask about off-season discounts. MC, V. Nearby parking 10€–28€ ($12–$32). Bus: D, 11, 36, or 37. **Amenities:** Concierge; tour desk; limited room service (breakfast); babysitting; laundry service; dry cleaning. *In room:* A/C in 8 units, TV in 5 units and on request, hair dryer.

Pensione Sorelle Bandini ✹ *Value*   This pensione occupies a landmark Renaissance palazzo on one of the city's great squares. You can live like the nobles of yore in rooms with 15-foot ceilings whose 10-foot windows and oversize antique furniture are proportionately appropriate. Room 9 sleeps five and offers a Duomo view from its bathroom window; room B is a double with a fantastic cityscape out the window. On closer inspection, you'll see the resident cats have left their mark on common-area sofas, and everything seems a bit ramshackle and musty. But that seems to be the point. The highlight is the monumental roofed veranda where Mimmo, the English-speaking manager, oversees breakfast and encourages brown-bag lunches and the chance to relax and drink in the views. Franco Zeffirelli used the pensione for some scenes in *Tea with Mussolini*. Quite frankly, their fame as a "typical old-fashioned" pensione has gone a bit to their heads—and to the prices, which have slowly crept rather higher than they should be for a budget-class hotel.

Piazza Santo Spirito 9, 50125 Firenze. ✆ **055-215-308.** Fax 055-282-761. pensionebandini@tiscali.it. 13 units, 5 with bathroom. Single rate on request. 108€ ($124) double without bathroom, 130€ ($150) double with bathroom. Extra person 35% more. Rates include continental breakfast (subtract about 9€/$10 per person if you opt out). No credit cards (but they're expecting to accept them "soon"). Bus: D, 11, 36, or 37. **Amenities:** Concierge; tour desk; car-rental desk; limited room service (breakfast); babysitting. *In room:* No phone.

Silla ✹   On a shaded riverside piazza, this 15th-century palazzo's second-floor patio terrace is one of the city's nicest breakfast settings (in winter, there's a breakfast salon with chandeliers and oil paintings). The Silla's most recent renovation was in 2001, with a few rooms redone in 1997. Many overlook the Arno and, when winter strips the leaves off the front trees, the spire of Santa Croce on the opposite bank. Every room is unique—some with beamed ceilings and parquet floors, others with floral wallpaper and stylish furnishings. The attention to detail and friendly skilled staff should make this hotel better known; word-of-mouth keeps it regularly full in pricey Florence despite its refreshing low profile.

Via dei Renai 5 (on Piazza Demidoff, east of Ponte delle Grazie), 50125 Firenze. ✆ **055-234-2888.** Fax 055-234-1437. www.hotelsilla.it. 35 units. 170€ ($196) double; 220€ ($253) triple. Rates include buffet breakfast. Ask about off-season discounts. AE, DC, MC, V. Parking in hotel garage 16€ ($18). Often closes late Nov to late Dec. Bus: C, D, 12, 13, or 23. **Amenities:** Concierge; tour desk; limited room service; nonsmoking rooms. *In room:* A/C, TV, minibar, hair dryer, safe.

IN THE HILLS
VERY EXPENSIVE

Villa San Michele ⭐ The peaceful air this place exudes recalls its origins in the 15th century as a Franciscan monastery, but I doubt the good friars had a heated outdoor pool or Jacuzzis in their cells. The facade was reputedly designed by Michelangelo, and everything is in shades of creamy yellow with soft gray *pietra serena* accents. The antique furnishings are the epitome of simple elegance, and some rooms come with canopied beds and linen sheets; others are fitted with wrought-iron headboards and antiques. The regular rooms are all in the main buildings, with modern junior suites dug into the hillside behind it, snuggled into the slopes between the terraces that host the swimming pool and formal gardens (several junior suites enjoy their own mini-gardens or terraces). They've recently converted the tiny hillside chapel into a cozy honeymoon suite with sweeping views, and the limonaia (where potted citrus trees once spent the frosty winters) into a grander suite. The monks never had it this good.

Via Doccia 4 (just below Fiesole off Via Fra' Giovanni Angelico), 50014 Fiesole (FI). ℂ **800/237-1236** in the U.S., or 055-567-8200 in Italy. Fax 055-567-8250. www.villasanmichele.com. 41 units. 843€–990€ ($969–$1,139) double; 1,351€–1,601€ ($1,554–$1,841) jr. suite; 2,001€ ($2,301) suite. Rates include breakfast. For half-pension add 73€ ($84), full pension add 138€ ($159). AE, DC, MC, V. Closed mid-Nov to mid-Mar. Free parking. Bus: 7 (ask driver for stop, because you get off before Fiesole); free hourly shuttle bus from Piazza del Duomo. **Amenities:** Restaurant; frescoed piano bar; heated outdoor pool; bike rental; concierge; tour desk; car-rental desk; shuttle bus to/from town center; small business center and secretarial services; 24-hr. room service; massage; babysitting; laundry service; same-day dry cleaning; extensive park with nature trails and jogging track. *In room:* A/C, TV/VCR (front desk has free movies), dataport, minibar, hair dryer.

EXPENSIVE

Torre di Bellosguardo ⭐⭐⭐ *(Finds)* This castle was built around a 13th-century tower sprouting from a hillside on the southern edge of Florence. Spend a few days here above the city heat and noise, lazing by the pool, hiking the olive orchard roads, or sitting on a garden bench to enjoy the intimate close-range vista of the city. Don't come expecting another climate-controlled and carpeted bastion of luxury. With its echoey halls, airy loggias, and imposing stone staircases, the Bellosguardo feels just a few flickering torches shy of the Middle Ages—exactly its attraction. It's packed with antiques, and the beds from various eras are particularly gorgeous. Some rooms have intricately carved wood ceilings, others sport fading frescoes, and many have views, including a 360-degree panorama in the romantic tower suite. It's a 15-minute stroll down the hill to Alla Vecchia Bettola (reviewed on p. 131).

Via Roti Michelozzi 2, 50124 Florence. ℂ **055-229-8145.** Fax 055-229-008. www.torrebellosguardo.com. 16 units. 280€ ($322) double; 330€–380€ ($380–$437) suite. Breakfast 20€ ($23). AE, DC, MC, V. Free parking. Bus: 12 or 13 to Piazza Tasso (then taxi up hill). **Amenities:** Outdoor pool (June–Sept), small indoor pool; small exercise room; Jacuzzi; sauna; concierge; tour desk; car-rental desk; 24-hr. room service (bar, no food); massage; babysitting; laundry service; same-day dry cleaning. *In room:* A/C in 3 suites, dataport, hair dryer.

MODERATE

Pensione Benescistà ⭐⭐ *(Kids)* This comfortable and quiet family-run pensione in a rambling 14th-century villa gets you the same view and escape from the city as the Villa San Michele above it at one-fifth the price. Antiques abound, and the elegantly cluttered salons are straight out of an E.M. Forster novel. Many accommodations have big old chests of drawers, and some open onto the pretty little garden. The dining room has a view of Florence, but in summer take in the vista by breakfasting on the terrace. Although service from the staff is occasionally off-handed, the owners are friendly and truly consider you a guest in their home. They also expect to be treated as hosts and require you to stay for most dinners. (I recommend trading one dinner for a lunch to try the nearby Trattoria le Cave di Maiano; see p. 133.)

Via Benedetto da Maiano 4 (just below Fiesole off the main road), 50014 Fiesole (FI). ℂ and fax **055-59-163**. 40 units. 176€ ($202) double. Rates include required half pension (full pension available for small supplement). Breakfast included. No credit cards. Free parking. Bus: 7 to Villa San Michele, then backtrack onto side road following signs. **Amenities:** Restaurant; limited room service (breakfast only). *In room:* Hair dryer.

HOSTELS & CAMPING

Both hostels below are immensely popular, especially in summer. If you aren't able to write or fax to reserve a space—months ahead, if possible—show up when they open. Also check out the private hostel Archi Rossi, listed above (along with its sister hotel Mia Cara) under the Santa Maria Novella/Mercato Central neighborhood.

Campeggio Michelangelo   Back in the good old days of yore when my family was wont to do "Europe on $5 a Day in an Ugly Orange VW Camper-van," this was our Florentine parking spot *de choix*. Here we could sleep with a select 1,000 of our fellow campers and have almost the same vista that the tour buses get up above on Piazzale Michelangiolo. (Sadly, a stand of trees blocks the Duomo.) Of course, you're packed in like sardines on this small plateau with very little shade (in Aug, arrive early to fight for a spot along the tree-lined fringe), but you get a bar, a minimart, a laundromat, and that killer view.

Viale Michelangelo 80 (about two-thirds of the way up to Piazzale Michelangiolo), 50125 Firenze. ℂ **055-681-1977**. Fax 055-689-348. www.ecvacanze.it/michelangelo/info.htm. Open camping (sleeps 1,000). 8€ ($9.20) per person plus 5€ ($5.75) per tent and 4.50€ ($5.20) per car. Rented tents 11€ ($13). No credit cards. Closed Nov to 1 week before Easter. Bus: 12 or 13. **Amenities:** Bar; coin-op laundry. *In room:* No phone.

Instituto Gould *(Kids)*   These are the best hostel-like accommodations in Florence, without a curfew, lockout period, or shower charge but with brand-new furnishings in plain but immaculate rooms—like a college dorm that's never seen a frat party. It's technically not a hostel, though it looks and operates like one. Most rooms are doubles or triples (all with buttonless phones to receive calls), and unless you opt for a five-person room, you're unlikely to bunk with strangers. The institute's real work is caring for orphans, and the proceeds from your room fee go to help needy children. Reception is open Monday through Friday from 9am to 1pm and 3 to 7pm, Saturday from 9am to 1pm (you can stay over and prepay in order to check out during the weekend, but you can't check in).

Via dei Serragli 49 (near Santo Spirito), 50124 Firenze. ℂ **055-212-576**. Fax 055-280-274. gould.reception@dada.it. 33 units, 27 with bathroom. Depending on how many beds are in room (1–4): 17€–28€ ($20–$32) per person without bathroom; 20€–34€ ($23–$39) per person with bathroom. No credit cards. Bus: 11, 36, or 37. *In room:* No phone.

Villa Camerata (Ostello della Gioventù)   Florence's IYH hostel is a ways outside the city center but worth it for the budget-strained. The name doesn't lie—this really is a countryside villa, with an outdoor loggia and is surrounded by greenery. The rooms are regulation hostel bland but livable. You can check in after the lockout (9am–2pm in summer, 9am–3pm in winter), and curfew is midnight. They also offer 180 tent sites for cool camping amid their wooded acres for 5€ ($5.75) per person plus 4€ to 6€ ($4.60–$6.90) per tent.

Viale Augusto Righi 2–4 (3.5km/2 miles northwest of the city center; above Campo di Marte), 50137 Firenze. ℰ **055-601-451.** Fax 055-610-300. www.ostellionline.org. 322 beds. 16€ ($18) per person; 17€ ($19) per person in 3-person family room; 19€ ($22) per person in 2-person family room. Meals 8€ ($9.20). Rates include breakfast. No credit cards. Bus: 17B (30-min. ride; 17A and 17C take longer). **Amenities:** Coin-op laundry. *In room:* No phone.

LONG-TERM STAYS

Many of the agencies listed under "Tips on Accommodations, Villa Rentals & Farm Stays" in chapter 2 also handle villas in Florence's hills and apartments in town. One of the most reputable specialists in Florence is **Florence and Abroad,** Via San Zanobi 58 (ℰ **055-487-004;** fax 055-490-143; www.florenceand abroad.com), which matches different tastes and budgets to a wide range of apartments starting at about $650 per week—though note they take a commission (10% for 1-month rentals, less for longer periods). Another reputable agency for short-term apartment and house rentals (weekly and monthly) is **Windows on Tuscany,** Via Tornabuoni 2 or Via della Vigna Vecchia 2 (ℰ **055-268-510;** fax 055-238-1524; www.windowsontuscany.com). To go it alone, check out the classifieds in the biweekly *Le Pulce,* available at newsstands.

Palazzo Antellesi   Here's your chance to set up housekeeping in a chunk of the Renaissance. Many people passing through Piazza Santa Croce notice Giovanni di Ser Giovanni's 1620 graffiti frescoes on the overhanging facade of no. 21, but few realize they can actually stay there. The 16th-century palazzo is owned by the gracious Signora Piccolomini, who rents out truly spacious apartments to anyone who has ever dreamed of lying in bed next to a roaring fire under a 17th-century frescoed ceiling (the Granduca, sleeping two or three) or sipping tea in a living room surrounded by trompe-l'oeil Roman ruins with a 16th-century wood ceiling above (the Donatello, sleeping six to eight). Even in the more standard rooms the furnishings are tasteful, with wicker, wood, or wrought-iron bed frames; potted plants; and the occasional 18th-century inlaid wood dresser to go with the plush couches and chairs. The fourth-floor rooms (the Miravista and Mimi) are booked seasons in advance by those who love the private penthouse terraces overlooking the lively piazza. The kitchens are sizable and fully equipped. Author R. W. B. Lewis wrote extensively about the Antellesi in the final chapter of *The City of Florence.*

Piazza Santa Croce 21–22, 50122 Firenze. ℰ **212/932-3480** in the U.S., and 055-244-456 in Italy. Fax 212/932-9039 in the U.S. and 055-234-5552 in Italy. www.palazzoantellesi.com. 13 apts. sleeping 2–6. 1,800€–4,000€ ($2,070–$4,600) per week; 3,960€–8,800€ ($4,244–$10,120) per month. Heating included in some, but most utilities extra. No credit cards. Parking 16€ ($18) in garage. Bus: B, 13, 23, or 71. **Amenities:** Babysitting; non-smoking rooms. *In room:* A/C, TV, VCR on request, dataport, kitchen, fridge, coffeemaker, hair dryer, safe.

3 Where to Dine

Florence is thick with restaurants, though many in the most touristy areas (around the Duomo and Piazza della Signoria) are of low quality, charge high prices, or do both. I'll point out the few that aren't. The highest concentrations of excellent *ristoranti* and *trattorie* are around Santa Croce and across the river in the Oltrarno. For a more complete Florentine dining primer, see "A Taste of Tuscany & Umbria" in Appendix A and "From Antipasti to Zuppa Inglese: Italian Menu Terms" in Appendix B.

NEAR THE DUOMO
MODERATE

Da Ganino FLORENTINE   The tiny family-run Ganino has long been a major destination for hungry tourists because it's across from the American

Express office as well as halfway between the Duomo and the Uffizi. This has caused the place to jack its prices to eyebrow-raising levels but not sacrifice its friendly service and good food, from the big ol' chunk of mortadella that accompanies your bread basket through the tasty *ribollita* or *gnocchi al pomodoro* (ricotta-and-spinach gnocchi in tomato sauce) to the *filetto all'aceto basalmico* (veal filet cooked in balsamic vinegar) or *coniglio in umido* (rabbit with boiled potatoes on the side) that rounds out your meal.

Piazza de' Cimatori 4r (near the Casa di Dante). ℭ **055-214-125.** Reservations recommended. Primi 6€–12€ ($6.90–$14); secondi 10€–20€ ($12–$23). AE, DC, MC, V. Mon–Sat 12:30–3pm and 7:30–10pm. Closed Aug. Bus: 14.

Paoli TUSCAN   Paoli has one of the most *suggestivo* (oft-used Italian word for "evocative") settings in town, with tables under a 14th-century vaulted ceiling whose ribs and lunettes are covered with fading 18th-century frescoes. It's in the heart of the sightseeing zone, meaning the prices are as high as they can reasonably push them; very few Italians drop by, but the food is actually quite good. The *ravioli verdi alla casalinga* (spinach ravioli in tomato sauce) may not be inspired, but it's freshly made and tasty. In mushroom season you can order *risotto ai funghi,* and year-round the scrumptious secondo *entrecôte di manzo arlecchino* (a thick steak in cognac-spiked cream sauce with peppercorns and sided with mashed potatoes).

Via dei Tavolini 12r. ℭ **055-216-215.** Reservations highly recommended. Primi 6€–12€ ($6.90–$14); secondi 14€–18€ ($16–$21); fixed-price menu with wine 20€ ($23). AE, MC, V. Wed–Mon noon–3pm and 7pm–midnight. Bus: A.

Ristorante Casa di Dante (da Pennello) ⚜ TUSCAN/ITALIAN   This is one of Florence's oldest restaurants, housed since the late 1400s in a palazzo that once belonged to Renaissance artist Albertinelli (Cellini, Pontormo, and Andrea del Sarto used to dine here). Its claim to fame is the antipasto table, groaning under the day's changing array of two dozen appetizers. Prices vary, but expect to spend 5€ to 8€ ($5.75–$9.20) for a good sampling. The best of the primi are under the handwritten *lo chef consigla* (the chef recommends) and *pasta fresa* (handmade pasta) sections of the menu. They do a perfectly grilled pork chop and, if the antipasti and pasta have done you in, several light omelets for secondo.

Via Dante Alighieri 4r (between Via dei Calzaiuoli and Via del Proconsolo). ℭ **055-294-848.** Reservations suggested. Primi 5.50€–8€ ($6.30–$9.20); secondi 7.50€–13€ ($8.65–$15); menù turistico 20€ ($23) without wine. AE, DC, V. Tues–Sat noon–3pm and 7–10:30pm. Closed Aug.

INEXPENSIVE

Cantinetta del Verrazzano ⚜ *Value* WINE BAR   Owned by the Castello di Verrazzano, one of Chianti's best-known wine-producing estates, this wood-paneled *cantinetta* with a full-service bar/*pasticceria* and seating area helped spawn a revival of stylish wine bars as convenient spots for fast-food breaks. It promises a delicious self-service lunch or snack of focaccia, plain or studded with peas, rosemary, onions, or olives; buy it hot by the slice or as *farcite* (sandwiches filled with prosciutto, arugula, cheese, or tuna). Try a glass of their full-bodied chianti to make this the perfect respite. Platters of Tuscan cold cuts and aged cheeses are also available.

Via dei Tavolini 18–20r (off Via dei Calzaiuoli). ℭ **055-268-590.** Focaccia sandwiches .95€–2.85€ ($1.10–$3.30); glass of wine 1.30€–8€ ($1.50–$9.20). AE, DC, MC, V. Mon–Sat 8am–9pm.

I Fratellini ⚜ SANDWICHES & WINE   Just off the busiest tourist thoroughfare lies one of the last of a dying breed: a *fiaschitteria* (derived from the

Where to Dine in Florence

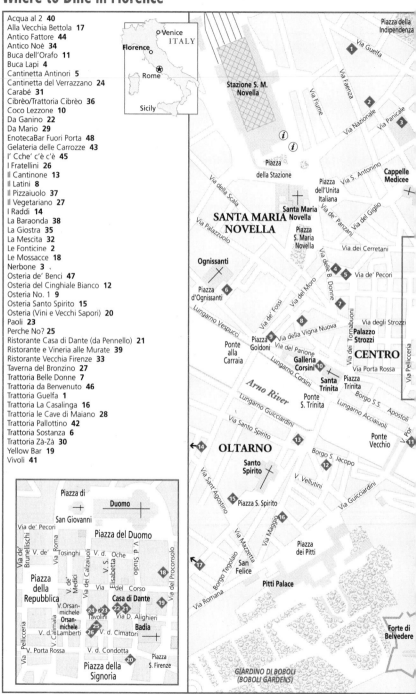

Booked aisle seat.

Reserved room with a view.

With a queen – no, make that a king-size bed.

With Travelocity, you can book your flights and hotels together, so you can get even better deals than if you booked them separately. You'll save time and money without compromising the quality of your trip. Choose your airline seat, search for alternate airports, pick your hotel room type, even choose the neighborhood you'd like to stay in.

Travelocity

Visit www.travelocity.com
or call 1-888-TRAVELOCITY

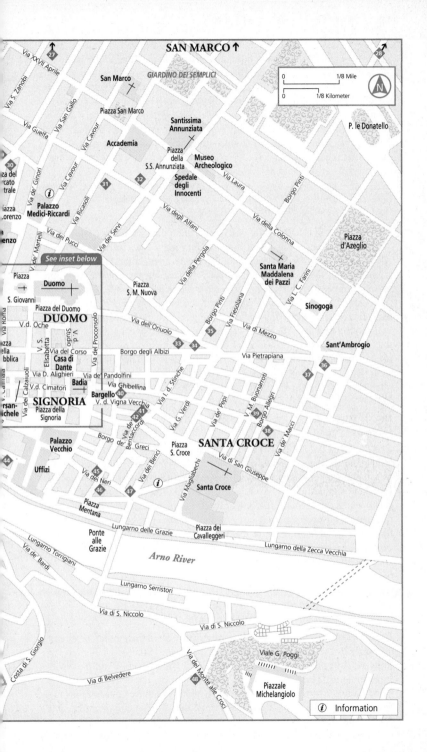

word for a flask of wine). It's the proverbial hole in the wall, a doorway about 5 feet deep with rows of wine bottles against the back wall and Armando and Michele Perrino busy behind the counter, fixing sandwiches and pouring glasses of vino. You stand munching and sipping on the cobblestones of the narrow street surrounded by Florentines on their lunch break and a few bemused tourists. The *cinghiale piccante con caprino* (spicy raw wild boar sausage with creamy goat cheese) is excellent. Otherwise, choose your poison from among 30 stuffing combinations—the menu posted on the doorjamb has English translations—and accompany it with either a basic *rosso* (red) wine or point to any bottle to try *un bicchiere* (a glass).

Via dei Cimatori 38r (2 blocks from Piazza della Signoria, off Via Calzaiuoli). ✆ **055-239-6096.** Sandwiches 2.10€–2.60€ ($2.40–$3); wine from 1.30€ ($1.50) a glass. No credit cards. Daily 8am–8:30pm (July–Aug closed Sat–Sun). Closed Aug 10–20 and 2 wks in Mar. Bus: 14, 23, or 71.

Le Mossacce FLORENTINE   Delicious, cheap, abundant, fast home cooking: This tiny *osteria*, filled with lunching businesspeople, farmers in from the hills, locals who've been coming since 1942, and a few knowledgeable tourists, is authentic to the bone. The waiters hate breaking out the printed menu, preferring to rattle off a list of Florentine faves like *ribollita, spaghetti alle vongole, crespelle,* and *lasagne al forno.* Unlike in many cheap joints catering to locals, the secondi are pretty good. You could try the *spezzatino* (goulashy beef stew) or a well-cooked, and for once cheap, *bistecca alla fiorentina,* but I put my money on the excellent *involtini* (thin slices of beef wrapped tightly around a bread stuffing and artichoke hearts, then cooked to juiciness in tomato sauce).

Via del Proconsolo 55r (a block south of the Duomo). ✆ **055-294-361.** Reservations suggested for dinner. Primi 4.20€–4.70€ ($4.80–$5.40); secondi 4.70€–14€ ($5.40–$16). AE, MC, V. Mon–Fri noon–2:30pm and 7–9:30pm.

NEAR PIAZZA DELLA SIGNORIA
MODERATE

Acqua al 2 SLIGHTLY ADVENTUROUS ITALIAN   Under a barrel-vaulted ceiling and dim sconce lights, diners sit elbow to elbow at tightly packed tables to sample this innovative restaurant's *assaggi* (tastings) courses. Acqua al 2 is proud of its almost cultish status, attained through the success of its *assaggio di primi,* which offers you a sampling of five flavorful pastas or *risotti.* If you order the *assaggio* for two, you both just may have room left over for a grilled portobello mushroom "steak," one of the many veal dishes, or something more cross-cultural, like *couscous d'agnello* (lamb). They also offer *assaggi* of salads, cheese, and desserts. Tour companies have started bringing in tourists by the busload on occasion, but the crowd still remains a good mix of locals and travelers.

Via della Vigna Vecchia 40r (at Via dell'Acqua). ✆ **055-284-170.** www.acquaal2.com. Reservations required. Primi 7€–8€ ($8.05–$9.20); secondi 7€–17€ ($8.05–$20); *assaggio* 8€ ($9.20) for pasta, 5€ ($5.75) for dessert. AE, MC, V. Daily 7:30pm–1am. Closed 1 wk in Aug. Bus: 14.

Antico Fattore FLORENTINE   The Antico Fattore was a literary watering hole early in the 20th century and remained a favorite trattoria just a few steps from the city's premier museum until the 1993 Uffizi bomb went off a few feet from its doors. The interior has been rebuilt and the restaurant reopened, but many claim it isn't what it used to be. Although it has indeed put on a few more airs, you can't deny they still make a tantalizing *lombatina all'aceto basalmico* (one of the thickest and most tender veal chops you'll ever find, cooked in balsamic vinegar). You can precede this with a *ribollita* (more souplike than usual)

(Kids) Family-Friendly Restaurants

It'd be a sin for any family to visit Florence and not drop by one of its premier gelato parlors to sample the rich Italian equivalent of ice cream. See "A Big Step Above Ice Cream: Florentine Gelato" on p. 124. If the kids mutiny and absolutely insist on a hamburger, try the slightly American-style restaurant **Yellow Bar,** Via del Proconsolo 39r (© **055-211-766**). But be warned: The hamburger doesn't come with a bun (a form of blasphemy among certain preteens). They also serve pizzas.

Il Cantinone (p. 132)   This noisy old wine cellar is popular with students and has long tables where your family can spread out and bite deep into *crostone* (slabs of peasant bread piled with your choice of toppings like a pizza).

Il Latini (p. 126)   This can be one of the most fun places to eat in Florence—you're seated at communal tables under battalions of hanging ham hocks and treated to huge portions of the Tuscan bounty. No food is too fancy or oddball to offend suspicious young palates, the waiters love to ham it up, and a festive atmosphere prevails.

Il Pizzaiuolo (p. 130)   When the kids are hankering for a pizza, turn it into a learning experience by visiting the only pizza parlor in Florence run by a Neapolitan. The "plain pizza," called *pizza margherita* in Italy, was invented about 100 years ago by a Naples chef who wanted to honor Italy's Queen Margherita with a pizza done in patriotic colors. For the newly created Kingdom of Italy, this meant red (tomatoes), white (mozzarella), and green (fresh basil)—the colors of the new flag. If someone at the table prefers pepperoni, order the pizza with *salame piccante* (hot salami slices); *pepperoni* in Italian are bell peppers.

Ristorante Vecchia Firenze (p. 130)   This roomy restaurant has a long menu sure to satisfy everyone's appetites. They love children here, and this was my family's favorite Florentine restaurant when I was 12. The owner, tickled pink one night that a little American boy was struggling to speak Italian, took over our meal, had all the wonders of Tuscan cuisine brought to our table, introduced us to grappa, and kept me up well past my bedtime.

Trattoria da Benvenuto (p. 122)   The dishes here are simple and homey—they're sure to have a plate of plain spaghetti and tomato sauce to please finicky youngsters.

or a traditional Tuscan *pappardelle sul cinghiale* (wide noodles in wild boar sauce). If veal's not your style, try their specialty *piccione* (grilled pigeon).

Via Lambertesca 1–3r (between the Uffizi and the Ponte Vecchio). © **055-288-975**. www.mega.it/antico. fattore. Reservations recommended. Primi 5.70€–8€ ($6.60–$9.20); secondi 8.80€–14€ ($10–$14). AE, DC, MC, V. Mon–Sat 12:15–3pm and 7:15–10:30pm. Bus: 23 or 71.

Buca dell'Orafo FLORENTINE   A *buca* is a cellar joint with half a dozen crowded tables serving good, basic Florentine fare. Here a few locals hang on every night, but Orafo's years in the guidebooks have made Americans its base of customers—Florentines aren't willing to give this place up yet, though, and you can still find it packed with locals if you reserve a late seating. However, the heavy tourism has jacked its prices above what you'd expect for peasant food. That food is still very well prepared, however, and the location can't be beat. You can't go wrong with the thick *ribollita*. If it's on the menu, go for the *paglia e fieno alla boscaiola* (a "hay and straw" mix of both egg and spinach fettuccine in mushroom-meat sauce). Orafo's best secondo is *arista di maiale con patate* (roast pork loin with potatoes), while candied stewed pears round out the meal nicely.

Volta dei Girolami 28r (under the arched alley left of the Ponte Vecchio). ✆ **055-213-619**. Reservations strongly recommended (or show up early for a spot at a communal table). Primi 6€–10€ ($6.90–$12); secondi 11€–20€ ($13–$23). No credit cards. Tues–Sat noon–2:30pm and 7:30–9:45pm. Bus: 23 or 71.

I' Cche' c'è c'è ✦✦ TUSCAN The name is a dialect variant on "What you see is what you get." What you see is a room with modern art prints and shelves of ancient wine bottles on the walls. What you get is good Tuscan cooking from Gino Noci, who trained in the kitchens of London before returning here to open a traditional trattoria. The scrumptious *ravioli rosée* (in creamy tomato sauce) faces serious competition from the *tagliatelle all boscaiola* (same sauce with giant slices of forest mushrooms added). *Topini* are Florentine potato gnocchi, topped with spinach and cream or four cheeses. Follow up with the grilled salmon or one of their specialties, *stracotto al chianti* (beef stuffed with celery and carrot and smothered in a chianti gravy served with fried polenta and an artichoke heart).

Via Magalotti 11r (just east of Via Proconsolo, 2 blocks from the Arno). ✆ **055-216-589**. Reservations recommended (not available for set-price menu at lunch). Primi 4€–9€ ($4.60–$10); secondi 9€–15€ ($10–$17); fixed-price menu without wine 11€ ($13). AE, MC, V. Tues–Sun 12:30–2:30pm and 7:30–10:30pm. Closed Aug 10–17.

Osteria (Vini e Vecchi Sapori) FLORENTINE/TUSCAN Within a block of the Palazzo Vecchio squats an authentic *osteria* with a wood-beamed ceiling, brick floor, the end of a giant chianti barrel embedded in one wall, and a handwritten menu that starts *Oggi C'è* ("Today we got . . ."). As the sign proudly proclaims, this one-room joint is devoted to "wine and old flavors," which means lunch could consist of anything from a rib-sticking stewlike *ribollita* and a *frittata rustica* (a darkly fried omelet thick with potatoes and vegetables) to an excellent crostini assortment and *scamorza e speck al forno* (smoked mozzarella melted with ham in a bowl, to scoop out and slather onto bread). The paunchy owner will continue pacing back and forth, passing around the lone menu, and welcoming people in off the street until he feels like going home.

Via dei Magazzini 3r (the alley off Piazza della Signoria to the left of the Palazzo Vecchio). ✆ **055-293-045**. Primi 6€–8€ ($6.90–$9.20); secondi 10€–14€ ($12–$16). No credit cards. Tues–Sat 9am–11pm; Sun noon–2:30pm. Bus: 14, 23, or 71.

Trattoria da Benvenuto ✦ *Kids* TUSCAN HOME COOKING This is a no-nonsense place, simple and good, and Gabriella is a no-nonsense lady who'll get exasperated if you're not ready with your order when she's ready to take it. Da Benvenuto's is basically a neighborhood hangout that somehow found its way into every guidebook over the years. Yet it continues to serve adequate helpings of tasty Florentine home cooking to travelers and locals seated together at long tables in two brightly lit rooms. This is always my first stop on any trip to Florence, where I usually order ravioli or *gnocchi* (potato-dumpling pasta)— both served in tomato sauce—and follow with a *veal scaloppa alla Livornese* or a *frittata* (an omelet filled at the whim of Loriano, Gabriella's husband and cook).

Via Mosca 16r (at the corner of Via dei Neri; walk around the right of the Palazzo Vecchio, under the arch, and it's in front of you after 4 short blocks). ✆ **055-214-833.** Primi 4.50€–9.50€ ($5.20–$11); secondi 5.50€–15€ ($6.30–$17). No credit cards. Mon–Tues and Thurs–Sat 12:30–3pm and 7pm–10:30. Bus: 23 or 71.

NEAR SAN LORENZO & THE MERCATO CENTRALE
MODERATE

Da Mario ✪ *Value* FLORENTINE   This is down-and-dirty Florentine lunchtime at its best, an *osteria* so basic the little stools don't have backs and a communal spirit so entrenched the waitresses will scold you if you try to take a table all to yourself. Since 1953, their stock in trade has been feeding market workers, and you can watch the kitchen through the glass as they whip out a wipe board menu of simple dishes at lightning speed. Hearty primi include *tortelli di patate al ragù* (ravioli stuffed with potato in ragù), *minestra di farro e riso* (emmer-and-rice soup), and *penne al pomodoro* (pasta quills in fresh tomato sauce). The secondi are basic but good; try the *coniglio arrosto* (roast rabbit) or *girello di vitello ai carciofi* (veal rolled around artichoke hearts, then stewed).

Via Rosina 2r (at the north corner of Piazza Mercato Centrale). ✆ **055-218-550.** www.trattoriamario.com. Reservations not accepted. Primi 3.10€–3.40€ ($3.55–$3.90); secondi 4€–10.50€ ($4.60–$12). No credit cards. Mon–Sat noon–3:30pm. Closed Aug. Bus: 10, 12, 25, 31, 32, or 91.

Le Fonticine TUSCAN/BOLOGNESE   Modern paintings carpet the walls like a jigsaw puzzle. Silvano Bruci has taken as much care over the past 40 years selecting the works of art as his Bologna-born wife Bruna Grazia has teaching these Tuscans the finer points of Emilia-Romagna cuisine. Even with the art, this place still feels a bit like a country trattoria. If you can, ask to sit *in dietro* (in the back), if only so you get to walk past the open kitchen and grill. There are so many good primi it's hard to choose, but you can't go wrong with lasagne, *penne al prosciutto punte d'asparagi* (stubby pasta with diced prosciutto and wild asparagus tips), or *ribollita*. Afterward, set to work on the *cinghiale maremmana cipolline* (stewed wild boar with caramelized baby onions) or *baccalà alla livornese* (salt cod covered in tomatoes and served with chickpeas in oil).

Via Nazionale 79r (at Via dell'Ariento, north end of the Mercato San Lorenzo). ✆ **055-282-106.** www.lefonticine.com. Reservations recommended. Primi 6€–12€ ($6.90–$14); secondi 8€–16€ ($9.20–$18). AE, DC, MC, V. Tues–Sat noon–2:30pm and 7–10pm. Closed July 25–Aug 25. Bus: 12, 25, 31, or 32.

Trattoria Zà-Zà ✪ TUSCAN CASALINGA (HOME COOKING)   This place serves many of the food market workers from across the way—people who appreciate the importance of using simple, fresh ingredients to make filling dishes. Ask to sit downstairs in the brick barrel vault of the old *cantina* if you want some privacy; if you want company (they make even the small wooden tables communal), sit upstairs, where you can gaze at the dozens of photos of the restaurant's more (but mostly less) famous patrons. The *antipasto caldo alla Zà-Zà* has a bit of everything. If you don't want *ravioli strascicati* (in creamy ragù), brace yourself for a *tris di minestre* (three soups: *ribollita, pappa al pomodoro,* and *fagioli con farro*). *Bocconcini di vitella alla casalinga con fagioli all'uccelletto* (veal nuggets with tomato-stewed beans) makes an excellent second course.

Piazza Mercato Centrale 26r. ✆ **055-215-411.** www.trattoriazaza.it. Reservations recommended. Primi 5.30€–10€ ($6.10–$12); secondi 10€–18€ ($12–$21); menù turistico without wine 13€ ($15). AE, DC, MC, V. Mon–Sat noon–3pm and 7–11pm. Closed Aug.

INEXPENSIVE

Nerbone ✪ *Moments* FLORENTINE   Nerbone has been stuffing stall owners and market patrons with excellent Florentine *cucina povera* ("poor people's

A Big Step Above Ice Cream: Florentine Gelato

Gelato is a Florentine institution—a creamy, sweet, flavorful food item on a different level entirely from what Americans call "ice cream." Fine Florentine gelato is a craft taken seriously by all except the tourist-pandering spots around major attractions that serve air-fluffed bland "vanilla" and nuclear-waste pistachio so artificially green it glows.

Here's how to order gelato: First, pay at the register for the size of *coppa* (cup) or *cono* (cone) you want, then take the receipt up to the counter to select your flavors (unlike in America, they'll let you stuff multiple flavors into even the tiniest cup). Prices are fairly standardized, with the smallest serving at around 1.50€ ($1.75) or 2€ ($2.30) and prices going up in .50€ (60¢) increments for six or eight sizes. A warning: Gelato is denser than ice cream and richer than it looks. There's also a concoction called *semifreddo,* somewhere on the far side of the mousse family, in which standard Italian desserts like tiramisu are creamed with milk and then partially frozen.

There are plenty of quality gelaterie besides the ones listed here. A few rules of thumb: Look for a sign that proudly proclaims *produzione propria* (homemade) and take a look at the gelato itself—no matter what kind you plan to order, make sure the banana is gray, the egg-based *crema* (egg-based "vanilla," though there's nary a vanilla bean in it) yellow, and the pistachio a natural, pasty pale olive.

Of all the centrally located gelaterie, **Festival del Gelato,** Via del Corso 75r, just off Via dei Calzaiuoli (*©* **055-239-4386**), has been the only serious contender to the premier Vivoli (below), offering about 50 flavors along with pounding pop music and colorful neon. It's open Tuesday through Sunday: summer 8am to 1am and winter 11am to 1am.

Vivoli, Via Isole delle Stinche 7r, a block west of Piazza Santa Croce (*©* **055-239-2334**), is still the city's institution. Exactly how renowned is this bright gelateria? Taped to the wall is a postcard bearing only "Vivoli, Europa" for the address, yet it was successfully delivered to this world capital of ice cream. It's open Tuesday through Sunday 9am to 1am (closed Aug and Jan to early Feb).

food") since the Mercato Centrale opened in 1874. You can try *trippa alla fiorentina, pappa al pomodoro,* or a plate piled with boiled potatoes and a single fat sausage. But the mainstay here is a *panino con bollito,* a boiled beef sandwich that's *bagnato* (dipped in the meat juices). Eat standing with the crowd of old men at the side counter, sipping glasses of wine or beer, or fight for one of the few tables against the wall.

In the Mercato Centrale, entrance on Via dell'Ariento, stand no. 292 (ground floor). *©* **055-219-949.** All dishes 3.50€–7€ ($4.05–$8.05). No credit cards. Mon–Sat 7am–3pm.

NEAR PIAZZA SANTA TRÍNITA
VERY EXPENSIVE
Cantinetta Antinori FLORENTINE/TUSCAN The Antinori *marchesi* started their wine empire 26 generations ago, and, taking their cue from an ancient vintner tradition, installed a wine bar in their 15th-century palazzo 30

One of the major advantages of the always crowded **Gelateria delle Carrozze,** Piazza del Pesce 3–5r (✆ 055-23-96-810), is its location at the foot of the Ponte Vecchio—if you're coming off the bridge and about to head on to the Duomo, this gelateria is immediately off to your right on a small alley that forks off the main street. In summer, it's open daily 11am to 1am; in winter, hours are Thursday through Tuesday 11am to 8pm.

A block south of the Accademia (pick up a cone after you've gazed upon *David*'s glory) is what local purists insist is Vivoli's only deserving contender to the throne as gelato king: **Carabé,** Via Ricasoli 60r (✆ **055-289-476**). It offers genuine homemade Sicilian gelato in the heart of Florence, with ingredients shipped in from Sicily by the hard-working Sicilian owners. Taste for yourself and see if Florentines can hope to ever surpass such scrumptiousness direct from the island that first brought the concept of ice cream to Europe. May 16 through September, it's open daily 10am to midnight; February 15 through May 15 and October through November 15, hours are Tuesday through Sunday 10am to 8pm.

In 1946, the first ice-cream parlor in the city's heart, **Perche No?** ⭐, Via dei Tavolini 19r, off Via del Calzaiuoli (✆ **055-239-8969**; Bus: 14, 23, or 71), introduced a novelty: the glass display case filled with tubs of flavors that have become standard in ice cream stores the world over. Wedged into an alley off Via dei Calzaiuoli between Piazza della Signoria and the Duomo, Perche No? has done an admirable job over the years of being many a harried tourist's first introduction to quality Florentine gelato. During World War II when the American army reached Florence after the Nazi withdrawal, they had the power grid specially reconnected so that Perche No?'s gelato production—and G.I. consumption—could continue. Try their *ciocolato bianco* (white chocolate studded with chunks of the main ingredient) or one of the semifreddi, a moussing process they helped invent. It's open Wednesday through Monday from 10am to midnight.

years ago. Most ingredients come fresh from the Antinori farms, as does all the fine wine. Start with the *fettucini all'anatra* (noodles in duck sauce) or the *ribollita*, and round out the meal with the *trippa alla fiorentina* or the mighty *gran pezzo* (thick slab of oven-roasted Chiana beef). If you choose this worthy splurge as a secondo, skip the first course and instead follow your steak with *formaggi misti*, which may include pecorino and mozzarella made fresh that morning. Their *cantucci* (Tuscan biscotti) come from Prato's premier producer.

Palazzo Antinori, Piazza Antinori 3 (at the top of Via Tornabuoni). ✆ **055-292-234.** www.antinori.it. Reservations strongly recommended. Primi 10€–16€ ($12–$18); secondi 14€–24€ ($16–$27). AE, DC, MC, V. Mon–Fri 12:30–3pm and 6:30–10:30pm. Closed Aug, Dec 24–Jan 6. Bus: 6, 11, 36, 37, or 68.

Osteria No. 1 TUSCAN "Osteria" belies this place's status as a full-fledged restaurant with some of the finer dining in Florence. Well-dressed Italians and Americans sit at well-spaced tables under the vaulted ceilings surrounded by painted coats of arms, musical instruments, and original art. Many opt for a *cocktail di gambereti* (shrimp cocktail) before their first course, which may include *zuppa di fagioli e farro* (bean-and-emmer soup) or the more imaginative *sfogliatine* (giant ravioli stuffed with cheese and carrots in basil-cream sauce). The secondi, all flavorful, range from tasty *sogliola griglia* (grilled sole) and adventurous *cervello* (fried calves' brains with artichokes) to a huge and succulent *bistecca alla fiorentina*. The one major drawback here is that, though service is friendly it's often hurried—fine if you're in a rush, but very un-Italian.

Via del Moro 22 (near the Ponte alla Carraia). ℂ 055-284-897. www.osterianumero1.it. Reservations recommended. Primi 9€–18€ ($10–$21); secondi 8€–35€ ($9.20–$40). AE, DC, MC, V. Tues–Sat noon–2:30pm and 7–11pm; Mon 7pm–12:30am. Closed Aug. Bus: A, C, 6, 9, 11, 36, 37, or 68.

EXPENSIVE

Buca Lapi TUSCAN   The vaulted ceiling is carpeted with travel posters, the cuisine is carefully prepared, and the wine comes from the Antinori vineyards (this was once part of their cellars). This place's prices have recently risen astronomically, and for no apparent reason, but the quality is still spot-on. An interesting start is the *filetto di cinghiale all'olio di rosmarino* (wild boar slices cured like prosciutto and served with rosemary-scented olive oil). One specialty is the *cannelloni gratinati alla Buca Lapi* (pasta canapés stuffed with ricotta and spinach served in a cream sauce of boar and mushrooms). A light secondo could be *coniglio disossato ripieno* (stuffed rabbit), or you can go all out on a masterful *bistecca chianina* (grilled steak, for two only). The desserts are homemade, including a firm and delicate *latte portugese* (a kind of crème caramel) and a richly dense chocolate torte.

Via del Trebbio, 1r (just off Piazza Antinori at the top of Via Tornabuoni). ℂ 055-213-768. Reservations essential. Primi 10€–12€ ($12–$14); secondi 20€–25€ ($23–$29). AE, DC, MC, V. Tues–Sat 12:30–2:30pm; Mon–Sat 7:30–10:30pm. Bus: 6, 11, 14, 17, 22, 36, 37, or 68.

Coco Lezzone FLORENTINE   This tiny trattoria hidden in a tangle of alleys near the Arno consists of long communal tables in a couple of pocket-size rooms wrapped around a cubbyhole of a kitchen whose chef, according to the restaurant's dialect name, is a bit off his rocker. The place is popular with local intellectuals, journalists, and the city soccer team. While enjoying your *ribollita* (known here as a "triumph of humility") or *rigatoni al sugo* (in a chunky ragù), look at where the yellow paint on the lower half of the wall gives way to white: That's how high the Arno flooded the joint in 1966. If you want a *bistecca alla fiorentina*, call ahead first. Friday is *baccalà* (salt cod) day, and every day their *involtini* (thin veal slice wrapped around vegetables) and *crocchette di filetto* (veal-and-basil meatloaf smothered in tomato sauce) are good.

Via del Parioncino 26r (at the corner of Via Purgatorio). ℂ 055-287-178. Reservations recommended. Primi 6.50€–13€ ($7.50–$15); secondi 9.50€–16€ ($11–$18). No credit cards. Mon and Wed–Sat noon–2:30pm and 7–10pm; Tues noon–2:30pm. Closed late July–Aug and Dec 23–Jan 7. Bus: C, 6, 11, 14, or 17.

MODERATE

Il Latini 🏆🏆🏆 *Kids* FLORENTINE   Uncle Narcisso Latini opened this cheap locals' eatin' joint in 1950, though it now gets as many tourists as Florentines. Arrive at 7:30pm to get in the crowd massed at the door, for even with a reservation you'll have to wait as they skillfully fit parties together at the communal tables. In fact, getting thrown together with strangers and sharing a common meal is part of the fun here. Under hundreds of hanging prosciutto ham hocks, the waiters try their hardest to keep a menu away from you and serve instead a filling, traditional set meal with bottomless wine. This usually kicks off with *ribollita* and *pappa al pomodoro* or *penne strascicate* (in a ragù mixed with cream). If everyone agrees on the *arrosto misto,* you can get a table-filling platter heaped high with assorted roast meats. Finish off with a round of *cantucci con vin santo* for everyone.

Via del Palchetti 6r (off Via della Vigna Nuova). ✆ **055-210-916.** Reservations strongly recommended. Primi 6€ ($6.90); secondi 8€–16€ ($9.20–$18); unofficial fixed-priced full meal with limitless wine 30€–35€ ($35–$40). AE, DC, MC, V. Tues–Sun 12:30–2:30pm and 7:30–10:30pm. Closed 15 days in Aug and Dec 24–Jan 6. Bus: C, 6, 11, 36, 37, or 68.

Trattoria Belle Donne TUSCAN   Tucked away on a narrow street (whose name refers to the women of the night who once worked this then-shady neighborhood) parallel to exclusive Via dei Tornabuoni, this packed-to-the-gills lunch spot (with no identifying sign) immediately drew the area's chic boutique owners and sales staff. It now tries to accommodate them and countless others in a rather brusque style—no lingering over lunch; dinner isn't as rushed. Tuscan cuisine gets reinterpreted and updated by the talented young chef, who placates the local palate without alienating it: Traditional dishes appear in the company of innovative alternatives like cream of zucchini and chestnut soup or lemon-flavored chicken. The regulars seem inured to the occasional rush job, so don't take it personally.

Via delle Belle Donne 16r (north off Via della Vigna Nuova). ✆ **055-238-2609.** www.osteriabelledonne.com. Reservations not accepted. Primi 5.50€–7.50€ ($6.30–$8.65); secondi 8€–12€ ($9.20–$14). MC, V. Mon–Fri 12:30–2:30pm and 7:15–10:30pm. Closed most of Aug.

NEAR SANTA MARIA NOVELLA
MODERATE

Trattoria Guelfa FLORENTINE/TUSCAN   Always crowded and always good, the Guelfa has lots of paintings hanging on its walls and a random trattoria decor—pendulous gourds, wine bottles, and an old oxen yoke rule over the tightly packed noisy tables. The kitchen is very traditional, offering *spaghetti alla rustica* (in a cheesy, creamy tomato sauce) and *risotto ai 4 formaggi* (a gooey rice dish made with four cheeses) as proud primi. For a main course, you can go light with the *pinzimonio di verdure crude* (a selection of seasonally fresh raw veggies with oil to dip them in) or indulge your taste buds with the *petti di pollo alla Guelfa* (a chicken breast rolled around a stuffing of prosciutto, cheese, and truffled cream served with a side of olive oil–drenched oven-roasted potatoes).

Via Guelfa 103r (near the Fortezza, beyond Via Nazionale). ✆ **055-213-306.** Reservations strongly recommended. Primi 5€–8€ ($5.75–$9.20); secondi 6€–15€ ($6.90–$17); menù turistico with wine 9€ ($10). AE, MC, V. Thurs–Tues noon–2:30pm and 7–10:30pm. Bus: 4, 10, 13, 14, 23, 25, 28, 31, 32, 33, 67, or 71.

Trattoria Sostanza FLORENTINE   Sostanza is popularly called Il Troia (the trough) because people have been lining up at the long communal tables since 1869 to enjoy huge amounts of some of the best traditional food in the city. The primi are very simple: pasta in sauce, *tortellini in brodo* (meat-stuffed pasta in chicken broth), and *zuppa alla paesana* (peasant soup ribollita). The secondi don't steer far from Florentine traditions either, with *trippa alla fiorentina* or their mighty specialty *petti di pollo al burro* (thick chicken breasts fried in butter). It's an extremely unassuming place, so laid-back you may not realize you're meant to be ordering when the waiter wanders over to chat. They also frown on anybody trying to cheat his or her own taste buds out of a full Tuscan meal.

Via Porcellana 25r (near the Borgo Ognissanti end). ✆ **055-212-691.** Reservations strongly recommended. Primi 6.20€–7.30€ ($7.15–$8.40); secondi 6.80€–180€ ($7.80–$20). No credit cards. Mon–Fri noon–2:15pm and 7:30–9:45pm. Closed Aug.

NEAR SAN MARCO & SANTISSIMA ANNUNZIATA
MODERATE
Il Vegetariano VEGETARIAN   Come early to Florence's only vegetarian restaurant and use your coat to save a spot at one of the communal wood tables before heading to the back to get your food. You pay at the start of the meal, after choosing from the daily selections penned on the wipe board, and take your dishes self-service style from the workers behind the counter. The menu changes constantly but includes such dishes as risotto with yellow squash and black cabbage; a soupy, spicy Tunisian-style couscous with vegetables; a quiche-like pizza rustica of ricotta, olives, tomatoes, and mushrooms; or a plate with *farro* (emmer) and a hot salad of spinach, onions, sprouts, and bean-curd chunks sautéed in soy sauce. You can mix and match your own salad, and they make a good chestnut flour cake stuffed with hazelnut cream for dessert.

Via delle Ruote 30r (off Via Santa Reparata near Piazza Indipendenza). ℂ 055-475-030. Reservations not accepted. Primi 5€–6€ ($5.75–$6.90); secondi 7.50€–8€ ($8.65–$9.20). No credit cards. Tues–Fri 12:30–2:30pm; Tues–Sun 7:30pm–midnight. Closed 2–3 weeks in Aug and Dec 24–Jan 2. Bus: 12, 91, or anything to San Marco.

La Mescita SANDWICHES & HOME COOKING   This tiny *fiaschetteria* is immensely popular with local businesspeople and students from the nearby university. Lunch can be a crushing affair, and they have signs admonishing you to eat quickly to give others a chance to sit. You'll be eating with Italians, and it's not for the timid because you have to take charge yourself: securing a seat, collecting your own place setting, and getting someone's attention to give your order before going to sit down. They offer mainly sandwiches, though there are always a few simple meat and pasta dishes ready as well. *Melanzana* (eggplant) is overwhelmingly the side dish of choice, and you can look to the cardboard lists behind the counter to select your wine, although the house wine is very good, and a quarter liter of it is cheaper than a can of soda.

Via degli Alfani 70r (near the corner of Via dei Servi). ℂ 347-795-1604. All sandwiches and dishes 4€–7€ ($4.60–$8.05). No credit cards. Mon–Sat 11am–4pm. Closed Aug. Bus: 6, 31, or 32.

Taverna del Bronzino FINE TUSCAN   The 1580 house where Santi di Tito spent the last years of his life painting is now inhabited by polite, efficient, and very accommodating waiters who will show you to a table in the vaulted-ceiling dining room or on the arbor-shaded patio. Among the delectable antipasti are *salmone Scozzese selvatica* (wild Scottish salmon) and *petto d'oca affumicato e carciofi* (thin slices of smoked goose breast on a bed of sliced artichokes drowned in olive oil). The *risotto agli asparagi* is a bit light on the asparagus but still very creamy and tasty. You can also try the excellent *ravioli alla Senese* (ricotta and spinach–stuffed pasta in creamy tomato sauce) or *tagliolini ai pesci* (noodles with fish). To stick with the sea you can order *branzino* (sea bass simmered in white wine) next or select the *paillard di vitella all'ortolana* (a grilled veal steak wrapped around cooked vegetables).

Via delle Ruote 27r (between Piazza Indipendenza and San Marco). ℂ 055-495-220. Reservations strongly recommended. Primi 12€–15€ ($14–$17); secondi 21€–25€ ($24–$29). AE, DC, MC, V. Mon–Sat 12:30–2:30pm and 7:30–10:30pm. Closed 3 weeks in Aug. Bus: 12, 91, or anything to San Marco.

NEAR SANTA CROCE
VERY EXPENSIVE
Cibrèo ⭐ REFINED TUSCAN   There's no pasta and no grilled meat—can this be Tuscany? Rest assured that while Benedetta Vitale and Fabio Picchi's culinary

creations are a bit out of the ordinary, most are based on antique recipes. Cibrèo's actually has a split personality; this is a review not of the trattoria branch (p. 131), but of the fan-cooled main restaurant room, full of intellectual babble, where the elegance is in the substance of the food and the service, not in surface appearances. Waiters pull up a chair to explain the list of daily specials, and those garlands of hot peppers hanging in the kitchen window are a hint at the cook's favorite spice. All the food is spectacular, and dishes change regularly, but if they're available try the yellow pepper soup drizzled with olive oil, the soufflé of potatoes and ricotta spiced and served with pecorino shavings and ragù, or the roasted duck stuffed with minced beef, raisins, and pinoli.

Via Andrea del Verrocchio 8r (at the San Ambrogio Market, off Via de' Macchi). © **055-234-1100.** Reservations required. Primi 18€ ($21); secondi 34€ ($39). AE, DC, MC, V. Tues–Sat 12:30–2:30pm and 7:30–11:15pm. Closed July 26–Sept 6. Bus: B or 14.

Ristorante e Vineria alle Murate TUSCAN & CUCINA CREATIVA   Soft illumination, soft jazz, and soft pastels rule in this trendy spot owned by chef Umberto Montano. Alle Murate was one of the first places in the city to experiment with nouvelle cuisine. It tries, however, to balance *cucina creativa* with traditional Tuscan techniques and dishes. You could start with *zuppa di fagioli e gamberi* (soup of creamed white beans with shrimp) or the lasagne. The best fish dish is sea bass on a bed of fried potatoes topped with diced tomatoes, and for a main course you could go in for the *anatra disossata alle erbete e scorze di arancia* (duck à l'orange). The *brasato di Chiana* (steak) in Brunello wine, however, was disappointing. For these prices, the portions could be larger and the presentation better, but the food is good and the antipasti, *contorni* (side dishes), aperitifs, and dessert wines are included in the price of your meal. The *vineria* half—really just a small room off the main one—offers an abbreviated menu at abbreviated prices.

Via Ghibellina 52r (near Borgo Allegri). © **055-240-618.** www.caffeitaliano.it. Reservations strongly recommended (specify *vineria* or *ristorante*). Primi 18€ ($21); secondi with side dish 22€–24€ ($25–$27); menu degustazione without wine 52€–60€ ($60–$69). AE, DC, MC, V. Tues–Sun 7:30–11pm. Bus: 14.

EXPENSIVE

Antico Noè SANDWICHES & WINE   A *fiaschitteria* with superior sandwiches masquerading as a regular bar, the Antico Noè is popular with students and shopkeepers for its well-stuffed panini and cheap glasses of quaffable wine—perfect for a light lunch on the go. The place is rather hidden, but you'll know you've found it when you see a small crowd gathered around a door in the shade of a covered alley—though, I should warn you, the alley and tiny piazza off it have of late begun hosting a small community of vagrants and bums. You can order your sandwich from the list, invent your own, or (better yet) let them invent one for you. They surprised me on my last trip with a rather tasty combination of stuffed chicken and sliced porcini mushrooms topped with a slightly spicy creamy tomato spread. The sit-down osteria next door serves simple Tuscan dishes.

Volta di San Piero 6r (the arched alley off Piazza San Pier Maggiore). © **055-234-0838.** Sandwiches 2.50€–5€ ($2.90–$5.75); wine .75€–2€ (85¢–$2.30) per glass; primi and secondi 7€–15€ ($8.05–$17). No credit cards. Mon–Sat 8am–midnight (often open Sun, too). Bus: B, 14, 23, or 71.

La Giostra ★★★ ADVENTUROUS TUSCAN   This is one of two restaurants I visit every time I come to town. The chef/owner is Dimitri d'Asburgo Lorena, a Hapsburg prince (with some local Medici blood for good measure) who opened this restaurant merely to indulge his love of cooking. They start you off with a complimentary flute of *spumanti* before you plunge into the tasty *crostini misti* and exquisite primi. Among my favorites are *tortelloni alla Mugellana* (handmade potato-stuffed pasta in ragù), *gnocchetti alla Lord Reinolds* (potato dumplings in a sauce of stilton and Port), homemade *tagliatelle* with tiny wild asparagus spears, and ravioli stuffed with brie in a sauce with thinly sliced, lightly fried artichokes. For an encore, try the *nodino di vitella ai tartufi bianchi* (veal slathered in eggy white truffle sauce with fresh truffle grated on top) or the lighter *spianata alle erbe aromatiche di Maremma* (a huge platter of spiced beef pounded flat and piled with a salad of rosemary sprigs, sage, and other herbs). Don't leave without sampling the sinfully rich Viennese Sachertorte, made from an old Hapsburg family recipe. This place has become (justifiably) popular, and even with a reservation there's often a short wait—laudably, they don't rush anybody to empty up tables—but it's worth it.

Borgo Pinti 10r (off Piazza Salvemini). ✆ 055-241-341. www.ristorantelagiostra.com. Reservations recommended. Primi 10€–14€ ($12–$16); secondi 14€–21€ ($16–$24). AE, DC, MC, V. Daily noon–2:30pm and 7pm–midnight. Bus: A, B, C, 6, 14, 23, 31, 32, or 71.

MODERATE

Il Pizzaiuolo ⭐ *Kids* NEAPOLITAN/PIZZA   Despite their considerable skill in the kitchen, Florentines just can't make a decent pizza. It takes a Neapolitan to do that, so business has been booming ever since Naples-born Carmine opened this pizzeria. Even with a reservation, you'll probably have to wait for a spot at a long, crowded, and noisy marble table. Save the pizza for a main dish; start instead with a Neapolitan first course like *fusilli c'a ricotta* (homemade pasta spirals in creamy tomato-and-ricotta sauce). Of the pizzas, you can't go wrong with a classic *margherita* (mozzarella, tomatoes, and fresh basil), or spice up your evening with a *pizza diavola,* topped with hot salami and olives.

Via de' Macci 113r (at the corner of Via Pietrapiana). ✆ 055-241-171. Reservations required for dinner. Pizza 4.50€–10€ ($5.20–$12); primi 6.50€–13€ ($7.50–$15); secondi 7.50€–13€ ($8.65–$15). No credit cards. Mon–Sat 12:30–3pm and 7:30pm–midnight. Closed Aug. Bus: B or 14.

Osteria de' Benci INVENTIVE TUSCAN   This popular trattoria serves enormous portions (especially of secondi) on beautiful hand-painted ceramics under high ceiling vaults echoing with the conversation of Florentine trendoids. The menu changes monthly, but you can always be assured of excellent *salumi*—they come from Falorni, the famed butcher of the Chianti (see "Wine Tasting in the Chianti," in chapter 5). The *eliche del profeta* are fusiloni tossed with ricotta, olive oil, oregano, and fresh tomatoes sprinkled with *parmigiano.* The unique *spaghetti dell'ubriacone* is bright crimson spaghetti that takes its color from being cooked in red wine, sauced with garlic, pepperoncino, and parsley sautéed in olive oil. And the *cibrèo delle regine* is a traditional rich Florentine dish of chopped chicken livers and gizzards served on toast.

Via de' Benci 13r (at the corner of Via de' Neri). ✆ 055-234-4923. Reservations highly recommended. Primi 6€–9€ ($6.90–$10); secondi 5€–16€ ($5.75–$18). AE, DC, MC, V. Mon–Sat 1–2:45pm and 7:45–10:45pm. Bus: B, 23, or 71.

Ristorante Vecchia Firenze ⭐ *Kids* FLORENTINE/TUSCAN   I first dined here with my parents when I was 12, and the place hasn't changed much since. It's set in a 15th-century palazzo, so avoid sitting in the boring front room in favor of the more intimate back rooms or the rowdier stone-lined cantina downstairs full of Florentine students. The *zuppa pavese* is a good vegetable soup, but try the *penne Vecchia Firenze* (pasta quills in a subtle creamy mushroom sauce with tomatoes). By all means order the *bistecca alla fiorentina*, but if your appetite runs more to *coniglio alla griglia* (grilled rabbit) or *branzino alla griglia* (grilled sea bass), you won't be disappointed.

Borgo degli Albizi 76–78r. ✆ **055-234-0361**. Primi 5€–7€ ($5.75–$8.05); secondi 7€–10€ ($8.05–$10); pizza 5€–7€ ($5.75–$8.05); fixed-price menus without wine 13€–15€ ($15–$17). AE, DC, MC, V. Tues–Sun 11am–3pm and 7–10pm. Bus: 14, 23, or 71.

Trattoria Cibrèo FLORENTINE   This is the casual trattoria of celebrated chef-owner Fabio Picchi; its limited menu comes from the same creative kitchen that put on the map his premier and more than twice as expensive *ristorante* next door. The trattoria moved from its back alley location to the main street in 1999, and this higher visibility has only made the lines longer. Picchi takes his inspiration from traditional Tuscan recipes, and the first thing you'll note is the absence of pasta. After you taste the velvety *passata di peperoni gialli* (yellow bell-pepper soup), you won't care much. The stuffed roast rabbit demands the same admiration. My only complaint: They rush you through your meal in an un-Italian fashion in order to free up tables. Enjoy your after-dinner espresso at the Caffè Cibrèo across the way.

Via de' Macci 122r. ✆ **055-234-1100**. Primi 6€ ($6.90); secondi 13€ ($15). AE, DC, MC, V. Tues–Sat 1–2:30pm and 7–11:15pm. Closed July 26–Sept 6. Bus: B or 14.

Trattoria Pallottino FLORENTINE   One long room with a few long tables on the cobblestone floor and a second room on the side are all there is to this local favorite, so reserve early or you won't get a seat. The cook makes a mean *bruschetta al pomodoro* (toasted bread topped with tomatoes over which you are invited to drizzle the olive oil liberally). For a first course, I look no further than the *spaghetti alla fiaccheraia,* with a tomato sauce mildly spiked with hot peppers. You might follow it with the *peposo* (beef stew loaded with black pepper). Skip dessert and pop next door for a Vivoli gelato (see the box, "A Big Step Above Ice Cream: Florentine Gelato," on p. 124).

Via Isola delle Stinche 1r. ✆ **055-289-573**. Reservations required for dinner. Primi 5€–8€ ($5.75–$9.20); secondi 7€–14€ ($8.05–$16). AE, DC, MC, V. Tues–Sun 12:30–2:30pm and 7:30–10:30pm. Closed Aug 5–21.

IN THE OLTRARNO
EXPENSIVE
Osteria Santo Spirito NOUVELLE TUSCAN   Some of the hippest dining in the Oltrarno fills these deep-red rooms with undulating track lighting stacked on top of each other. Funk and dance music pounds from the speakers as they serve up excellent dishes with a modern twist. You can start with a salad like *pollo pinoli e uvetta con dressing* (chicken, pine nut, and raisin), or for pasta try *orecchiette Santo Spirito* (pasta in spicy tomato sauce with ricotta) or *gnocchi di patate gratinati* (oven-baked gnocchi swimming in a bubbling hot mix of soft cheeses flavored with truffle). Afterward, fill up on *filetto di manzo à tartufo* (beef filet with truffles) or the *coscie d'anatre con la panna* (very meaty roasted duck in cream sauce with carrots and bacon).

Piazza Santo Spirito 16r. ✆ **055-238-2383**. Reservations recommended. Primi 6€–14€ ($6.90–$16); secondi 12€–25€ ($14–$29). AE, DC, MC, V. Daily 12:45–2:30pm and 8pm–midnight. Bus: B, 11, 36, 37, or 68.

MODERATE
Alla Vecchia Bettola FLORENTINE   Founded by the owners of Nerbone in the Mercato Centrale (see review on p. 123), this simple room right on the piazza may not look it, but it's one of the city's premier restaurants in town for

ultratraditional Florentine food. It fills up very early with food-loving Florentines, who choose from an always-changing menu that may include *penne alla Bettola* in spicy cream tomato sauce, rigatoni dressed with crushed olives, or *riso sulle testicciole d'agnello* (a "local's" rice dish cooked in a halved sheep's head). Secondi range from *anatra ripiena tartufata* (stuffed duck in truffle sauce) to the superlative *carpaccio con rucola*—pounded disks of beef piled high with arugula and tissue-thin slices of pecorino cheese. As far as wine goes, you simply pay for however much you finish of the light and tangy house wine on the table.

Viale Vasco Pratolini 3/7 (on Piazza Tasso). ✆ **055-224-158.** Reservations required. Primi 6€–7€ ($6.90–$8.05); secondi 8€–12€ ($9.20–$14). No credit cards. Tues–Sat noon–2:30pm and 7:30–10:30pm. Closed 3 weeks in Aug, Dec 23–Jan 2, Easter. Bus: 12 or 13.

Il Cantinone 🎈 *Kids* TUSCAN   With tourists and large groups of locals all seated at long tables under the low arc of a brick ceiling, the convivial noise can sometimes get a bit overwhelming. But the feeling of having walked into a party is part of the charm of this place. The specialty is *crostini,* slabs of peasant bread that act as vehicles for toppings like prosciutto, tomatoes, mozzarella, and sausage. The wine list is excellent—due perhaps to this locale's past incarnation as a Chianti cellar—and the best way to sample it is through the menù degustazione. You and your companion get an antipasto, two primi (usually pasta dishes), and a secondo, which might be a tender and tasty wild boar stew. With each course you get a different wine, building from something like a light Orvieto *secco* through a well-chosen chianti to a brawny Brunello for the meat dish.

Via Santo Spirito 6r (off Piazza Santa Trinita). ✆ **055-218-898** or 055-225-955. Primi and *crostoni* 5.50€–8€ ($6.30–$9.20); secondi 6€–20€ ($6.90–$23). AE, MC, V. Tues–Sun 12:30–2:30pm and 7:30–10:30pm. Bus: D, 8, 11, 36, or 37.

I Raddi 🎈 TUSCAN   Luccio's trattoria hidden in the heart of the Oltrarno is a true find—excellent cooking at reasonable prices in a city rapidly overpricing itself. The beamed ceiling and Tuscan standbys on the menu give it a grounding in tradition while the young staff and light touch in the kitchen lend a fresh bohemian air. The specialty is *tagliolini ardiglione* (with sausage and aromatic herbs), but they also make a mean *crespelle alla fiorentina* (pasta crepes layered with cheese). They do a fine *cibrèo,* a tasty *peposo alla fornacina con spinaci* (beef baked in wine with lots of pepperoncino and served with spinach), and a spicy *fagioli all'uccelletto con salsiccia.*

Via Ardiglione 47r (off Via dei Serragli, near Piazza delle Carmine). ✆ **055-211-072.** www.iraddi.com. Reservations recommended. Primi 7€ ($8.05); secondi 10€–15€ ($12–$17). AE, MC, V. Mon–Sat noon–3pm and 7–11pm. Closed 10 days in Feb and a week in mid-Aug. Bus: D, 11, 36, 37, or 68.

Osteria del Cinghiale Bianco TUSCAN   Massimo Masselli will sooner turn people away at the door than rush you though your meal. The place does a good repeat business of locals (including cooks from other restaurants) and tourists alike who come for the delicious *taglierini* (wide noodles) with pesto or the famous *strozzapreti* ("priest-chokers" made of the spinach-and-ricotta mix normally found inside ravioli, served with melted butter). You can't go wrong ordering anything made of the restaurant's namesake *cinghiale* (wild boar)—from the cold boar slices as an appetizer to *cinghiale alla maremmana con polenta* (wild boar stew cozied up to creamy, firm polenta) as a main course. Set in the base of a 12th-century tower, this place milks its medieval look with exposed stone, odd iron implements hanging everywhere, and lights hidden in suspended cauldrons or the pigeonholed walls. Note that dishes with truffles in them might raise the maximum prices below by about 5€ ($5.75).

Borgo Sant' Jacopo 43r. ℭ 055-215-706. www.cinghialebianco.it. Reservations required on weekends. Primi 5€–10€ ($5.75–$12); secondi 9.50€–16€ ($11–$18). MC, V. Thurs–Tues 6.30–11pm (Sat–Sun also noon–3pm). Closed July 10–Aug 1. Bus: D, 8, 11, 36, or 37.

INEXPENSIVE

EnotecaBar Fuori Porta ENOTECA/CROSTONI   You can dine out on the sidewalk in nice weather, or sit on the benches at tiny wooden tables inside to taste the excellent pizzalike crostini here. Start with the *pappa al pomodoro* or gnocchi with broccoli rabe and sausage. The *crostoni* are divided by cheese—mozzarella, sharp pecorino, creamy goat-cheese *caprino*—along with a list of the toppings to accompany them. My fave is *caprino con prosciutto arrosto e pomodori secchi* (with goat cheese, roasted prosciutto, and sun-dried tomatoes). The wine is a key part of your meal; the list draws from the more interesting vineyards in Tuscany and beyond. This place is a bit out of the way but worth the trip.

Via del Monte alle Croci 10r (near San Niccolò, through the gate at Via San Miniato). ℭ 055-234-2483. www.fuoriporta.it. Sandwiches and appetizers 2€–7€ ($2.30–$8.05). AE, MC, V. Mon–Sat 12:30–3:30pm and 7pm–1am. Bus: C, D, 12, 13, or 23.

Trattoria La Casalinga FLORENTINE   Their recent expansion sadly removed the last wisps of Renaissance aura from La Casalinga, replacing it with a crowded, almost cafeteria-like feeling—but the home cooking of its name is still some of the most genuine in town. The *ribollita* is thick, the *ravioli al sugo di coniglio* (in a rabbit sauce) rich, and the *pasta della nonna* (short, hollow pasta in a sauce of tomatoes, sausage, and onions) excellent. Don't expect anything fancy in the secondi department either, just solid favorites like *bollito misto* (a mix of boiled meats with green sauce), *trippa alla fiorentina*, and *galletto ruspante al forno* (half a young oven-baked chicken). The starving artists and local artisans have been all but driven out by the tourist hordes, but if you want to stuff yourself on huge portions of Oltrarno workman's food, this is the place to come.

Via Michelozzi 9r (between Via Maggio and Piazza Santo Spirito). ℭ 055-267-9243. Primi 3.50€–4€ ($4.05–$4.60); secondi 5€–10€ ($5.75–$12). Mon–Sat noon–2:30pm and 7–10pm. AE, DC, MC, V. Bus: D, 8, 11, 36, or 37.

IN THE HILLS
MODERATE

Trattoria le Cave di Maiano ✿ TUSCAN   This converted farmhouse is the countryside restaurant of choice for Florentines wishing to escape the city heat on a summer Sunday afternoon. You can enjoy warm-weather lunches on the tree-shaded stone terrace with a bucolic view. In cooler weather, you can dine inside several large rustic rooms with haphazard paintings scattered on the walls. The *antipasto caldo* of varied *crostini* and fried polenta is a good way to kick off a meal, followed by a *misto della casa* (for two only) that gives you a sampling of primi. This may include *penne strascicate* (stubby pasta in cream sauce and tomato ragù), or *riso allo spezzacamino* (rice with beans and black cabbage). The best secondo is the *pollastro al mattone* (chicken roasted under a brick with pepper) or the *lombatina di vitello alla griglia* (grilled veal chop).

Via Cave di Maiano 16 (in Maiano, halfway between Florence and Fiesole east of the main road). ℭ 055-59-133. Reservations required. Primi 7€–10€ ($8.05–$12); secondi 10€–15€ ($12–$17). AE, DC, MC, V. Daily 12:30–3:30pm and 7:30pm–midnight. Bus: 7 (get off at Villa San Michele, then turn around and take the road branching to the left of the winding one your bus took; continue on about ¾ mile up this side road, past the Pensione Benecistà); a taxi is a better idea.

4

Exploring Florence

Florence is the Renaissance city— home to Michelangelo's *David*, Botticelli's *Birth of Venus*, and Raphael's Madonnas. It's where Fra' Angelico painted delicate *Annunciations* in bright primary colors and Giotto frescoed monks wailing over the *Death of St. Francis*. The city is so dense in art, history, and culture that even a short visit can wear out the best of us. Take a hint from that great pragmatist Mark Twain, who, after acknowledging the genius of Michelangelo, said "I do not want Michelangelo for breakfast—for luncheon—for dinner—for tea—for supper—for between meals. I like a change occasionally."

Don't necessarily pass up the Uffizi or take a rain check on *David* and the Accademia, but do take the time to enjoy the simple pleasures of Florence—wander the medieval streets in Dante's old neighborhood, sip a cappuccino on Piazza della Signoria and people-watch, haggle for a leather jacket at the street market around San Lorenzo, or immerse yourself in the greenery of the Boboli Gardens.

1 Seeing the Sights

Cenacolo di Santo Spirito
Museum, p. 174
Galleria dell'Accademia (Academy
Gallery) ✷✷, p. 161
Gallerie degli Uffizi (Uffizi
Galleries) ✷✷✷, p. 145
Museo Archeologico (Archaeological
Museum) ✷✷, p. 166
Museo Horne, p. 169
Museo di Santa Maria Novella ✷,
p. 160
Museo di Storia della Scienza
(Science Museum) ✷, p. 153

Museo dell'Opera del Duomo
(Duomo Works Museum) ✷,
p. 142
Museo dell'Opera di Santa Croce
✷, p. 169
Museo Nazionale del Bargello
(Bargello Museum) ✷✷, p. 155
Museo Opificio delle Pietre Dure,
p. 165
Museo Stibbert, p. 177
Museo Zoologico La Specola,
p. 176

ON PIAZZA DEL DUOMO

The cathedral square is filled with tourists and caricature artists during the day, strolling crowds in the early evening, and knots of students strumming guitars on the Duomo's steps at night. Though it's always crowded, the piazza's vivacity and the glittering facades of the cathedral and the baptistery doors keep it an eternal Florentine sight.

At the corner of the busy pedestrian main drag, Via Calzaiuoli, sits the pretty little **Loggia del Bigallo** (1351–58). Inside is a small museum of 14th-century works, which is unfortunately almost always closed. Call ☎ **055-215-440** if you're interested in trying to make an appointment to get in to see the 1342 *Madonna della Misericordia* by the school of Bernardo Daddi, which features the earliest known cityscape view of Florence.

Note that just south of the Duomo, hidden in the tangle of medieval streets toward Piazza della Signoria, is a 14th-century Florentine house restored and converted into the **Casa di Dante** (☎ **055-219-416**), a small museum chronicling the life and times of the great poet. But, this isn't likely the poet's actual house. The entrance is up the side alley of Via Santa Margherita, and it's open Monday and Wednesday through Saturday from 10am to 6pm (to 4pm in winter) and Sunday from 10am to 2pm. Admission has nearly tripled this year to a ludicrous 6.50€ ($7.50), so only diehard fans should bother.

Tips The Best Times to Sightsee

Museums Open on Mondays: Palazzo Vecchio, Museo Bardini, Museo di Firenze Com'Era, Museo di Santa Maria Novella, Casa Buonarroti, Casa di Dante, Opera di Santa Croce, Museo dell'Opera del Duomo, Campanile di Giotto, Duomo's cupola, Opificio Pietre Dure, Museo Stibbert, Instituto e Museo di Storia di Scienza, Palazzo Medici-Riccardi, Museo Horne, Cappella Brancacci, Synagogue, Spedale degli Innocenti, Roman Amphitheater, and Museo Archeologico (Fiesole).

Sights Open During Il Riposo (1–4pm): Uffizi, Accademia, Palazzo Vecchio, Duomo and its cupola, Museo dell'Opera del Duomo, Campanile di Giotto, Baptistery, Palazzo Vecchio, Santa Croce, Galleria Palatina (Pitti Palace), Forte di Belvedere and Boboli Gardens, Cappella Brancacci, Roman Amphitheater, and Museo Archeologico (Fiesole).

What to See & Do in Florence

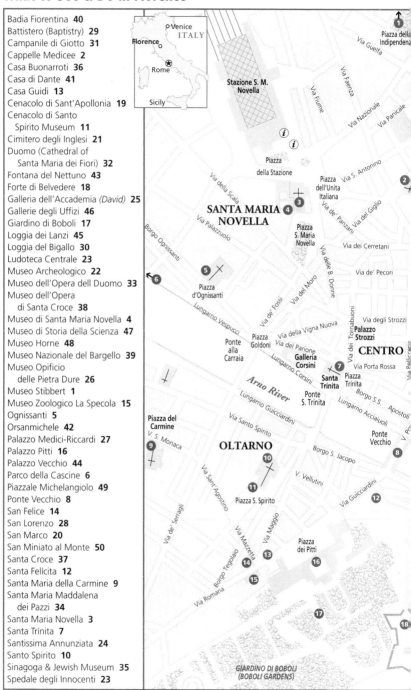

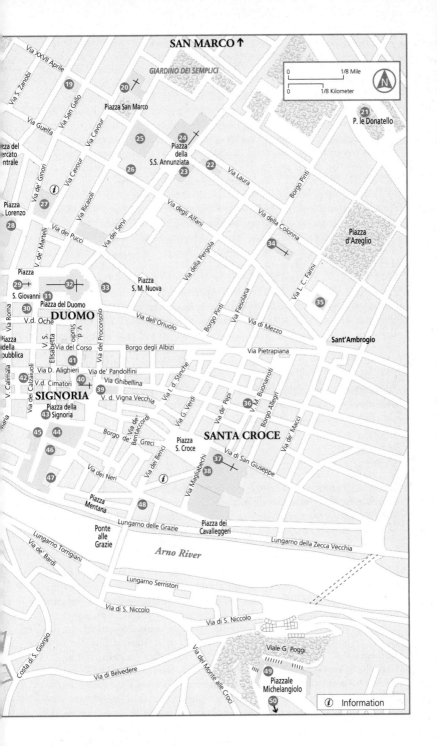

SAN MARCO ↑

GIARDINO DEI SEMPLICI

Piazza San Marco

P. le Donatello

Piazza della S.S. Annunziata

Via Laura

Borgo Pinti

Via della Colonna

Piazza d'Azeglio

Via degli Alfani

Via della Pergola

Piazza S. M. Nuova

Via dell'Oriuolo

Piazza del Duomo

DUOMO

V.d. Oche

Via del Corso

Borgo degli Albizi

Via Pietrapiana

Sant'Ambrogio

Via di Mezzo

Via Fiesolana

Borgo Pinti

Via L. C. Farini

Via Pietrapiana

Via D. Alighieri

Via de' Pandolfini

Via Ghibellina

SIGNORIA

V. d. Vigna Vecchia

Piazza della Signoria

Via G. Verdi

Via de' Pepi

V. M. Buonarroti

Borgo Allegri

Via de' Macci

SANTA CROCE

Piazza S. Croce

Via di San Giuseppe

Borgo de' Bentaccordi

Greci

Via de' Benci

Via Magliabechi

Via dei Neri

Piazza Mentana

Ponte alle Grazie

Lungarno delle Grazie

Piazza dei Cavalleggeri

Lungarno della Zecca Vecchia

Lungarno Torrigiani

Via de' Bardi

Arno River

Lungarno Serristori

Via di S. Niccolo

Via di S. Niccolo

Costa di S. Giorgio

Via di Belvedere

Via del Monte alle Croci

Viale G. Poggi

Piazzale Michelangiolo

ⓘ Information

Duomo (Cathedral of Santa Maria dei Fiori) ⭐⭐ For centuries, people have commented that Florence's cathedral is turned inside out, its exterior boasting Brunelleschi's famous dome, Giotto's bell tower, and a festive cladding of white, green, and pink marble, but its interior left spare, almost barren.

By the late 13th century, Florence was feeling peevish: Its archrivals Siena and Pisa sported huge new Duomos filled with art while it was saddled with the tiny 5th- or 6th-century Santa Reparata as a cathedral. So, in 1296, the city hired Arnolfo di Cambio to design a new Duomo, and he began raising the facade and the first few bays before his death in 1302. Work continued under the auspices of the Wool Guild and architects Giotto di Bondone (who concentrated on the bell tower) and Francesco Talenti (who finished up to the drum of the dome and in the process greatly enlarged Arnolfo's original plan). The facade we see today is a neo-Gothic composite designed by Emilio de Fabris and built from 1871 to 1887 (for its story, see the Museo dell'Opera del Duomo, below).

The Duomo's most distinctive feature is its enormous **dome** ⭐⭐⭐, which dominates the skyline and is a symbol of Florence itself. The raising of this dome, the largest in the world in its time, was no mean architectural feat, tackled admirably by Filippo Brunelleschi between 1420 and 1436 (see "A Man & His Dome," on p. 140). You can climb up between the two shells of the cupola for one of the classic panoramas across the city. At the base of the dome, just above the drum, Baccio d'Agnolo began adding a balcony in 1507. One of the eight sides was finished by 1515, when someone asked Michelangelo—whose artistic opinion was by this time taken as cardinal law—what he thought of it. The master reportedly scoffed, "It looks like a cricket cage." Work was immediately halted, and to this day the other seven sides remain rough brick.

The Duomo was actually built around **Santa Reparata** so it could remain in business during construction. For more than 70 years, Florentines entered their old church through the freestanding facade of the new one, but in 1370 the original was torn down when the bulk of the Duomo—except the dome—was finished. Ever the fiscal conservatives, Florentines started clamoring to see some art as soon as the new facade's front door was completed in the early 1300s—to be sure their investment would be more beautiful than rival cathedrals. Gaddo Gaddi was commissioned to mosaic an *Enthronement of Mary* in the lunette above the inside of the main door, and the people were satisfied. The stained-glass windows set in the facade were designed by Lorenzo Ghiberti, and Paolo Uccello, a painter obsessed by the newly developed perspective, frescoed the huge *hora italica* clock with its four heads of Prophets in 1443.

At a right-aisle pier are steps leading down to the excavations of the old Santa Reparata. In 1972, a tomb slab inscribed with the name Filippo Brunelleschi was discovered there (visible through a gate). Unless you're interested in the remains of some ancient Roman houses and parts of the paleo-Christian mosaics from Santa Reparata's floor, the 3€ ($3.45) admission isn't worth it.

Against the left-aisle wall are the only frescoes besides the dome in the Duomo. The earlier one to the right is the greenish ***Memorial to Sir John Hawkwood*** ⭐ (1436), an English *condottiere* (mercenary commander) whose name the Florentines mangled to Giovanni Acuto when they hired him to rough up their enemies. Before he died, or so the story goes, the mercenary asked to have a bronze statue of himself riding his charger to be raised in his honor. Florence solemnly promised to do so, but, in typical tightwad style, after Hawkwood's death the city hired the master of perspective and illusion, Paolo Uccello, to paint an equestrian monument instead—much cheaper than casting a statue in bronze. Andrea Castagno copied this painting-as-equestrian-statue idea 20 years later when he frescoed a *Memorial to Niccolò da Tolentino* next to Uccello's work. Near the end of the left aisle is Domenico di Michelino's *Dante Explaining the Divine Comedy* (1465).

In the back left corner of the sanctuary is the **New Sacristy.** Lorenzo de' Medici was attending Mass in the Duomo one April day in 1478 with his brother Giuliano when they were attacked in the infamous Pazzi Conspiracy. The conspirators, egged on by the pope and led by a member of the Pazzi family, old rivals of the Medici, fell on the brothers at the ringing of the sanctuary bell. Giuliano was murdered on the spot—his body rent with 19 wounds—but Lorenzo vaulted over the altar rail and sprinted for safety into the New Sacristy, slamming the bronze doors behind him. Those doors were cast from 1446 to 1467 by Luca della Robbia, his only significant work in the medium. Earlier, Luca had provided a lunette of the *Resurrection* (1442) in glazed terra cotta over the door, as well as the lunette Ascension over the south sacristy door. The interior of the New Sacristy is filled with beautifully inlaid wood cabinet doors.

The frescoes on the **interior of the dome** were designed by Giorgio Vasari but painted mostly by his less-talented student Frederico Zuccari by 1579. The frescoes were subjected to a thorough cleaning completed in 1996, which many people saw as a waste of restoration lire when so many more important works throughout the city were waiting to be salvaged. The scrubbing did, however, bring out Zuccari's only saving point—his innovative color palette.

Piazza del Duomo. ℂ **055-230-2885.** www.operaduomo.firenze.it. Admission to church free; Santa Reparata excavations 3€ ($3.45); cupola 6€ ($6.90), free for children under 6. Church Mon–Wed and Fri 10am–5pm; Thurs 10am–3:30pm; 1st Sat of month 10am–3:30pm, other Sat 10am–4:45pm; Sun 1:30–4:30pm. Free tours every 40 min. daily, 10:30am–noon and 3–4:20pm. Cupola Mon–Fri 8:30am–6:20pm; Sat 8:30am–5pm (first Sat of month to 3:20pm). Bus: 1, 6, 17, 14, 22, 23, 36, 37, or 71.

Battistero (Baptistery) ★★★   In choosing a date to mark the beginning of the Renaissance, art historians often seize on 1401, the year Florence's powerful wool merchant's guild held a contest to decide who would receive the commission to design the **North Doors** ★ of the Baptistery to match the Gothic **South Doors** cast 65 years earlier by Andrea Pisano. The era's foremost Tuscan sculptors each designed and cast a bas-relief bronze panel depicting his own vision of The Sacrifice of Isaac. Twenty-two-year-old Lorenzo Ghiberti, competing against the likes of Donatello, Jacopo della Quercia, and Filippo Brunelleschi, won hands down. He spent the next 21 years casting 28 bronze panels and building his doors. Although limited by his contract to design the scenes within Gothic frames as on Pisano's doors, Ghiberti infused his figures and compositions with an unmatched realism and classical references that helped define Renaissance sculpture. (Ghiberti stuck a self-portrait in the left door, the 4th head from the bottom of the middle strip, wearing a turban.)

The result so impressed the merchant's guild—not to mention the public and Ghiberti's fellow artists—they asked him in 1425 to do the **East Doors** ★★★, facing the Duomo, this time giving him the artistic freedom to realize his Renaissance ambitions. Twenty-seven years later, just before his death, Ghiberti finished 10 dramatic life-like Old Testament scenes in gilded bronze, each a masterpiece of Renaissance sculpture and some of the finest low-relief perspective in Italian art. The panels now mounted here are excellent copies; the originals are displayed in the Museo dell'Opera del Duomo (see below). Years later, Michelangelo was standing before these doors and someone asked his opinion. His response sums up Ghiberti's life accomplishment as no art historian ever

A Man & His Dome

Filippo Brunelleschi, a diminutive man whose ego was as big as his talent, managed in his arrogant, quixotic, suspicious, and brilliant way to literally invent Renaissance architecture. Having been beaten by Lorenzo Ghiberti in the famous contest to cast the baptistery doors (see below), Brunelleschi resolved he'd rather be the top architect than the second-best sculptor and took off for Rome to study the buildings of the ancients. On returning to Florence, he combined subdued gray *pietra serena* stone with smooth white plaster to create airy arches, vaults, and arcades of classically perfect proportions in his own special variant on the ancient Roman orders of architecture. Apart from designing the serene San Lorenzo, Santo Spirito, and the elegant Ospedale degli Innocenti, his greatest achievement by far was erecting the dome over Florence's cathedral.

The Duomo, then the world's largest church, had already been built, but nobody had been able to figure out how to cover the daunting space over its center without spending a fortune and without filling the church with the necessary scaffolding—plus no one was sure whether they could create a dome that would hold up under its own weight. One of the many ridiculous solutions was making it of pumice (so it would be light) and filling the church with dirt studded with small coins. (After the work was done, the populace would be invited to dig for the money and thus remove the dirt.) Brunelleschi kept insisting he had the answer, but he wouldn't share it, fearful others would use his ideas and get the job over him.

After becoming so heated during several meetings of the Dome Erection Committee that he had to be carried out, he finally came in bearing an egg and issued a challenge (or so Vasari says). He bet he was the only one of the learned architects and councilmen in the room who

could: "They are so beautiful that they would grace the entrance to Paradise." They've been called the Gates of Paradise ever since.

The Baptistery is one of Florence's oldest, most venerated buildings. Florentines long believed it was originally a Roman temple, but it most likely was raised somewhere between the 4th and 7th centuries on the site of a Roman palace. The octagonal drum was rebuilt in the 11th century, and by the 13th century it had been clad in its characteristic green-and-white Romanesque stripes of marble and capped with its odd pyramid-like dome.

The interior is ringed with columns pilfered from ancient Roman buildings and is a spectacle of mosaics above and below. The floor was inlaid in 1209, and the ceiling was covered between 1225 and the early 1300s with glittering **mosaics** ★★. Most were crafted by Venetian or Byzantine-style workshops, which worked off designs drawn by the era's best artists. Coppo di Marcovaldo drew sketches for the over 7.8m (26-ft.) high, ape-toed Christ in Judgment and the Last Judgment that fills over a third of the ceiling.

To the right of the altar is the 1425 wall **tomb of Antipope John XXIII,** designed by Michelozzo and Donatello, who cast the bronze effigy of the deceased, deposed pontiff.

could make an egg stand on its end. A marble slab was procured for the balancing act but, try as they might, the others couldn't get the egg to stay vertical. Brunelleschi took the egg in his hand, and with one quick movement slammed it down on the marble, smashing its end—but leaving it standing. The others protested that they, too, could have easily done that, to which Brunelleschi replied they would say the same thing if he showed them his plans for the dome. He was granted the commission and revealed his ingenious plan—which may have been inspired by close study of Rome's Pantheon.

He built the dome in two shells, the inner one thicker than the outer, both shells thinning as they neared the top, thus leaving the center hollow and removing a good deal of the weight. He also planned to construct the dome of giant vaults with ribs crossing over them, with each of the stones making up the actual fabric of the dome being dovetailed. In this way, the walls of the dome would support themselves as they were erected. In the process of building, Brunelleschi found himself as much an engineer as architect, constantly designing remarkable new winches, cranes, and hoists to carry the materials faster and more efficiently up to the level of the workmen. He was even farsighted enough to build in drainage systems for the rain and iron hooks to support interior scaffolding for future cleanings or paint jobs.

His finished work speaks for itself, 45m (150 ft.) wide at the base and 90m (300 ft.) high from drum to lantern—Florentines proudly claim they've lived their whole lives within sight of the dome. For his achievement, Brunelleschi was accorded a singular honor: He's the only person ever buried in Florence's cathedral, under his ingenious and revolutionary dome.

Piazza di San Giovanni. ℂ **055-230-2885.** www.operaduomo.firenze.it. Admission 3€ ($3.45), free for children under 6. Mon–Sat noon–6:30pm; Sun 8:30am–1:30pm. Bus: 1, 6, 17, 14, 22, 23, 36, 37, or 71.

Campanile di Giotto (Giotto's Bell Tower) ★★   In 1334, Giotto started the cathedral bell tower (clad in the same three colors of marble gracing the Duomo) but completed only the first two levels before his death in 1337. He was out of his league with the engineering aspects of architecture, and the tower was saved from falling in on itself by Andrea Pisano, who doubled the thickness of the walls. Andrea, a master sculptor of the Pisan Gothic school, also changed the design to add statue niches—he even carved a few of the statues himself—before quitting the project in 1348. Francesco Talenti finished the job between 1350 and 1359— he exchanged the heavy solidity of the base for a lighter, airier effect.

The **reliefs** and **statues** in the lower levels—by Andrea Pisano, Donatello, and others—are all copies, the weatherworn originals now housed in the Museo dell'Opera del Duomo (see below). You can climb the 414 steps to the top of the tower. What makes the 84m- (25-ft.-) high view different from what you get out of the more popular climb up the cathedral dome, besides a cityscape vista, are great views of the Baptistery as you ascend and the best close-up shot in the whole city of Brunelleschi's dome.

Around Piazza della Signoria

When the medieval Guelf party finally came out on top of the Ghibellines, they razed part of the old city center to build a new palace for civic government. It's said the Guelfs ordered architect Arnolfo di Cambio to build what we now call the Palazzo Vecchio in the corner of this space, but to be careful that not one inch of the building sat on the cursed former Ghibelline land. This odd legend was probably fabricated to explain Arnolfo's quirky off-center architecture.

The space around the palazzo became the new civic center of town, the L-shaped **Piazza della Signoria** ⭐⭐, named after the oligarchic ruling body of the medieval city. Today, it's an outdoor sculpture gallery, teeming with tourists, postcard stands, horses and buggies, and outdoor cafes.

The statuary on the piazza is particularly beautiful, starting on the far left (as you're facing the Palazzo Vecchio) with Giambologna's equestrian statue of *Grand Duke Cosimo I* (1594). To its right is one of Florence's favorite sculptures to hate, the *Fontana del Nettuno* (*Neptune Fountain;* 1560–75), created by Bartolomeo Ammannati as a tribute to Cosimo I's naval ambitions but nicknamed by the Florentines *Il Biancone,* "Big Whitey." Michelangelo, to whom many a Renaissance quip is attributed, took one look at it and shook his head, moaning "Ammannato, Ammannato, what a beautiful piece of marble you've ruined." The highly mannerist bronzes surrounding the basin are much better, probably because a young Giambologna had a hand in most of them.

Note the **porphyry plaque** set in the ground in front of the fountain. This marks the site where puritanical monk Savonarola held the Bonfire of the Vanities: With his fiery apocalyptic preaching, he whipped the Florentines into a reformist frenzy, and hundreds filed into this piazza, arms loaded with paintings, clothing, and other effects that represented their "decadence." They consigned it all to the flames of a roaring pile. However, after a few years the pope (not amused by Savonarola's criticisms) excommunicated first the monk and then the entire city for supporting him. On May 23, 1498, the Florentines decided they'd had enough of the rabid-dog monk, dragged him and two followers to the torture chamber, pronounced them heretics, and led them into the piazza for one last day of fire and brimstone. In the very spot where they once burnt their luxurious belongings, they put the torch to Savonarola himself. The event is commemorated by an anonymous painting kept in Savonarola's old cell in San Marco and by the plaque here.

Piazza del Duomo. © **055-230-2885.** www.operaduomo.firenze.it. Admission 6€ ($6.90). Daily 8:30am–6:50pm. Bus: 1, 6, 17, 14, 22, 23, 36, 37, or 71.

Museo dell'Opera del Duomo (Duomo Works Museum) ⭐ This museum exists mainly to house the sculptures removed from the niches and doors of the Duomo group for restoration and preservation out of the elements. The dusty old museum was completely rearranged from 1998 to 2000.

To the right of the Neptune Fountain is a long, raised platform fronting the Palazzo Vecchio known as the *arringheria,* from which soapbox speakers would lecture to crowds before them (we get our word "harangue" from this). On its far left corner is a copy (original in the Bargello) of Donatello's **Marzocco,** symbol of the city, with a Florentine lion resting his raised paw on a shield emblazoned with the city's emblem, the *giglio* (lily). To its right is another Donatello replica, **Judith Beheading Holofernes.** Farther down is a man who needs little introduction, Michelangelo's **David,** a 19th-century copy of the original now in the Accademia. Near enough to David to look truly ugly in comparison is Baccio Bandinelli's **Heracles** (1534). Poor Bandinelli was trying to copy Michelangelo's muscular male form but ended up making his Heracles merely lumpy.

At the piazza's south end, beyond the long U that opens down the Uffizi, is one of the square's earliest and prettiest embellishments, the **Loggia dei Lanzi** ★★ (1376–82), named after the Swiss guard of lancers *(lanzi)* Cosimo de' Medici stationed here. The airy loggia was probably built on a design by Andrea Orcagna—spawning another of its many names, the Loggia di Orcagna (another is the Loggia della Signoria). The three huge arches of its simple, harmonious form were way ahead of the times, an architectural style that really belongs to the Renaissance. This open arcade is filled with statuary, though as we go to press much of it is encased in big wooden boxes as they restore the pieces. At the front left corner stands Benvenuto Cellini's masterpiece in bronze, **Perseus** ★★ (1545), holding out the severed Medusa's head before him, restored from 1996 to 2000. On the far right of the loggia has stood Giambologna's **Rape of the Sabines** ★★, one of the most successful mannerist sculptures in existence, a piece you must walk all the way around to appreciate, catching the action and artistry from different angles. Sadly, once it was boxed up and examined for restoration, authorities determined that the outdoors had wreaked intolerable damage, and the original statue will soon be removed to the Accademia (to take the place of its plaster model long anchoring the museum's first room) with a marble copy to take its place here.

Across the piazza, on the north end at no. 5, is the **Raccolta della Ragione** (© 055-283-078), a gallery of mainly late-19th- and 20th-century art with some nice second-story views over the piazza. Usually open Wednesday through Saturday from 9am to 4pm and Sunday from 8am to 1pm, the gallery is temporarily closed.

The courtyard has now been enclosed so as to show off—under natural daylight, as they should be seen—Lorenzo Ghiberti's original gilded bronze panels from the Baptistery's **Gates of Paradise** ★★★, which are being displayed as they're slowly restored. Ghiberti devoted 27 years to this project (1425–52), and you can now admire up close his masterpiece of *schiacciato* (squished) relief—using

---

Tips **Reserving Tickets for the Uffizi & Other Museums**

You can bypass the hours-long ticket line at the **Uffizi Galleries** by reserving a ticket and an entry time in advance by calling **Firenze Musei** at © **055-294-883** (Mon–Fri 8:30am–6:30pm, Sat until 12:30pm) or at www.firenze musei.it (24/7). By March, entry times can be booked more than a week in advance. You can also reserve for the **Accademia Gallery** (another interminable line, to see _David_), as well as the **Galleria Palatina** in the Pitti Palace, the **Bargello,** and several others. There is a 1.55€ ($1.80) fee (worth every penny), and you can pay by credit card.

---

the Donatello technique of almost sketching in perspective to create the illusion of depth in low relief.

On the way up the stairs, you pass **Michelangelo's _Pietà_** ✰ (1548–55), his second and penultimate take on the subject, which the sculptor probably had in mind for his own tomb. The face of Nicodemus is a self-portrait, and Michelangelo most likely intended to leave much of the statue group only roughly carved, just as we see it. Art historians inform us that the polished figure of Mary Magdalene on the left was finished by one of Michelangelo's students, while storytellers relate that part of the considerable damage to the group was inflicted by the master himself when, in a moment of rage and frustration, he took a hammer to it.

The top floor of the museum houses the **Prophets** carved for the bell tower, the most noted of which are the remarkably expressive figures carved by Donatello: the drooping aged face of the _Beardless Prophet;_ the sad fixed gaze of _Jeremiah;_ and the misshapen ferocity of the bald _**Habakkuk**_ ✰ (known to Florentines as _Lo Zuccone_—pumpkin head). Mounted on the walls above are two putti-encrusted marble _**cantorie**_ **(choir lofts).** The slightly earlier one (1431) on the entrance wall is by Luca della Robbia. His panels (the originals now displayed at eye level, with plaster casts set in the actual frame above) are in perfect early Renaissance harmony, both within themselves and with each other, and they show della Robbia's mastery of creating great depth within a shallow piece of stone. Across the room, Donatello's _**cantoria**_ ✰ (1433–38) takes off in a new artistic direction as his singing cherubs literally break through the boundaries of the "panels" to leap and race around the entire _cantoria_ behind the mosaicked columns.

The room off the right stars one of Donatello's more morbidly fascinating sculptures, a late work in polychrome wood of _**The Magdalene**_ ✰ (1453–55), emaciated and veritably dripping with penitence.

The new exit corridor leading off from the Prophets room houses some of the **machines** used to build the cathedral dome, **Brunelleschi's death mask** as a grisly reminder of its architect, and the **wooden model proposals** for the cupola's drum and for the facade. The original Gothic facade was destroyed in 1587 to make room for one done in High Renaissance style, but the patron behind the work—Grand Duke Francesco de' Medici—died before he could choose from among the submissions by the likes of Giambologna and Bernardo Buontalenti. The Duomo remained faceless until purses of the 18th century, heavy with money and relentless bad taste, gave it the neo-Gothic facade we see today.

Piazza del Duomo 9 (directly behind the dome end of the cathedral). © **055-230-2885.** www.operaduomo.firenze.it. Admission 6€ ($6.90), free for children under 6. Mon–Sat 9am–7:30pm; Sun 9am–2pm; last admission 30 min. before close. Bus: 6, 11, 14, 17, or 23.

Gallerie degli Uffizi (Uffizi Galleries) ★★★   The Uffizi is one of the world's great museums, and the single best introduction to Renaissance painting, with works by Giotto, Masaccio, Paolo Uccello, Sandro Botticelli, Leonardo da Vinci, Perugino, Michelangelo, Raphael Sanzio, Titian, Caravaggio, and the list goes on. The museum is deceptively small. What looks like a small stretch of gallery space can easily gobble up half a day—many rooms suffer the fate of containing nothing but masterpieces.

Know before you go that the Uffizi regularly shuts down rooms for crowd-control reasons—especially in summer, when the bulk of the annual 1.5 million visitors stampedes the place. Of the more than 3,100 artworks in the museum's archives, only about 1,700 are on exhibit. As they restore the building from the 1993 bombing (see "Rising from the Blast," below), they're also making new exhibition spaces available, but this process has taken years and we've yet to see these new exhibition spaces (just new ticketing and gift shop areas).

The painting gallery is housed in the structure built to serve as the offices (*uffizi* is Florentine dialect for *uffici,* or "offices") of the Medici, commissioned by Cosimo I from Giorgio Vasari in 1560—perhaps his greatest architectural work. The painting gallery was started by Cosimo I as well and is now housed in the second-floor rooms that open off a long hall lined with ancient statues and frescoed with grotesques.

The first room off to your left after you climb Vasari's monumental stairs (**Room 2;** Room 1 is perennially closed) presents you with a crash course in the Renaissance's roots. It houses three huge altarpieces by Tuscany's greatest late-13th-century masters. On the right is Cimabue's *Santa Trínita Maestà* (1280), still very much rooted in the Byzantine traditions that governed painting in the early Middle Ages—gold-leaf crosshatching in the drapery, an Eastern-style inlaid throne, spoonlike depressions above the noses, highly posed figures, and cloned angels with identical faces stacked up along the sides. On the left is Duccio's *Rucellai Maestà* (1285), painted by the master who studied with Cimabue and eventually founded the Sienese school of painting. The style is still thoroughly medieval but introduces innovations into the rigid traditions. There's a little more weight to the Child Madonna holds, and the Madonna's face has a more human, somewhat sad, expression.

In the center of the room is Giotto's incredible ***Ognissanti Maestà*** ★★★ (1310), by the man who's generally credited as the founding father of Renaissance painting. It's sometimes hard to appreciate just how much Giotto changed when he junked half the traditions of painting to go his own way. It's mainly in

---

Tips for Seeing the Uffizi

If you have the time, make two trips to the museum. On your first, concentrate on the first dozen or so rooms and pop by the Greatest Hits of the 16th Century, with works by Michelangelo, Caravaggio, Raphael, and Titian. Return later for a brief recap and continue with the rest of the gallery.

Be aware that the **gift shop** at the end of the galleries closes 20 minutes before the museum. You can visit it without reentering the museum at any time; if you plan to stay in the collections until closing, go down to the shop earlier during your visit and get the guards' attention before you pass through the exit turnstile, so they'll know you're just popping out to buy a few postcards and will recognize you when you ask to be let back in.

The Uffizi

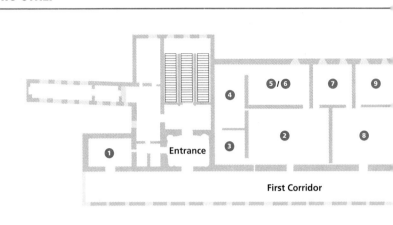

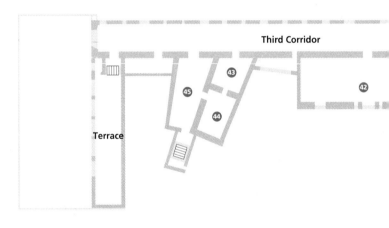

Rising from the Blast

On May 27, 1993, a car bomb ripped through the west wing of the Uffizi, seriously damaging it and some 200 works of art and destroying three (thankfully lesser) Renaissance paintings. The bomb killed five people inside, including the museum curator and her family. While everything from a Mafia hit to a government conspiracy was blamed, the motive for the bombing, and the perpetrators, remain unknown to this day.

In December 1998, Italy unveiled what it called the New Uffizi, a $15-million renovation that repaired all damaged rooms, added more than 20,000 square feet of new museum space, and displayed more than 100 works that had never been seen before—part of a larger project to triple exhibit space. Several branches of the book/gift shop were added to the ticketing areas on the ground floor, and the old outdoor cafe at the end of the galleries, atop the Loggia dei Lanzi with a view of the Palazzo Vecchio's tower, was reopened.

the very simple details, the sorts of things we take for granted in art today, such as the force of gravity, the display of basic emotions, the individual facial expressions, and the figures that look like they have an actual bulky body under their clothes. (See "The Genius of Giotto" on p. 395 for more on Giotto and his art.) Giotto's Madonna sways slightly to one side, the fabric of her off-white shirt pulling realistically against her breasts as she twists. Instead of floating in mysterious space, Giotto's saints and angels stand on solid ground.

Room 3 pays homage to the 14th-century Sienese school with several delicately crafted works by Simone Martini and the Lorenzetti brothers. Here is Martini's *Annunciation* ✸ (1333). Note that Mary, who in so much art both before and after this period is depicted as meekly accepting her divine duty, looks reluctant, even disgusted, at the news of her imminent Immaculate Conception. Pietro and Ambrogio Lorenzetti helped revolutionize Sienese art and the Sienese school before succumbing to the Black Death in 1348. Of their work here, Ambrogio's 1342 *Presentation at the Temple* is the finest, with a rich use of color and a vast architectural space created to open up the temple in the background.

Room 4 houses the works of the 14th-century Florentine school, where you can clearly see the influence Giotto had on his contemporaries. **Rooms 5 and 6** represent the dying gasps of International Gothic, still grounded in medievalism but admitting a bit of the emergent naturalism and humanist philosophy into their works. Lorenzo Monaco's *Coronation of the Virgin* (1413) is particularly beautiful, antiquated in its styling but with a delicate suffused coloring.

In **Room 7,** the Renaissance proper starts taking shape, driven primarily by the quest of two artists, Paolo Uccello and Masaccio, for perfect perspective. On the left wall is Uccello's *Battle of San Romano* (1456), famously innovative but also rather ugly. This painting depicts one of Florence's great victories over rival Siena, but for Uccello it was more of an excuse to explore perspective—with which this painter was, by all accounts, positively obsessed.

In the far corner is the only example of Masaccio's art here (he died at 27), the *Madonna and Child with St. Anne,* which he helped his master, Masolino, paint in 1424. Masaccio's earthy realism and sharp light are evident in the figures of Mary and the Child, as well as in the topmost angel peeking down. In the center of the room is Piero della Francesca's **Portrait of Frederico da Montefeltro and Battista Sforza** ★★, painted around 1465 or 1470 and the only work by this remarkable Sansepolcran artist to survive in Florence. The fronts of the panels depict the famous duke of Urbino and his wife, while on the backs are horse-drawn carts symbolic of the pair's respective virtues. Piero's incredibly lucid style and modeling and the detailed Flemish-style backgrounds need no commentary, but do note he purposefully painted the husband and wife in full profile—without diluting the realism of a hooked nose and moles on the duke—and mounted them face to face, so they'll always gaze into each other's eyes.

Room 8 is devoted to Filippo Lippi, with more than half a dozen works by the lecherous monk who turned out rich religious paintings with an earthy quality and a three-dimensionality that make them immediately accessible. His most famous painting here is the *Madonna and Child with Two Angels* (1455–66). Also here are a few works by Filippo's illegitimate son, Filippino. **Room 9** is an interlude of virtuoso paintings by Antonio del Pollaiolo, plus a number of large Virtues by his less-talented brother, Piero. These two masters of anatomical verisimilitude greatly influenced the young Botticelli, three of whose early works reside in the room. This introduction to Botticelli sets us up for the next room, invariably crowded with tour-bus groups.

The walls separating **Rooms 10 to 14** were knocked down in the 20th century to create one large space to accommodate the resurgent popularity of Sandro Filipepi—better known by his nickname, Botticelli ("little barrels")—master of willowy women in flowing gowns. Fourteen of his paintings line the walls, along with works by his pupil (and illegitimate son of his former teacher) Filippino Lippi and Domenico Ghirlandaio, Michelangelo's first artistic master. But everybody flocks here for just two paintings, Botticelli's *Birth of Venus* and his *Primavera (Allegory of Spring)*. Though in later life Botticelli was influenced by the puritanical preachings of Savonarola and took to cranking out boring Madonnas, the young painter began in grand pagan style. Both paintings were commissioned between 1477 and 1483 by a Medici cousin for his private villa, and they celebrate not only Renaissance art's love of naturalism but also the humanist philosophy permeating 15th-century Florence, a neo-Platonism that united religious doctrine with ancient ideology and mythological stories.

In the **Birth of Venus** ★★, the love goddess is born of the sea on a half shell, blown to shore by the Zephyrs. Ores, a goddess of the seasons, rushes to clothe her. Some say the long-legged goddess was modeled on Simonetta Vespucci, a renowned Florentine beauty, cousin to Amerigo (the naval explorer after whom America is named) and not-so-secret lover of Giuliano de' Medici, Lorenzo the Magnificent's brother). The **Primavera** ★★ is harder to evaluate, since contemporary research indicates it may not actually be an allegory of spring influenced by the humanist poetry of Poliziano but rather a celebration of Venus, who stands in the center, surrounded by various complicated references to Virtues through mythological characters. Also check out Botticelli's *Adoration of the Magi,* where the artist painted himself in the far right side, in a great yellow robe and golden curls.

Room 15 boasts Leonardo da Vinci's **Annunciation** ★★★, which the young artist painted in 1472 or 1475 while still in the workshop of his master, Andrea del Verrocchio; however, he was already fully developed as an artist. The solid yet light figures and sfumato airiness blurring the distance render remarkably life-like figures somehow suspended in a surreal dreamscape. Leonardo helped Verrocchio on the *Baptism of Christ*—most credit the artist-in-training with the angel on the far left as well as the landscape, and a few art historians think they see his hand in the figure of Jesus as well. The *Adoration of the Magi,* which Leonardo didn't get much beyond the sketching stage, shows how he could retain powerful compositions even when creating a fantasy landscape of ruinous architecture and incongruous horse battles. The room also houses works by Lorenzo di Credi and Piero di Cosimo, fellow 15th-century maestros, and a *Pietà* that shows Perugino's solid plastic style of studied simplicity. (This Umbrian master would later pass it on to his pupil Raphael.) Uffizi officials use **Room 18, the Tribune,** as a crowd-control pressure valve. You may find yourself stuck shuffling around it slowly, staring at the mother-of-pearl discs lining the domed ceiling; studying the antique statues, such as the famous *Medici Venus* (a 1st-c. B.C. Roman copy of a Greek original); and scrutinizing the Medici portraits wallpapering the room. The latter include many by the talented early baroque artist Agnolo Bronzino, whose portrait of **Eleonora of Toledo** ✦, wife of Cosimo I, with their son Giovanni de' Medici (1545), is particularly well worked. It shows her in a satin dress embroidered and sewn with velvet and pearls. When the Medici tombs were opened in 1857, her body was found buried in this same dress (it's now in the Pitti Palace's costume museum).

Also here are Raphael's late *St. John the Baptist in the Desert* (1518) and mannerist Rosso Fiorentino's 1522 Angel Musician, where an insufferably cute little *putto* (cherub) plucks at an oversized lute—it's become quite the Renaissance icon in the recent spate of angel mania.

Room 19 is devoted to both Perugino, who did the luminous *Portrait of Francesco delle Opere* (1494), and Luca Signorelli, whose *Holy Family* (1490–95) was painted as a tondo set in a rectangle, with allegorical figures in the background and a torsion of the figures that were to influence Michelangelo's version (in a later room). **Room 20** is devoted to Dürer, Cranach, and other German artists who worked in Florence, while **Room 21** takes care of 16th-century Venetians Giovanni Bellini, Giorgione, and Carpaccio. In **Room 22** are Flemish and German works by Hans Holbein the Younger, Hans Memling, and others, and **Room 23** contains Andrea Mantegna's triptych of the *Adoration of the Magi, Circumcision, and Ascension* (1463–70), showing his excellent draftsmanship and fascination with classical architecture. Now we move into the west wing, still in the throes of restoration following the bombing (see "Rising from the Blast," above). **Room 25** is overpowered by Michelangelo's **Holy Family** ✦✦✦ (1506–08), one of the few panel paintings by the great master. The glowing colors and shocking nudes in the background seem to pop off the surface, and the torsion of the figures was to be taken up as the banner of the mannerist movement. Michelangelo also designed the elaborate frame.

Room 26 is devoted to Andrea del Sarto and High Renaissance darling Raphael. Of Raphael we have the *Madonna of the Goldfinch* (1505), a work he painted in a Leonardesque style for a friend's wedding, and several important portraits, including *Pope Leo X with Cardinals Giulio de' Medici and Luigi de' Rossi* and *Pope Julius II,* as well as a famous *Self-portrait.* Del Sarto was the most important painter in Florence in the early 16th century, while Michelangelo and Raphael were off in Rome. His consciously developed mannerist style is evident in his masterful *Madonna of the Harpies* (1515–17).

Room 27 is devoted to works by Del Sarto's star mannerist pupils, Rosso Fiorentino and Pontormo, and by Pontormo's adopted son, Bronzino.

Fiorentino's **Moses Defends the Daughters of Jethro** ✩ (1523) owes much to Michelangesque nudes but is also wholly original in the use of harsh lighting that reduces the figures to basics shapes of color.

Room 28 is split between honoring the great Venetian Titian, of whose works you'll see a warm full-bodied **Flora** ✩✩ and a poetic **Venus of Urbino** ✩ languishing on her bed; Sienese High Renaissance painter Sebastiano del Piombo (his *Death of Adonis* and *Portrait of a Woman* are both strong works); and a few mediocre works by Palma il Vecchio.

Tiny **Rooms 29-30**, ostensibly honoring works by several Emilian artists, are totally dominated by late mannerist master Il Parmigianino, who carried the mannerist movement to its logical extremes with the almost grotesquely elongated bodies of the **Madonna of the Long Neck** ✩ (1534). **Room 31** continues to chart the fall of painting into decorative grace with Paolo Veronese's *Martyrdom of St. Justine* (1573), which is less about the saint being stabbed than it is a sartorial study in fashion design.

Room 32 is a nice break provided by the dramatic and visible brushstrokes that boldly swirled rich, somber colors of several lesser works by Venetian master Tintoretto. All the better, as these must see you through the treacle and tripe of **Rooms 33-34,** stuffed with substandard examples of 16th century paintings by the likes of Vasari, Alessandro Allori, and other chaps who grew up in Michelangelo's shadow and desperately wished they could paint like him (note: They couldn't).

Popping back out in the main corridor again, you visit the last several rooms one at a time as each opens off the hall. **Room 35** features the taffeta, cotton candy oeuvre of baroque weirdo Frederico Barocci (whose works are currently coming into vogue—why, I've no idea). Continue right past that exit staircase, because they save a few eye-popping rooms for the very end.

Room 41 is all about Rubens and his famously ample nudes, along with some works by his Flemish cohorts (Van Dyck, Sustermans). **Room 42** is a lovely side hall flooded with sunlight and graced by more than a dozen Roman statues that are copies of Hellenic originals, most of them of the dying Niobids.

And so we come to **Room 43** and the caravaggieschi. Caravaggio was the baroque master of *chiaroscuro*—painting with extreme harsh light and deep shadows. The Uffizi preserves his painting of the severed head of *Medusa,* a *Sacrifice of Isaac,* and his famous **Bacchus** ✩✩. Caravaggio's work influenced a generation of artists—the caravaggieschi—including Artemisia Gentileschi, the only female painter to make a name for herself in the late Renaissance/early baroque. Artemisia was eclipsed in fame by her slightly less talented father, Orazio, and she was the victim and central figure in a sensational rape trial brought against Orazio's one-time collaborator. It evidently had an effect on her professional life; among her paintings here is the violent *Judith Slaying Holofernes.*

Duck through the end of this room to pay your respects to Rembrandt in **Room 44,** where he immortalized himself in two *Self-portraits,* one done as a youth and the other as an old man. Hang a right to exit back into the corridor again via **Room 45,** a bit of a let-down after the last two rooms, but still engaging (if you've any art-appreciation energies left after all this) for its Greatest Hits of the 18th Century artists—Giuseppe Maria Crespi, Giovanni Paolo Pannini, Il Canaletto, Francesco Guardi, and Tiepolo—plus a Spanish twist to end it all with two paintings by Francisco Goya.

That's it. The Uffizi is finished. Treat yourself to a cappuccino al fresco in the loggia-top bar just beyond the last room; you've earned it.

Did I say finished? Not quite. Cosimo I de' Medici, after he moved to the Pitti Palace across the river in the Oltrarno, needed a way to get to and from his home and his office without mingling with the peons on the streets. So he had Giorgio Vasari build him the **Corridorio Vasariano (Vasarian Corridor)** in 1565. It took only 5 months to complete this aboveground tunnel running along the Arno, across the tops of the Ponte Vecchio shops, and then zigzagging its way to the Pitti. The corridor, hung with paintings and poked through with lots of windows, has finally reopened to visitors. (Following the 1993 bombing it was closed for restoration and rearrangement.) Tours of the corridor are available on Tuesday and Wednesday and Friday through Sunday. Call ℂ 055-265-4321 for required reservations.

Piazzale degli Uffizi 6 (off Piazza della Signoria). ℂ **055-238-8651,** or ℂ 055-294-883 to reserve tickets. www.uffizi.firenze.it (gallery info) or www.firenzemusei.it (to reserve tickets). Admission 8.50€ ($9.80). Tues–Sun 8:15am–7pm. Ticket window closes 45 min. before museum. Bus: A, B, 23, or 71.

Palazzo Vecchio ⭐   Florence's imposing fortresslike town hall was built from 1299 to 1302 on the designs of Arnolfo di Cambio, Gothic master builder of the city. Arnolfo managed to make it solid and impregnable-looking yet still graceful, with thin-columned Gothic windows and two orders of crenellations—square for the main rampart and swallow-tailed on the 94m- (313-ft.-) high bell tower.

The palace was once home to the various Florentine republican governments (and today to the municipal government). Cosimo I and his ducal Medici family moved to the palazzo in 1540 and engaged in massive redecoration. Michelozzo's 1453 **courtyard** just through the door was left architecturally intact but frescoed by Vasari with scenes of Austrian cities to celebrate the 1565 marriage of Francesco de' Medici and Joanna of Austria. The grand staircase leads up to the **Sala dei Cinquecento,** named for the 500-man assembly that met here in the pre-Medici days of the Florentine Republic and site of the greatest fresco cycle that ever wasn't. Leonardo da Vinci was commissioned in 1503 to paint one long wall with a battle scene celebrating a famous Florentine victory. He was always trying new methods and materials and decided to mix wax into his pigments. Leonardo had finished painting part of the wall, but it wasn't drying fast enough, so he brought in braziers stoked with hot coals to try to hurry the process. As others watched in horror, the wax in the fresco melted under the intense heat and the colors ran down the walls to puddle on the floor. Michelangelo never even got past making the preparatory drawings for the fresco he was supposed to paint on the opposite wall—Pope Julius II called him to Rome to paint the Sistine Chapel, and the master's sketches were destroyed by eager young artists who came to study them and took away scraps. Eventually, the bare walls were covered by Vasari and assistants from 1563 to 1565 with blatantly subservient frescoes exalting Cosimo I de' Medici and his dynasty.

Off the corner of the room (to the right as you enter) is the **Studiolo di Francesco I,** a claustrophobic study in which Cosimo's eldest son and heir performed his alchemy and science experiments and where baroque paintings hide secret cupboards. Against the wall of the Sala dei Cinquecento, opposite the door you enter, is Michelangelo's statue of *Victory* ⭐, carved from 1533 to 1534 for the Julius II tomb but later donated to the Medici. Its extreme torsion—the way the body twists and spirals upward—was to be a great influence on the mannerist movement.

The first series of rooms on the second floor is the **Quartiere degli Elementi,** again frescoed by Vasari. The **Terrazza di Saturno,** in the corner, has a view over the Uffizi to the hills across the Arno. Crossing the balcony overlooking the Sala dei Cinquecento, you enter the **Apartments of Eleonora di Toledo,** decorated for Cosimo's Spanish wife. Her small private chapel is a masterpiece of mid-16th-century painting by Bronzino. Farther on, under the sculpted ceiling of the **Sala dei Gigli,** are Domenico Ghirlandaio's fresco of *St. Zenobius Enthroned* with ancient Roman heroes and Donatello's original *Judith and Holofernes* ✦ bronze (1455), one of his last works.

During the summer evening hours, the following sections, normally closed, are open: the **Loeser Collections,** with paintings by Pietro Lorenzetti and Bronzino and sculptures by Tino di Camaino and Jacopo Sansovino, and, perhaps more fun, the outdoor **Balustrade** running around the roof behind the crenellations—it offers a unique panorama of the city and the piazza below.

Piazza della Signoria. ✆ 055-276-8465. Admission 6€ ($6.90). Fri–Wed 9am–7pm; Thurs 9am–2pm. Bus: A, B, 23, or 71.

Ponte Vecchio (Old Bridge) ✦✦✦

The oldest and most famous bridge across the Arno, the Ponte Vecchio we know today was built in 1345 by Taddeo Gaddi to replace an earlier version. The characteristic overhanging shops have lined the bridge since at least the 12th century. In the 16th century, it was home to butchers until Cosimo I moved into the Palazzo Pitti across the river. He couldn't stand the stench as he crossed the bridge from on high in the Corridorio Vasariano every day, so he evicted the meat cutters and moved in the classier gold- and silversmiths, tradesmen who occupy the bridge to this day.

A bust of the most famous Florentine goldsmith, the swashbuckling autobiographer and *Perseus* sculptor Benvenuto Cellini, stands off to the side of the bridge's center, in a small piazza overlooking the Arno. From this vantage point Mark Twain, spoiled by the Mighty Mississippi, once wryly commented, "It is popular to admire the Arno. It is a great historical creek, with four feet in the channel and some scows floating about. It would be a very plausible river if they would pump some water into it. They call it a river, and they honestly think it is a river . . . They even help out the delusion by building bridges over it. I do not see why they are too good to wade."

The Ponte Vecchio's fame saved it in 1944 from the Nazis, who had orders to blow up all the bridges before retreating out of Florence as Allied forces advanced. They couldn't bring themselves to reduce this span to rubble—so they blew up the ancient buildings on either end instead to block it off. The Arno flood of 1966 wasn't so discriminating, however, and severely damaged the shops. Apparently, a private night watchman saw the waters rising alarmingly and called many of the goldsmiths at home, who rushed to remove their valuable stock before it was washed away.

Via Por Santa Maria/Via Guicciardini. Bus: B or D.

Museo di Storia della Scienza (Science Museum) ✦

The mainframe computer and multifunction calculator don't hold a candle to this collection's beautifully engraved intricate mechanical instruments. Galileo and his ilk practiced a science that was an art form of the highest aesthetic order. The cases display such beauties as a mechanical calculator from 1664—a gleaming bronze sandwich of engraved disks and dials—and an architect's compass and plumb disguised as a dagger, complete with sheath.

In the field of astronomy, the museum has the lens with which Galileo discovered four of the moons of Jupiter (which he promptly and prudently named after his Medici patrons) and, alongside telescopes of all sizes and complexity, a tiny "lady's telescope" made of ivory that once came in a box of beauty products. There's also a somewhat grisly room devoted to medicine, with disturbingly realistic wax models of just about everything that can go wrong during childbirth. And what Italian institution would be complete without a holy relic? In this case, it's the middle finger of Galileo's right hand, swiped while he was en route to reinterment in Santa Croce. He was allowed burial in a Christian church only in the 18th century, after he was posthumously vindicated against the Inquisition for supporting a heliocentric view of the universe.

Piazza dei Giudici 1 (next to the Uffizi at the Arno end of Via dei Castellani). (C) 055-265-311. www. imss.fi.it. Admission 6.50€ ($7.50), 4.50€ ($5.20) ages 15–25, free for ages 6–14 and over 65. June–Sept Mon and Wed–Fri 9:30am–5pm, Tues and Sat 9:30am–1pm, last Thurs of June and Aug, and first Thurs of July and Sept 9–11pm; Oct–May Mon and Wed–Sat 9:30am–5pm, Tues 9:30am–1pm, and second Sun of every month 10am–1pm. Bus: 23.

Orsanmichele ⭐⭐   This tall structure halfway down Via dei Calzaiuoli looks more like a Gothic warehouse than a church—which is exactly what it was, built as a granary/grain market in 1337. After a miraculous image of the Madonna appeared on a column inside, however, the lower level was turned into a chapel. The city's merchant guilds each undertook the task of decorating one of the outside nichelike Gothic tabernacles around the lower level with a statue of their guild's patron saint. Masters such as Ghiberti, Donatello, Verrocchio, and Giambologna all cast or carved masterpieces to set here. Since 1984, these have been removed and are being replaced by casts as the originals are slowly cleaned and exhibited up on the second story.

Unfortunately, the church now keeps erratic hours due to a lack of personnel, so there are no set opening hours, however you may get lucky and find the doors thrown open when you pass by (or, though this may take even more luck, someone might actually answer the phone number below and give you details on when it will next open). Since it's pretty nifty, and there's a chance you'll be able to pop in, I'll go ahead and describe it all.

In the chapel's dark interior (emerged in 1999 from a long restoration and entered around the "back" side on Via dell'Arte della Lana) are recently restored 14th- to 16th-century paintings by the likes of Lorenzo di Credi and Il Poppi. The elaborate Gothic *Tabernacle* ⭐ (1349–59) by Andrea Orcagna looks something like a miniature church, covered with statuettes, enamels, inset colored marbles and glass, and reliefs. It protects a luminous 1348 *Madonna and Child* painted by Giotto's student Bernardo Daddi. The prominent statue of the *Madonna, Child, and St. Anne* to its left is by Francesco da Sangallo (1522).

Across Via dell'Arte della Lana from the Orsanmichele's main entrance is the 1308 Palazzo dell'Arte della Lana. This Gothic palace was home to medieval Florence's most powerful body, the guild of wool merchants, which employed about one third of Florence in the 13th and 14th centuries. Up the stairs inside you can cross over the hanging walkway to the first floor (American 2nd floor) of Orsanmichele. These are the old granary rooms, now housing a **museum of the statues** ⭐ that once surrounded the exterior. A few are still undergoing restoration, but eight of the original sculptures are here, well labeled, including Donatello's marble *St. Mark* (1411–13); Ghiberti's bronze *St. John the Baptist* (1413–16), the first life-size bronze of the Renaissance; and Verrocchio's *Incredulity of St. Thomas* (1473–83). This museum, too, does not always adhere to its posted hours, as those are dependent on someone being around to honor them. Still, it's at least worth a try.

Via Arte della Lana 1/Via de' Calzaiuoli. Ⓒ **055-284-944**. Free admission. Church open erratic hours (though never open during *riposo*). Museum daily 9–9:45am, 10–10:45am, 11–11:45am (plus Sat–Sun 1–1:45pm); closed the 1st and last Mon of month. Bus: A.

Museo Nazionale del Bargello (Bargello Museum) ☆☆ Inside this 1255 Gothic palazzo is Florence's premier sculpture museum, with works by Michelangelo, the della Robbias, and Donatello.

In the palazzo's old **armory** are 16th-century works, including some of Michelangelo's earliest sculptures. Carved by a 22-year-old Michelangelo while he was visiting Rome, *Bacchus* ☆☆ (1497) was obviously inspired by the classical antiquities he studied there but is also imbued with his own irrepressible Renaissance realism—here is a (young) God of Wine who's actually drunk, reeling back on unsteady knees and holding the cup aloft with a distinctly tipsy wobble. Michelangelo polished and finished this marble in the traditional manner, but from 1503 to 1505, soon after finishing his famous *David* with a high polish, he carved the *Pitti Tondo* ☆ here, a *schiacciato* Madonna and Child scene in which the artist began using the textures of the partially worked marble itself to convey his artistic message. One of his weaker works here is the so-called *Apollo-David* (art historians can't agree on which hero the unfinished work was meant to be), but the master is back in top form with the bust of *Brutus* (ca. 1539). Some people like to see in this sculpture an idealized portrait of Michelangelo himself; a more accurate and less contentious representation sits nearby, the famous and oft-cast bronze bust of *Michelangelo* by his pupil Daniele da Volterra. Also in this room is Giambologna's *Flying Mercury* ☆ (ca. 1564), looking for all the world as if he's on the verge of taking off from the ground—justifiably one of this mannerist's masterpieces.

The palazzo's inner **courtyard**—one of the few medieval cortile in Florence to survive in more-or-less its original shape—is studded with the coats of arms of various past *podestà* and other notables. The grand stairwell leads up to a second-story loggia filled with a flock of whimsical bronze birds cast by Giambologna for the Medici's gardens. The doorway leads into the old **Salone del Consiglio Generale (General Council Room)** ☆☆, a vast space with a high ceiling filled with glazed terra-cotta Madonnas by Luca della Robbia and his clan, and some of the most important sculptures of the early Renaissance.

Donatello dominates the room, starting with a mischievously smiling *Cupid* (ca. 1430–40). Nearby is his polychrome bust of *Niccolò da Uzzano,* a bit of hyperrealism next to two much more delicate busts of elfin-featured characters by Desiderio da Settignano. Donatello sculpted the *Marzocco,* lion symbol of the Florentine Republic, out of pietra serena between 1418 and 1420. The marble *David* (1408) is an early Donatello, but the bronze *David* ☆☆ (1440–50) beyond it is a much more mature piece, the first freestanding nude since antiquity. The figure is a nubile, almost erotic youth, with a shy, detached air that has little to do with the giant severed head at his feet. Against the far wall is *St. George* ☆, carved in 1416 for a niche of Orsanmichele. The relief below it of the saint slaying his dragon is an early example of the sculptor's patented *schiacciato* technique, using thinly etched lines and perspective to create great depth in a very shallow space.

In the back right corner of this room are two bronze relief panels by Brunelleschi and Ghiberti of the *Sacrifice of Isaac,* finalists in the famous 1401 competition for the commission to cast the Baptistery's doors (see "A Man & His Dome," on p. 140). Ghiberti's panel won for the greater dynamism and flowing action in his version.

Out the other end of the room is the **Islamic Collection,** a testament to Florence's wide and profitable trade network. Decorative arts from the Roman era through the 16th century fill the long corridor, at the end of which is the small **Cappella Maddalena,** where condemned prisoners spent their last moments praying for their souls; it was frescoed by Giotto's studio. A perpendicular corridor houses the largest collection of ivories in the world, from the 5th to 17th centuries.

Upstairs are rooms with glazed terra cottas by Andrea and Giovanni della Robbia and another room devoted to the sculptural production of Leonardo da Vinci's teacher Verrocchio, including yet another *David* (1465), a haughty youth with a tousle of hair inspired by the Donatello version downstairs.

Via del Proconsolo 4. ✆ **055-238-8606.** www.sbas.firenze.it. (Reserve tickets at ✆ 055-294-883 or www.firenzemusei.it.) Admission 4€ ($4.60). Daily 8:30am–1:50pm. Closed 2nd and 4th Mon and 1st, 3rd, and 5th Sun of each month. Bus: A, 14, or 23.

Badia Fiorentina   The slender pointed bell tower of this Benedictine abbey founded in A.D. 978 is one of the landmarks of the Florentine skyline. Sadly, the bells Dante wrote of in his *Paradiso* no longer toll the hours. Serious structural problems have silenced the tower. In the now-baroque interior, some say Dante first laid eyes on his beloved Beatrice, and Boccaccio, of *Decameron* fame, used to lecture on Dante's Divine Comedy here. The church's most arresting sight is a 1485 Filippino Lippi painting of the *Madonna Appearing to St. Bernard.* The box to shed light on it parcels out a measly 10 seconds for each coin, so feed it only the smallest pieces. For a nominal "donation," the sacristan will throw on the lights to the *trompe l'oeil* ceiling.

Via Dante Alighieri and Via del Proconsolo. ✆ **055-287-389.** Free admission. Thurs–Tues 5–7pm (sometimes also in the morning). Bus: A, 14, or 23.

Santa Trínita ✦   Beyond Bernardo Buontalenti's late-16th-century **facade** lies a dark church, rebuilt in the 14th century but founded by the Vallombrosans before 1177. The third chapel on the right has what remains of the detached frescoes by Spinello Aretino (viewable by push-button light), which were found under Lorenzo Monaco's excellent 1422 frescoes covering the next chapel down.

In the right transept, Domenico Ghirlandaio frescoed the **Cappella Sassetti** ✦ in 1483 with a cycle on the *Life of St. Francis* (coin-op lights), but true to form he set all the scenes against Florentine backdrops and peopled them with portraits of the notables of the day. The most famous is *Francis Receiving the Order from Pope Honorius,* which in this version takes place under an arcade on the north side of Piazza della Signoria—the Loggia dei Lanzi is featured in the middle, and on the left is the Palazzo Vecchio. (The Uffizi between them hadn't been built yet.) It's also full of contemporary portraits: In the little group on the far right, the unhandsome man with the light red cloak is Lorenzo the Magnificent.

The chapel to the right of the main altar houses the miraculous *Crucifix* that once hung in San Miniato al Monte. One day the nobleman Giovanni Gualberto was storming up the hillside in a rage, on his way to wreak revenge on his brother's murderer. Gualberto paused at San Miniato and after some reflection decided to pardon the assassin, whereupon this crucifix bowed its head in approval. Gualberto went on to found the Vallombrosan order of monks, who later established this church.

The south end of the piazza leads to the **Ponte Santa Trínita,** one of Italy's most graceful bridges. In 1567, Ammannati built a span here that was set with four 16th-century statues of the seasons in honor of the marriage of Cosimo II.

After the Nazis blew up the bridge in 1944, it was rebuilt, and all was set into place again—save the head on the statue of Spring, which remained lost until a team dredging the river in 1961 found it by accident. From the bridge you get a great view upriver of the Ponte Vecchio and downriver of the **Ponte alla Carraia** (another postwar reconstruction), where in 1304 so many people gathered to watch a floating production of Dante's *Inferno* that it collapsed and all were drowned. Florentine wits were quick to point out that all the people who went to see Hell that day found what they were looking for.

Piazza Santa Trínita. Ⓒ **055-216-912**. Free admission. Mon–Sat 8am–noon and 4–6pm; Sun 4–6pm. Bus: A, B, 6, 11, 36, 37, or 68.

AROUND SAN LORENZO & THE MERCATO CENTRALE

The church of San Lorenzo is practically lost behind the leather stalls and souvenir carts of Florence's vast **San Lorenzo street market** (see "Shopping," later in this chapter). In fact, the hawking of wares and bustle of commerce is what characterizes all the streets of this neighborhood, centered around both the church and the nearby **Mercato Centrale food market.** This is a colorful scene, but one of the most pickpocket-happy in the city, so be wary.

San Lorenzo ⊕   A rough brick anti-facade and the undistinguished stony bulk of a building surrounded by the stalls of the leather market hide what is most likely the oldest church in Florence, founded in A.D. 393. San Lorenzo was the city's cathedral until the bishop's seat moved to Santa Reparata (later to become the Duomo) in the 7th century. More important, it was the Medici family's parish church, and as those famous bankers began to accumulate their vast fortune, they started a tradition of lavishing it on this church that lasted until the clan died out in the 18th century. Visiting the entire church complex at once is tricky: Though interconnected, the church proper, the Old Sacristy, and the Laurentian Library have different open hours. The Medici tombs, listed separately below, have a separate entrance around the back of the church and have still different hours.

The first thing Giovanni di Bicci de' Medici, founder of the family fortune, did for the church was hire Brunelleschi to tune up the **interior,** rebuilding according to the architect's plans in 1426. At the end of the aisle is a Desiderio da Settignano marble tabernacle that's a mastery of *schiacciato* relief and carefully incised perspective. Across the aisle is one of the two bronze 1460 **pulpits** ⊕⊕—the other is across the nave—that were Donatello's last works. His patron and the first great consolidator of Medici power, which at this early stage still showed great concern for protecting the interests of the people, was Cosimo il Vecchio, Lorenzo the Magnificent's grandfather. Cosimo, whose wise behind-the-scenes rule made him popular with the Florentines, died in 1464 and is buried in front of the high altar. The plaque marking the spot is simply inscribed PATER PATRIAE—father of his homeland.

Off the left transept is the **Sagrestia Vecchia (Old Sacristy)** ⊕, one of Brunelleschi's purest pieces of early Renaissance architecture. In the center of the chapel Cosimo il Vecchio's parents, Giovanni di Bicci de' Medici and his wife, Piccarda Bueri, rest in peace.

On the wall of the left aisle is Bronzino's huge fresco of the *Martyrdom of San Lorenzo* ⊕. The 3rd-century namesake saint of this church, San Lorenzo was a flinty early Christian and the treasurer of the Roman church. When commanded by the Romans to hand over the church's wealth, Lorenzo appeared before Emperor Valerian's prefect with "thousands" of sick, poor, and crippled people saying "Here is all the church's treasure." The Romans weren't amused and decided to martyr him on a gridiron over hot coals. Feisty to the last, at one point while Lorenzo lay there roasting he called out to his tormentors through gritted teeth, "Turn me over, I'm done on this side."

Near this fresco is an entrance to the cloister and just inside it a stairwell to the right leading up to the **Biblioteca Laurenziana (Laurentian Library)** 🌟🌟, which can also be entered admission free without going through—and paying for—the church (the separate entrance is just to the left of the church's main doors). Michelangelo designed this library in 1524 to house the Medici's manuscript collection, and it stands as one of the most brilliant works of mannerist architecture. The vestibule is a whacked-out riff on the Renaissance, all *pietra serena* and white plaster walls like a good Brunelleschi piece, but turned inside out. There are phony piers running into each other in the corners, pilaster strips that support nothing, and brackets that exist for no reason. On the whole, however, it manages to remain remarkably coherent. Its star feature is a *pietra serena* flight of curving stairs flowing out from the entrance to the reading room. This actual library part, however—filled with intricately carved wood and handsomely illuminated manuscripts—was closed indefinitely in 1999 until "urgent maintenance" is completed.

Piazza San Lorenzo. ⓒ **055-216-634.** Admission 2.50€ ($2.90). Church Mon–Sat 10am–5pm. Old Sacristy (usually) Sept–July Mon, Wed, Fri, and Sat 10–11:45am; Tues and Thurs 4–5:45pm. Laurentian Library Mon–Sat 9am–1pm. Bus: 1, 6, 7, 11, 14, 17, 23, 67, 68, 70, or 71.

Cappelle Medicee (Medici Chapels) 🌟🌟   When Michelangelo built the New Sacristy between 1520 and 1533 (finished by Vasari in 1556), it was to be a tasteful monument to Lorenzo the Magnificent and his generation of fairly pleasant Medici. When work got underway on the Chapel of the Princes in 1604, it was to become one of the world's most god-awful and arrogant memorials, dedicated to the grand dukes, some of Florence's most decrepit tyrants. The **Cappella dei Principi (Chapel of the Princes)** 🌟 is an exercise in bad taste, a mountain of cut marbles and semiprecious stones—jasper, alabaster, mother-of-pearl, agate, and the like—slathered onto the walls and ceiling with no regard for composition and still less for chromatic unity. The pouring of ducal funds into this monstrosity began in 1604 and lasted until the rarely conscious Gian Gastone de' Medici drank himself to death in 1737 without an heir—but teams kept doggedly at the thing, and they were still finishing the floor in 1962. The tombs of the grand dukes in this massive marble mistake were designed by Pietro Tacca in the 17th century, and off to the left and right of the altar are small treasuries full of gruesome holy relics in silver-bedecked cases. The dome of the structure, seen from the outside, is one of Florence's landmarks, a kind of infant version of the Duomo's.

Michelangelo's **Sagrestia Nuova (New Sacristy)** 🌟🌟, built to jibe with Brunelleschi's Old Sacristy in San Lorenzo proper, is much calmer. (An architectural tidbit: The windows in the dome taper as they get near the top to fool you into thinking the dome is higher.) Michelangelo was supposed to produce three tombs here (perhaps four) but ironically got only the two less important ones done. So Lorenzo de' Medici the Magnificent—wise ruler of his city, poet of note, grand patron of the arts, and moneybags behind much of the Renaissance—ended up with a mere inscription of his name next to his brother Giuliano's on a plain marble slab against the entrance wall. Admittedly, they did get one genuine Michelangelo sculpture to decorate their slab, a *Madonna and Child* that's perhaps the master's most beautiful version of the theme (the other two statues are later works by less talented sculptors).

The Master's Doodles

On the walls around the small altar in the Medici Chapels are some recently uncovered architectural graffiti that have been attributed to Michelangelo. Even more important are some 50 charcoal drawings and sketches the master left on the walls in the sepulchral chamber below. The drawings include a sketch of the legs of Duke Giuliano, Christ risen, and the Laocoön. Michelangelo found himself hiding out here after the Medici reconquered the city in 1530—he had helped the city keep the dukes out with his San Miniato defenses and, probably rightly, feared a reprisal. You need an appointment to see the sketches; ask at the ticket office.

On the left wall of the sacristy is Michelangelo's *Tomb of Lorenzo* ⚜, duke of Urbino (and Lorenzo the Magnificent's grandson), whose seated statue symbolizes the contemplative life. Below him on the elongated curves of the tomb stretch *Dawn* (female) and *Dusk* (male), a pair of Michelangelo's most famous sculptures, where he uses both high polish and rough cutting to impart strength, texture, and psychological suggestion to the allegorical works. This pair mirrors the similarly fashioned and equally important *Day* (male) and *Night* (female) across the way. One additional point *Dawn* and *Night* brings out is that Michelangelo really wasn't too adept at the female body—he just produced softer, less muscular men with slightly elongated midriffs and breasts sort of tacked on at funny angles.

Piazza Madonna degli Aldobrandini (behind San Lorenzo, where Via Faenza and Via del Giglio meet). ℰ 055-238-8602. Admission 6€ ($6.90); call Firenze Musei ℰ 055-294-883 for reservations. Daily 8:15am–5pm. Closed 1st, 3rd, and 5th Mon and 2nd and 4th Sun of each month. Bus: 1, 6, 7, 11, 14, 17, 23, 67, 68, 70, or 71.

Palazzo Medici-Riccardi ⚜ The Palazzo Medici-Riccardi was built by Michelozzo in 1444 for Cosimo de' Medici il Vecchio; it's the prototype Florentine palazzo, on which the more overbearing Strozzi and Pitti palaces were later modeled. It remained the Medici private home until Cosimo I more officially declared his power as duke by moving to the city's traditional civic brain center, the Palazzo Vecchio. A door off the right of the entrance courtyard leads up a staircase to the **Cappella dei Magi,** the oldest chapel to survive from a private Florentine palace; its walls are covered with gorgeously dense and colorful Benozzo Gozzoli **frescoes** (1459–63). Rich as tapestries, the walls depict an extended *Journey of the Magi* to see the Christ child, who's being adored by Mary in the altarpiece. Gozzoli is at his decorative best here, inheriting an attention to minute detail in plants and animals from his old teacher Fra' Angelico.

Via Cavour 3. ℰ 055-276-0340. Admission 4€ ($4.60). Thurs–Tues 9am–7pm. Number of visitors limited; arrive early or call to book a time to visit. Bus: 1, 6, 7, 11, 14, 17, 23, 67, 68, 70, or 71.

ON OR NEAR PIAZZA SANTA MARIA NOVELLA

Piazza Santa Maria Novella boasts patches of grass and a central fountain. The two squat obelisks, resting on the backs of Giambologna tortoises, once served as the turning posts for the "chariot" races held here from the 16th to the mid–19th century. However, these days the piazza sees more action as a roving ground for the few Gypsies picking tourists' pockets in Florence and the hangout for the city's economically depressed small immigrant population and even smaller cache of itinerants. Several bars and pubs have tried to infuse the area with some life, but the night still leans toward the seedy around here.

Santa Maria Novella ⭐⭐ Of all Florence's major churches, the home of the Dominicans is the only one with an original **facade** ⭐ that matches its era of greatest importance. The lower Romanesque half was started in the 14th century by architect Fra' Jacopo Talenti, who had just finished building the church itself (started in 1246). Leon Battista Alberti finished the facade, adding a classically inspired Renaissance top that not only went seamlessly with the lower half but also created a Cartesian plane of perfect geometry.

The church's interior underwent a massive restoration in the late 1990s, returning Gioto's restored *Crucifix* to pride of place, hanging in the nave's center—and becoming the first church in Florence to charge admission. Against the second pillar on the left of the nave is the pulpit from which Galileo was denounced for his heretical theory that Earth revolved around the Sun. Just past the pulpit, on the left wall, is **Masaccio's *Trinità*** ⭐⭐⭐ (ca. 1428), the first painting in the world to use perfect linear mathematical perspective. Florentine citizens and artists flooded in to see the fresco when it was unveiled, many remarking in awe that the coffered ceiling seemed to punch a hole back into space, creating a chapel out of a flat wall. The **transept** is filled with spectacularly frescoed chapels. The **sanctuary** ⭐ behind the main altar was frescoed after 1485 by Domenico Ghirlandaio with the help of his assistants and apprentices, probably including a very young Michelangelo. The left wall is covered with a cycle on *The Life of the Virgin* and the right wall with the *Life of St. John the Baptist.* The works have a highly polished decorative quality and are less biblical stories than snapshots of the era's fashions and personages, full of portraits of the Tornabuoni family who commissioned them.

The **Cappella Gondi** to the left of the high altar contains the *Crucifix* carved by Brunelleschi to show his buddy Donatello how it should be done (see the Santa Croce review on p. 167 for the story). At the end of the left transept is a different **Cappella Strozzi,** covered with restored **frescoes** ⭐ (1357) by Nardo di Cione, early medieval casts of thousands where the Saved mill about Paradise on the left and the Damned stew in a Dantean inferno on the right.

Piazza Santa Maria Novella. ✆ **055-215-918.** 2.50€ ($2.90) adults, 1.50€ ($1.75) ages 12–18. Mon–Thurs and Sat 9:30am–5pm; Fri and Sun 1–5pm. Bus: A, 6, 11, 12, 36, 37, or 68.

Museo di Santa Maria Novella ⭐ The cloisters of Santa Maria Novella's convent are open to the public as a museum. The **Chiostro Verde,** with a cypress-surrounded fountain and chirping birds, is named for the greenish tint in the pigment used by Paolo Uccello in his **frescoes** ⭐⭐. His works line the right wall of the first walkway; the most famous is the confusing, somewhat disturbing first scene you come to, where the *Flood and Recession of the Flood and the Drunkenness and Sacrifice of Noah* (1446) are all squeezed onto one panel as the story lines are piled atop one another and Noah appears several times. The two giant wooden walls on either side are meant to be the Ark, shown both before and after the Flood, seen in extreme, distorting perspective.

The **Cappella degli Spagnoli (Spanish Chapel)** ⭐ got its name when it became the private chapel of Eleonora of Toledo, recently arrived in Florence to be Cosimo de' Medici's bride. The pretty chapel was entirely frescoed by Andrea da Firenze and his assistants in a kind of half Florentine–half Sienese style around 1365.

Piazza Santa Maria Novella (entrance to the left of the church facade). ✆ **055-282-187.** Admission 1.40€ ($1.60). Sat and Mon–Thurs 9am–2pm; Sun 8am–1pm. Bus: A, 6, 11, 12, 36, 37, or 68.

Ognissanti ⭐ Founded in 1256 by the Umiliati, a wool-weaving sect of the Benedictines whose trade helped establish this area as a textile district, the present

Ognissanti was rebuilt by its new Franciscan owners in the 17th century. It has the earliest baroque **facade** in Florence, designed by Matteo Nigetti in 1627 and rebuilt in travertine in 1872.

Ognissanti was the parish church of the Vespucci family, agents of the Medici bank in Seville. A young Domenico Ghirlandaio portrayed several of the family members in his *Madonna della Misericordia* (1470) on the second altar to the right. The lady under the Madonna's left hand may be Simonetta Vespucci, renowned beauty of her age, mistress of Giuliano de' Medici (Lorenzo's brother), and the possible model for Venus in Botticelli's *Birth of Venus*. The young man with black hair to the Madonna's right is said to be Amerigo Vespucci (1454–1512), whose letters about exploring the New World in 1499 and again from 1501 to 1502 would become so popular that a cartographer used a corruption of Amerigo's name on an influential set of maps to describe the newly discovered continent. Sorry, Columbus. The family tombstone (America's namesake rests in peace underneath) is to the left of this altar.

Between the third and fourth altars is Botticelli's fresco of a pensive *St. Augustine in His Study* (1480), a much more intense work than its matching *St. Jerome in His Study* by Ghirlandaio across the nave. Botticelli, whose real name was Sandro Filipepi, is buried under a round marker in the second chapel in the right transept. In the left transept's second chapel is the habit St. Francis was wearing when he received the stigmata. You can enter the convent to the left of the church facade at Borgo Ognissanti 42. In the refectory here is Domenico Ghirlandaio's **Last Supper** ⊛, painted in 1480 with a background heavy on Christian symbols.

Piazza Ognissanti. ⓒ **055-239-8700.** Free admission. Church daily 8am–noon and 4–6:30pm. Convent Mon, Tues, and Sat 9am–noon. Bus: B, D, or 12.

NEAR SAN MARCO & SANTISSIMA ANNUNZIATA

Galleria dell'Accademia (Academy Gallery) ⊛⊛   Though tour-bus crowds flock here just for Michelangelo's *David*, anyone with more than a day in Florence can take the time to peruse some of the Accademia's paintings as well.

The first long hall is devoted to Michelangelo and, though you pass his *Slaves* and the entrance to the painting gallery, most visitors are immediately drawn down to the far end, a tribune dominated by the most famous sculpture in the world: **Michelangelo's *David*** ⊛⊛⊛. A hot young sculptor fresh from his success with the *Pietà* in Rome, Michelangelo offered in 1501 to take on a slab of marble that had already been worked on by another sculptor (who had taken a chunk out of one side before declaring it too strangely shaped to use). The huge slab had been lying around the Duomo's workyards so long it earned a nickname, *Il Gigante* (the Giant), so it was with a twist of humor that Michelangelo, only 29 years old, finished in 1504 a Goliath-size David for the city.

There was originally a vague idea that the statue would become part of the Duomo, but Florence's republican government soon wheeled it down to stand on Piazza della Signoria in front of the Palazzo Vecchio to symbolize the defeated tyranny of the Medici, who had been ousted a decade before (but would return

---

⌐Tips Seeing *David*

The wait to get in to see *David* can be up to an hour if you didn't reserve ahead. Try getting there before the museum opens in the morning or an hour or two before closing time.

with a vengeance). During a 1527 anti-Medicean siege on the palazzo, a bench thrown at the attackers from one of the windows hit David's left arm, which reportedly came crashing down on a farmer's toe. (A young Giorgio Vasari came scurrying out to gather all the pieces for safekeeping, despite the riot going on around him, and the arm was later reconstituted.) Even the sculpture's 1873 removal to the Accademia to save it from the elements (a copy stands in its place) hasn't kept it entirely safe—in 1991, a man threw himself on the statue and began hammering at the right foot, dislodging several toes. The foot was repaired, and *David's* Plexiglas shield went up.

The hall leading up to *David* is lined with perhaps Michelangelo's most fascinating works, the four famous *nonfiniti* ("unfinished") **Slaves,** or **Prisoners** ★★★. Like no others, these statues symbolize Michelangelo's theory that sculpture is an "art that takes away superfluous material." The great master saw a true sculpture as something that was already inherent in the stone, and all it needed was a skilled chisel to free it from the extraneous rock. That certainly seems to be the case here, as we get a private glimpse into Michelangelo's working technique: how he began by carving the abdomen and torso, going for the gut of the sculpture and bringing that to life first so it could tell him how the rest should start to take form. Whether he intended the statues to look the way they do now or in fact left them only half done has been debated by art historians to exhaustion. The result, no matter what the sculptor's intentions, is remarkable, a symbol of the master's great art and personal views on craft as his Slaves struggle to break free of their chipped stone prisons.

Nearby, in a similar mode, is a statue of **St. Matthew** ★★ (1504–08), which Michelangelo began carving as part of a series of Apostles he was at one point going to complete for the Duomo. (The *Pietà* at the end of the corridor on the right is by one of Michelangelo's students, not by the master as was once thought.)

Off this hall of *Slaves* is the first wing of the painting gallery, which includes a panel, possibly from a wedding chest, known as the **Cassone Adimari** ★, painted by Lo Scheggia in the 1440s. It shows the happy couple's promenade to the Duomo, with the green-and-white marbles of the Baptistery prominent in the background.

In the wings off *David's* tribune are large paintings by Michelangelo's contemporaries, mannerists over whom he had a very strong influence—they even say Michelangelo provided the original drawing from which Pontormo painted his amorous *Venus and Cupid.* Off the end of the left wing is a long 19th-century hall crowded wall to wall and stacked floor to ceiling with **plaster casts** of hundreds of sculptures and busts—the Accademia, after all, is what it sounds like: an academy for budding young artists, founded in 1784 as an offshoot of the Academy of Art Design that dates from Michelangelo's time (1565).

Via Ricasoli 58–60. ✆ **055-238-8609** or 055-238-8612. www.sbas.firenze.it/accademia. (Reserve tickets at ✆ **055-294-883** or www.firenzemusei.it.) Admission 6.50€ ($7.50) adults, 3.25€ ($3.75) children. Tues–Sun 8:15am–6:50pm; last admission 30 min. before close. Bus: 1, 6, 7, 10, 11, 17, 25, 31, 32, 33, 67, 68, or 70.

San Marco ★★   In 1437, Cosimo de' Medici il Vecchio, grandfather of Lorenzo the Magnificent, had Michelozzo convert a medieval monastery here into a new home for the Dominicans, in which Cosimo also founded Europe's first public library. From 1491 until he was burned at the stake on Piazza della Signoria in 1498, this was the home base of puritanical preacher Girolamo Savonarola. The monastery's most famous friar, though, was early Renaissance

Michelangelo: The Making of a Renaissance Master

Irascible, moody, and manic-depressive, Michelangelo was quite simply one of the greatest artists of all time. Many feel he represents the pinnacle of the Italian Renaissance, a genius at sculpture, painting, and architecture, and even a master poet.

In 1475, Michelangelo Buonarotti was born near Arezzo in the tiny town of Caprese, where his Florentine father was serving a term as a *podestà* (visiting mayor). He grew up on the family farm at Settignano, outside Florence, and was wet-nursed by the wife of a local stonecutter—he used to joke that he sucked his skill with the hammer and chisel along with the mother's milk. He was apprenticed early to the fresco studio of Domenico Ghirlandaio who, while watching the young apprentice sketching, once remarked in shock, "This boy knows more about it than I do." After just a year at the studio, Michelangelo was recruited by Lorenzo the Magnificent de' Medici to become part of his new school for sculptors.

Michelangelo learned quickly, and soon after his arrival at the school took a chunk of marble and carved it to copy the head of an old faun from an ancient statue in the garden. Lorenzo happened by and saw the skill with which the head was made, but when he saw Michelangelo had departed from his model and carved the mouth open and laughing with teeth and a tongue, he commented only "But you should have known that old people never have all their teeth and there are always some missing." The young artist reflected on this. When Lorenzo returned a while later, he found Michelangelo waiting anxiously, eager to show he had not only chipped out a few teeth but also gouged down into the gums of the statue to make the tooth loss look more realistic. Impressed, Lorenzo decided to take the boy under his wing and virtually adopted him into the Medici household.

After his success at age 19 with the *Pietà* sculpture in Rome, Michelangelo was given the opportunity by the city council to carve the enormous block of marble that became *David*. He worked on it behind shuttered scaffolding so few saw it until the unveiling. Legend has it that when Soderini, the head of the city council, came to see the finished work, he remarked the nose looked a tad too large. Michelangelo, knowing better but wanting to please Soderini, climbed up to the head (out of view), grabbed a handful of leftover plaster dust, and while tapping his hammer lightly against his chisel, let the dust sprinkle down gradually as if he were actually carving. "Much better," remarked Soderini when Michelangelo climbed down again and they stepped back to admire it. "Now you've really brought it to life."

painter Fra' Angelico, and he left many of his finest works, devotional images painted with the technical skill and minute detail of a miniaturist or an illuminator but on altarpiece scale. While his works tended to be transcendently spiritual, Angelico was also prone to filling them with earthy details with which any peasant or stonemason could identify.

The museum rooms are entered off a pretty cloister. The old Pilgrim's Hospice has been converted into a **Fra' (Beato) Angelico Gallery** ✹✹, full of altarpieces and painted panels. Also off the cloister is the **Reffetorio Grande (Great Refectory),** with 16th- and 17th-century paintings, and the **Sala del Capitolo (Chapter House),** frescoed from 1441 to 1442 with a huge *Crucifixion* by Fra' Angelico and his assistants. The door next to this leads past the staircase up to the Dormitory (see below) to the **Sala del Cenacolo (Small Refectory),** with a long fresco of the *Last Supper* by Domenico Ghirlandaio.

The **Dormitorio (Dormitory)** ✹✹ of cells where the monks lived is one of Fra' Angelico's masterpieces and perhaps his most famous cycle of frescoes. In addition to the renowned *Annunciation* ✹✹ at the top of the stairs to the monks' rooms, Angelico painted the cells themselves with simple works to aid his fellow friars in their meditations. One of these almost anticipates surrealism—a Flagellation where disembodied hands strike at Christ's face and a rod descends on him from the blue-green background. Angelico's assistants carried out the repetitious Crucifixion scenes in many of the cells. At the end of one of the corridors is the suite of cells occupied by Savonarola when he was here prior. In the first are two famous portraits of him by his devout follower and talented painter Fra' Bartolomeo, along with an anonymous 16th-century painting of *Savonarola Burned at the Stake* on Piazza della Signoria. The **Biblioteca (Library)** off the corridor to the right of the stairs was designed by Michelozzo in 1441 and contains beautifully illuminated choir books.

Piazza San Marco 3. ⓒ **055-238-8608.** Admission 4€ ($4.60) adults, 2€ ($2.30) children. Mon–Fri 8:30am–1:50pm; Sat–Sun 8:15am–7pm. Closed 1st, 3rd, and 5th Sun and 2nd and 4th Mon of each month. Bus: 1, 6, 7, 10, 11, 17, 20, 25, 31, 32, 33, 67, 68, or 70.

Cenacolo di Sant'Apollonia ✹

There are no lines at this former convent and no crowds. Few people even know to ring the bell at the nondescript door. What they're missing is an entire wall covered with the vibrant colors of Andrea del Castagno's masterful *Last Supper* (ca. 1450). Castagno used his paint to create the rich marble panels that checkerboard the *trompe l'oeil* walls and broke up the long white tablecloth with the dark figure of Judas the Betrayer, whose face is painted to resemble a satyr, an ancient symbol of evil.

Via XXVII Aprile 1. ⓒ **055-238-8607.** Free admission. Daily 8:30am–1:50pm. Closed 1st, 3rd, and 5th Sun and 2nd and 4th Mon of each month. Bus: 1, 6, 7, 10, 11.

Santissima Annunziata

In 1230, seven Florentine nobles had a spiritual crisis, gave away all their possessions, and retired to the forests to contemplate divinity. They returned to what were then the fields outside the city walls and founded a small oratory, proclaiming they were Servants of Mary, or the Servite Order. The oratory was enlarged by Michelozzo (1444–81) and later baroqued. Under the facade's **portico,** you enter the **Chiostro dei Voti (Votice Cloister),** designed by Michelozzo with Corinthian-capitaled columns and decorated with some of the city's finest mannerist frescoes (1465–1515). Rosso Fiorentino provided an *Assumption* (1513) and Pontormo a *Visitation* (1515) just to the right of the door, but the main works are by their master, Andrea del Sarto, whose *Birth of the Virgin* ✹ (1513) in the far right corner is one of his finest works. To the right of the door into the church is a damaged but still fascinating *Coming of the Magi* (1514) by del Sarto, who included a self-portrait at the far right, looking out at us from under his blue hat.

The **interior** is excessively baroque. Just to the left as you enter is a huge tabernacle hidden under a mountain of flowers and *ex votos* (votive offerings). It was designed by Michelozzo to house a small painting of the *Annunciation.* Legend holds that this painting was started by a friar who, vexed that he couldn't paint the Madonna's face as beautifully as it should be, gave it up and took a nap. When he awoke, he found an angel had filled in the face for him. Newlywed brides in Florence don't toss their bouquets—they head here after the ceremony to leave their flowers at the shrine for good luck.

The large circular **tribune** was finished for Michelozzo by Leon Battista Alberti. You enter it from its left side via the left transept, but first pause to pay your respects to Andrea del Sarto, buried under a floor slab at the left-hand base of the great arch.

From the left transept, a door leads into the **Chiostro dei Morti (Cloister of the Dead;** track down a sacristan to open it), where over the entrance door is another of Andrea del Sarto's greatest frescoes, the *Madonna del Sacco* ✸, and, a *Rest on the Flight into Egypt* scene that got its name from the sack Joseph is leaning against to do a little light reading. Also off this cloister is the **Cappella di San Luca (Chapel of St. Luke),** evangelist and patron saint of painters. It was decorated by late Renaissance and mannerist painters, including Pontormo, Alessandro Allori, Santi di Tito, and Giorgio Vasari. On the **piazza** ✸✸ outside, flanked by elegant porticos (see Spedale degli Innocenti, below), is an equestrian statue of *Grand Duke Ferdinando I,* Giambologna's last work; it was cast in 1608 after his death by his student Pietro Tacca, who also did the two little fountains of fantastic mermonkey-monsters. The piazza's beauty is somewhat ruined by the car and bus traffic routed through both ends, but it's kept lively by students from the nearby university, who sit on the loggia steps for lunch and hang out here in the evenings.

Piazza Santissima Annunziata. ✆ **055-266-181.** Free admission. Daily 7:30am–12:30pm and 4–6:30pm. Bus: 6, 31, or 32.

Spedale degli Innocenti Europe's oldest foundling hospital, opened in 1445, is still going strong as a convent orphanage, though times have changed a bit. The lazy Susan set into the wall on the left end of the arcade—where once people left unwanted babies, swiveled it around, rang the bell, and ran—has since been blocked up. The colonnaded **portico** ✸ (built 1419–26) was designed by Filippo Brunelleschi when he was still an active goldsmith. It was his first great achievement as an architect and helped define the new Renaissance style he was developing. Its repetition by later artists in front of other buildings on the piazza makes it one of the most exquisite squares in all Italy. The spandrels between the arches of Brunelleschi's portico are set with glazed **terra-cotta reliefs** of swaddled babes against rounded blue backgrounds—hands-down the masterpieces of Andrea della Robbia.

Piazza Santissima Annunziata 12. ✆ **055-249-1708.** www.istitutodeglinnocenti.it. Admission 2.60€ ($3). Thurs–Tues 8:30am–2pm. Bus: 6, 31, or 32.

Museo Opificio delle Pietre Dure In the 16th century, Florentine craftsmen perfected the art of *pietre dure,* piecing together cut pieces of precious and semi-precious stones in an inlay process, and the Medici-founded institute devoted to the craft has been in this building since 1796.

Long ago misnamed a "Florentine mosaic" by the tourism industry, this is a highly refined craft in which skilled artisans (artists, really) create scenes and boldly colored intricate designs in everything from cameos and tabletops to never-fade stone "paintings." Masters are adept at selecting, slicing, and polishing stones so that the natural grain or color gradations in the cross sections will, once cut and laid in the design, become the contours, shading, and molding that give good *pietre dure* scenes their depth and illusion of three-dimensionality.

The collection in this museum is small, but the pieces are uniformly excellent. Souvenir shops all over town sell modern *pietre dure* items—much of it mass-produced junk, but some very nice. The best contemporary maestro is Ilio de Filippis, whose workshop is called Pitti Mosaici (see "Shopping," later in this chapter).

Via degli Alfani 78. ✆ **055-265-1357** or 055-294-883 for ticket reservations (not necessary). www.opificio. arti.beniculturali.it. Admission 2€ ($2.30), free for children under 6. Mon–Sat 8:15am–2pm (Thurs until 7pm). Bus: 6, 11, 17, 31, or 32.

Museo Archeologico (Archaeological Museum) ⋆⋆

This embarrassingly rich collection is often overlooked by visitors in full-throttle Renaissance mode. It conserves Egyptian artifacts, Roman remains, many Attic vases, and an important Etruscan collection. Parts of it have been undergoing restoration and rearrangement for years and are closed indefinitely, including the garden. The relics to be on the lookout for start in the first ground-floor room with an early-4th-century B.C. bronze **Chimera** ⋆⋆, a mythical beast with a lion's body and head, a goat head sprouting from its back, and a serpent for a tail (the tail was incorrectly restored in 1785). The beast was found near Arezzo in 1553 and probably made in a Chiusi or an Orvieto workshop as a votive offering. The legend that claims Benvenuto Cellini recast the left paws is hogwash; the feet did have to be reattached, but they had the originals to work with. Ground-floor room III contains a **silver amphora** studded with concave medallions, a work from Antioch (ca. A.D. 380).

In room III on the upper floor is an extraordinarily rare **Hittite wood-and-bone chariot** from the 14th century B.C. Room XIV upstairs has a cast bronze *Arringatore,* or orator, found near Perugia. It was made in the 1st century B.C. and helps illustrate how Roman society was having a great influence on the Etruscan world—not only in the workmanship of the statue but also in the fact that the Etruscan orator Aule Meteli is wearing a Roman toga. Room XIII contains the museum's most famous piece, the *Idolino* ⋆. The history of this nude bronze lad with his outstretched hand is long, complicated, and in the end a bit mysterious. The current theory is that he's a Roman statue of the Augustan period (around the time of Christ), with the head perhaps modeled on a lost piece by the Greek master Polycleitus. The rub: *Idolino* was originally probably part of a lamp stand used at Roman banquets. The male torso displayed here was fished out of the sea near Livorno. It was made in Greece around 480 to 470 B.C.—the earliest known Greek bronze cast using the lost wax method. The horse's head also in this room once belonged to the Medici, as did much of this museum's collections, and tradition holds that it was a source of inspiration for Verrocchio and Donatello as they cast their own equestrian monuments. It was probably once part of a Hellenistic sculpture from the 2nd or 1st century B.C.

As we go to press, rooms IX, X, and the garden are under reconstruction.

Via della Colonna 38. ✆ **055-23-575**. Admission 4€ ($4.60). Mon 2–7pm; Tues and Thurs 8:30am–7pm; Wed and Fri–Sun 8:30am–2pm. Closed 2nd and 4th Mon of month. Bus: 6, 31, or 32.

Cimitero degli Inglesi (Protestant Cemetery)

When this plot of green was nestled up against the city's medieval walls, it was indeed a quiet, shady, and reflective spot. When those walls were demolished in the late 19th century and the boulevard Viale put in their place, it became a traffic circle instead. We can only hope that frail and gentle Elizabeth Barrett Browning can block out the noise from her tomb off the left of the main path. The **sepulcher** was designed by her husband and fellow poet Robert Browning after her death in Florence in 1861.

Piazzale Donatello 38. (*C*) **055-582-608**. www.florin.ms/cemetery.html. Free admission, donation suggested (ring at the gate). Easter–Oct Mon 9am–noon, Tues–Fri 3–6pm; Oct–Easter Mon 9am–noon, Tues–Sat 2–5pm. Bus: 6, 8, 33.

AROUND PIAZZA SANTA CROCE

Piazza Santa Croce is pretty much like any in Florence—a nice bit of open space ringed with souvenir and leather shops and thronged with tourists. Its most unique feature (aside from the one time a year it's covered with dirt and violent Renaissance soccer is played on it) is the **Palazzo Antellisi** on the south side. This well-preserved, 16th-century patrician house is owned by a contessa who rents out a bunch of peachy apartments.

Santa Croce ⭐⭐   The center of the Florentine Franciscan universe was begun in 1294 by Gothic master Arnolfo di Cambio in order to rival the huge church of Santa Maria Novella being raised by the Dominicans across the city. The church wasn't completed and consecrated until 1442, and even then it remained faceless until the neo-Gothic **facade** was added in 1857 (and cleaned in 1998–99). The cloisters are home to Brunelleschi's Cappella de' Pazzi (see the Museo dell'Opera, below), the convent partially given over to a famous leather school (see "Shopping," later in this chapter), and the church itself a shrine of 14th-century frescoes and a monument to notable Florentines, whose tombs and memorials litter the place like an Italian Westminster. The best artworks, such as the Giotto frescoes, are guarded by euro-gobbling lightboxes; bring plenty of change.

The Gothic **interior**—for which they now charge a premium admission (it was free until recently)—is wide and gaping, with huge pointed stone arches creating the aisles and an echoing nave trussed with wood beams, in all feeling vaguely barnlike (an analogy the occasional fluttering pigeon only enforces). The floor is paved with worn tombstones—because being buried in this hallowed sanctuary got you one step closer to Heaven, the richest families of the day paid big bucks to stake out small rectangles of the floor. On the right aisle is the first tomb of note, a mad Vasari contraption containing the bones of the most venerated of Renaissance masters, **Michelangelo Buonarroti,** who died of a fever in Rome in 1564 at the ripe age of 89. The pope wanted him buried in the Eternal City, but Florentines managed to sneak his body back to Florence. Past Michelangelo is a pompous 19th-century cenotaph to Florentine **Dante Alighieri,** one of history's greatest poets, whose *Divine Comedy* codified the Italian language. He died in 1321 in Ravenna after a long and bitter life in exile from his hometown (on trumped-up embezzlement charges), and that Adriatic city has never seen fit to return the bones to Florence, the city that would never readmit the poet when he was alive.

Against a nave pillar farther up is an elaborate **pulpit** (1472–76) carved by Benedetto di Maiano with scenes from the life of St. Francis. Next comes a wall monument to **Niccolò Machiavelli,** the 16th-century Florentine statesman and author whose famous book *The Prince* was the perfect practical manual for a powerful Renaissance ruler.

Past the next altar is an *Annunciation* (1433) carved in low relief of *pietra serena* and gilded by Donatello. Nearby is Antonio Rossellino's 1446 tomb of the great humanist scholar and city chancellor **Leonardo Bruni** (d. 1444). Beyond this architectural masterpiece of a tomb is a 19th-century knockoff honoring the remains of **Gioacchino Rossini** (1792–1868), composer of the *Barber of Seville* and the *William Tell Overture.*

Around in the right transept is the **Cappella Castellani** frescoed by Agnolo Gaddi and assistants, with a tabernacle by Mino da Fiesole and a *Crucifix* by Niccolò Gerini. Agnolo's father, Taddo Gaddi, was one of Giotto's closest followers, and the senior Gaddi is the one who undertook painting the **Cappella Baroncelli** ✸ (1332–38) at the transept's end. The frescoes depict scenes from the Life of the Virgin, and to the left of the window is an *Angel Appearing to the Shepherds* that constitutes the first night scene in Italian fresco. The altarpiece *Coronation of the Virgin* is by Giotto. To the left of this chapel is a doorway, designed by Michelozzo, leading to the *sagrestia* (sacristy) past a huge *Deposition* (1560) by Alessandro Allori that had to be restored after it incurred massive water damage when the church was inundated during the 1966 flood. Past the gift shop is a leather school and store.

In the right transept, Giotto frescoed the two chapels to the right of the high altar (for an explanation of Giotto's art, see "The Genius of Giotto" on p. 395). The frescoes were whitewashed over during the 17th century but uncovered from 1841 to 1852 and inexpertly restored. The **Cappella Peruzzi** ✸✸ on the right is a late work and not in the best shape. The many references to antiquity in the styling and architecture of the frescoes reflect Giotto's trip to Rome and its ruins. His assistant Taddeo Gaddi did the altarpiece. Even more famous, if only as the setting for a scene in the film *A Room with a View,* is the **Cappella Bardi** ✸✸ immediately to the right of the high altar. The key panels here include the *Trial by Fire Before the Sultan of Egypt* on the right wall, full of telling subtlety in the expressions and poses of the figures. One of Giotto's most well-known works is the lower panel on the left wall, the *Death of St. Francis,* where the monks weep and wail with convincing pathos. Alas, big chunks of the scene are missing from when a tomb was stuck on top of it in the 18th century. Most people miss seeing *Francis Receiving the Stigmata,* which Giotto frescoed above the outside of the entrance arch to the chapel.

Agnolo Gaddi designed the stained-glass windows, painted the saints between them, and frescoed a *Legend of the True Cross* cycle on the walls of the rounded **sanctuary** behind the high altar. At the end of the left transept is another Cappella Bardi, this one housing a legendary *Crucifix* ✸ by Donatello. According to Vasari, Donatello excitedly called his friend Filippo Brunelleschi up to his studio to see this *Crucifix* when he had finished carving it. The famed architect, whose tastes were aligned with the prevailing view of the time that refinement and grace were much more important than realism, criticized the work with the words, "Why Donatello, you've put a peasant on the cross!" Donatello sniffed, "If it was as easy to make something as it is to criticize, my Christ would really look to you like Christ. So you get some wood and try to make one yourself." Secretly, Brunelleschi did just that, and one day he invited Donatello to come over to his studio for lunch. Donatello arrived bearing the food gathered up in his apron. Shocked when he beheld Brunelleschi's elegant *Crucifix,* he let the lunch drop to the floor, smashing the eggs, and after a few moments turned to Brunelleschi and humbly offered, "Your job is making Christs and mine is making peasants." Tastes change, and to modern eyes this "peasant" stands as the stronger work. If you want to see how Brunelleschi fared with his Christ, visit it at Santa Maria Novella.

Past a door as you head back down the left aisle is a 16th-century *Deposition* by Bronzino. A bit farther along, against a pier, is the roped-off floor tomb of Lorenzo Ghiberti, sculptor of the baptistery doors. Against the wall is an altarpiece of the *Incredulity of St. Thomas* by Giorgio Vasari. The last tomb on the right is that of **Galileo Galilei** (1564–1642), the preeminent Pisan scientist who figured out everything from the action of pendulums and the famous law of bodies falling at the same rate (regardless of weight) to discovering the moons of Jupiter and asserting that Earth revolved around the Sun. This last one got him in trouble with the church, which tried him in the Inquisition and—when he wouldn't recant—excommunicated him. At the urging of friends frightened his obstinacy would get him executed as a heretic, Galileo eventually kneeled in front of an altar and "admitted" he'd been wrong. He lived out the rest of his days under house arrest near Florence and wasn't allowed a Christian burial until 1737. Giulio Foggini designed this tomb for him, complete with a relief of the solar system—the Sun, you'll notice, is at the center. The pope finally got around to lifting the excommunication in 1992. Italians still bring him fresh flowers.

Piazza Santa Croce. ℂ 055-244-619. Admission 4€ ($4.60). Mon–Sat 9:30am–5:30pm; Sun 1–5:30pm. Bus: B, 13, 23, or 71.

Museo dell'Opera di Santa Croce 👁

Part of Santa Croce's convent has been set up as a museum, mainly to harbor artistic victims of the 1966 Arno flood, which buried the church under tons of mud and water. You enter through a door to the right of the church facade, which spills into an open-air courtyard planted with cypress and filled with bird song.

At the end of the path is the **Cappella de' Pazzi** 👁, one of Filippo Brunelleschi's architectural masterpieces (faithfully finished after his death in 1446). Giuliano di Maiano probably designed the porch that now precedes the chapel, set with glazed terra cottas by Luca della Robbia. The rectangular chapel is one of Brunelleschi's signature pieces and a defining example of (and model for) early Renaissance architecture. Light gray *pietra serena* is used to accent the architectural lines against smooth white plaster walls, and the only decorations are della Robbia roundels of the *Apostles* (1442–52). The chapel was barely finished by 1478, when the infamous Pazzi Conspiracy got the bulk of the family, who were funding this project, either killed or exiled.

From back in the first cloister you can enter the museum proper via the long hall of the **refectory.** On your right as you enter is the painting that became emblematic of all the artworks damaged during the 1966 flood, Cimabue's *Crucifix* 👁, one of the masterpieces of the artist who began bridging the gap between Byzantine tradition and Renaissance innovation, not the least by teaching Giotto to paint.

Piazza Santa Croce 16. ℂ 055-244-619. Admission included with San Croce; hours same. Bus: B, 13, 23, or 71.

Museo Horne

Of the city's several small once-private collections, the one formed by Englishman Herbert Percy Horne and left to Florence in his will has perhaps the best individual pieces, though the bulk of it consists of mediocre paintings by good artists. In a 15th-century palazzo designed by Cronaca (not Sangallo, as had once been believed), the collections are left, unlabeled, as Horne arranged them; the reference numbers on the handout they give you correspond to the stickers on the wall, not the numbers on the frames. The best works are a *St. Stephen* by Giotto and Sienese mannerist Domenico Beccafumi's weirdly colored tondo of the *Holy Family.*

Via dei Benci 6. ℂ 055-244-661. Admission 5€ ($5.75). Mon–Sat 9am–1pm; in summer also Tues 8:30–11pm. Bus: B, 13, 23, or 71.

Casa Buonarroti

Though Michelangelo Buonarroti never actually lived in this modest palazzo, he did own the property and left it to his nephew Lionardo.

Lionardo named his own son after his famous uncle, and this younger Michelangelo became very devoted to the memory of his namesake, converting the house into a museum and hiring artists to fill the place with frescoes honoring the genius of his great uncle.

The good stuff is upstairs, starting with a display case regularly rotating pages from the museum's collection of original drawings. In the first room off the landing are Michelangelo's earliest sculptures: the *Madonna of the Steps,* carved before 1492 when he was a 15- or 16-year-old student in the Medici sculpture garden. A few months later, the child prodigy was already finished carving another marble, a confused tangle of bodies known as the *Battle of the Centaurs and Lapiths.* The sculptural ideals that were to mark his entire career are already evident here: a fascination with the male body to the point of ignoring the figures themselves in pursuit of muscular torsion and the use of rough "unfinished" marble to speak sculptural volumes.

Via Ghibellina 70. (𝄞 **055-241-752.** www.casabuonarroti.it. Admission 6.50€ ($7.50). Wed–Mon 9:30am–2pm. Bus: A, 14, or 23.

Santa Maria Maddalena dei Pazzi   The entrance to this church is an unassuming, unnumbered door on Borgo Pinti that opens onto a pretty cloister designed in 1492 by Giuliano da Sangallo, open to the sky and surrounded by large *pietra serena* columns topped with droopy-eared Ionic capitals. The interior of the 13th-century church was remodeled in the 17th and early 18th centuries and represents the high baroque at its restrained best. At the odd hours listed below, you can get into the chapter house to see the church's hidden main prize, a wall-filling fresco of the ***Crucifixion and Saints*** ☝ (1493–96) by Perugino, grand master of the Umbrian school. Typical of Perugino's style, the background is drawn as delicately in blues and greens as the posed figures were fleshed out in full-bodied volumes of bright colors.

Entrance next to Borgo Pinti 58. (𝄞 **055-247-8420.** Free admission to church and Perugino *Crucifixion* 1€ ($1.15) "donation." Church daily 9am–noon; Mon–Fri 5–5:20pm and 6–6:50pm; Sat 5–6:20pm; Sun 5–6:50pm. Perugino *Crucifixion,* ring bell at no. 58 9–10am or enter through sacristy (knock at the last door on the right inside the church) at 5pm or 6:15pm. Bus: A, 6, 14, 23, 31, 32, or 71.

Sinagoga (Synagogue) and Jewish Museum   The center of the 1,000-strong Jewish community in Florence is this imposing Moorish-Byzantine synagogue, built in the 1870s. In an effort to create a neo-Byzantine building, the architects ended up making it look rather like a church, complete with a dome, an apse, a pulpit, and a pipe organ. The intricate polychrome arabesque designs, though, lend it a distinctly Eastern flavor, and the rows of prayer benches facing each other, and the separate areas for women, hint at its Orthodox Jewish nature. Though the synagogue is technically Sephardic, the members of the Florentine Jewish community are Italian Jews, a Hebrew culture that has adapted to its Italian surroundings since the 1st century B.C. when Jewish slaves were first brought to Rome. (The Florentine community dates from the 14th c.)

Via Farina 4. (𝄞 **055-234-6654.** www.firenzebraica.net. Admission 4€ ($4.60) adults, 3€ ($3.45) students. June–Aug Sun–Thurs 10am–6pm; April, May, Sept, and Oct Sun–Thurs 10am–5pm; Nov–March Sun–Thurs 10am–3pm.; obligatory 45-min. guided tours every 25 min. Bus: 6, 31, 32, or C.

IN THE OLTRARNO

Santa Felícita   The 2nd-century Greek sailors who lived in this neighborhood brought Christianity to Florence with them, and this little church was probably the second to be established in the city, the first edition of it rising in the late 4th century. The current version was built in the 1730s. The star works are in the first chapel on your right, paintings by mannerist master Pontormo (1525–27). *The Deposition* and frescoed *Annunciation* are rife with his garish color palette of oranges, pinks, golds, lime greens, and sky blues. The four round paintings of the *Evangelists* surrounding the dome are also by Pontormo, except for the *St. Mark* (with the angel), which was probably painted by his pupil Bronzino.

Piazza Santa Felícita (2nd left off Via Guicciardini across the Ponte Vecchio). ℭ **055-213-018**. Free admission. Daily 8am–noon and 3:30–6:30pm. Bus: B or D.

Palazzo Pitti & Giardino Boboli (Pitti Palace & Boboli Gardens) ✫✫✫

Though the original, much smaller Pitti Palace was a Renaissance affair probably designed by Filippo Brunelleschi, that palazzo is completely hidden by the enormous mannerist mass we see today. Inside are Florence's most extensive set of museums, including the Galleria Palatina, a huge painting gallery second in town only to the Uffizi, with famous works by Raphael, Andrea del Sarto, Titian, and Rubens. When Luca Pitti died in 1472, Cosimo de' Medici's wife, Eleonora of Toledo, bought this property and unfinished palace to convert into the new Medici home—she hated the dark, cramped spaces of the family apartments in the Palazzo Vecchio. They hired Bartolomeo Ammannati to enlarge the palazzo, which he did starting in 1560 by creating the courtyard out back, extending the wings out either side, and incorporating a Michelangelo architectural invention, "kneeling windows," on the ground floor of the facade. (Rather than being visually centered between the line of the floor and that of the ceiling, kneeling windows' bases extend lower to be level with the ground or, in the case of upper stories, with whatever architectural element delineates the baseline of that story's 1st level.) Later architects finished the building off by the 19th century, probably to Ammannati's original plans, in the end producing the oversize rustication of its outer walls and overall ground plan that make it one of the masterpieces of Florentine mannerist architecture.

The ticket office for the painting gallery—the main, and for many visitors, most interesting of the Pitti museums—is off Ammannati's excellent **interior courtyard** ✫ of gold-tinged rusticated rock grafted onto the three classical orders.

GALLERIA PALATINA ✫✫✫   If the Uffizi represents mainly the earlier masterpieces collected by the Medici, the Pitti Palace's painting gallery continues the story with the High Renaissance and later eras, a collection gathered by the Medici, and later the Grand Dukes of Lorraine. The works are still displayed in the old-world fashion, which hung paintings according to aesthetics—how well, say, the Raphael matched the drapes—rather than that boring academic chronological order. In the first long **Galleria delle Statue (Hall of Statues)** are an early Peter Paul Rubens's *Risen Christ,* Caravaggio's *Tooth-puller* ✫, and a 19th-century tabletop inlaid in *pietre dure,* an exquisite example of the famous Florentine mosaic craft. The next five rooms made up the Medici's main apartments, frescoed by Pietro da Cortona in the 17th-century baroque style—they're home to the bulk of the paintings.

The **Sala di Venere (Venus Room)** is named after the neoclassical *Venus,* which Napoléon had Canova sculpt in 1810 to replace the *Medici Venus* the Emperor had appropriated for his Paris digs. Four masterpieces by the famed early-16th-century Venetian painter Titian hang on the walls. Art historians still argue whether *The Concert* ✫ was wholly painted by Titian in his early 20s or by Giorgione, in whose circle he moved. However, most now attribute at most the fop on the left to Giorgione and give the rest of the canvas to Titian. There

are no such doubts about Titian's *Portrait of Julius II,* a copy of the physiologi-
cally penetrating work by Raphael in London's National Gallery (the version in
the Uffizi is a copy Raphael himself made), or the *Portrait of a Lady (La Bella).*
Titian painted the *Portrait of Pietro Aretino* for the writer/thinker himself, but
Aretino didn't understand the innovative styling and accused Titian of not having completed the work. The painter, in a huff, gave it to Cosimo I as a gift. The
room also contains Rubens's *Return from the Hayfields,* famous for its classically
harmonious landscape.

The **Sala di Apollo (Apollo Room)** has another masterful early *Portrait of an
Unknown Gentleman* by Titian as well as his sensual, luminously gold **Mary Magdalene** ✩, the first in a number of takes on the subject the painter was to make
throughout his career. There are several works by Andrea del Sarto, whose late
Holy Family and especially *Deposition* display the daring chromatic experiments
and highly refined spatial compositions that were to influence his students Pontormo and Rosso Fiorentino as they went about mastering Mannerism.

The **Sala di Marte (Mars Room)** is dominated by Rubens, including the
enormous **Consequences of War** ✩✩, which an aged Rubens painted for his
friend Sustermans at a time when both were worried that their Dutch homeland
was on the brink of battle. Rubens's **The Four Philosophers** ✩ is a much more
lighthearted work, in which he painted himself at the far left, next to his seated
brother Filippo.

The star of the **Sala di Giove (Jupiter Room)** is Raphael's **La Velata** ✩✩,
one of the crowning achievements of his short career and a summation of what
he had learned about color, light, naturalism, and mood. It's probably a portrait
of his Roman mistress called La Fornarina, a baker's daughter who sat for many
of his Madonnas.

Raphael is the focus of the **Sala di Saturno (Saturn Room)** ✩✩, where the
transparent colors of his *Madonna*s and probing portraits show the strong influence of both Leonardo da Vinci (the *Portrait of Maddalena Strozzi Doni* owes
much to the *Mona Lisa*) and Raphael's old master Perugino, whose *Deposition*
and a *Mary Magdalene* hang here as well. The **Sala dell'Iliade (Illiad Room)** has
another Raphael portrait, this time of a **Pregnant Woman** ✩, along with some
more Titian masterpieces. Don't miss *Mary Magdalene* and **Judith** ✩, two paintings by one of the only female artists of the late Renaissance era, Artemesia Gentileschi, who often turned to themes of strong biblical women.

From here, you enter a series of smaller rooms with smaller paintings. The
Sala dell'Educazione di Giove (Room of Jupiter's Education) has two famous
works: one a 1608 **Sleeping Cupid** ✩✩ Caravaggio painted while living in exile
from Rome (avoiding murder charges) on the island of Malta; and the other
Cristofano Allori's **Judith with the Head of Holofernes** ✩, a Freudian field day
where the artist depicted himself in the severed head, his lover as Judith holding
it, and her mother as the maid looking on.

APARTAMENTI REALI ✩   The other wing of the *piano nobile* is taken up
with the Medici's private apartments, which were reopened in 1993 after being
restored to their late-19th-century appearance when the kings of the House of
Savoy, rulers of the Unified Italy, used the suites as their Florentine home. The
over-the-top sumptuous fabrics, decorative arts furnishings, stuccoes, and frescoes reflect the neo-baroque and Victorian tastes of the Savoy kings. Amid the
general interior-decorator flamboyance are some thoroughly appropriate
baroque canvases, plus some earlier works by Andrea del Sarto and Caravaggio's

Portrait of a Knight of Malta ✦. January through May, you can visit the apartments only by guided tour Tuesday and Saturday (and sometimes Thurs) hourly from 9 to 11am and 3 to 5pm (reserve ahead at ℂ **055-238-8614;** inquire about admission fees).

GALLERIA D'ARTE MODERNA ✦   Modern art isn't what draws most people to the capital of the Renaissance, but the Pitti's collection includes some important works by the 19th-century Tuscan school of art known as the Macchiaioli, who painted a kind of Tuscan Impressionism, concerned with the *macchie* (marks of color on the canvas and the play of light on the eye). Most of the scenes are of the countryside or peasants working, along with the requisite lot of portraits. Some of the movement's greatest talents are here, including Silvestro Lega, Telemaco Signorini, and Giovanni Fattori, the genius of the group. Don't miss his two white oxen pulling a cart in ***The Tuscan Maremma*** ✦.

GALLERIA DEL COSTUME & MUSEO DEGLI ARGENTI   These aren't the most popular of the Pitti's museums, and the **Museo degli Argenti** has what seems like miles of the most extravagant and often hideous *objets d'art* and housewares the Medici and Lorraines could put their hands on. If the collections prove anything, it's that as the Medici became richer and more powerful, their taste declined proportionally. Just be thankful their **carriage collection** has been closed for years. The **Costume Gallery** is more interesting. The collections concentrate on the 18th to 20th centuries but also display outfits from back to the 16th century. The dress in which Eleonora of Toledo was buried, made famous by Bronzino's intricate depiction of its velvety embroidered silk and in-sewn pearls on his portrait of her in the Uffizi, is usually on display.

GIARDINO BOBOLI (BOBOLI GARDENS) ✦✦   The statue-filled park behind the Pitti Palace is one of the earliest and finest Renaissance gardens, laid out mostly between 1549 and 1656 with box hedges in geometric patterns, groves of ilex, dozens of statues, and rows of cypress. In 1766, it was opened to the Florentine public, who still come here with their families for Sunday-morning strolls. Just above the entrance through the courtyard of the Palazzo Pitti is an oblong **amphitheater** modeled on Roman circuses. Today, we see in the middle a **granite basin** from Rome's Baths of Caracalla and an **Egyptian obelisk** of Ramses II, but in 1589 this was the setting for the wedding reception of Ferdinando de' Medici's marriage to Christine of Lorraine. For the occasion, the Medici commissioned entertainment from Jacopo Peri and Ottavio Rinuccini, who decided to set a classical story entirely to music and called it *Dafne*—the world's first opera. (Later, they wrote a follow-up hit *Erudice,* performed here in 1600; it's the 1st opera whose score has survived.)

Around the park, don't miss the rococo **Kaffehaus,** with bar service in summer, and near the top of the park the **Giardino del Cavaliere,** the Boboli's prettiest hidden corner—a tiny walled garden of box hedges with private views over the wooded hills of Florence's outskirts. At the north end of the park, down around the end of the Pitti Palace, are some fake caverns filled with statuary, attempting to invoke some vaguely classical sacred grotto. The most famous, the **Grotta Grande,** was designed by Giorgio Vasari, Bartolomeo Ammannati, and Bernardo Buontalenti between 1557 and 1593, dripping with phony stalactites and set with replicas of Michelangelo's unfinished *Slave* statues. (The originals were once placed here before being moved to the Accademia.) All the grottoes are being restored, but you can visit them by appointment by calling ℂ **055-218-741.** Near the exit to the park is a Florentine postcard fave, the ***Fontana di Bacco***

(**Bacchus Fountain;** 1560), a pudgy dwarf sitting atop a tortoise. It's actually a portrait of Pietro Barbino, Cosimo I's potbellied dwarf court jester.

Piazza Pitti. **Galleria Palatina:** ⓒ **055-238-8614;** reserve tickets at ⓒ **055-294-883** or www.firenzemusei.it; admission 6.50€ ($7.50) adults, 3.25€ ($3.75) children; Easter–Oct Tues–Sat 8:30am–10pm, Sun 8:30am–8pm and winter Tues–Sat 8:30am–6:50pm, Mon 8:30am–1:50pm; last admission 45 minutes before close. **Galleria d'Arte Moderna:** ⓒ **055-238-8601;** admission 5€ ($5.75) adults, 2.50€ ($2.90) children, cumulative ticket with Galleria del Costume available; daily 8:15am–1:50pm, closed 1st, 3rd, and 5th Mon and 2nd and 4th Sun of each month. **Galleria del Costume:** ⓒ **055-238-8713;** admission 5€ ($5.75) adults, 2.50€ ($2.90) children, cumulative ticket with Galleria d'Arte Moderna available; daily 8:15am–1:50pm, closed 1st, 3rd, and 5th Mon and 2nd and 4th Sun of each month. **Museo degli Argenti:** ⓒ **055-238-8709;** admission 4€ ($4.60) adults, 2€ ($2.30) children, cumulative ticket with Giardino Boboli available; Nov–Feb daily 8:15am–4:30pm, March daily 8:15am–5:30pm, April–May and Oct daily 8:15am–6:30pm, and June–Sept daily 8:15am–7:30pm. **Giardino Boboli:** ⓒ **055-265-1816;** admission 4€ ($4.60) adults, 2€ ($2.30) children, cumulative ticket with Museo degli Argenti available; Nov–Feb daily 8:15am–4:30pm, March daily 8:15am–5:30pm, April–May and Oct daily 8:15am–6:30pm, and June–Sept daily 8:15am–7:30pm. Bus: D, 11, 36, 37, or 68.

Santo Spirito ✯   One of Filippo Brunelleschi's masterpieces of architecture, this 15th-century church doesn't look like much from the outside (no true facade was ever built), but the **interior** ✯ is a marvelous High Renaissance space—an expansive landscape of proportion and mathematics worked out in classic Brunelleschi style, with coffered vaulting, tall columns, and the stacked perspective of arched arcading. Good late-Renaissance and baroque paintings are scattered throughout, but the best stuff lies up in the transepts and in the east end, surrounding the extravagant **baroque altar** with a ciborium inlaid in *pietre dure* around 1607.

The **right transept** begins with a *Crucifixion* by Francesco Curradi. Against the back wall of the transept, the first chapel holds an early-15th-century *Madonna del Soccorso* of uncertain authorship. Two chapels down is one of Filippino Lippi's best works, a *Madonna and Child with Saints and Donors.* The background seen through the classical arches was painted with an almost Flemish exacting detail. In the east end of the church, the center two chapels against the back wall contain Alessandro Allori altarpieces: *The Martyred Saints* (1574) on the right has a predella view of what the Palazzo Pitti looked like before its enlargement; and the *Christ and the Adulteress* on the left is extremely advanced in style, already almost a work of the late baroque. In the **left transept,** the first chapel on the right side is a late-15th-century *Madonna Enthroned with Child and Saints.* Next to this is the highly skilled *St. Monica and Augustinian Nuns,* an almost monochrome work of black and pale yellow, faintly disturbing in its eerie monotony and perfection of composition. It's now usually attributed to the enigmatic Andrea del Verrocchio, one-time master of Leonardo da Vinci.

The famed **piazza** outside is one of the focal points of the Oltrarno, shaded by trees and lined with trendy cafes that see some bar action in the evenings. It's not quite the pleasant hangout it once was, however—especially since the heroin set moved in a few years ago, making it a less than desirable place to be after midnight (though early evening is still fine). Stop by Bar Ricci at no. 9r, where more than 300 facade designs for faceless Santo Spirito line the walls, the product of a fun-loving contest the bar held in 1980.

Piazza Santo Spirito. ⓒ **055-210-030.** Free admission. Daily 8am–noon; Thurs–Tues 4–6pm. Bus: D, 6, 11, 36, 37, or 68.

Cenacolo di Santo Spirito Museum   The dark and haphazard museum in the church's old refectory (entrance to the left of Santo Spirito's facade) has a gathering of Romanesque and paleo-Christian stone sculptures and reliefs. The main reason to drop by is the end wall frescoed by Andrea Orcagna and his brother Nardo di Cione in 1360 with a *Last Supper* (of which only 1.5 apostles and a halo are left) and above it a beautiful *Crucifixion,* one of 14th-century Florence's masterpieces.

Piazza Santo Spirito 29. ℂ **055-287-043**. Admission 2.20€ ($2.55). Tues–Sat 10:30am–1:30pm (until 2pm Apr–Nov). Bus: D, 6, 11, 36, 37, or 68.

Santa Maria della Carmine ★★★

Following a 1771 fire that destroyed everything but the transept chapels and sacristy, this Carmelite church was almost entirely reconstructed and decorated in high baroque style. Ever since a long and expensive restoration of the famous frescoes of the **Cappella Brancacci** in the right transept, they've blocked off just that chapel and you have to enter through the cloisters (doorway to the right of the church facade) and pay admission. The frescoes were commissioned by an enemy of the Medici, Felice Brancacci, who in 1424 hired Masolino and his student Masaccio to decorate it with a cycle on the life of St. Peter. Masolino probably worked out the cycle's scheme and painted a few scenes along with his pupil before taking off for 3 years to serve as court painter in Budapest, during which time Masaccio kept painting, quietly creating one of his masterpieces and some of the early Renaissance's greatest frescoes. Masaccio left for Rome in 1428, where he died at age 27. The cycle was completed between 1480 and 1485 by Filippino Lippi, who faithfully imitated Masaccio's technique.

Even before Lippi's intervention, though, the frescoes had been an instant hit. People flocked from all over the city to admire them, and almost every Italian artist of the day came to sketch and study Masaccio's mastery of perspective, bold light and colors, and unheard-of touches of realism. Even later masters like Leonardo da Vinci and Michelangelo came to learn what they could from the young artist's genius. A 1980s restoration cleaned off the dirt and dark mold that had grown in the egg-based pigments used to "touch up" the frescoes in the 18th century and removed additions like the prudish ivy leaves trailing across Adam and Eve's privates.

Masolino was responsible for the *St. Peter Preaching,* the upper panel to the left of the altar, and the two top scenes on the right wall, which shows his fastidiously decorative style in a long panel of *St. Peter Healing the Cripple* and *Raising Tabitha,* and his *Adam and Eve.* Contrast this first man and woman, about to take the bait offered by the snake, with the **Expulsion from the Garden** ★★ across from it painted by Masaccio. Masolino's figures are highly posed models, expressionless and oblivious to the temptation being offered. Masaccio's Adam and Eve, on the other hand, burst with intense emotion and forceful movement. The top scene on the left wall is also by Masaccio, and it showcases both his classical influences and another of his innovations, perfect linear perspective. On the end wall, Masaccio painted the lower scene to the left of the altar of *St. Peter Healing the Sick with His Shadow,* unique at the time for its realistic portrayal of street beggars and crippled bodies. The two scenes to the right of the altar are Masaccio as well, with the *Baptism of the Neophytes* taking its place among his masterpieces. Most of the rest of the frescoes were painted by Filippino Lippi. The left transept chapel, which isn't blocked off, is one of Florence's most harmonious examples of the baroque (1675–83), with a ceiling painted by Luca Giordano.

Piazza della Carmine. ℂ **055-238-2195**. Free admission to church; Brancacci chapel 4€ ($4.60), cumulative ticket with Palazzo Vecchio available. Daily 10am–5pm; Sun 1–5pm. Bus: D, 6, 11, 36, 37, or 68.

Museo Zoologico La Specola   Italy has very few zoos, but this is the largest zoological collection, rooms full of insects, crustaceans, and stuffed birds and mammals—everything from ostriches and apes to a rhinoceros. The museum was founded here in 1775, and the collections are still displayed in the style of an old-fashioned natural sciences museum, with specimens crowded into beautiful old wood-and-glass cases. The last 10 rooms contain an important collection of human anatomical wax models crafted between 1775 and 1814 by Clemente Susini for medical students. The life-size figures are flayed, dissected, and disemboweled to varying degrees and are truly disgusting, but fascinating.

Via Romana 17. (📞 **055-228-8251.** www.specola.unifi.it. Admission 5€ ($5.75) adults, 2.50€ ($2.90) children 6–18, free for children under 6. Thurs–Tues 9am–1pm. Bus: C, D, 11, 36, or 37.

San Felice   This tiny Gothic church just south of the Pitti Palace sports a High Renaissance facade by Michelozzo (1457) and a *Crucifixion* over the high altar recently attributed to Giotto. Also peek at the remnants of Niccolò Gerini's early-15th-century *Pietà* fresco over the first altar on the right.

At no. 8 on the piazza is the entrance to the **Casa Guidi,** where from 1846 English poet Elizabeth Barrett Browning lived with her husband, Robert, moving in just after their secret marriage. When the unification of Italy became official in Florence, Elizabeth recorded the momentous event in a famous poem, "Casa Guidi Windows": "I heard last night a little child go singing / 'Neath Casa Guidi windows, by the church, / O bella libertà, O bella!" Mrs. Browning died in this house on June 18, 1861.

Piazza di San Felice. No phone. Free admission. Bus: D, 11, 36, 37, or 68.

IN THE HILLS

Piazzale Michelangiolo ⍟   This panoramic piazza is a required stop for every tour bus. The balustraded terrace was laid out in 1885 to give a sweeping vista of the entire city, spread out in the valley below and backed by the green hills of Fiesole beyond. The monument to Michelangelo in the center of the piazza is made up of bronze replicas of *David* and his Medici chapel sculptures.

Viale Michelangelo. Bus: 12 or 13.

San Miniato al Monte ⍟⍟   High atop a hill, its gleaming white-and-green facade visible from the valley below, San Miniato is one of the few ancient churches of Florence to survive the centuries virtually intact. San Miniato was an eastern Christian who settled in Florence and was martyred during Emperor Decius's persecutions in A.D. 250. The legend goes that the decapitated saint picked up his head, walked across the river, climbed up the hillside, and didn't lie down to die until he reached this spot. He and other Christians were buried here, and a shrine was raised on the site as early as the 4th century.

The current building began to take shape in 1013, under the auspices of the powerful Arte di Calimala guild, whose symbol, a bronze eagle clutching a bale of wool, perches atop the **facade** ⍟⍟. The Romanesque facade is a particularly gorgeous bit of white Carrara and green Prato marble inlay. Above the central window is a 13th-century mosaic of *Christ Between the Madonna and St. Miniato* (a theme repeated in a slightly later mosaic filling the apse inside).

The **interior** has a few Renaissance additions, but they blend in well with the overall medieval aspect—an airy, stony space with a raised choir at one end, painted wooden trusses on the ceiling, and tombs interspersed with inlaid marble symbols of the zodiac paving the floor.

Catching *Calcio* Fever

To Italians, *calcio* (soccer) is something akin to a second religion. You don't know what a "fan" is until you've attended a soccer match in a country like Italy, and an afternoon at the football stadium can offer you as much insight (if not more) into Italian culture as a day in the Uffizi. Catch the local team, the Fiorentina, Sundays September through May at the Stadio Comunale, Via Manfredi Fanti 4 (© **055-262-5537** or 055-50-721; www. acfiorentina.it). Tickets go on sale at the stadium box office 3 hours before each game.

Below the choir is an 11th-century **crypt** with small frescoes by Taddo Gaddi. Off to the right of the raised choir is the **sacristy,** which Spinello Aretino covered in 1387 with cartoonish yet elegant frescoes depicting the *Life of St. Benedict* ★. Off the left aisle of the nave is 15th-century **Cappella del Cardinale del Portogallo** ★★, a brilliant collaborative effort by Renaissance artists built to honor young Portuguese humanist Cardinal Jacopo di Lusitania, who was sent to study in Perugia but died an untimely death at 25 in Florence. Brunelleschi's student Antonio Manetti started the chapel in 1460 but soon died, and Antonio Rossellino finished the architecture and carving by 1466. Luca della Robbia provided the glazed terra-cotta dome, a cubic landscape set with tondi of the four *Virtues* surrounding the *Holy Spirit* to symbolize the young scholar's devotion to the church and to humanist philosophy. It stands as one of della Robbia's masterpieces of color and classical ideals. The unfinished **bell tower** seen from the outside was designed by Baccio d'Agnolo. In 1530 the combined troops of Charles V and Medici Pope Clement VII, who had recently reconciled with each other, lay siege to the newly declared Republic of Florence in an attempt to reinstate the Medici dukes. San Miniato al Monte was one of the prime fortifications, and an artilleryman named Lapo was stationed up in the tower with two small cannons—he was basically bait, stuck there to draw the fire of the enemy where it would do little harm. The man in charge of the defenses was Michelangelo, who, the authorities figured, was so good at everything else, why not military fortifications? After throwing up dirt ramparts and cobbling together defensible walls out of oak timbers, Michelangelo helped poor Lapo out by devising an ingenious way to protect the tower: He hung mattresses down the sides to absorb the shock of the cannonballs fired at it and left the tower (and, more important, Lapo) still standing.

The siege was eventually successful, however, and the Florentine Republic fell, but while it lasted, Michelangelo spent his day up here and referred to the church of **San Salvatore al Monte** just below as "my pretty country maid." It's a simple 1400 church built by Cronaca, with a Giovanni della Robbia *Deposition* and a Neri di Bicci Pietà inside.

Via del Monte alle Croci/Viale Galileo Galilei (behind Piazzale Michelangiolo). © **055-234-2731.** Free admission. Easter to early Oct daily 8am–7:30pm; winter Mon–Sat 8am–1pm and 2:30–6pm, Sun 8am–6pm. Bus: 12 or 13.

Museo Stibbert   Half Scotsman, half Italian, Frederick Stibbert was nothing if not eccentric. A sometime artist, intrepid traveler, voracious accumulator, and even hero in Garibaldi's army, he inherited a vast fortune and this villa from his Italian mother. He connected the house to a nearby villa to create an eclectic museum housing his extraordinary collections, including baroque canvases, fine porcelain, Flemish tapestries, Tuscan crucifixes, and Etruscan artifacts. The museum was partially rearranged in past decades to try and make some sense out of 57 rooms stuffed with over 50,000 items. More recently, however, the city has come to appreciate this rare example of a private 19th-century museum and is busily setting it all back the way Stibbert originally intended.

Stibbert's greatest interest and most fascinating assemblage is of **armor** ⍟— Etruscan, Lombard, Asian, Roman, 17th-century Florentine, and 15th-century Turkish. The museum has the largest display of Japanese arms and armor in Europe and a new exhibit of porcelain. The high point of the house is a remarkable grand hall filled with an entire cavalcade of mannequins in 16th-century armor (mostly European, but with half a dozen samurai foot soldiers thrown in for good measure). Stibbert even managed to get some seriously historic Florentine armor, that in which Medici warrior Giovanni delle Bande Nere was buried.

Via Stibbert 26. ☏ 055-475-520. www.museostibbert.com. Admission 5€ ($5.75) adults, 2€ ($2.30) children. Mon–Wed 10am–4pm; Fri–Sun 10am–6pm. Bus: 4.

PARKS & GARDENS

Florence's best park is the Medici grand dukes' old backyard to the Pitti Palace, the **Giardino Boboli** (p. 171). Less scenic, but free and more jogger-friendly, is the **Parco della Cascine** along the Arno at the west end of the historic center. Originally a wild delta of land where the Arno and Mugnone rivers met, the area later became a Medici hunting reserve and eventually a pasture for the grand duke's milk cows. Today, the Cascine is home to tennis courts, pools, a horse racetrack, and some odd late-18th- and early-19th-century features like an incongruous pyramid and funky neoclassical fountains. There's a flea market here every Tuesday morning. Though perfectly safe in the daylight, this park becomes a den of thieves and a hangout for heroin addicts after dark, as do most sections of the Arno's banks, so steer clear.

2 Shopping

THE SHOPPING SCENE

The cream of the crop of Florentine shopping lines both sides of the elegant **Via de' Tornabuoni,** with an extension along **Via della Vigna Nuova** and other surrounding streets. Here you'll find big names like Gucci, Armani, Ferragamo, and Mila Schön ensconced in old palaces or modern minimalist boutiques.

On the other end of the shopping spectrum is the haggling and general fun of the colorful and noisy **San Lorenzo street market.** Antiques gather dust by the truckload along **Via Maggio** and other Oltrarno streets. Another main corridor of stores somewhat less glitzy than those on the Via de' Tornabuoni begins at **Via Cerretani** and runs down **Via Roma** through the Piazza della Repubblica area; it keeps going down **Via Por Santa Maria,** across the **Ponte Vecchio** with its gold jewelry, and up **Via Guicciardini** on the other side. Store-laden side tributaries off this main stretch include **Via della Terme, Borgo Santissimi Apostoli,** and **Borgo San Jacopo.**

General Florentine **shopping hours** are daily from 9:30am to noon or 1pm and 3 or 3:30pm to 7:30pm, though increasingly, many shops are staying open through that mid-afternoon *riposo* (especially the larger stores and those around tourist sights).

SHOPPING A TO Z

Here's **what to buy in Florence:** leather, high fashion, shoes, marbleized paper, hand-embroidered linens, lace, lingerie, Tuscan wines, gold jewelry, *pietre dure* (aka Florentine mosaic, inlaid semiprecious stones), and Renaissance leftovers and other antiques. Here's where to buy it.

ART & ANTIQUES

The antiques business is clustered where the artisans have always lived and worked: the Oltrarno. Dealers' shops line Via Maggio, but the entire district is packed with venerable chunks of the past. On "this side" of the river, Borgo Ognissanti has the highest concentration of aging furniture and art collectibles.

The large showrooms of **Gallori-Turchi,** Via Maggio 14r (© **055-282-279**), specialize in furnishings, paintings, and weaponry (swords, lances, and pistols) from the 16th to 18th centuries. They also offer majolica and ceramic pieces and scads of excellent desks and writing tables of hand-carved and inlaid wood. Nearby you'll find **Guido Bartolozzi Antichità,** Via Maggio 18r (© **055-215-602**), under family management since 1887. This old-fashioned store concentrates on the 16th to 19th centuries. They might be offering a 17th-century Gobelin tapestry, an inlaid stone tabletop, or wood intarsia dressers from the 1700s. The quality is impeccable: The owner has been president of Italy's antiques association and secretary of Florence's biannual antiques fair. There's another showroom at Via Maggio 11.

For the serious collector who wants his or her own piece of Florence's cultural heritage, the refined showroom at **Gianfranco Luzzetti,** Borgo San Jacopo 28A (© **055-211-232**), offers artwork and furniture from the 1400s to 1600s. They have a gorgeous collection of 16th-century Deruta ceramics and majolica, canvases by the likes of Vignale and Bilivert, and on last visit even a glazed terracotta altarpiece from the hand of Andrea della Robbia. Bring sacks of money.

BOOKS

Even the smaller bookshops in Florence these days have at least a few shelves devoted to English-language books. **Feltrinelli International,** Via Cavour 12–20 (© **055-219-524;** www.lafeltrinelli.it), is one of the few of any size.

For English-only shops, hit **Paperback Exchange,** Via Fiesolana 31r (© **055-247-8154;** www.papex.it); it's not the most central, but it is the best for books in English, specializing in titles relating in some way to Florence and Italy. Much of their stock is used, and you can't beat the prices anywhere in Italy—dog-eared volumes and all Penguin books go for just a few euros. You can also trade in that novel you've already finished for another. **BM Bookshop,** Borgo Ognissanti 4r (© **055-294-575**), is a bit smaller but more central and carries only new volumes. They also have a slightly more well-rounded selection—from novels and art books to cookbooks and travel guides. A special section is devoted to Italian- and Tuscany-oriented volumes.

G. Vitello, Via dei Servi 94–96r (© **055-292-445**), sells coffee table–worthy books on art and all things Italian at up to half off the price you'd pay in a regular bookstore. Other branches are at Via Verdi 40r (© **055-234-6894**) and Via Pietrapiana 1r (© **055-241-063**). **Libreria Il Viaggio,** Borgo degli Albizi 41r (© **055-240-489**), is a cozy niche specializing in specialty travel guides, related literature, and maps, with a sizable selection in English.

DEPARTMENT STORES

Florence's central branch of the national chain **Coin,** Via Calzaiuoli 56r (© **055-2 80-531;** www.coin.it), is a stylish multifloored display case for upper-middle-class fashions—a chic Macy's. **La Rinascente,** Piazza della Repubblica 2 (© **055-219-113;** www.rinascente.it), is another of Italy's finer department stores. This six-floor store serves as an outlet for top designers (Versace, Zegna, Ferré, and so on). It also has areas set up to sell traditional Tuscan goods (terra cotta, alabaster, olive oils, and wrought iron).

DESIGN, HOUSEWARES & CERAMICS

Viceversa ⭐, Via dello Stell 3 (© **055-696-392;** www.viceversashop.com), offers one of the largest selections of the latest Robert Graves–designed teakettle or any other whimsical Alessi kitchen product. The friendly staff will also point out the Pavoni espresso machines, Carl Merkins' totemic bar set, the Princess motorized gadgets, and shelf after shelf of the best of Italian kitchen and houseware designs.

Tiny **La Botteghina,** Via Guelfa 5r (© **055-287-367;** www.labotteghina.it), is about the best and most reasonably priced city outlet for true artisan ceramics I've found in all Italy. Daniele Viegi del Fiume deals in gorgeous hand-painted ceramics from the best traditional artisans working in nearby Montelupo, the famed Umbrian ceramics centers of Deruta and Gubbio, and Castelli, high in the Abruzzi mountains.

If you can't make it to the workshops in the hill towns themselves, La Botteghina's the next best thing. If you like the sample of pieces by **Giuseppe Rampini** you see here (or in his Chianti workshop; see chapter 5) and want to invest in a full table setting, Rampini has its own classy showroom at Borgo Ognissanti 32–34 (right at Piazza Ognissanti; © **055-219-720;** www.chianti net.it/rampiniceramics).

For big-name production-line china and tablewares, visit **Richard Ginori,** Via Giulio Cesare 21 (© **055-420-491;** www.richardginori1735.com). Colorful rims and whimsical designs fill this warehouselike salesroom of the firm that has sold Florence's finest china since 1735. Other houseware bigwigs are represented as well—Alessi coffeepots, Nason and Meretti Murano glass, and Chrisofle flatware.

FASHION & CLOTHING

Although Italian fashion reached its pinnacle in the 1950s and 1960s, the country has remained at the forefront of both high (Armani, Gucci, Pucci, Ferragamo, just to name a few) and popular (as evidenced by the spectacular success of Benetton in the 1980s) fashion. Florence plays second fiddle to Milan in today's Italian fashion scene, but the city has its own cadre of highly respected names, plus, of course, outlet shops of all the hot designers. Also see "Leather, Accessories & Shoes," below.

FOR MEN & WOMEN   Cinzia, Borgo San Jacopo 22r (© **055-298-078**), is a grab bag of hand-knit, usually bulky wool sweaters offered by an elderly couple who've been sending their creations around the world for more than 30 years. **Luisa Via Roma,** Via Roma 19–21r (© **055-217-826;** www.luisaviaroma.com), is a famed gathering place for all the top names in avant-garde fashion, including Jean Paul Gaultier, Dolce & Gabbana, and Issey Miyake. Men can hand over their wallets upstairs, and women can empty their purses on the ground floor. Service can be chilly.

The address may be a hint that this isn't your average fashion shop: **Emilio Pucci,** Palazzo Pucci, Via de' Pucci 6 (© **055-283-061;** www.pucci.com). Marchese Emilio Pucci's ancestors have been a powerful banking and mercantile family since the Renaissance, and in 1950 the marchese suddenly turned designer and shocked the fashion world with his flowing silks in outlandish colors. His women's silk clothing remained the rage into the early 1970s and had a Renaissance of its own in the 1990s club scene. The design team is now headed by daughter Laudomia Pucci. If you don't wish to visit the showroom in the ancient family palace, drop by the shop at Via dei Tornabuoni 20–22r (© **055-265-8082**).

Then there's **Giorgio Armani,** Via Tornabuoni 48r (© **055-219-041; www.giorgioarmani.com**), Florence's outlet for Italy's top fashion guru. The service and store are surprisingly not stratospherically chilly (the Official Armani Attitude at the moment is studied, casual indifference). The **Emporio Armani** branch at Piazza Strozzi 16r (© **055-284-315; www.emporioarmani.com**) is the outlet for the more affordable designs. The merchandise is slightly inferior in workmanship and quality and greatly inferior in price—you can actually dig out shirts for less than $1,000.

But the biggest name to walk out of Florence onto the international catwalk has to be **Gucci,** with the world flagship store at Via de' Tornabuoni 73r (© **055-264-011; www.gucci.com**). This is where this Florentine fashion empire was started by saddlemaker Guccio Gucci in 1904, now run by a gaggle of grandsons. You enter through a phalanx of their trademark purses and bags. Forget the cheesy knock-offs sold on street corners around the world; the stock here is elegant.

Nearby is another homegrown fashion label, **Enrico Coveri,** Via Tornabuoni 81r (© **055-211-263; www.coveri.com**). Enrico started off in the nearby textile town of Prato and has a similar penchant for bright colors as contemporary Emilio Pucci. The major difference is that Enrico Coveri's firm produces down-scale fashion that fits the bods and wallets of normal folk—not just leggy models. Some of the men's suits are particularly fine, but the children's collection may be best left alone. There's another tiny branch at Via Tornabuoni 81r.

FOR WOMEN   Loretta Caponi, Piazza Antinori 4r (© **055-213-668**), is world famous for her high-quality intimates and embroidered linens made the old-fashioned way. Under Belle Epoque ceilings are nightgowns of all types, bed and bath linens of the highest caliber, curtains, and feminine unmentionables. There's also a large section for the little ones in the back. Peek through the pebble-glassed doors to see the workshop.

STOCK HOUSES   To get your high fashion at bargain-basement prices, head to one of the branches of **Guardaroba/Stock House Grandi Firme.** The store at Borgo degli Albizi 78r (© **055-234-0271**) carries mainly the past season's models, while the Via dei Castellani 26r branch (© **055-294-853**) carries spring/summer remaindered collections, and the Via Verdi 28r (© **055-247-8250**) and Via Nazionale 38r (© **055-215-482**) store outfits from the past winter. **Stock House Il Giglio,** Via Borgo Ognissanti 86 (no phone), also carries big name labels at 50% to 60% off.

GIFTS & CRAFTS

Florentine traditional "mosaics" are actually works of inlaid stone called *pietre dure.* The creations of young Ilio de Filippis and his army of apprentices at **Pitti Mosaici,** Piazza Pitti 16r and 23–24r (© **055-282-127; www.pittimosaici.it**), reflect traditional techniques and artistry. Ilio's father was a *pietre dure* artist, and his grandfather was a sculptor. (The family workshop was founded in 1900.) Besides the pieces on display down the road toward the Arno at Via Guicciardini 80r and across the river at Lungarno Vespucci 36r, the firm will custom make works to your specifications.

Professore Agostino Dessi presides over the traditional Venetian Carnevale–style maskmaking at **Alice Atelier,** Via Faenza 72r (© **055-287-370**). All masks are made using papier-mâché, leather, and ceramics according to 17th-century techniques, hand-painted with tempera, touched up with gold and silver leaf, and polished with French lacquer.

JEWELRY

If you've got the financial solvency of a small country, the place to buy your baubles is the Ponte Vecchio, famous for its gold- and silversmiths since the 16th century. The craftsmanship at the stalls is usually of a very high quality, and so they seem to compete instead over who can charge the highest prices. A more moderately priced boutique is Milan-based **Mario Buccellati,** Via de' Tornabuoni 71r (✆ **055-239-6579**), which since 1919 has been making thick, heavy jewelry of high quality.

Florence is also a good place to root around for interesting costume jewelry. The audacious bijoux at **Angela Caputi,** Borgo San Jacopo 82r (✆ **055-212-972;** www.angelacaputi.com), aren't for the timid. Much of Angela's costume jewelry—from earrings and necklaces to brooches and now even a small clothing line—is at least oversize and bold and often pushes the flamboyance envelope.

LEATHER, ACCESSORIES & SHOES

It has always been a buyers' market for leather in Florence, but these days it's tough to sort out the jackets mass-produced for tourists from the high-quality artisan work. The most fun you'll have leather shopping is without a doubt at the outdoor stalls of the **San Lorenzo** market, even if the market is rife with mediocre goods (see "Markets," below). Never accept the first price they throw at you; sometimes you can bargain them down to almost half the original asking price. The shops below should guarantee you at least quality merchandise, but not the bargaining joys of the market. (See also "Fashion & Clothing," above.)

Anna, Piazza Pitti 38–41r (✆ **055-283-787**), is a fine store for handcrafted leather coats and clothing set in the remains of a 14th-century tower. You can also pick up discounted Versace purses and funky colorful Missioni sweaters. For the best of the leather, head down the stairs in the back where you'll find fur-collared coats, suede jackets, and supple pigskin vests. They'll do alterations and even full tailoring in 24 hours. **John F.,** Lungarno Corsini 2 (✆ **055-239-8985;** www.johnf.it), is a purveyor of high-quality leather goods as well as Missioni sweaters, Krizia purses, and Bettina bags.

More fun, but no less expensive, is to watch the artisans at work at the·**Scuola del Cuoio (Leather School) of Santa Croce.** You enter through Santa Croce church (right transept), Piazza Santa Croce 16, or on Via San Giuseppe 5r on Sunday morning (✆ **055-244-533** or 055-244-534; www.leatherschool.it). The very-fine-quality soft-leather merchandise isn't cheap.

In the imposing 13th-century Palazzo Spini-Feroni lording over Piazza Santa Trínita are the flagship store, museum, and home of **Ferragamo,** Via de' Tornabuoni 4–14r (✆ **055-292-123;** www.ferragamo.it). Salvatore Ferragamo was the man who shod Hollywood in its most glamorous age and raised footwear to an art form. View some of Ferragamo's funkier shoes in the second-floor museum (call ahead at ✆ **055-336-0456**) or slip on a pair yourself in the showrooms downstairs—if you think your wallet can take the shock.

If you prefer to buy right from the cobbler, head across the Arno to **Calzature Francesco da Firenze,** Via Santo Spirito 62r (✆ **055-212-428**), where handmade shoes run 80€ to 165€ ($92–$190), and you can hear them tap-tapping away on soles in the back room.

For more made-in-Florence accessorizing, head to **Madova Gloves,** Via Guicciardini 1r (✆ **055-239-6526;** www.madova.com). Gloves are all they do in this tiny shop, and they do them well. The grandchildren of the workshop's founders do a brisk business in brightly colored, supple leather gloves lined with cashmere and silk. Although they display a bit of everything at **Beltrami,** Via de' Tornabuoni 48r (© **055-287-779**), their forte is still beautiful well-built footwear, bags, briefcases, and luggage. Beltrami is based in Florence, so prices are as low here as you're going to find.

MARKETS

Haggling is accepted, and even expected, at most outdoor markets (but don't try it in stores). The queen of Florentine markets is the **San Lorenzo street market,** filling Piazza San Lorenzo, Via del Canto de' Nelli, Via dell'Ariento, and other side streets. It's a wildly chaotic and colorful array of hundreds of stands hawking T-shirts, silk scarves, marbleized paper, Gucci knockoffs, and lots and lots of leather. Many of the stalls are merely outlets for full-fledged stores hidden behind them. Haggling is tradition here, and though you'll find plenty of leather lemons, there are also great deals on truly high-quality leather and other goods—you just have to commit to half a day of picking through it all and fending off sales pitches. March through October, most stalls are open daily about 8am to 8pm (it varies with how business is doing); November through February, the market is closed Mondays and Sundays, except for the 2 weeks or so around Christmas, when it remains open daily.

Somewhere in the center of this capitalist whirlwind hides the indoor **Mercato Centrale food market** (between Via dell'Ariento and Piazza del Mercato Centrale). Downstairs you'll find meat, cheese, and dry goods. There's one stall devoted to tripe aficionados, a second piled high with *baccalà* (dried salt cod), and a good cheap eatery called **Nerbone** (p. 123). The upstairs is devoted to fruits and veggies—a cornucopia of fat eggplants, long yellow peppers, stacks of artichokes, and pepperoncini bunched into brilliant red bursts. In all, you couldn't ask for better picnic pickings. The market is open Monday through Saturday from 7am to 2pm and Saturday also 4 to 7:30pm.

As if two names weren't enough, the **Mercato Nuovo (Straw Market)** is also known as Mercato del Porcellino or Mercato del Cinghiale because of the bronze wild boar statue at one end, cast by Pietro Tacca in the 17th century after an antique original now in the Uffizi. Pet the well-polished porcellino's snout to ensure a return trip to Florence. Most of the straw stalls disappeared by the 1960s. These days, the loggia hawks mainly poor-quality leather purses, mediocre bijoux, souvenirs, and other tourist trinkets. Beware of pickpockets. In summer it's open daily around 9am to 8pm, but in winter it closes at 5pm and all day Sunday and Monday.

MUSIC

Although restrictions are ever tightening, Italy still remains one of the best places in Western Europe to get bootlegs. Quality, obviously, can vary drastically (most places will let you listen before you buy). Some of the more "reputable" pirate labels include Pluto, Great Dane, Bugsy, On Stage, Teddy Bear, Beech Marten, and Red Line. **Data Records,** Via dei Neri 15r (© **055-287-592**), is a hip place with a sassy funk attitude, knowledgeable staff, plenty of cutting-edge music (Italian and international), and scads of good bootlegs. They also run a more mainstream outlet, **Super Records** (© **055-234-9526;** www.superecords.com), in the pedestrian passage leading from Santa Maria Novella train station, with some of the best prices in town on first-run presses from major labels. Both are closed in August.

PAPER & JOURNALS

Giulio Giannini and Figlio, Piazza Pitti 36–37r (© **055-212-621;** www.giulio giannini.it), offers an expensive but quality selection of leather-bound notebooks, fine stationery, and the shop's specialty, objects garbed in decorative papers. This was one of the first stores to paste marbleized sheets onto desktop items, but its real trademark is objects sheathed in genuine 17th- to 19th-century manuscript and choir-book sheets. **Il Papiro,** Via dei Tavolini 13r (© **055-213-823;** www. madeinfirenze.it/papiro_e.htm), is now a modest Tuscan chain of jewel box–size shops specializing in marbled and patterned paper, as plain gift-wrap sheets or as a covering for everything from pens and journals to letter openers or full desk sets. There are several branches, including the head office at Via Cavour 55r (no phone) and shops at Piazza del Duomo 24r (no phone), Lungarno Acciaiuoli 42r (© **055-215-262**), and Piazza Rucellai 8r (© **055-211-652**).

Scriptorium, Via dei Servi 5–7r (© **055-211-804**), is my own journal supplier, a small shop that's one of the few fine stationery stores in Florence with very little marbleized paper. Come here for hand-sewn notebooks, journals, and photo albums made of thick paper—all bound in soft leather covers. With classical music or Gregorian chant playing in the background, you can also shop for calligraphy and signet wax sealing tools. There's a new branch in the Oltrarno at Piazza de' Pitti 6 (© **055-238-2272;** www.scriptoriumfirenze.com).

PRINTS

Little Bottega delle Stampe, Borgo San Jacopo 56r (© **055-295-396**), carries prints, historic maps, and engravings from the 1500s through the Liberty-style and Art Deco prints of the 1930s. You can dig out some Dürers here, as well as original Piranesis and plates from Diderot's 1700 Encyclopedia. There are Florence views from the 16th to 19th centuries, plus a fine collection of 18th-century French engravings.

TOYS

Since 1977, Florence's owner-operated branch of national chain **La Città del Sole,** Borgo Ognissanti 37r (© **055-219-345;** www.cittadelsole.it), has sold old-fashioned wooden brain teasers, construction kits, hand puppets, 3-D puzzles, science kits, and books. There's nary a video game in sight.

WINE & LIQUORS

The front room of the **Enoteca Alessi,** Via dell'Oche 27–31r (© **055-214-966;** www.enotecaalessi.it), sells boxed chocolates and other sweets, but in the back and in the large cellars, you can find everything from prime vintages to a simple-quality table wine. This large store, 2 blocks from the Duomo, also offers tastings. The **Enoteca Gambi Romano,** Borgo SS. Apostoli 21–23r (© **055-292-646**), is another central outlet for olive oil, vin santo, grappa, and (upstairs) lots of wine.

3 Florence After Dark

THE PERFORMING ARTS

Florence doesn't have the musical cachet or grand opera houses of Milan, Venice, or Rome, but there are two symphony orchestras and a fine music school in Fiesole. The city's public theaters are certainly respectable, and most major touring companies stop in town on their way through Italy. Get tickets to all cultural and musical events at the city's main clearinghouse, **Box Office,** Via Alamanni 39 (© **055-210-804;** www.boxoffice.it). In addition to tickets for year-round events of all genres, they handle the summertime Calcio in Costume folkloric festival and the Maggio Musicale.

Many concerts and recitals staged in major halls and private spaces across town are sponsored by the **Amici della Musica** (© **055-607-440** or 055-608-420; www.amicimusica.fi.it), so contact them to see what "hidden" concert might be on while you're in town. When Florentines really want a fine night out at the theater, they skip town and head to nearby Prato for the **Teatro Metastasio,** one of Italy's finest (see chapter 6 for more information).

CHURCH CONCERTS   Many Florentine churches fill the autumn with organ, choir, and chamber orchestra concerts, mainly of classical music. The tiny **Santa Maria de' Ricci** (© **055-215-044**) on Via del Corso seems always to have music wafting out of it; slipping inside to occupy a pew is occasionally free, but sometimes there's a small charge. Around the corner at Santa Margherita 7, the **Chiesa di Dante** (© **055-289-367**) puts on quality concerts of music for, and often played by, youths and children (tickets required). **The Florentine Chamber Orchestra,** Via E. Poggi 6 (© **055-783-374**), also runs an autumn season in the Orsanmichele; tickets are available at Box Office (see above) or at the door an hour before the 9pm shows.

CONCERT HALLS & OPERA   One of Italy's busiest stages, Florence's contemporary **Teatro Comunale,** Corso Italia 12 (© **055-213-535** or 055-211-158; www.maggiofiorentino.com), offers everything from symphonies to ballet to plays, opera, and concerts. The large main theater seats 2,000, with orchestra rows topped by horseshoe-shaped first and second galleries. Its smaller Piccolo Teatro seating 500 is rectangular, offering good sightlines from most any seat. The Teatro Comunale is the seat of the annual prestigious Maggio Musicale.

The **Teatro Verdi,** Via Ghibellina 99–101 (© **055-212-320** or 055-263-877; www.teatroverdi.com), is Florence's opera and ballet house, with the nice habit of staging Sunday-afternoon shows during the January-through-April season. **The Orchestra della Toscana** (© **055-280-670;** www.orchestradellatoscana.it) plays classical concerts here December through May. Like the Teatro Comunale, they do a bit of theater, but not of the caliber of La Pergola (see below).

THEATER   The biggest national and international touring companies stop in Florence's major playhouse, the **Teatro della Pergola,** Via della Pergola 12 (© **055-226-4335;** www.pergola.firenze.it). La Pergola is the city's chief purveyor of classical and classic plays from the Greeks and Shakespeare through Pirandello, Samuel Beckett, and Italian modern playwrights. Performances are professional and of high quality, if not always terribly innovative (and, of course, all in Italian).

THE CLUB & MUSIC SCENES

Italian clubs are rather cliquey—people usually go in groups to hang out and dance only with one another. There's plenty of flesh showing, but no meat market. Singles hoping to find random dance partners will often be disappointed.

LIVE MUSIC   For live bands you can dance to in the center, head to **Dolce Zucchero,** Via dei Pandolfini 36–38r (© **055-247-7894**). "Sweet Sugar" is one of the better recent efforts to spice up Florence's nightlife and is popular with all ages. Under high ceilings are a long bar and a small dance floor with a stage for the nightly live musicians, usually a fairly talented cover act cranking out American and Italian dance songs for the packed crowd.

DANCE CLUBS & NIGHTCLUBS   Florence's clubs have a "minimum consumption" charge of 10€ to 16€ ($12–$18). The big hit of 2002 was **Universale,**

Cafe Culture

Florence no longer has a glitterati or intellectuals' cafe scene, and when it did—from the late-19th-century Italian *Risorgimento* era through the *dolce vita* of the 1950s—it was basically copying the idea from Paris. Although they're often overpriced tourist spots today, Florence's high-toned cafes are fine if you want designer pastries and hot cappuccino served to you while you sit on a piazza and people-watch.

At the refined, wood-paneled, stucco-ceilinged, and very expensive 1733 cafe **Gilli**, Piazza della Repubblica 36–39r/Via Roma 1r (© 055-213-896), tourists gather to sit with the ghosts of Italy's *Risorgimento*, when the cafe became an important meeting place of the heroes and thinkers of the unification movement from the 1850 to the 1870s. The red-jacketed waiters at **Giubbe Rosse**, Piazza della Repubblica 13–14r (© 055-212-280), must have been popular during the 19th-century glory days of Garibaldi's red-shirt soldiers. This was once a meeting place of the Florentine futurists, but aside from organized literary encounters on Wednesdays, today, it too is mainly a tourists' cafe with ridiculous prices.

Once full of history and now mainly full of tourists, **Rivoire**, Piazza della Signoria/Via Vacchereccia 5r (© 055-214-412), has a chunk of prime real estate on Piazza della Signoria. Smartly dressed waiters serve smartly priced sandwiches to cappuccino-sipping patrons. **Giacosa**, Via de' Tornabuoni 83r (© 055-239-6226), was a 19th-century hangout for literati and intellectual clutches as elegant as any of the others, but today it's really more of a high-class bar, with no outside tables. It makes a good shopping break, though, with panini, pastries, cold salads, and hot pasta dishes.

Via Pisana 77r (© **055-221-122;** www.universalefirenze.it), housed in a converted 1940s cinema and successfully managing to draw everyone from folks in their early 20s to those pushing 50 (how they manage to keep collegians cutting loose from running into their young-at-heart parents here is a miracle). From 8pm it's a popular restaurant in the balcony and a pizzeria on the main floor. Around 11pm a live band takes the main floor stage for an hour or so, after which a DJ comes on board to conduct the disco until 3am.

In the city center near Santa Croce, **Full-Up,** Via della Vigna Vecchia 25r (© **055-293-006**), is a long-enduring disco/piano bar that's one of the top (and more restrained) dance spaces in Florence for the postcollegiate set. There are plenty of theme evenings (revival, samba, punk), so call to find out what's on.

Forever known as Yab Yum but recently reincarnated with a new attitude is **Yab,** Via Sassetti 5r (© **055-215-160**), just behind the main post office on Piazza della Repubblica. This dance club for 20-somethings is a perennial favorite, a relic of a 1980s disco complete with rope line and surly bouncers.

A balanced combination of visitors and Italians—teenagers, students, and an under-30 crowd—fill the two-floor **Space Electronic**, Via Palazzuolo 37 (© **055-293-082**). On the first floor are a video karaoke bar, a pub, an American-style bar, and a conversation area. Head upstairs for the dance floor with laser lights and a flying space capsule hovering above.

PUBS, BARS & WINE BARS

PUBS & BARS There's an unsurprising degree of similarity among Florence's half dozen **Irish-style pubs** dark, woody interiors usually with several back rooms and plenty of smoke; and a crowd (stuffed to the gills on weekends) of students and 20- and 30-something Americans and Brits along with their Italian counterparts. The better ones are the Florence branch of the successful Italian chain **Fiddler's Elbow,** Piazza Santa Maria Novella 7r (© **055-215-056**); **The Old Stove,** Via Pellicceria 4r (© **055-284-640**), just down from Piazza della Repubblica; and, under the same management, **The Lion's Fountain,** Borgo Albizi 34r (© **055-234-4412**), on the tiny but lively Piazza San Pier Maggiore near Santa Croce. You'll find plenty of others around town—they pop up like mushrooms these days, but often disappear just as quickly.

Red Garter, Via de' Benci 33r (© **055-234-4904**), is a speakeasy attracting a 20s-to-30s crowd of Italians and some Americans, Australians, and English. There's a small bi-level theater room in the back with live music some nights—once when I stopped in, it was a one-man band with a synth kit playing American and Italian rock hits with some blues mixed in.

WINE BARS The most traditional wine bars are called *fiaschetterie,* after the word for a flask of chianti. They tend to be hole-in-the-wall joints serving sandwiches or simple food along with glasses filled to the brim—usually with a house wine, though finer vintages are often available. The best are listed in chapter 3 under "Where to Dine," including **I Fratellini,** Via dei Cimatori 38r (© **055-239-6096**); **Antico Noè,** off Piazza S. Pier Maggiore (© **055-234-0838**); and **La Mescita,** Via degli Alfani 70r (© **347-795-1604**). There's also a traditional wine shop in the Oltrarno called simply **La Fiaschetteria,** Via de' Serragli 47r (© **055-287-420**), which, like many, doubles as a small locals' wine bar.

A more high-toned spot is the **Cantinetta Antinori,** Piazza Antinori 3 (© **055-292-234**), also listed in chapter 3. It's housed in the palace headquarters of the Antinori wine empire at the top of Florence's main fashion drag, Via Tornabuoni. For a trendier wine bar focusing on handpicked labels offered with plates of cheese and other snacks, head to the Oltrarno and a real oenophile's hangout, **Il Volpe e L'Uva,** Piazza de' Rossi, behind Piazza Santa Felícita off Via Guicciardini (© **055-239-8132**). The Avuris, who run the Hotel Torre Guelfa (p. 107), have recently opened a great little wine bar right across from the Pitti Palace called **Pitti Gola e Cantina,** Piazza Pitti 16 (© **055-212-704**), with glasses of wine from 4€ to 9€ ($4.60–$10) to help unwind from a day of museums. They also have light dishes, meat and cheese platters, and cakes for 7€ to 15€ ($8.05–$17).

THE GAY & LESBIAN SCENE

The gay nightlife scene in Florence isn't much, and for lesbians it's pretty much just the Thursday through Saturday nights mixed gay-and-lesbian party at the **Flamingo Bar,** Via Pandolfini 26r (© **055-243-356**), whereas the rest of the week it's men only. The main bar is downstairs, where an international gay crowd shows up in everything from jeans and tees to full leather. Upstairs are a lounge and a theater showing videos and the occasional show. September through June, the ground floor becomes a dance floor Friday and Saturday nights pumping out commercial pop and lots of disco. The bar is open Sunday through Thursday from 10pm to 4am (until 6am Fri–Sat).

Florence's dark room is the **Crisco Bar,** Via Sant'Egidio 43r east of the Duomo (© **055-248-0580;** www.crisco.it), for men only. Its 18th-century building contains a bar and a dance floor open Wednesday through Monday from 9pm to 3am (until 5am weekends). They also have male strippers and drag shows some weekends.

The only real gay dance floor of note is at the **Tabasco Bar,** Piazza Santa Cecilia 3r (© **055-213-000;** www.tabascogay.it). Italy's first gay disco attracts crowds of men (mostly in their 20s and 30s) from all over the country. The music is techno, disco, and retro rock, but entertainment offerings also include cabaret, art shows, and the occasional transvestite comedy. In summer, foreigners arrive in droves. It's open Sunday through Thursday from 10pm to 3 or 4am (until 6am Fri and Sat). Tuesday, Friday, and Saturday it's all disco; Wednesday is leather night. They've also recently opened up a gay cruising bar called **Silver Stud,** Via della Fornace 9 (© **055-688-466**).

Cover charges vary, but it's generally 10€ ($12) or less and often includes the first drink.

4 A Side Trip to Fiesole: A Perfect Summer Escape

Although it's only a city bus ride away from Florence, Fiesole is very proud of its status as an independent municipality. In fact, this hilltop village high in the wash of green above Florence predates that city in the valley by centuries.

An Etruscan colony from Arezzo probably founded a town here in the 6th century B.C. on the site of a Bronze Age settlement. By the time Caesar set up a Roman retirement colony on the banks of the Arno below, Faesulae was the most important Etruscan center in the region. It butted heads with the upstart Fiorentina in the valley almost right from the start. Although it eventually became a Roman town, building a theater and adopting Roman customs, it always retained a bit of the Etruscan otherness that has kept it different from Florence throughout the ages. Following the requisite barbarian invasions, it became part of Florence's administrative district in the 9th century, yet continued to struggle for self-government. Medieval Florence put an end to it all in 1125 when it viciously attacked Fiesole and razed the entire city, save the cathedral and bishop's palace.

Becoming an irrelevant footnote to Florentine history has actually aided Fiesole in the end. Modern upper-middle-class Florentines have decided it's posh to buy an old villa on the hillside leading up to the town and maintain the villa's extensive gardens. This means that the oasis of cultivated greenery separating Florence from Fiesole has remained. Even with Florence so close by, Fiesole endures as a Tuscan small town to this day, entirely removed from the city at its feet and hence the perfect escape from summertime crowds. It stays cool all summer long, and sitting at the outside tables of a cafe on Piazza Mino, sipping an iced cappuccino, can make the lines at the Uffizi and pedestrian traffic jam of the streets around the Duomo seem very distant indeed.

ESSENTIALS

GETTING THERE   Take bus no. 7 from Florence, which after a scenic ride through the greenery above Florence, lets you off in the town's main square, Piazza Mino.

VISITOR INFORMATION   The **tourist office** is at Piazza Mino 36–37 (© **055-598-720;** fax 055-598-822; www.comune.fiesole.fi.it; it's open Mon–Sat 8:30am–1:30pm). If it's closed, as it sometimes is from October to Easter, there's

A Countryside Stroll in the City

Take the afternoon to **walk back down to Florence from Fiesole** 🌟. As you exit Piazza Mino, just as the main road makes its big downward curve to the left, look straight ahead where Via Vecchia Fiesolana, the narrow old road linking the two cities, forks right. It's steep, winding, and banked by high walls along many parts over which occasionally peek olive trees or more exotic plantings from the private gardens planted by rich eccentrics of the 18th century. A few of these gardens are open to the public; free admission. Among them are the **Villa Medici** (📞 **800-414-240**; open Mon–Fri 8:15am–1pm—you can just drop by, but it's best to call ahead), the first major entrance on your left; and the **Villa Le Balze** (📞 **055-59-208**; call Mon–Fri 9am–5pm to reserve a visit) at no. 26, now owned by Georgetown University. Every so often along the road is a break in the cypress where a Florence panorama opens before you—a scene you share only with yourself and the occasional passing nun.

another small office (📞 **055-596-1257**) just to the left inside the 14th-century Palazzo Pretorio—still the town hall whose loggia is covered in the coats of arms of Fiesole's past *podestà*—at no. 26 at the top of the square.

FESTIVALS & MARKETS   Fiesole's biggest event is cultural: Two months of music, ballet, film, and theater from late June to August called the **Estate Fiesolana** 🌟. Cooling off from the Florentine heat has never been more pleasant as you sit back under the stars in the restored 1st-century A.D. Roman theater and listen to Mozart and Verdi. You can get information and tickets in Florence at Box Office (see "Florence After Dark," earlier in this chapter) or at the Roman Theater itself after 4:30pm the day of the show. The **Festa di San Romulo** on July 6 brings processions and partying all day and fireworks in the evening. Call 📞 **055-59-611** for info. There's a market every Saturday in Piazza Mino.

EXPLORING FIESOLE

Fiesole's two museums and its Teatro Romano archaeological site keep the same hours and use a single admission ticket, costing 6.50€ ($7.50) adults and 4.50€ ($5.20) students and over 65s. They all open Easter through October daily from 9:30am to 7pm, in winter Wednesday through Monday from 9:30am to 5pm. For more, call 📞 **055-59-118** or visit www.fiesolemusei.it.

Cattedrale   The cathedral's 13th-century **bell tower,** with its comically over-size crenellations added in the 18th century, can be spotted for miles around. The cathedral is a pleasingly plain medieval church, built in 1028 using columns from nearby Roman buildings. There are coin-op lights to illuminate the nave and presbytery and another set for the half-submerged crypt, so bring pocket change. The **crypt** is supported by slender columns with primitive carvings on the capitals. The remains of St. Romolo, Fiesole's patron, reside under the altar, and the 15th-century lunette frescoes tell his story. There's a spot near the front of the crypt where you can see through the floor to a bit of Roman road and column bases, discovered during restoration in the early 1990s.

Piazzetta della Cattedrale/Piazza Mino. No phone. Free admission. Daily 9am–noon and 3–6pm. Bus: 7.

Teatro Romano (Roman Theater & Archaeological Museum) ⟨★★⟩ If you're in the Florence area during the summertime Estate Fiesolana music concerts, by all means try to get a ticket for a night of music under the stars in this 1st-century B.C. **Roman Theater.** The *cavea,* of which the right half is original and the left rebuilt in the 19th century when this area was first excavated, seats 3,000. This archaeological area is romantically overgrown with grasses, amid which sit sections of column, broken friezes, and other remnants of architectural elements. A grove of olive trees grows in the center. Beyond the theater to the right, recognizable by its three rebuilt arches, are the remains of the 1st-century A.D. **baths.** Near the arches is a little cement balcony over the far edge of the archaeological park. From it, you get a good look at the best stretch that remains of the 4th-century B.C. **Etruscan city walls.** At the other end of the park from the baths are the floor and steps of a 1st-century B.C. **Roman Temple** built on top of a 4th-century B.C. Etruscan one. To the left are some oblong **Lombard tombs** from the 7th century A.D. when this was a Gothic necropolis.

Among the collections in the **Museum,** recently reopened after a prolonged rearrangement, are the bronze "she-wolf," a fragment of the back of what was probably a statue of a lion, lots of Etruscan urns and Roman architectural fragments, and Bronze Age remains found atop the hill now occupied by San Francesco. The Constantini collection of beautiful Greek vases includes significant works from Greek colonies in Apulia that span the 8th to 4th centuries B.C., as well as many red- and black-figure vases and amphorae, 7th-century B.C. Corinthian vases, and some black Bucchero ware.

Via Portigiani 1. ⟨C⟩ 055-59-118. www.fiesolemusei.it. For admission and hours, see above.

Museo Bandini This modest museum to the left of the Roman Theater entrance has a good small collection of 13th- to 15th-century Florentine paintings arranged chronologically. There are works by the likes of Bernardo Daddi, Taddeo and Agnolo Gaddi, Nardo di Cione, Bicci di Lorenzo, and Neri di Bicci, plus a pair of altar doors by the bottega of Filippino Lippi.

Via Duprè 1. ⟨C⟩ 055-59-118. www.fiesolemusei.it. For admission and hours, see above.

San Francesco The road up here is intimidating, rising steeply to a sharp bend, which you round only to discover you're not even near the end. You can take a break halfway up in the small ilex-planted **panoramic gardens** ⟨★★⟩, which offer a postcard view of Florence. This garden is called the Park of Remembrance, and there's an odd, dangerously sharp-looking modern memorial set up near the edge in honor of the three *carabinieri* who laid down their lives before a Nazi firing squad in exchange for the safety of Fiesole civilians.

At the top of the hill, the ancient focal point of the Etruscan and Roman cities, are the church and convent of **San Francesco.** The 14th-century church has been largely overhauled, but at the end of a small nave hung with baroque canvases is a fine *Crucifixion and Saints* altarpiece by Neri di Bicci. Off the cloisters is a quirky but interesting little archaeological/ethnographic museum.

Via San Francesco (off Piazza Mino). ⟨C⟩ 055-59-175. Free admission. Church daily 8am–noon and 3–6pm. Museum Mon–Sat 10am–12pm and 3–6pm; Sun 9–11am and 3–6pm (until 7pm daily in summer). Bus: 7.

EN ROUTE FROM FLORENCE TO FIESOLE

San Domenico ⟨★⟩ Halfway between Fiesole and Florence's outskirts, this crossroads hamlet grew around two religious buildings: the **Badia** and the 15th-century **church and convent of San Domenico.** Soon after the convent opened, one Giovanni da Fiesole came knocking on the door wanting to put on the Dominican habit, take his vows, and start painting altarpieces. He moved along with many other friars to San Marco in Florence a little later, and we now know him as Fra' Angelico. He did leave his old convent a few works, such as a beautiful *Crucifixion* (1430) and a detached *Madonna and Child* in the Chapter House. (Ring at no. 4, to the right of the church, between 9am and noon, the earlier the better.)

Inside the church are *pietra serena*–accented chapels. Verrocchio's student Lorenzo di Credi painted the *Baptism of Christ* in the second chapel on the right. In the first chapel on the left is a rich **Madonna and Saints** ✦ by Fra' Angelico, recently restored to its fully ripe colors and modeling. (There's a light switch on the right.) Lorenzo di Credi filled in the background landscape in 1501.

Via San Domenico. No phone. http://sandomenicofiesole.op.org. Free admission. Daily 8am–noon and 3:30–5pm. Bus: 7.

5

The Chianti, Siena & the Western Hill Towns

Siena, a great banking and textile rival of Florence in the Middle Ages, slumbered through the Renaissance. As a result, it has preserved dozens of Gothic palaces and churches, and its museums are filled with a distinctive and decorative style of painting. Many visitors zip south from Florence to Siena on the train or along the autostrada and end up missing one of Tuscany's most picturesque regions: the castle-topped hills and Arcadian vineyards of the **Chianti,** Italy's most famous wine district.

Siena is also the center of hill town territory, a landscape of small mountains and river-fed valleys watched over by stony medieval towns perched on the taller peaks. (Those south of Siena are covered in chapter 8.) West of the city, in some of the tallest mountains of central Tuscany, hide two of the more famous hill towns: **San Gimignano** still sprouts more than a dozen medieval towers, and **Volterra** is an ancient Etruscan center and modern workshop of alabaster artisans. Nearby, but seldom visited, **Massa Marittima** makes a great excursion off the beaten path into a city from the Dark Ages.

1 Wine Tasting in the Chianti

You can find many people's idea of earthly paradise in the 167 sq. km (65 sq. miles) plot of land between Florence and Siena, known as the Chianti. In fact, the British have such a history of buying up old farmhouses and settling here it's often referred to as Chiantishire. It isn't hard to see why they come—the tall, closely gathered hills are capped by ancient cities and medieval castles, and the stream-fed valleys are dotted with expanding market towns. All is often shrouded in a light mist that renders the blue-gray distance inscrutable and cloaks the hills in a mysterious rural magic. Many of the rolling slopes are planted with olive groves that shimmer dark green and dusty silver, but some 4,000 hectares (10,000 acres) are blanketed with marching vines. The grapes that grow from these gnarled woody question marks form the primary capital in the region's bacchanalian economy.

This is the world's definitive wine region, in both history and spirit; these hills have been an enological center for several thousand years. In fact, one local grape, the Canaiolo nero—one of the varietals that traditionally goes into Chianti Classico—was known to the ancients as the "Etruscan grape." The name Chianti, probably derived from that of the local noble Etruscan family Clantes, has been used to describe the hills between Florence and Siena for centuries, but it wasn't until the mid–13th century that Florence created the **Lega del Chianti** to unite the region's three most important centers—Castellina, Radda, and Gaiole—which chose the black rooster as their symbol. By 1404 the red wine long produced here was being called chianti as well, and in 1716 a grand ducal

The Chianti Region

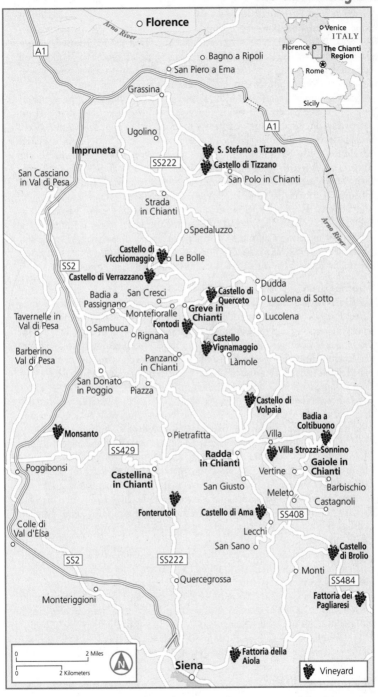

Florence

Arno River

A1

Bagno a Ripoli

San Piero a Ema

Grassina

Ugolino

Impruneta

SS222

San Casciano
in Val di Pesa

Strada
in Chianti

Spedaluzzo

Castello di
Vicchiomaggio

Le Bolle

SS2

Castello di Verrazzano

Badia a
Passignano

San Cresci

Montefioralle

Tavernelle in
Val di Pesa

Sambuca

Rignana

Fontodi

Barberino
Val di Pesa

Panzano
in Chianti

San Donato
in Poggio

Piazza

Monsanto

Poggibonsi

SS429

Castellina
in Chianti

Pietrafitta

Radda
in Chianti

Fonterutoli

Castello di Ama

Colle di
Val d'Elsa

SS2

SS222

Quercegrossa

Monteriggioni

S. Stefano a Tizzano

Castello di Tizzano

San Polo in Chianti

A1

Arno River

Castello di
Querceto

Dudda

Lucolena di Sotto

Greve in
Chianti

Lucolena

Castello
Vignamaggio

Làmole

Castello di
Volpaia

Badia a
Coltibuono

Villa

Villa Strozzi-Sonnino

Vertine

Gaiole in
Chianti

San Giusto

Meleto

Barbischio

Castagnoli

SS408

Lecchi

San Sano

Castello
di Brolio

Monti

SS484

Fattoria dei
Pagliaresi

Fattoria della
Aiola

Siena

0   2 Miles

0   2 Kilometers

N

Vineyard

The Chianti Region

Venice
ITALY

Florence

Rome

Sicily

193

decree defined the boundaries of the Chianti and laid down general rules for its wine production, making it the world's first officially designated wine-producing area. In the 19th century, one vintner, the "Iron Baron" Ricasoli, experimented with varietals using the sangiovese grape as his base. Working off centuries of refinement, he eventually came up with the perfect balance of grapes that became the unofficial standard for all chianti.

Soon the title "chianti" was being taken in vain by hundreds of poor-quality, vino-producing hacks, both within the region and from areas far flung, and the international reputation of the wine was besmirched. To fight against this, Greve and Castelnuovo Berardenga joined the original Lega cities and formed the **Consorzio del Gallo Nero** in 1924, reviving the old black rooster as their seal. The *consorzio* (still active—their members produce about 80% of the Chianti Classico bottled) pressed for laws regulating the quality of chianti wines and restricting the Chianti Classico name to their production zone. When Italy devised its DOC and DOCG laws in the 1960s, chianti was one of the first to be defined as DOCG, guaranteeing its quality as one of the top wines in the country. Today, of the 100 sq. km (39 sq. miles.) of vineyards in the hills between Florence and Siena, some 6,972 hectares (17,430 acres) are devoted to the grapes that will eventually become Chianti Classico and carry the seal of the black rooster.

ESSENTIALS

GETTING AROUND   The only way to explore the Chianti effectively is to **drive.** But know that many of the roads off the major SS222 (aka the Chiantigiana) are unpaved and sometimes heavily potholed. **Biking** through the Chianti can be one of Tuscany's most rewarding and scenic strenuous workouts. See "Special-Interest Vacations" in chapter 2 for tour companies or go on your own by renting a bike in Greve at **Ramuzzi Marco,** Viale Falsettacci 6 (© **055-853-037;** turn right at tourist office; it's down on the left); the cost is 13€ to 16€ ($15–$18) per day (scooters 16€–23€/$18–$26 per half day or 26€–39€/$30–$45 per full day), though the daily price goes down the longer you keep it. The region's low mountains and stands of ancient forest are also excellent for **hiking.**

For exploring by any means, you'll need a good map; both the huge Edizione Multigrafic (EMG) 1:50,000 map and the smaller free 1:70,000 sheet called "Il Chianti" put out by the Florentine tourist board are excellent for back road exploring. (***Drivers be warned:*** These maps do, on occasion, mark dry streambeds as "unpaved roads.") I'd have to give the edge to the free map for detailed accuracy, but reading it involves a lot more squinting than with the EMG sheet, which is widely available in bookshops and souvenir stores in the Chianti, Siena, and Florence.

You can visit the major towns by **bus,** but be prepared to stay a while until the next ride comes along. **SITA** (© **055-214-721;** www.sita-on-line.it) from Florence services Strada (40 min. from Florence), Greve (65 min.), Panzano (75 min.), Radda or Castellina (95 min.), and Gaiole (2 hr.); it leaves at least hourly for stops up through Greve and Panzano and at least one to three times a day all the way through to Gaiole. About eight (Mon–Sat) **Tra-in** buses (© **0577-204-111;** www.comune.siena.it/train) from Siena hit Radda, Gaiole, and Castellina; and, you can get to Impruneta with a **CAP** bus (© **055-214-637;** www.capautolinee.it) from Florence.

VISITOR INFORMATION   You can pick up some information on the Chianti at the **Florence tourist office** (see "Essentials" in chapter 3 for details) or the **Siena tourist office** (see "Siena: A Taste of the Tuscan Middle Ages," later in this chapter). The unofficial capital of the area is Greve in Chianti, and its **tourist office** (© **055-854-6287;** fax 055-854-4149), is in a modern little shack on the right just as you arrive in Greve coming from the north, makes an effort to provide some Chianti-wide info. From Easter to October, it's open Monday through Friday from 10am to 1pm and 3 to 7pm, Saturday from 10am to 1pm. In winter, it might keep shorter hours. You can also try **www.chianti.it/turismo,** a site with links to many hotels and restaurants in the area.

WINE FESTIVALS   The second weekend in September, Greve in Chianti hosts the main annual **Rassegna del Chianti Classico,** a bacchanalia festival of food and dancing that showcases wine from all the region's producers. Call © **055-853-295** for more information. **Radda** sponsors its own **wine festival** the last weekend in May, where buying the commemorative glass lets you sample 50 to 60 wines for free. There's also a free concert, snacks, and a communal grappa tasting.

ON THE ROAD IN THE FLORENTINE CHIANTI
EN ROUTE TO GREVE

Cross Florence's eastern Ponte San Niccolò and follow the signs from Piazza Ferrucci on the other side toward Grassina and the SS222 Chiantigiana. At **Ponte a Ema,** take a 1km (½-mile) detour to the left to the **Oratorio di Santa Caterina dell'Antella,** which has a wall fresco cycle of the *Life of St. Catherine* (1390) by Spinello Aretino. The apse frescoes are also of St. Catherine and were painted by the "Master of Barberino" around 1360.

Continuing on to **Grassina,** you'll find a side road leading 9km (6 miles) to terra-cotta-producing **Impruneta** (tourist info: © **055-231-3729**). The Collegiata church on the main piazza was restored to its Renaissance appearance after World War II bomb damage. On the right aisle are some good baroque works—*Martyrdom of St. Lawrence* by Cristofano Allori, *Birth of the Virgin* by Il Passignano, and a Giambologna bronze *Crucifix* in the chapel. The most revered bits are kept in a pair of chapels designed by Michelozzo and decorated with excellent glazed terra cottas by Luca della Robbia. Another byroad swings back onto the Chiantigiana at Santa Caterina. South on the SS222 takes you through **Strada in Chianti,** where a Donatello-school crucifix rests in the church of San Cristofano.

At the bend in the road called Le Bolle is a right turnoff for **Vicchiomaggio** ✦ (© **055-854-079;** fax 055-853-911; www.vicchiomaggio.it). This A.D. 957 Lombard fortress was modified in the 15th century and is today one of the best preserved of the typical Chianti castles. Its estate, under British ownership, produces well-regarded wines, including Ripa delle More, a sangiovese/cabernet sauvignon whose 1997 vintage won "three glasses" from Gambero Rosso (the Italian oenological equivalent of two Michelin stars). You can taste for free at the roadside Cantinetta San Jacopo wine shop (on the SS222 right at the turnoff for the castle) daily from 9am to 12:30pm and 2:30 to 6:30pm (as late as 7:30pm in summer). Sadly, visits to the cellars, parts of which date to the 10th century, are now limited only to groups, though it's worth the short drive up here just to look at the castle exterior and for the countryside views. They do, however, offer cooking courses (anywhere from 1 hr. or 2 hr. to several days) and rent rooms (see "Where to Stay in the Florentine Chianti," below).

A bit farther along on the right is the turnoff for the **Castello di Verrazzano** ✦✦ (© **055-854-243** or 055-290-684; fax 055-854-241; www.verrazzano.com), the 12th-century seat of the Verrazzano family. Young Giovanni Verrazzano, born here in 1485, became restless with viticultural life and sailed out of the Chianti to discover New York. The estate has been making wine at least since 1170, and you can sample it Monday through Friday from 8am to 6pm. Their 100% sangiovese is called Sasello, while the "Bottiglia Particolare" ("Particular Bottle") is 70% sangiovese/30% cab. Tours of the gardens and cellars run Monday through Friday starting at 11am (lasting until 3pm); book ahead at least a day in advance, a week or more in advance in high season (May and June especially). The cost is 10€ ($12) for a tour and tasting of three wines, and 32€ ($37) if you take the light lunch as well (you'll get a few more wines, too). On weekends, you can buy the wine at the small stand on SS222 (© **055-853-211**).

GREVE IN CHIANTI ✦✦
Throughout the Dark Ages and Middle Ages, the Chianti castles and their heavily fortified princelings ruled the patchwork of fiefdoms that made up this area. As alliances sweetened castle-to-castle relations in the later Middle Ages, trade began flowing. Valley crossroads became market towns; and one such town began growing along the tiny river Greve in the 13th or 14th century. As trade became increasingly important, so did that market town. Today, as Greve in Chianti, the oversize village is the center of the wine trade and the unofficial capital of Chianti.

The central **Piazza Matteotti** is a rough triangle surrounded by a mismatched patchwork arcade—each merchant had to build the stretch in front of his own shop. The statue in the center is of the intrepid **Giovanni Verrazzano,** and the narrow end of the piazza spills into the tiny **Piazzetta Santa Croce,** whose pretty little church houses an *Annunciation* by Bicci di Lorenzo and a 13th-century triptych.

Greve is the host of Chianti's annual September wine fair, and there are, naturally, dozens of wine shops in town. Some of the better ones are the **Bottega del Chianti Classico,** Via Cesare Battisti 2–4 (© **055-853-631;** www.chianticlassico shop.com), and the **Enoteca del Chianti Classico,** Piazzetta Santa Croce 8 (© **055-853-297**). At Piazza Matteotti 69–71 is one of Italy's most famous butchers, **Macelleria Falorni** (© **055-854-363;** www.falorni.it), established in 1700 and still a cornucopia of hanging prosciutti and hundreds of other cured meats, along with a decent wine selection. For **visitor information,** see the beginning of this chapter.

NEAR GREVE
One kilometer (half-mile) east of (and almost as high above) Greve perches the solid stone 14th-century medieval hamlet of **(Castello di) Montefioralle** ✦, where the circular main street and enticing alleyways have only a few electric cables to remind you you're still in the 21st century. Don't miss the prettily isolated 10th-century Pieve di San Cresci, located outside the walls.

The road beyond Montefioralle continues over several miles of winding, often potholed dirt roads to the **Badia a Passignano** ✦ (© **055-807-1622**), dramatically situated amid a cypress grove atop its vineyards and olive groves. The monastery was established in 1049 by Benedictine St. Giovanni Gualberto, who founded the Vallombrosan order. Gualberto died here in 1073 and is buried in what was originally the small Romanesque church of San Michele. The church is the meeting spot for tours of the rest of the monastery that leave Sundays around 3pm. The tour's highlight is the Ghirlandaio brothers' (Davide and Domenico) fresco of the *Last Supper* (1476) in the refectory, though it's hard to ignore the attraction of the kitchen with its massive fireplace and dozens upon dozens of Bundt cake pans nailed to the walls. If you show up Monday through Friday when the monastery is closed, you can visit the **osteria** (© **055-807-1278**) to buy the wines produced by the Badia's vineyards (owned by the powerful and well-regarded Antinori empire) and tour their cellars.

A Vino Break

The **Enoteca Baldi,** Piazza Bucciarelli 25, on the main traffic triangle at the Chiantigiana (© **055-852-843**), is an excellent wine shop cum tasting spot offering snacks, a dart board, and good vintages of Chianti Classico, vin santo, and other Tuscan wines, grappe, and olive oils.

South of Greve, the SS222 takes you past the left turn for **Villa Vignamaggio** ★★ (© **055-854-661;** fax 055-854-4468; www.vignamaggio.com), a russet-orange villa surrounded by cypress and elegant gardens that might seem suspiciously similar to Signor Leonato's home in the 1993 movie *Much Ado About Nothing.* Kenneth Branagh's choice of movie sets wasn't the first time this 14th- or 15th-century villa garnered fame: Lisa Gherardini, who grew up to pose for Leonardo da Vinci's *Mona Lisa,* was born here in 1479. The estate's wine was famous in the past and in 1404 became the first red wine of these hills to be referred to as "Chianti" in written record. Long derelict in reputation, Vignamaggio wines have been stunningly revived by the new owners, who have made it one of the top vineyards in the region. Book ahead at least 1 week in advance and you can tour the cellar and ornate gardens Tuesdays and Thursdays and sample five wines with simple snacks for 35€ ($40). They also rent rooms (see "Where to Stay in the Florentine Chianti," below).

The Chiantigiana next cuts through the town of **Panzano in Chianti** ★; the tourist office is **InfoChianti,** Via Chiantigiana 6 (© **055-852-933;** www.infochianti.com; Tues–Fri 10am–1pm and 3–7pm, Sat 10am–12:30pm and 3:30–7:30pm, Sun 10am–1pm). The town is known for its embroidery and for another famed butcher, **Antica Macelleria Cecchini,** Via XX Luglio 11 (© **055-852-020**), where Dario Cecchini loves to entertain visitors with classical music and tastes of his products. (Something of a local character, Dario has been featured on more than one TV program in Italy; he held a large, well-publicized mock funeral for the *bistecca fiorentina* on the day it was temporarily outlawed in 2001 during Europe's mad cow disease outbreaks.)

Just south of town is the turnoff for the Romanesque **Pieve di San Leolino.** Beyond the 16th-century portico, this simple church conserves several 14th- and 15th-century Sienese altarpieces, including a *Madonna with Sts. Peter and Paul* (1260–80) attributed to Meliore di Jacopo on the left aisle and a pretty little brick-columned courtyard off the right aisle. The SS222 continues south toward Castellina in Chianti (see "On the Road in the Sienese Chianti," below).

WHERE TO STAY IN THE FLORENTINE CHIANTI

Besides the choices below, the **Castello Vicchiomaggio** wine estate (© **055-854-079;** fax 055-853-911; www.vicchiomaggio.it), just north of Greve, offers seven basic self-catering apartments in a National Monument Renaissance castle. Each sleeps two to six and has a kitchenette, TV, hair dryer, iron, and safe. Most have a countryside view, and while there are no phones, there is a pool on a panoramic terrace. Prices start at 100€ ($115) per night for two people. During high season, they often require a 1-week minimum stay.

March through November, **Castello di Verrazzano** (© **055-853-211;** fax 055-854-241; www.verrazzano.com) also rents seven double rooms, breakfast included, at 77€ ($89) for one person, 103€ ($118) for two people, and 129€ ($148) for three people. Two apartments with kitchenette are available; one, for two people, is 103€ ($118), while the apartment for four people is 129€ ($148).

The apartments require a stay of at least 3 nights. All units have TV and access to the gardens.

Hotel Giovanni da Verrazzano The Verrazzano hotel/restaurant sits across from its namesake's statue on Greve's triangular central piazza. The rooms are on the smallish side, the furnishings functional but nice, with painted wrought-iron bed frames with firm mattresses, dark wood furniture, terra-cotta floors, spotless bathrooms installed in 2001, and a handful of wood-beamed ceilings. Those on the front overlook the mismatched arcades of the piazza, while the back rooms have tiny terraces with late-morning sun, potted plants, and a view over lichen-spotted roof tiles to the Chianti hills. The four-sleeper in the attic is perfect for families, and the restaurant (www.ristoranteverrazzano.it) serves hearty portions of highly recommendable Tuscan fare in a laid-back trattoria atmosphere, with alfresco summer dining at tables on a terrace atop the arcades.

Piazza G. Matteotti 28, 50022 Greve in Chianti (FI). ✆ **055-853-189.** Fax 055-853-648. www.verrazzano.it. 10 units, 8 with bathroom (shower only). 77€ ($89) double without bathroom; 89€ ($102) double with bathroom; triple 105€ ($121); quad 122€ ($140). Half and full pension available. Breakfast 9€ ($10). AE, DC, MC, V. Closed Jan 15–Feb 15. **Amenities:** Restaurant; pool; concierge; limited room service; laundry service; dry cleaning. *In room:* TV, minibar, hair dryer.

Villa Rosa di Boscorotondo ★★ This villa offers wonderful countryside seclusion at perfectly modest prices—a rarity in the Chianti. Giancarlo and Sabina Avuri, who own Florence's Hotel Torre Guelfa, opened this huge pink villa as a roadside inn in 1998, retaining the original features and roominess while modernizing with an elegance that lends it an antique rustic air. The curtained beds on wrought-iron frames rest under gorgeous beamed ceilings, and rooms along the front open onto two huge terraces that drink in views of the small valley in which the villa nestles. There are a series of small drawing rooms, a pool with a view, and a path that leads through the vineyards all the way to San Leolino church outside Panzano. Famed butcher Cecchini provides the meat for fixed-price dinners (25€/$29 not including wine) on the terra-cotta terrace in summer.

Via San Leolino 59 (on the SS222 between Panzano and Radda), 50022 Loc. Panzano in Chianti (FI). ✆ **055-852-577.** Fax 055-856-0835. www.resortvillarosa.com. 15 units. 80€–125€ ($92–$144) double; 100€–140€ triple ($115–$161). Rates include breakfast. AE, MC, V. Free parking. Closed mid-Nov to Apr. **Amenities:** Small restaurant; outdoor pool; concierge; limited room service; massage; babysitting; laundry service; dry cleaning. *In room:* A/C, TV, minibar, hair dryer.

Villa Vignamaggio ★★ You can't actually stay in the room where Mona Lisa grew up, but you can certainly make do with suites, each with a tiny kitchenette and complimentary bottle of the estate's award-winning chianti. This is one of the most comfortable *agriturismi* on the market, offering hotel-style amenities such as daily maid service. The heavy wood-beam ceilings and the comfortable rustic furnishings mesh well with the contemporary designer lights, spanking-new bathrooms, and cast-iron bed frames; four suites even have Jacuzzi tubs and air-conditioning. You can stay in one of several suites in the villa, rent the small cottage next door, or shack out in a suite in one of the old stone peasant houses dotting the property on either side of the road.

Villa Vignamaggio (5km/3 miles southeast of Greve), Greve in Chianti (FI). ✆ **055-854-661.** Fax 055-854-4468. www.vignamaggio.com. 4 units, 16 apts. 150€ ($173) double; 210€ ($242) triple; 250€–450€ ($288–$518) apt. Minimum 2-night stay; 10% discount for stays of a week or longer. Continental breakfast 10€ ($12); brunch buffet 15€ ($17). AE, DC, MC, V. Turn off the SS222 just south of Greve onto the Lamole road, then follow the signs. **Amenities:** Restaurant (only twice a week; days vary); 2 outdoor pools (1 heated); outdoor tennis court (lit for night play); small exercise room with Jacuzzi shower; free bikes; children's playground; game room; limited room service (breakfast); massage; laundry service; nonsmoking rooms. *In room:* A/C (for now, not in villa rooms), TV, fax on request, kitchenette in apts., minibar, coffeemaker, hair dryer, safe.

WHERE TO DINE IN THE FLORENTINE CHIANTI

Beside the restaurants below, don't miss the hearty meals at **Hotel Giovanni da Verrazzano** (see above). Also in Greve, the **Enoteca Bar Gallo Nero,** Via C. Battisti 9 (© **055-853-734**), is a good pizza and pasta place (order the *affettati misti* appetizer) popular with locals and families—and cheaper than most Chianti spots. It's open Friday through Wednesday from noon to 10pm (closed Jan 6–31).

Bottega del Moro ☆ TUSCAN   Modern art and a view over the tiny Greve River are the backdrop at this pleasant trattoria in the center of Greve. After *bruschetta al pomodoro,* dig into the light *maltagliati del Moro* (wide noodles with slivers of porcini and prosciutto in butter-and-sage sauce) or the richer *crespelle alla fiorentina* (pasta crepes stuffed with ricotta and spinach and served in a cheesy béchamel garnished with tomato purée). For an encore, try *coniglio al forno* (tender, meaty rabbit baked with spices and black olives). The local specialty is *zampone con puree* (stewed pigs' feet). Whatever you order, see if they're offering *pecorino con pere* as a *contorno* (side dish)—the creamy, firm, fresh sheep's cheese pairs excellently with the soft, sweet slices of ripe pear.

Piazza Trieste 14r (a tiny park on the east side of the main road near the south end of Greve). © **055-853-753**. www.greve-in-chianti.com/il-moro.htm. Reservations recommended. Primi 5€–7.50€ ($5.75–$8.05); secondi 11€–15€ ($13–$17). AE, DC, MC, V. Thurs–Tues 12:15–2:15pm and 7:15–9:15pm. Closed 1st week of May and Nov.

La Cantinetta di Rignana ☆☆ TUSCAN   From Greve, follow the signs to Montefioralle, then toward Badia a Passignano until the signposted turnoff. A medieval ramble of stone houses at the end of a long dirt road hides La Cantinetta, one of the Chianti's most genuine countryside trattorie. You can have lunch on the glassed-in patio with a sweeping view of the vineyard, but I prefer ducking under the hanging bunches of sausages and pendulous prosciutto ham hocks to eat inside. Here a congregation of reproduction Madonna and Child icons on one wall stare down the small armada of hammered copper pots and lanterns across the way. The staff is given to warbling snatches of folk songs and opera as they prepare handmade pasta (ravioli, gnocchi, or tagliolini) with your pick of rich sauces—the thick, pasty *noci* nut sauce is excellent. Grilled meats top the main courses (*coniglio,* rabbit, is charred to perfection), or try the delicious *involtini di manzo* (beef slices rolled up with vegetables). The white-chocolate mousse is legendary. If the beautifully isolated setting appeals to you, the attached farm also offer seven basic country-style rooms from April to early November for 95€ ($1.10) for a double, including breakfast (minimum 3 nights; book at © **055-852-065**; www.rignana.it).

Loc. Rignana, Greve in Chianti. © **055-852-601**. www.lacantinettadirignana.it. Reservations strongly recommended. Primi 6.50€–8€ ($7.50–$9.20); secondi 8.50€–11€ ($9.80–$13). AE, DC, MC, V. Wed–Mon 12:30–2:15pm and 7:30–10:30pm. Closed Nov 30–Dec 22.

La Cantinetta di Spedaluzzo ☆☆ TUSCAN   Atop a rise in the Chianti-giana, this countryside trattoria offers friendly service and excellent Tuscan dishes. The *crostini caldi al fornello* are do-it-yourself affairs—spread the pâté of your choice onto slabs of toasted peasant bread. The *ribollita* is especially tasty, with some meat for flavor, and comes with an enormous urn of olive oil to ladle over it. *Pipe al sugo ricco* are large maccheroni in a duly rich sauce of pork, mutton, beef, and strips of tomato. The stars of the secondi are the *involtini ai porcini* (veal rolls cooked in a sauce of concentrated porcini mushrooms), the *salsicce al tartufo* (a pair of salty sausages with white truffles chopped into the mix), and the huge *bistecca alla fiorentina.* Don't leave without ordering their homemade tiramisù for dessert, one of the best I've ever tasted. They've added a glassed-in veranda with a fireplace for three-seasons dining with a view.

Via Mugnana 93, Loc. Spedaluzzo (halfway between Strada and Greve on SS222). (C) **055-857-2000.** Reservations required. Primi 8€–12€ ($9.20–$14); secondi 7€–15€ ($8.05–$17); children's menu 12€ ($14). AE, DC, MC, V. Tues–Sun 12:30–2:30pm and 7:30–10:30pm. Closed for 3 weeks in late Feb to early Mar.

Oltre Il Giardino ⊛ TUSCAN   Stefano Cozzi got tired of being a Florentine attorney and decided to indulge his love of fine cooking and the Chianti countryside. You can dine on the terrace in warm weather or ensconce yourself in the intimate second-floor dining room, lit by table candles and a fireplace, with great Chianti-side views (so long as you don't look straight down from the window, where Panzano's mini urban sprawl festers). The daily handwritten menu includes primi like *tagliatelle al ragù di anatra* (they don't skimp on the duck in the ragù!) and *maltagliati ai carciofi* (sheets of fresh-cut pasta with artichoke hearts, tomatoes, celery, and carrots). The meat that goes into the excellent *stracotto al chianti* (beef strewed in chianti wine and served with sautéed spinach) and *maiale al senape* (suckling pig with mustard and pearl onions) comes from neighbor and famed butcher Dario Cecchini.

Piazza G. Bucciarelli 42 (a few steps toward the old town from the central traffic triangle), Panzano in Chianti. (C) **055-852-828.** Reservations highly recommended. Primi 8€ ($9.20); secondi 12€–13€ ($14–$15), fixed-price menu without wine 35€ ($40). AE, DC, MC, V. Tues–Sun 12–3pm and 7–10pm. Closed Dec 8–Feb.

ON THE ROAD IN THE SIENESE CHIANTI
EN ROUTE TO RADDA IN CHIANTI
An Etruscan center later fortified by the Florentines as an outpost against rival Siena, **Castellina in Chianti** ⊛ is one of the more medieval-feeling hill towns of the region and a triumvirate member of the old Lega del Chianti. The closest thing to a tourist office is the **Colline Verdi** travel agency, Via della Rocca 12 ((C) and fax **0577-740-620**). Castellina's medieval walls survive almost intact, and the central piazza is dominated by the imposing crenellated **Rocca** fortress. The nearby **Via delle Volte** is an evocative tunnel street with open windows facing out to the valley below—it's a soldiers' walk from the town's days as a Florentine bastion. You can taste a few drops of *vino* at **La Castellina**'s enoteca and shipping point in the ground floor of the family palazzo at Via Ferrucio 26 ((C) **0577-740-454**). The **Bottega del Vino,** Via della Rocca 13 ((C) **0577-741-110;** www.enobottega.it), is a good wine shop.

Outside town on the road to Radda is a 6th-century B.C. Etruscan tomb, the **Ipogeo Etrusco di Montecalvario** ⊛. It's a perfect example of its type, a little green beanie of a hill surrounded by pines, topped with a pair of cypress, and slashed with stone-walled tunnels leading to the burial chambers beneath. Push the button on the little fuse box–looking thing on your right as you enter the gate to flip the lights on inside.

From Castellina, you can take a long but rewarding detour on the road to Poggibonsi into the Val d'Elsa to visit the vineyards of **Monsanto** ⊛⊛ ((C) **055-805-9000**), which produces my favorite Chianti wine. (Their Classico Riserva 1995 is about the best I've ever tasted.) At this medieval estate, Dr. Laura Bianchi carries on her father Fabrizio's often iconoclastic oenological traditions—after buying Monsanto in 1961, he was among the first to produce a 100% sangiovese chianti, and using only *sangiovese grosso* grapes at that. (Because this was illegal back in 1974, they still listed all the unused grapes on the labels.) Aside from their exquisite "Chardonnay" (aged half in steel and half in wood, so that its fruitiness isn't overpowered with oak but still has its body and longevity), they use native grapes as much as possible. The result is a suite of remarkable and singular wines, like Il Poggio, a full-bodied elixir made with 90% sangiovese and 10% Colorino and Canaiolo (aged in Slovenian-wood *barriques*), or Tinscvil, a sangiovese-cabernet Supertuscan whose name, in Etruscan, means "Gift to the gods." They started bottling that last one after discovering an Etruscan tomb on the property, which also inspired them to extend their vast cellars with a huge hall built using a low Etruscan-style arch. Down here and in the original 18th-century cellars are stored thousands of bottles from every year of production—many still for sale. They do tastings and direct sales Monday through Friday from 8:30am to 12:30pm and 1:30 to 6pm; reserve a tour of the cellars for 16€ ($18) per person at least a few days in advance.

If you're tired of these wine-sodden hills, you can shoot down the Chiantigiana from here to Siena, an 18km (11-mile) trip. It takes you past the medieval village of **Fonterutoli** ⋆ (© **0577-740-212;** www.fonterutoli.com)—a working *borgo* that has been supporting the winemaking business of the Mazzei Marquis since 1435. Fonterutoli produces some of the most highly regarded wines in the region, including an excellent Chianti Classico and Chianti Classico riserva, Supertuscans Siepi and Brancaia (the latter a sangiovese and merlot cru), the rich berry-flavored Belguardo (a Morellino di Scansano cru), and the superb fruity I.G.T. Badiola, a sangiovese wine (with 3% each of merlot and cabernet) meant to be drunk young, after about 2 years. The direct sales office in town is usually locked; follow the signs for the *ristorante* to find the easygoing, old-fashioned bar where you can sample their bounty (and get the *barrista* lady to fetch a few cases from that direct sales office when you're ready to buy). You can taste and buy daily from 10am to 10:30pm. While you're there, be sure to buy a bottle or two of Fonterutoli's olive oil, also superb.

The road continues on to Siena, passing through **Quercegrossa,** the birthplace of Siena's great sculptor Jacopo della Quercia. But if you want to explore what many consider the best of the Chianti, it's time to cut east into the rugged, mountainous heart of the old Lega del Chianti along the SS429 toward Radda.

Just before you hit Radda, a signposted right turn will take you a winding 7km (4 miles) past the Romanesque **San Giusto** to the **Castello di Ama,** a top-rated winery whose Frenchified methods are seen by some as bucking homegrown tradition—they not only produce a Merlot *vino di tavola* but also age almost all their more traditional Tuscan wines in—gasp—French oak *barriques.* The quality of their oakey Chianti can't be disputed, however, and they also produce an excellent barrel-aged pinot grigio along with silky olive oils. Direct sales (year-round) and tastings (Easter–Sept) are available down the road in the hamlet of **Lecchi** at the **Rinaldi Palmira** shop (© **0577-746-021**) on Via San Martino 8. (If there's no one inside, ask at their little grocery store next door.)

RADDA IN CHIANTI & ENVIRONS

Radda in Chianti ⋆, one of the three players in the original Lega del Chianti and still an important wine center, retains its medieval street plan and a bit of its walls. The center of town is the 15th-century **Palazzo del Podestà,** studded with the mayoral coats of arms of past *podestà;* it contains the tourist office (© and fax **0577-738-494;** www.chiantinet.it; open Mon–Sat 10am–1pm and 3–7pm, Sun 10am–1pm; in winters, mornings only). Again we have a local butcher who's a true artisan, in Radda's case **Luciano Porciatti** and his sister; they'll give you a taste of traditional salamis and cheeses at their alimentari on Piazza IV Novembre 1 at the gate into town (© 0577-738-055). They also sell local products, from wines to pasta, at their enoteca along Radda's tunnel-like old soldier's wall walk.

Seven kilometers (4 miles) north of Radda on a secondary road is the **Castello di Volpaia** ★★ (© 0577-738-066; fax 0577-738-619; www.volpaia.com), a first-rank wine estate with a medieval stone heart. The castle here was a Florentine holding buffeted by Sienese attacks and sieges from the 10th to 16th centuries. The still-impressive central keep is all that remains, but it's surrounded by an evocative 13th-century *borgo* (village) containing the Renaissance La Commenda church. You can tour the winery—installed in a series of buildings throughout the little village (with an eye to preserving its medieval visual charm, owner Giovannella Stanti Mascheroni is busily having the electrical wires and high-tech plumbing through which the wine flows buried seamlessly inside the stone walls)—for 11€ to 23€ ($13–$26) per person (Sun–Fri) depending on the size of the group (cheaper for larger groups), and included tasting of the wines and their fantastic olive oil. Call ahead, preferably a week in advance. The central tower has an enoteca (open 10am–6pm; closed Feb) for drop-in tastings and direct sales of some of the wines that helped found the Chianti Consorzio in 1924, plus award-winning (and scrumptious) olive oils and the only farm-produced vinegars in the Chianti. They also rent apartments and two small villas and lease out a small hotel on a neighboring hill of the estate (see "Where to Stay in the Sienese Chianti," below, for details).

Three kilometers (2 miles) east of Radda, get on the left byroad for a 19km (12-mile) trip to the beautifully isolated **Badia a Coltibuono** ★ (© 0577-749-498 or 0577-74-481; fax 0577-749-235; www.coltibuono.com). The abbey's core was founded in A.D. 770, but the monastery was owned and expanded by the Vallombrosan Order from the 12th century to 1810, when the Napoleonic suppressions passed it into private hands and it became an agricultural estate. You can visit the 11th-century San Lorenzo church only during daily Mass (open 4:30pm in summer, 3:30pm in fall, 3pm in winter, and 4pm in spring). Today, the estate is owned by the Stucci-Prinetti family, which oversees the wine production; try their Sangioveto label, a 100% sangiovese wine. The family's most famous member, international cookbook maven Lorenza de' Medici, started a famed (and egregiously overpriced) culinary school here in summers, though it's now run by an acolyte (see "Special-Interest Vacations" in chapter 2 for details), and her son, Paolo, runs the fine and oft-acclaimed on-site restaurant (© 0577-749-424; closed Mon and Nov–Feb). There's a direct sales office for their products called the **"osteria"** (© 0577-749-479) down at the main road. March through December, the osteria is open Tuesday through Saturday from 9:30am to 1pm and 2 to 6:30pm, and Mondays from 2 to 6:30pm.

EN ROUTE TO SIENA

Follow the scenic road leading south out of Radda toward Siena along the valley of the Piana stream and you'll immediately see the 17th-century **Villa Strozzi-Sonnino** crowning a steep hillside of **Vistarenni** vines to your left (© 0577-738-476; www.villavistarenni.com). They offer direct sales weekdays from 8:30am to 5:30pm and will set up tastings for small groups (book at least a day in advance) as well as tours of 18th-century cellars. They are also now offering, as are most other vineyards these days, apartments and villas for long-term rental; visit the website for details and photos.

A bit farther south on this road, on the left side, you'll see the **ceramic workshop** ★★★ and showroom of master Giuseppe Rampini (© 0577-738-043;

www.chiantinet.it/rampiniceramics). Here the Gubbio-born *maestro* (who still remembers gathering clay from the Tiber riverbed for his father when he was 8) and his assistants create hand-painted ceramics based on antique Florentine motifs or inspired by the Renaissance art of Venetian painter Archimboldo. The front space is full of pattern displays; the back room has individual pieces for sale.

Heading south directly from Badia a Coltibuono on the SS408 will take you through **Gaiole in Chianti,** the third member of the Lega del Chianti. The tourist office is at Via Ricasoli 50 (© **0577-749-411;** gaiole@chiantinet.it; open Mon–Sat 9:30am–1pm and 3–6:30pm). This is an ancient market town like Greve but is basically modernized without much to see, aside from the wine shops: the **Cantina Enoteca Montagnani,** Via B. Bandinelli 13–17 (© **0577-749-517**), and **La Cantinetta del Chianti,** Via F. Ferruci 20 (© **0577-749-125**).

A side road here leads west past the 12th-century **Castello di Spaltenna** (now a hotel; see below) 3km (2 miles) to the 13th-century **Castello di Vertine,** an imposing castle surrounded by a 9th-century village.

East of Gaiole, an unfinished road winds up to the fortified medieval hamlet of **Barbischio.** For more castle viewing, head south of Gaiole to the turnoff for Meleto and Castagnoli. **Castello di Meleto**'s twin circular towers stand mighty at either expanse of a long blank wall to watch over the estate's vineyards. The poor castle cum villa was built in the 1100s, partially dismantled by the Sienese in the 15th century, rebuilt by the Florentines, and then smashed by the Sienese again in the 16th century before a 1700s restoration transformed it to the villa we see today. Farther up this road is the hamlet of **Castagnoli,** wrapped around the thick, squat walls of an early medieval castle.

Farther south of Gaiole, the SS484 branches east toward Castelnuovo Berardenga and the famous **Castello di Brolio** ★★ (© **0577-749-066;** www.ricasoli.it; pull the bell rope and wait). The Chianti as a region may date to the 1200s, but Chianti Classico as a wine was born here in the mid–19th century. The Brolio castle has been in the Ricasoli family since 1141, though its vineyards date from at least 1007; the current fortress was rebuilt in 1484. "Iron Baron" Bettino Ricasoli inherited it in 1829 at age 20 and, before he went off in 1848 to help found a unified Italy and become its second prime minister, spent his days here, teaching— really dictating—scientific farming methods to his peasants. He also whiled the time tinkering with grape varietals. By the mid–19th century, he'd arrived at a quaffable formula balancing sangiovese, canaiolo, trebbiano, and malvasia grapes that was used when Italy's wine-governing DOC and DOCG laws were written in the 1960s. You can visit the castle grounds, including the small chapel (Bettino rests in peace in the family crypt) and the gardens, and walk along the wall for a good view of the lower Chianti valleys. Admission is 3€ ($3.45). In summer, the gardens are open daily 9am to noon and 3 to 6pm; in winter, from 9am to noon and 2 to 5pm.

After years of being passed from larger to larger corporate ownership, Brolio declined as a winery; then in 1993 the Baron Francesco Ricasoli bought it from Seagram's and brought it back into the family. He effected a drastic turnaround, investing billions of lire, replanting vines, and rigorously revising the philosophy to rocket Brolio back to superstardom and respect on the Italian wine scene, winning acclaim and awards once again. They now produce several wines, including the newest—a single Castello di Brolio, 100% sangiovese Chianti Classico— they're going for the French châteaux concept, where the wine is associated with a place, not a brand. To buy their award-winning wines, visit wine shop (© **0577-7301**) from Monday to Friday between 9am and 7:30pm, Saturday and Sunday from 11am to 6:30pm. They offer cantina tours by appointment (call at least a few days in advance) with a wine tasting at the end, for 21€ ($24) per person for up to five people (11€/$12 per person if the group is larger). On the side of the private road up to the *castello* is also a quite good **Osteria del Castello** restaurant (© **0577-747-277**).

The westerly byroad out of here leads most quickly to join the SS408 as it heads south, out of the land of the black rooster and into Siena.

WHERE TO STAY IN THE SIENESE CHIANTI

Beside the choices below, the medieval **Castello di Volpaia** (© **0577-738-066; fax 0577-738-619; www.volpaia.com**), listed above as a winery, rents out five agriturismo apartments with kitchenettes and TVs and, in a few, working fireplaces (bookable from the estate) in the stony buildings of its 13th-century village for 570€ to 930€ ($656–$1,070) per week for two people, or 1,000€ to 2,070€ ($1,150–$2,381) for the one that sleeps six. Guests can take part in various programs, from self-guided hikes to cooking lessons, wine tastings, or dinner with the owner. They also rent two lovely villas (sleeping up to 8 or 11) with private gardens and pools with views (bookable only via the private agency Salogi in Lucca at © **0583-48-717** or fax 0583-48-727), and lease a *casa colonica* on a nearby hillock amid the estate's vineyards to a hotelier who operates it as the classy-rustic **La Locanda** hotel (© and fax **0577-738-833; www.lalocanda.it**), with 180€–235€ ($207–$270) doubles and 235€–250€ ($270–$288) suites, breakfast included.

Borgo Argenina ★★   From the flagstoned terrace of Elena Nappa's new hilltop B&B (she bought the whole medieval hamlet), you can see the farmhouse where Bertolucci filmed *Stealing Beauty* in 1996. Against remarkable odds (she'll regale you with the anecdotes), she has created the rural retreat of her (and your) dreams. When you arrive, you'll likely find Elena upstairs next to a roaring fire in the kitchen, sewing. Elena's design talents (she was a fashion stylist in Milan) are amazing, and the guest rooms boast antique wrought-iron beds, deluxe mattresses, handmade quilts, hand-stitched lace curtains, and timeworn terra-cotta tiles. The bathrooms are made to look old-fashioned, though the plumbing is modern. Since the place isn't easy to find, English-speaking Elena will fax you directions when you reserve. In addition to four doubles, Elena offers accommodation in two suites, two small houses (for two or three people), and the Villa Oliviera (for four people). When faced with all the questions foreign guests often inundate her with when booking (Do you have air-conditioning? Is there parking? How much of a deposit do I need to make?), Elena replies, "Don't worry. Just come!" Good advice.

Loc. Argenina (near San Marcellino Monti), 53013 Gaiole in Chianti. © **0577-747-117**. Fax 0577-747-228 (they prefer faxes, and will respond within the day). www.borgoargenina.it. 4 units, 2 suites, 2 small houses, 1 villa. 130€ ($150) double; 160€ ($184) suite for 2 people, 180€ ($207) suite for 3 people; 180€ ($207) house for 2 people, 200€ ($230) house for 3 people; 400€ ($460) villa for 4 people. 3-night minimum stay. Rates include country breakfast. AE, DC, MC, V. Free parking. Ask for directions when reserving. **Amenities:** Limited room service (breakfast); laundry service. *In room:* Minibar, hair dryer.

Castello di Spaltenna ★   The Spaltenna is one of the Chianti's most famous luxury hotels, a converted medieval castle from before the 12th century set in a grassy field. The rooms have a simple but tasteful decor, with reproduction and genuine country-style antiques, including some massive wooden desks and wrought-iron 19th-century bed frames. Most have ancient worn terra-cotta tile floors and views of the valley below, but a few look over the unfortunate housing developments of modern Gaiole creeping up the hill. No room is overly spacious, but the semi-lofted corner suites in the main building are sizable, with fantastic cross ribbing of heavy hewn wood beams on the ceilings. Suites in the outbuilding, such as no. 28, are particularly nice, with two rooms and their own little terraces overlooking the hotel's vineyards. Rooms of the deluxe category and above have Jacuzzi tubs in the modernized bathrooms, many with double sinks.

53013 Gaiole in Chianti (SI; on a small hill west of Gaiole). © **0577-749-483**. Fax 0577-749-268. www. spaltenna.com. 38 units. Apr 1–Nov 4 and Dec 28–Jan 1 240€–320€ ($276–$368) double, 380€–2,600€ ($437–$2,990) suite; Jan 2–Mar 31 and Nov 5–Dec 27 204€–272€ ($235–$313) double, 323€–2,200€ ($317–$2,530). Half-pension 62€ ($71). AE, DC, MC, V. Free parking. **Amenities:** Restaurant (in an old stone wine cellar or, in summer, in the central courtyard around an old stone well); indoor heated pool and 2 outdoor pools overlooking grape vines; tennis courts; tiny exercise room (just a Stairmaster, bike, and treadmill); sauna; free bikes; game room (billiards); concierge; tour desk; car-rental desk; room service; babysitting; laundry service. *In room:* A/C, TV, minibar, hair dryer, safe.

Hotel Il Colombaio ☙   This modest, excellently priced hotel sits in a 16th-century stone house at the edge of Castellina (near the Etruscan tomb and a 5-min. walk into town for restaurants) and once housed shepherds who spent the night after selling their sheep at market. The good-size rooms with their sloping beam-and-tile ceilings, terra-cotta floors, and iron bed frames seem to belong to a well-to-do 19th-century farming family. Upstairs accommodations are lighter and airier than the ground-floor rooms (formerly stalls) and enjoy better views over the vineyards (a few overlook the road). Six of the rooms are in an annex across the road. The house's old kitchen has been converted into a comfy rustic reading room. You breakfast in winter under stone vaults and in summer on a terrace sharing its countryside vistas with the pool.

Via Chiantigiana 29, 53011 Castellina in Chianti (SI). © **0577-740-444**. Fax 0577-740-402. www.albergoil colombaio.it. 21 units. 87€–103€ ($100–$118) double. Rates include continental breakfast. AE, DC, MC, V. Free parking. Closed 2 weeks in winter. **Amenities:** Restaurant (a block away); outdoor pool (June–Sept); concierge; tour desk; car-rental desk; limited room service (breakfast); massage; babysitting; laundry service. *In room:* TV, hair dryer.

Podere Terreno ☙☙   Paris-born Silvie, who used to run a Florentine art gallery, and her Italian husband, Roberto, are your gracious hosts at their small 16th-century farmstead turned agriturismo topping a hillock between Radda and Volpaia. They and their son, Francesco, treat you like family—the last one to go to bed has to turn out the lights, the wonderful home-cooked dinner is served promptly at 7:30pm, and they'll scold you if you aren't being a good guest. With this quiet countryside retreat slowly growing in fame, the nightly extended family can get quite multinational. Most who sign up for just a night or two in the simple, comfortably rustic rooms with old peasant furnishings and firm beds on terra-cotta floors return the following year to stay for a week. Breakfast includes salami, excellent homemade marmalades and jams, and soft sheep cheese; and, the scrumptious dinner is accompanied by their own velvety chianti, consistently rated among the top 25 in the Classico region.

Strada per Volpaia (2km/1 miles north of Radda off the road to Volpaia), 53017 Radda in Chianti (SI). © **0577-738-312**. Fax 0577-738-400. www.podereterreno.it. 7 units. 95€ ($109) per person, including breakfast and obligatory dinner half-pension. AE, MC, V. Free parking. **Amenities:** Home-cooked dinners in living room; 2 swimming ponds; free bikes; game room (billiards); tour desk; massage on request. *In room:* Hair dryer on request, no phone.

WHERE TO DINE IN THE SIENESE CHIANTI

Albergaccio ☙ CREATIVE TUSCAN   On the outskirts of Castellina, this place offers an excellent mix of fine cuisine and rustic timbered atmosphere with valley views. Francesco Cacciatori glides through the place serving a changing roster of dishes steeped in local traditions but enlivened by the creativity of chef Sonia Visman. Among the tasty combinations I've sampled recently, I heartily recommend the *bavette con timo e pecorino di fossa* (thin noodles with tomatoes, thyme, and specially aged pecorino cheese), *gnocchi di ricotta con tartufo marzolo* (dollops of ricotta with shaved truffles and thyme leaves). The *rollé di maiale con cavolo nero* (pork involtini made with black cabbage, tomatoes, and wild fennel) and *piccione speziato con fichi caramelati al marsala* (stuffed pigeon with figs caramelized in Marsala wine) are fine secondi. They also rent five rooms across the street for 73€ ($84) per double, including breakfast (call ✆ **0577-741-166**).

Via Fiorentina 63, Castellina in Chianti (just outside the walls along the road toward San Donato). ✆ **0577-741-042**. www.albergacciocast.com. Reservations highly recommended. Primi 11€–13€ ($13–$15); secondi 16€–19€ ($18–$22). Tasting menus 45€ ($52). MC, V. Mon–Sat 12:30–2:15pm and 7:30–9:30pm. Closed last 2 weeks of Nov and 1st week of Dec.

Le Vigne TUSCAN   The aptly named Le Vigne is tucked between the rows of vines washing the slopes southeast of Radda. You can watch vintners working the vines as you sip your wine and sample such well-turned dishes as *pici all'aglione* (hand-rolled spaghetti with tomatoes, leeks, and a dab of pancetta), bready *ribollita,* boned duck stuffed with porchetta, and excellent *agnello alla griglia* (tender lamb chops grilled with aromatic herbs). Definitely order the homemade *patate fritte,* thinly sliced discs of potato fried in olive oil.

Podere Le Vigne (off the SS408 to Villa just east of Radda in Chianti). ✆ **0577-738-640**. Reservations recommended. Primi 5€–9.50€ ($5.75–$11); secondi 8.50€–14€ ($9.80–$16) AE, DC, MC, V. Wed–Mon 12–2:30pm and 7:15–9:30pm (open daily in summer). Closed Nov 15–Mar 15.

2 Siena: A Taste of the Tuscan Middle Ages

70km (43 miles) S of Florence; 232km (144 miles) N of Rome

Siena is a medieval city of brick. From a vantage point such as the Palazzo Pubblico's tower, its sea of roof tiles blends into a landscape of steep, twisting stone alleys. This cityscape hides dozens of Gothic palaces and pastry shops galore, unseen neighborhood rivalries, and altarpieces of unsurpassed beauty.

Siena is proud of its past. It trumpets the she-wolf as its emblem, a holdover from its days as *Saena Julia,* the Roman colony founded by Augustus about 2,000 years ago (though the official Sienese myth has the town founded by the sons of Remus, younger brother of Rome's legendary forefather). Siena still parcels out the rhythms of life, its rites of passage and communal responsibilities, to the 17 *contrade* (neighborhood wards) formed in the 14th century. It makes a point of offering an image of Tuscany different from that of Florence, its old medieval rival: Siena is as inscrutable in its culture, decorous in its art, and festive in its life attitude as Florence is forthright, precise, and serious on all counts. Where Florence produced hard-nosed mystics like Savonarola, Siena gave forth saintly scholars like St. Catherine (1347–80) and St. Bernardino (1380–1444).

Its bankers, textile magnates, and wool traders put 12th-century Siena in direct competition with Florence, and the two cities kept at each other's throats for more than 400 years. When Florence went Guelf, Siena turned Ghibelline and soundly thrashed Florence at the 1260 Battle of Montaperti. Unfortunately for Siena, the battle was fought in alliance with ousted Florentine Ghibellines, who refused to allow the armies to press the advantage and level Florence. Within 10 years, Charles of Anjou had crushed the Sienese Ghibellines.

With Siena now Guelf again, Sienese merchants established in 1270 the Council of Nine, an oligarchy that ruled over Siena's greatest republican era,

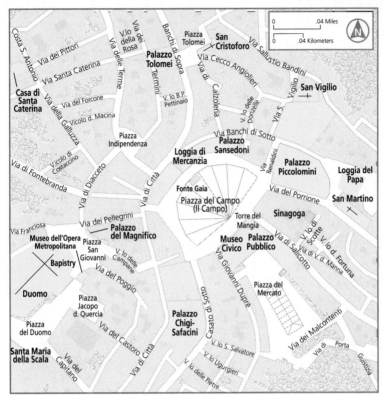

when civic projects, the middle-class economy, palace building, and artistic prowess reached their greatest heights. Artists like Duccio, Simone Martini, and the Lorenzetti brothers invented a distinctive Sienese art style, a highly developed Gothicism that was an excellent artistic foil to the emerging Florentine Renaissance (see "Art & Architecture 101" in Appendix A).

Then, in 1348, the Black Death hit the city like a Fury, killing more than three quarters of the population, decimating the social fabric, and devastating the economy. The Council of Nine soldiered on, but Charles IV attacked Siena from 1355 to 1369, and though Siena again trounced Florence in 1526, the Spanish took control in 1530 and later handed Siena over to Ducal Florence.

To subdue these pesky Sienese once and for all, Cosimo I sent the brutal marquis of Marignano, who besieged the city for a year and a half, destroying its fields and burning its buildings. By the time he stormed the city in 1555, the marquis had done more damage than even the Black Death—only 8,000 out of a population of 40,000 had survived—and the burned and broken city and countryside bore an uncanny resemblance to the *Effects of Bad Government*, half of Ambrogio Lorenzetti's fresco in Siena's Palazzo Pubblico. Some 2,000 fiercely independent Sienese escaped to Montalcino, where they kept the Sienese Republic alive, in name at least, for another 4 years. Then Montalcino too was engulfed by Florence. Siena became, on paper and in fact, merely another part of Grand Ducal Tuscany.

Siena

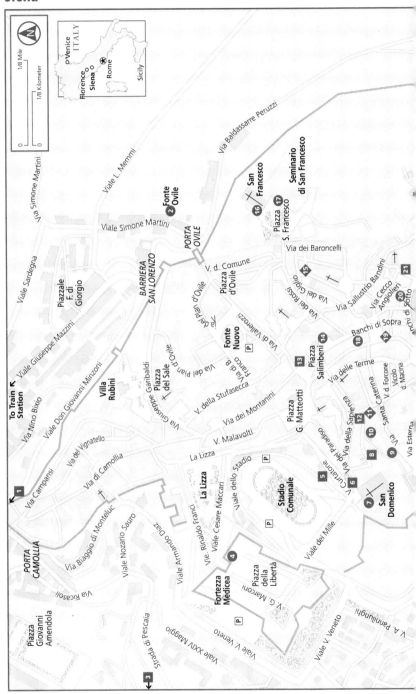

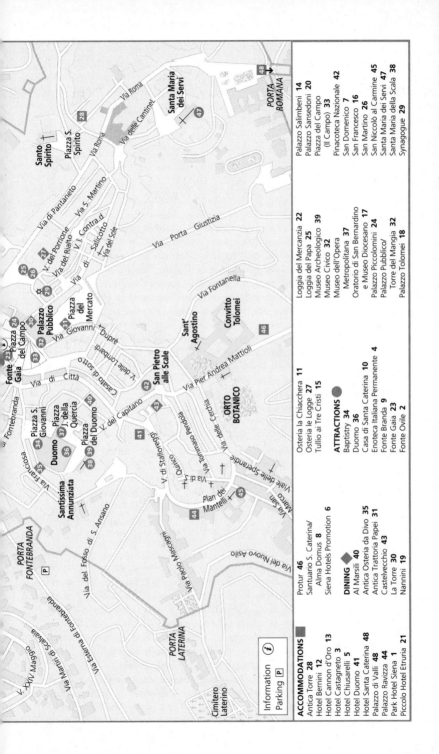

Information (i)

Parking P

ACCOMMODATIONS
Antica Torre **28**
Hotel Bernini **12**
Hotel Cannon d'Oro **13**
Hotel Castagneto **3**
Hotel Chiusarelli **5**
Hotel Duomo **41**
Hotel Santa Caterina **48**
Palazzo di Valli **48**
Palazzo Ravizza **44**
Park Hotel Siena **1**
Piccolo Hotel Etruria **21**

Protur **46**
Santuario S. Caterina/
Alma Domus **8**
Siena Hotels Promotion **6**

DINING ◆
Al Marsili **40**
Antica Osteria da Divo **35**
Antica Trattoria Papei **31**
Castelvecchio **43**
La Torre **30**
Nannini **19**

Osteria la Chiacchera **11**
Osteria le Logge **27**
Tullio ai Tre Cristi **15**

ATTRACTIONS ●
Baptistry **34**
Duomo **36**
Casa di Santa Caterina **10**
Enoteca Italiana Permanente **4**
Fonte Branda **9**
Fonte Gaia **23**
Fonte Ovile **2**

Loggia del Mercanzia **22**
Loggia del Papa **25**
Museo Archeologico **39**
Museo Civico **32**
Museo dell'Opera
Metropolitana **37**
Oratorio di San Bernardino
e Museo Diocesano **17**
Palazzo Piccolomini **24**
Palazzo Pubblico/
Torre del Mangia **32**
Palazzo Tolomei **18**

Palazzo Salimbeni **14**
Palazzo Sansedoni **20**
Piazza del Campo
(Il Campo) **33**
Pinacoteca Nazionale **42**
San Domenico **7**
San Francesco **16**
San Martino **26**
San Niccolò al Carmine **45**
Santa Maria dei Servi **47**
Santa Maria della Scala **38**
Synagogue **29**

Since the plague of the 14th century, Siena was so busy defending its liberty it had little time or energy to develop as a city. As a result, it has remained one of the largest Tuscan cities to retain a distinctively medieval air and offers your best chance in Italy to slip into the rhythms and atmosphere of the Tuscan Middle Ages.

ESSENTIALS

GETTING THERE   By Train   The bus is often more convenient, because Siena's train station is outside town. Some 19 trains daily connect Siena with **Florence** (90 min.–2¼ hr.). There's also a line to **Chiusi–Chianciano Terme** (90 min.) passing through **Asciano** and **Montepulciano** (see chapter 8 for more information). Siena's **train station** (© **0577-280-115**) is at Piazza Fratelli Roselli, about 3km (2 miles) north of town. Take the C minibus to Piazza Gramsci in Terza di Camollia or a taxi.

By Car   There's an autostrada highway direct from **Florence** (it has no route number; follow the green autostrada signs toward Siena), or you can take the more scenic routes, down the old Via Cassia SS2 or the Chiantigiana SS222 through the Chianti (see "Wine Tasting in the Chianti," earlier in this chapter). From **Rome** get off the A1 north at the Val di Chiana exit and follow the SS326 west for 50km (31 miles). The SS223 runs 70km (43 miles) here from **Grosetto** in the Maremma. From **Pisa** take the highway toward Florence and exit onto the SS429 south at Empoli (100km/62 miles total).

Trying to drive into the one-way and pedestrian-zoned center isn't worth the massive headache. Siena **parking** (© **0577-22-871**; www.sienaparcheggi.com) is now coordinated, and all the lots charge 1.50€ ($1.75) per hour or—and this price just scandalously shot up by 50%—36€ ($41) per day. Luckily, almost every hotel has a discount deal with the nearest lot for anywhere from 40% to 100% off. All are well signposted, with locations just inside city gates' Porta Tufi (the huge and popular Il Campo lot, though it's a 20-min. walk from the Campo!), Porta San Marco, and Porta Romana; under the Fortezza (another large lot) and around La Lizza park (the latter closed market Wed and soccer Sun); and at Piazza Amendola (just outside the northern gate Porta Camollia). Ask your hotel about parking when booking—many have deals with one of these lots to get you anywhere from 50% to 100% off. You can **park for free** a bit farther away around the unguarded back (northwest) side of the Fortezza all week long. There's also free parking outside the southeast end of town at Due Ponti (beyond Porta Pispini) and Coroncina (beyond Porta Romana); from both you can get a *pollicino* (minibus) into the center (see below).

By Bus   Because buses from **Florence** are faster and let you off right in town, they're more convenient than trains. **Tra-in** runs express (19 daily; 75 min.) and slower buses (18 daily; 90 min.–2 hr.) from **Florence**'s SITA station to Siena's Piazza San Domenico or Piazza Gramsci. Siena is also connected with **San Gimignano** (hourly Mon–Sat; change in Poggibonsi; 55–65 min. not including layover), **Volterra** (three daily; change in Colle di Val d'Elsa; 40 min. each leg), **Massa Marittima** (three daily; 80 min.), **Perugia** (two to four daily; 85 min.), and **Rome**'s Tiburtina station (five to seven daily; 2 hr. 47 min.).

Follow the signs to Siena's **Tra-in bus ticket office,** underneath Piazza Gramsci in the pedonale della Lizza (© **0577-204-246** or 0577-204-225; www.trainspa. it), and there's another small office in the city's train station (© **0577-204-245**).

CITY LAYOUT   Siena is splayed out like a "Y" along three ridges with deep valleys in between, effectively dividing the city into thirds, called *terze.* The *terze* are each drawn out along three main streets following the spines of those ridges. The southern arm, **Terza di San Martino,** slopes gently down around **Via Banchi di Sotto** (and the various other names it picks up along the way). To the west is **Terza di Città** (home to the Duomo and Pinacoteca), centered on **Via di Città. Terza di Camollia** runs north around **Via Banchi di Sopra.** These three main streets meet at the north edge of **Piazza del Campo,** Siena's gorgeous scallop-shaped central square.

Tip for the footsore: Each *terza's* main ridge-top street is relatively flat—for Siena—while off either side medieval alleyways drop precipitously. If you hate climbing hills, the shortest (or at least less strenuous) distance between two points in Siena isn't a straight line but a curve that follows the three main drags as much as possible.

GETTING AROUND   Although it often looks and feels like a small Tuscan hill town, Siena truly is a city (albeit a small one), and its sites are widely spread. There is no efficient public transport system in the center, so it's up to your feet to cover the territory. There are plenty of steep ups and downs and no shortcuts from one *terza* to another without a serious workout.

The city does run **minibuses,** called *pollicini* (© 0577-204-246), which dip into the city center from 6am to 9pm. The B services the Terza di San Martino and out the Porta Pispini gate, as does bus 5 (there's also an N night bus on this route 9pm–1am). Confusingly, there are four A buses, differentiated by color. *A pink* goes around Terza di San Martino (and out the Porta Romana gate), as does bus no. 2; *A green* and *A yellow* cover Terza di Città (green from Porta Tufi to the Duomo, yellow from Porta San Marco to the Duomo); and *A red* takes care of the southerly part of Terza di Camollia (from Piazza della Indipendenza out Porta Fontebranda).

You can call for a radio **taxi** at © 0577-49-222 (7am–9pm only); they also queue at the train station and in town at Piazza Matteotti.

VISITOR INFORMATION   The **tourist office,** where you can get a great free map, is at Piazza del Campo 56 (© 0577-280-551; fax 0577-270-676; www.siena.turismo.toscana.it). From March 21 to November 11, it's open Monday through Friday from 8:30am to 1pm and 3 to 7pm, and Saturday from 8:30am to 1pm; winter hours are Monday through Saturday from 8:30am to 7:30pm. For help finding a hotel, see the agencies under "Where to Stay," later in this section.

FESTIVALS & MARKETS   Aside from the two annual **Palio races** ✦✦✦ (see "The Palio delle Contrade," below), Siena throws a **pottery fair** in honor of the Festa di Santa Lucia on December 13. The prestigious **Accademia Musicale Chigiana** music center, Via di Città 89 (© 0577-22-091; www.chigiana.it), sponsors concerts and opera year-round (the website has a schedule), culminating in the week of the **Settimana Musicale Senese** in July or August. **St. Cecilia** is celebrated on November 22 with church concerts. The extensive main city **market** is held Wednesday from 8am to 1pm, filling the streets around the Fortezza Medicea and La Lizza park.

IL CAMPO: THE HEART OF SIENA

Via Banchi di Sopra, Via Banchi di Sotto, and Via di Città all meet at the **Loggia della Mercanzia,** begun from Sano di Matteo's plans in 1417. Here Siena's merchants argued cases before a commercial tribunal so impartial that foreign governments came to have them settle financial differences.

From here, several tunnel-like stepped alleys lead down into **Piazza del Campo** (aka **Il Campo**) ★★★, arguably the most beautiful piazza in all Italy. Crafted like a sloping scallop shell, the Campo was first laid out in the 1100s on the site of the Roman forum. The herringbone Siena brick pavement is divided by white marble lines into nine sections representing the city's medieval ruling body, the Council of Nine. The Campo's tilt, fan shape, and structure are all a calibrated part of the city's ancient water system and underground canal network. At the top of the Campo is a poor 19th-century replica of Jacopo della Quercia's 14th-century masterpiece fountain, the **Fonte Gaia** ★★. Some of the very badly eroded original panels are kept in the Palazzo Pubblico (see below).

The only surviving medieval buildings on the square are, at the top, the curving facade of the battlemented 13th-century **Palazzo Sansedoni** and at the fan's base, the city's focal point, the **Palazzo Pubblico** ★★ (1297–1310). This crenellated town hall is the city's finest Gothic palace, and the Museo Civico inside is home to Siena's best artwork (see below). When the Black Death finally abated in 1348, the city built a loggia chapel, the **Cappella della Piazza,** at the left end of the palazzo's base to give thanks that at least parts of the city had been spared. Rising above it is the slender 100m (337-ft.) tall brick **Torre del Mangia** ★ (1338–48), crowned with a Lippo Memmi–designed cresting in white travertine. It was the second-tallest tower in medieval Italy and was named after a slothful bell ringer nicknamed *Mangiaguadagni,* or "profit eater." (There's an armless statue of him in the courtyard.)

If you fancy climbing 503 steps and aren't particularly claustrophobic, the tower offers an unforgettable view across Siena's cityscape and the rolling green countryside beyond. Admission is 5€ ($5.75) with a reservation and 5.50€ ($6.30) without. You can reserve a time to climb the tower by calling ℭ **0577-41-169,** faxing 0577-226-265, or e-mailing moira@comune.siena.it. The tower (entrance in the courtyard) is open from November 1 to March 15 from 10am to 4pm and from March 16 to October 31 from 10am to 7pm.

Museo Civico ★★★   Don't be put off by the first rooms of mediocre 16th- to 18th-century works; the museum's pride comes later with the masterpieces of Sienese painting giants Simone Martini and Ambrogio Lorenzetti. The fifth room, the **Sala del Risorgimento,** was painted (1887–90) to celebrate the career of Italy's first king, Vittorio Emanuele II. A detour up the wide staircase leads up to an open-air **loggia** with Jacopo della Quercia's eroded panels from the original Gaia fountain.

The **Sala di Balìa** ★ beyond the foot of the stairs was frescoed (1407) by Spinello Aretino and his son Parri, with scenes from the *Life of Pope Alexander III,* including an exceptional naval battle. The **Anticamera del Concistoro** has a detached Ambrogio Lorenzetti fresco on the entrance wall and a Matteo di Giovanni *Madonna and Child.* The **Sala del Concistoro** was frescoed (1529–35) by Domenico Beccafumi in his best mannerist style, illustrating the heroic feats of ancient Greece and Rome in order to give the government authorities who met here a backbone.

The **vestibule** has a 1429 gilded bronze she-wolf, Siena's republican symbol and link to its Roman founding. The **Anticappella** was frescoed by Taddeo di Bartolo with ancient Greek and Roman heroes, along with the *Virtues* and a giant *St. Christopher.* The **Cappella** is difficult to see through Jacopo della Quercia's iron screen, but it was also frescoed by Domenico di Bartolo (1407–08). The altarpiece is a dark *Madonna and Child with Saints* by Sodoma.

Siena's Cumulative Tickets

Siena has several **reduced-price cumulative ticket** combos you can pick up at any of the participating museums or sites. One, valid for 2 days, covers civic museums—**Museo Civico, Santa Maria della Scala,** and the contemporary art gallery in the **Palazzo delle Papesse** on Via di Città (where admission is usually 4€–5€/$4.60–$5.75)—for 9€ ($10) total.

There are also two combined tickets that are valid for 7 days and are seasonally based. From November to March 14, you can get a 13€ ($15) 7-day ticket that includes all the sites listed above on the 2-day ticket, and also gives you access to **Museo Dell' Opera Metropolitana, Baptistery,** and **Libreria Piccolomini.** From March 15 to October for 16€ ($18), the same ticket covers all seven sites listed above plus **S. Bernardino** and **Museo Diocesano.**

Additionally, some attractions sell their own cumulative tickets, as the one for admission to both the **Museo Civico** and **Torre del Mangia**—a savings of 1.50€ ($1.75) over separate admission tickets.

The **Sala del Mappamondo** off the chapel—named after a now lost Ambrogio Lorenzetti painting of the world—contains two of Simone Martini's greatest works. On the left is his masterpiece, **_Maestà_** ⭑⭑. Incredibly, this was his very first painting, finished in 1315 (he went over it again in 1321). Cleaned and restored in the early 1990s, it's the next generation's answer to Duccio's groundbreaking work on the same theme painted just 4 years earlier and now in the Museo dell'-Opera Metropolitana (p. 215). Martini's paintings tend to be characterized by richly patterned fabrics, and the gown of the enthroned Mary is no exception.

Those fabrics can be seen again across this great hall in Simone Martini's other masterwork, the fresco of **_Guidoriccio da Fogliano_** ⭑⭑⭑, where the captain of the Sienese army rides his charger across the territory he has just conquered (Montemassi, in 1328). Recently, iconoclastic U.S. art historians have disputed the attribution of this work to Martini, claiming that it was either a slightly later work or even a 16th-century fake. Part of what sparked the debate was the 1980 discovery of another, slightly older scarred fresco lower on the wall here. This earlier painting depicts two figures standing in front of a wooden-fenced castle. Some claim this is the fresco Martini painted, while those who support the authenticity of the _Guidoriccio_ attribute this older fresco to Duccio, Pietro Lorenzetti, or Memmo di Filipuccio.

The **Sala della Pace** was where the Council of Nine met, and to keep them mindful of how well they needed to govern, the city commissioned Ambrogio Lorenzetti (1338) to fresco the walls with his masterpiece and the single most important piece of secular art to survive from medieval Europe, the **_Allegory of Good and Bad Government and Their Effects on the Town and Countryside_** ⭑⭑⭑. Good government is represented by a bearded old man surrounded by virtues (starting with a languid, sexy Peace on the left). The good effects of this government are played out on the entrance wall. A prosperous 14th-century Siena is pictured here—easily recognizable by its towers, battlemented houses, and the Duomo squeezed into the corner. The painted city wall breaks the scene in half so that the countryside—with its cultivated hillsides watched over by winged

Serenity—runs the length of the Sienese territory all the way to their seaport Talamone.

The bad government frescoes are, perhaps appropriately, in a high state of ruin. Monstrous Tyranny reigns with the help of such henchman as Cruelty, Fraud, and the creaturelike Deceit. The city under their rule is literally falling into ruin, soldiers must patrol constantly, the shops are abandoned, and citizens are robbed on the streets. The countryside, over which flies Terror, fares as badly, with scorched, lifeless fields and armed highwaymen scaring travelers off the roads.

The **Sala dei Pilastri** beyond contains a 1330 stained-glass window of St. Michael the Archangel designed by Ambrogio Lorenzetti and a *Maestà* by Guido da Siena painted in the 1270s (despite the date on it of 1221, which was perhaps used to commemorate the year St. Domenic had died). The main prize is Matteo da Giovanni's ***Massacre of the Innocents*** ★, a richly painted but highly disturbing work. They sometimes display this painting in the Sala Mappamondo.

In the Palazzo Pubblico, Piazza del Campo. ✆ **0577-292-226.** www.comune.siena.it. Admission on cumulative ticket with Torre Mangia 9€ ($10) with reservation, 9.50€ ($11) without a reservation (for other cumulative ticket options, see "Siena's Cumulative Tickets," below), or 6€ ($6.90) adults with a reservation, 6.50€ ($7.50) adults without a reservation; 3.50€ ($4.05) students and seniors over 65 with a reservation, 4€ ($4.60) students and seniors without a reservation; free for under 11. Nov 1–Mar 15 daily 10am–6:30pm; Mar 16–Oct 31 daily 10am–7pm. Bus: A (pink), B, N, 22, 25, 26, or 27.

ON PIAZZA DEL DUOMO

Duomo ★★★   Siena's cathedral is a rich treasure house of Tuscan art. Despite being an overwhelmingly Gothic building, the Duomo has one eye-popping Romanesque holdover: its 1313 **campanile** with its mighty black-and-white banding. The Duomo was built from around 1215 to 1263, involving Gothic master Nicola Pisano as architect at some point. His son, Giovanni, drew up the plans for the lower half of the **facade,** begun in 1285. Giovanni Pisano, along with his studio, also carved many of the statues decorating it (most of the originals are now in the Museo dell'Opera Metropolitana, below). The facade's upper half was added in the 14th century and is today decorated with gold-heavy, 19th-century Venetian mosaics.

The city was feeling its oats in 1339. Having defeated Florence 80 years earlier, Siena was by now its rival's equal as a middle-class-ruled republic. It began its most ambitious project yet: to turn the already huge Duomo into merely the transept of a new cathedral, one that would dwarf St. Peter's in Rome and trumpet Siena's political power, spiritual devotion, and artistic prowess. The city started the new nave off the Duomo's right transept but completed only the fabric of the walls when the Black Death hit in 1348, decimating the population and halting building plans forever. The **half-finished walls** remain—a monument to Siena's ambition and one-time wealth.

You could wander inside the Duomo for hours, just staring at the **flooring** ★, a mosaic of 59 etched and inlaid marble panels (1372–1547). Some of the top artists working in Siena lent their talents, including Domenico di Bartolo, Matteo di Giovanni, Pinturicchio, and especially Beccafumi, who designed 35 scenes (1517–47)—his original cartoons are in the Pinacoteca. The ones in the nave and aisles are usually uncovered, but the most precious ones under the apse and in the transepts are protected by cardboard flooring and uncovered from August 23 to October 3 in honor of the Palio (when admission to the cathedral is charged). The only floor panel usually visible in the Duomo's center, in the left transept, is Matteo di Giovanni's fantastic 1481 *Massacre of the Innocents* (a theme with which the painter was obsessed, leaving us disturbing paintings of it in the Palazzo Pubblico and Santa Maria dei Servi).

At the entrance to the right transept, the small octagonal **Cappella Chigi** 🟊 was designed by Roman baroque master Gian Lorenzo Bernini in 1659. It houses the *Madonna del Voto,* a fragmentary late-13th-century painting by a follower of Guido da Siena. The work fulfilled a vow the Sienese made on the eve of the Montaperti battle that they would devote their city to the Madonna should they win the fight against Florence (they did). Five times since, in times of dire need, the Sienese have placed the keys to the city in front of the miraculous Madonna and prayed for deliverance, most recently in June 1944 during Nazi occupation. Two weeks later, the city was liberated. The *St. Jerome* and *St. Mary Magdalene* statues cradling their heads in the niches nearest the door are also by Bernini, who did the organ outside the chapel as well.

At the entry to the left transept is Nicola Pisano's masterpiece **pulpit** 🟊🟊 (1265–68), on which he was assisted by his son, Giovanni, and Arnolfo di Cambio. The elegantly Gothic panels depict, as do the Pisanos' other great pulpits in Pisa and Pistoia, the life of Christ in crowded, detailed turmoil, divided by figures in flowing robes. The columns are supported on the backs of lions with their prey and cubs, and the base of the central column is a seated congregation of philosophers and figures representing the liberal arts. In the left transept's far right corner is Tino di Camaino's **tomb of Cardinal Petroni** (1313), which set the new standard for tomb design in the 14th century.

Umbrian master Pinturicchio is the star in the **Libreria Piccolomini** 🟊🟊🟊, built in 1485 by Cardinal Francesco Piccolomini (later Pope Pius III—for all of 18 days before he died in office) to house the library of his famous uncle, Pope Pius II. The marble entrance was carved by Marrina in 1497, above which Pinturicchio was commissioned to paint a large fresco of the *Coronation of Pius III* (1504). In the center of the room is a Roman copy of the Greek Praxiteles' *Three Graces,* which Pinturicchio, Raphael, and Canova studied as a model. Pinturicchio and assistants covered the ceiling and walls with 10 giant frescoes (1507) displaying Pinturicchio's rich colors, delicate modeling, limpid light, and fascination with mathematically precise, but somewhat cold, architectural space. The frescoes celebrate the life of Aeneas Silvio Piccolomini, better known as the humanist Pope Pius II. The next-to-last scene on the left wall records the act Siena most remembers the pope for, canonizing local girl Catherine as a saint in 1461.

Next door to the library's entrance is the **Piccolomini Altar** 🟊, designed by Andrea Bregno around 1480. The *Madonna and Child* above may be Jacopo della Quercia's earliest work (1397–1400). A young, squash-nosed Michelangelo carved the statuettes of *Sts. Peter, Pius, Paul,* and *Gregory* in the other niches here (1501–04).

Piazza del Duomo. 📞 **0577-283-048.** www.operaduomo.it. Admission to church free, except when floor uncovered in Sept–Oct, then 5.50€ ($6.30); Libreria Piccolomini on cumulative ticket, or 1.50€ ($1.75). Mar 15–Oct daily 9am–7:30pm; Nov–Mar 14 daily 10am–1pm and 2:30–5pm.

Museo dell'Opera Metropolitana 🟊🟊

Housed in the walled-up right aisle of the Duomo's abortive new nave, Siena's Duomo museum contains all the works removed from the facade for conservation as well as disused altarpieces, including Duccio's masterpiece. It also offers one of the city's best views. The **ground floor** has the fascinating but weatherworn facade **statues by Giovanni Pisano** and his school (1284–96), remarkable for their Gothic plasticity and craned, elongated necks. (When they were 50 ft. up in niches, these protruding necks made sure their faces were visible from the ground.) In the center of the room is Jacopo della Quercia's last work, a 1438 marble panel of *Cardinal Casini Presented to the Virgin by St. Anthony Abbot.* Also here is a luminous marble tondo of the **Madonna and Child** ⭐ carved in refined *schiacciato* relief. Most scholars now agree it's the work of Donatello. There are more statues out a side door, but that leads to the exit, so first head up the stairs.

Upstairs is the museum's, if not the city's, masterpiece, **Duccio's *Maestà*** ⭐⭐⭐. It's impossible to overstate the importance of this double-sided altarpiece, now separated and displayed on opposite sides of the intimate room. Not only did it virtually found the Sienese school of painting, but it has also been considered one of the most important late medieval paintings in all Europe since the day it was unveiled. When Duccio finished the work on June 9, 1311, it was reportedly carried in procession from the painter's workshop to the Duomo's altar by the clergy, government officials, and every last citizen in Siena. The centuries have, all told, been unusually kind to it. Although eight of the predella panels are in foreign museums and one is lost (12 pinnacle angels suffered similar fates), it's otherwise remarkably intact and in great shape. The central scene of the *Maestà,* or Virgin Mary in Majesty enthroned and surrounded by saints, became the archetypal grand subject for a Sienese painter. Her dark bulk and the gorgeous inlaid throne contribute to the Madonna's majesty, while the soft folds of her robes and her gentle features bring out her humanity.

On the wall is an early Duccio *Madonna and Child.* Almost overlooked here is Pietro Lorenzetti's incredible ***Birth of the Virgin*** ⭐⭐. The perspective in the piece may be a bit off, but Lorenzetti broke traditions and artistic boundaries with his fabrics, his colors, and (most important) the architectural space he created. Instead of painting a triptych with a central main scene and two unrelated side panels of saints, as was the norm, Lorenzetti created a single continuous space by painting vaulted ceilings that seem to grow back from the pointed arches of the triptych's frame. Pietro never got a chance to develop these ideas; this is the last work he painted before succumbing to the plague.

The upper floor's **Treasury Room** has a remarkable early *Crucifix* by Giovanni Pisano (ca. 1280), a 13th-century gilded silver reliquary containing the head of St. Galgano, and paintings by Domenico Beccafumi, Sassetta, and Vecchietta kept in a usually locked side room. In the **Sala della Madonna degli Occhi Grossi,** the namesake *Madonna of the Big Eyes,* which got nudged off the cathedral's high altar by Duccio's *Maestà,* was painted in 1220s by the "Maestro di Tressa." Also here are some Ambrogio Lorenzetti *Saints* (and a few by Il Sodoma), and *Madonna and Child* works by Matteo di Giovanni, Sano di Pietro, and the "Master of Città di Castello."

If you take the stairs (past rooms of baroque canvases and church vestments) that lead up to the walkway atop the would-be facade of the "New Duomo," you get the best visualization of how the enlarged Duomo would have looked as well as sweeping **views** ⭐⭐ across the city's rooftops with the Torre del Mangia towering over the Palazzo Pubblico.

Piazza del Duomo 8. Ⓒ 0577-42-390 or 0577-283-048. www.operaduomo.siena.it. Admission on cumulative ticket, or 5.50€ ($6.30). Mar 15–Sept daily 9am–7:30pm; Oct daily 9am–6pm; Nov–Mar 14 daily 9am–1pm.

Baptistery ⭐ The Duomo's baptistery was built in the 14th century beneath the cathedral's choir and supports a Gothic facade left unfinished by Domenico di Agostino (1355). The upper walls and vaulted ceilings inside were **frescoed by Vecchietta** and his school in the late 1440s (look for the alligator) but "touched up" in the 19th century. What you're here to see, though, is the **baptismal font** ⊛ (1417–30). The frames are basically Gothic, but the gilded brass panels were cast by the foremost Sienese and Florentine sculptors of the early Renaissance. Starting on the side facing the altar, Siena's master Jacopo della Quercia did the *Annunciation to Zacharias.* Giovanni di Turino did the next two, the *Birth of the Baptist* and the *Preaching of the Baptist.* The *Baptism of Christ* is by the author of the Baptistery doors in Florence, Lorenzo Ghiberti, who collaborated with Giuliano di Ser Andrea on the *Arrest of St. John.* The final panel is perhaps the greatest, Donatello's masterful early study of precise perspective and profound depth in the *Feast of Herod.*

Piazza San Giovanni (down the stairs around the back right flank of the Duomo). ℭ **0577-283-048.** www. operaduomo.it. Admission on cumulative ticket, or 2€ ($2.30). Mar 15–Sept daily 9am–7:30pm; Oct daily 9am–6pm; Nov–Mar 14 daily 10am–5pm.

Ospedale di Santa Maria della Scala ⊛   The hospital across from the Duomo entrance cared for the infirm from the 800s up until the 1990s, when it began to restructure as a museum and exhibition space. At press time, temporary shows were being held, and they've incorporated the city's archaeological collections, but there are plans to perhaps move here the Pinacoteca's paintings. The original decorations of the hospital itself, inside, however, merit a visit on their own. And if the round stained-glass window from the cathedral's apse is still under restoration here, by all means check it out—it's your only chance to see up close the oldest stained glass of Italian manufacture, designed by Duccio in 1288.

The first fresco you see, just after the ticket booth, is Domenico Beccafumi's luridly colored **Meeting at Porta Andrea** (after 1512). Off to the left, just past the bookshop, is the entrance to the **Sala del Pellegrinaio** ⊛, which held hospital beds until just a few years ago. The walls were frescoed in the 1440s with scenes from the history of the hospital and its good works (all labeled). Most are vivid masterpieces by Domenico di Bartolo, richly colored and full of amusing details. However, Vecchietta did the upwardly mobile orphans over the exit door; Jacopo della Quercia's less talented and little known brother, Priamo, did a cartoonish scene on the left wall; and a pair of mannerist hacks filled in the spaces at the room's end.

Downstairs are rooms documenting the restoration of Jacopo della Quercia's Fonte Gaia with plaster casts, and the **Oratorio di Santa Caterina della Notte.** This latter was decorated mainly in the 17th century by Rustici and Rutilio Manetti but also contains a rich *Madonna and Child with Saints, Angels, and Musicians* by Taddeo di Bartolo (ca. 1400) in the back room. Exit through the church of **Santissima Annunziata,** with a bronze *Risen Christ* by Vecchietta over the high altar and an apse-covering fresco by Sebastiano Conca (1732).

The collection in Siena's new modern **archaeology museum,** recently incorporated into the Santa Maria della Scala complex, is small, and while there's nothing of earth-shattering significance, there are some surprisingly good pieces for a museum hardly anyone knows exists. Wander past fading frescoes to examine local Etruscan bronzes, black *bucchero* vases, funerary urns in terra cotta and alabaster, and some Roman pocket change.

Piazza del Duomo 2. ℭ **0577-49-153;** www.santamaria.comune.siena.it. Admission on cumulative ticket, or 4.70€ ($5.40) with reservations, 5.20€ ($6) without reservations. Mar 15–Nov 5 Mon–Sat 10am–6:30pm; Nov 6–14 Mar Mon–Sat 10:30am–4:30pm.

THE PALIO DELLE CONTRADE

No other festival in Italy is as colorful, as intense, or as spectacular as **Siena's Palio** ⊛⊛⊛. Twice a year, Siena packs the Piazza del Campo with dirt and runs a no-holds-barred bareback horse race around it, the highlight of a full week of trial runs, feasts, parades, spectacles of skill, and solemn ceremonies. The tradition, in one form or another, goes back to at least 1310.

The Palio is a deadly serious competition, and while Siena doesn't mind if visitors show up (you may, in fact, find yourself adopted into the *contrada* of the 1st person you make friends with and invited to the communal feasts), but in the end visitors are peripheral. The Palio is for the Sienese.

To understand the Palio—really, to understand Siena—you must know something of the *contrada* system. In the 14th century there were about 42 *contrade,* neighborhood wards that helped provide militia support for Siena's defense. The number of wards was successively reduced until the current 17 *contrade* were fixed in 1675. Each ward is named after an animal or object—*Drago* (Dragon), *Giraffa* (Giraffe), *Istrice* (Porcupine), *Onda* (Wave), *Torre* (Tower)—and each has its own headquarters, social club, museum, and church.

Each *contrada* has always been responsible for its own. You are born into the *contrada* of your parents, are baptized in your *contrada's* open-air font, learn your *contrada's* allies and enemies at an early age, go to church in your *contrada's* oratory, almost invariably marry within your *contrada,* spend your free time hanging out in the *contrada* social club, and help elect or serve on your *contrada's* governing body. Even your funeral is sponsored by the *contrada,* which mourns your passing as family. In a way, it's like a benevolent form of Hollywood's mythical Mafia—but no *contrada* tolerates unlawfulness, and as a result Siena has a shockingly low crime rate.

Ten *contrade* are chosen by lot each year to ride in the **July 2** Palio (established in 1659). The other seven, plus three of the July riders, run the even bigger Palio on **August 16** (which dates from 1310). Although both races are technically equal in importance, the August Palio gets the most attention, partly because it's older but mainly because it's a sort of rematch, the last chance to win for the year. Actually, chance really is what wins the Palio: Your opportunity to ride, the horse you're given, and the order you're lined up on the track are each chosen by separate lots; even your jockey is a wild card. He's always imported—traditionally a Maremma horseman, but many come these days from Sardegna and Sicily as well—and you'll never know how well he'll ride, whether the bribe one of your rival *contrade* may slip him will outweigh the wages you paid, or if he'll even make it to the race without being ambushed. If your jockey does turn on you, you'd better hope he's thrown quickly. The Palio, you see, is a true horse race—the horse is the one that wins (it's hoped no rivals have drugged it), whether there's a rider still on it or not. The jockey's main job is to hang onto the horse's bare back and thrash the other horses and their riders with the stiff ox-hide whip he's given for the purpose. The Palio may at this point seem pretty lawless, but there actually is one rule: No jockey can grab another horse's reins.

At the two 90-degree turns of the Campo, almost every year a rider or two—and occasionally an entire horse—goes flying out of the racetrack to land among the stands or slams up against the mattresses prudently padding the palazzi walls. Sienese lore, however, maintains that no one has ever died in the running of a Palio. What is the prize for all this? A *palio,* a banner painted with the image of the Virgin Mary, in whose name the race is run. That, and the honor of your *contrada.* The Sienese refer to the *palio* banner offhandedly as *il cencio* (the rag), trying their best to sound flippant about the single greatest object of their collective desires and aspirations.

The Palios really start on June 29 and August 13, when the lots are drawn to select the 10 lucky racers and the trial races begin. Over the next 2 days, morning and afternoon trial runs are held, and on the evening before each Palio, the *con-trade* hold an all-night feast and party lasting more or less until the 7:45am Jockey's Mass in the Cappella della Piazza on the Campo. There's a final heat at 9am, then everybody dissolves to his or her separate *contrada* for last-minute preparations. The highlight is the 3pm (3:30pm in July) Blessing of the Horse in each *contrada*'s church—a little manure dropping at the altar is a sign of good luck—at which the deacon ends with a resounding command to the horse: "Go forth, and return a winner!"

Unless invited by a *contrada,* you're probably not going to get into any of the packed churches for this, so your best strategy is to stick around the Campo all day. Because standing in the center of the Campo for the race is free (the grand-stands require tickets; see below), you should ideally stake out a spot close to the start-finish line before 2pm. Just before 5pm, the pageantry begins, with pro-cessions led by a contingent from Montalcino in honor of it harboring the last members of the Sienese Republic in the 16th century. The *palio* banner is drawn about the piazza in the War Chariot (a wagon drawn by two snowy white oxen), and *contrada* youths in Renaissance costume juggle huge, colorful banners in the *sbandierata* flag-throwing display.

At 7:30pm (7pm in July) the horses start lining up between two ropes. Much care is taken to get the first nine in some indeterminate perfect order. After count-less false starts and equine finagling, suddenly the tenth horse comes thundering up from behind, and as soon as he hits the first rope the second one is dropped and the race is on. Three laps and fewer than 90 seconds later, it's over. The win-ning *contrada* bursts into songs celebrating its greatness, losers cry in each other's arms, and those who suspect their jockeys of double-crossing them chase the hap-less men—whose horses don't stop running at the finish line—through the streets, howling for blood. The banquets that night, at long tables laid out on the streets of each *contrada,* are more solemn than the feasts of the night before, with only the winners truly living it up—their party goes on for several days.

If standing in the middle of the hot and crowded Campo doesn't attract you—and anyone with a small bladder might want to think twice, as there are no facilities and no one is allowed in or out from just before the procession until the race is over (about 3½ hr.)—you can try to buy a ticket for a seat in the grandstands or at a window of one of the buildings surrounding the piazza. These are controlled by the building owners and the shops in front of which the stands are set up and cost anywhere from 348€ ($400) for a single seat to 1,217€ ($1,400) for a window seating four people. They sell out sometimes up to 6 months before the race itself. **Palio Viaggi,** Piazza Gramsci 7 (© **0577-280-828**), can help you score a few, and the tourist office has all the contacts for the individual shops and buildings if you want to negotiate directly for a seat. If you show up late and sans ticket, make your way up Via Giovanni Duprè to the Piazza del Mercato behind the Palazzo Pubblico; the police stationed there will often allow people into the Campo between the processions and the race itself.

SEEING THE REST OF SIENA
IN TERZA DI CITTÀ
Pinacoteca Nazionale ⍟   Siena's painting gallery houses the most representa-tive collection of the Sienese school of art. It wouldn't be fair to label it a museum of second-rate paintings by first-rate artists, but the supreme masterpieces of Siena do lie elsewhere. It's laid out more or less chronologically starting on the second floor, though the museum is constantly rearranging (especially the last

bits), and there are rumors that all the collections will eventually be moved to the Ospedale di Santa Maria della Scala (p. 217).

Room 1 contains the first definite work of the Sienese school, a 1215 altar frontal by the "Maestro di Teresa," and one of the earliest known paintings on canvas, Guido da Siena's *Scenes from the Life of Christ* (late 1200s). Rooms 3 and 4 have works by the first great Sienese master, Duccio, including an early masterpiece showing Cimabue's influence, the tiny 1285 *Madonna dei Francescani* (in poor condition; kept under glass). Rooms 5 to 8 pay homage to the three great early-14th-century painters, Simone Martini and the brothers Pietro and Ambrogio Lorenzetti. Of Martini, be sure to look at the *Madonna and Child* (1321) from the Pieve di San Giovanni Battista and the *Altar of Beato Agostino Novello.* Martini's brother-in-law Lippo Memmi weighs in with a fresco fragment of the *Madonna and Child with Saints,* and there's a gold-heavy *Ascension* by the "Maestro di Ovile." The best Lorenzetti works are in the small side rooms off room 7, including a *Madonna Enthroned* and a *Madonna of the Carmelites* by Pietro; also look for Ambrogio's small cityscapes of castles and cities, and his last dated work, a 1344 *Annunciation.*

In the atrium corridor are some 14th-century Sienese and Florentine works, then rooms 13 to 19 feature 15th-century Sienese paintings by the likes of Giovanni di Paolo, including a 1440 *Crucifixion* and two of the *Presentation at the Temple.* Matteo di Giovanni is also represented here before passing to the work of Sano di Pietro, Vecchietta, and Francesco di Giorgio Martini. The third floor houses a small, formerly private collection of 16th- and 17th-century paintings, including a Durer *St. Jerome.*

The regular collections continue on the first floor, which is often rearranged. Among the paintings are two by the "Maestro di Volterra," a Pinturicchio *Holy Family,* and Girolama Genga's 1509 frescoes *Ransom of Prisoners* and the *Flight of Aeneas from Troy.* The museum sometimes displays in the next rooms its many works by mannerist master Domenico Beccafumi, including a *Trinity with Saints,* a *Stigmata of St. Catherine,* a *Birth of the Virgin,* and a particularly fine *Christ Descending into Limbo.* Also look for Beccafumi's huge **cartoons** 🎨🎨, from which many of the panels in the Duomo floor were made. Beccafumi's 16th-century rival, who painted more in the classicist branch of the High Renaissance rather than the mannerist, was Sodoma, also well represented here. If it's on display, you can compare the two painters by looking at Sodoma's take on *Christ in Limbo;* it's a brighter work with a better use of color but lacks Beccafumi's weird mastery of light and experimentation with form. The detached fresco of Sodoma's *Christ at the Column* is remarkably realistic and has a fascinating use of rich colors, as does his large and detailed *Deposition,* where parts of the scene are reflected in the soldier's armor and helm.

Via San Pietro 29. 📞 **0577-281-161.** Admission 4€ ($4.60). Mon 8:30am–1:30pm; Tues–Sat 8:15am–7:15pm; Sun 8:15am–1:15pm.

San Niccolò al Carmine (aka Santa Maria del Carmine)
This 14th-century church on the edge of town was remodeled by Sienese master architect Baldassare Peruzzi in 1517 and contains some good baroque works. Search out especially Domenico Beccafumi's eerily luminous *St. Michael,* on the right wall's altar. The chapel holds Sodoma's dark *Birth of the Virgin.* The left side of the church has—to balance the Beccafumi—a beat-up but well-done *Ascension* by Girolamo del Pacchia.

Pian dei Mantellini. No phone. Free admission. Bus: A (green, yellow).

IN TERZA DI SAN MARTINO

Palazzo Piccolomini   This 1469 palace is a touch of Florence peeking into the southeast corner of the Campo. It was designed by Bernardo Rossellino in the Florentine Renaissance style and is now home to the *Archivio di Stato* (head down the corridor off the left of the courtyard to grab the elevator to the 4th floor). The state archives (closed at press time for renovations) preserve, among other notable documents, Boccaccio's will and Jacopo della Quercia's contract for the Fonte Gaia. But the main thing to see is a remarkable set of wooden covers made for the city's account books, called the **Tavolette di Biccerna** ⊛, painted from the 13th to 17th centuries with religious scenes and important events in Siena's history—Sano di Pietro, Vecchietta, Domenico Beccafumi, and Ambrogio Lorenzetti even did a few.

Via Banchi di Sotto 52 (between Via Banchi di Sotto and Via del Porrione at Via Rinaldini). ℂ 0577-247-145. www.comune.siena.it. Free admission. Currently closed for renovations (previous hours were Mon–Sat 9am–1pm). Bus: A (pink), B, N, 22, 25, 26, or 27.

San Martino   Beyond a 1613 facade by Giovanni Fontana, this little church, whose founding dates from before the 8th century, retains a few good late Renaissance paintings. The second altar on the right has a Guido Reni *Circumcision* (1636), and beyond it is a severely darkened Il Guercino *Martyrdom of St. Bartholomew*. The high altar is a fair baroque job by Giuseppe Mazzuoli, and as you leave take a good look at Domenico Beccafumi's mannerist *Nativity* on the third altar of the left aisle.

Just to the facade's left is the Renaissance **Loggia del Papa** (1462), built for Pius II. When you exit San Martino, head left down Via delle Scotte to no. 14 to see the 18th-century **Synagogue,** a remnant of the Jewish ghetto that existed behind the Campo from 1571 to 1796. You can visit by guided tour only (for a donation of about 2.60€/$3) every 40 minutes on Sundays from 10am to 1pm and 2 to 5pm (to 4pm Nov–Mar); book at the Florentine number ℂ **055-234-6654** (for more info, in Italian, see www.fol.it/sinagoga/sienai.htm).

Off Via Banchi di Sotto. No phone. Free admission. Bus: A (pink), B, N, 22, 25, 26, or 27.

Santa Maria dei Servi   Beyond some cypress and a small patch of green grass, this huge 13th-century church sits facadeless, with mute rough brick climbing up the front next to an enormous campanile. The second chapel on the right aisle houses the church's masterpiece, a late Byzantine-style **Madonna del Bordone** ⊛ by Coppo di Marcovaldo, signed in 1261. The third chapel jumps ahead to the baroque with Rutilio Manetti's *Birth of the Virgin,* and the Renaissance is represented in the fifth chapel with Matteo di Giovanni's stupendous and frightening *Massacre of the Innocents* (1491). The right transept has another take on the subject in the second chapel to the right of the altar; this *Massacre* was probably frescoed by Francesco di Segna with the help of Niccoló di Segna and Pietro Lorenzetti. Across the transept are a painted *Crucifix* by Niccoló di Segna in the chapel and an *Annunciatory Angel* by Francesco Vanni (the *Mary Annunciate* half is in the left transept). The second chapel to the left of the high altar has frescoed scenes from the *Life of St. John the Baptist,* again by the di Segnas and Pietro Lorenzetti; Taddeo di Bartolo did the *Nativity* altarpiece in 1404.

Piazza A. Manzoni. No phone. Free admission. Bus: A (pink), B, N, 22, 25, 26, or 27.

IN TERZA DI CAMOLLIA

Siena's northern third spreads off either side of the palace-lined **Via Banchi di Sopra.** Two blocks up on the left is the oldest Gothic palace in the city, the

Palazzo Tolomei, begun in 1208 and now home to the Cassa di Risparmio di Firenze bank. The piazza out front is where the city council met from the 11th century until the Palazzo Pubblico was built. Two blocks farther is the piazza formed by the Gothic **Palazzo Salimbeni** and its tributary palaces, linked to form the seat of the Monte di Paschi di Siena, Siena's powerhouse bank founded in 1472 and still a strong player in Italian finance (and the city's largest employer).

San Francesco   A late Gothic church (1326–1475), Siena's Franciscan barn was badly damaged in a 1655 fire and used as a military barracks for a long time before being reconstructed in the 1880s. On the inside of the entrance wall you can see what happens to frescoes that are left out under the elements at city gates. Remounted here are heavily deteriorated works that once graced tabernacles at the Porta Romana (on the left, painted by Sassetta and Sano di Pietro) and the Porta Pispini (on the right, by Sodoma). On the right wall are 14th- or 15th-century Sienese school frescoes. In the second chapel to the right of the altar is a tomb with a *schiacciato* effigy carved by Urbano da Cortona (1462–87); the chapel to its left has a late-14th-century *Madonna and Child* by St. Catherine's friend Andrea Vanni. The first chapel to the left of the altar contains a detached *Crucifixion* by Pietro Lorenzetti, whose brother Ambrogio did the excellent frescoes, now in poor condition, kept in the third chapel down. What's left of these early 1330s works, Ambrogio's first fresco attempt, depict the *Martyrdom of Franciscan Missionaries at Ceuta* and *St. Louis d'Angou Taking Leave of Pope Boniface VIII,* where Lorenzetti makes you, the viewer, part of the papal court looking on. The last choir chapel has a *Madonna and Child Enthroned* attributed to Jacopo di Mino.

Piazza San Francesco. No phone. Free admission. Daily 7am–noon and 3:30–7pm.

Oratorio di San Bernardino e Museo Diocesano ⚐   The church of San Francesco was where St. Bernardine first donned his monkish robes. The exact spot where he prayed and began preaching is now marked by the **Oratory of San Bernardino,** built in the late 15th century. The lower of the oratory's two levels was frescoed by the best 17th-century Sienese artists—including Francesco Vanni, Rutilio and Domenico Manetti, and Ventura Salimbeni—and houses a little *Madonna* by Sano di Pietro. The upper level has higher-quality **frescoes** ⚐ by 16th-century artists Sodoma, Domenico Beccafumi, and Girolamo del Pacchia. The rooms that make up the **Diocesian Museum** contain mostly unremarkable paintings and churchly artifacts.

Via del Comune doglegs off Via dei Rossi just down from Piazza San Francesco and leads to the 14th-century double city gate **Porta Ovile,** which preserves a tabernacle frescoed by Sano di Pietro. Just outside the gate you'll find the 1262 **Fonte Ovile,** one of the city's most picturesque public fountains.

Piazza San Francesco 18. ℂ **0577-283-048**; www.operaduomo.siena.it. Admission 2.50€ ($2.90). Mar 15–Oct daily 10:30am–1:30pm and 3–5:30pm. Closed Nov–March 14.

Casa di Santa Caterina ⚐   The remarkable Caterina Benincasa, daughter of a rich Sienese dyer, took a nun's veil (but never an order's vows) in 1355 at the age of 8 after her first of many visions of Christ. In 1375, a Crucifix in Pisa cinched her holiness by giving her the stigmata of Christ's wounds. Her name and reputation for devout wisdom and saintly life spread, and in 1378 she was chosen as Siena's ambassador to Pope Gregory XI in Avignon. There, her eloquent letter writing and sharp, argumentative mind eventually succeeded in doing what no amount of traditional political finagling had been able to accomplish for 73 years: She persuaded the pope to leave civilized Avignon and return the papal seat to Rome, which was then a medieval backwater rife with the armed squabbles of noble clans. Caterina died in Rome in 1380, at age 33, and was canonized 80 years later. In 1939, she was declared patron saint of Italy, and in 1970, together with St. Teresa of Avila, received the highest honor the church can bestow. Saints Catherine and Teresa became the first women ever elevated to Doctor of the Church.

The house where she was born was converted into a sanctuary in 1466, and it remains a peaceful, reflective spot. The entrance is a small brick-lined courtyard where you can occasionally see a pair of Goose *contrada* teenagers practicing the complicated art of flag tossing for the Palio. Beyond this is a small but pretty little loggia built in 1533 by Peruzzi or his student Giovanni Battista Pelori.

To the left is the old family kitchen transformed into an **oratory** and decorated in the 16th and 19th centuries with paintings by Il Pomarancio, Il Riccio, Francesco Vanni, and others. The majolica-tiled floor is 16th century. The **church** opposite the oratory was built in 1623 over Catherine's orchard to house the 12th-century Pisan-school *Crucifixion* in front of which the saint received the stigmata. Back under the loggia, the stairs lead down past Catherine's **cell,** frescoed in 1896, toward the Goose *contrada*'s church, the **Oratorio dell'Oca** (seldom open, but containing works by Sodoma).

At the bottom of Via Santa Caterina below, nestled amid the remaining green of the narrow valley between San Domenico and the Duomo, is the brick 1246 **Fonte Branda,** a public washhouse battlemented like a tiny fortress.

Costa di San Antonio (between Via della Sapienza and Via Santa Caterina). 🕐 **0577-247-393.** www. caterinati.org. Free admission. Easter–Oct daily 9am–12:30pm and 3–6pm; winter daily 9am–12:30pm and 3:30–6pm. Bus: A (red), 2, 5.

San Domenico 🐦★ The Dominican's Siena home is an enormous, severe, and vaguely unattractive pile of bricks (1226), jutting above a modern section of town. There are good views here, though, of the Duomo and Siena's rooftops. The raised chapel off the west end (to the right as you enter) preserves the only genuine *Portrait of St. Catherine,* painted by her friend and contemporary Andrea Vanni.

The **Cappella di Santa Caterina (Chapel of St. Catherine)** halfway down the right wall was frescoed with scenes from the saint's life. All except the right wall (where in 1593 Francesco Vanni painted Catherine performing an exorcism) were frescoed by Sodoma in 1526. The large work on the left wall of her interceding on behalf of a condemned man as well as the other scenes of her in ecstasy and swooning are some of Sodoma's best work. Drop some coins in the light box and the frescoes as well as Catherine's venerated head, in a gilt reliquary case, on the altar light up.

At the end of the nave, on the right, is a *Nativity* by Francesco di Giorgio Martini dominated by a crumbling Roman triumphal arch in the background and a *Pietà* above. The first chapel to the right of the altar is home to a *Madonna and Child with Saints* by Matteo di Giovanni, one of whose masterpieces, *St. Barbara Enthroned with Angels and Sts. Mary Magdalen and Catherine,* is in the second chapel of the left transept. An altar on the right as you leave has a 14th-century *Madonna and Child Surrounded by Four Saints and God* by Sodoma, with a 16th-century Siena skyline above the tiny-paneled predella.

Piazza San Domenico. No phone. Free admission. Apr–Oct 7am–12:55pm and 3–6:30pm; Nov–Mar 9am–12:55pm and 3–6pm. Bus: 1, 3, 6, 10, 18, 30, 31, 37, or 106.

Enoteca Italiana 🐦🐦 The 16th-century Fortezza Medicea has been turned into a public park. Its courtyard is an open-air theater, its ramparts are a place for a stroll and a view, and its vaults are filled with Italy's national wine museum.

Seated at small tables in the tunnel-like brick halls or out on the terraces in summer, you can sample a choice selection of Tuscan and Italian wines by the glass or go all out on an entire bottle from their extensive *cantine* (more than 1200 labels cool their heels here). It wouldn't be fair to say this is a truly representative collection, because not all vintners choose to take part, but it has been Italy's official state-mandated *museo del vino* since 1950. Out of Italy's some 4,000 wines, it preserves at least all 266 kinds of DOC, each of the 17 DOCG labels, and every last one of Italy's 128 IGT wines.

Fortezza Medicea. ☏ **0577-288-497.** www.enoteca-italiana.it. Free admission; glass of wine 2€–5€ ($2.30–$5.75). Cold plate of typical regional foods 7.50€–12€ ($8.65–$14). Mon noon–8pm; Tues–Sat noon–1am. Closed Dec 25–Jan 6.

SHOPPING

ANTIQUES   The best antiques shop in town is the **Antichità Monna Agnese** (☏ **0577-282-288**), with a main branch at Via di Città 60 and another across the street at no. 45 that specializes in jewelry.

BOOKS & PAPER   The **Libreria Senese,** Via di Città 62–66 (☏ **0577-280-845**), has the largest selection of English-language books, though it's now getting competition from the chain store **Feltrinelli,** with store entrances at Via Banchi di Sopra 52 and 64–66 (☏ **0577-271-104** or 0577-44-009). For art and coffee-table books, often at a discount, hit **Arte & Libri,** Via di Città 111 (☏ **0577-221-325**). The Siena branch of Florence's **Il Papiro,** Via di Città 37 (☏ **0577-284-241**), carries fine stationery, marbleized paper products, and wonderful journals (leather-bound and otherwise).

CERAMICS & HOUSEWARES   Though lots of ceramics shops line Via di Città, they're mainly only of souvenir quality. The work of **Ceramiche Artistiche Santa Caterina,** with showrooms at Via di Città 51, 74, and 76 (☏ **0577-283-098**) and a workshop outside town at Via P.A. Mattioli 12 (☏ **0577-45-006**), is not. Maestro Marcello Neri trained at Siena's art school and in the ceramics workshops of Montelupo Fiorentino, Tuscany's foremost ceramics center, before taking over this studio in 1961, aided by his talented wife, Franca Franci, and now their adult son, Fabio, also an art school grad. Look especially for their wares painted in "Sienese style" using only black, white, and *terra di Siena* reddish brown (what we call burnt sienna) with designs inspired by the oldest pavement panels in the Duomo.

Muzzi Sergio, Via dei Termini 97 (☏ **0577-40-439**), is a friendly designer housewares shop, perfect for that set of grappa glasses or Alessi kitchen gadget.

CLOTHING   For men's and women's high fashion, bring your credit cards along for a date with Armani, Gucci, Versace, Burberry, Missoni—and some more affordable labels—at **Cortecci,** Via Banchi di Sopra 27 (☏ **0577-280-096;** www.corteccisiena.it). There's also a branch on Il Campo at 30–31 (☏ **0577-280-984**).

For something a bit more unique, drop by Fioretta Bacci and her pair of giant looms taking up most of the room at **Tessuti a Mano,** Via San Pietro 7 (☏ **0577-282-200**). Fioreta weaves all her incredible scarves, shawls, and sweaters by hand.

Fabrics and linens, both as raw materials and made into sheets, curtains, or embroidered hand towels, are the stock in trade of Debora Loreni's **Antiche Dimore,** Via di Città 115 (☏ **0577-45-337**). Signora Bruna Brizi Fontani is a bundle of energy and full of stories in her little embroidery and needlepoint store, **Siena Ricama,** Via di Città 61 (☏ **0577-288-339**). She spends so much time amiably gabbing with visitors to her workroom and shop, I wonder when she finds the time to finish the wonderful lampshades and other objects—every one stitched by Fontani herself. They're inspired by medieval Sienese art: the Duomo floor, illuminated manuscripts, the frescoes of the Lorenzetti brothers, and anything else that catches her fancy from art history books and local museums.

FOOD   Siena's classiest stop for foodies is the glass-and-wood-shelved shop of the **Antica Drogheria Manganelli,** Via di Città 71–73 (✆ **0577-280-002**), since 1879 making its own *panforte* (one of the few left) and delicious soft *ricciarelli* almond cookies. It also carries the tops in Tuscan products, like vinegar from Castello di Volpaia and cured meats from Greve in Chianti's Falorni butchers.

For less touristy (and cheaper) pickings of traditional regional foods, head to one of the spots where many Sienese come to stock up. **La Terra di Siena,** Via G. Duprè 32 (✆ **0577-223-528**), looks like a bargain basement–type place with stacks of regional products like Sienese cookies and area wines, honeys, cheeses, and meats, but it actually carries quality merchandise (at great prices). The supermarket-like **Consorzio Agrario Siena,** Via Piangiani 9 (✆ **0577-2301**), has been a farmer's co-op since 1901; most of the produce comes direct from the farm, and much of the packaged goods were packaged locally.

For fresh pastries, you can't beat **Pasticceria Bini,** behind the left flank of the Duomo at Via dei Fusari 9–13 (✆ **0577-280-207**), where since 1943 they've filled the neighborhood with irresistible scents as they make their delicious sweets on-site—you can watch them at work through the next window down the street.

WHERE TO STAY

For help finding a room, there are two private agencies. Stop by the **Siena Hotels Promotion** booth on Piazza San Domenico (✆ **0577-288-084;** fax 0577-280-290; www.hotelsiena.com), where for 1.50€ to 4€ ($1.75–$4.60), depending on the category of hotel, they'll find you a room and reserve it. The booth is open Monday through Saturday from 9am to 7pm (until 8pm in summer). In the underground office of Parcheggio il Campo parking lot, Via Fontanella 4, is **Protur** (✆ **0577-45-900;** fax 0577-283-145; www.protur.it), which will book you a room for free; it also runs guided tours of Siena and its province.

VERY EXPENSIVE

Park Hotel Siena ⚐   The great Sienese Renaissance architect Peruzzi built this villa on a ridge northwest of the city in 1530 for the Gori family. It even has a small-scale replica of Siena's Campo, with a view of the tower over the real one far in the distance. The inside, however, has mostly been redone—the salons and bar area in a Belle Epoque style and the rooms in an uninspired but plush modern style. With these prices, the bathrooms could stand an overhaul. It is, however, one of the few hotels in Tuscany with its own golf course, and the hotel keeps a few well-manicured gardens.

Via Marciano 18, 53100 Siena. ✆ **0577-44-803.** Fax 0577-49-020. www.parkhotelsiena.it. 69 units. 255€–412€ ($293–$474) double; 473€–819€ ($544–$942) suite. Breakfast 26€ ($30). AE, DC, MC, V. Free parking. **Amenities:** Restaurant opens onto a garden in summer; bar service in lush old-fashioned salons; outdoor pool; 6-hole golf course; tennis court; bike rental; concierge; tour desk; car-rental desk; shuttle bus into town; in-room massage; babysitting; room service; laundry service; dry cleaning; nonsmoking rooms. *In room:* A/C, TV, minibar, hair dryer, safe.

EXPENSIVE

Hotel Chiusarelli   This vaguely neoclassical palm-fronted villa in need of an exterior face-lift (and an elevator) is just a 5-minute hike from the Campo yet only half a block from the bus depot; it's not a particularly pretty area but certainly convenient. The rooms are functionally nondescript, with linoleum or parquet floors and firm beds, and a recent renovation has prettied them up a bit—though certainly not to 225€ ($259) levels!—and the bathrooms have been redone with shower/tubs. The rooms look over either the noisy road or the clipped lawn of the soccer stadium out back. Monday through Saturday, the latter are the quietest rooms in the house; come Sunday in soccer season, however, you're in for a noisy, but entertainingly educational, afternoon. This is a "proper" hotel with a bar, a breakfast terrace, a restaurant (avoid the half- or full-board option that requires you to eat here and go to one of my suggestions below), and tour groups.

Viale Curtatone 15 (near San Domenico), 53100 Siena. ✆ **0577-280-562**. Fax 0577-271-177 www. chiusarelli.com. 49 units, 48 with bathroom. 225€ ($259) double with bathroom; 153€ ($175) triple with bathroom; 187€ ($214) quad with bathroom. Rates include breakfast. AE, MC, V. Free parking (8 spaces) or around 18€ ($21) in garage. **Amenities:** Restaurant; concierge; tour desk; limited room service; Internet access. *In room:* A/C, TV, hair dryer, safe.

MODERATE

Antica Torre 🐞🐞 The very friendly Patrizia Landolfo and her family run one of Siena's most simply elegant hotels, installed in a 16th-century tower house atop a brick-lined 600-year-old potter's workshop, which now serves as a minuscule breakfast room. A travertine staircase leads to rooms that are on the cozy side of small, with marble flooring, iron filigree headboards, old writing desks, and gauzy curtains. The rooms on the street are a smidgen larger, but those in back are quieter. The best rooms are the two on the top levels with a view over the Sienese rooftops to rolling green hills. The old tower is on a residential side street near the Porta Romana, a 10-minute stroll down Via Banchi di Sotto from the Campo.

You may also be interested in the **Palazzo di Valli** 🐞, Via Enea Silvio Piccolomini 135 (✆ **0577-226-102**), the Landolfo's new 12-room countryside hotel converted from a 17th-century villa set amid olive trees and flower gardens that lies a half-mile from Porta Romana gate (a bus carries you to the Campo in 5 min.). Doubles here go for 100€ to 130€ ($115–$150), including breakfast, bathroom, TV (on request), minibar, and phone. It's open April through the July Palio, then again August through October.

Via di Fieravecchia 7, 53100 Siena. ✆ and fax **0577-222-255**. 8 units. 90€–107€ ($104–$123) double. Prices lower in slow periods. Breakfast 7€ ($8.05). AE, DC, MC, V. Parking in streets around hotel or public lot nearby. *In room:* TV on request, hair dryer.

Hotel Castagneto This 200-year-old brick farmhouse owned by the Franconi brothers sits on a ridge northwest of the city and has good views down the valley over their olive grove and up to Siena beyond. You get the vista from all but two rooms, and several even enjoy a small terrace. The accommodations are all good-size and comfortable, with tile floors and those soft cradling Italian beds of dubious spring power. It's a friendly, homey, and very quiet place to escape from the city a bit without going too far—a city bus stop is right outside the gates (or take a taxi into town for about 10€/$12). There's also a good bar up the road if you want a cheaper breakfast.

Via dei Cappuccini 39, 52100 Siena. ✆ **0577-45-103**. Fax 0577-283-266. 11 units. 130€ ($150) double; 150€ ($173) triple. Rates include continental breakfast. No credit cards. Free parking. Bus: 1. Closed Dec–Mar 15. **Amenities:** Concierge; tour desk; limited room service; laundry service. *In room:* TV, hair dryer.

Hotel Duomo 🐞🐞 This hotel, excellently located just south of its namesake, is housed in a 12th-century palazzo that once served as barracks to host medieval troops, though the only reminders of this are the Renaissance central staircase and the ancient brickwork in the basement breakfast room. Most carpeted accommodations are of a modest size but not cramped, and the modern furnishings are as tasteful as functional gets, some with worn veneer units, others with newer wicker-and-wood pieces. The bathrooms are tiny, but the mattresses lie on wood-slat orthopedic frames. If you want to secure one of the 12 "panoramic" rooms with a view of the Duomo, be sure to ask when booking. The friendly staff is polished and professional.

Via Stalloreggi 34–38 (halfway between the Duomo and Il Campo), 53100 Siena. © **0577-289-088.** Fax 0577-43-043. www.hotelduomo.it. 23 units. 130€ ($150) double; 171€ ($197) triple; 186€ ($214) quad. 20%–40% less in slow periods. Rates include buffet breakfast. AE, DC, MC, V. Parking free in nearby garage. Bus: A (green, yellow). **Amenities:** Concierge; limited room service; laundry service. In room: A/C, TV, dataport, hair dryer.

Hotel Santa Caterina ★   You'll find some of the friendliest hoteliers in Siena here, and they've been slowly reinvesting in the place since they took it over more than 10 years ago. The rooms have tile floors (antique terra-cotta flooring in some), soft beds, and furniture made of old wood; and, many have a view down one of the most verdant, unspoiled valleys around Siena. (Most of the other vales in the area have been filled with housing developments.) In summer you can breakfast in the pretty little garden; there's a new glassed-in breakfast veranda for winter dining.

Via Enea Silvio Piccolomini 7 (just outside the Porta Romana), 53100 Siena. © **0577-221-105.** Fax 0577-271-087. www.hscsiena.it. 22 units. 144€ ($166) double; 195€ ($224) triple. Rates include buffet breakfast. AE, DC, MC, V. Free parking along street or 12€ ($14) in small lot. Bus: A (pink), N, or 2. **Amenities:** Bike rental; concierge; tour desk; limited room service; massage; babysitting; laundry service; dry cleaning; non-smoking rooms. In room: A/C, TV, dataport, minibar, hair dryer.

Palazzo Ravizza ★   The Santi-Ravizza family has run this hotel in a 17th-century Renaissance palazzo since the 1920s. It's a bit overpriced in the high season, when you have to take dinner here, but an excellent deal in winter. (Make sure to call ahead, as some years they close for a month to renovate.) The rooms tend to be large, with high ceilings—some gorgeously frescoed, a few with painted details around the wood beams. "Superior" rooms are a bit bigger with a small sitting area. Those on the front catch some traffic noise, but on the back you'll hear only birdsong and the splashing fountain in the grave garden with sublime countryside vistas. It's outside the center but still inside the city walls, offering a good Sienese neighborhood experience away from the tourist bustle.

Pian dei Mantellini 34 (near Piazza San Marco). © **0577-280-462.** Fax 0577-221-597. www.palazzoravizza. it. 30 units. Mar 31–Nov 21 and Dec 26–Jan 6 required half pension 160€ ($184) standard double, 180€ ($207) superior double, 220€–270€ ($253–$311) suite; low season without pension: 130€ ($150) standard double; 150€ ($173) superior double; 180€–230€ ($207–$265) suite. 10% discount for stays of more than three nights. Rates include breakfast. AE, DC, MC, V. Free parking. Bus: A (green, yellow). **Amenities:** Restaurant (closed Jan–Feb); concierge; tour desk; car-rental desk; room service (24-hr. bar service; limited restaurant service); babysitting; laundry service; dry cleaning. In room: A/C, TV, minibar in suites, hair dryer.

INEXPENSIVE

Hotel Bernini ★ (Value)   Mauro and Nadia oversee a very amiable, homey set of clean and, for the price, surprisingly comfortable rooms decorated with the odd antique. The firm beds rest on patterned tiling and are surrounded by whitewashed walls curving into the ceilings. (A few have painted wood beams.) Some accommodations are hung with printed curtains in the archways. A pair of rooms has a distant view of the Duomo's flank, and all are mouse quiet, as the place sits atop St. Catherine's house cum convent. The bathrooms are all brand new. If you ask, they'll let you go up on the terrace for views of the city and valley. This is a family environment; on rainy days, Mauro breaks out his accordion to entertain guests.

Via della Sapienza 15 (near San Domenico), 53100 Siena. ℂ and fax **0577-289-047**. www.albergo bernini.com. 9 units, 4 with bathroom. 62€ ($71) double without bathroom; 82€ ($94) double with bathroom; 87€ ($100) triple without bathroom; 107€ ($123) triple with bathroom. Sometimes rates are discounted up to 20% in slow periods. Breakfast 7€ ($8.05). No credit cards. Parking in public lots. Closed Dec 1–28. Bus: A (red), C, 2, or 10. **Amenities:** Limited room service (breakfast); nonsmoking rooms. *In room:* A/C in 2 units, hair dryer on request, no phone.

Hotel Cannon d'Oro *(star) (Kids)* It's just a few short blocks up the shop-lined Via Banchi di Sopra (its name changes to Via Montanini) to this 15th-century palazzo. Most rooms are plain but large, though the decor is livened up in some rooms with old-fashioned bevel-glass mirrors in the wardrobe doors or an antique chest of drawers. A few are quite pleasant indeed, with painted wrought-iron bed frames in a 19th-century country style and worn terra-cotta floors or medieval stonework walls. The bathrooms are very compact, with amusing anachronisms—they've installed heated towel racks but haven't yet been hit with the fuzzy towel revolution. The beds are mercifully firm, and while there's some moped and chatter noise outside most windows, it usually disappears by bedtime.

Via Montanini 28 (a few blocks north of Il Campo), 53100 Siena. ℂ **0577-44-321**. Fax 0577-280-868. www.cannondoro.it. 30 units. Easter–Oct 90€ ($104) double, 116€ ($133) triple; Oct–Easter 70€ ($81) double, 90€ ($104) triple. Continental breakfast 6€ ($6.90). AE, MC, V. Parking 13€ ($15) in nearby garage. Bus: C. **Amenities:** Concierge. *In room:* TV, hair dryer on request.

Piccolo Hotel Etruria *(star)(star) (Finds)* This small family-run hotel could veritably thumb its nose at the big corporate chains, as it offers equally comfortable modernity with twice the character and one third the price. In both the main building and the *dipendenza* across the street, the rooms have tiled floors; brand-new, wood-toned built-in furnishings with stone-topped desks and end tables; and leather strap chairs. The bathrooms are immaculately new, and everything is kept spotless. This place gets a star for being as clean, comfortable, and central as you're ever going to find, especially at these prices. Book early. The only real drawback is the 12:30am curfew.

Via delle Donzelle 3 (off Via Banchi di Sotto), 53100 Siena. ℂ **0577-288-088**. Fax 0577-288-461. hetruria@ tin.it. 13 units. 75€ ($86) double; 99€ ($114) triple. Continental breakfast 5€ ($5.75). AE, DC, MC, V. Closed around Dec 10–27. Bus: A (red), B, or N. **Amenities:** Limited room service (breakfast). *In room:* TV, hair dryer, safe.

Santuario S. Caterina/Alma Domus *(Kids)* Down below San Domenico church in an untouristy part of Siena, this simple, cheap hotel is run by the nuns of St. Catherine, so there's a certain monastic quality, but also a kindly hospitality and meditative calm. Many of the midsize rooms have balconies with great views of the Duomo across the little valley. The furnishings are a mix of modular and old-fashioned, with a few wrought-iron bed frames (but soft mattresses). The showers lack curtains, but they're clean and come with fuzzy towels. They have installed A/C in some of the rooms, and will probably charge a bit extra for those in summer. While you can receive calls only on your room phone (plans are afoot to make the phones fully operational in the near future), there are four pay phones. Guests share a common living room and a TV room—and a lamentable 11:30pm curfew.

Via Camporeggio 37 (the steep street down off Piazza San Domenico), 53100 Siena. ℂ **0577-44-177**. Fax 0577-47-601. 40 units. 55€ ($63) double; 70€ ($81) triple; 85€ ($98) quad. Breakfast 6€ ($6.90). No credit cards. Bus: 1, 3, 6, 10, 18, 30, 31, 37, or 106. *In room:* Hair dryer on request.

WHERE TO DINE

Siena has a pretty good **cafe culture,** and during the *passeggiata,* Sienese cozy up to the bar of the cafes lining Via Banchi di Sopra and Via di Città to gulp down espresso and sample finger-size pastries and slices of *panettone* (dry cake) and Siena's famous, dense, barlike *panforte.* (It comes in many types, most a variation on a thick honey paste binding nuts and bits of candied fruit, a holdover from the cane sugar–less Middle Ages.)

For pastry makers and specialty food shops, see "Shopping," above. Or, sample the bounty at Siena's top cafe, the bustling **Nannini,** Via Banchi di Sopra 22–24 (© **0577-41-591**), which also has a *gelateria* branch several blocks farther along at Via Banchi di Sopra 99 (no phone). The cafe is open Monday from 6:30am to 8:30pm, Tuesday through Saturday from 6:30am to midnight, and Sunday from 8am to 8:30pm. Its pastry and *panforte* "factory" is outside the walls at Via Massetana Romana 42 (© **0577-285-208**).

Few smaller operations turn out *panforte* anymore, leaving this traditional sweet to be mass-produced by Sapori and Nannini—though recently, Nannini gave over its *panforte* production to Sapori, so while they're still labeled separately and the formulas may differ slightly, in effect they're all the same now.

EXPENSIVE

Al Marsili INVENTIVE SIENESE   Under massive cross-vaulted ceilings of rough old brick, Al Marsili's soft yellow plaster walls are pocketed with a few very private alcoves. This is the most elegant place in town, complete with bow-tied waiters and a very well chosen, if pricey, wine list. Standout primi are *pici alla casareccia* (fat spaghetti in meat-and-mushroom sauce) and *conchiglie alla rustica* (shell pasta in a strong spinach-and-sausage sauce). For your second course, try *scaloppine al dragoncello* (veal scallops with tomatoes and tarragon), or their best dish, *faraona alla Medici* (meaty guinea hen cooked with pine nuts, almonds, and prunes).

Via del Castoro 3 (between Via di Città and the Duomo). © **0577-47-154**. www.ristorantealmarsili.it. Reservations recommended. Primi 7.75€–9.50€ ($8.90–$11); secondi 9.50€–16€ ($11–$18). AE, DC, MC, V. Tues–Sun 12:30–2:15pm and 7:30–10pm. Bus: A (green, yellow).

Antica Osteria da Divo ★★ *Finds* CREATIVE SIENESE   This former trattoria has gone midscale and greatly improved its menu to offer excellent innovative dishes rooted in Sienese traditions in a classy, but not frosty, atmosphere of soft jazz. The main dining room is a crazy medieval mélange of stone, brick, wood supports, and naked rock, while the rooms in back and in the basement are actually Etruscan tombs carved from the tufa. *Pici al ragout di lepre* (thick hand-rolled pasta strands in hare ragù) and *gnochetti di patate con erbe cipollina e pecorino di fossa* (gnocchi with chives on a parmigiana pastry crust swimming in melted pecorino cheese) are palate-pleasing primi. For the main course, they ascribe to the growing school of Italian cooking wherein a side dish is included with each secondo (making a meal here less costly than the prices below would suggest). A perfect example: the exquisite *petto d'anatra al vin santo con patate allo zafferano* (duck breast with crisp balls of saffron-kissed mashed potatoes).

Via Franciosa 25-29 (behind the left flank of the Duomo). © **0577-284-381**. Reservations recommended. Primi 7€–10€ ($8.05–$12); secondi with side dish 16€–22€ ($18–$25). MC, V. Daily noon–2:30pm and 7–10pm. Bus: A (green, yellow).

Osteria le Logge ★★★ SIENESE/TUSCAN   Le Logge is many a local's choice for a special night out, offering excellent cooking in a sedate, yet not sedated, atmosphere. The *taglierini al tartufo* has a light butter sauce that doesn't mask the delicate flavor of the black truffles. Heavier primi include *malfatti all'Osteria* (spinach-and-ricotta balls in a creamy tomato sauce) and *ravioli ripieni di* *pecorino e menta* (ravioli stuffed with sheep's-milk cheese and mint in a sauce flavored with port). The staff is friendly and very accommodating. I once visited with a vegetarian, and our waitress quickly established his eating parameters (does he eat fish? cheese?), proceeded to mark everything on the menu he could order, and then had the kitchen concoct for him a suitable secondo of all the veggies they had on hand. Meatier palates can enjoy the *bistecche di vitello* (tender veal steaks) or delicate *carpaccio di pesce spada affumicato* (smoked swordfish sliced and pounded into thin disks).

Via del Porrione 33 (just off the Campo). ☎ **0577-48-013**. Reservations recommended. Primi 7€–10€ ($8.05–$12); secondi 14€–18€ ($16–$21); tasting menu 40€ ($46). AE, DC, MC, V. Mon–Sat noon–2:45pm and 7–10:30pm. Closed Jan 1–Feb 7. Bus: A (pink) B, or N.

MODERATE

Antica Trattoria Papei ☆ SIENESE   Although tourists now know to filter behind the Palazzo Pubblico to this large family-run trattoria, locals still hang on vigorously, returning for the simple but good Sienese fare. In summer, you can dine alfresco on the unsightly piazza with a view of the Terza di San Martino. If you're eating inside, head to the left of the door or upstairs for wood-ceilinged ambience—the modern room to the right is where they try to stick all the tourists. The *pappardelle al sugo di cinghiale* (noodles in wild boar sauce) is a traditional dish, while the *pici alla cardinale* (chewy fat spaghetti in tomato sauce with hot peppers and chunks of pancetta) is a bit more original. Keep it spicy with *coniglio all'arabbiata* (rabbit cooked in white wine, rosemary, and sage with a pinch of pepperoncino), or try *anatra alla Tolomei* (duck stewed with tomatoes).

Piazza del Mercato 6 (behind the Palazzo Pubblico). ☎ **0577-280-894**. Reservations suggested. Primi 6.20€ ($7.10); secondi 6.50€–10€ ($7.50–$12). AE, MC, V. Tues–Sun noon–3pm and 7–10:30pm.

Castelvecchio ☆☆ CREATIVE TUSCAN/VEGETARIAN   This intimate and very personable little restaurant has a devoted following of regulars who enjoy Simone Romi's skilled service and Mauro Lombardini's daily changing menu of creative Tuscan cuisine. There's at least one meatless dish nightly, and on vegetarian Wednesdays there's only one meat dish available. On my last visit I had an excellent risotto of zucchini, mint, and basil, a delicious lentil-and-turnip soup, *pennette* in tomato sauce sprinkled with crunchy cream, vegetable pie with a mashed-potato crust, and chicken with peppers and onions.

Via Castelvecchio 65 (off Via San Pietro). ☎ **0577-49-586**. www.osteriacastelvecchio.com. Reservations recommended. Primi 6€–7€ ($6.90–$8.05); secondi 9€–11€ ($10–$13); tasting menu without wine 25€ ($29) each for 2 people only. AE, DC, MC, V. Apr–Sept 12:30–2:30pm and 7:30–9:30pm; Oct–Mar Wed–Mon 12:30–2:30pm and 7:30–9:30pm. Bus: A (green, yellow).

La Torre *Value* TUSCAN   You can usually trust a place that doesn't hide its kitchen. La Torre's is in plain view, next to a dozen tightly packed tables under an undulating brick ceiling. It's a popular place, so reserve ahead or show up early. All the pasta is homemade (none more deliciously than the *pici* and the plump tortellini) and served with the sauce of your choice and a generous heap of Parmesan cheese on top. Afterward, try the *vitello arrosto* (slices of roast veal) or *piccione al forno* (oven-baked pigeon).

Via Salicotto 7–9 (9m/30 ft. off Il Campo to left of the Palazzo Pubblico). ☎ **0577-287-548**. Reservations recommended. Primi 6€–8€ (6.90–$9.20); secondi 9€–10€ ($10–$12); menù turistico with wine 18€ ($21). AE. Fri–Wed noon–3pm and 7–10pm. Closed Aug 17–Sept 1. Bus: A (pink), B, or N.

Tullio ai Tre Cristi SIENESE   A staunchly traditional trattoria in the heart of Giraffe territory since 1830, Tullio has a distinctly taverna feel. The two long dining rooms are ribbed with brick arches and hung with painted plaques representing the *contrade,* and the tables are lined up along creaky wall benches as if waiting to be set for a medieval feast. The *antipasto Tre Cristi* is a fan of assorted large crostini and prosciutto rolls, and if *pici al porcino* (homemade fat spaghetti with porcini mushroom sauce) or *pappardelle alla lepre* (noodles in hare ragù) don't catch your fancy, try *penne alla carrettiera* (in a spicy hot garlic and pepperoncino tomato sauce). Afterward, go for the *medaglione al burro verde* (veal medallion cooked in herbed butter) or the *cappelle di porcini* (grilled caps of porcini mushrooms—the traditional poor Tuscan's steak).

Vicolo di Provenzano 1 (follow the signs down Via Rossi off Via Banchi di Sopra). ✆ **0577-280-608**. Reservations recommended. Primi 5€–8€ ($5.75–$9.20); secondi 7€–18€ ($8.05–$21). MC, V. Thurs–Tues 12:30–2:30pm and 7:30–10:30pm. Closed last 15 days Dec. Bus: A (red) or C.

INEXPENSIVE
Osteria la Chiacchera SIENESE CUCINA POVERA   This is a tiny joint with worn wooden tables, terra-cotta floors, and barrel ends embedded everywhere. "The Chatterbox" proudly serves Sienese poor people's food. Couples come here to make moon eyes at each other and save money on the date (not only is it cheap, but there's no cover charge or service fee—tips are greatly appreciated). A choice first course is the *pici boscaiola* (long strands of fat, hand-rolled pasta in tomato-and-mushroom sauce), though the *penne arrabbiata* (in piquant tomato sauce) goes pretty quickly, too. Secondi are simple peasant dishes like *salsicce e fagioli* (grilled sausages with beans) and *stracotto* (beef and boiled potatoes in piquant tomato sauce). They also do a mean chocolate pie.

Costa di Sant'Antonio 4 (near San Domenico, off Via della Sapienza under the Hotel Bernini). ✆ **0577-280-631**. Reservations recommended. Primi 3.60€–6€ ($4.05–$6.90); secondi 4.50€–7€ ($5.20–$8.05). No credit cards. Daily noon–3pm and 7–midnight.

EN ROUTE TO SAN GIMIGNANO
Monteriggioni ✸✸, 20km (12 miles) northwest of Siena along the SS2, is one of the most perfectly preserved fortified villages in all Italy. The **tourist office** is at Largo Fontebranda 5 (✆ **0577-304-810**). You've probably seen aerial photos of this place at postcard stands. The town was once a Sienese outpost; the city's soldiers patrolled the walls and kept an eye out for Florentine troops from the vantage points of Monteriggioni's towers. All 14 of these have survived more or less intact since the day Dante likened them to the circle of Titans guarding the lowest level of Hell. Although more day-trippers are stopping by every year and there's even a board-rated four-star hotel (**Hotel Monteriggioni;** ✆ **0577-305-009;** www.hotel monteriggioni.net; doubles 210€/$242) hidden in one of the buildings, Monteriggioni remains a sleepy little place. Most of the village is taken up with gardens and a few olive trees. Monteriggioni is content to offer you a lunch at one of its two restaurants, and sell you a few postcards from the shops on the central piazza.

Another 10km (6 miles) along a secondary road takes you to **Colle di Val d'Elsa,** the medieval birthplace of master Gothic architect Arnolfo di Cambio, who designed Florence's Palazzo Vecchio and Duomo. The **tourist office** is at Via Campana 43 (✆ **0577-922-791;** fax 0577-922-621). Buses run here from Siena and San Gimignano, and you can also get a train on the Siena to Empoli line (with connections to Florence) that stops in Poggibonsi, from which buses connect to Colle di Val d'Elsa. Don't enter Colle's old city at the east end; instead, circle around the small center to come in the west side for the proper introduction, passing over a short bridge and under the yawning arch of Baccio d'Agnolo's mannerist **Palazzo Campana** (1539) gate. If you're driving and want to get out to explore, park beneath the walls at the lot off the SS68 and walk up the steps to the old town.

The main road of the old town, Via del Castello, leads to **Piazza del Duomo.** The cathedral contains one of the nails supposedly used to crucify Christ in a Mino da Fiesole tabernacle in the left transept and a bronze *Crucifix* designed by Giambologna and cast by his student Pietro Tacca over the high altar. Next door is the **Palazzo Pretorio,** which houses a small **archaeology museum** (C 0577-922-954) with a rather bland Etruscan collection and some 14th- and 15th-century frescoes. The communists jailed here in the 1920s scrawled political graffiti on some of the walls. April through September, it's open Tuesday through Friday from 10am to noon and 5 to 7pm and Saturday and Sunday from 10am to noon and 4:30 to 7:30pm; October through April, hours are Tuesday through Friday from 3 to 5pm and Saturday and Sunday from 10am to noon and 3 to 6pm. Admission is 1.55€ ($1.80). A fine set of Sienese-school paintings resides in the nearby **Museo Civico e d'Arte Sacra,** Via del Castello 31 (C 0577-923-888), housed in the graffiti-covered **Palazzo dei Priori.** It's open April through October Tuesday through Sunday from 10am to noon and 4 to 7pm; November through April, hours are Saturday and Sunday only from 10am to noon and 3:30 to 6:30pm. Admission is 2.60€ ($3).

3 San Gimignano: The Medieval Manhattan ⋆⋆

40km (24 miles) NW of Siena; 57km (34 miles) SW of Florence; 270km (167 miles) NW of Rome

The scene that hits you when you pass through the Porta San Giovanni gate inside the walls of San Gimignano and walk the narrow flagstone Via San Giovanni is thoroughly medieval. Okay, so the crossbows, flails, and halberds in shop windows are miniature souvenir versions and the small Romanesque church facade halfway up the street today hides a modern wine shop. But, if you can mentally block out the racks of postcards, you've got a stage set straight out of Tolkien.

At the top of Via San Giovanni is the center of town, formed by two interlocking triangular piazze: **Piazza della Cisterna** ⋆⋆, centered around a 1237 well, and **Piazza del Duomo,** flanked by the city's main church and civic palace. Both spaces are guarded by the tall medieval towers that have made San Gimignano, "city of the beautiful towers," the poster child for Italian hill towns everywhere. No one can agree how many stone skyscrapers remain in the Medieval Manhattan—so many have been chopped down it's a tough call whether they're still officially towers or merely tall skinny houses—but the official tower count the tourist office gives is 14. There were at one time somewhere between 70 and 76 of the things spiking the sky above this little village. The spires started rising in the bad old days of the 1200s, partly to defend against outside invaders but mostly as command centers for San Gimignano's warring families. Several successive waves of the plague that swept through the town and region (1348, 1464, and 1631) caused the economy (based on textiles and hosting passing pilgrims) to crumble, and San Gimignano became a provincial backwater. Because there was no impetus for new building, by the time tourism began picking up in the 19th century, visitors found a preserved medieval village of crumbling towers.

San Gimignano is by far the most popular Tuscan hill town, a day-trip destination for masses of tour buses coming from Siena and Florence. The town is best enjoyed in the evening, after the tour buses leave, especially in the off-season and on spring nights: The alleyways are empty, and you can wander in the yellow light of street lamps.

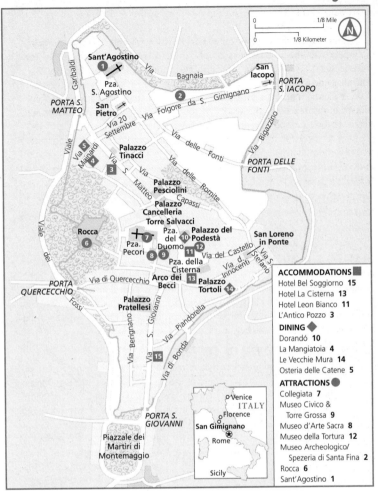

ACCOMMODATIONS ■
Hotel Bel Soggiorno **15**
Hotel La Cisterna **13**
Hotel Leon Bianco **11**
L'Antico Pozzo **3**

DINING ◆
Dorandó **10**
La Mangiatoia **4**
Le Vecchie Mura **14**
Osteria delle Catene **5**

ATTRACTIONS ●
Collegiata **7**
Museo Civico &
   Torre Grossa **9**
Museo d'Arte Sacra **8**
Museo della Tortura **12**
Museo Archeologico/
   Spezieria di Santa Fina **2**
Rocca **6**
Sant'Agostino **1**

ESSENTIALS

GETTING THERE   By Train   The 20 or so daily trains on the line between **Siena** (trip time: 20–45 min.) and Empoli, where you can connect from **Florence** (60–75 min.)—stop at Poggibonsi (© **0577-933-646** or 0577-936-462). From **Poggibonsi,** 19 buses make the 25-minute run to San Gimignano Monday through Saturday, but only nine buses run on Sunday.

By Car   Take the Poggibonsi exit off the **Florence-Siena** autostrada or the SS2. San Gimignano is 12km (8 miles) from Poggibonsi. Another secondary road meets this coming up from Colle di Val d'Elsa.

By Bus   You almost always have to **transfer buses at Poggibonsi** (see "By Train," above). SITA (© **055-47-821;** www.sita-on-line.it) runs 26 buses daily from **Florence** to Poggibonsi (50–90 min.), 13 of which meet right up with the connection to San Gimignano. There's also a **Sunday direct bus from Florence** (80 min.) at 8:30am. **Tra-in** (© **0577-204-246;** www.trainspa.it) runs about 33

Tips **Take a Hike**

The tourist office sponsors guided walks through the countryside April through October, 2 to 3 days a week (usually weekends), costing 10€ to 15€ ($12–$17) per person. Because the country edges right up to San Gimignano's walls, you could also easily set out on your own to wander with a good map—the tourist office also sells a map and catalog marked with suggested hikes and walks, or you can pick up a regional map from any of the local souvenir stands.

---

daily buses from **Siena** to Poggibonsi (35–45 min.), stopping at **Colle di Val d'Elsa** on the way. In San Gimignano, buy tickets at the tourist office.

VISITOR INFORMATION The **tourist office** is at Piazza Duomo 1 (© 0577-940-008; fax 0577-940-903; www.sangimignano.com). It's open daily: March through October from 9am to 1pm and 3 to 7pm and November through February from 9am to 1pm and 2 to 6pm.

FESTIVALS & MARKETS The citizens dress up in elaborate masks and costumes for a **Carnival** parade just before Lent (late Jan or early Feb). **Sangimignanese Summer** has, since 1924, brought some lightweight culture to town on the last weekend in July, with open-air opera recitals, classical concerts, and film screenings in the ruins of the Rocca fortress. Thursday and Saturday morning see a bustling **market** on Piazza del Duomo.

EXPLORING THE TOWN OF TOWERS

You can buy a **cumulative ticket** that covers the Torre Grossa and its Museo Civico; little Pinacoteca painting gallery in the Palazzo Pubblico; the tiny Museo Archeologico detailing the region's Etruscan era and the adjacent Spezeria Santa Fina (a preserved Renaissance pharmacy); the new Galleria d'Arte Moderna modern art gallery; and the weird little Museo Ornithologico, a couple of glass cases stuffed with stuffed birds in the dimly lit confines of a tiny, deconsecrated church—basically all the museums in town *except* the Collegiata, the Museo d'Ate Sacra, and the privately run Torture Museum. The ticket costs 7.50€ ($8.65) adults and 5.50€ ($6.30) ages 6 to 18 and over 65. Prices listed below are for individual entries to each.

Collegiata ★★ The main church in town—it no longer has a bishop, so it's no longer officially a duomo (cathedral)—was started in the 11th century and took its present form in the 15th century. It's not much from the outside, but the interior is smothered in 14th-century frescoes, making it one of Tuscany's most densely decorated churches.

The right wall was frescoed from 1333 to 1341—most likely by Lippo Memmi—with three levels of **New Testament scenes** (22 in all) on the life and Passion of Christ along with a magnificent *Crucifixion.* In 1367, Bartolo di Fredi frescoed the left wall with 26 scenes out of the **Old Testament,** and Taddeo di Bartolo provided the gruesome *Last Judgment* frescoes around the entrance wall in 1410. Benozzo Gozzoli wins the "Prickliest *St. Sebastian* in Tuscany" prize for his colorful and courtly 1464 rendition on the entrance wall.

In 1468, Giuliano da Maiano built the **Cappella di Santa Fina** ★★ off the right aisle, and his brother Benedetto carved the relief panels for the altar. Florentine Renaissance master Domenico Ghirlandaio decorated the tiny chapel's walls with some of his finest, airiest works. With the help of assistants (his brother Davide and Sebastiano Mainardi), Ghirlandaio in 1475 frescoed two scenes summing up the life of Santa Fina, a local girl who, though never officially canonized, is one of San Gimignano's patron saints. Little Fina, who was very devout and wracked with guilt for having committed the sin of accepting an orange from a boy, fell down ill on a board one day and didn't move for 5 years, praying the whole while. Eventually, St. Gregory appeared to her and announced her death, whereupon the board on which she lay miraculously produced flowers. When her corpse was carried solemnly to the church for a funeral, the city's towers burst forth with yellow pansies and angels flew up to ring the bells. At the church, a blind choirboy and Fina's nurse, who had a paralyzed hand, found themselves miraculously cured merely by touching her body. The town still celebrates their child saint every year on March 12, when the pansies on San Gimignano's towers naturally bloom.

Piazza del Duomo. ℂ 0577-940-316. Admission on cumulative ticket, or 3.50€ ($4.05) adults, 1.50€ ($1.75) ages 6–18. Mar 9:30am–5pm; Apr–Oct Sun–Fri 9:30am–7:30pm, Sat 9:30am–5pm; Nov–Jan 26 Mon–Sat 9:30am–5pm, Sun 1–5pm. Closed Jan 27–Feb 28.

Museo Archeologico/Spezeria di Santa Fina
San Gimignano's modest Etruscan collection proves the town's roots run deeper than the Middle Ages. Atop one of the funerary urns, a reclining figure representing the deceased is holding the cup of life—now empty of all but a single coin to pay his way into the afterlife. This museum is now installed in the 1253 pharmacy branch of the medieval Santa Fina hospital (though the painted druggery vases and other accouterments on display are largely 15th–18th c.). There's also a small modern art gallery here.

Via Folgore 11. ℂ 0577-940-384. Admission on cumulative ticket, or 3.50€ ($4.05) adults, 2.50€ ($2.90) ages 6–18 and over 65. Daily 11am–6pm. Closed Jan 7–Mar 31.

Museo Civico & Torre Grossa ⭑
In the late 13th century, the city government moved from the Palazzo del Podestà across from the Collegiata to the brand-new **Palazzo del Comune** (or del Popolo). You can climb its **Torre Grossa** ("Big Tower") ⭑⭑⭑, finished in 1311, for one of the best tower-top views of the cityscape and rolling countryside in all Tuscany. Before the step workout, though, check out the worthy **civic painting gallery** on the palace's second floor.

The small museum was built around a large fresco in the Sala del Consiglio of the *Maestà* (1317) by the Sienese Lippo Memmi. Up the stairs is the Pinacoteca, but before entering it, duck through the door to the left to see perhaps San Gimignano's most famous **frescoes** ⭑. Painted in the 14th century by Memmo di Filippucio, they narrate a rather racy story of courtship and love in quite a departure from the usual religious themes of the era. The most oft-reproduced scenes are of a couple taking a bath together and then getting into bed for their wedding night.

The first work in the painting gallery across the hall is a Coppo di Marcovaldo Crucifix surrounded by Passion scenes, one of the true masterpieces of 13th-century Tuscan art. Benozzo Gozzoli's *Madonna and Child with Saints* (1466) has an almost surreal Deposition scene with a delicate landscape running the length of the

---

A Great Point of View

Behind the Collegiata, the remains of the city's 14th-century fortress, the **Rocca** ⭑, are now a public park. Climb atop the crumbling ramparts for a view of the surrounding farmland and the best panorama of San Gimignano's towers.

predella. A 25-year-old Filippino Lippi painted the matching tondos of the *Annunciation* in 1482, and the huge early-16th-century *Madonna in Glory with Sts. Gregory and Benedict* with its wild Umbrian landscape is a late work by Pinturicchio. That psychedelic almond-shaped rainbow of cherub heads over which Mary is hovering was one of Pinturicchio's favorite painterly devices to symbolize virginity.

Two works here tell the stories of the city's most popular patron saints. Lorenzo di Nicoló Gerini did a passable job in 1402 on the *Tabernacle of Santa Fina,* built to house the teen saint's head and painted with scenes of the four most important miracles of her brief life. In the late 14th century, Taddeo di Bartolo painted the *Life of St. Gimignano* as an altarpiece for the Collegiata; the saint himself sits in the middle, holding in his lap the town he was constantly invoked to protect.

This city, you see, was founded by the Etruscans and originally called Castel di Selva. When Totila the Goth was rampaging through the area in the 6th century A.D., the town decided to pray—no one is quite sure why—to Gimignano, an obscure martyred bishop from the far-off city of Modena. The sanctified bishop came riding out of the clouds clad in golden armor, and the Goths took to their heels and left the city alone. The town gratefully changed its name and has kept St. Gimignano on call ever since against plagues and other natural disasters.

Piazza del Duomo. ℂ **0577-940-340** (ask for museo). Admission on cumulative ticket, or 5€ ($5.75) adults, 4€ ($4.60) kids and seniors. Mar–Oct daily 9:30am–7:20pm; Nov–Feb daily 10am–5:50pm (until 1:30pm Dec 24–31).

Museo d'Arte Sacra

Museo d'Arte Sacra The archway to the left of the Collegiata's facade leads to a pretty brick courtyard called Piazza Pecori. On one side, under brick vaulting, is a fresco of the *Annunciation* painted in 1482 by either Domenico Ghirlandaio or his brother-in-law and pupil Sebastiano Mainardi. Inside the small museum across the piazza, the sacred art collection includes a *Madonna and Child* triptych painted by Bartolo di Fredi and some illuminated choir books. The Etruscan museum that was once here has been moved (see Museo Archeologico, above).

Piazza Pecori (the courtyard through the arch to the left of the church entrance). ℂ **0577-942-226.** Admission 3€ ($3.45) adults, 1.50€ ($1.75) ages 6–18. Apr–Oct Mon–Fri 9:30am–7:30pm, Sat 9:30am–5pm, Sun 1–5pm; Nov–Mar Mon–Sat 9:30am–5pm, Sun 1–5pm. Closed Jan 21–Feb 28.

Museo della Tortura (Torture Museum)

Museo della Tortura (Torture Museum) The Torture Museum (aka the Museum of Medieval Criminology and the Inquisition) is serendipitously installed in the medieval **Torre del Diavolo (Devil's Tower).** Its iron maidens, racks—both the spiked and unspiked varieties—chastity belts, various bone-crunching manacles, breast-rippers, and other medieval party favors are accompanied by engrossingly dispassionate descriptions of their uses and history. If nothing else, the kids might think it's cool (though the historical etchings and watercolors showing the torture instruments at work are definitely R-rated).

Via del Castello 1 (just off Piazza della Cisterna). ℂ **0577-942-243.** Admission 8€ ($9.20) adults, 5.50€ ($6.30) students. Mar 16–July 18 daily 10am–7pm; July 19–Sept 17 daily 10am–midnight; Sept 18–Nov 1 daily 10am–8pm; Nov 2–Mar 15 Mon–Fri 10am–6pm, Sat–Sun 10am–7pm.

Sant'Agostino

Sant'Agostino 🏛 This 13th-century church at the north end of town is full of good 15th-century frescoes. In 1464, a plague swept the town and the citizens prayed to their patron saint to end it. When the sickness passed, they dutifully hired Benozzo Gozzoli to paint a thankful scene on the nave's left wall showing St. Gimignano and his cloak full of angels stopping and breaking the plague arrows being thrown down by a vengeful God and his angelic hosts. The city liked the results, so they commissioned Gozzoli to spend the next 2 years frescoing the choir behind the main altar floor to ceiling with scenes from the *Life of St. Augustine.*

Against the main entrance wall to the left is a chapel filled with an elaborate marble tomb (1495) by Benedetto di Maiano. Sebastiano Mainardi painted the frescoes on the chapel's vaults and the *Saints Gimignano* (holding his city), *Lucy, and Nicholas of Bari* to the left of the tomb. Next to the cloister door on the nave's left wall is another fresco by Sebastiano Mainardi, this one of an enthroned St. Gimignano blessing three of the city's dignitaries.

Piazza Sant'Agostino. ℂ **0577-907-012.** Free admission. Daily 7am–noon and 3–7pm (Oct–Apr closes at 6pm).

WHERE TO STAY

Hotels in this most popular hill town aren't cheap. The **Siena Hotels Promotion** office, Via San Giovanni 125 (ℂ or fax **0577-940-113;** www.hotelsiena. com), will help you find a room. It's open daily: March through October from 9:30am to 7pm and November through February from 9am to 12:30pm and 3 to 6:30pm. Those watching their euros might want to stay in the more modern satellite community of **Santa Chiara,** just a few minutes' walk from Porta San Giovanni. You can check out pictures of all the hotels below (and others) at **www.sangimignano.com**.

Hotel Bel Soggiorno   Owned and run by the Gigli family since 1886, the Bel Soggiorno rooms provide views of the countryside below (three share a panoramic terrace) or of the ultramedieval, if souvenir-ridden, main street in town. The modern, medium-size accommodations are mostly fitted with cheap, functional furniture and beds verging on the over-soft. Little of the original 13th-century structure shows through, and its general lack of antique charm makes it the least desirable of the hotels within the walls. But the friendly family management and highly recommendable restaurant, serving Tuscan fare in a half-medieval, half-plate-glass panoramic environment, keep the Bel Soggiorno in the running. Many of the amenities, such as a swimming pool, are available at their countryside sister hotel, Pescille, 4km (2 miles) from town.

Via San Giovanni 91 (near Porta San Giovanni), 53037 San Gimignano. ℂ **0577-940-375.** Fax 0577-907-521. www.hotelbelsoggiorno.it. 22 units. 100€ ($115) double; 140€ ($161) suite. Rates include continental breakfast. AE, DC, MC, V. Parking 15€ ($17) in garage outside walls. Closed Jan or Feb; restaurant closed Jan 7–Feb 28. **Amenities:** Restaurant; pool (at Pescille); tennis (at Pescille); Jacuzzi (at Pescille); concierge; car-rental desk; laundry service; dry cleaning. *In room:* A/C, TV, VCR in suites, minibar in 11 units, hair dryer on request.

Hotel La Cisterna ⭐   The rooms in this hotel, installed in the bases of 14th-century tower stumps, vary in size; some are quite large and others seem almost cramped, but all are comfortable, with firm beds and a tastefully uncluttered decor. The place was scenic enough to serve as a set for the film version of E. M. Forster's novel *Where Angels Fear to Tread.* You have a choice of views: the piazza side with its towers vista or the verdant valley out back. (Don't go for the cheapest rooms with no view at all; you get at least a vista, if not a balcony, starting at 115€/$132.) The breakfast room and bar sit in the well-preserved brick- and tufa-walled base of one of the towers.

Piazza della Cisterna 23–24, 53037 San Gimignano. ℂ **0577-940-328.** Fax 0577-942-080. www.hotel cisterna.it. 49 units. 90€–95€ ($104–$109) double without view; 105€–110€ ($121–$127) double with view; 115€–120€ ($132–$120) double with view and balcony; 128€–133€ ($147–$153) suite. Half and full pensione available. Rates include continental breakfast. AE, DC, MC, V. Parking 15€ ($17) in lot. Closed Jan 8–Mar 8; restaurant closed Jan 8–Mar 8. **Amenities:** One of best Tuscan restaurants in town (closed Tues and lunch Wed); concierge; limited room service (bar); laundry service. *In room:* A/C in 17 units, TV, minibar in suites, hair dryer, safe.

Hotel Leon Bianco ⭐   Typical of a 500-year-old building turned hotel, the rooms here can't seem to agree on a style or decor scheme, but most retain some element from the 14th-century palazzo—a painted wood beamed ceiling here, an old stone wall in a bathroom there, or a brick barrel vault filling one room. Accommodations look out over the pretty well of the tower-lined piazza out front or across a garden next door and rooftops to a glimpse of the countryside. (A few, however, overlook the partially glassed-in courtyard of the lobby.) "Superior" rooms are merely larger and come with minibars. The rooms are smaller and less well appointed and posh than those at La Cisterna across the square or the Antico Pozzo up the block, but this place has more vestigial Renaissance charm than the Bel Soggiorno, plus the most central location in town (beating out La Cisterna by a couple of yards).

Piazza della Cisterna 8, 53037 San Gimignano. © **0577-941-294.** Fax 0577-942-123. www.leonbianco.com. 26 units. 90€ ($104) standard double; 100€ ($115) standard double with view; 125€ ($144) superior double; 135€ ($155) triple. Rates include breakfast. AE, DC, MC, V. Parking 15€ ($17) in lot. Closed 20 days before Christmas and Jan 7 to early Feb. **Amenities:** Limited room service; laundry service. *In room:* A/C, TV, minibar in superior rooms, hair dryer, safe.

L'Antico Pozzo ★★ L'Antico Pozzo is the choicest inn within the walls, a 15th-century palazzo converted to a hotel in 1990 with careful attention to preserving the structural antiquity without sacrificing modern convenience (guests even have Internet access). The subdued elegance and comfort offer the most medieval-feeling experience in this most medieval of cities. Over the building's colorful history it has hosted Dante, the Inquisition trials, a religious community, and an 18th-century salon. Accommodations vary in size and decor, but none is small, and the huge junior suites have large writing desks, wood ceilings, and spumanti waiting for you. Throughout, the furnishings are simple wooden 19th-century pieces, and the firm beds are surrounded by cast-iron frames—the junior suites come with canopies. "Superior" doubles have 17th-century ceiling frescoes and the smaller "standard" rooms on the third floor have wood floors and a view of the Rocca and a few towers, while other rooms look over the street or the rear terrace (where breakfast is served in summer).

Via San Matteo 87 (near Porta San Matteo), 53037 San Gimignano. © **0577-942-014.** Fax 0577-942-117. www.anticopozzo.com. 18 units. 130€ ($150) double; 150€ ($173) superior double. Rates include breakfast. AE, DC, MC, V. Parking 15€ ($17) in nearby garage or lot. Closed Feb. **Amenities:** Concierge; car-rental desk; room service; in-room massage; babysitting; laundry service; same-day dry cleaning. *In room:* A/C, TV, dataport, minibar, hair dryer, safe.

WHERE TO DINE

Few of San Gimignano's restaurants are outstanding, but its white wine certainly is. **Vernaccia di San Gimignano,** probably the best white in Tuscany, is a slightly peppery, dry wine old enough to have been cited in Dante's *Divine Comedy.*

Bar I Combattenti, Via San Giovanni 124 (© **0577-940-391**) has been serving coffee since 1924 just inside the gates of town. Try their creamy gelato: the award-winning *ricciarello di Siena* made with the Sienese cookies, or even a local saffron-tinged flavor.

Dorandó ★★★ TUSCAN   The Dorandó is an elegant splurge tucked away just off Piazza Duomo, where the stone-walled rooms, alabaster platters, and knowledgeable waiters create a backdrop for San Gimignano's best dining. The menu doesn't just list dishes but describes each one's history in detail as the chef attempts to keep the oldest traditions of Sangimignanese cooking alive—many of the dishes purport to be medieval, some even Etruscan, in origin—while balancing nouvelle cuisine philosophy with hearty home-cookin' quality. Dishes vary with the season and market, though if the excellent *cibreo* (chicken livers and giblets scented with ginger and lemon) makes it back onto the menu, by all means order it. The desserts are excellent, too.

Vicolo dell'Oro 2. ✆ 0577-941-862. www.ristorantedorando.it. Reservations highly recommended. Primi 12€–15€ ($14–$17); secondi 18€–20€ ($21–$23); tasting menus 47€ ($54). AE, MC, V. Tues–Sun 12:30–2:30pm and 7:30–9:30pm. Closed mid-Jan to mid-Mar.

La Mangiatoia ★★ TUSCAN   "The Eatin' Trough" is a quirky mix of largish but still cozy rooms with heavily stuccoed stone walls inset with backlit stained-glass cabinet doors. This place is fond of Latin quips and dramatic classical music, and the staff is friendly and helpful. Alas, the food's a mix too—stick to the more unusual dishes, intriguing and excellently prepared choices where the cook seems to try harder. The *gnocchi deliziose* (spinach gnocchi in a delicious Gorgonzola sauce) is good, as is the *tagliatelle dell'amore* (with prosciutto, cream, tomatoes, and a little hot spice). Afterward, try the *coniglio in salsa di carciofi* (rabbit with artichokes), but I'd choose the more adventurous *cervo in dolce et forte,* an old Sangimignanese recipe of venison cooked with pine nuts and a strong sauce of pinoli, raisins, vinegar, and chocolate—traditionally used to cut the gaminess of several-day-old venison. The desserts are excellent.

Via Mainardi 5 (near Porta San Matteo). ✆ **0577-941-528.** Reservations recommended. Primi 8€–12€ ($9.20–$14); secondi 12€–15€ ($14–$17). MC, V. Wed–Mon 12:30–2:30pm and 7:30–10pm. Closed early Nov to early Dec.

Le Vecchie Mura *(Value* TUSCAN/ITALIAN   Even better than holing up in the cavernous 18th-century former stalls, with worn terra-cotta bricks cross-vaulting the ceiling, is booking a table on the wall-top panoramic terrace in summer. Inside, the bench-lined tables get crowded even in winter, as locals, tourists, and families show up for the simple home cooking at reasonable prices. The satisfying *ribollita* comes with sliced pungent red onion on the side, but the *tagliatelle al cinghiale* (noodles with wild boar) offers it serious competition. The house specialty is *cinghiale alla vernaccia* (chunks of tender wild boar marinated in vernaccia white wine and served with green sauce and black olives), or you can try *cervo in bianco* (venison in white-wine sauce). They also rent out two simple double rooms, with bathroom, for 49€ ($56).

Via Piandornella 15 (a twisty walk down the first right off Via San Giovanni as you walk up from Porta San Giovanni). ✆ **0577-940-270.** www.vecchiemura.it. Reservations recommended. Primi 6.50€–7.50€ ($7.50–$8.65); secondi 8€–13€ ($9.20–$14). AE, DC, MC, V. Wed–Mon 6–10pm. Closed Dec–Feb.

Osteria delle Catene ★ *(Finds* TUSCAN   This is an *osteria* true to its name, a small gathering place offering ultratraditional dishes to accompany its well-priced selection of local wines. The decor can only be described as minimalist medieval, with contemporary paintings and modern lighting in concert with an abbreviated barrel vault made of hand-cast bricks. A great appetizer to pair with your Vernaccia is the *piatto misto di prosciutto* (with both pig and boar ham) along with *formaggi Toscani* (Tuscan cheeses). The *ribollita* adds a purée of cannellini beans to the usual mix, and the *penne al porro* (stubby pasta quills in cheesy cream sauce) and *pipe coi broccoli* (maccheroni with broccoli-based vegetable purée cut with onions) are eminent pasta choices. If you're still hungry, try the Tuscan standbys *salsicce con fagioli all'uccelletto* (grilled sausage with beans stewed with tomatoes) and *stracotto al chianti* (beef muscle cooked in Chianti wine).

Via Mainardi 18 (near Porta San Matteo). ✆ 0577-941-966. Reservations recommended. Primi 7€–9€ ($8.05–$10); secondi 12€–14€ ($14–$16); fixed-price menu without wine 17€ ($20). AE, DC, MC, V. Thurs–Tues 12:30–2pm and 7:30–9:30pm. Closed occasionally Dec–Feb.

4 Volterra: City of Alabaster

29km (18 miles) SW of San Gimignano; 50km (31 miles) W of Siena; 72km (45 miles) SW of Florence; 300km (186 miles) NW of Rome

Volterra is, in the words of the writer D. H. Lawrence, "on a towering great bluff that gets all the winds and sees all the world." The city seems to rear higher than any other in Tuscany, rising a precipitous 540m (1,800 ft.) above the valley below. It's a fortresslike town, drawn out thinly along a narrow ridge with a warren of medieval alleys falling steeply off the main piazza.

Lawrence came here to study the Etruscans, who took the 9th century B.C. town established by the Villanovian culture and by the 4th century B.C. had turned it into *Velathri,* one of the largest centers in Etruria's 12-city confederation. The Etruscans left some hauntingly beautiful bronzes and a stupefying collection of alabaster funerary urns. The art of carving the translucent white alabaster still flourishes today in artisan workshops scattered throughout the city, but modern Volterra has only recently moved beyond the shrunken womb of its medieval inner circle of walls to fill in the abandoned extent of Velathri's 4th-century B.C. defensive belt.

ESSENTIALS

GETTING THERE   **By Train**   Volterra isn't very convenient by train, with a station only at **Saline di Volterra** (© **0588-86-150**) 10km (6 miles) away, to which five daily trains run on a secondary line from Cécina (trip time: 30–40 min.) on the coast. You can transfer at Cécina from one of the coastal-line trains between **Rome** (17 trains daily; 3 hr.) and **Pisa** (26 daily; 40–75 min.). Buses meet the incoming trains for the 20-minute ride up to Volterra.

By Car   Volterra is on the SS68 about 30km (19 miles) from where it branches off the Colle di Val d'Elsa exit on the Florence–Siena autostrada. From San Gimignano, head southwest on the secondary road to Castel di San Gimignano, which is on the SS68.

By Bus   From **Siena,** there are 16 daily SITA buses (www.sita-on-line.it) that make the 20- to 30-minute trip to **Colle di Val d'Elsa,** from which there are five daily buses to Volterra (50 min.). From **San Gimignano,** you have to first take a bus to Poggibonsi (20 min.), four of which daily link up with buses to Colle di Val d'Elsa for the final transfer. From **Florence,** SITA has two mid-afternoon direct runs (2½ hr.), or you can take one of five daily buses (three on Sun) to Colle di Val d'Elsa and transfer there (2½–3 hr.). Six to 10 APT buses run here Monday through Saturday from **Pisa** (change in Pontedera; 2–2½ hr. total). **Tickets** and information in Volterra are available at the tourist office. Buses run to and from Piazza Martiri della Libertà.

VISITOR INFORMATION   Volterra's helpful **tourist office,** Piazza dei Priori 19–20 (© **0588-87-257;** fax 0588-86-099; www.volterratur.it), offers both tourist information and free hotel reservations. April through October, it's open daily from 10am to 1pm and 2 to 6pm; November through March, hours are Monday through Saturday from 10am to 1pm and 2 to 5pm and Sunday from 10am to 1pm only.

FESTIVALS & MARKETS   **Volterrateatro** is a July theater festival. On the first Sunday of September, Volterrans dress up in medieval costume to engage in a bit of **flag-tossing** on Piazza dei Priori. On the last Saturday of September, the town hosts the **International Festival of Choral Singing.** The sizable **weekly market** is Saturday morning.

In Search of Alabaster

Volterrans have been working the watery, translucent calcium sulfate stone found around their mountain for almost 3,000 years. The Etruscans turned the **alabaster** into the tiny sarcophagi that fill the Guarnacci museum; the industry revived in the late 19th century, mainly to crank out lampshades for the exploding market in electric lights. The working of alabaster is taken very seriously in town, and you can major in it at the local art school. Among the producers are the roadside workshops outside town that use machines and trained hacks to churn out chess sets, life-size reproductions of famous Italian sculptures, and such follies as alabaster kitchen sinks; and then there are the craftsmen in town who put a great deal of skill and pride into their bowls and statuettes.

The *comune* has put Plexiglas plaques at the workshops of some of the most traditional artisans, the ones who still handwork every stage. Via di Sotto has a good run of them, including the workshop of **Lido Baroncini** at no. 7; he welcomes visitors to peek in his window and watch him work. His stuff is among the many items sold at the large **Gallerie Agostine**, Piazza XX Settembre 3–5 (✆ **0588-86-868**). **Renzo Gazzanelli and Roberto Guerrieri's** workshop is at Via del Mandorlo 42, and the larger **Alabastri Rossi** (✆ **0588-86-133**) outfit works out of a shop at the end of the block, where the street turns for the Roman theater panoramic walk.

There's a good **figure-carving workshop** based at Via Gramsci 60, and Via Porta all'Arco has several fine shops, including the shop of the town's top artiste, **Paolo Sabatini** at no. 45 (✆ **0588-87-594**). For some of the better craft objects, the **Società Cooperativa Artieri Alabastro**, Piazza dei Priori 4–5 (✆ **0588-87-590**), has been a cooperative showroom and sales outlet for artisans who don't have big enough operations to open their own shop since 1895.

WHAT TO SEE & DO

One **cumulative admission ticket** covers all three major museums—Museo Etrusco Guarnacci, Museo d'Arte Sacra, and Pinacoteca e Museo Civico. It costs 7€ ($8.05) adults, 5€ ($5.75) students and seniors over 60, 15€ ($17) family of four (children under six are admitted free). All museums' summer hours run from March 16 to October 15.

San Francesco   Just inside the 14th-century Porta San Francesco, Volterra's 13th-century Franciscan church has one overwhelming reason to visit: Halfway up the right aisle is the **Cappella Croce del Giorno** 🏛🏛, frescoed with the *Legend of the True Cross* in medieval Technicolor by Cenni di Francesco. (The light switch is outside the chapel entrance.) Cenni painted this story in 1410, creating an unmatched example of early-15th-century narrative art. His vivid and unusual color palette, eye for detail, and painterly tailoring has also left us a valuable record of the dress and architecture of his era.

Piazza San Francesco (off Via San Lino). No phone. Free admission.

Volterra

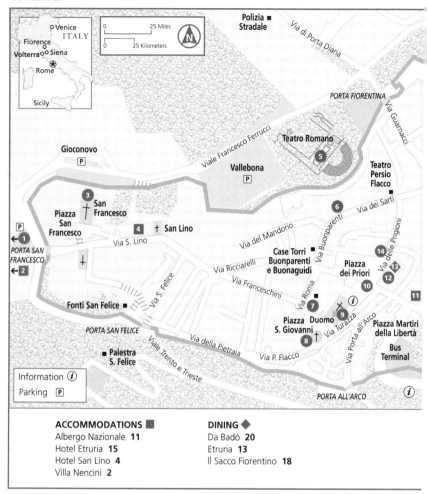

ITALY
Venice
Florence
Volterra • • Siena
• Rome
Sicily

0 — 25 Miles
0 — 25 Kilometers

Polizia ■
Stradale

Via di Porta Diana

PORTA FIORENTINA

Via Guarnacci

Gioconovo
P

Teatro Romano
5

Viale Francesco Ferrucci

Vallebona
P

Teatro
Persio
Flacco

San
Francesco
3

Piazza
San
Francesco

San Lino
4

6

Via dei Sarti

Via del Mandorlo

Via Buonparenti

Via delle Prigioni

P
← 1

PORTA SAN
FRANCESCO
← 2

Via S. Lino

Via Ricciarelli

Case Torri
Buonparenti
e Buonaguidi

Via Roma

14
13
Piazza
dei Priori
12
10

Via S. Felice

Via Franceschini

11

Fonti San Felice ■

7
Piazza Duomo
S. Giovanni
8

i

9

PORTA SAN FELICE

Via della Pietraia

Via Porta all'Arco

Via Turazza

Piazza Martiri
della Libertà

Viale Trento e Trieste

Via P. Flacco

Bus
Terminal

■ Palestra
S. Felice

PORTA ALL'ARCO

i

Information ⓘ
Parking P

ACCOMMODATIONS ■
Albergo Nazionale **11**
Hotel Etruria **15**
Hotel San Lino **4**
Villa Nencini **2**

DINING ◆
Da Badò **20**
Etruria **13**
Il Sacco Fiorentino **18**

Palazzo dei Priori   The Palazzo dei Priori (1208–57) is the oldest building of
its kind in Tuscany, the Gothic town hall on which Florence's Palazzo Vecchio
and most other civic buildings in the region were modeled. Walk up to the first
floor to see the town council chamber, which aside from getting a new vaulted
ceiling in 1516 has pretty much looked the same over its 740 years of continuous use. The end wall was frescoed with an *Annunciation* by Jacopo di Cione or
his brother Orcagna in 1383.

Volterra's civic palace sits on a medieval rectangle of a piazza. The **Piazza dei
Priori** ✿ is laid with mason-cut stone and surrounded on all sides with 13th-
and 14th-century buildings, some crenellated, some with Gothic two-light windows, and some just implacably old and stony. It's particularly evocative at night
under the moonlight. Across from the Palazzo dei Priori is the **Palazzo Pretorio,** sprouting the rough old **Torre del Porcellino**—a tower named after the
weather-beaten little sculpted boar jutting out near the top window. The only
impostor on this perfectly medieval piazza was built to blend in very well—the

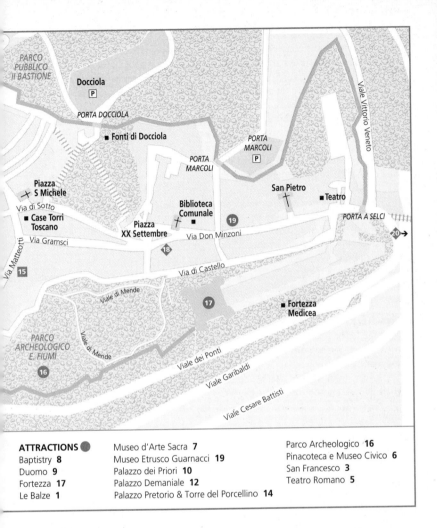

modern **Palazzo Demaniale** on the southeast end. Next to the Palazzo dei Priori on the piazza, a bit of imitation Romanesque striped marble (added in 1937) tucked into a corner announces the back entrance to the Duomo (see below).

Piazza dei Priori. ☎ 0588-86-050. Free admission. Summer Mon–Sat 10am–1pm and 3–4pm; winter Mon–Sat 10am–1pm.

Duomo   Beyond the 13th-century Pisan-style facade, the first thing that strikes you in this 12th-century church is its magnificent **ceiling.** It was carved and embossed with gold and azure in 1580 and is filled with portraits of Volterran saints, including St. Linus, a truly venerable native son who became the world's second pope, filling St. Peter's shoes in A.D. 67.

Volterra's Duomo is filled with well-done baroque paintings, but few stand out. Among those that do is the first altarpiece on the right, Belgian mannerist Pieter de Witte's *The Presentation of Volterra to the Virgin,* with a 1578 view of the city. In the right transept, above the door to the Chapel of the Holy Sacrament, is a 1611 *Crucifixion* ✶ by Francesco Curradi—a good baroque study of light and fabric. Across the transept from this chapel is a life-size sculpted wood group of the *Deposition* ✶, painted in bright primaries and heavy gold. It looks vaguely mid–20th century but was actually carved around 1228 by anonymous masters, artists who were bridging the gap between stiff Byzantine traditions and the more fluid, emotional art of the Romanesque era.

The **Cappella degli Inhirami** at the end of the left transept was built in 1607 and dedicated to St. Paul with some good paintings from the 1620s, including the central *Conversion of St. Paul* by Domenichino. In the left aisle of the church is a **pulpit** assembled from 13th-century Pisan relief panels in the 16th century; the *Last Supper* on the front is particularly arresting for its visual style and whimsical detail.

In the **Cappella dell'Addolorata (Lady Chapel)** ✶ off the end of the left aisle are a pair of niches made for anonymous 15th-century terra-cotta sculptures. On the left wall, in the niche housing the *Nativity* terra cottas, Benozzo Gozzoli frescoed an intimate backdrop for the scene, placing it in a rocky pass bursting with foliage and the horse train of the Magi riding in from the distance (viewable by coin-op lights).

Piazza San Giovanni (also entrance on Piazza dei Priori). No phone. Free admission. Summer daily 7am–7pm; winter daily 7am–12:30pm and 2–6pm.

Baptistery   The baptistery drum, with its one side of distinctive black-and-white marble bands, was built in 1283, but the dome was added in the 16th century. Just inside the door is an Etruscan funerary urn recycled as a holy water stoup, and in the center is an 18th-century font. This polychrome affair replaced the smaller, more elegant **marble font** Andrea Sansovino carved with simple reliefs in 1502, now against the right wall.

Piazza San Giovanni. No phone. Free admission. Summer daily 7am–7pm; winter daily 7am–12:30pm and 2–6pm.

Porta all'Arco ✶   At the end of Via Porta all'Arco stands the main gateway to Etruscan Volterra, a huge arch of a gate that has survived since the 4th century B.C.—with a bit of Roman-era rebuilding in the 1st century B.C. On the outside of the arch are mounted three basalt heads—worn by well over 2,000 years of wind and rain to featurelessness—said to represent the Etruscan gods Tinia (Jupiter), Uni (Juno), and Menvra (Minerva). In 1944, just before intense fighting began against the Germans laying siege to the city, Volterran partisans saved the gate from destruction by filling it overnight with stones—both for structural support and to keep it from being a focus of attack.

No phone. Free admission.

Museo d'Arte Sacra   The medieval and early Renaissance fragments salvaged from an older version of the cathedral and other Volterran churches along with a few good paintings make this small museum a good half-hour stopover. Among the sculptural pieces are some works by Tino di Camaino and Romanesque elements fitted with Roman friezes. Giovanni della Robbia may have crafted the painted terra-cotta *Bust of San Lino,* while Antonio Pollaiolo created the hyperrealist silver-and-gilt reliquary *Bust of San Ottaviano.* Of the paintings, keep an eye out for Rosso Fiorentino's mannerist *Madonna of Villamagna* (1521) and a *Madonna of Ulignano* (1545) by Daniele "da Volterra" Ricciarelli.

Palazzo Vescovile, Via Roma 13. ℂ **0588-86-290.** www.diocesivolterra.it. Admission by cumulative ticket. Daily 9am–1pm; Mar 16–Nov 1 also 3–6pm.

Pinacoteca e Museo Civico   Volterra's worthy small painting gallery contains some pick-of-the-litter works by artists working in Volterra between the 12th and 17th centuries. Room 4 has a remarkably intact polyptych of the *Madonna with Saints* (1411), complete with pinnacles, predella, and all, signed by Taddeo di Bartolo; the guy in the red cape and beard in the tiny left tondal is Santa Claus (St. Nicholas of Bari). Room 5 preserves a polyptych by Cenni di Francesco, and in the following room hangs a polyptych by Portuguese immigrant Alvaro Pirez d'Evora (1430), who mixed Spanish traditions with early Renaissance Sienese styles. In room 11 is an *Apothesis of Christ with Saints* (1492), the last great work from the brush of Florentine Domenico Ghirlandaio. The figures create a perfectly oval architectural frame for the Flemish-inspired landscape detailing of the background—if you look hard, you can spot a giraffe, recently acquired by the Medici for their menagerie, being led along the road.

Room 12 pulls out all the stops and hits you with two large 1491 Luca Signorelli paintings, including a remarkably colored *Annunciation,* and an early masterpiece by Rosso Fiorentino. A 26-year-old Rosso Fiorentino painted the ***Deposition*** 🟊🟊 here (1521). The late Renaissance instruction of his teacher Andrea del Sarto shows through in the young artist's work, as do the influences of other contemporary masters, like Filippino Lippi, from whom Rosso lifted the basic composition, and Michelangelo, from whom he copied the pose of the mourning St. John on the right. (It's Eve expelled from the garden on the Sistine Chapel ceiling.) But Rosso's supremely odd color palette and exaggerated use of light are purely his own, and the work's tense action and the rhythm created by the ladders and alternately calmly posed or violently contorted figures have helped set it among the masterpieces of the mannerist movement. Try to picture it hanging amid the bright Cenni frescoes in San Francesco church, where it originally sat atop the altar.

Palazzo Minucci Solaini, Via dei Sarti 1. 🕿 **0588-87-580.** Admission by cumulative ticket. Mar 16–Nov 2 daily 9am–7pm; Nov 3–Mar 15 daily 9am–2pm.

Teatro Romano (Roman Theater & Baths) 🟊   A left turn off Via Guarnacci as you head steeply down toward Porta Fiorentina takes you to a walkway atop the medieval ramparts overlooking the impressive remains of Volterra's Roman theater and baths. There are some of the best-preserved Roman remains in Italy, dating back to the 1st century B.C. The view from up here is the best way to see it all, but there's an entrance down on Viale Francesco Ferrucci if you want to wander among the ruins.

Viale Francesco Ferrucci. 🕿 **0588-86-050.** Free admission. Mar 16–Nov 2 daily 11am–5pm. Closed when raining.

Tips **A Cappuccino Break**

Right on the main square, with a few tables outside, sits the very friendly little **Bar Priori**, Piazza Priori 2 (no phone). The **Vecchia Osteria dei Poeti,** Via Matteotti 55 ([tel **0588-86-029**), is a narrow, stand-up bar with good panini, snacks laid out on the bar during *passeggiata* hour, and the thickest hot chocolate you ever stuck a fork in. Its neighbor, newcomer **L'Incontro,** Via Matteoti 18 (🕿 **0588-80-500**), makes for a more relaxed pit stop, with music playing to small wooden tables and a marble bar scattered under high medieval ceilings, with homemade pastries (they specialize in mini tarts) and *panini* made fresh at the deli counter.

The Encroaching Edge of Town

A 15-minute walk down Borgo San Stefano and Borgo San Giusto east out of Porta San Francesco leads to **Le Balze** ⟨⟨, a bowl-shaped broken landscape where fast-paced erosion of the clay is gobbling up the edges of Etruscan Volterra. It's one of Italy's more quietly frightening scenes. Helped along by periodic earthquakes, this erosion has already exposed and then destroyed much of the Etruscan necropoli at this end of town and now threatens the medieval Badia church, which was abandoned after an 1846 quake brought the erosion to its doorstep.

Museo Etrusco Guarnacci ⟨⟨   Volterra has managed to hold on to a horde of valuable remains from its rich past in one of Italy's most important and fascinating Etruscan museums. Besides the prehistoric section with its Villanovian tombs and some Roman busts and mosaic floors, the lion's share of this museum is taken up with more than 600 **Etruscan funerary urns** ⟨. Most of these date from the 3rd century B.C., but there are some entire tomb finds gathered from as early as the 9th century B.C. The urns—rectangular boxes about 3 feet long, the oldest ones in plain terra cotta, but most carved of alabaster or other stone with a relief on the front and capped with a lid sculpted with the reclining figure of the deceased—are grouped by their many styles and types. The effect of room after room lined with these intricate studies on the Etruscans' views of life and death is fascinating.

The reliefs and reclining effigies often show a primitive naturalism unmatched even by the Renaissance, and because many of the panels depict the symbolic departure of the deceased to the realm of the dead—on horseback, in wagons, aboard ships, riding centaurs, driving chariots—there's room for plenty of touching episodes where friends and family are shown waving their last goodbyes. One of the finest is a striking bit of portraiture: an early-1st-century B.C. **sarcophagus lid** carved with the figures of a husband and wife, both very old, somewhat dour-faced and full of wrinkles, but staying together even in death. Also here, among the bronzes, is an early-3rd-century B.C. votive figure of an exceedingly elongated young boy known as the *Shadow of the Evening* ⟨.

Via Don Minzoni 15. ⟨ **0588-86-347.** Admission 8€ ($9.20), or by cumulative ticket. Mar 16–Nov 2 daily 9am–7pm; Nov 3–Mar 15 daily 9am–2pm.

Parco Archeologico   Volterra's public park calls itself "archaeological" after the jumbled remains of a Roman-era *piscina* reservoir partially excavated in one corner, but it's really just a grassy space spotted with trees and crossed by hedge-lined gravel paths. It's good for picnics, sightseeing breaks, and napping in the sun. Guarding it at one end is the **Fortezza** (1343–1475), used since the Medici times as a prison, a function it still performs admirably.

Via del Castello. No phone. Free admission. Mar 16–Nov 2 daily 11am–5pm. Closed when raining.

WHERE TO STAY

Albergo Nazionale   Built atop medieval stalls a few yards from Piazza dei Priori and opened as a hotel in 1890, the Nazionale has hosted the likes of Gabriele d'Annunzio and D. H. Lawrence, who stayed here while researching *Etruscan Places*. The furniture is pretty mix and match, with a few Art Deco bed frames, 19th-century chairs or dressers, and some contemporary cast-iron crafted tables alongside functional pieces. The beds are firm, and most of the bathrooms redone. There are some pretty ceramic-patterned floors throughout, and the rooms on the front side of the top floor have a panorama of the countryside below Volterra's rocky crag. In all, you'll find a slightly erratic gaggle of accommodations maybe one notch above those at the nearby Etruria (see below). Half- and full-pension options are available (48€–61€/$55–$70).

Via dei Marchesi 11 (at Piazza Martiri di Libertà), 56048 Volterra (Pisa). ✆ **0588-86-284.** Fax 0588-84-097. www.albergonazionalevolterra.it. 36 units. 60€–68€ ($69–$78) double; 72€–80€ ($83–$92) triple. Breakfast 6€ ($6.90). AE, DC, MC, V. Parking in nearby lot 10€ ($12). **Amenities:** Restaurant (in winter, only on request); concierge; laundry service; dry cleaning. *In room:* TV, hair dryer.

Hotel Etruria *Kids*

The elevator-less Etruria is housed in an 18th-century palazzo on one of the town's main drags, which is packed with strolling Volterrans every evening. The rooms are very basic, with soft beds, smallish bathrooms, and functional furnishings of contemporary or 1970s vintage, but the family that runs the place keeps it all spotless. There are some hidden treats, such as the stretch of 5th-century B.C. Etruscan wall up on the second floor. A rooftop garden overlooks the terra-cotta roofs of Volterra and hides a gate opening directly into the city's manicured public gardens, the Parco Archeologico. Seventeen of the rooms have TVs, and only one double has no bathroom. The rates reflect season, and in winter they prefer you take bed and breakfast.

Via Matteotti 32 (in the center of town), 56048 Volterra (Pisa). ✆ **0588-87-377** or 0588-81-606. 22 units, 19 with bathroom. 52€ ($60) double without bathroom, 67€ ($77) double with bathroom. Breakfast 6€ ($6.90). MC, V. **Amenities:** Concierge; limited room service (breakfast and bar). *In room:* TV in 17 units.

Hotel San Lino ★

The San Lino is the best hotel in town, a 13th-century palazzo that until 1978 was a cloistered convent. The older rooms on the first floor, reserved mainly for students and groups, have battle-scarred functional furniture and subcompact bathrooms of the curtainless shower persuasion. The accommodations on the second floor (and those on the 1st that stretch alongside the large terrace with its small pool) are what garner the hotel four stars. These rooms feature air-conditioning, minibars, nicer built-in appointments, curtained windows, and larger, new bathrooms. The San Lino isn't as central as the other hotels listed here (still, it's only a 2-min. walk up to the main piazza), but it is definitely more comfortable.

Via San Lino 26 (near Porta San Francesco), 56048 Volterra (Pisa). ✆ **0588-85-250.** Fax 0588-80-620. www.hotelsanlino.com. 44 units. 73€–81€ ($84–$93) standard double; 89€–99€ ($102–$114) superior double. Rates include breakfast. AE, DC, MC, V. Parking 11€ ($13) in garage next door. Closed 3 weeks in Nov. **Amenities:** Restaurant (Apr, Aug, and Sept); outdoor pool; concierge; tour desk; limited room service (breakfast and bar); laundry service; same-day dry cleaning; nonsmoking rooms; Internet access. *In room:* A/C, TV, minibar, hair dryer.

Villa Nencini ★ *Finds*

This converted 17th-century farmhouse may be a 10-minute walk from the city, but it's got great countryside views, and Mario Nencini, an ex-trattoria owner, is passionate about wine and keeps a private—and recently renovated—enoteca downstairs (put together a group of at least six hotel guests for a tasting with snacks). In 2000, Mario overhauled the rooms in the original building with unvarnished wood furnishings and antique-style painted wood bed frames, but the brown tiled bathrooms are beginning to age. Rooms in the newer wing, which wrap around the pool, feature stylish wood units, carpeting, colorful bedspreads, and firmer mattresses. Ground-floor rooms of this newer wing are larger, with independent entrances (the reception closes 12:30am–7am) but no real views.

Borgo Santo Stefano 55 (a 10–15-min. walk from Porta San Francesco, outside the walls), 56048 Volterra (Pisa). ✆ **0588-86-386.** Fax 0588-80-601. www.villanencini.it. 36 units, 33 with bathroom. 68€ ($78) double without bathroom, 83€ ($95) double with bathroom; 86€ ($99) triple without bathroom, 112€ ($129) triple with bathroom; 165€ ($190) suite. AE, DC, MC, V. Breakfast included. **Amenities:** Restaurant; outdoor pool; concierge; tour desk; courtesy car; 24-hr. room service (breakfast and bar); laundry service; same-day dry cleaning; nonsmoking rooms. *In room:* TV, dataport, minibar, hair dryer.

WHERE TO DINE

Da Badò ⚓ VOLTERRANA   In the satellite village of San Lazzero, the small and simple Badò is loved and respected by locals for its unwavering commitment to Volterran cuisine, which means improvising dishes based on the freshest ingredients available while sticking to traditional recipes. The thick-sliced prosciutto in the *antipasto misto* is gorgeously soft, flaky, and salty. The *zuppa alla Volterrana* is a ribollita with fresh veggies, and the *papparedelle alla lepre* are wide homemade egg noodles in hare sauce. Bunnies pop up again for the *coniglio à modo nostro* (rabbit cooked with onions and tomatoes), but Badò's true specialty secondo, for those who can stomach tripe, is *trippa alla Volterrana,* stewed with tomatoes and herbs.

Borgo San Lazzero (just outside the walls). ✆ 0588-86-477. Reservations recommended. Primi 4€–8€ ($4.60–$9.20); secondi 6€–12€ ($6.90–$14). MC, V. Thurs–Tues noon–2:30pm and 7–9:30pm. Closed Feb 10–28 and Nov 15–30.

Etruria TUSCAN   The only worthwhile restaurant inside Volterra's walls sits right on the main piazza. Its kitchen—under the guidance of the acclaimed late owner Beppino Raspi—drew actors, artists, and heads of state to its frescoed vaulted ceilings and well-priced food. The cooking is still excellent and abundant. Start with a *fantasia di crostini* (a huge plate piled with a rich assortment of crostini). The *poker d'assi* allows you and a companion to sample three primi, which may be *pappardelle di lepre* (noodles in hare sauce), *riso salsiccia e funghi* (rice with mushrooms and sausage), or *farfalle all'Etrusca* (spinach bow ties with spinach-Gorgonzola sauce underneath and tomato purée on top).

Piazza dei Priori 6–8. ✆ 0588-86-064. Reservations recommended. Primi 2.50€–9€ ($2.90–$10); secondi 9.50€–17€ ($11–$19); menù turistico without wine 13€ ($14); fixed-price menus with wine 13€–20€ ($15–$22). AE, DC, MC, V. Thurs–Tues noon–3pm and 7–10pm.

Il Sacco Fiorentino TUSCAN   Though it keeps changing ownership, Il Sacco only gets better with each reinvention. The young couple that runs it now have spiced up the Tuscan menu with international touches while toning down the former chilly atmosphere to make it into a moderately priced and friendly neighborhood hangout. The polenta served with wild boar and porcini ragù is excellent, as is the odd *tagliatelle de sacco,* the noodles enveloped in saffron-chicken sauce studded with fresh veggies. For a secondo, try *costolette d'agnello gratinate con carciofi* (broiled lamb chops with artichokes).

Piazza XX Settembre 18. ✆ 0588-88-537. Reservations recommended. Primi 6€–7.75€ ($6.90–$8.90); secondi 8.50€–11€ ($9.80–$13). AE, DC, MC, V. Thurs–Tues noon–2:30pm and 7–9:30pm. Closed Jan.

5 Massa Marittima: An Overlooked Gem

70km (43 miles) S of Volterra; 65km (40 miles) SW of Siena; 115km (71 miles) SW of Florence; 230km (143 miles) NW of Rome

Massa Marittima, sitting stately atop its 356m (1,188-ft.) mount with a sweeping view over the farmland far below and Metalliferous Hills beyond, is an Etruscan grandchild. It's a medieval mining town that's heir to ancient Pupolónia, now little more than fragmentary remains 40 miles away on the coast (see "Livorno" in chapter 7 for more information). When St. Cerbone moved his bishop's seat here in the 9th century, he kicked off Massa's Middle Ages prosperity, based on mining

Massa Marittima

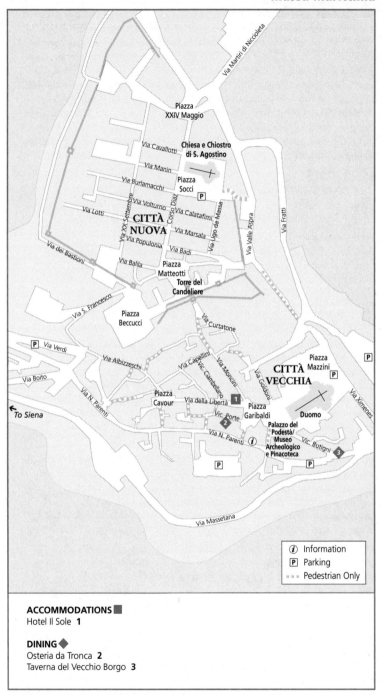

Information

ⓘ Information
Ⓟ Parking
░░░ Pedestrian Only

ACCOMMODATIONS ▪
Hotel Il Sole **1**

DINING ◆
Osteria da Tronca **2**
Taverna del Vecchio Borgo **3**

the metal-rich hills around it. It established a republic in 1225 and grew fat on mine proceeds—unfortunately attracting the attentions of the nearby Sienese.

In 1335, Siena attacked and subdued Massa, taking the upper half of town and fortifying it as their Città Nuova (New Town). In its heyday, the city produced both religious heritage (St. Bernardine of Siena was born and died here) and civic legacy. (The first mining code in European history was drawn up here in the 14th c., one of the most important legislative documents from the Middle Ages.)

Today, Massa is an overlooked gem of the western Tuscan hill towns. The Germans are the only ones who come in droves in the summer, but aside from them, the fewer than 10,000 inhabitants, and the occasional bike tour whizzing through, Massa and its gorgeous cathedral lie empty for exploration.

ESSENTIALS

GETTING THERE   By Train   Massa Marittima doesn't have its own train station, but there's a stop 27km (17 miles) away at Follonica (© **0566-902-016**) on the main line between **Rome** (10 daily; 2½ hr.) and **Pisa** (15 daily; 1 hr. 20 min.). Buses meet incoming trains for the ride to Massa.

By Car   Massa sits where the SS439 from Volterra meets the SS441 coming up from the coast at Follonica and continues on to just past San Galgano, where it meets up with the SS73 coming down from Siena.

By Bus   Three to four daily buses run from **Volterra** (you have to change in Monterotondo), one from **Grosseto,** and two from **Florence** and **Siena.**

VISITOR INFORMATION   The private agency Amatur (© **0566-902-756;** fax 0566-940-095; www.amatur.it) acts as the official **tourist information center** at Via N. Parenti 22. It'll also offer help finding a hotel or signing up for courses (usually weeklong) in artisan crafts like ceramics, leather, wood inlay, and cooking. It's open Sunday and Tuesday through Friday from 9:30am to 12:30pm (in summer also 3:30–7pm), Saturday from 9:30am to 12:30pm and 3:30 to 6pm. There's also a small **information stand** (© **0566-902-289;** fax 0566-902-052) at the museum desk inside the Palazzo del Podestà at Piazza Garibaldi 1. It has a few pamphlets and maps for sightseeing.

FESTIVALS & MARKETS   The **Balestro del Girifalco** involves a crossbow competition, processions, and displays of complex flag juggling all done in 13th-century costume. It's put on twice a year, on May 20 or the following Sunday and on the second Sunday in August. March through October, there are **chamber music concerts,** and in July there's an international **mineralogical fair** held in the cloisters of Sant'Agostino. There's a Wednesday **market** on Viale Risorgimento and a Saturday one on Piazza XXIV Maggio.

WHAT TO SEE & DO
EXPLORING THE CITTÀ VECCHIA

The Old Town focuses around triangular **Piazza Garibaldi.** Today, the medieval buildings guard over sleepy cafes with tables out on the flagstones or shaded under arcades. The square is anchored at one end by the steeply angled off-kilter steps of the **Duomo** ★★, turned slightly as if to show off its good side and bell tower (open daily 8am–noon and 3–6pm). The bulk of the building was raised in travertine in the early 13th century with Pisan-Romanesque blind arcading, but the Gothic style had hit town by the time they got to the top half of the facade, so it was crowned with an architecturally agile arcade of slender columns and pink and white marbles. Above the main door lintel, a 12th-century Pisan sculptor carved a relief panel celebrating the miracle-ridden life of Massa's patron saint and one-time bishop, 9th-century African immigrant San Cerbone, to whom the cathedral is dedicated.

The interior is supported by fat travertine columns with flowing Corinthian capitals. Just inside the entrance is a font carved with *St. John the Baptist* scenes by Giroldo da Como from a single block of travertine (1267). The tabernacle balancing above it is an anonymous 15th-century Sienese work. On the entrance wall to the left of the main door are several spellbinding **early medieval reliefs** 🟉 carved from a dark chestnut-brown stone. These pre-Romanesque images of Christ and his apostles and a riveting *Massacre of the Innocents* scene, with skull-faced figures wearing stiffly pleated robes, are of unknown provenance and by an unknown hand and are unique in the Maremma province.

In the apse behind the altar is the **Arco di San Cerbone** 🟉. This marble urn sheltering the remains of the town patron is covered with reliefs depicting the saint's life carved in 1324 by little-known Sienese Gothic talent Goro di Gregorio. Across the piazza from the Duomo is the 13th-century **Palazzo del Podestà**—recognizable by the old mayoral coats of arms. Inside you'll find Massa's minuscule **Museo Archeologico e Pinacoteca** (℗ **0566-902-289;** www. coopcollinemetallifere.it/musei). Down the corridor to the right off the entrance room is Massa's main art treasure, **Ambrogio Lorenzetti's *Maestà*** 🟉 painted in the late 1330s. Sitting at the feet of Mary nuzzling her baby is a glowing reddish Lorenzetti angel, and amid the stacks of saintly halos on the right is black-robed St. Cerbone, his geese milling about his feet. During the baroque era, which didn't care for these early "crude" paintings, the city lost track of the work, and it wasn't rediscovered until 1867, by which point it had been divided into five pieces and, nailed together, was serving as an ash bin for a stove. The museums are open Tuesday through Sunday from 10am to 12:30pm and 3:30 to 7pm (3–5pm Nov–Feb). Admission is 3€ ($3.45) adults and 1.50€ ($1.75) children under 14 and seniors over 60.

From the narrow end of Piazza Garibaldi, Via Moncini branches steeply up from Via della Libertà toward the "New Town."

EXPLORING THE CITTÀ NUOVA

The upper part of town is only "new" by virtue of the fact that the conquering Sienese revamped it after 1335. You enter the New Town through the **Porta alla Silici,** part of the *cassero* fortifications built by the Sienese (1337–38). The gate's back side sprouts a narrow **flying arch** framing the trees of the tiny park beyond—though built as a viaduct for the Sienese garrisons, it was made more for show than for sound military purposes. The arch connects the fortress ramparts to the 1228 **Torre del Candeliere** (℗ **0566-902-289;** www.coopcollinemetallifere.it/musei/musei/torre.html), a clock tower since 1443 and still impressive at two thirds of its original 60m (200 ft.). You can climb it for **views** 🟉 over the ramparts. April through October, it's open from 10am to 1pm and 3 to 6pm; November through March, it's open 11am to 1pm and 2:30 to 4:40pm. Admission is 2.50€ ($2.90) adults and 1.50€ ($1.75) children under 14 and seniors over 60. Around the right side, through the small park, is an always-open entrance to the ramparts' lower level and a cityscape view over the Città Vecchia below.

WHERE TO STAY

Hotel Il Sole   Since it opened in 1990 at the center of town, Il Sole has been the best choice in Massa, stealing much steam from older peripheral board-rated two-stars like the Duca del Mare. Persian runners line the halls, and the carpeted rooms are of a simple low-key elegance with carved wood furnishings that vaguely recall the Liberty style, plus small but modern bathrooms.

Via della Libertà 43, 58024 Massa Marittima (GR). C **0566-901-971.** Fax 0566-901-959. hotelilsole@tin.it. 50 units. 85€ ($98) double; 115€ ($132) triple. Rates include breakfast. AE, DC, MC, V. Parking 15€ ($17) in garage. Closed mid-Jan to mid-Feb. **Amenities:** Concierge; tour desk; car-rental desk; courtesy car; 24-hr. room service; babysitting; laundry service; same-day dry cleaning. *In room:* TV, hair dryer.

WHERE TO DINE

Osteria da Tronca ⭐ *Finds* MAREMMANA   This restaurant, known by most people simply as L'Osteria, is split-level medieval—all stone walls, brick arches, and hand-hewn wood ceiling beams but spread over two floors with open spaces in between. An explanation of any dish begins "Oh, that's 'X' the way we make it." "We" seems to incorporate the jocular restaurateurs, the septuagenarian cook who steadfastly prepares food the way her mamma taught her, and Massans in general. Kick off your meal with *tortelli alla maremmana* (giant ravioli stuffed with ricotta and Swiss chard in meaty ragù) or *zuppa dell'Osteria* (a cannellini bean and cabbage soup poured over toasted garlic bread). Follow with *cinghiale alla cacciatore* (wild boar huntsman style, stewed with mushrooms—but no olives, which, they sniff, are only "for making oil") or an *arista di maiale* (slices of roast pork with potatoes).

Vicolo Porte 5 (parallel to Via della Libertà; from Piazza Garibaldi, take left turn after Hotel Il Sole, then left again). C **0566-901-991.** Reservations recommended. Primi 5.50€–7€ ($6.30–$8.05); secondi 6€–9€ ($6.90–$10). MC, V. Thurs–Tues 7–10:30pm. Closed Jan–Feb.

Taverna del Vecchio Borgo MAREMMANA   Step inside under the low vaulted stone rooms and you may see owner Claudio Bindi at the corner fireplace, roasting an entire pig on a spit. His wife, the felicitously named Grazia Innocenti ("innocent grace"), is a skilled chef and devotee of traditional cooking. Her antipasti are unusual, like *spiedini di polenta gratinati con pancetta* (fried polenta cubes speared with pancetta ham and cheese and grilled). The classic Maremma poor man's soup is *acqua cotta dei butteri* (celery, onions, tomatoes, and chicken stock poured over stale bread), named for the lonely cowboys who roam this region. More festive is the *gnocchi di patate con zucchini e speck di anatra fumé* (gnocchi in a rich sauce of zucchini and smoked duck). Two people can split a *tris di primi* and sample three of Grazia's creations. For a main course, stick with the excellent *grigliata mista* (fresh meats grilled) or *agnello scottaditto* (succulent lamb chops).

Via Norma Parenti 12. C **0566-903-950.** Reservations highly recommended. Primi 5.20€–7.80€ ($6–$9); secondi 7.80€–35€ ($9–$40); fixed-price menu without wine 23€ ($26) per person for 2 people only. AE, DC, MC, V. Tues–Sun 7:30–10pm. Closed Feb 15–Mar 15.

Lucca & Northwestern Tuscany

The strip of Tuscany riding along the Apennines and the Emilia–Romagna border doesn't hold to most people's image of Tuscany and remains relatively undiscovered despite being wedged between Florence and Pisa, favorites of guided tours. Florence's close neighbors **Prato,** with its renowned theater and friendly folk and the best *cantucci* in Tuscany, and **Pistoia,** known in the Middle Ages for its murderous tendencies but today for Romanesque churches and booming economy, have rich histories and artistic patrimonies that can keep you steeped in Tuscan culture just a few dozen kilometers from Florence but a world away from its summer crowds.

Beyond them stretches a land of genteel spas like **Montecatini Terme** and tall alpine mountains buried in green forest and capped with snow. Tuscany's northern coast catches the southern extreme of the Riviera attitude in resort towns like **Viareggio** and **Forte dei Marmi,** while just inland from them tremendous peaks around the **Garfagnana Valley** rise jaggedly, hiding the marble of Michelangelo, a hotbed of the anarchy movement, and some of the most extensive caves in Italy.

Lucca, the region's main city, lies in the plains just south of these mountains. It's a considerably more interesting town than Pisa, just a 15-minute train ride to the south, yet it doesn't get one-tenth of Pisa's hordes. This regally refined burg of bicyclists is home to beautiful Romanesque churches and the mightiest set of walls of any medieval Italian metropolis—now tamed into a city park and planted with trees to shade Sunday strollers.

1 Prato & the Virgin Mary's Girdle

17km (10 miles) NW of Florence; 333km (206 miles) N of Rome

Poor Prato is overlooked by too many sightseers simply because it seems too close to Florence to be different. What they're missing is one of northern Tuscany's most open, friendly, and lively cities, one with a modest repository of heavyweight art treasures from the likes of Donatello and Filippo Lippi as well as a glittering collection of early Renaissance altarpieces. The city was probably an Etruscan campsite and later meadow (*prato* in Italian) market site that quickly developed into a stable Lombard town around A.D. 900. It has always been a thriving trade center and was a free commune from 1140 until 1351, when Florence bought it from its nominal lord and set it up as an ally state. Prato is the region's fastest-growing city, a hard-working community that helps debunk the myth of the lackadaisical Italian with a millennium of serious commitment to its economy. The Pratese also know how to roll up their sleeves and enjoy themselves, with festivals, lively bars, and what is perhaps Tuscany's top theater.

The textile industry has been important since the Middle Ages and was the foundation of the medieval wealth of early Pratese capitalists like Francesco Datini, the famous Merchant of Prato; it's going stronger than ever today, as is other light industry. The town is proud to assume the moniker "Prato: Industrial City," which is nicer than its Anglo nickname, snorted somewhat derisively, the "Manchester of Tuscany." And the Pratese are positively elated that their expanding economic empire has allowed the city to become the third largest in Tuscany, in recognition of which regional officials in 1992 carved out a sliver of a new province with Prato as its capital.

ESSENTIALS

GETTING THERE   By Train   Prato is on the Florence–Lucca–Viareggio and the Florence–Bologna lines, with more than 50 trains daily from Florence (about 30 min.). All trains stop at **Prato Centrale station,** a 10-minute walk southeast from the center, but only the former line stops at the **Prato Porta Serraglio station,** outside the gate just a few blocks north of the Duomo. For train information, call ℭ **0574-26-617** or 0574-28-398.

By Car   If you're taking the A11 from Florence or Pistoia, Prato Est is the exit you want. The best place to **park** is on Piazza Mercatale (free parking along the edges, payment by the hour in the central lot).

By Bus   Lazzi and CAP buses make the trip from Florence in about 30 minutes. The half-hourly **CAP** buses from Florence drop you off at the train station (ℭ **0574-608-218** in Prato; 055-214-637 in Florence at Largo F.lli Alinari 11; www.capautolinee.it). **Lazzi** buses (ℭ **055-215-1558** in Florence; www.lazzi.it) from Florence, Pistoia, Lucca, Pisa, and Siena terminate in Prato at Piazza San Francesco.

VISITOR INFORMATION   The well-stocked and helpful **tourist office** (ℭ and fax **0574-24-112;** Mon–Sat 9am–1:30pm and 4–6:30pm [until 6pm Sat]), is at Piazza Santa Maria delle Carceri 15. The monthly **events calendar,** available here and at many hotels and restaurants, is called *Pratomese.* Additionally, Prato's tourism website (www.prato.turismo.toscana.it) features an event search by date, so you can learn what's happening during your visit—or plan your trip around a particular festival.

FESTIVALS & MARKETS   The town's main event is the **display of the Virgin's girdle** 𝓕𝓕, which is done five times yearly—Easter, May 1, August 15, September 8, and December 25. This girdle is actually Mary's belt, which she removed and passed down to that ever-doubting St. Thomas whilst she was being Assumed into Heaven (rather than have Mary suffer the pain and indignity of mortal death, God decided to Assume her, or lift her bodily, up into the afterlife right at the point of her death; Thomas, as usual, didn't believe his eyes, and Mary did this to convince him it was really her rising into the sky—you'll see the moment captured in paint, marble, and inlaid wood all over town).

The holy artifact, which was passed down to generations of Thomas's family, came to Prato at the time of the Crusades, when a local boy fighting in the Holy Land married Thomas' descendent and got the girdle as part of her dowry. The strip of dark green cloth is now preserved in a glass and gilt case which is kept inside nesting boxes within its own chapel in the Duomo under a series of locks that only keys kept by the bishop, mayor, and local chief of *carabinieri* can open, which they do with much pomp and Renaissance-style ceremony during the five yearly High Masses to celebrate the relic. The prelate, amid swirling incense and chanting, shows the girdle three times each to the parishioners inside the church and to the crowds massed on the piazza outside (there's a special exterior pulpit solely for this purpose), the faithful chosen to be so blessed line up to kneel and kiss the case with the girdle in it, and the relic is then locked away until the next celebratory mass. A costumed parade with lots of drumming and fifing then follows. The best, most Byzantine celebrations are held for the Christmas viewing.

The **Festa degli Omaggi** is a costumed historical pageant held on September 8. The renowned **Teatro Metastasio's season** runs October through April, and the main **market** is held on Mondays at the Mercato Nuovo.

EXPLORING THE CITY

Duomo ⚜ There was once the Pieve di Santo Stefano in the center of the Prato of the 900s, but between 1211 and 1457 a new building with Romanesque green-and-white striping rose on the site to become Prato's Duomo. The facade has a glazed terra cotta *Madonna and Sts. Stefano and Lorenzo* (1489) by Andrea della Robbia above the main door. The beautiful *Pulpit of the Sacred Girdle* hangs off the facade's right corner, from which Prato's most revered relic, the Virgin Mary's girdle, is displayed five times yearly. The pulpit is a Michelozzo (design) and Donatello (sculpted friezes) collaborative effort (1434–38). The frolicking cherubs around the base are cast replacements for Donatello's badly weathered originals, now kept in the Museo dell'Opera dell Duomo (see below).

Inside the church on the left is the **Cappella della Cintola (Chapel of the Sacred Girdle),** entirely frescoed (1392–95) by Agnolo Gaddi. On top of the altar stands one of Giovanni Pisano's finest sculptures, a small marble *Madonna and Child* (1317). Alas, popping a few coins in the box doesn't buy much light, and the frescoes are hard to see through the bronze screen, though you may find a sacristan to flip on a few more lights for you.

The nave **pulpit** was carved by Mino da Fiesole and Antonio Rossellino (1469–73). To the right of the high altar is the **Cappella dell'Assunzione (Chapel of the Assumption),** frescoed with scenes from the lives of St. Stephen and the Virgin.

The **frescoes** ⚜⚜ (1452–66) covering the walls of the choir behind the high altar—the *Life of St. Stephen* on the left wall and *St. John the Baptist* on the right—comprise one of the masterpieces of Filippo Lippi. This randy monkish painter asked if a certain Lucrezia Buti, a beautiful young novice from the nearby convent, could model for his Madonnas. The nuns agreed, Filippo promptly seduced her, and the two ran off, eventually having a son, Filippino Lippi, who became an important painter in his own right. Supposedly Filippo did actually use Lucrezia in the paintings—she's the graceful flowing figure of Salome dancing into the banquet of Herod on the right wall. Lippi portrayed himself, along with Fra' Diamante and others of the assistants who helped him here, on the left wall among the crowd mourning the passing of St. Stephen. (They're the little red-hatted group on the far right; Filippo is 3rd in from the end.) Sadly, the choir has been closed to visitors since the mid-1990s, when someone armed with a paintbrush decided to add his own touch to Lippi's works, and it's extremely difficult to see the frescoes well from the gate. The frescoes are also currently undergoing a multiyear restoration. However, rather than just cut us off from them, the tourist office and restorers have provided the unique opportunity to examine the frescoes (and the art of restoration) up close by ascending the scaffolding for guided hour-long visits on weekends. The visits—which are limited to 12 people, in Italian unless a bunch of English speakers show up, and cost 8€ ($9.20), and must be booked in advance—are on Saturday at 10am, 11am, 4pm, and 5pm, and Sunday at 10am and 11am. To make a booking, call 0574-24-116 weekdays 9am to 1pm, or stop

---

Cumulative Ticket

Prato sells a 5€ ($5.75) ticket that covers the Museo dell'Opera dell Duomo, Galleria Comunale e Museo Civico, Museo di Pittura Murale in San Domenico, and the Castello dell'Imperatore and Cassero.

---

by the Museo del Opera dell Duomo (see below); see also www.restauro filippolippi.it for lots more info.

Piazza del Duomo. (C) **0574-26-234**. Free admission. July–Sept daily 7:30am–12:30pm and 4–7:30pm; Oct–June daily 7am–12:30pm and 3–6:30pm (until 8pm Sun).

Museo dell'Opera del Duomo   The pickings here are fairly slim, though the admission price is worth it if only for the smog-coated and worn originals of Donatello's dancing putti friezes from the Duomo's outdoor *Pulpit of the Sacred Girdle*. First, however, you pass through a room with early-14th-century works, including Bettino di Corsino's *Madonna del Parto*—the pregnant Mary is an extremely rare subject in early Italian art. Through the cloister, the rooms with the Donatellos also contain Fra' Diamante's *Annunciation,* a *St. Lucy* sprouting a huge sword from her neck by Filippino Lippi, a possible Paolo Uccello in the detached fresco of *Jacopone da Todi,* and a 15th-century reliquary case for the Holy Girdle worked by Maso di Bartolomeo. (Apparently dancing putti were *de rigueur* for girdle-associated artworks.)

Piazza del Duomo 49 (left of the Duomo entrance). (C) **0574-29-339**. Admission on cumulative ticket. Mon and Wed–Sat 9:30am–12:30pm and 3–6:30pm; Sun 9:30am–12:30pm.

Galleria Comunale e Museo Civico ⭐   Inside the tall crenellated 14th-century Palazzo Pretorio in Prato's civic heart, the communal museum kicks off with a World War II–damaged 1498 **Filippino Lippi tabernacle** he frescoed for his mother, Lucrezia, and a *Portrait of Baldo Magini* by Ridolfo del Ghirlandaio. Through the large salon of 16th- and 17th-century canvases you can get to the stairs up to the good stuff. A long, poorly lit hall glitters with the gold-leaf backgrounds of one of the finest collections of **polyptych** ⭐ altarpieces in Tuscany. Among the masterpieces is a predella by Bernardo Daddi telling the story of the Holy Girdle cartoon-strip style. Most of the works, though, are various takes on the Madonna theme (with Child, with Saints, Enthroned, and so on) by Pietro di Miniato, Lorenzo Monaco, Luca Signorelli, both Filippo and Filippino Lippi, Raffelino di Garbo, Andrea di Giusto, and Botticini.

On the piazza outside is a **statue of Francesco Datini** (see Palazzo Datini, below) with bronze plaques showing the man's life accomplishments—besides making obscene amounts of money in the 14th-century textile business, he founded the charitable Ospedale del Ceppo.

Note: The museum closed for restoration in 1998 and is expected to reopen in 2006. In the meantime, the collection of excellent 14th- and 15th-century polyptychs and paintings is on display at the Museo di Pittura Murale in San Domenico (see below).

Piazza del Comune. (C) **0574-616-302**. Currently closed for restoration. Admission on cumulative ticket. Mon and Wed–Sat 9:30am–12:30pm and 3–6:30pm; Sun 9:30am–12:30pm.

Santa Maria delle Carceri   This was the first centrally planned templelike church of the High Renaissance (1485–1506), a not entirely successful exercise in Brunelleschian theoretical architecture by Giuliano da Sangallo. The light plaster walls with *pietra serena* accents and Andrea della Robbia friezes and tondi are still pleasantly evocative, but the place somehow leaves you cold. The interior contains a St. John the Baptist statue over the font by the architect's son, Francesco, and the miraculous small 14th-century fresco of the *Madonna with Child and Two Saints* the church was built to house. The basilica's stained-glass windows were designed by Domenico Ghirlandaio.

Piazza Santa Maria delle Carceri. ✆ **0574-27-933**. Free admission. Daily 7am–noon and 4–7pm.

Castello dell'Imperatore   Hohenstaufen Emperor Frederick II's sharp-lined and blindingly white stone citadel was inspired by the Norman-style fortresses in Puglia. Frederick II built it here in the 1240s to remind the Pratese who was boss and to defend the route from his homelands in Germany to his realm in southern Italy. While these days the inside is bare, you can climb onto what's left of the broken-toothed ramparts for a view of the city. Nearby is the newly restored 14th-century tower **Cassero,** once connected to the defensive wall by a viaduct until modern roads cut through it.

Piazza Santa Maria delle Carceri. ✆ **0574-38-207**. Admission on cumulative ticket or 2€ ($2.30) with Cassero. Mar–Apr and Oct daily 10am–5pm; May–Sept daily 10am–7pm; Nov–Feb daily 10am–4pm.

San Francesco   The earthly remains of Prato's late medieval financial genius, Francesco Datini (see "Palazza Datini," below), are laid to rest at the altar's steps. There's a pretty tomb erected after 1460 by Bernardo Rossellino on the left wall. Off the cloister (also accessible through a door in the sacristy) is the **Cappella Migliorati,** entirely frescoed in 1395 by Niccolò di Pietro Gerini with the lives of St. Anthony Abbot and St. Matthew played out in medieval Technicolor around a large Crucifixion.

Piazza San Francesco. ✆ **0574-31-555**. Free admission. Daily 8am–noon and 3:30–6:30pm.

Palazzo Datini ⟲   This was the home of Francesco di Marco Datini (1330–1410), a textile magnate and secular patron saint of capitalism whose life was drawn so vividly by Italian-American author Iris Oriogo that he's become known by the title of her book, *The Merchant of Prato.* Datini, almost single-handedly responsible for Prato's late medieval trade prosperity, was the inventor of the promissory note, and he kept scrupulous records of all his business activities—the basis for Oriogo's book—and inscribed each one of his financial ledgers with an accountant's battle cry: "For God and Profit."

One of the few places he allowed himself to spend money was on the decoration of his home, hiring Niccolò Gerini and Arrigo di Niccolò di Prato for the job. The outside frescoes have faded to reveal their fascinating *sinopia* sketches underneath, but many paintings on the interior walls remain. The de facto ticket room retains bucolic scenes bubbling with plant and animal life, and a side room contains a portrait of Datini dressed in red. Next to the main door, as in many medieval houses, is a giant St. Christopher, which Datini glanced at daily to protect against sudden death while he was out and about conducting business.

Via Mazzei 33/Via Rinaldesca. ✆ **0574-21-391**. Free admission. Mon–Sat 9am–noon; Wed and Fri also 4–6pm.

Galleria degli Alberti   Just up the street from the Palazzo Datini, the pinkish Palazzo degli Alberti houses the Cassa di Risparmio di Prato bank, which keeps its good little painting collection above the pit where they carry on Datini's money-making tradition. Giovanni Bellini crucified his beautifully modeled ***Christ*** ⟲ in the middle of a Jewish graveyard and painted an amalgamated fantasy city in the background. Next to this masterpiece hangs a small *Madonna col Bambino* against a scallop-shelled niche by Filippo Lippi, and a few

Italy's Best Biscotti & Tuscany's Top Theater

Prato is known throughout Italy for making the finest of those twice-baked hard almond crescent cookies called *cantucci*. To pick up a bag of these **biscotti di Prato,** stop by the award-winning shop **Antonio Mattei,** Via Ricasoli 20–22 (② 0574-257-56; www.antoniomattei.it), which has been selling Prato's famous *cantucci* and the vin santo in which to dunk them since 1858. The shop is open Tuesday through Friday from 8am to 8pm, and weekends from 8am to 1pm and 3:30 to 7:30pm (closed Sun afternoon).

For an evening at one of Tuscany's, and even Italy's, most innovative theaters, pick up a brochure at the tourist office for the **Teatro Metastasio** ⑉, Via B. Cairoli 59 ② 0574-608-501 for tickets; www.metastasio.it). The box office is open Monday through Friday from 10am to 1pm and 3:30 to 7pm. You can also visit **Dischi Niccoli** at Via Cairoli 19 (② 0574-27-890). The theater dates from 1830 and puts on contemporary and classic plays and music concerts ranging from classical orchestral pieces to modern jazz acts.

paintings later we get the large canvas of *Christ Crowned with Thorns,* the crowning apparently being done by Roman soldier triplets—Caravaggio must have used the same model for the different poses.

Via Alberti 2. ② **0574-617-359.** Free admission, but you must book ahead. Mon–Fri 8:30am–12:30pm and 3–4pm.

Museo di Pittura Murale in San Domenico Inside this barnlike Dominican church finished by Giovanni Pisano in 1322 is a Niccolò Gernini *Crucifix* on the second altar on the right, a pair of Matteo Rosselli works (*Madonna and St. Filippo Neri* on the 2nd altar on the right and an *Annunciation* on the 5th altar), and an Il Poppi *Crucifix Speaking to St. Thomas Aquinas* on the fourth altar on the right. The chapter house off the cloister has some excellent 15th-century fresco bits by Pietro di Minato rescued from under the whitewash in the 1980s.

Also housed here are the 14th- and 15th-century altarpieces from the Museo Civico and the **Museo di Pittura Murale.** The latter contains works, many of them damaged, by Niccolò Gerini, Pietro di Miniato, Agnolo Gaddi, and a nice Taddeo Gaddi *San Domenico,* along with anonymous 15th-century graffiti decorations saved from the gardens of the Palazzo Vaj.

Piazza San Domenico. ② **0574-440-501.** Admission on cumulative ticket. Mon–Sat 10am–6pm; Sun 10am–1pm.

Sant'Agostino This 13th-century church holds 17th-century paintings by the likes of Empoli and Lorenzo Lippi. Off the cloister is the Cappella di San Michele, with the remains of a 14th-century frescoed police lineup of saints and, in the next tiny chapel, a *Pietà* from the same era.

If you've got some more time, head down Via Convenevole and detour up Via Seminario. Ring at no. 28 and ask *posso vedere* ("can I see") **San Fabiano,** one of the oldest churches in Prato. The interior is modernized, but they do preserve bits of the early medieval mosaic floor mounted on the walls. Some, such as the siren figure, were probably adopted straight from pagan symbolism and hint at a possible older cultish temple on this site.

Piazza Sant'Agostino 19. ✆ **0574-37-629**. Free admission. Mon–Sat 7am–1pm and 3:30–7:30pm; Sun 8am–1pm and 3:30–7:30pm.

WHERE TO STAY

With tourist juggernaut Florence just a few kilometers down the road, Prato doesn't bother offering much in the way of hotels. If you're traveling by rail and staying at the Hotel Giardino, ask the conductor if the train stops at Prato's secondary station, Prato Porta al Serraglio, and get off there, because it's closer. For the hotels San Marco and Flora, get off at the main station, Prato Centrale.

Besides the choices below, you might try the **San Marco,** Piazza San Marco 48 (✆ **0574-21-321;** fax 0574-22-378; www.hotel-sanmarco.com), a modern but not new hotel overlooking the Henry Moore sculpture halfway between the train station and the Castello; doubles run 90€ to 95€ ($104–$109).

Hotel Flora   The Flora is on a central but quiet street between the Castello and the Galleria Comunale. The rooms are uninspiringly contemporary but very livable, with amenities like double-glazed windows and personal climate control. The owners keep the place in tiptop shape—after all, they live on the top floor, just across from the glassed-in terrace with a view over Santa Maria delle Carceri and the Palazzo Pretorio and where in warm weather you can enjoy breakfast.

Via Cairoli 31, 50047 Prato. ✆ **0574-33-521**. Fax 0574-400-289. www.pratohotels.it. 31 units. 140€ ($161) double. Rates include breakfast. AE, DC, MC, V. Parking 10€ ($12) in garage. **Amenities:** Concierge; limited room service; laundry service; dry cleaning. *In room:* A/C, TV/VCR, minibar, hair dryer, safe.

Hotel Giardino   The Giardino is right on the corner of Piazza del Duomo, but you can't see the Duomo itself. On the plus side, this once heavily trafficked corner has recently become blessedly pedestrianized. The Giardino is the center's most modern hotel, restructured in 1990 with built-in furniture, new carpeting in all the rooms, and large, firm beds. Another plus is the family that runs it: an extremely friendly bunch who keep their little inn in great shape.

Via Magnolfi 2–6, 50047 Prato. ✆ **0574-26-189**. Fax 0574-606-591. 28 units. 130€ ($150) double; 156€ ($179) triple. Rates include breakfast. AE, DC, MC, V. Free parking in Piazza del Duomo or 11€ ($13) in garage. **Amenities:** Concierge; tour desk; limited room service; laundry service; same-day dry cleaning. *In room:* A/C, TV, dataport, minibar, hair dryer, safe.

WHERE TO DINE

The restaurant scene fares better than hotels in Prato, and many local restaurateurs have taken advantage of the city's proximity to Florence's airport to partake of the daily infusions of fresh fish flown in from the coast.

Besides the places below, try **Tonio,** Piazza Mercatale 161 (✆ **0574-21-266;** Tues–Sat 12:30–2:30pm and 7:30–10:30pm), a formal place with very good seafood dishes. Another excellent choice is **Baghino,** Via dell'Accademia 9 (✆ **0574-27-920;** Tues–Sat noon–2:30pm and 7:30–10:30pm, Mon 7:30–10:30pm), a moderately priced trattoria serving Tuscan specialties like *minestra di pane* (a scrumptious ribollita) and *ravioli alle sienese* in spinach-cream sauce.

Il Borbottino TUSCAN/SEAFOOD   A pair of creamy rooms done in straight contemporary lines with floral chairs and soft music make up Il Borbottino, which took over (but refused to change) the restaurant called Osvaldo Baroncelli which occupied this site for more than 40 years. There's still a modest nouvelle touch applied to solidly traditional Tuscan foods, and still a concentration on seafood, but since the menu itself and the selection of dishes appearing on it are still being tested and fine tuned by the new owners, I'm afraid it's impossible to list some sample dishes as you never know what you'll find on offer. Still, it's almost guaranteed to be good.

Via Fra' Bartolomeo 13 (just south of the city walls off Piazza San Marco). © **0574-23-810**. Reservations strongly recommended. Primi 6€–12€ ($6.90–$14); secondi 12€–20€ ($14–$23). AE, MC, V. Mon–Fri 12:30–3pm and 7:30–10pm; Sat 7:30–10pm. Closed 3 weeks in Aug.

Il Piraña ⭐⭐ SEAFOOD   Hard to believe, but this refined modern restaurant landlocked in an industrial suburb of Prato is one of Tuscany's bastions of fine seafood. They leave you no doubt as to their purpose: When you open the door you come face-to-fish with an aquarium of the flesh-eating critters after which the place is named. After you target the fresh specimen you want grilled for a second course from the ample selection, take your seat and start with a scampi salad or a "fantasy of crustaceans" with asparagus and tartar sauce. Select primi include *gnocchetti di patate con scampi e fiori di zucca* (potato dumplings with shrimp and served with stuffed squash blossoms) or *riso con crema di scampi* (a large portion of shrimpy, creamy rice). Secondi include the baked *rombo con patate olive nere capperi e pomodoro* (turbot with potatoes and a salsa of black olives, capers and tomatoes). A small selection of vegetarian primi is also available. The Piraña is popular enough to warrant reservations even midweek, but service, while very competent, can make a glacier look speedy.

Via Valentini 110 (south of the walls near A11). © **0574-25-746**. Reservations strongly recommended. Primi 6€–10€ ($6.90–$12); secondi 13€–24€ ($15–$27); tasting menu (fresh fish and vegetables) without wine 37€–47€ ($43–$54). AE, DC, MC, V. Mon–Fri 12:30–2:30pm and 8–10:30pm; Sat 8–10:30pm. Closed Aug 5–Sept 5. Bus 3.

2 Pistoia: Where Romanesque Meets Renaissance

17km (10 miles) NW of Prato; 35km (21 miles) NW of Florence; 336km (208 miles) N of Rome

An ancient Roman town (Catiline and his conspirators were defeated here in 62 B.C.) built against the foothills of the Apennines, Pistoia is another city whose proximity to Florence causes many travelers to pass it by on their way to Lucca or Pisa. Its pretty churches, small but worthy art collections, and well-preserved dark medieval alleyways make it a worthwhile stop—and hint at its unusual historic situation. Halfway between rivals Pisa and Florence, it inherited beautiful Romanesque churches and Gothic sculpture through the influence of the former and the best of the Renaissance from its proximity to the latter.

However, the machinations of these eternally feuding Tuscan rivals, with some 14th-century meddling by Lucca thrown in, also left their mark on Pistoia's medieval character. After the city's Ghibelline *comune* was conquered by Guelf Florence in 1254, the Pistoians were reportedly the ones who began the schism between Black and White Guelfs. One day, a Pistoiese child of the ancient Neri (Black) family was playing at wooden swords with a friend from the Bianchi (White) household and one—the legend doesn't say which—was injured. When the perpetrator was sent by his father to apologize to the other boy, the hurt child's father responded by hacking off the offending youth's hand, declaring, "Iron, not words, is the remedy for sword wounds." The ensuing conflict spread to Florence as noble households waged secret wars and occasional all-out street battles against one another. This political plague was so devastating and devious that Michelangelo later stigmatized the Pistoiese as the "enemies of Heaven."

Pistoians already had a nasty reputation. Political arguments in Pistoia were historically decided by secret assassinations, performed with the aid of the daggers,

called *pistolese,* produced by the city's famous metalworking industry. As times advanced and science allowed men to kill one another in increasingly effective ways, the city began producing handheld firearms that adopted the dagger's old name: pistol.

Modern-day Pistoia, aside from its art treasures, has little to do with its notorious past. Today, the metal industry's chief products are the train cars and buses made by the Breda works, which outfitted the Washington, D.C., Metro. The town's biggest modern industry is horticultural, and Pistoia's peripheral "industrial zone" is a Dr. Seuss miniature landscape of ornamental trees and shrubbery lined up in orderly rows.

ESSENTIALS

GETTING THERE   By Train   Pistoia is on the Florence–Lucca–Viareggio line, with more than 35 trains daily from **Florence** (45–55 min.). There are also sixteen daily local trains from **Bologna** (a 2-hr. trip), most of which connect in

Prato. Pistoia's **train station** (© 0573-20-789) is on Piazza Dante Alighieri, a short walk south of the town center on Via XX Settembre.

By Car   Take the A11 from **Florence,** past Prato. The SS64 leads here from **Bologna.** You can park off Via Pacinotti (just outside the south wall) at the ex-Officine Meccaniche Breda.

By Bus   Lazzi/COPIT buses (© 0573-363-243 or 0573-21-170; www.copitspa. it) run to Via XX Settembre 71 (near the train station) from Florence (75 min.), Prato (30 min.), Montecatini Terme, Lucca, Viareggio, Pisa, Livorno, and other destinations. COPIT buses also run from Piazza San Francesco 4 to service Pistoia province (Abetone, Cutigliano, and nearby areas) and Florence. You can buy tickets onboard from the driver.

VISITOR INFORMATION   The helpful **tourist information office** (© **0573-21-622;** fax 0573-34-327; www.pistoia.turismo.toscana.it, though you'll find more info regarding museums and such on the city website at www. comune.pistoia.it.) is open daily 9am–1pm and 3–6pm at Via Roma 1/Piazza del Duomo 4 (cater-cornered to the Baptistery).

FESTIVAL & MARKETS   In 1300, the **Giostra del Orso** was a real Joust of the Bear, a bearbaiting event in which horsemen ceremonially took on the captive ursine. Revived in 1947, the wildly popular July 25 event is these days more humane. The highlight in a day of general costumed pageantry is the joust, when mounted knights circle opposite each other around a track and score points by slamming their lances into stylized bear targets. There are **daily fruit and veggie markets** (except Sun) on Piazza della Sala and Via Ciliegiole, and a **Wednesday and Saturday morning market** on Piazza del Duomo.

EXPLORING THE CITY

Ospedale del Ceppo ⟨⋆⟩   Pistoia's star attraction is the facade of the Ospedale del Ceppo, one of the best works by the often disappointing Giovanni della Robbia and Pistoia's answer to the Ospedale degli Innocenti in Florence, which was decorated by Giovanni's father, Andrea. Here, Giovanni was in top form, creating a frieze (1514–25) of glazed terra-cotta panels to surmount a Michelozzo-designed loggia. Because this is a hospital, founded in 1277 and still going strong, the six well-preserved della Robbia panels, plus a decaying one added later by Filippo Paladini, represent the seven acts of mercy, divided by the cardinal and theological Virtues.
Piazza Giovanni XXIII.

San Domenico   This 1280 church squats a block inside the southern walls of town. The first item on the right as you enter is the **tomb of Filippo Lazzari,** one of Dante's best friends. The scholar lectures on eternally in the relief panel below. (I like to think his young follower Boccaccio, said to be one of the students here, is the kid stifling a yawn on the right.) The chapel to the left of the high altar contains a Cristofano Allori canvas of *St. Domenic Receiving the Rosary,* interesting not so much for the painting itself, but for the argument in the background between the artist and the church sacristan over payment for the picture. Benozzo Gozzoli, who died of the plague while on a fresco job here in 1497, is buried in the cloister, which also gives access to several rooms housing detached **13th-century frescoes.** The refectory and attached tiny museum house the remaining fragments of Gozzoli's last work, a *Journey of the Magi,* and a possible early Verrochio *St. Jerome.* To see all the above if the cloister isn't open, hunt down a sacristan or ring the bell at Piazza San Domenico 1.
Piazza San Domenico. © **0573-28-158.** Free admission. Daily 7–11:50am and 4:30–6pm (Sun to 8pm).

Cappella del Tau ★★   This remarkable chapel was built in 1360 by a branch of the Franciscan order that cared for the sick and disabled and whose members wore a Greek Tau as their symbol. In the 1500s a private citizen bought it and whitewashed over the 1372 **fresco cycle by Niccolò di Tommaso** that covered every inch of the walls and ceiling. In the process of stripping the whitewash in 1968, many of the frescoes were seriously damaged, but what remains of the *Life of St. Anthony Abbot* and (on the ceiling) the stories of *Creation* and *Original Sin* is stupendous. The colors on the few in the upper corners of the back give some idea of how vivid the original effect must have been.

Corso Silvano Fedi 70. ℂ **0573-32-204**. Free admission. Mon–Sat 9am–1pm.

San Giovanni Fuoricivitas   The **side facade** ★ of this tiny but supremely Romanesque church is one of the most photographed sites in Pistoia, an orderly festival of blind arcades, inlaid diamond lozenges, and stripes to put a zebra to shame. Inside is a giant 13th-century crucifix, a *Visitation* in white terra cotta by Luca della Robbia, and a Giovanni Pisano holy water stoup. The main attraction, however, is the **pulpit** ★ (1270) by Fra' Guglielmo da Pisa (a student of Nicola Pisano). Of the three major pulpits in Pistoia (see San Bartolomeo in Pantano and Sant'Andrea, both below), this is the most solidly Romanesque.

Via Cavour. ℂ **0573-24-784**. Free admission. Daily 8am–noon and 5–6:30pm.

Duomo (Cattedrale di San Zeno) ★   The current incarnation of San Zeno dates from 1220, soon after which an old defensive tower close by, bristling with Ghibelline swallowtail crenellations, was given a respectable church clothing of Romanesque striped arches and converted to the cathedral bell tower. The glazed **terra-cotta decorations** of the barrel vault in the entrance arcade and the lunette above the main door are Andrea della Robbia creations.

On the inside right wall is a tomb by Cellino di Nese (1337) and a good Byzantine painted crucifix by Coppo di Marcovaldo (1275). Just past that is the Capella di San Jacopo and the Duomo's greatest treasure, the **Altare di San Jacopo (Altar of St. James)** ★. Close to a ton of partially gilded silver is molded into medieval saints (the upper half), early Renaissance biblical scenes (the front and flanks), and a pair of Brunelleschi prophets around on the left side. Started in 1287 and not finished until the 15th century, this altar outlasted a number of silversmiths, including a handful, such as Leonardo di Ser Giovanni, who also worked on the only other comparable altar, a similar pile of silvery holiness now in Florence's Museo dell'Opera del Duomo.

The **Il Passignano frescoes** inside the dome are hard to see. Pop down into the **crypt** for the remains of the 5th-century church and marvelously medieval bits of a **Guido da Como pulpit** (1199), dismembered in the 17th century. Get the custodian from the St. James altar to pull aside the curtain and turn on the lights in the chapel to the left of the high altar so you can see the 1485 *Madonna di Piazza,* a brightly colored work, including a fantastically rich carpet under the Virgin's feet, that has been declared the only documented painting by Verrochio (though some are now trying credit it to his protégé Leonardo da Vinci—or even Leonardo's student Lorenzo di Credi).

Piazza del Duomo. ℂ **0573-25-095**. Admission to Duomo free; Cappella di San Jacopo 4€ ($4.60) adults, 3€ ($3.45) children. Duomo daily 8:30am–12:30pm and 3:30–7pm. Cappella di San Jacopo Mon–Sat 10am–12:30pm and 3–5:30pm; Sun 8–9:30am, 11–11:30am, and 4–5:30pm.

Baptistery This baptistery was built in those strong Pistoian bands of dark green and white by Cellino di Nesi between 1337 and 1359, based on a design by Andrea Pisano. The Gothic pulpit set to the right of the entrance was added in 1399, and the *Madonna* above the door is the work of Tommaso and Nino Pisano. The spare interior, with bare bricks showing off the bulk of the dome, contains a reconstituted baptismal font (1226) of carved and intarsia marble panels by Lanfranco da Como that date from an earlier version of the baptistery.

Piazza del Duomo. No phone. Free admission. Tues–Sat 9:30am–12:30pm and 3–6pm; Sun 9:30am–12:30pm.

Museo San Zeno A local bank now owns the old Bishop's Palace wedged between the Duomo and the Baptistery, but they keep their archaeological and Duomo-related collections open to the public via a guided tour (see below). The highlights of the excavation are bits of a **Roman house** and an **Etruscan furnace.** There is also a pair of **Etruscan tomb markers** and a precious **alabaster funerary urn** carved with a chariot scene in high relief. The placard declares it Roman of the 2nd century A.D., but a team of American art historians has declared it was more likely of Etruscan origin. There's a **gold reliquary case** (1407) by Lorenzo Ghiberti and his workshop in the room that was once used as the Duomo's sacristy and treasury. In the 13th century, Vanni Pucci—one of those bad seeds who helped cement Pistoia's evil reputation—broke into this room looking for politically damaging documents. While inside, Pucci also helped himself to some of the church's riches, a despicable act that caused Dante to stick Pucci, surrounded by snakes and cursing God, in a fairly low circle of Hell. The tour also takes you past the bishop's private chapel, devoted to San Niccolò, with badly damaged **14th-century fresco fragments,** and a room specially built to receive the detached dry tempera frescoes from a nearby villa, painted in 1868 by Macchiaioli artist Giovanni Boldini.

Via Roma 1, Palazzo dei Vescovi (Piazza del Duomo). ✆ 0573-369-277. Admission 4€ ($4.60) adults, 2€ ($2.30) children over 1m (3 ft., 4 in.) and seniors. Open by reservation on a guided tour only: Mon–Sat 8am–12:30pm and 3:30–7pm, Sun 8am–1pm and 3:30–7pm. Tours meet at the tourist office.

Museo Civico Pistoia's most worthwhile museum is housed in the 1294 **Palazzo del Comune,** sprouting a hard-to-see basalt black head from the early 14th century that local legends make out to be either a Moorish king of Mallorca enslaved by pirating Pistoians or a traitorous citizen who sold his city out to Lucca. The museum's first floor boasts a Lucchese-style panel painting of *St. Francis* surrounded by his life story (1260s), a 14th-century *Lamentation* by Lippo di Benivieni, a polyptych of the *Madonna and Child with Saints* by the anonymous Master of 1310, and four early-16th-century *Sacred Conversations* with heavy colors of deep saturation. Two of the Conversations are by local boy Gerino Gerini, and one each came from the brushes of Florentines Lorenzo di Credi and Ridolfo del Ghirlandaio. The collection continues upstairs but goes downhill from here, with a glut of 17th- to 19th-century efforts on the third floor.

Piazza del Duomo 1. ✆ 0573-3711 or 0573-371-296. Admission 2.60€ ($3) adults, 1.30€ ($1.50) children; free to all Sat afternoon. Tues–Sat 10am–7pm; Sun 9am–12:30pm.

San Bartolomeo in Pantano "St. Bartholomew in the Swamp" is a 12th-century enlargement of an 8th-century church that has been sinking slowly into its namesake bog for more than a millennium. In the very dark interior, you may be able to make out the **13th-century fresco** in the apse, and you'll certainly stumble over the **pulpit** ✿ by Guido da Como (1250), one of the quirkier

---

Tips **A Cappuccino Break**

Valiani, Via Cavour 55 (© **0573-23-034**), is a cafe and pastry shop installed in 1831 under the high, vaulted ceilings behind a striped Romanesque facade next to San Giovanni Fuoricivitas. There are also a few tables outside.

---

medieval sculptors. The crouching figure supporting one of the back columns is said to be a self-portrait.

Piazza San Bartolomeo. © **0573-24-297**. Free admission. Daily 8:30am–noon and 4–6pm.

Sant'Andrea 🎨   Pistoia's other artistic heavyweight is Giovanni Pisano's **pulpit** 🎨🎨 (1298–1301) in this 12th-century church. The third of the four great Pisano pulpits (the others are in Pisa and Siena) and the first carved by Giovanni without the help of his dad, Nicola, this is the work with which the Pisan sculptor brought his art to absolute Gothic perfection. The reliefs are so deeply carved that the figures seem to come out at us. Because the naturalism of the Renaissance hadn't yet come into vogue, Giovanni relied on narrative density (the Annunciation, two takes on the Nativity, and the angels averting the shepherds in their fields are all crammed into the 1st panel) and exaggerated expression to bring his works to life. But the reliefs do foreshadow later movements, especially where Giovanni breaks the borders of the panels to carry the artistic narrative across real space. Notice how the angel of the Magi panel is pointing back to the Nativity scene as it wakes the three wise men to go adore the baby Jesus. There are also two **wood crucifixes,** one behind the pulpit by Gerino Gerini (early 1500s) and another by Giovanni Pisano across the nave. Feed the light box one coin at a time; otherwise, you'll waste your euros lighting the whole church instead of just the good bits.

Via Sant'Andrea. © **0573-21-912**. Free admission. Daily 8am–12:30pm and 3:30–6pm (to 7pm in summer).

San Francesco   Pistoia's barnlike Franciscan church contains lots of good **14th-century frescoes,** the best of which are in the chapels along the transept. Behind the high altar is a fresco cycle on the *Life of St. Francis* by a Giotto copycat (perhaps a student) who mimicked his master's formulae for most of the scenes. The chapel to the left has a Sienese-school cycle of an *Allegory of the Triumph of St. Augustine.* After giving a nod to the frescoes in the second chapel to the right of the high altar, go through the door at the transept's end for a peek at more 14th-century works in the **sacristy.** If it's open (if you're quiet about it, you can lift the blockade bar yourself), pass though the door into the **chapter house** beyond for even better frescoes, including a giant *Tree of Life* that just might be by the hand of Sienese master Pietro Lorenzetti.

Piazza San Francesco. © **0573-368-096**. Free admission. Daily 7:30am–noon and 4–7pm.

WHERE TO STAY

With just a few business travelers and a handful of tourists staying the night, Pistoia doesn't have a particularly scintillating crop of hotels. An additional choice to the ones below is the **Hotel Leon Bianco,** Via Panciatichi 2 (© **0573-26-675** or 0573-26-676; fax 0573-26-704; www.hotelleonbianco.it), a block from the Patria and very comparable, only with thicker quilts, smaller rooms, and newer bathrooms. Doubles cost roughly the same (75€–100€/$86–$115), but breakfast is free (except in highest season, when it's 8€/$9.20) if you flash this Frommer's guide. All hotels listed provide a permit to park free on the surrounding streets.

Albergo Firenze *(Value* Pistoia's only central budget choice is run by an American/Italian couple who keep the spacious, plain rooms very clean. The floors are stone linoleum tile and the beds sway-backed, but there's at least a sink-and-bidet affair in the corner of bathroom-less rooms (the shared bathroom bears an uncanny resemblance to a chapel, with a box shower as the altar). A few of the largest units have extra beds thrown in for families on a shoestring.

Via Curtatone e Montanara 42 (between the Duomo and San Francesco), 51100 Pistoia. *(C)* and fax **0573-23-141.** www.hotel-firenze.it. 20 units, 18 with bathroom. 70€ ($81) double without bathroom, 85€ ($98) double with bathroom; 20€ ($23) more for a triple. Breakfast included. AE, DC, MC, V. Bus: 10. *In room:* AC and TV in units with bathrooms.

Hotel Il Convento *(Finds* A friendly Florentine family runs this 18th-century convent turned countryside inn on the lower slopes of the Apennines northeast of the city. The decor hasn't been updated since they transformed it into a hotel in 1969, so much remains in an unfortunate 1960s style—but mercifully not all the rooms have matching curtains and quilts covered with brown, blue, and orange blobs or the olive green "son of Astroturf" carpeting. The hotel was overhauled in 2001, installing minibars, dataports, and safes in the rooms, generally freshening the place up, and adding eight new rooms to the mix. The best bits are the public areas—arcaded salons with overstuffed sofas, a panoramic terrace with a view stretching all the way down to Prato, a beautifully landscaped pool with a view, and an extremely intimate restaurant in the former monks' cells on the first floor. Each cell has only three tables, or you can dine like the *frate* did in the tiny old refectory.

Via San Quirico 33 (4km/2½ miles northeast of town), 51030 Pontenuovo (Pistoia). *(C)* **0573-452-651** or 0573-452-652. Fax 0573-453-578. 32 units. 95€ ($109) double without view, 120€ ($133) double with view. Breakfast 7€ ($8.05). MC, V. Restaurant closed Jan–Mar. **Amenities:** Restaurant; outdoor pool (May–Sept); concierge; limited room service; laundry service. *In room:* TV, minibar, hair dryer, safe.

Hotel Patria This is the most pleasant option in the historic center, a modern hotel with built-in lacquered headboards and furniture, carpeting on the floors and the walls, and recently renovated bathrooms. Its location can't be beat: just a few blocks from the train station but also only three doors down from the Romanesque stripes of San Giovanni Fuoricivitas and a minute's walk from the Duomo.

Via F. Crispi 8, 51100 Pistoia. *(C)* **0573-25-187.** Fax 0573-368-168. www.patriahotel.com. 28 units. 80€–105€ ($92–$121) double. Rates include buffet breakfast. AE, DC, MC, V. Free parking on street (ask hotel for pass). **Amenities:** Concierge; tour desk; car-rental desk. *In room:* TV, minibar, hair dryer.

WHERE TO DINE

Besides the choices below, you can get a good and fairly inexpensive pasta and pizza meal at perennially packed **La Sala "Da Ale,"** Via San Anastasio 4 *(C)* **0573-24-108;** Fri–Wed noon–2:30pm and 7pm–midnight), at the edge of Piazza della Sala. For excellent midpriced meals under brick vaults, go to **San Jacopo,** Via Crispi 15 *(C)* **0573-27-786;** Wed–Sun 12:15–2:30pm and 7–10pm, Tues 7–10pm), for *panzerotti gratinati* (a pasta casserole with mozzarella, tomatoes, mortadella, and prosciutto).

Lo Storno *(Value* TUSCAN This tiny and ever-popular place on a side street of medieval-era shops boasts a pedigree as a restaurant/inn dating from 1395. The radio and TV simultaneously compete to add noise to the already crowded rooms, and the weekly changing menu limits itself to about four primi and half a dozen secondi—all usually excellent preparations of hearty peasant food. The classic starter is *gran farro sui fagioli* (barley-and-bean soup), or try their homemade pasta of the day, which might be *penne all'arrabbiata* (piccante). Main courses also don't deviate too much from simple Tuscan standards, with choices like *arista di maiale al forno* (thinly sliced oven-baked pork) or *scallopine ai carciofi freschi* (veal scallops cooked with fresh artichokes).

Via del Lastrone 8 (a few steps off Piazza del Duomo). ℂ 0573-26-193. Reservations recommended. Primi 6€–6.50€ ($6.90–$7.50); secondi 6€–8€ ($6.90–$9.20). No credit cards. Mon–Sat noon–3pm and 7:45–9:30pm.

Rafanelli ⓐ PISTOIESE/TUSCAN   This countryside trattoria has become hidden in the midst of a growing "industrial zone"—serendipitously consisting mainly of carefully tended gardens feeding Pistoia's midget tree trade—but that hasn't diminished its popularity as a spot for Pistoian city slickers to come out for a big Sunday lunch in one of the large modernized rooms. The *papardelle alle lepre* (wide noodles with hare) and *risotto ai funghi porcini* (rice with porcini mushrooms) are perennial favorites, as is the local dish *maccheroni Pistoiese* (pasta in duck sauce). You can go all out on a *tris di primi* (three primi chosen at the chef's discretion). The *cinghiale alla Maremmemana* is wild boar cooked with black olives, while their grilled meats selections include a *bistecca fiorentina* and *scotta-ditto d'agnello*.

Via Sant'Agostino 47 (Loc. Sant'Agostino, just east of the city walls). ℂ 0573-532-046. Reservations recommended. Primi 6€–8€ ($6.90–$9.20); secondi 13€–18€ ($15–$21). AE, DC, MC, V. Tues–Sat noon–2:30pm and 7:30–9:30pm; Sun noon–2:30pm. Closed Aug and 1 week in Jan.

3 Montecatini Terme & Monsummano Terme: Spas & Saunas

15km (9 miles) W of Pistoia; 46km (29 miles) W of Florence; 330km (205 miles) N of Rome

The curative powers coursing through the sulfurous underground hot springs and steaming vaporous caverns of the Valdinevole west of Pistoia have been renowned for centuries. This "Valley of Mists" is home to Montecatini Terme, the grande dame of Italian spas, and Monsummano Terme, with eerie natural sauna caves. Though modern thermal centers aimed at relaxing your body and emptying your wallet have begun filling the valley, the hillsides remain beautiful. Capped with tiny medieval villages, the hills are a joy to wander—the SS633 twists its way into the mountains north of Montecatini, providing an especially gorgeous route for Sunday drivers. If you're heading here hell-bent on heavy relaxation, know that both Montecatini and Monsummano become veritable ghost towns from mid-October to Easter.

ESSENTIALS
GETTING THERE   By Train   The Florence–Viareggio train, which pauses at Pistoia on the way, stops at Montecatini (19 daily; 50–70 min. from Florence, 10 min. from Pistoia). If you're staying in Montecatini, get off at the second stop in town, Montecatini Succursale. If you're heading to Monsummano Terme, get off at Montecatini Terme–Monsummano or Centrale.

By Car   Take the A11 from Florence or Pistoia to the Montecatini exit.

By Bus   Hourly Lazzi (ℂ 055-363-041; www.lazzi.it) buses run from Florence (52 min.). From Pistoia, it's best to take the train.

VISITOR INFORMATION   Montecatini Terme's **tourist office** is at Viale Verdi 66 (ℂ 0572-772-244; fax 0572-70-109; apt@montecatini.turismo.toscana. it; no official site, but the following are all useful: www.termemontecatini.it, www. montecatini-terme.it, and www.montecatini-alto.it). It's open Monday through

Saturday from 9am to 12:30pm and 3 to 6pm and Sunday from 9am to noon; closed Sundays from December to Easter. For Monsummano, contact Grotta Giusti (below) directly.

TAKING THE WATERS

MONTECATINI TERME   Montecatini is a mecca for well-heeled spa-goers who like to do a bit of shopping to unwind after spending long hours wrapped in mud packs, drinking mineral-laden waters, getting radioactive vapors steamed into their faces, and lying about doing nothing. This town's on permanent *riposo,* and its nucleus is the **Parco dei Termi,** a long park of neoclassical temples each expanding over the sources of various underground hot springs and vaporous crevices.

The oldest is **Terme Tettuccio** (*©* **0572-778-501**), written of as early as 1370 and visited by the high-strung merchant of Prato, Francesco Datini, in 1401. The spa wasn't really exploited until Grand Duke Leopold I took an interest in developing the terme of the town in the 1700s. Reconstructed from 1919 to 1927, the long neoclassical facade opens onto the 20th-century ideal of a Roman bathhouse, decorated with murals, ceramics, and statues by Italy's Art Nouveau Liberty masters, like Galileo Chini and Ezio Giovannozzi. Drinking the waters here will supposedly do wonders for the liver you've been rotting with all that Chianti Classico.

The **Terme Leopoldine** (*©* **0572-778-551**) at the park's entrance goes so far as to dedicate itself as a neoclassical (1926) temple to Asculapius, the god of health, as if its mineral mud baths could cure all ills. These and most of the other spas are open May through October only, but one remains open to the ailing, aching public year-round: the neo-Renaissance-meets-modernism house of the **Excelsior** (*©* **0572-778-509**).

All the spas charge in the neighborhood of 4€ to 8.50€ ($4.60–$9.80) for half a day's entrance and water to sip and anywhere from 21€ to 104€ ($24–$120) for mud baths and more serious treatments, depending on season. Tickets are sold at the **Società delle Terme** office, Viale Verdi 41 (*©* **0572-7781** or 0572-778-487 for reservations; www.termemontecatini.it), outside the park entrance.

For a very light cultural workout to wring out your spa-sodden brain, you can drop by the **Accademia d'Arte** on Viale Diaz (no phone) during afternoons to see Macchiaioli and Liberty-style works by the likes of Giovanni Fattori and Galileo Chini as well as some Salvador Dalí surrealism and the piano on which Verdi composed *Otello* while taking the waters here. The hill sloping up behind the Parco delle Terme contains the wooded **Parco della Panteraie,** good for strolls through the woods and deer reserve, and a dip in the swimming pool.

May through October, a funicular makes a 10-minute trip from Viale Diaz up to **Montecatini Alto** (*©* **0572-766-862;** www.montecatini-alto.it) about every half-hour daily from 10am to 1pm and 3pm to midnight (in case all the relaxation has made the 5km/3-mile climb by foot daunting). It costs 3€ ($3.45) one-way and 5€ ($5.75) round-trip. The old town offers not much more than a few outdoor (in summer) cafes on its diminutive main piazza and fine views across the Valdinevoli, but it's a pleasant break from the languorous wallet-draining hedonism and general flatness of the modern spa town below. It's also a base for short hikes into the surrounding valley, especially to visit the stalactites of the **Grotta Maona** caverns nearby (*©* **0572-74-581**), open April through November Tuesday through Sunday from 9am to noon and 2:30 to 6:30pm. Admission is 4.50€ ($5.20) adults, 2.50€ ($2.90) for kids 6 to 12. The surrounding complex includes a bar that becomes a disco and dance hall some evenings.

MONSUMMANO TERME   One of the eeriest spas in Italy lies just south of Montecatini at Monsummano Terme. In 1849, the Giusti family discovered on their lands a series of stalactite- and stalagmite-laden caves with a sulfurous lake at the bottom and hot mineral-laden vapors permeating the air. By 1852, they had built a spa around it dubbed the **Grotta Giusti Terme** ⭐ and converted their adjacent villa into a luxury hotel (see below).

You don't have to stay at the inn to visit the spa at Via Grotta Giusti 171 (© **0572-90-771;** fax 0572-907-7300; www.grottagiustispa.com), where you can don a white shift and a dun-colored robe—like a member of some hedonistic monastic order—and descend through a series of increasingly hot and steamily dripping caverns named, of course, Paradiso, Purgatorio, and Inferno, after Dante (the scalding sulfur pool below is the Lake of Limbo). It costs 40€ ($46) to steam in the caves for 1 hour, but you can also go in for a whole regimen of treatments (such as full-body massages, starting at 28€ for 20 min. or 53€ ($61) for a 50-min. Swedish massage; mud baths; and cellulite-reduction programs) or stay for a weeklong "cure." Half-day package treatments start at 110€ ($127); full-day treatments from 200€ ($230). From April to the first weekend of November, the *terme* are open from 9am to noon (last entry 11am) and 3 to 6pm (last entry 5pm). The shuttle bus for the Hotel Grotta Giusti (below) will take you here from the Montecatini train station free of charge.

The town of Monsummano Terme doesn't offer much more than the small 16th-century **Santa Maria della Fontenuova** on the main piazza, with a frescoed wraparound portico and a tiny museum (opened on request) containing some 17th-century paintings and an ivory crucifix reputedly by Giambologna. In front of the church is a statue of the town's only citizen of historical note, poet Giuseppe Giusti.

Follow the yellow signs for the steep, twisty road through groves of chestnuts, olives, and pines up to the old village of **Monsummano Alto,** all but abandoned since the population moved down to the valley in the 1500s. Founded in the Dark Ages, the village is mostly in ruins, but still intact are half a guard tower (the 1st thing you come to) and, down to the right of it, one of the crumbling town gates. A path of crushed gravel and grass slowly becomes stone as you arrive at the few houses and tiny church—with an inexplicable small pine sprouting out halfway up the facade—that huddle around the small piazza, surrounded by the junglelike ruins of the rest of town. Only three of the houses are continuing concerns, home to a handful of old residents, several loud dogs, and a dozen lazing cats. Beyond the church are some excavated 15th-century house foundations. The views of the surrounding valleys are excellent.

WHERE TO STAY & DINE
IN MONTECATINI TERME

I sometimes wonder where Montecatinians live, because almost every building that isn't a restaurant, store, or spa seems to be an *albergo* (hotel). With more than 300 hotels in town, you should have no difficulty finding a room—Montecatini's tourist office spends half its time hunting them up for vacationers. Most hotels require you to take half or full board, and the vast majority are closed completely from mid-October to Easter. If you can escape your hotel's pension requirement, head to the **Enoteca da Giovanni,** Via Garibaldi 25 (© **0572-71-695**), for an excellent, but far from cheap, meal of innovative Tuscan fare and game dishes.

Grand Hotel & La Pace ⭐⭐   In a town where half the hotels use the name "Grand," this one should adopt the moniker "Monumental." From the palatial lounges to the 2-hectare (5-acre) wooded grounds to the frescoed restaurant that could host a UN conference, La Pace keeps early-20th-century formal elegance alive and very well cared for; it has been *the* place to stay in town since 1870. The guest rooms are more subdued but still create a sense of comfort, with shiny wood floors, high ceilings, and tasteful furnishings, including some new polished granite bathrooms. Renovations of the bar and some of the guest rooms are planned for 2004. Monday through Saturday, a wide range of spa treatments is available in *Centro Benessere* (the Natural Health Center).

Via della Torretta 1 (off Via Verdi), 51016 Montecatini Terme (PT). ✆ 0572-9240. Fax 0572-78-451. www. grandhotellapace.it. 150 units. 300€ ($345) double; 390€ ($449) jr. suite; 440€ suite ($506). Continental breakfast 13€ ($15), buffet breakfast 20€ ($23). AE, DC, MC, V. Free parking in hotel lot. Closed Nov 1–Mar 30. **Amenities:** 2 restaurants (1 formal and 1 low-key poolside open June–Sept); 2 bars; heated outdoor pool; nearby 18-hole golf course (60% discount); outdoor clay tennis court; health club; spa; Jacuzzi; sauna; bike rental; concierge; tour desk; car-rental desk; courtesy car; limited room service; massage; babysitting; laundry service; same-day dry cleaning. *In room:* A/C, TV, dataport, minibar, hair dryer, safe in suites.

IN MONSUMMANO TERME

Hotel Grotta Giusti ✦ Converted from a family villa in the 1850s, this hotel has hosted Garibaldi, Verdi, and Liz Taylor on relaxing escapes. The rooms are well sized if bland, but they're comfortable, have thermal bathwater on tap, and come with robes and shifts for descending into the grottoes. A few accommodations downstairs have frescoed ceilings, and some on the third floor have balconies, but steer clear of the boring modern rooms in the new wing. The ceiling frescoes are repeated in the sunny breakfast rooms and in the vaulted lounges off the lobby. They also have a 42-hectare (105-acre) forest with a fitness path. The hotel's Spa and Wellness Center offers many therapeutic treatments (see "Taking the Waters," above).

Via Grotta Giusti 1411, 51015 Monsummano Terme (PT). ✆ **0572-90-771.** Fax 0572-907-7200. www.grotta giustispa.com. 64 units. 250€–350€ ($288–$403) "charm" double; 280€–380€ ($322–$437) "elegance" double; 390€–510€ ($449–$587) suite. Required half board included in prices; for full board add 10€ ($12) per person. Children under 10 get 30% discount. AE, DC, MC, V. Free parking. Closed Jan 8–Mar 20. From Montecatini Terme–Monsummano station, take a free shuttle bus (3 run in morning, 3 run in afternoon); a blue LAZZI bus from in front of train station; buy ticket at newsstand in station and make sure it's the tiny bus for Grotta Giusti, not the larger one to Monsummano Terme itself); or take a taxi (try to bargain the fare down to 12€/$14). **Amenities:** Restaurant; frescoed lounges; small bar; chilly outdoor pool; driving range on grounds or nearby golf course; outdoor tennis court; small exercise room; health spa; natural sauna; concierge; tour desk; car-rental desk; courtesy shuttle (train station); business center and secretarial services; salon; room service; massage; babysitting; laundry service; dry cleaning. *In room:* A/C, TV w/pay movies (and Internet access in some units), minibar, hair dryer, safe.

La Cantina (da Caino) ITALIAN/GAME Caino bustles out of the kitchen carrying a plate of shriveled mushrooms, joins a table of regulars under the wood-beamed ceiling, and launches into a discourse on the merits of various *tartufi* (truffles). He holds each one up, invoking its city of origin as he turns it like a gem in the light of the bright globe lamps. He excuses himself but returns with a wooden crate packed with regiments of dead sparrows—his catch from that morning. Though the menu is long, this place really excels in game, fish, and the produce of the forests. So forgo standard Italian dishes for anything with *cinghiale* (wild boar), *coniglio* (rabbit), *lepre* (hare), *uccelini* (Caino's sparrows), or fresh *pesce* (fish). In warm weather, you can dine in the arbor-covered garden or on the open-windowed terrace.

Via Picasso 55. ✆ **0572-53-173.** Primi 6€–7€ ($6.90–$8.05); 8€–12€ ($9.20–$14); pizza 5€–7€ ($5.75–$8.05). AE, DC, MC, V. Tues–Sun noon–3pm and 7pm–midnight. Closed Aug 16–30. From Hotel Grotta

(Kids Pinocchio's Park

Another 5km (3 miles) along the road from Pescia takes you to **Collodi**, family home village of 19th-century Florentine novelist Carlo Lorenzini, who visited the village often as a child and took the pen name Collodi when he wrote *The Adventures of Pinocchio* (1881). Although it's one of the world's most beloved children's stories (translated into more than 60 languages), Italians of all ages have an especially fierce love of and devotion to the tale. The **Parco di Pinocchio** (© **0572-429-342;** www. pinocchio.it) was built here in 1956 to celebrate it, with a bronze *Pinocchio* by Emilio Greco, mosaicked scenes from the story by Futurist Venturino Venturi, a restaurant designed by Liberty master Giovanni Michelucci, and a museum, hedge maze, and other diversions for the kids. It's open daily from 8:30am to sunset; admission is 8.50€ ($9.80), adults, 6.50€ ($7.50) ages 3 to 14 and over 65.

Giusti, exit property and take 1st left (just before Albergo La Speranza). La Cantina is the last building on the right.

EN ROUTE TO LUCCA: THE LAND OF PINOCCHIO

Pescia, stretched along the Pescia River 12km (7½ miles) west of Montecatini along the SS435, is Italy's capital of flowers, second in Europe only to Holland in flower production. Its huge market daily ships out millions of carnations, gladioli, lilies, and chrysanthemums—all before 8am. Pescia's horticultural industry also produces excellent asparagus, olive oil, and cannellini beans. Art aficionados will enjoy dropping by its 13th-century **San Francesco,** frescoed by Bonaventura Berlinghieri (1235) with a cycle of the *Life of St. Francis*—Berlinghieri was a close friend of Francis, who had died a mere 9 years earlier, and many hold that these may be some of the most accurate portraits of Assisi's famous mystic.

4 Lucca & Its Mighty Medieval Walls

26km (16 miles) W of Montecatini; 72km (45 miles) W of Florence; 335km (208 miles) NW of Rome

Lucca is the most civilized of Tuscany's cities, a stately grid of Roman roads snug behind a mammoth belt of tree-topped battlements. It's home to Puccini and soft pastel plasters, an elegant landscape of churches and palaces, delicate facades, and Art Nouveau shop fronts on wide promenades. The sure lines of the churches here inspired John Ruskin to study architecture, and though the center isn't the traffic-free Eden many other guidebooks would lead you to believe, cars truly are few and far between. Everyone from rebellious teens to fruit-shopping grandmothers tools around this town atop bicycles.

Lucca's greatest cultural contribution has been musical. The city had a "singing school" as early as A.D. 787, and this crucible of musical prodigies gave the world Luigi Boccherini (1743–1805), the composer who revitalized chamber music in the 18th century with such compositions as his widely famous Minuet no. 13, and most famously the operatic genius Giacomo Puccini (1858–1924), whose *Tosca, Madame Butterfly, Turnadot,* and *La Bohème* have become some of the world's favorite operas.

Lucca boasts some pretty heavyweight history. Its plains were inhabited more than 50,000 years ago, and as a Roman *municipum*, it was the site of the First Triumvirate between Julius Caesar, Pompey, and Crassus in 56 B.C. Bishop

Paulinas, one of St. Peter's disciples, brought a third-generation Christianity here in A.D. 47, making Lucca the first Tuscan city to convert. It was a major pit stop for pilgrims and crusaders coming from northern Europe along the Francigiana road, and in 588 local clergy shanghaied one passing Irish pilgrim, the abbot Finnian, and pronounced him bishop as "Frediano."

When Pisa conquered Lucca in 1314, hometown adventurer Castruccio Castracani fought back until Lucca regained its liberty. Over the next 10 years, Castracani went on to conquer Pisa and expanded a Luccan empire over western Tuscany. Both Pistoia and Volterra fell, but in 1328, just as Castracani was training his sights on Florence, malaria struck him down. Disgruntled Pisa took over again until 1369, when Charles IV granted Lucca its independence. The proud, if relatively unimportant, city stayed a free *comune*—occasionally under powerful bosses such as Paolo Guinigi (1400–30)—for 430 years. Napoléon gave it to his sister Elisa Baciocchi as a principality in 1805, and in 1815 it was absorbed into the Tuscan Grand Duchy.

ESSENTIALS

GETTING THERE   By Train   Lucca is on the Florence–Viareggio train line, with 21 trains daily passing through **Florence** (trip time: 70–90 min.), **Pistoia** (50 min.), and **Montecatini Terme** (35 min.). The short hop from **Pisa** takes about 20 to 30 minutes (24 trains daily, 12 on Sun). The **station** (✆ 848-888-088) is a short walk south of Porta San Pietro, or you can take *navetta* minibus no. 16 into town.

By Car   The A11 runs from Florence through Prato, Pistoia, and Montecatini before hitting Lucca. The SS12 runs straight up here from Pisa.

By Bus   Lazzi buses (✆ 0583-584-876; www.lazzi.it) run hourly from Florence (70 min.) and Pisa (50 min.) to Lucca's Piazzale Verdi. Lazzi also services Bagni di Lucca, Forte dei Marmi, Lago di Torre Puccini, Livorno, and Viareggio. **CLAP** buses (✆ 0583-587-897; also based on Piazzale Verdi) run between Lucca and Bagni di Lucca, Barga, Castelnuovo di Garfagnana, Collodi, Forte dei Marmi, Massa, Pescia, and Viareggio.

GETTING AROUND   A set of *navette* (electric minibuses) whiz dangerously down the city's peripheral streets, but the flat town is easily traversable on foot.

To really get around like a Lucchese, though, you need to **rent a bike.** There are four main rental outfits. There's the **city-sponsored stand** on Piazzale Verdi (✆ 0583-442-937; closed Nov to mid-Mar), and **Cicli Barbetti** near the Roman amphitheater at Via Anfiteatro 23 (✆ 0583-954-444; Mon–Fri 9am–12:30pm and 2:30–6pm, Sat 2:30–6pm; also open Sat morning and Sun if the weather is nice). Only one bicycle shop in town is open all day: **Antonio Poli,** Piazza Santa Maria 42 (✆ 0583-493-787; www.biciclettepoli.com; daily 8:30am–7:30pm; closed Sun mid-Nov to Feb and Mon mornings year-round). There you can rent a bike for 2.10€ ($2.40) for 1 hour or for 11€ ($12) for a full day; a mountain bike is 3.10€ ($3.50) per hour or 16€ ($18) for a full day. You can also try **Cicli Bizzarri** next door at Piazza S. Maria 32 (✆ 0583-496-031; www.cicli bizzarri.com; Mon–Sat 8:30am–1pm and 2:30–7:30pm and Sun Mar to mid-Sept). Bizzarri's rates are 11€ ($13) for 1 day; mountain bikes are 16€ ($18) per day. **Taxis** rank at the train station (✆ 0583-494-989), Piazza Napoleone (✆ 0583-492-691), and Piazzale Verdi (✆ 0583-581-305).

VISITOR INFORMATION   The main **tourist information office** is just inside the east end of the city walls at Piazza Santa Maria 35 (✆ 0583-919-931;

0 — 1/8 Mile
0 — 1/8 Kilometer

ACCOMMODATIONS	Hotel Rex **14**	DINING ◆	Da Leo **8**
Albergo Diana **12**	Hotel Universo **11**	Amadeo Giusti **7**	La Buca di Sant'Antonio **10**
Fattoria Maionchi **16**	Locanda Elisa **14**	Antico Caffè delle Mura **13**	Pizzeria da Felice **6**
Hotel Ilaria **15**	Ostello S. Frediano **1**	Antico Caffè di Simo **5**	
Hotel La Luna **4**	Piccolo Hotel Puccini **9**	Da Giulio **2**	
Hotel Moderno **14**	Villa la Principessa **14**	Da Giudo **3**	

fax 0583-469-964; www.luccaturismo.it; summer daily 9am–7pm; Nov–Mar daily 9am–1pm and 3–6pm). It provides an excellent free pocket map and good pamphlets on Lucca and the Garfagnana. The comune also has a small **local info office** on Piazzale Verdi (☎ **0583-442-944**), which keeps similar hours.

For **events** and theater, pick up the English-language monthly *Grapevine* for 1.50€ ($1.75) at most newsstands. Another good, private website for lots of Lucca info is www.in-lucca.it.

FESTIVALS & MARKETS   **Musical festivals** celebrate the town's melodious history. April through June, the churches take part in a **Festival of Sacred Music.** All September long, the **Settembre Lucchese** brings concerts and Puccini operas to the theater where many premiered, the Teatro Comunale on Piazza del Giglio. On September 13, an 8pm candlelit procession from San Frediano to the Duomo honors Lucca's most prized holy relic, the **Volto Santo** statue of Christ that tradition holds was carved by Nicodemus himself.

A huge **antiques market,** one of Italy's most important, is held the third Sunday (and preceding Sat) of every month in Piazza Antelminelli and the streets around the Duomo. It's great fun but also leaves rooms hard to find and restaurants booked, especially at lunch (even those normally closed Sun reopen for this one). It's spawned a local **art market** on Piazza del Arancio on the same dates, and the final Sunday of the month sees an **artisans' market** on Piazza San Giusto. A cute little **Christmas market** is held on Piazza dell'Anfiteatro from

December 8 to 26, and September 13 to 29 brings an **agricultural market** to Piazza San Michele featuring Lucca's wines, honeys, and olive oils.

DISCOVERING LUCCA'S TREASURES

Cattedrale di San Martino 🜲🜲 The **facade** 🜲 of Lucca's Duomo is an excellent and eye-catching example of the Pisan–Lucchese Romanesque school of architecture. Long lines of baby columns—every variety imaginable—backed by discreet green-and-white Romanesque banding are stacked into three tiers of arcaded loggias. Signed in 1204 by Guidetto da Como, the facade is technically unfinished, lacking the topmost loggia and a tympanum. The carved great arches making up the portico underneath include a dwarfish third partner, probably made smaller to accommodate the preexisting (1060) base of the bell tower, the crenellated marble top half of which was finished in 1261. The pillar abutting the tower is carved with a circular 12th-century **labyrinth,** a symbol of the long, torturous road to salvation. Such mazes once pointedly graced the entrance to many medieval churches.

The 13th-century **reliefs under the portico** 🜲 are beautiful examples of medieval stonework, a few of them carved by Guido da Como. Around the central door are the months of the year and stories from the life of St. Martin. Martin of Tours was a 4th-century Hungarian soldier in the Roman army who famously divided his cloak to share with a beggar and, after converting, preached against capital punishment (panel 1), cured lepers with kisses (panel 2, though here he's not puckering), raised a few dead (panel 3), and was made bishop (panel 4) before becoming the first saint to die of natural causes instead of martyrdom. Bedecking the left portal are an *Adoration of the Magi* and *Deposition* that may be early Nicola Pisano works. Few visitors know to wander around the back of the church to admire the arcaded **exterior of the apse,** which sits in a small grassy park.

In the 14th- to 15th-century **interior,** talented local sculptor Matteo Civitali designed the **pavement** as well as the holy water stoups and the **pulpit** along the aisles. Against the entrance wall is the original 13th-century statue of St. Martin dividing his cloak to give to a beggar (outside is a replica). Among the fine baroque works in the right aisle is (3rd altar) a *Last Supper* (1590–91) by Tintoretto and his assistants.

On the right aisle just past a few steps is the entrance to the former sacristy (for admission, see below), containing an altarpiece of the *Madonna Enthroned with Saints* by Domenico Ghirlandaio over a predella by his pupil Bartolomeo di Giovanni and surmounted by a lunette of the *Deposition* by a follower of Filippo Lippi. The sacristy is also home to the Duomo's masterpiece, Jacopo della Quercia's **tomb of Ilaria Carretto Guinigi** 🜲🜲🜲 (long-term plans are to move it to the Museo della Cattedrale, below). Married in 1403 to Paolo Guinigi and dead 2 years later at age 26, Ilaria del Carretto had only a brief moment in the limelight. But her rich husband also happened to be the town boss, so she was guaranteed everlasting fame as the subject of Jacopo della Quercia's masterpiece marble tomb. Jacopo barely had time to finish it in 1407 before Guinigi married again. Della Quercia's International Gothic style is influenced here by French models— the lying-in-state look with folded hands and with a little pug dog at her feet to symbolize fidelity. But he also started to introduce Renaissance elements that look back to antiquity, like the sarcophagal friezes of putti and garlands around the sides; the natural and accurate representation of Ilaria's face; and the flowing, limpid lines full of grace and repose. The tomb is famous, if for nothing else, because the young lady was quite obviously very beautiful, and Jacopo's chisel has kept her beauty alive. Incidentally, Ilaria is actually buried, and always has been, in the Guinigi chapel of Santa Lucia in San Francesco; Paolo Guinigi had the tomb placed in the cathedral just to show off what he could buy.

In the right transept are more Matteo Civitali works, including the 1472 **tomb of Pietro Noceto** and the tomb of Domenico Bertini. In the far right transept chapel, Civitali gave up the two praying angels flanking the tabernacle, and the chapel next to the choir has his Altar of St. Regolo (1484). The first chapel in the left transept houses Giambologna's mannerist altar that includes the Risen Christ, Sts. Peter and Paul, and a very low **bas-relief of Lucca's skyline** as it appeared in 1577, complete with towers and the newly finished city walls. The baroque canvases decorating the left aisle are fine, the only outstanding one being Bronzino's 1598 *Presentation of Mary at the Temple,* full of gorgeously rich fabrics appropriate to this textile town; it's on the second altar from the door.

Halfway down this aisle is Civitali's octagonal **Tempietto** (1482), built of white Carrara and red porphyry marble, with a St. Sebastian on the backside. It houses Lucca's most holy relic, the **Volto Santo** ✸. This thick-featured, bug-eyed, time-blackened wooden statue of Jesus crucified was rumored to have been started by Nicodemus—who would've known what he was carving since he was the one who actually took Jesus off the Cross—but was miraculously completed. Hidden during the persecutions and eventually stuck on a tiny boat by itself and set adrift, it found its way to the Italian port of Luni in 782, where the local bishop was told in a dream to place it in a cart drawn by two wild oxen, and wherever they went, there the Holy Image would stay. The ornery beasts, miraculously submitting meekly to the yoke, wandered over to Lucca and hit the brakes, and the miraculous image has been planted here ever since.

The city was famous for its Holy Visage throughout the Middle Ages—not many cathedrals could claim a bona fide portrait of Christ. Lucca's mints turned out coinage stamped with its image; the medieval French invented a St. Vaudeluc out of corruption of its Latin name (sanctum vultum de Lucca); and King William Rufus of England even swore oaths by it. In truth, however, the simple sculpture was probably carved in a 13th-century Lombard workshop to replace a lost 11th-century version that may have been copied from a Syrian statue of the 700s. Every September 13 and 14 (and again May 3) the Luccans dress their Christ up in kingly jewel-encrusted medieval vestments (kept in the Museo della Cattedrale) and hold a solemn procession in its honor.

Piazza San Martino. ✆ **0583-957-068.** Admission to church free; Ilaria tomb (in sacristy) 2€ ($2.30) adults, 1.50€ ($1.75) children 6–12. Cumulative ticket for tomb, Museo, and San Giovanni 5.50€ ($6.80) adults, 3€ ($3.45) children 6–12. Daily 9:30am–5:45pm (to 6:45pm Sat).

Museo della Cattedrale   The highly successful architectural marriage of the town's 12th- to 15th-century buildings with the cast-iron-and-glass modernity of this new museum is almost more interesting than the collections themselves (though if the long-term plans to move the tomb of Ilaria del Carretto here from inside the Duomo are carried out, it'll be well worth the admission). The first floor contains a bit of Matteo Civitali's late-15th-century **choir screen,** removed from the Duomo in 1987 despite vehement local protest. The second floor starts with 16th-century paintings and a pair of too-realistic wooden carvings of St. John the Baptist's head on a plate. Past an early-17th-century Francesco Vanni *Crucifixion* and a stretch of priestly vestments is a room with sculptures from the Duomo's facade, such as Jacopo della Quercia's huge early-15th-century *St.*

Walking the Walls

The walls are what make Lucca, Lucca, and they comprise a city park more than 4km (3 miles) long but only about 18m (60 ft.) wide, filled with avenues of plane, chestnut, and ilex trees planted by Marie Louise Bourbon in the 19th century. The shady paved paths of Lucca's formidable bastions are busy year-round with couples walking hand in hand, tables of old men playing unfathomable Italian card games, families strolling, children playing, and hundreds of people on bicycles, from tykes to octogenarians.

Rent a bike 👫👫 (see "Getting Around," above) and take a Sunday afternoon spin, peering across Lucca's rooftops and down into its palace gardens and narrow alleys, gazing toward the hazy mountains across the plane, and checking out the 11 bastions and 6 gates. The 1566 **Porta San Pietro,** the southerly and most important gate into town, still has a working portcullis, the original doors, and Lucca's republican motto, "Libertas," carved above the entrance. You can also visit a photo archive and some of the **tunnels under the bastions** daily from 10am to noon and 4 to 6pm. You must make an appointment in advance (8am–2pm) with CISCU, the International Center for the Study of Urban Walls (© **0583-496-257;** www.ciscu.it), located in the gatehouse at no. 21 near the San Paolino bastion (south of Piazzale Verdi on the west end of town).

The defensive walls you see today—a complete kidney-shaped circuit built from 1544 to 1654—are Lucca's fourth and most impressive set and perhaps the best preserved in all Italy. About 12m (40 ft.) high and 30m (100 ft.) wide at their base, the ramparts bristled with 126 cannons until the Austrian overlords removed them. The walls were never put to the test against an enemy army, though it turned out they made excellent dikes—there's no doubt the walls saved the city in 1812 when a massive flood of the Serchio River inundated the valley. Elisa Bonaparte Baciocchi was governing Lucca at the time from her villa outside the walls, and when she tried to get into the city for safety, the people didn't want to open the gates for fear of the surging waters. Lest they let their princess—and, more important, the sister of Europe's emperor—drown, however, they hoisted her highness over the walls rather unceremoniously with the help of a crane.

John the Evangelist 👫. At the end of the route are the jewelry and baubles the Volto Santo wears on the days he's specially venerated.

Via Arcivescovado (next to the cathedral). © **0583-490-530.** Admission 3.50€ ($4.05) adults, 2€ ($2.30) children 6–12. Cumulative ticket for Ilaria tomb, Museo, and San Giovanni 5.50€ ($6.30) adults, 3€ ($3.45) children 6–12. Mar–Oct daily 10am–6pm, Nov–Mar Mon–Fri 10am–3pm and Sat–Sun 10am–6pm.

Chiesa e Battistero di San Giovanni e Santa Reparata   The Duomo's Romanesque neighbor has a 16th-century facade and a 12th-century body, but recent excavations have revealed the structure is actually five layers deep. It sits atop a much older Lombard church that served until the early 700s as Lucca's cathedral, which in turn was built atop a 4th- to 5th-century A.D. paleo-Christian church that took the place of a Roman temple built atop Roman houses. In all, 12 centuries of history jumble together in a confusing but interesting mélange beneath the pavement inside (well signed, nonrestrictive use with a handout to help you figure it all out).

Piazza San Giovanni. © 0583-490-530. Admission is 2.50€ ($2.90), or get the cumulative ticket for Ilaria tomb, Museo, and San Giovanni 5.50€ ($6.30) adults, 3€ ($3.45) children 6–12. Hours same as Museo della Cattedrale; see above.

San Michele in Foro ✮ This church is as beautiful as a 12th-century Romanesque church can get. It boasts a Pisan-inspired **facade** ✮ of blind arches with lozenges and colonnaded arcades stacked even higher than San Martino's, and it's smack in the center of town—on top of the ancient Roman forum, in fact, hence the name—and yet this isn't the Duomo. Past the marvelous facade, with its orderly rows of doggedly unique columns topped by a Romanesquely flattened St. Michael, however, the **interior** of the church doesn't have too much to hold our attention. The original Matteo Civitali *Madonna and Child* sculpture from the facade is wedged in the right corner as you enter. (Its replacement doppelgänger basks in gilded beams of holy light on the outside corner of the church.) Another take on the same theme in glazed **terra cotta** by Andrea della Robbia (some now say it was by his uncle Luca) is inset on the first altar on the right. The church's best art hangs on the far wall of the right transept, a painting of *Sts. Roch, Sebastian, Jerome, and Helen* ✮ by Filippino Lippi, whose figures are more humanly morose but every bit as graceful as those of his famous teacher Sandro Botticelli. As you leave, check out the **medieval graffiti drawings** scratched on the columns of the left aisle (especially the 3rd and 4th from the door).

Two generations of Puccinis played the organ in this church, and the third, one young master Giacomo, sang in the choir as a boy. He didn't have far to walk, for the young **Giacomo Puccini,** who was to become one of Italy's greatest operatic composers, was born in 1858 just down the block at Via Poggio no. 30 (plaque). Around the corner at Corte San Lorenzo 9 is the entrance to a small museum installed in his birth home (© **0583-584-028**). Along with the usual composer memorabilia, it includes the piano on which he composed *Turnadot*. Admission is 3€ ($3.45) adults, 2€ ($2.30) for kids under 14. It's open daily June through September from 10am to 6pm, in winter Tuesday through Sunday from 10am to 1pm and 3 to 6pm; closed January and February. The nearby heavily baroque church of **San Paolino** is where the boy Puccini got his first crack at twiddling an organ's keyboard.

Piazza San Michele. © 0583-48-459. Free admission. Daily 7:30am–noon and 3–6pm.

Torre Guinigi ✮ Only one of the two towers sprouting from the top of the 14th-century palace home of Lucca's iron-fisted ruling family still stands, but it certainly grabs your attention. Historians tell us that many of Lucca's towers once had little gardens like this on top—the city was civilized even in its defenses—but that doesn't diminish the delight at your first glance at this stack of bricks 44m (146 ft.) high with a tiny forest of seven holm oaks overflowing the summit. For a closer look, climb the tower (230 steps) for a spectacular **view** ✮✮ of Lucca's skyline with the snow-capped Apuan Alps and the Garfagnana mountains in the distance. Up here, you can also see the oval imprint the Roman amphitheater left on the medieval buildings of Piazza Anfiteatro (see below).

Via Sant'Andrea, at Via Chiave d'Oro. © 0583-48-524 or 0583-491-205. Admission 3.50€ ($4.05) adults, 2.50€ ($2.90) children 6–12 and seniors over 65 (a cumulative ticket with Torre dell Ore is also offered).

Mar–May daily 9am–7:30pm; June–Sept 15 daily 9am–midnight; Sept 16–Oct daily 9:30am–8pm; Nov–Feb daily 9:30am–5:30pm.

Santa Maria Forisportum   This church was built in the 12th century outside the gates, hence the name, with a Pisan-style facade from the 1200s. Inside are two late-17th-century Guercino paintings: *St. Lucy* on the fourth altar on the right, a simple composition with Lucia holding her eyes daintily on a plate, and a smoke-blackened *Assumption* in the north transept. There's also a ciborium in *pietre dure* in the left transept (1680) and a 1386 Giottesque *Assumption* by Angelo Puccinelli with angels emerging from cocoonlike clouds in the sacristy (ring for the custodian). Just beyond the church is the sandstone **Porta San Gervasio,** a gate preserved from the medieval walls of 1260. Out the other side of the gate, running down the center of **Via del Fosso,** is the **former moat** of the wall, now demoted to charming canal status.

Via Santa Croce and Via della Rosa. (C) **0583-467-769.** Free admission, donation suggested. Mon–Sat 9am–noon and 3:15–6:30pm. Tours by appointment.

Museo Nazionale Villa Guinigi   The early-15th-century palace built for Paolo Guinigi on the occasion of his second marriage is now home to the best gallery in Lucca's poor museum crop. The collections start with **archaeological finds** that are well labeled—alas, only in Italian. Among the scraps from the Iron Age of the 10th century B.C. through the 8th-century-B.C. Villanovan period and 6th- to 3rd-century-B.C. Etruscan era are some reconstructed 3rd-century-B.C. Ligurian tombs that look like miniature versions of Fred Flintstone's suburban Bedrock home. There are some fascinating **medieval carvings** and capitals and a **coin collection** that proves just how important a symbol the Volto Santo has been throughout the ages.

Upstairs are some **14th- and 15th-century paintings,** including panels by Ugolino Lorenzetti and Francesco Traini, and a Zainobi Machiavelli *Madonna and Child with Saints.* The **15th-century wood inlays** show Luccan scenes as well as the Devil's Bridge at Borgo a Mozzano (see "North of Lucca: The Garfagnana & the Lunigiana," below). Fra' Bartolomeo is represented here by a classically simple *The Eternal Father with Saints* and a Raphael-influenced *Madonna della Misericordi.*

Via della Quarquonia. (C) **0583-496-033.** Admission 4€ ($4.60) adults, 2€ ($2.30) children under 18 and seniors over 65 (cumulative ticket with Museo Nazionale di Palazzo Mansi available). Tues–Sat 9am–7pm; Sun 9am–2pm.

Piazza Anfiteatro ⚜   Near the north end of Via Fillungo, a series of houses were built during the Middle Ages into the remains of a 1st- or 2nd-century A.D. Roman amphitheater, which had been used for centuries as a quarry for raw materials to raise the city's churches and palaces. The outline of the stadium was still visible in the 1930s when Duke Ludovico asked local architect Lorenzo Nottolini to rearrange the space and bring out the ancient form better. Nottolini pulled down the few structures that had been built inside the oval, restructured the ground floors of each building, and inserted four tunneled entranceways,

---

Cumulative Ticket

Museums in both the Villa Guinigi and the Palazzo Mansi are covered by a cumulative ticket. It costs 6.50€ ($7.50) for adults and 3.25€ ($3.75) for children under 18 and seniors over 65.

The Patron Saint of Ladies-in-Waiting

Just beyond the font inside San Frediano, is the **Cappella di Santa Zita (Chapel of St. Zita),** built in the 17th century to preserve the glass-coffined body of the saint and painted with her miracles by Francesco del Tintore. Zita is the patron saint of ladies-in-waiting and maids everywhere who, as a serving girl in the 13th-century Fatinelli household, was caught sneaking out bread in her apron to feed poor beggars on the street. Her suspicious master demanded to know what she was carrying, to which she answered, "Roses and flowers." She opened her apron and, with a little Divine Intervention, that's what the bread had become. Every April 26, the Lucchesi carpet the piazza outside with flowers to celebrate the miracle and bring out her shrunken body to kiss and caress.

but he retained the jumbled medieval look the differing heights of the tower stumps and houses give the place. Nothing other than the occasional market and kids playing soccer interrupts the oval space ringed with lazy cafes and a few shops. The floor of the amphitheater is about 3m (10 ft.) underground, but you can make a circuit of the piazza's outer edge to see the imprint of the stadium's ancient arcade and poke your head into the entrance halls of apartments, a few of which contain interrupted spans of tufa arches and other Roman remnants.

Piazza Anfiteatro. No phone. Free admission. Daily 24 hr.

San Frediano ✫   Especially on a sunny day, San Frediano's **facade** vies with those of the Duomo and San Michele as the most attention-grabbing in town, with a glittering 13th-century mosaic two stories high taking the place of the other churches' stacks of columns. Berlinghiero Berlinghieri designed it in a Byzantine/medieval style and threw just enough color into the apostles and Ascending Christ to balance the tens of thousands of gold-leaf tiles solid in the background for a truly eye-popping effect. The original church here was built by Irish Bishop Frediano in the 6th century, and when the current structure was rebuilt (1112–47), it was rededicated to the by-then sanctified Frediano. Bring euro for the light boxes.

All the interior works are well labeled, and the highlight is just inside the entrance, a Romanesque **baptismal font** in the right aisle from around the 12th century, dismantled and squirreled away in the 18th century and discovered and reassembled only a few decades ago. Three master carvers probably worked on it. A Lombard sculptor gave us the stories of Moses on the large lower basin, and one Maestro Roberto signed the last two panels of the Good Shepherd and six prophets. The small tempietto sprouting out of the top was carved by a Tuscan master, with the apostles and months of the year on the lid. Behind this work, high up on the wall, is a glazed terra-cotta lunette attributed to Andrea dell Robbia of the *Annunciation* framed by garlands of fruit and a chorus line of winged putti heads. Matteo Civitali carved the 15th-century polychrome *Madonna Annunciata* in the corner.

Up to the left of the high altar is a massive **stone monolith,** probably pilfered from the nearby Roman amphitheater. The Cappella Trenta, fourth in the left aisle, contains another Jacopo della Quercia masterpiece, an **altar** carved with the help of his assistant Giovanni da Imola (1422) as well as a pair of tombstones from the master's chisel.

A long restoration was recently finished on **Lucca's finest fresco cycle** ✿ in the second chapel of the left aisle, painted by Amico Aspertini (1508–09). In the *Miracles of St. Frediano,* the Irish immigrant bishop saves Lucca from a flood in a realistic way—though he symbolically performs a miracle in the middle ground by raking a new path for the water to be diverted away from the city, naked-torsoed workmen take the prudent pragmatic step of building a dam as well; the group of noblemen on the left (who aren't doing the least bit to help) are probably portraits of Luccan bigwigs of the day as well as the artist himself. In the *Arrival in Lucca of the Volto Santo,* opposite, the legend says the pair of heifers drag the holy statue, which washed ashore at the port of Luni in the background, to Lucca of their own volition, accompanied only by Luni's bishop. But here they're joined by a crowd of singing monks, townsfolk, and a wonderfully stooped old lady in voluminous red robes who steals the show down in front.

Around the left side of the church and down Via Battisti, at Via degli Asili 33, is the 17th-century **Palazzo Pfanner** (✆ **0583-491-243**), whose sumptuous 18th-century walled garden out back was featured in Jane Champion's 1996 film *Portrait of a Lady.* In 1999, the palace reopened to visitors to house a costume collection and offers a peek inside those fabulous gardens. Admission is 2.50€ ($2.90) each to visit the gardens or the palazzo (in other words, 5€/$5.75 for both). It's open March 1 to November 15 daily from 10am to 6pm. If you tool around the city's ramparts you can look down into the gardens for free.

Piazza San Frediano. ✆ **0583-493-627.** Free admission. April to mid-Nov Mon–Sat 7:30am–noon and 3–5pm; Sun 10:30am–5pm.

Museo Nazionale di Palazzo Mansi　This museum is worth the admission price if only to see the ridiculously sumptuous tapestries, frescoes, and other decorations of this 16th- to 19th-century palace. The collection isn't large or particularly spectacular, but be on the lookout for Luca Giordano's *St. Sebastian,* Domenico Beccafumi's wildly colored *Scipio,* Jacopo Vignale's *Tobias and the Angel,* and Rutilio Manetti's *Triumph of David.* In the second room is one of several versions of Agnolo Bronzino's definitive *Portrait of Cosimo I* and Pontormo's mannerist *Portrait of a Boy.* The third room has a *Madonna and Child* by Correggio and Il Sodoma's *Christ with the Cross,* along with some portraits by Tintoretto and Luca Giordano.

Via Galli Tassi 43. ✆ **0583-55-570.** Admission 4€ ($4.60) adults, 2€ ($2.30) children under 18 or seniors over 65 (cumulative ticket with Museo Nazionale Villa Guinigi available). Tues–Sat 8:30am–7pm; Sun 8:30am–1pm.

SHOPPING

Lucca's main shopping promenades are the elite **Via Fillungo** and more proletarian **Via Santa Lucia,** both epicenters of the evening *passeggiata.* To pick up a bottle of DOC Vino Rosso delle Colline Lucchesi, divine Lucca olive oil, Garfagnana honey, and other local edibles, head to **Lucca in Tavola,** Via San Paolino 130–132 (✆ **0583-581-002**). For a less commercial venture, drop by the famous ultratraditional dried beans and seed shop **Antica Bottega di Prospero,** Via Santa Lucia 13 (no phone; www.bottegadiprospero.it). Since 1965, the best wine cellar in town has been the **Enoteca Vanni,** Piazza del Salvatore 7 (✆ **0583-491-902;** www.enotecavanni.com), with hundreds of bottles of local and Tuscan vintage lining the cryptlike rooms under the tiny storefront. And who can pass up the heavenly rich chocolates at the **Cioccolateria Canoparoli,** Via San Paolino 96, at the corner of Via Galli Tassi (✆ **0583-53-456**).

Lucca has lots of jewelry stores but none more gorgeous than **Carli,** Via Fillungo 95 (© **0583-491-119**), specializing in antique jewelry, watches, and silver from its high vaulted room frescoed in 1800.

WHERE TO STAY

There are only four hotels within the walls, so unless you book ahead you may have to make do with one of the fully amenitied bland modern joints near the train station. These include the **Rex,** Piazza Ricasoli 19 (© **0583-955-443;** fax 0583-954-348; www.hotelrexlucca.com), where doubles run 100€ ($115), and the **Moderno,** Via V. Civitali 38 (© **0583-55-840;** fax 0583-53-830; www. albergomoderno.com), where doubles cost 65€ ($75).

I hesitate to recommend the **Albergo Diana,** Via del Molinetto 11 (© **0583-492-202;** fax 0583-467-795; www.albergodiana.com), which has nine passable plain doubles with bathroom, phone, and TV for around 52€ to 67€ ($60–$77), and six rather nicer rooms in the *dipendence* around the corner for 83€ to 114€ ($95–$131), and is just half a block from the Duomo. But the staff can turn from seemingly friendly to downright nasty at the drop of a hat. It is, however, the cheapest thing going within the walls.

Another economical option is the new **Ostello S. Frediano,** Via della Cavallerizza (© **0583-469-957;** fax 0583-461-007; www.ostellolucca.it). It has 140 beds in 20 multi-bed rooms and 8 mini-apartments sleeping six. The cost is 16€ ($18) per day for a bunk in a multi-bed room. Space in the mini-apartments is 39€ ($45) for two people, 58€ ($67) for three, 78€ ($90) for four. Lock-out is noon to 3:30pm; curfew is at midnight.

If you have 1,180€ to 2,951€ ($1,357–$3,394) to spare, you can buy a night in one of the 10 sumptuous suites of the **Locanda Elisa,** Via Nuova per Pisa 1952 (© **0583-379-737;** fax 0583-379-019; www.relaischateaux.fr), about 5km (3 miles) south of town, with all the amenities: a beautifully landscaped pool, and fine restaurant in a glass gazebo. Considerably less expensive are the 240€ to 290€ ($276–$334) doubles at the Locanda Elisa's almost equally elegant sister hotel, the **Villa la Principessa,** Via Nuova per Pisa 1616, across the road (© **0583-370-037;** fax 0583-379-136; www.hotelprincipessa.com).

Fattoria Maionchi 🌟 *Kids*   Fitted into the olive-blanketed hills where Lucca's valley rises to Le Pizzorne mountains, the *agriturismo* of Fattoria Maionchi offers you the chance to stay in an outbuilding of a 17th-century farming estate—with concessions to modernity like fully outfitted kitchens and a pool overlooking the grapevines. A motley assortment of antiques acquired over the centuries are scattered throughout the spacious multifloor apartments, but the overall scheme manages to remain rustic. Recent renovations, such as those to the old mill, have not only doubled the accommodations, but are also more modern in appearance. The friendly owners will show you their cellars and let you sample their wine—good enough to be the house red of Lucca's top restaurant, La Buca di Sant'Antonio (see below). A stay here (must be at least a week) makes a perfect escape in the country; you're close enough for easy excursions into Lucca (15 min. by car; 16€ by taxi) as well as trips into the Garfagnana mountains.

Località Tofori (13km/8 miles east of Lucca), 55012 Camigliano (LU). © **0583-978-194** or 0583-978-138. Fax 0583-978-345. www.fattoriamaionchi.it. 11 efficiency apts (sleeping 4–5). Weekly rates July–Aug, Easter and Christmas 670€–982€ ($771–$1,129); June and Sept 530€–878€ ($610–$1,010); May and Oct 413€–568€ ($475–$653); other months 370€–568€ ($426–$653) per week (Sat afternoon–Sat morning). AE, DC, MC, V. Free parking. **Amenities:** Restaurant (Fri, Sat dinner, Sun lunch); 2 outdoor pools (1 private to a single apartment); free bikes; children's center; babysitting. *In room:* TV, kitchenette, coffeemaker, no phone.

Hotel Ilaria ⭐ Seven years ago this was just a facade that said "Hotel" in front of a great big roofless hole in the ground (every travel writer's worst nightmare). The new Ilaria that arose from that rubble in 2000 is a classy deluxe hotel entered from a jasmine-scented courtyard. The modern rooms are fitted simply but stylishly with cherry veneer built-in units. The rooms with double-paned windows—you don't even need them on this quiet street—opening onto the little canal out front are nice, but even better views are over the gravelly tree-filled garden out back. Three of these rooms even open onto a shared terrace, and there's also a public terrace dotted with potted camellias and shaded by a giant sycamore. The same group owns three restaurants in town, including the Buca di Sant'Antonio, highly recommended below, and you can work out a pension deal. They've recently completed renovations to a nearby medieval church, creating six junior suites, one suite, and four wheelchair-accessible doubles. They've also jacked up their prices by over 25%, which is a shame.

Via del Fosso 25, 55100 Lucca. ⓒ 0583-469-200. Fax 0583-991-961. www.hotelilaria.com. 41 units. 230€ ($265) double; 250€ ($288) triple. Rates include breakfast. AE, DC, MC, V. Free parking. **Amenities:** Free bikes; concierge; tour desk; car-rental desk; courtesy car; limited room service (breakfast and bar); babysitting; laundry service; same-day dry cleaning. *In room:* A/C, TV, dataport, minibar, hair dryer, safe.

Hotel La Luna *(Kids)* This hotel is divided between two buildings on a dead-end street off Lucca's main shopping promenade and just a few steps from the medieval houses following the curves of the Roman amphitheater. The rooms are mostly furnished in circa-1980s style, but a few lush 17th-century frescoes grace the second-floor rooms in the older half of the hotel—including no. 242, a family-perfect quad. The bathrooms range from spacious to cramped, from tub plus box shower to a curtainless wall nozzle, but all have fluffy towels. The accommodating owners keep the place very clean and well maintained.

Corte Compagni 12 (off Via Fillungo near the amphitheater), 55100 Lucca. ⓒ 0583-493-634. Fax 0583-490-021. www.hotellaluna.com. 30 units. 105€ ($121) double; 170€ ($196) suite. Breakfast 11€ ($12). AE, DC, MC, V. Parking 11€ ($12) in garage. Closed Jan 6–Feb 6. **Amenities:** Concierge. *In room:* A/C, TV, minibar, hair dryer.

Hotel Universo ⭐ A huge rambling hotel that since 1857 has hosted luminaries like John Ruskin, the Universo is installed in a 15th-century palace across the square from Lucca's premier opera house/theater. No two rooms are alike—though refurbishments have begun to standardize the accommodations. There are still a few decorative holdovers from the 1960s, but most rooms enjoy renovated bathrooms (waffle towels, alas) and generally pleasant, if lackluster, built-in furnishings. The majority are carpeted and have heavy curtains framing the windows. The few rooms that tend toward the tiny side are decorated with floral-print fabrics in a charming country style.

Piazza del Giglio 1 (off Piazza Napoleone), 55100 Lucca. ⓒ 0583-493-678. Fax 0583-954-854. www.lunet.it/aziende/hoteluniverso. 57 units. 150€ ($173) double. Breakfast included. MC, V. 10 free parking spaces or nearby paid lots. **Amenities:** Restaurant; bar; concierge; tour desk; car-rental desk; limited room service; babysitting; nonsmoking rooms. *In room:* A/C in about 20 units, TV, hair dryer on request.

Piccolo Hotel Puccini ⭐⭐ *(Value)* This tiny hotel boasts Lucca's best location: just off the central piazza of San Michele. Your neighbor is the ghost of Puccini, who grew up across the street. The prices are fantastic for the location and comfort. And Paolo and his staff are the friendliest hoteliers in town. Most of the rooms are smallish, but they have been renovated with firm beds, compact bathrooms, floral-print wallpaper, carpeting, and reproduction opera playbills framed on the walls. (Renovations of the bathrooms were planned for 2004.)

From the 12 rooms along the front (this street sees very little traffic), you can lean out and see a sliver of the fabulous San Michele facade half a block away. The hotel doesn't allow smoking in any rooms, and is planning to install small fridges (empty, because he doesn't want to have to overcharge for the contents as most hotels do). The Puccini fills quickly, so be sure to book ahead.

Via di Poggio 9 (just off Piazza San Michele), 55100 Lucca. (✆ **0583-55-421.** Fax 0583-53-487. www. hotelpuccini.com. 14 units. 80€ ($92) double. Breakfast 3.50€ ($4.05). AE, DC, MC, V. Free parking nearby. **Amenities:** Bike rental; concierge; tour desk; car-rental desk; 24-hr. room service; massage; babysitting; laundry service; same-day dry cleaning; nonsmoking rooms. *In room:* TV, dataport, hair dryer, safe.

WHERE TO DINE

Gastronomically, Lucca is famous above all for its divine extra-virgin olive oil, a light-green elixir with a fresh olive taste that's drizzled on just about every dish in these parts. The most typically Luccan dish is the creamy, filling *zuppa di farro,* a soup made with spelt, an emmer or barleylike wheaty grain cooked *al dente.* The Lucca area is also known for its asparagus, strawberries, and honey. Accompany any dish with Lucca's excellent and little-known DOC **wines,** Rosso delle Colline Lucchesi and Montecarlo.

If you just want to grab a slice and a Coke for 4.55€ ($5.25), try the **Pizzeria da Felice,** Via Buia 12 (✆ **0583-494-986;** Tues–Sat 9:30am–2pm and 4–8:30pm, Mon 11am–2pm and 4–8:30pm), which serves generous slices of real wood-oven pizza and where you can also sample two Lucchese specialties: *cecina* (a flat bread made of ceci beans) and *castagnaccio* (a sort of chestnut flour pita, split with each half wrapped around sweetened fresh ricotta).

People line up to wait for the bakery **Amadeo Giusti,** Via Santa Lucia 18–20 (✆ **0583-496-285**) to reopen at 4:30pm (it's open daily 7am–1pm and 4:30–7:45pm, but closed Sat afternoons), and the shop has installed a window on the street just to distribute its immensely popular focaccia, which is used by many local restaurants in their bread baskets.

Antico Caffè delle Mura INVENTIVE TUSCAN   Built atop the city's formidable bastions in 1860, the Old Cafe of the Walls offers the most elegant dining in town in an intimate room filled with piano music and a giant fresco of Lucca's skyline. The *insalata del Caffè no. 1* is concocted of chicken, artichokes, pinoli, and shredded arugula. *Papardelle al baluardo* (homemade wide noodles in a sauce of vegetables, tomatoes, sausage, and a pinch of hot pepper) and the *zuppa di farro* (barley soup) are tempting first courses. Afterward, enjoy the light *petto di anatra agli aromi* (duck breast cooked in balsamic vinegar) or the *bocconcini di coniglio al dragoncello* (rabbit scallops scented with tarragon). The Antico Caffè has less character than La Buca di Sant'Antonio (see below) but is more refined; and though it doesn't quite revive the Belle Epoque, it at least sings it a graceful swan song.

Piazzale Vittorio Emanuele II (at the south end of Via Vittorio Veneto). (✆ 0583-467-962. Reservations required. Primi 7€–9€ ($8.05–$10); secondi 14€–16€ ($16–$18). AE, DC, MC, V. Wed–Mon noon–2pm and 8–10:30pm. Closed 20 days in Jan.

Da Giulio ✦ LUCCHESE/TUSCAN HOME COOKING   This cavernous and very popular trattoria is short on antique charm but long on antique tradition. Don't let the modern decor put you off—the friendly service and genuine peasant cuisine are as trattoria as they come. The soups are superb, such as the *farro con fagioli* (emmer and beans) and the *farinata* (a creamy soup of polenta corn grain with beans and veggies), or you can try the *maccheroni tortellati* (large pasta squares in ricotta, tomatoes, and herbs). *Pollo al mattone* (chicken breast roasted under a heated brick) is the secondo most in demand, but *spezzatino con olive* (stewed beef with olives) runs just behind. They also have plenty of local specialties—tripe, horse tartar, and veal snout—to whet your appetite. The homemade tiramisù is positively heavenly.

Via Conce 45, Piazza San Donato (nestled in the very northwest corner of the walls). (C) **0583-55-948.** Reservations recommended. Primi 4.15€–5.15€ ($4.70–$5.90); secondi 7€–25€ ($8.05–$23). AE, DC, MC, V. Tues–Sat and 3rd Sun of month noon–3pm and 7–11:30pm. Closed 10 days in Aug and 10 days around Christmas.

Da Guido *(Value* LUCCHESE/TUSCAN   I must admit I have a weakness for this sort of joint: a small locals' hangout, run by an extended family, that's not much more than an overgrown bar but offers the cheapest, truest meals in town. Although the Big Brother TV in the corner is annoying, the food is divine. Start with the homemade *tortelli della casa* (meat ravioli in a ragù), *penne all'arrabbi-ata* (in a spicy hot tomato sauce), or *riso ai funghi* (rice with porcini mushrooms) before digging into the *coniglio arrosto* (roast rabbit) or *spezzatino di vitella* (veal scallops) served with beans.

Via Cesare Battisti 28 (near Piazza Sant'Agostino and San Frediano, west of the Roman amphitheater). (C) **0583-476-219.** Primi 2.60€–3.80€ ($3–$4.35); secondi 4.15€–5€ ($4.70–$5.75); menù turistico with wine 11€ ($13). AE, MC, V. Mon–Sat noon–2:30pm and 7:30–10pm. Closed 3–4 weeks in Aug.

Da Leo TUSCAN/LUCCHESE   It isn't often a homespun trattoria dramatically improves its cooking while retaining its low prices and devoted following of local shopkeeps, groups of students, and solitary art professors sketching on the butcher paper place mats between bites. This place is now good enough to recommend for the best cheap meals in the center. There's usually an English menu floating around somewhere—the good-natured waiters are used to dealing with foreigners who've discovered one of the most authentic Lucchese dining spots in town, run by the amiable Buralli family. This isn't as much a bare-bones tavern as Guido's, not quite as polished an operation as the well-regarded Giulio's, but still as beloved by a devoted local following nonetheless. Its location, two steps from the central Piazza San Michele, draws tourists who happen by, lured into the peach-colored rooms by the aroma of roasting meats and the scent of rosemary. The food isn't fancy, but they do traditional dishes well: *minestra di farro, spaghetti pancetta piselli* (with pancetta bacon and sweet peas), *arrosto di manzo con patate arrosto* (roast beef and potatoes), and the excellent *zuppa ai 5 ceriali* (a soup with emmer, red and green lentils, barley, a cousin to black-eyed peas, and cannellini beans).

Via Tegrimi 1 (just north of Piazza San Michele). (C) **0583-492-236.** www.trattoriadaleo.it. Reservations recommended. Primi 4.70€ ($5.40); secondi 8.80€–16€ ($10–$18). No credit cards. Mon–Sat noon–2:30pm and 7:30–10:30pm.

La Buca di Sant'Antonio *(★★★* LUCCHESE   Since before 1782, La Buca has been the premier gastronomic pit stop inside Lucca's walls. It's a maze of a place with copper pots and musical instruments hanging everywhere. It's attracted the likes of Puccini, Ezra Pound, and others who in times past just wanted to read the restaurant's secret stock of banned books. They like to keep it formal but friendly and pour you a glass of spumanti before bringing out your *coppa Garfagnana con crostini della casa* (Lucchese salami with excellent fried crostini). The first course is a tossup between the *ravioli di ricotta alle zucchine* (fresh ricotta-stuffed ravioli in rich butter sauce, topped with julienned zucchini) and the *tortelli Lucchesi al sugo* (meat-filled ravioli in a scrumptious ragù). For a secondo, though, do try the house specialty *capretto nostrale al forno con* *patate alla salvia* (tender spit-roasted kid with roasted sage potatoes). This is one of the few pricey Tuscan restaurants I personally return to year after year.

Via della Cervia 3 (a hidden alley just west of Piazza San Michele; follow the signs). © **0583-55-881**. Reservations highly recommended. Primi 6€–7€ ($6.90–$8.05); secondi 12€–13€ ($14–$15). AE, DC, MC, V. Tues–Sat 12:30–3pm and 7:30–10:30pm; Sun 12:30–3pm. Closed 1st week of Jan and 1st week of July.

AFTER DARK: THEATER

The important 19th-century opera houses the **Teatro del Giglio,** Piazza del Giglio 13–15 (© **0583-467-521;** www.teatrodelgiglio.it), where Rossini premiered his *William Tell* in 1831 (Paganini was in the orchestra, little realizing that the dramatic Overture he was playing would one day be better known as *The Lone Ranger Theme*). Today it presents mainly classic plays—Greek, Shakespearean, and Italian—along with a few contemporary Italian works from mid-November to mid-March. It also hosts concerts year-round and is remaining open while undergoing a much-needed face-lift. In spring and summer especially, check at the tourist office to see if various villas in the surrounding countryside are presenting opera or chamber music in honor of Puccini and other Lucca musical sons.

5 North of Lucca: The Garfagnana & the Lunigiana

The Garfagnana region north of Lucca along the Serchio River is heavily wooded and mountainous, peppered with Romanesque churches, medieval Alpine villages, and good hiking trails. (The regional tourist office is in Castelnuovo di Garfagnana; see below.) It's home to the eastern slopes of the Alpi Apuane, now a natural park protecting the wildlife (over one quarter of the plants known in Italy grow here) of these massive Apuan Alps. It's also a good bird-watching region, with more than 165 species wheeling in the skies above the mountains, including peregrine falcons and golden eagles. The **Lunigiana** to the north, a Ligurian land that's part of Tuscany in name only, preserves some remarkable prehistoric carvings in the communal museum of Pontrémoli.

GETTING AROUND BY BUS & TRAIN

If you don't have your own wheels, **CLAP** buses (© **0583-5411** or 0583-587-897) service most of the Garfagnana, and **Lazzi** buses (© **0583-584-877;** www.lazzi.it) hit the major towns of **Bagni di Lucca** (trip time from Lucca: 40 min.), **Barga** (1 hr.), and **Castelnuovo** (90 min.). In Lucca, both lines are based at Piazzale Verdi. A **scenic railway line** (12 runs daily from Lucca) ducks in and out of tunnels alongside the Serchio River—you ride under an arch of the Devil's Bridge—and goes out onto the Lunigiana plain to Aulla, where you can change for a train to Pontrémoli.

A DRIVE UP THE GARFAGNANA

The main SS12 road north toward Barga and Castelnuovo splits to go up either side of the steep-valleyed Serchio just south of Ponte a Moriano. You want to stay on the east (right) branch because there's no parking on the other side of the river when you get to Borgo a Mozzano (20km/12 miles) and the **Ponte del Diavolo (Devil's Bridge),** sometimes called the Ponte della Maddalena. This impossibly narrow humpbacked 11th-century bridge of fitted stone was built under the auspices of the area's iron-fisted ruler, Countess Matilda. Much more fun to believe, however, is the legend that Satan agreed to build the span for the townspeople if they'd grant him the first soul to cross it. The morning after the bridge was completed—diabolical work crews move fast—the villagers outwitted Lucifer by sending a hapless dog trotting over.

Two and a half kilometers (1½ miles) farther along, the SS12 diverges east up the Lima valley for **Bagni di Lucca;** the **tourist office** is at Viale Umberto I 139 (© **0583-805-754** or 0583-805-813; fax 0583-809-937; www.prolocobagni dilucca.it). This was one of Europe's most famous spas in the 19th century. It hosted nobles and moneyed princes from the 17th century onward and a veritable stampede of British Romantics at the height of its popularity. Napoléon's sister Elisa Baciocchi, whom he made the princess of Lucca, helped its heyday along by turning it into her summer residence. As you enter the lower part of town, known as **Ponte a Serraglio,** take the lower road to the left along the tree-shaded river to see the **Casino,** one of Europe's first licensed gaming houses and the birthplace of roulette.

Back in the Serchio valley, the main road now becomes the SS445 and runs another 18km (11 miles) to the turnoff to **Barga** set up on the mountainside; the tourist office is at Piazza Angelio 3 (© **0583-723-499**). Barga is home to a gaggle of **della Robbian terra cottas** (on the main entrance gate, in the 15th-c. Conservatorio di Sant'Elizabetta, and in the Duomo), and dominated by the outsized battlemented bell tower of its cathedral. The facade of the 9th- to 14th-century **Duomo** is made from local white stone called albarese and covered with medieval and Romanesque low reliefs. The interior houses a reddish-toned 13th-century **pulpit** ✪ by the quirky Lombard carver Guido Bigarelli da Como, full of medieval symbolism. The red marble columns are supported by a pug-nosed dwarf (evil) and the Lion of Giudea (representing Jesus), who under one pillar conquers a dragon (evil) and under another is simultaneously killed and stroked worshipfully by a man (supposedly representing the fact that man, who once crucified Christ, later came to love him). Don't miss the 10th-century painted wooden St. Christopher and the della Robbian terra cottas in a right-hand chapel.

Next take the road heading directly back down to the Serchio, cross under the railroad tracks, cross over the river and under the main road on the other side, proceed through the hamlet of Gallicano, and climb alongside the Turrite stream into the **Parco Naturale delle Alpi Apuane.** After about 9km (6 miles) up the slopes of the 1,800m (6,000-ft.) "Queen of the Apuan Alps," Pania della Croce, you'll come to Fornovolasco and the **Grotta del Vento (Cave of the Winds)** ✪ (© **0583-722-024;** www.grottadelvento.com). It's one of the best and most easily visited caverns of the system that honeycombs these mountains, a grotto network offering the best caving in all Italy. The cave is a fascinating subterranean landscape of tunnels, stalactites, bottomless pits, eerie pools of water, and polychromatic rivers of rock that seem to flow in sheets and cascade down stony shoots. April through September, it's open daily with 1-hour guided tours (6.50€/$7.50 adults, 5€/$5.75 children under 10) on the hour from 10am to noon and 2 to 6pm; 2-hour jaunts (10.50€/$12 adults, 8.50€/$9.80 children) at 11am, 3pm, 4pm, and 5pm; and 3-hour explorations (15€/$17 adults, 12€/$13 children) leaving at 10am and 2pm. October through March, it's open Sundays only. Go as early as possible to miss the crowds.

The stony capital of the Garfagnana, **Castelnuovo di Garfagnana,** lies about 11km (7 miles) north of Barga. For tourist information, visit the **Comunità Montana Garfagnana** off Piazza delle Erbe (© and fax **0583-644-473**); Castelnuovo itself is covered next to the Rocca at Loggiato Porta 10 (© **0583-641-007;** fax 0583-644-354). There's not much to see other than the 14th-century **Rocca** castle, a stronghold of the Este dukes of Ferrara. You can't even get into the Rocca anymore, so the best Castelnuovo is good for is views of the mountains and valley, and as an information office for hikes into the Apuan Alps and the Orecchiella mountains.

At Castelnuovo, you can branch off into the **Parco Naturale Orecchiella (Orecchiella Natural Park)** on the east (Apennine) side of the valley by heading up one of the most scenic winding roads in this part of Tuscany toward Villa, San Pellegrino in Alpe, and the Emilia–Romagna border.

Otherwise, keep heading along the main road for another 58km (36 miles) or so to **Aulla,** lorded over by the 16th-century Brunella fort. You're now in the **Lunigiana,** a northern spur of Tuscany wedged between Liguria and Emilia–Romagna. The chief town and main point of interest here is the sleepy, partly medieval city of **Pontrémoli** on the Magra River 22km (14 miles) north of Aulla (the tourist office is on Piazza Municipio). Tuscany's northernmost city has a baroque church of **San Francesco,** the rare Tuscan rococo church of **Nostra Donna,** and a baroque **Duomo** hitched up to the **Torre del Campanone,** the only remnant of the fortress Castruccio Castracani built in 1322 to keep the town's two feuding factions from ripping each other to shreds.

The city's most important attraction though, almost worth the whole trip up here, is the **Museo delle Statue Stele di Pontremoli (Castello del Piangnaro;** ② **0187-831-439;** www.lunigiana.com/pontremoli/stele.htm), housed in a 14th-century castle and created to show off some 20-odd prehistoric **statue-stele** ★★ and casts of 30 or so others whose originals are elsewhere. The stylized menhirs look sort of like tombstones carved to resemble humans and were created by a long-lived Lunigiana cult that existed from about 3000 to 200 B.C. The earliest (3000–2000 B.C.) have just a "U" for a head and the mere suggestion of arms and a torso, the next group (2000–800 B.C.) has more features and realism, and the most recent (700–200 B.C.) are developed to the point where many of them carry weapons in both hands. It's open daily from 9am to 1pm and 2:30 to 6:30pm (in winter Tues–Sun 9am–noon and 2–5pm). Admission is 3.50€ ($4.05) for adults, 1.50€ ($1.75) for children ages 12 to 16.

7

Pisa, Tuscany's Coast & the Maremma

The ancient maritime republic of **Pisa** is one of Italy's grand cities. This somewhat sleepy university town boasts one of the most peaceful and beautiful piazze in all Italy, an expansive grassy lawn studded with serene Gothic-Romanesque buildings of white- and gray-banded marble and delicate colonnaded arcading. But it'll forever be known chiefly for that square's cathedral bell tower: It just can't for the life of itself stick straight up.

The brawny Medici-created port of **Livorno** to the south is Tuscany's second-largest city, but is perhaps unique in the region for its lack of art (beyond some Tuscan "impressionists") and dearth of decorative churches. The seafood in its restaurants, though, is some of the best in the country, and its back-street canals add a quasi-Venetian romantic touch to this Tuscan city.

The green islands of the Tuscan archipelago sitting off the **Etruscan Riviera** shoreline are dotted with some fine beaches and fantastic nature preserves. Most, however, are off-limits unless you're doing 10 to 20 in one of their high-security prisons. But the granddaddy of the group, **Elba,** is a high-power summer tourist destination. It's Italy's third-largest island and a veritable mineral horde that has been mined since before the Etruscans. Elba is famous as the short-lived kingdom of exiled ex-emperor Napoléon and popular for its colorful fishing towns, island cuisine, inland hiking, and beaches.

The **Maremma** is Tuscany's deep south, a little-visited province with deep Etruscan roots, crumbling ancient hill towns built atop dramatic tufa outcrops, and snow-white cattle watched over by the *butteri,* some of the world's last true-grit cowboys.

THE VALDARNO FROM FLORENCE TO PISA

MONTELUPO FIORENTINO The old SS67 and a newer superhighway link ancient rivals Florence and Pisa down the industrialized Arno valley. Along the way, the road passes through the village of **Montelupo Fiorentino** (www.comune.montelupo-fiorentino.fi.it), famous in the 15th and 16th centuries for producing some of Mediterranean's finest ceramics as well as the father and son sculptor/architects Baccio and Raffaello di Montelupo. Today, the village is worth a brief stop for Botticelli's *Madonna Enthroned with Saints* in the church of **San Giovanni Evangelista** on Via Baccio di Montelupo (open daily 9am–8pm) and the **Museo Archeologico e della Ceramica,** Via Sinibaldi 43 (© **0571-51-352;** www.museomontelupo.it). The latter is an eclectic small-town collection of archaeological finds, 15th-century frescoes, and a detailed exhibit on ceramics production. It's open Tuesday through Sunday from 9am to 6pm, and the ticket (5€/$5.75 adults, 3.50€/$4.05 children 6–14 and seniors over 65, free for children under 6) also gets you into Empoli's Museo della Collegiata di Sant'Andrea and Vinci's Museo.

A Central Tourist Office

The **Ufficio Turistico Intercomunali,** Via della Torre 11, 50059 Vinci (FI; *©* **0571-568-012;** fax 0571-567-930; www.terredelrinascimento.it), is the central tourism office for **Vinci, Montelupo Fiorentino,** and **Empoli.** In summer, it's open daily from 2 to 7pm; winter hours are often shorter. **Montelupo Fiorentino** maintains its own info point at Via Sinibaldi 43 (*©* **0571-518-993;** fax 0571-911-421), open Tuesday through Sunday from 10am to 6pm.

EMPOLI   The modern market town of **Empoli** gave forth in 1551 a talented baroque painter christened Jacopo Chimenti but known by the name of his hometown. The town today manufactures green-glass chianti jugs and raincoats for the rest of Italy. Although World War II bombs wreaked havoc on much of the town, the historic main piazza, Piazzetta della Propositura, is still graced with the **Collegiata di Sant'Andrea,** an 8th-century church with a harmonious green-and-white Romanesque facade. The facing is original 12th century in the bottom half, but the top was finished off in a seamless imitation style in the 19th century; even that had to be rebuilt following World War II damage.

The inside doesn't live up to the exterior, but its **Museo della Collegiata di Sant'Andrea** ✿, Piazza Prepositura 3 (*©* **0571-76-284**), entered through the courtyard to the right, certainly is. It was one of Tuscany's first community museums when it opened in 1859, and the collections include a Bernardo Rossellino 1447 font, a detached Masolino *Pietà* fresco (1424–25), a Francesco di Valdambrino polychrome wood statue of *St. Stephen* (1403), a tiny Filippo Lippi *Madonna,* and works by Lorenzo Monaco, like his 1404 *Madonna dell'Umilità with Saints.* The museum is open Tuesday through Sunday from 9am to noon and 4 to 7pm, and the ticket (5€/$5.75 adults, 3.50€/$4.05 children 6–14 and seniors over 65, free for children under 6) is also valid for the Montelupo's ceramics museum (see above) and Vinci's Museo Leonardino (see below).

VINCI   Leonardo fans can jog east to take a 9km (6-mile) detour north to visit his hometown, Vinci. The village honors the original Renaissance man with a minuscule **Museo Leonardino,** Via della Torre 2 (*©* **0571-56-055**), in the 13th-century castle of the Guidi counts. It has no original Leonardos but does contain models of some of the machines he invented and reproductions of his drawings. It's open daily from 9:30am to 6pm (until 7pm in summer), and the admission (5€/$5.75 adults, 3.50€/$4.05 children 6–14 and seniors over 65, free for children under 6) is split with museums in Montelupo and Empoli. You can also see the baptismal font where he was baptized in **Santa Croce** church and drop by the **Biblioteca Leonardina,** Via Giorgio la Pira 1 (*©* **0571-56-540**), preserving copies of anything printed relating to Leonardo. The biblioteca is open Tuesday through Friday from 3 to 7pm. Hike or drive 3km (2 miles) up the hill to the tiny hamlet of Anchiano to see **Leonardo's modest birth house** (free admission; open Mar–Oct daily 9:30am–7pm, Nov–Feb till 6pm).

SAN MINIATO   More diverting than Vinci is a trip southeast of Empoli to the other major town of the Arno valley, **San Miniato.** The tourist office is at Piazza del Popolo (*©* **0571-418-739;** www.sanminiatotartufo.it and www.comune.san-miniato.pi.it; open June to mid-Sept daily 9:30am–1pm and 3:30–7:30pm; in winter Mon–Sat 9am–1pm and 3–6:30pm, Sun 10am–1pm and 3–7:30pm). The hilltop old town of this large village is famous these days mainly for its kite-flying championships (the weekend after Easter) and the white **truffles** hiding under the soil of the surrounding valley. San Miniato's long history, though, puts it as a former outpost of the Holy Roman Empire and countryside seat of emperors from Otto I to Frederick II. The latter left the town a 1240 **Rocca** (rebuilt entirely after it was bombed in World War II), the taller remaining tower of which rises gracefully above the village and the shorter of which serves as the bell tower for the Duomo.

On Piazza del Castello is the **Duomo,** open daily from 8am to 12:30pm and 3 to 6:30pm. Few of its original 12th-century Romanesque features remain, save the facade, unusually inset with ceramic North African bowls. A few of those bowls have been removed and are kept next door in the **Museo Diocesano** (*© 0571-418-071*), along with a Sienese school *Maestà,* a Neri di Bicci *Madonna and Child,* a Verrocchio terra-cotta bust of the *Redeemer,* and some baroque works upstairs. Admission is 2.50€ ($2.90). Summer hours are Tuesday through Sunday from 10am to 1pm and 3 to 6pm and winter hours Saturday and Sunday from 9am to noon and 2:30 to 5pm. The town's other worthwhile church is **San Domenico,** Piazza del Popolo, with works ranging from 14th-century Masolino-school frescoes to early-20th-century Art Deco frescoes. It's open daily from 8:30am to noon and 4 to 7pm (3–7pm in winter). The church of **San Francesco,** Piazza San Francesco, also has some frescoes in the style of Masolino and is open daily from 8am to 12:30pm and 3 to 6:30pm.

1 Pisa & Its Tipsy Tower

22km (14 miles) S of Lucca; 81km (50 miles) W of Florence; 334km (208 miles) NW of Rome

Pisa is the ultimate Tuscan day trip. Millions of people descend annually on the Leaning Tower and its neighboring architectural miracles on Campo dei Miracoli square. Few visitors, however, venture beyond this monumental grassy square into the rest of the city.

The city began as a seaside settlement around 1000 B.C. and was expanded into a naval trading port by the Romans in the 2nd century B.C. By the 11th century, Pisa had grown into one of the peninsula's most powerful maritime republics, along with Venice, Amalfi, and Genoa. Its extensive trading in the Middle East helped import advanced Arabic ideas (decorative and scientific), and its wars with the Saracens led it to create an offshore empire of Corsica, Sardegna, and the Balearics. It lay waste to rival Amalfi in 1135 and, riding a high tide of wealth in the late Middle Ages, created its monumental buildings. In 1284, Pisa's battle fleet was destroyed by Genoa at Meloria (off the Livorno coast), a staggering defeat allowing the Genoese to take control of the Tyrrhenian Sea and forcing Pisa's long slide into twilight. Its Ghibelline nature gave Florence the excuse it needed to take control in 1406. Despite a few small rebellions, Florence stayed in charge until Italian unification in the 1860s.

Pisa's main claim to fame since the end of its naval power has been its university, established in 1343 and one of Italy's top schools. Pisa was also the birthplace of one of Western history's greatest physicists and astronomers, Galileo Galilei (1564–1642), a man prone to dropping uneven weights from the Leaning Tower and making blasphemous statements about Earth revolving around the Sun.

ESSENTIALS

GETTING THERE   By Train   There are more than 20 trains daily from **Rome** (3 hr.). From **Florence,** 40 daily trains make the trip (80–90 min.). Three to four trains an hour run from nearby **Livorno** (15 min.); and there are trains

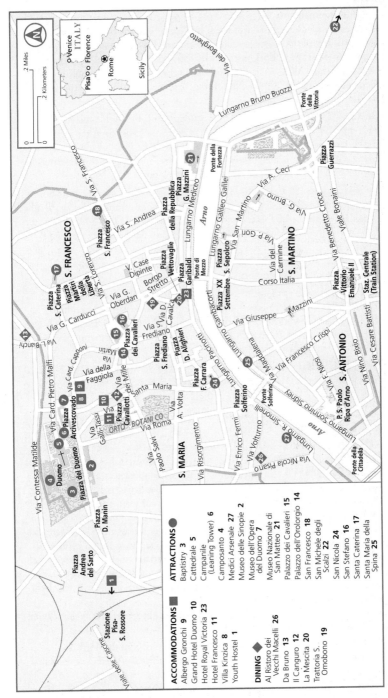

Pisa

ACCOMMODATIONS ■

Albergo Gronchi **9**
Grand Hotel Duomo **10**
Hotel Royal Victoria **23**
Hotel Francesco **11**
Villa Kinzica **8**
Youth Hostel **1**

DINING ◆

Al Ristoro dei
  Vecchi Macelli **26**
Da Bruno **13**
Il Canguro **12**
La Mescita **20**
Trattoria S.
  Omobono **19**

ATTRACTIONS ●

Baptistry **3**
Cattedrale **5**
Campanile
  (Leaning Tower) **6**
Camposanto **4**
Medici Arsenale **27**
Museo delle Sinopie **2**
Museo dell'Opera
  del Duomo **7**
Museo Nazionale di
  San Matteo **21**
Palazzo dei Cavalieri **15**
Palazzo dell'Orologio **14**
San Francesco **18**
San Michele degli
  Scalzi **22**
San Nicola **24**
San Stefano **16**
Santa Caterina **17**
Santa Maria della
  Spina **25**

running approximately every hour from **Siena** (100–110 min.). **Lucca** zips 24 runs here every day (20–30 min.). On the Lucca line, day-trippers (and anyone staying in any of the hotels listed here except the Royal Victoria) should get off at the **San Rossore station,** just a few blocks west of Piazza del Duomo and its Leaning Tower. All other trains, and the Lucca one eventually, pull into **Pisa Centrale station** (② **050-41-385**). From here, bus no. 1, 3, or 11 will take you to Piazza del Duomo.

By Car   There's a Florence–Pisa autostrada along the Arno valley. Take the SS12 or S12r from Lucca; the A12 comes down the coast from the north, and the SS1 runs north and south along the coast. **Park** just outside Porta Santa Maria, either along Via A. Pisano (metered; 1€/$1.15 per hour 8am–8pm) or in the nearby lot at Via C. S. Cammeo 51 (same rates).

By Bus   **Lazzi** (② **0583-584-876;** www.lazzi.it), Via d'Azeglio, runs hourly buses from **Florence** (2–2½ hr.), but you have to connect through Lucca (hourly runs; 20–30 min.). **CPT,** Via Nino Bixio (② **050-505-511** or 800-012-773 in Italy; www.cpt.pisa.it), has routes from **Volterra** (10 daily connect through Pontenedra for a 2–2½-hr. total trip), **Livorno** (half-hourly; 40–55 min.), and towns along the coast. The bus **station** is at Piazza Vittorio Emanuele II, just north of the main train station.

By Plane   Tuscany's main international airport, **Galileo Galilei** (general info ② **050-500-707;** www.pisa-airport.com), is just 3km (2 miles) south of Pisa. Trains zip you downtown to the train station in 5 minutes (1€/$1.15). A taxi ride to town will cost 4€ to 8€ ($4.60–$9.20). For more information, see "Getting There" in chapter 2.

GETTING AROUND   **By Bus**   **CPT** (② **050-505-511** or 800-012-773 in Italy; www.cpt.pisa.it) runs the city's buses. Bus nos. 1, 3, and 11 run most directly to Campo dei Miracoli from the main train station.

By Taxi   Taxis rank on Piazza Stazione and Piazza del Duomo. Call a radio taxi at ② **050-541-600.**

VISITOR INFORMATION   The main **tourist office** is just outside Porta Santa Maria on the west end of Campo dei Miracoli at Via C. Cammeo 2 (② **050-560-464** or 050-830-253; www.pisa.turismo.toscana.it; open daily May–Oct 9am–7:30pm, until 5:30pm Nov–Apr). A small office is to the left as you exit the train station (② **050-42-291**). Either can hand out maps and pamphlets, but they're oddly uninformed on the city of Pisa. Considerably more knowledgeable "Custodians of the Duomo" usually hang around the Museo dell'Opera del Duomo desk. The administrative **APT** office is at Via Pietro Nenni 24 (② **050-929-777;** fax 050-929-764). A helpful **private tourism consortium** (supported by the state) shares office space with the Via C. Cammelo tourist office (② **050-830-253;** fax 050-830-243; www.pisae.it); among other services, it will book rooms for free.

To find out what's going on in town, pick up a copy of the free weekly *Indizi e Servizi* (at some newsstands and hotels).

FESTIVALS & MARKETS   Since the 1400s, teams from the north and south sides of the Arno have dressed in Renaissance costumes and tried their darnedest to run one another over with a giant 7-ton decorated cart on the Ponte di Mezzo, site of the city's old Roman bridge. This inverse tug-of-war, the **Gioco del Ponte** (✸, is held on the last Sunday in June. Also in June is the **Festa di San Ranieri,** when Pisans honor their patron saint by lining the Arno with torches on the 16th, then running a boat race on the 17th. There's an excellent **daily food market** on Piazza delle Vettovaglie, described under "Other Attractions in Pisa" later in this section.

THE LEANING TOWER & OTHER PISAN MIRACLES

On a grassy lawn wedged into the northwest corner of the city walls, medieval Pisans created one of the most beautiful squares in the world. Historically dubbed the **Campo dei Miracoli (Field of Miracles)** ⚘⚘⚘, Piazza del Duomo contains an array of elegant buildings that heralded the Pisan Romanesque style.

But Piazza del Duomo isn't Pisa Central, not the central plaza in town as in most Tuscan cities. When it was built between the 11th and 13th centuries, the square was against the city walls, surrounded by farmland. But this peripheral location also somehow plays a role in the piazza's uniqueness. A very large but hidden part of its appeal, aside from the beauty of the buildings, is its spatial geometry. The piazza's medieval engineers knew what they were doing. If you take an aerial photo of the square and draw connect-the-dot lines between the centers, doors, and other focal points of the buildings and the spots where streets enter the piazza, you'll come up with all sorts of perfect triangles, tangential lines of mathematical grace, and other unfathomable hypotenuses.

Incidentally, only the tourist industry calls it Campo dei Miracoli. Pisans think that's just a bit too much and refer to it, as they always have, as Piazza del Duomo. I recommend visiting the Camposanto after the two museums, since both contain exhibits that'll help you appreciate the loss of the Camposanto frescoes.

Baptistery ⚘⚘   Italy's biggest baptistery (104m/348 ft. in circumference), it was begun in 1153 by Diotisalvi, who gave it its lower Romanesque drum. Nicola and Giovanni Pisano Gothicized the upper part between 1277 and 1297 and Cellino di Nese capped it with a Gothic dome in the 1300s. Most of the exterior statues and decorative elements by Giovanni Pisano are now kept in the Museo dell'Opera del Duomo (see below), and only a few have been replaced here with casts. It may not look it, but if you include the statue on top, this building is actually taller than the Leaning Tower across the square. The interior is surprisingly plain but features the first of the great Pisano pulpits as well as a large baptismal **font,** carved and inlaid by the idiosyncratic Guido Bigarelli da Como and sprouting a 20th-century statue of St. John.

Nicola Pisano was the founder of a great line of Gothic sculptors who liberated their art from the static iconography of medievalism to a new level of dynamic action and intense expressiveness that would influence Ghiberti and Donatello and so pave the road for the Renaissance. The **pulpit** ⚘ Nicola carved for the

---

Campo dei Miracoli Admissions

Admission charges for the group of monuments and museums on the campo are tied together in a needlessly complicated way. The Cattedrale alone costs 2€ ($2.30). Any other single sight is 5€ ($5.75). Any two sights are 6€ ($6.90). The Cattedrale plus any two other sights is 8€ ($9.20). An 8.50€ ($9.80) ticket gets you into the Baptistery, Camposanto, Museo dell'Opera del Duomo, and Museo delle Sinopie, while a 10.50€ ($12) version throws in the Cattedrale as well. Children under 10 enter free. For more information, visit their collective website at www.opapisa.it. Admission to the Leaning Tower (17€/$20) is by advance reservation only; see "Pisa's Perpendicularly Challenged Tower" on p. 296.

baptistery (1255–60) is his masterpiece and the prototype for a series he and his son Giovanni carried out over the years (the last, Giovanni's greatest work, is in Pisa's Duomo; the other two are in Pistoia and Siena). Heavily influenced by classical works—including the Roman sarcophagi and Greek vase now in the Camposanto—Nicola's high-relief panels (a synopsis of Christ's life) include pagan gods converted to Christianity as Madonnas and saints.

The other main attraction of the baptistery is its renowned **acoustics.** When it's crowded in summer, you may have to bribe a guard to warble, but when there are fewer people (come early in the morning), lean over the ropes to get as near to center as possible and let fly a clear loud note, listening to it echo around the room as it fades. Even better, sing two notes a half-octave apart and listen for their echoing atonal mingling. When a choir sings here, you can hear it for miles.

Piazza del Duomo. ℭ **050-560-547.** www.opapisa.it. For admission fees, see "Campo dei Miracoli Admissions." Apr–Sept daily 8am–7:30pm; Mar and Oct daily 9am–5:30pm; Nov–Feb daily 9am–4:30pm. Bus: 1, 3, or 11.

Cattedrale ✸✸   Buscheto, the architect who laid the cathedral's first stone in 1063, kicking off a new era in art by building what was to become the model for the Pisan Romanesque style, is buried in the last blind arch on the left of the facade. All the elements of the nascent Romanesque style are here on the **facade** ✸, designed and built by Buscheto's successor, Rainaldo: alternating light and dark banding, rounded blind arches with Moorish-inspired lozenges at the top and colored marble inlay designs, and Lombard-style open galleries of tiny mismatched columns stacked to make the facade (currently being restored) much higher than the church roof. A disastrous 1595 fire destroyed most of the works inside the church, but luckily the 16th-century Pisans recognized and hired some of the better late- and post-Renaissance artists for the refurbishing.

In summer, you sometimes enter through the **main door,** one of three cast by students of Giambologna after the 1595 fire destroyed the originals. The normal entrance to the church is usually on the back of the right transept, across from the bell tower, where the fourth original bronze **Door of San Ranieri** ✸ still survives. It was cast (along with the now-lost facade doors) by Bonnano Pisano in 1180 while he was working on the soon-to-be-listing bell tower. Inside the right transept (which you enter through this door), you'll find another work that survived the fire, the **tomb of Emperor Henry VII** by Tino da Camaino (1315) surmounted by a pair of Ghirlandaio angels. Henry VII was a hero to the Ghibelline Pisans, who supported his successful bid for Holy Roman Emperor.

On the north side of the nave, Giovanni Pisano's masterpiece **pulpit** ✸ (1302–11) has regained its rightful place. After the fire, the baroquies decided the nasty old Gothic pulpit was an eyesore, so they dismantled it and crated it up; it wasn't found and reassembled until 1926. It's the last of the famed Pisano pulpits and arguably the greatest.

Hanging low near the pulpit is a large **bronze lamp** that, according to legend, a bored Galileo was staring at one day during Mass, watching it sway gently back and forth, when his law of the pendulum suddenly hit him. Spoilsports like to point out the lamp was cast in 1586, a few years after Galileo's discovery, but the legend may still be salvaged: Another lamp probably hung here before this one. Beneath the frescoed oval dome is what remains of the **Cosmatesque pavement** of parti-colored marble designs. The **bronze angels** (1602) flanking the choir entrance and the **crucified Christ** over the altar are by the baroque master of bronze Giambologna, and on the entrance pier to the choir is Andrea del Sarto's almost Leonardesque *St. Agnes with her Lamb* ✸, painted in High Renaissance style. In the apse is the last of the major survivors of the fire, an enormous 13th-century mosaic *Christ Pancrator,* completed in 1302 by Cimabue, who added the St. John the Evangelist on the right.

Piazza del Duomo. ⓒ 050-560-547. www.opapisa.it. For admission fees, see "Campo dei Miracoli Admissions." Apr–Sept Mon–Sat 10am–7:30pm, Sun 1–7:30pm; Mar and Oct Mon–Sat 10am–5:30pm, Sun 1–5:30pm; Nov–Feb Mon–Sat 10am–12:45pm and 3–4:30pm, Sun 3–4:30pm. Bus: 1, 3, or 11.

Camposanto   Begun in 1278 by Giovanni di Simone to house the shiploads of holy Golgotha dirt (the mount where Christ was crucified) brought back by an archbishop from the Crusades, the Camposanto has been burial ground for Pisan bigwigs ever since. Most funerary monuments are recycled Roman sarcophagi or neoclassical confections installed in the peacefully arcaded corridor encircling the patches of green in the center.

The walls were once covered with important 14th- and 15th-century frescoes by Taddeo Gaddi, Spinello Aretino, and Benozzo Gozzoli, among others. On July 27, 1944, however, American warplanes launched a heavy attack against the city (which was still in Nazi hands) and the cemetery was bombed. The wooden roof caught fire, and its lead panels melted and ran right down over the frescoes, destroying most of the paintings and severely damaging the few that remained. When the surviving frescoes were detached to be moved, workers discovered the artists' preparatory sketches *(sinopie)* underneath. These, along with the *sinopie* of the destroyed frescoes, are housed in the Museo delle Sinopie (see below).

A doorway off one corridor leads to an exhibit of photos of the frescoes from before 1944 and of the devastation wreaked by the bombing. Also here is a 2nd-century B.C. **Greek vase** that inspired the Pisan Gothic sculptors. Then come the few damaged frescoes that made it through the bombing. The most fascinating is the 14th-century *Triumph of Death* ✯. The attribution to any one artist is so contested that the work's painter has been dubbed, somewhat melodramatically, "The Master of the Triumph of Death." Liszt was so moved by it that he sat down and wrote his famous *Totentanz.*

Piazza del Duomo. ⓒ 050-560-547. www.opapisa.it. For admission fees, see "Campo dei Miracoli Admissions." Apr–Sept daily 8am–7:30pm; Mar and Oct daily 9am–5:30pm; Nov–Feb daily 9am–4:30pm. Bus: 1, 3, or 11.

Museo delle Sinopie ✯   This museum houses the *sinopie* sketches that were discovered underneath the charred remains of the Camposanto's ruined frescoes (see above). Placards reproducing Carlo Lasinio's 19th-century engravings of the finished frescoes sit in front of each *sinopie* to help you reconstruct what the final work once looked like. The two most interesting things are how different artists used the *sinopia* stage of the fresco process (some sketched just rough outlines to guide their later work, others went as far as shading the drapery and detailing facial features) and to see where the master changed his mind between sketch and finished work—like a giant academic's game of "One of These Things Is Not Like the Other."

Piazza del Duomo. ⓒ 050-560-547. www.opapisa.it. For admission fees, see "Campo dei Miracoli Admissions." Apr–Sept daily 8am–7:30pm; Mar and Oct daily 9am–5:30pm; Nov–Feb daily 9am–4:30pm. Bus: 1, 3, or 11.

Museo dell'Opera del Duomo ✯   The old Chapter House cum convent has been transformed into a storehouse for sculptures, paintings, and other works from the ecclesiastical buildings on Piazza del Duomo. Room 1 has **models** of the Duomo buildings and engraved glass plans showing the square's history and geometry. Room 3 has delicate 12th-century carvings and intarsia marble decoration displaying a strong Moorish influence and a massive 12th-century wooden crucifix from Burgundy, with a Christ styled so medievally naive that it

Pisa's Perpendicularly Challenged Tower

The fact is, most medieval towers still standing in Italy haven't been able to keep perpendicular over the centuries. But it's the **Leaning Tower of Pisa** that has captured the world's fascination and become international shorthand for Italy itself.

The tower's problem—that which has been the bane of Pisan engineers trying to overcome it for more than 800 years—is you can't stack that much heavy marble on top of a shifting subsoil foundation and keep it all on the up and up. It was started in 1173—the date on the wall of 1174 owes to an old Pisan quirk of starting the year with the date of the Virgin's conception—by Guglielmo and Bonnano Pisano (who also sculpted the Duomo's original bronze doors). They got as far as the third level in 1185 when they noticed the lean, at that point only about 3.8cm, but enough to worry them. Everyone was at a loss as to what to do, so work stopped for almost a century and wasn't resumed again until 1275 under the direction of Giovanni di Simone. He tried to correct the tilt by intentionally curving the structure back toward the perpendicular, giving the tower its slight banana shape. In 1284, work stopped yet again just before the belfry. In 1360, Tomasso di Andrea da Pontedera capped it all off at about 51m (170 ft.) with a slightly Gothic belfry that tilts jauntily to the side.

The only major blip in the tower's long career as a world-famous Italian freak show attraction came in 1590, when a hometown scientist named Galileo Galilei dropped some mismatched wooden balls off the leaning side to prove to an incredulous world his theory that gravity exerted the same force on two falling objects no matter what their relative weights. In the early 19th century, someone got it into his head to dig out around the base of the tower in order to see how the foundations were laid and perhaps find a way to correct the slipping lean, but all he accomplished was to remove what little stability the tower had acquired over the centuries, and it started falling faster than ever before (not that it was all that fast: about 1mm a year).

For several decades, a series of complicated and delicate projects has been directed at stabilizing the alluvial subsoil. In 1989, more than a million people climbed the tower, but by 1990 the lean was at about 15 feet

looks like modern art. But the main attraction is the Islamic 11th-century bronze **griffin** ✸, war booty from the Crusades, which long decorated the Duomo's cupola before it was replaced by a copy.

Room 6 has curving ranks of faded-to-facelessness 13th-century Giovanni Pisano statues from the baptistery. The treasury has two Pisanos: a wooden crucifix and a swaybacked ***Madonna col Bambino*** ✸ he carved from a curving ivory tusk (1299). Also here is a precious Pisan relic, the cross that led Pisans on the First Crusade.

The last few rooms house the precious legacy of Carlo Lasinio, who restored the Camposanto frescoes in the early 19th century and, fortunately for posterity, made a series of **etchings** ✸ of each fresco, the prints from which were colored out of plumb and, by order of a mayor's office concerned for safety, the tower was closed to the public. At 3:25pm on January 7, 1990, with the tower's bells sounding a death knell, the doors were closed indefinitely. In 1992, steel cables were belted around the base to prevent shear forces from ripping apart the masonry. In 1993, even the bells and their dangerous vibrations were silenced, and the same year a series of lead weights was rather unaesthetically stacked on the high side to try to correct the list. In 1997, engineers took a chance on excavating around the base again—this time carefully removing more than 70 tons of soil from the foundation of the high side so the tower could gradually tip back.

In December 2001, righted to its more stable lean of 1838 (when it was a mere 4m/13.5 ft. off its center), the tower reopened to the public. Now, however, the number of visitors is strictly controlled via compulsory 35- to 40-minute guided tours—and a massive admission charge. Visit www.opapisa.it/boxoffice to book tickets. It's wise to book well ahead; when I checked ticket availability in June, tours were sold out a full 16 days in advance. If you show up in Pisa without reservations, you will *not* be able to get into the tower.

The campanile, by the way, isn't the only edifice out of whack on the piazza. The same water-saturated and unsteady sandy soil under the Field of Miracles that causes the bell tower's poor posture has taken its toll on the other buildings as well. The baptistery lurches toward the north, and if you catch the Duomo's facade at the correct angle, you'll see it, too, is a few feet shy of straight. The nature of Pisa's alluvial plain has caused many of its older buildings to shift and settle in this manner, and a couple of other campanile about town have been nicknamed Pisa's "other leaning towers" (San Michele dei Scalzi is, if anything, even more weirdly askew than its more famous cousin; see "Other Attractions in Pisa," below).

Piazza del Duomo. © 050-560-547. www.opapisa.it/boxoffice. Admission by reservation only, 17€/$20 (15€ ticket plus 2€ advance sales fee). Children under 8 not permitted. Show printed proof of receipt at the ticket offices of Opera della Primaziale Pisa 1 hour prior to scheduled visit. Mon–Fri 8am–1:30pm. Bus: 1, 3, or 11.

by his son. Not only did the original publication of these prints have an important influence on the developing pre-Raphaelite movement at the time, but they're the best record we have of the paintings that went up in flames when the Camposanto was bombed in 1944.

Piazza Arcivescovado 6. © 050-560-547. www.opapisa.it. For admission fees, see "Campo dei Miracoli Admissions." Apr–Sept daily 8am–7:20pm; Mar and Oct 9am–5:20pm; Nov–Feb 9am–4:20pm. Bus: 1, 3, or 11.

OTHER ATTRACTIONS IN PISA

If you go down Via Santa Maria from Piazza del Duomo and take a left on Via dei Mille, you'll come out into **Piazza Cavalieri,** possibly the site of the Roman town's forum and later the square where the citizens of the medieval city-state met to discuss political issues. Giorgio Vasari remodeled the **Palazzo dei Cavalieri** in 1562

Pisa's Sunken Archaeological Treasure

A new museum in the old Medici Arsenale, Lungarno Simonelli, houses the finds in the remarkable ongoing excavation of the 10 **ancient Roman wooden ships** ⭐—spanning the 1st century B.C. to the Imperial Age, from riverboats to seafaring vessels—stumbled upon by workers expanding the San Rossore train station in 1998. Italy's Culture Minister proclaimed it to be a "marine Pompeii" as Pisa's forgotten port comes back to light. Buried by silt in the 12th century (which has since moved the shoreline 8km/5 miles west), these docks where the Arno met the sea were probably half marshy flatlands, half lagoon—much like modern-day Venice. Alas, this sort of harbor is prone to flash flooding during storms, a recurrent event that probably sank these ships at various times over the centuries.

Fortunately for us, their sudden demise also meant that much of their contents has survived, from holds filled with clay amphorae (whose seals have preserved shipments of olives, cherries, walnuts, and wine for 2,000 years) to sailor's quarters still kitted out with their belongings: leather sandals, sewing kits, even a wax writing board. In the half-decade since the discovery, maritime archaeologists had uncovered two more vessels, including what may be the only Roman warship ever recovered intact. The museum, **Museo Navi Antiche di Pisa** (ⓒ **050-21-441** or 055-321-5446; www.navipisa.it), currently displays the ships' contents (including a sailor's skeleton), and will soon let you watch the arduous restoration work on the vessels, which will be displayed here when the work is done. It's open Tuesday through Sunday from 10am to 1pm and 2 to 6pm (until 9pm in summer); admission is 3€ ($3.45) adults, 2.50€ ($2.90) seniors over 65, free for children under 10.

and decorated it with recently restored and very detailed graffiti; it now houses the renowned university college Scuola Normale Superiore. Next to the palace is the baroque **San Stefano,** housing some tempera paintings by the likes of Empoli, Cristofano Allori, and Vasari (open Mon–Fri 9am–12:30pm, Sat–Sun 9am–12:30pm and 3–6pm). Also on the piazza is the stubby clock tower of the **Palazzo dell'Orologio,** where Count Ugolino della Gherardesca, suspected of having betrayed his fellow Pisans in the fateful battle where Genoa decisively crushed Pisan naval might, was locked up to starve to death along with his sons and grandsons. The tragic story was immortalized by both Dante in his *Inferno* and Shelley in his *Tower of Famine.*

If you continue down Via Santa Maria toward the Arno, you'll come to the millennial church of **San Nicola** (ⓒ **050-24-677**), with a Francesco Traini *Madonna and Child* on the first altar on the right and a 1400 St. Nicholas of Tolentino *Protecting Pisa from the Plague.* To the left of the high altar is a gaunt *Jesus* being crucified carved by Giovanni Pisano. The church is also home to the second of Pisa's leaning towers, a 13th-century campanile whose spiral staircase inspired Renaissance architect Bramante for the stairs he installed in the Vatican. (Though the church is officially open daily 9am–noon and 5–8pm, you often need to seek out the sacristan to get in; ring the bell at the door next to the tower.)

To the northeast of Piazza Cavalieri lies **Santa Caterina** (© 050-552-883), with a Gothic facade from 1330 and the tomb of Archbishop Simone Saltarelli by Nino Pisano along with Francesco Triani's *Apotheosis of St. Thomas Aquinas.* It's open daily from 8am to 1pm. Southeast of this, near the city walls, **San Francesco** (© 050-544-091) contains some good baroque works by Empoli, Il Passignano, and Santi di Tito. The vault has 1342 frescoes by Taddeo Gaddi, and in the second chapel to the right of the high altar is a *Crucifixion with Saints* by Spinello Aretino. It's open daily from 7:30am to noon and 4 to 7:30pm.

Walk west along Via San Francesco to **Borgo Stretto,** Pisa's arcaded shopping street. Off Borgo Stretto near Piazza Garibaldi is hidden the arched **Piazza Vettovaglie,** which houses an old-fashioned **food market.**

A ways up the Arno near Ponte Fortezza is Pisa's only significant painting collection, the **Museo Nazionale di San Matteo** ✸✸, Lungarno Mediceo (© 050-541-865). To see the collection in chronological order, head immediately out into the pretty brick cloister and cross to ascend the central staircase on the opposite side. (If you mistake doors, you'll be in for a whole lot of medieval and Renaissance painted plates.) Poorly lit and sporadically labeled, the collections are constantly being rearranged, but you should be able to find the masterpieces amid the shuffle. The first large room of paintings has many good 14th- and 15th-century works by Turino Vanni, Taddeo di Bartolo, and Spinello Aretino, plus a pair of Agnolo Gaddi polyptychs. One of the prides of the collections is the Sienese master Simone Martini's polyptych of the *Virgin and Child with Saints.* In a side room they keep the originals of the Giovanni and Nino Pisano sculptures from Santa Maria della Spina, including Nino's masterpiece, *Madonna del Latte,* a very human mother in Gothic curving grace who smiles down at her nursing baby.

Other star works are a *St. Paul* by Masaccio, the greenishly aged *Madonna dell'Umiltà* by Gentile da Fabriano, and a *Madonna col Bambino* by Fra' Angelico. The Donatello gilded bronze reliquary *Bust of St. Rossone* (1427) is an important sculptural step from medieval to Renaissance style and is held by some to be a self-portrait. Take bus no. 5, 7, or 13 to get to the museum; it's open Tuesday through Saturday from 9am to 7pm and Sunday from 9am to 2pm; admission is 4€ ($4.60).

If you follow the north side of the Arno upstream about a mile past San Matteo (or take bus no. 14), you'll come to Pisa's third and perhaps most skewed "leaning tower." It almost looks as if the Pisans simply gave up on rulers and right angles when building **San Michele degli Scalzi.** Nothing stands straight up: not the outer walls, the tiers of columns dividing the nave from the aisles, the apse, the windows, or, of course, the bell tower. Take bus no. 13 (from Via San Michele degli Scalzi) back to the center.

The south bank of the Arno holds little of interest except for the Gothic gem **Santa Maria della Spina** ✸✸ (© 050-21-441), which sits along the river. The church is a collaborative Giovanni and Nino Pisano work of 1230 to 1323, dismantled and raised to current ground level (for fear of floods) in 1871. It was built to house a *spina* (thorn) from Christ's Passion crown brought back by a merchant from the Crusades. Much of the Pisano sculpture from the outside has been removed for safekeeping to the Museo Nazionale di San Matteo, as has the church's primary attraction, Nino Pisano's *Madonna del Latte.* However, for the first time since it closed 35 years ago, you can finally peek inside, Tuesday through Friday 11am to 1:30pm and 2:30 to 6pm, Saturday and Sunday from 11am to 8pm: October through March from 10am to 2pm (and 10am–1pm and 2:30–5pm on the 2nd Sun of those months); April, May, and September from 10am to 1:30pm and 2:30 to 6pm (7pm weekends); June through August from 11am to 1:30pm and 2:30 to 6pm (8pm weekends). Admission is 1.10€ ($1.30) adults, free for children under 10 and adults over 65.

WHERE TO STAY

Pisa is such a major day-trip site that few people stay here overnight, which helps keep hotel prices down but also limits selection. The hotel desk in the main tourist office will book you a room at no charge. The low season for most hotels in Pisa is July through August.

Albergo Gronchi   This is a very plain, *very* decrepit, but very cheap hotel that stays full (and stays in this book) both because of its location on the edge of Piazza del Duomo and for the fact that the rooms along the front have that ultimate Pisan hotel amenity: a view of the Leaning Tower (or at least the top half). The weak-springed beds and worn furniture of the fair-size rooms are redeemed by some frescoed ceilings on the first floor. Room 29 has a balcony with Leaning Tower views.

Piazza Arcivescovado 1 (just off Piazza del Duomo), 56126 Pisa. ✆ **050-561-823**. 23 units, 4 with shower and sink, none with bathroom. 35€ ($40) double. Small discounts for longer stays. No credit cards. Free parking nearby. Bus: 4. *In room:* No phone.

Grand Hotel Duomo   This is the best hotel near the Duomo, but pricey. Its outward appearance and public spaces aren't much to look at, but the rooms are pleasant enough, with parquet floors and built-in furniture in dark wood. Some of the rooms were refurbished in 1997 with marble flooring, and those along the front have views of the monuments on Campo dei Miracoli. The suites are large and have direct access onto the rooftop terrace. The rooms have large new bathrooms. An expanded continental breakfast, including cheese and ham, is served in the elegant dining room.

Via Santa Maria 94 (1½ blocks down from Piazza del Duomo), 56126 Pisa. ✆ **050-561-894**. Fax 050-560-418. www.grandhotelduomo.it. 93 units. 178€ ($205) double; 210€ ($242) junior suite. Half and full pension available. Rates include breakfast. AE, DC, MC, V. Parking around 16€ ($18). Bus: 4. **Amenities:** Restaurant; concierge; car-rental desk; limited room service; laundry service; same-day dry cleaning. *In room:* A/C, TV, minibar, hair dryer, safe.

Hotel Francesco   Carmela Corradino and her family care for this small, modern hotel. The rooms are smallish but not cramped, the ceilings high and vaulted, the mattresses firm, and the furnishings are new. Many of the rooms have a third bed, making them perfect for families, but I'd go for room 201 or 202 (which can be connected), sharing a lovely terrace overlooking the botanical gardens behind the hotel. In fact, any room on the back will be quieter than those on the busy street (though the windows' double glazing does muffle things somewhat). The small terrace where you can breakfast in summer glimpses the top half of the Leaning Tower. Corradino will arrange free transfer from the Pisa airport if you book at the Hotel Francesco for 3 nights or longer.

Via Santa Maria 129 (1½ blocks from Piazza del Duomo), 56126 Pisa. ✆ **050-554-109**. Fax 050-556-145. www.hotelfrancesco.com. 13 units. 115€ ($132) double; 130€ ($150) triple. Rates include breakfast. AE, DC, MC, V. Parking 5€ ($5.75). Bus: 4. **Amenities:** Restaurant; bike rental; concierge; tour desk; car-rental desk; courtesy car; nonsmoking rooms. *In room:* A/C, TV, minibar, coffeemaker; hair dryer.

Hotel Royal Victoria ⭐   "I fully endorse the above," wrote Teddy Roosevelt of this place in one of the antique guest books. It opened in 1839 as Pisa's first hotel, uniting several medieval towers and houses, and is Pisa's only inn of any real character. The rooms on the Arno tend to be larger, as do the quieter (and cooler) ones installed in the remains of a tower dating from the 980s. There are many frescoed ceilings, and one room is a triumph of *trompe l'oeil,* including fake curtains painted on the walls surrounding the bed. They have several rooms with common doors that can be turned into family suites for four (with two separate bathrooms). The new small, plant-filled terrace is a lovely place to take drinks or sun surrounded by roof tiles. Although some rooms are very small and plain, in all you'll probably find yourself, as Ruskin did in terse simplicity, "always very comfortable in this inn."

Lungarno Pacinotti 12 (near Ponte di Mezzo), 56126 Pisa. © 050-940-111. Fax 050-940-180. www.royal victoria.it. 48 units, 40 with bathroom. 72€ ($83) double without bathroom; 115€ ($132) double with bathroom; triple with bathroom 125€ ($144); 208€ ($239) family suites. 20% discount for a stay of 5 nights or longer. Rates include breakfast. AE, DC, MC, V. Parking 16€ ($18) in hotel garage. Bus: 1, 3, 4, or 7. **Amenities:** Bike rental; concierge; tour desk; car rental (they have their own Smartcar); 24-hr. room service (breakfast, bar, and food from nearby restaurant); babysitting; laundry service; same-day dry cleaning. *In room:* A/C in 17 units, TV, VCR on request, modem hook-up, hair dryer on request.

Villa Kinzica   The carpeted medium-size rooms in this middle-range hotel have modern wood furniture and tasteful art prints on the walls. Around the corner from the Leaning Tower, the Kinzica's rooms are mostly arranged on the front and east sides, so you can open your window and have a camera-ready shot of the campanile. Half the rooms have air-conditioning. The bathrooms are modern but small, and the price is excellent for the location and general comfort.

Piazza Arcivescovado 2 (just off Piazza del Duomo), 56100 Pisa. © 050-560-419. Fax 050-551-204. www. hotelvillakinzica.it. 34 units. 103€ ($118) double; 124€ ($143) triple. Rates include breakfast. AE, DC, MC, V. Free parking on street (ask for permit). Bus: 4. **Amenities:** Restaurant; concierge; tour desk; limited room service (24-hr. bar service; restaurant during kitchen hours); nonsmoking rooms. *In room:* A/C in some units, TV, hair dryer.

WHERE TO DINE

For a quick bite near Piazza del Duomo, or perhaps for a picnic in front of the Leaning Tower, **Il Canguro** (© **050-561-942**), a few short blocks down Via Santa Maria at no. 151, serves scrumptious sandwiches.

Al Ristoro dei Vecchi Macelli ⚑ SEAFOOD/PISAN   This is Pisa's finest restaurant, excelling at both fish and meat dishes but always local Tuscan at heart. It offers antipasto samplers either *di mare* (surf) or *di terra* (turf), and though the specialty primo is a *minestra fagioli rossi e frutti di mare* (a creamy purée of red beans with clams, cuttlefish, and mussels), they make their pasta in-house, so the *ravioli farciti di maiale* (pork ravioli in broccoli sauce) offers stiff competition for your palate. Sticking to land, you can follow your first course with the *coniglio disossato e farcito con salsa al tartufo* (slices of stuffed rabbit in cream-truffle sauce). The *spigola con salsa di cipolle e ostriche gratinate* (sea bass cooked with onions and oysters) makes a good fishy secondo.

Via Volturno 49 (at the corner of Via N. Pisano). © 050-20-424. Reservations strongly recommended. Primi 11€–13€ ($13–$15); secondi 16€–18€ ($18–$20); fixed-priced menus without wine 42€–60€ ($48–$69). AE, DC, MC, V. Thurs–Tues 12:30–3pm and 7:30–10pm; Sun 8–10pm. Bus: 5.

Da Bruno ⚑ CASALINGA PISANA   The decor is typical, cluttered trattoria—paintings of the Duomo, pictures of the owner with famous people and of the local soccer team, copper pots—for this is a typical trattoria that has been dignified to *ristorante* status only through its years of deserved success. It specializes in tried-and-true Pisan dishes. The *prosciutto con crostini* antipasto is as good as it comes, to be followed by *pasta e ceci* (pasta with garbanzo beans) or *zuppa pisana* (a very bready Pisan ribollita). Although you can order well-turned versions of *agnello arrosto* (roast lamb) or *coniglio al forno* (baked rabbit), the famous secondo here is a *Pisan baccalà con porri,* salt cod cooked with leeks and tomatoes. Try the tiramisù sundae, with chocolate chips and syrup on top.

Via Luigi Bianchi (outside Porta Lucca on the north end of town). 🕿 **050-560-818**; www.pisaonline.it/trattoriadabruno. Reservations recommended. Primi 8€–10€ ($9.20–$12); secondi 10€–15€ ($12–$17). AE, DC, MC, V. Wed–Sun noon–3pm and 7–10:30pm. Bus: 1 or 4.

La Mescita PISAN/ENOTECA   The marketplace location and simple decor of this popular spot belie its reputation for fine cuisine—although a recent expansion is a nod to its success. The menu changes each month, but includes the delicious likes of a *sformatino di melanzane* (eggplant soufflé in tomato sauce), to be followed by *ravioli di ceci con salsa di gamberetti e pomodoro fresco* (ravioli stuffed with a garbanzo bean pâté and served in shrimp-and-tomato sauce) or *strozzapreti al trevisano e gorgonzola* (a slightly bitter dish of pasta curlicues in a cheesy sauce topped with shredded red cabbage). You can stick to tradition with your secondo by ordering the *baccalà con patate e ceci* (salt cod with potatoes and garbanzo beans). Because the place operates as an *enoteca* after hours, the wine list is long and detailed.

Via D. Cavalca 2 (just off the market square of Piazza Vettovaglie). 🕿 **050-544-294.** Reservations recommended. Primi 9€–11€ ($11–$13); secondi 15€–16€ ($17–$18). AE, DC, MC, V. Tues–Sun 8–11pm, Sat and Sun 1–2:30pm. Closed 20 days in Aug. Bus: 1, 2, or 4.

Trattoria S. Omobono 🕿 CASALINGA PISANA   Around a column surviving from the medieval church that once stood here, locals gather to enjoy authentic Pisan home cooking. You can get away with a full meal, including wine, for under 20€ ($23), opening with something like *brachette alla renaiaola* (an antique Pisan dish consisting of large pasta squares in a purée of turnip greens and smoked fish) or *tagliatelle alla scarpara* (in a sausage ragù). The secondi are simple and straightforward: *baccalà alla livornese* (salt cod with tomatoes) or *maiale arrosto* (thinly sliced roast pork), with which you can order fried polenta slices or ultra-Pisan *ceci* (garbanzo) beans.

Piazza S. Omobono 6 (the piazza next to the market square Piazza Vettovaglie). 🕿 **050-540-847.** Reservations recommended. Primi 6€ ($6.90); secondi 8€ ($9.20). DC, MC, V. Mon–Sat 12:30–2:30pm and 7:30–10pm. Closed Aug 8–20. Bus: 1, 2, or 4.

A MONASTERY & A WILDLIFE AREA NEAR PISA

Twenty kilometers (32 miles) or so east of Pisa outside the town of Calci lies the largest and most interesting Carthusian monastery in Italy, the **Certosa di Calci** 🕿 (🕿 **050-938-430**). It was founded in 1366, but most of its current facade dates from the 18th and 19th centuries. You can see this huge complex of baroque frescoed chapels and cloisters during a fascinating guided tour leading you through 11 chapels, the main church, and a monk's "cell." The University of Pisa also keeps a **natural history museum** here (🕿 **050-936-193** or 050-937-092), with a large taxonomy collection, including a dinosaur and an articulated giraffe skeleton. The Certosa is open Tuesday through Saturday from 8:30am to 6:30pm, and Sunday from 8:30am to 12:30pm year-round. Admission is 4€ ($4.60), with guided tours on the hour. The natural history museum is open Tuesday through Saturday 9am to 5pm (Sun 9am–6pm), and admission is an additional 5€ ($5.75). The best way to get to the Certosa is by taking the APT bus to Montemagno, which lets you off at the gates, rather than the one to Calci. (Catch the bus in Pisa at Piazza Sant'Antonio, off Piazza Vittorio Emanuele II.)

Just west of Pisa, close enough that you can take city bus no. 11 (from Lungarno Gambacorti) to get there, begins the **Tenuta di San Rossore** 🕿 (🕿 **050-530-101;**

www.parcosanrossore.it). This was once the summer estate of Italy's president, but in 1988 it was turned into a publicly owned park system along with a few other areas along the coast. It now forms part of one of Tuscany's most precious protected wildlife areas, a coastal zone of dense pines with populations of wild deer, boars, and aquatic birds surrounding several beaches and some boggy wetlands. Although it isn't open to the public often, it is well worth the free visit, from Saturday to Sunday 8:30am to 5:30pm in winter, till 9:30pm in summer (they also run various guided tours for modest fees—in Italian naturally, but since they include walking, biking, and horseback visits, they can be fun even if you don't understand the language; the website has details). In 1822 at the beach at Gombo, now part of the park, the body of self-exiled English poet Percy Bysshe Shelley washed ashore (he drowned while sailing off the coast; many hold it was a pirate murder).

2 Livorno: A Busy Port City with Great Seafood

19km (12 miles) S of Pisa; 95km (59 miles) W of Florence; 315km (195 miles) NW of Rome

Livorno is like a blue-collar Tuscan Venice, a busy port city second only to Florence in size and graced with canals and some of the peninsula's best seafood. The city is perhaps unique in Tuscany because there are few sights to see, no churches to speak of, and just one measly museum of 19th- and 20th-century paintings by artists of the Macchiaioli movement, a Tuscan variant on French Impressionism.

You'll see posters in town of a ruinous tower sprouting from pale cobalt-blue waters apparently in the middle of the sea. Actually, this watchtower, **Meloria,** is resting on a barely submerged reef about 5km (3 miles) offshore. It was here, in 1284, that Genoa's navy thoroughly trounced the Pisan fleet, signaling the beginning of Pisa's slow decline under Genoese maritime dominance.

ESSENTIALS

GETTING THERE   By Train   The Arno valley line runs 24 trains daily from **Florence** (about 1½ hr.) through **Pisa** (14 min.) to **Livorno Centrale** (© **0586-400-456**), where you can catch the no. 1, 2, or 8 bus (and many others, though they don't make a beeline) to Piazza Grande in the center of town.

By Car   There's a highway from Florence that runs straight into town. From Pisa, the fastest way is to zip down the SS1. Convenient pay parking is along the Fosse Reale, on Via Magenta, and on Viale Carducci.

By Bus   Lazzi buses (© **0586-899-562;** www.lazzi.it) run from **Florence** and **Pisa** to the Livorno terminal at Piazza Manin on the Fosse Reale, just a hop away from the tourist office on Piazza Cavour. ATL buses (© **0586-884-262;** www.atl. livorno.it/WWW/ATL/index.html) run from Piazza Grande to service **Pisa** and

Masterpiece Theater

In 1884, bohemian sculptor Amadeo Modigliani was born here to an upper-middle-class family. In Paris, his womanizing was notorious, and he drank himself to death at age 35. Rumor held that a despondent Modigliani had thrown some of his works into a canal on his last visit to his hometown. In 1984, several sculptures were dredged up and trumpeted as his lost works. But just before they sold for millions of dollars, some school kids appeared on national TV showing how they'd made the works themselves—one of the most successful art hoaxes of the century.

Livorno's province down the coast, including Castiglioncello, Cecina, and Piombino.

VISITOR INFORMATION The **tourist info booth** is on Piazza Municipio (© **0586-204-629**), open Monday through Saturday 10am to 1pm and 3 to 6pm; these hours may change (they may eliminate or reduce afternoon hours, especially Sat). The administrative APT, which also has information, is tucked away on the second floor of an unassuming building at Piazza Cavour 6, on the south edge of the old city (© **0586-204-611;** fax 0586-896-173; www.livorno. turismo.toscana.it or www.comune.livorno.it). It's open Monday through Friday from 9:30am to 1:30pm and also 3 to 5pm, Saturday from 9:30am to 1:30pm. A **summer information booth** operates June through September at the main dock on Molo Mediceo (© **0586-895-320** or 0586-210-331) daily from 8am to 1pm, Monday through Thursday from 8am to 1pm and 3 to 9pm, Friday through Sunday from 8am to 1pm and 3 to 10pm.

EXPLORING THE PORT

Most of the interesting bits of Livorno are within the old **Porto Mediceo** part of town (laid out by Florentine architect Bernardo Buonatlenti in 1567 on behalf of the Medici), still surrounded by its five-sided **Fosso Reale canal.** The canal is bridged in the east by an enormous vault called the Voltone, better known today as the huge rectangular **Piazza della Repubblica,** off the north of which you can see the **Fortezza Nuova,** which today is home to the city's most popular, if somewhat downtrodden, public park (open daily 10am–7pm).

Via Grande leads west from Piazza della Repubblica, passing **Via Madonna** on the right, with its three baroque facades (no churches, just the facades) before spilling into Piazza Grande. The **Duomo** here, laid out in 1587, had to be almost entirely reconstructed after World War II bombing. The piazza used to be much longer, but a modern building has separated it from what's now Largo Municipio to the north, where you'll find the bell tower and double stairs of the 1720 **Palazzo Municipio** and, to the left, the 17th-century **Palazzo di Camera.**

Follow Via San Marco past a glassy school built into the rubble of a bombed-out palazzo to see the facade of the former **Teatro di San Marco,** where the Italian Communist Party was founded in 1921. Heading west toward the harbor is a bombed-out district with the church of **San Ferdinando** standing forlornly in the middle.

On the water is the **Fortezza Vecchia,** designed by Antonio da Sangallo (1521–34) and built into a 1377 Pisan fort with the stump of the 11th-century **Torre Matilda** poking perkily above it and hiding a Roman *castrum* in its bowels. The road along the harbor gives a good glimpse into the life of a still very much alive and functioning seaport, and where it hits the other end of Via Grande coming down from the Duomo is Livorno's prize sight, the mannerist **Monumento dei Quattro Mori** ⚜ (1623–26). It's the masterpiece of Giambologna's student Pietro Tacca and is much more famous for the four bronze Moorish slaves lunging and twisting in their bonds than the statue of Ferdinando I above them.

South of the old city, Livorno's modern art collections were consolidated in 1994 at the **Museo Civico Giovanni Fattori.** It's housed in the Villa Mimbelli, which is surrounded by a public park on Via San Jacopo in Acquaviva (© **0586-808-001**). The villa is a trip, designed by Liberty architect Vincenzo Micheli in 1865 for a local businessman; its sumptuous restored interior contains quite an eclectic grab bag of styles. The museum is almost entirely dedicated to the only Tuscan art movement of note over the past several hundred years, the Macchiaioli, whose painters were interested in the way a viewer perceived the marks of light and color on a painting and covered canvases with their own take on French Impressionism. The museum is dedicated to one of the Macchiaioli's greatest talents and Livorno native son, Giovanni Fattori, whose work spanned the 1860s to 1908. Admission is 4€ ($4.60) adults, or 2.50€ ($2.90) for students, children, and anyone who happens to have an FS train ticket less than 3 days old. The museum is open Tuesday through Sunday from 10am to 1pm and 4 to 7pm. You can grab bus no. 1, 3, or 8 out in this direction.

WHERE TO STAY

Hotel Europa   The tiny rooms here are 1970s-ish, even if they have been entirely redone in the past 10 years. The beds are firm, there's blue carpeting on everything (even the doors), and the modern furniture is pleasant—built-in desks and light wood armoires with smoked-glass doors. The four largest (that's a relative term) even come with minibars and safes. This remains one of the cleanest and most pleasant midrange hotels in town.

Via dell'Angiolo 23 (off Via Grande, 2 blocks east of the Duomo), 57123 Livorno. ☎ **0586-888-581.** Fax 0586-880-085. www.hoteleuropalivorno.it. 24 units. 80€ ($92) double; 90€ ($104) triple. Breakfast included. AE, DC, MC, V. Parking in nearby garage 5€ ($5.75). Bus: 1, 5, 8r, or 18. **Amenities:** Concierge; tour desk; courtesy car; limited room service; laundry service; dry cleaning. *In room:* A/C in some units, TV, hair dryer in most units.

Hotel Gran Duca   Overlooking the harbor and Pietro Tacca's Monument of the Four Moors, the Gran Duca is the nicest hotel in the center of town. Most accommodations are medium to small, with unassuming but comfortable furniture, and some rooms have futons that fold out to sleep up to four. The proprietors are in the process of overhauling the bathrooms and replacing the old cranky toilets (there are 83 cranky toilets, so this has taken them two editions of the guide so far, and they're still at it!). The rooms along the front have small terraces so you can sit and watch the shipping trade at your feet.

Piazza Micheli 16–18 (on the port at the end of Via Grande), 57123 Livorno. ☎ **0586-891-024.** Fax 0586-891-153. www.granduca.it. 83 units. 124€ ($143) double; 158€ ($181) triple; 187€ ($215) quad. Breakfast included. AE, DC, MC, V. Parking 13€ ($15) in garage. Bus: 1, 5, 8r, or 18. **Amenities:** Restaurant; American bar; compact health club; oversize Jacuzzi; sauna; concierge; tour desk; car-rental desk; limited room service; massages; babysitting; laundry service; same-day dry cleaning. *In room:* A/C, TV, minibar, hair dryer, safe in some units.

WHERE TO DINE

If you don't like seafood, you've come to the wrong town. Livorno's king of all seafood dishes is *cacciucco,* a poor man's soup of shellfish, squid, mollusks, fish, prawns, and other fruits of the sea in a tomato soup base spiked with hot peppers, garlic, and red wine, poured over stale bread.

Antico Moro LIVORNESE SEAFOOD   The place is sea shanty meets trattoria, with chianti flasks hanging from the wood ceiling beams, a postcard-clad bar, and various crustaceans nailed to the walls. The *antipasto mare* of shellfish and squid is brought out almost automatically, and you can follow it with *spaghetti alle vongole* (with clams) or *penne al favolo* (pasta in a slightly spicy tomato sauce made with minced shellfish and garnished with a scampi claw). Just two veal dishes sit lonely on the "meat" side of the menu—this is Livorno, after all—but there's a school of fishy secondi, from *fritto* (fried) and *griglia* (grilled) *misti* of various swimming things to *aragoste* (small lobsters) or any one of the daily catches cooked the way you like it. The *torta di pesca* (layers of spongecake, cream, and peach compote) is a particularly good dessert.

Via Bartelloni 59 (an alleyway near market). ℂ **0586-884-659.** Reservations recommended. Primi 7€–7.50€ ($8.05–$8.65); secondi 10€–20€ ($12–$23). AE, MC, V. Thurs–Sat and Mon–Tues 7:30–11pm; Sun and holidays noon–2:30pm and 7:30–11pm. Closed Sun lunch in summer and Aug 24–Sept 7. Bus: 1.

La Chiave ⚘ INVENTIVE TUSCAN & SEAFOOD   Along the moat surrounding the Fortezza Nuova, Livorno's finest restaurant has the air of a private club. Rough brick arches blend with smoothly modern white plaster walls, with Macchiaioli-style paintings and R&B music in the background. The menu changes biweekly and is good for all tastes, balancing the fruits of the sea (such as *riso con scampi al profumo di basilico,* risotto with shrimp, and the fish of the day cooked with an olive paste and pine nuts) with the fruit of the land *(gnocchi con gorgonzola e mela)*—the chopped walnuts and apple slices cut through the musky, heavy bitterness of the Gorgonzola—and *filetto di manzo in salso di capperi e cognac* (beef filet cooked with capers and cognac).

Scali delle Cantine 52 (off Piazza Garibaldi). ℂ **0586-888-609.** Reservations strongly recommended. Primi 8€–9€ ($9.20–$10); secondi 13€–21€ ($15–$24). AE, DC, MC, V. Thurs–Tues 8–10pm. Closed Aug. Bus: 1.

Trattoria il Sottomarino ⚘ LIVORNESE SEAFOOD   "The Submarine" is a die-hard nautical joint with model ships, naval paintings, and a board of ridiculously complicated sailing knots on the walls. The relentlessly friendly waiters serve a no-excuses selection of Livornese seafood, and the place doesn't start swinging until late—after 9:30pm or so. You could order the *riso nero sulle seppie* (risotto with squid blackened with their ink), followed by a mixed seafood fry of "the fish you see in the window." But, everybody flocks here for the spicy *cacciucco di mamma Vinicia,* so big as to make a full meal accompanied by nothing other than your basket of bread.

Via Terrazzini 48 (off Piazza della Repubblica). ℂ **0586-887-025.** Reservations recommended. Primi 7.50€ ($8.65); secondi 10€–16€ ($12–$18). No credit cards. Wed–Sun noon–3pm and 7:30–11pm. Closed July 4–Aug 7. Bus: 1.

EXPLORING THE COAST SOUTH OF LIVORNO

Although Livorno's tourist office has been trying valiantly to sell the idea that the stretch of coast south of it is an "Etruscan Riviera," few of the beaches are worthy, and those that are tend to teem with Italian vacationers in summer. The old Roman Via Aurelia SS1 down the coast has become a highway in some places and passes **Castiglioncello,** a popular resort town with a good pay beach at **Quercetano. Vada** is a modern center with passable sand, and **Marina di Cécina** has some good stretches of free sand.

Another 10km (6 miles) farther down the road, just south of the turnoff for **Bólgheri** village (known for its dry white and rosé wines, especially the Cabernet Sassicaia), is the right turn into the **Rifugio Faunisitco di Bólgheri** ⚘ (ℂ **0565-224-361,** reachable Mon–Fri 10am–noon and 3–7pm, Sat 10am–noon), Italy's first nature preserve, established when the land was deeded by its nature-loving owner to the World Wildlife Fund in 1962. Its 22 sq. km (8 sq. miles) of shoreline, marshland, and wooded areas constitute a microcosm of the Maremma region, one of the best places to glimpse native fauna and flora. Alas, to enjoy it you must reserve at the number above or by stopping by the Vigli Urbani office of **Castagneto Carducci** about 10km (6 miles) south on the SS329 byroad (ℂ **0565-777-125**). Only 20 people at a time are allowed into the park for 3-hour escorted visits at specific entry times: Fridays and Saturdays at 9am and again at 2pm. The cost is 5€ ($5.75) for adults, 3€ ($3.45) for kids under 14.

Back on the coastal road, you'll find that **Marina di Bibbona** has plenty of sand to go around, and if you don't mind crowds the busy and trendy resort of

San Vincenzo has even longer swaths of quality beach. Ancient **Pupolonia,** on its promontory beyond some excellent beaches, was an important center in the Etruscan world. On sunny days you get a great coastal view from its castle (open daily 9:30am–12:30pm and 2:30pm–dusk), and the town still retains bits of the walls the Etruscans built. The best archaeological materials discovered in the surrounding tombs were carted off to Florence, but you can still visit the tombs in the **Necropolis of Baratti/Populónia (San Cerbone)** off the road into town (✆ **0565-29-002;** www.parchivaldicornia.it/italiano/parcobp.htm). They're open Tuesday through Friday from 10am to 4pm, Saturday and Sunday from 9am to 2pm (open until sunset in spring, until 8pm in summer). At the south end of this promontory sits **Piombino,** a modern port most popular among travelers taking the ferry to Elba.

3 Elba: Tuscany's Island Resort

12km (7 miles) off the coast at Piombino; 86km (53 miles) S of Livorno; 179km (111 miles) SW of Florence; 231km (143 miles) NW of Rome

Elba is a proletarian resort, visited mainly by middle-class Italian families and German tourists, who together fill just about every available inch of hotel and camping space in August and September. What Elba lacks in the glamour department, it makes up for in variety. It's Italy's third-largest island, but at about 27km by 18km (17 miles by 11 miles), it's much smaller than Sicily or Sardinia. So while it has a tall mountainous interior speckled with ancient mining villages, the sea is never far away. Coastal fishing and port towns in soft pastels are interspersed with modest sandy beaches.

The Greeks founded the first large-scale settlements here in the 10th century B.C., calling the island *Aethalia* after the Greek word for sparks, a reference to the dozens of forges sailors could see winking throughout the night. The forges were smelting iron ore, one of the hundreds of minerals that make up the fabric of Elba. After an Etruscan interlude, the Romans, calling it *Ilva,* used its raw iron to forge the swords with which they conquered their empire. The island was raided by pirates (including Barbarossa) and split between Italian and Spanish rules until the 18th century, but mining remained at the core of Elban economy for about 3,000 years until the easily accessible iron finally ran out. The last iron mine shut down in 1984.

When would-be emperor of Europe Napoléon Bonaparte was first defeated, he was exiled to Elba to rule as the island's governor. Beginning May 3, 1814, the Corsican general busied himself with revamping the island's economy, infrastructure, and mining system—perhaps out of nation-building habit or merely to keep himself and his 500-man personal guard occupied. Napoléon managed to be a good boy until February 26, 1815, at which point the conquering itch grew too strong and he sailed ashore to begin the famous Hundred Days that ended in his crushing defeat at the Battle of Waterloo. The island is proud to have had, no matter how briefly, a resident of such considerable note, and preserves his two villas and various other mementos of the Napoleonic era.

ESSENTIALS
GETTING THERE   The easiest way to get to the island is by **ferry from Piombino** to Portoferraio, Elba's capital. In August and throughout the high season, it's best to reserve, especially if you're taking a car over. There are two major ferry companies, **Toremar** (✆ **199-123-1990,** or 565-31-100 in Piombino, 0565-918-080 in Portoferraio; www.toremar.it) and **Moby Lines,** also

known as **NAV.AR.MA** (© 0565-225-211 or 0565-221-212 in Piombino, 0565-914-133 in Portoferraio; www.mobylines.it). Both run regular ferries (*traghetto* or *nave*) that take about an hour. Toremar also offers slightly faster (40 min.) but almost twice as expensive hydrofoils *(aliscafo)* on which you can't take a car. Toremar has the most ferry runs daily, especially off season, with hourly runs April through August and six to eight daily in winter. Year-round, there are three or four hydrofoils daily to Cavo, on Elba's northeast coast, plus three to four direct to Portoferraio in summer only. You can compare both companies' schedules quickly and easily at www.traghetti.com.

You'll find uncrowded **ticket offices** on the right side of the road as you approach Piombino, more crowded offices just before the port on the right, and packed offices at the port itself (all well sign-posted). One-way ferry tickets are 5.64€ to 7.54€ ($6.50–$8.65), per passenger including tax (the price depends on the period). Cars with one person in them cost 27€ ($31).

Hydrofoils cost 6.74€ to 9.84€ ($7.75–$11) per passenger to Portoferraio or 5.24€ ($6) to Cavo. You can **park** at a number of garages and lots at the Piombino docks for 8€ to 12€ ($9.20–$14) per day.

Toremar's office in Portoferraio is at Calata Italia 23; Moby Lines' Portoferraio office is at Via Ninci 1. Toremar also runs boats to Elba's other ports (Cavo, Rio Marina, and Porto Azzuro) as well as a longer-haul **ferry from Livorno** to Elba once daily (plus an extra Sat run) from May 24 to September 14 that calls on Capraia (and sometimes also Gorgonza) along the way. Toremar in Livorno is at the Porto Mediceo (© **0586-896-113**).

GETTING AROUND Drivers will have no problem, as the island's road system is quite good. If you want to rent a car on Elba, contact **Hertz,** Viale Elba 4 (© **0565-917-148;** www.hertz.com); **Maggiore,** Calata Italia 8 (© 0565-930-222 or 0565-903-212; www.maggiore.it); or **Happy Rent,** Viale Elba 5 (© **0565-914-665;** www.renthappy.it).

To rent a scooter or bike—not a bad way to tool around—try these places in Portoferraio: **BW's Racing,** Via Manganaro 15 (© **0565-930-491;** www.bwsrent.com) or **Two Wheels Network,** Viale Elba 32 (© **0565-914-666**). Rates vary widely depending on season, but expect scooters to run 38€–49€ ($44–$56) per day and bikes and mountain bikes starting at 8€ ($9.20).

Elba is also blessed with an excellent **bus** network run by ATL (© **0565-914-392**). Buses leave Portoferraio from the main terminal at Viale Elba 20 in the new town (turn right out of the tourist office, then right again at the main street), servicing just about every town on the island. (If you know the name of a beach between villages where you want to be let off, tell the driver.) You can **store your bags** at the bus station for 1.30€ ($1.50) per bag per day. It's open daily: summer from 8am to 8pm and winter from 7:40am to 1:20pm and 4 to 6:05pm.

VISITOR INFORMATION Elba's main **tourist office** is in Portoferraio's new town at the ferry dock, Calata Italia 26, up the stairs (© **0565-914-671;** fax 0565-916-350; www.arcipelago.turismo.toscana.it; open Mon–Sat 8am–2pm and 3–6pm; in summer also sometimes Sun 8am–2pm). Two private websites are loaded with info and pictures (and paid for by local businesses, so take it all with a grain of salt): **www.elbacom.it,** mostly in Italian but with spiffy music; and **www.elbatuttanatura.com,** put up by an Elban hotel devoted to enjoying the natural wonders of the island (with a downloadable newsletter in English).

For help in the hotel hunt, head to the **Associazione Albergatori Isola d'Elba,** Calata Italia 20 (© **800-903-532** toll-free in Italy or 0565-914-754; fax

Elba

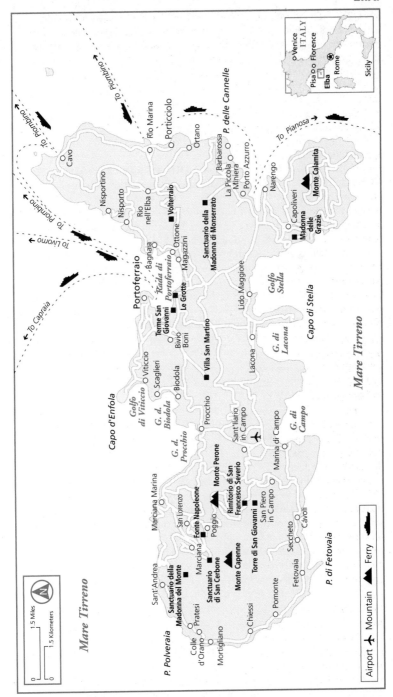

0565-917-865; www.albergatorielbani.it; open Mon–Fri 9am–1pm and 3–7pm, Sat 9:30am–12:30pm). Though it isn't an official body, its network does include most hotels on the island, and it'll be happy to give you a catalog and price list.

FESTIVALS & MARKETS   Elba puts on a **wine festival** the last week of July at Le Ghiaie beach behind Portoferraio. During the July and August high season, every town puts on some sort of **small** *festa;* in Marciana Alta, it's an August **medieval pageant** that robes the locals in costume and fills the streets with artisans offering old-fashioned crafts (call ⓒ **0565-901-215** for info). Portoferraio's weekly **Friday market** is held on Viale Zambelli.

TOURING THE ISLAND
NAPOLEON & MORE IN & AROUND PORTOFERRAIO
PORTOFERRAIO   Founded in 1548 by Medici grand duke Cosimo I, Portoferraio is Elba's capital and largest city. Ferries dock in the city's newer half to the west, but its core is still an old fishing village, a U-shaped amphitheater of streets terracing up the rocky promontory. It was guarded in Medici days by two massive fortresses, the **Forte Falcone** and the **Forte Stella.** You can explore the rambling battlements of both for free; the Forte Falcone to the west is open daily from 9am to 8pm (until midnight July–Aug); the Forte Stella is open daily from 9am to 8pm.

The old entrance to the city is through **Porta al Mare** at the base of Portoferraio's "U." In the town's upper reaches is the house where Napoléon lived in exile for 9 months: The **Villa dei Mulini** (ⓒ **0565-915-846**) doesn't excite much, but you do get to wander through the emperor's apartments and see the books he kept in his study. March through October, it's open Monday through Saturday from 9am to 7pm and Sunday from 9am to 1pm (it sometimes keeps longer hours in summer). Admission is 3€ ($3.45), though the 5€ ($5.75) cumulative ticket also gets you into Napoléon's summer villa just outside Portoferraio (see below); you have 3 days to use the other half of the ticket. There's a rocky little beach, **Le Viste,** signposted down the backside of the sheer cliff behind the villa. On your way back down toward the docks, stop off at the **Chiesa della Misericordia** (ⓒ **0565-914-009**) or **Santissimo Sacramento** (no phone)—both have copies of Napoléon's death mask.

NEAR PORTOFERRAIO   Cut through the edge of Portoferraio's new town to the north shore, past **Le Ghiaie,** Portoferraio's only real (but not great) beach. Farther beyond are better beaches at **Acquaviva, Sanzone,** and **Viticcio.** Barely connected to the rest of the island out here is the large green hump of **Capo d'Enfola,** closed to cars and a lovely place to take an easy hike.

South of Portoferraio, the road divides at Bivio Boni to head east and west. A short trip west (right) then off the main road, following the signs, will lead you to the entrance to the **Villa San Martino** ✦ (ⓒ **0565-914-688**), the more interesting of the two villas Napoléon left on the island. The pretentious neoclassical facade wasn't the ex-emperor's idea—his step-nephew had it constructed years after his death to honor him with its giant *N*'s all over. Head to the left to be escorted up a path to Napoléon's more modest cottage—for the former ruler of half the known world, he had surprisingly simple tastes. The only extravagance is the Egyptian Room, celebrating his most successful campaign with *trompe l'oeil* desert scenes glimpsed between hieroglyphic-painted walls and columns. For hours and admission, see the Villa dei Mulini under Portoferraio, above.

A left (east) at Bivio Boni will take you past the **Terme San Giovanni** (ⓒ **0565-914-680;** www.termelbane.com), offering spa treatments such as sulfurous mud

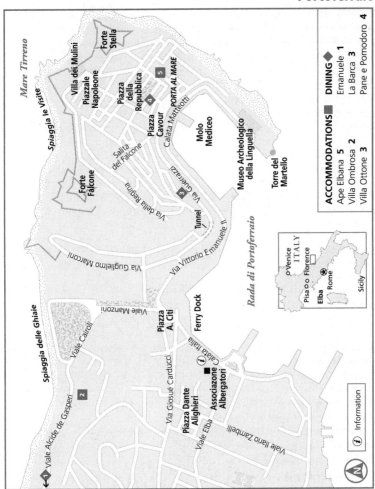

ACCOMMODATIONS ■
Ape Elbana **5**
Villa Ombrosa **2**
Villa Ottone **3**

DINING ◆
Emanuele **1**
La Barca **3**
Pane e Pomodoro **4**

Information

baths, massages, and seaweed body wraps for 8€ to 50€ ($9.20–$58). Just beyond are the ruins of a Roman villa overlooking Portoferraio's bay. Little remains of **Le Grotte** ⚐, but the crumbling walls of the now-buried rooms and patches of mosaic with their stunning bay view are rather romantic. It's open summer only daily from 9am to 6:30pm; admission is free.

You'll find a small beach at **Magazzini,** and a bit farther along is the turnoff for a dirt road detour to the 14th-century **Santo Stefano,** a pretty little Pisan Romanesque church perched on a small olive-planted hilltop. The main road leads north to the fine beaches at **Ottone** and **Bagnaia.**

EASTERN & WESTERN ELBA
On eastern Elba, visit the old Spanish capital of **Porto Azzurro,** with a 1603 fortress built so well they're still using it as a prison. Today, the fortified Spanish port is one of the island's major resort cities, but you can catch a whiff of the past in the shop fronts and bustle of the **old quarter** around Via d'Alarcon.

From Porto Azzurro, you can see the fortified Capo Focardo across the bay, with the nice resort beach of **Narengo** leading up to it.

South of Porto Azzurro lies eastern Elba's most picturesque town, the ancient mountainside village of **Capoliveri** ☆. It's full of twisty old streets, a large terracelike main **Piazza Matteotti,** and cavernlike bars like the **Enoteca Elba,** on the piazza's edge (© **0565-968-707**), where you can quaff Elba's wines by the glass until 2 or 3am. In fact, the town is known for its nightlife, as well as for its traditional Thursday market.

On western Elba, **Marciana** ☆, the island's oldest settlement, is the most attractive and the central base for exploring western Elba. It's a picturesque and very steep little town made of minuscule tree-shaded piazze and winding stepped-stone streets stacked atop one another. Aside from relaxing with a view, you can get in some light culture by popping into the small prehistoric and Roman collections of the **Museo Archeologico** (© **0565-901-215;** 2€/$2.30 admission; open Apr–Sept daily 9:30am–12:30pm and 3:30–7:30pm).

WHERE TO STAY

Elba is a resort island, chock-full of resort hotels. To find the perfect hotel to fit your needs, you can call, fax, or drop by the **Associazione Albergatori** office (see "Essentials," above).

Seasons on the island have seemingly infinite gradations. The highest season is August, when the island is packed with vacationing Italians and you'll find the highest prices and most hotels booked months in advance (and at most places at least half pension required). The second most crowded and expensive seasons are Easter and Christmas, again often with half pension obligatory. Then come various midseasons in June, July, late spring, and early fall. The lowest season is winter, when most places are closed but those that stay open often offer rack rates. To simplify matters, the prices below lump together the higher seasons and the lowest into ranges not including pension, with any period wherein pension is required quoted separately.

Campers will find plenty to satisfy them. Ask at the tourist office for a color catalog of campgrounds because sacking out on most beaches is frowned on, and you'll often get shooed away.

IN PORTOFERRAIO

Ape Elbana   One of the island's oldest inns, the Elban Bee is very simple but sits on the main square in Portoferraio's old town—best for those who didn't come exclusively for a beach vacation. The basic furniture is a bit worn, but the beds are firm, the tile floors clean, and the price as good as you're going to find, especially off season. Twelve of the rooms even have air-conditioning. Some look over the main piazza, while others spread their vista across the rooftops.

Salita Cosimo de' Medici 2 (in the center of the old town, on Piazza della Repubblica), 57037 Portoferraio (LI). © **0565-914-245.** Fax 0565-945-985. apelbana@elba2000.it. 24 units. Low season 60€–70€ ($69–$81) double; high season 80€–90€ ($92–$104) double; Aug 1–31 125€ ($144) double with half pension. Rates include breakfast. MC, V. Free parking on piazza. **Amenities:** Restaurant (Apr–Oct); limited room service (breakfast and bar). *In room:* A/C and TV in 12 units, dataport, hair dryer.

Villa Ombrosa   On the north shore behind Portoferraio, off Le Ghaie beach, the Ombrosa is one of the best all-around places in Portoferraio itself. A renovation completed in 1999 prettied both the public areas and the well-kept guest rooms. The furnishings and bathrooms vary from room to room, and while a few rooms push the small side of medium, most have plenty of space—they even have some rooms with a communicating door you can turn into a two-room family suite. Try by all means to get a sea-view room, most of which come with a balcony (a 4€–13€/$4.60–$15 supplement). Rates include a beach umbrella and lounge chairs. Half- and full-board options are available.

Via A. de Gasperi 3, 57037 Portoferraio, Elba (LI). ℂ **0565-914-363.** Fax 0565-915-672. www.villaombrosa.it. 38 units. Low season 69€–99€ ($79–$114) double; shoulder season 80€–138€ ($92–$159) double; high season 129€–139€ ($148–$160) double with half pension. Rates include breakfast. MC, V. Free parking. **Amenities:** Restaurant; concierge; tour desk; 24-hr. room service (bar); babysitting; laundry service. *In room:* TV, hair dryer.

Villa Ottone 🏨🏨   This genteel hotel's showpiece is a gorgeous 19th-century villa overlooking the bay, with basic furnishings but frescoed ceilings (in most rooms) and fantastic views from the front rooms. But the 1970s main building is also fine, renovated between 1997 and 1998 to add wicker units to rooms on the lower floors and 19th-century–style furnishings and Jacuzzi shower/bathtub combos to the nicer (and pricier) third-floor accommodations. All enjoy small terraces with at least a lateral sea view. Sit in the frescoed bar at the Villa's porch above the private beach and watch the sun set over Portoferraio across the waters. The hotel requires a minimum stay of 3 days and half pension, and rates are highly variable depending on the season, the view, and whether you can control the air-conditioning in your own room or whether, as in the original villa, it's centralized and hence not all that chilling.

Loc. Ottone (about 15–20 min. around the bay from Portoferraio), 57037 Portoferraio, Elba (LI). ℂ **0565-933-042.** Fax 0565-933-257. www.villaottone.com. 75 units. Apr 18–May31 and Sept 13–Oct 12 160€–232€ ($184–$267) double, 280€–330€ ($322–$380) suite; Jun 1–Jun 21 and Aug 30–Sept 12 186€–260€ ($214–$299) double, 320€–380€ ($368–$437) suite; Jun 22–Aug 2 and Aug 23–Aug 30 284€–314€ ($327–$361) double, 360€–460€ ($414–$529) suite. All rates include half pension. AE, DC, MC, V. Free parking. Closed Oct–Apr. **Amenities:** Restaurant; poolside lunch grill; 3 bars; small pool with bay view; golf (discount on course 3km/2 miles away); tennis court; watersports equipment; free bikes; car-rental desk; limited room service; babysitting; laundry service; dry cleaning. *In room:* A/C, TV, dataport, minibar, hair dryer on request, safe in some units.

IN MARCIANA

Bellavista 🏨 *(Finds)*   This is a secluded, semi-isolated oasis a 20-minute drive beyond Marciana, set above one of Elba's trendier, quieter villages. The family-run Bellavista is aptly named: Its position at the isthmus of a short peninsula gives most of the accommodations a "beautiful view" of the sea in three directions, and on clear days you can see the whole of the Tuscan coast, Gorgona, Capraia, and Corsica from many windows and the shared terrace. Most rooms still sport uninspired furnishings (though they were replacing those at press time) and cool tile flooring, but they have just finished restructuring the lower floor with new bathrooms and furniture, along with tiny terraces that overlook the owners' modest vineyards and gardens to the infant chestnut grove and wooded Sant'Andrea spur and blue sea beyond. Trails lead into these woods, down to the little Sant'Andrea beach in one direction, or to secluded shoals in the other. Only two rooms are without views.

Sant'Andrea, 57030 Marciana, Elba (LI). ℂ **0565-908-015.** Fax 0565-908-079. www.hotel-bellavista.it. 10 units. Low season 58€–64€ ($67–$74) double; high season 72€–90€ ($83–$104) double. Half pension (10€–24€/$12–$27 depending on the season) available. Small discounts for longer stays. Rates include breakfast. MC, V. Free parking. Closed 1 month sometime between Dec and Feb. **Amenities:** Restaurant; children's center; concierge; tour desk; courtesy car (from bus stop; call). *In room:* TV in most units (soon to be in all), minibar, hair dryer, safe.

WHERE TO DINE
IN & NEAR PORTOFERRAIO

When all I want is a quick sandwich in a split focaccia or a simple *tavola calda* dish such as lasagne, I stop by unpretentious **Pane e Pomodoro,** on Via Cavalieri di Vittorio Veneto in Portoferraio between the town gate and main square (C **0565-917-121**), a simple bar with a small glassed-in veranda off the side should you want to sit; panini go for about 2€/$2.90, main dishes and pizza for 4.50€ to 7€ ($5.20–$8.05).

Emanuele ★★ ELBAN/SEAFOOD   Behind a beach-bum bar facade hides what most Italian gastronomic critics agree is the best dining on Elba. Snuggled into the beach at the Enfola headland, friendly family-run Emanuele excels at marrying the catch of the day and pick of the crustaceans with fresh pastas and seasonal vegetables. Reserve ahead for one of a few tables on the pocket-size courtyard out back, strewn with gravel and shaded by pine trees and umbrellas just feet from the waves lapping at the pebble beach. The *gaganelli branzino e verdure* (sea bass scented with rosemary and tossed with zucchini, carrots, oil, and a bit of peperoncino) is outstanding, as is the simple *tagliolini bottarga e carciofi* (thin pasta strands twirled with grated tuna roe and artichoke hearts). For a secondo, have them grill or oven-roast the sea bream, grouper, or perch pulled in by local fishermen that morning, or try the island specialty *totani alla diavola* (small cuttlefish cooked up with oil and hot peppers). Save room for the *torta di mele* (warm caramelized apple torte drizzled with sweetened cream).

Loc. Enfola (15 min. west of Portoferraio along coast). C **0565-939-003.** Reservations highly recommended. Primi 7€–12€ ($8.05–$14); secondi 9.50€–18€ ($11–$21); fixed-price menu without wine 25€ ($29). MC, V. Daily noon–3:30pm and 7:30–11pm. Closed mid-Oct to Easter and Wed until June 15.

La Barca ELBAN   "The Boat" is one of Portoferraio's best restaurants. It sees its fair share of tourism but remains a place locals return to for well-prepared fish dishes and a friendly atmosphere. You can dine alfresco under an awning on the quiet street out front or inside surrounded by island art and with a fresh tulip on your table. The *gnocchi all'Elbana* is a good preparation of the potato dumpling pasta with a mix of tomato sauce and pesto, while the *spaghetti alla bottarga* is more traditional—thin spaghetti in butter with dried tuna eggs grated over it. For a secondo, try the catch of the day baked in the oven (the *spigola,* or sea bass, is good) or the *stoccafisso con patate* (dried cod cooked with potatoes, onions, and parsley).

Via Guerrazzi 60–62, Portoferraio (in the old city, a block up from the dock on the landward arm of the "U"). C **0565-918-036.** Reservations strongly recommended. Primi 7.50€–13€ ($8.65–$14); secondi 8€–16€ ($9.20–$18). AE, MC, V. Thurs–Tues 12:30–2pm and 7:30–10pm (June to mid-Sept, dinner is served daily). Closed mid-Jan to mid-Feb.

4 The Maremma: Tuscany's Deep South

The **Maremma** stretches along Tuscany's coast from Cecina to Monte Argentario and extends inward along mostly flat land toward the mountainous interior. The Maremma was once the heartbeat of the Etruscan world and preserves scant remains of some of their most important cities and miles of the mysterious sunken roads they carved more than 4m (12 ft.) into the tufa. The complex canal and drainage system built by those ancient Tuscans allowed them to turn the marshy flatlands into a breadbasket.

The conquering Romans, though, weren't as able as landscape administrators, and when the neglected drainage system broke down, marshes and bogland swamped the region and brought with them the malaria mosquito. Grand Duke Leopold I was the first to seriously attempt a large-scale reclamation of the land in 1828, and his canals still form an important part of the drainage network, but it wasn't until malaria was defeated here in the 1950s that the land became livable again.

Today, the Maremma puts forth a mixed image. It's part rugged new colony, where man has reconquered the land and cowboys called *butteri* watch over herds of white oxen. It's also part relic of the ancient past, where centuries of relative isolation have allowed Etruscan ruins and towns to decay romantically. You'll encounter very few other tourists as you explore archaic hill towns and grassy, mounded Etruscan tombs.

ESSENTIALS

GETTING AROUND   By Train   The slowest trains on the main **Rome–Pisa** line stop at Follonica, Grosseto, Albarese, and Ortobello (for Monte Argentario). The faster ones pause at Grosseto and Ortobello, but IC trains take the time to hit only Grosseto. There's also a train from **Florence** that passes through **Siena** on its way to Grosseto and Ortobello.

By Bus   Maremma's **RAMA** bus network (℃ **0564/454-169**) runs from Grosseto to Florence, Siena, Marina di Grosseto, Castiglione, Alberese, Follonica, Scansano, and Massa Marittima. It also services Ortobello to Monte Argentario's main towns.

EXPLORING THE MAREMMA

GROSSETO   The Maremma's capital isn't a promising introduction to the region. Grosseto certainly doesn't invite lingering, but the region's website, **www. gol.grosseto.it**, offers a few options for visitors. The tourist office is at Via Monterosa 206 (℃ **0564/462-611;** fax 0564/454-606; www.grosseto.turismo.toscana. it; open Mon–Fri 8:30am–1:30pm and 3–6pm, Sat 8:30am–12:30pm). Grosseto's a fairly scuzzy burg, with the highest drug-use rate per capita in Italy. I suggest taking a quick gander at its few worthwhile sights in the old center and moving on. The main sight is the **Museo Civico Archeologico e d'Arte della Maremma,** Piazza Baccarini 3 (℃ **0564-488-752;** open Tues–Sun: May–Oct 10am–1pm and 5–8pm; Nov–Feb 9am–1pm, plus 4:30–7pm Sat and Sun; Mar–Apr 9:30am–1pm and 4:30–7pm). The Maremma is particularly rich in prehistoric, Etruscan, and Roman remains, and this museum's archaeological collections bring together almost all the major finds from across the province. Upstairs is a small painting collection from local churches. The collection's prima donna is a 13th-century *Last Judgment* by Guido da Siena. Admission is 5€ ($5.75).

HITTING THE BEACH   Along the southern stretch of Tuscany's coast are several beaches and resorts. **Follónica** represents the huge down-market brand of beach with lots of city folk who've dashed to the shore for the day. There's lots of sand, but little of it is special. From here you can turn 19km (12 miles) inland to **Massa Marittima** (see chapter 5). **Punta Ala** is a posh spot, with luxury hotels and a well-heeled vacationing crowd sunning on the modern bay side. **Castiglione della Pescaia** ⚓ is more middle-of-the-road and perhaps the best all-around. The beach isn't great but passable, the prices are lower, and it has only a touch of the resort air about it, relying instead on an old fishing village atmosphere and the ancient old town up on the hill as attractions. **Marina di Grosseto** is a bland town, but the beach is clean and surprisingly good.

Tuscany's most southerly point is along the coast at the resort peninsula of **Monte Argentario** 🗗. The city of Ortobello, sitting in the middle of a lagoon between Monte Argentario and the mainland, serves as the gateway to L'Argentario. The lagoon surrounding Ortobello is partly protected by the World Wildlife Fund (WWF) as a natural oasis called the **Laguna di Ortobello** (© **0564-820-297**), which together with the WWF nature reserve **Lago di Burano** (© **0564-898-829**), a bit farther down the main coast, comprises Italy's most important birding center, where an estimated 200 of the 450 species that call the country home live or pass through every year. Both are open September through April by guided visit only: Ortobello, Thursday through Sunday at 10am and 2pm; and Burano, Sundays between 10am and 3pm.

HIKING IN THE MOUNTAINS OF THE LITTLE BIRD   Just 15 kilometers (9 miles) southwest of Grosseto, a 15km stretch of hilly coastline is protected as the **Parco Naturale della Maremma** 🗗 (www.parco-maremma.it or www.parks.it/parco.maremma). It's called "one of the last earthly paradises in Italy" and incorporates the **Monti dell'Uccellina** capped by crumbling medieval towers. The "Mountains of the Little Bird" are actually hills some 390m (1,300 ft.) high, covered with the almost unbroken carpet of an umbrella pine forest, though you'll also find ilex, oak, elms, juniper, and the occasional dwarf palm, Italy's only native-growing palm tree. Rustling around in the myrtle and juniper *macchia* brush are families of Italy's small native wild boar, herds of roe deer, foxes, crested porcupines, and the occasional feral cat. Larger critters include a famous pack of semiwild horses and long-horned white cattle, both of which are wrangled by the Maremma's famous but dwindling breed of cowboy, the *butteri.* Seaside, there are wondrous stretches of sand dune beaches in the center, rising to a rocky cliff toward the south and petering into marshy bog land to the north. The latter is the park's best bird-watching area, where you might even spot flamingos, peregrine falcons, and osprey among the scores of migratory and water birds that spend time here.

The park entrance is at **Alberese** (© **0564-407-098**), sight of the annual August *butteri* rodeo. An hourly bus takes you from Alberese into the closed-to-traffic park and drops you off at the trailheads. The park office's map is pretty bad; buy an Instituto Geografico Militare 1:25,000 map or something similar in town. The path marked STRADA DEGLI OLIVI leads straight to the beach. Trail 1 is 6km (4 miles) in its entirety and involves the most rugged, but most rewarding, climbing; it leads past the evocative ruins of the 11th-century San Rabano abbey. Trail 2 runs for 5km (3 miles) past abandoned medieval watchtowers toward the rocky southern coast with the best vistas of the pine forests along the way. Trail 3 follows 8km (5 miles) of sandy pine woods and visits caves once inhabited by prehistoric man. Trail 4 is 11km (7 miles) and takes you along cliffs, down on the coast, and up hills. They also offer guided visits by foot, canoe, or horseback, as well as (pricey) nighttime excursions. The park is open Wednesday, Saturday, and Sunday from 7am (9am Oct–June 14) to dusk. Admission ranges from 6€ to 8€ ($6.90–$9.20).

8

Southern Tuscany

The hill towns and valleys south of Siena comprise perhaps Tuscany's most enchanting and downright picturesque region. It's a land of medieval castles guarding narrow road passes, isolated farmhouses sitting atop long, eroded limestone ridges, clusters of cypress and ribbons of plane trees against a bucolic backdrop, and thermal spas enjoyed by both the Medici and the modern proles. The region has a few small patches of forest on the steeper slopes of its river valleys, but most of it has been landscaped to a human scale over thousands of years, turning the low, rolling hills into farmlands and vineyards that produce Tuscany's mightiest red wines.

Southern Tuscany's cities are textbook Italian hill towns. **Chiusi** dwells deep in its Etruscan roots, still remembering a time when King Lars Porsena was one of the few leaders of the Etruscan confederation who had the audacity to take on Rome. Roman settlements like **Montalcino** and **Montepulciano** grew into medieval cities and today produce two of Italy's top red wines, the powerhouse Brunello di Montalcino and the noble Vino Nobile di Montepulciano. And the gemlike village of **Pienza,** famed for its pecorino sheep's cheese, shelters within its tiny ring of walls a Renaissance core of the most perfect proportions and planning.

Much of the area is filled with the expansive and beautiful **Val d'Orcia**—many people's idealized picture of Tuscany because well over half the souvenir-stand postcards and cover shots of coffee-table books with "Tuscany" in the title were snapped here. From many parts of it, especially the zone around Montalcino and Pienza, you can see the broken tooth of the **Rocca d'Orcia.** From the 11th to the 14th century, the castle was a stronghold and strategic watchtower of the Aldobrandeschi clan, formidable toll collectors along the Francigena pilgrim road through these parts. The castle juts from its crag to the south, still keeping an eye on its valley.

EN ROUTE TO MONTALCINO

The SS438 leads 26km (16 miles) from Siena to **Asciano,** a small town still partially girded by its 1351 Sienese walls. The tourist office is at Corso Matteotti 18 (© **0577-719-510** for all sights), open Tuesday through Saturday from 10am to noon and 3 to 6pm, Sunday from 10am to noon.

The 14th-century **Palazzo Corboli,** Corso Matteotti 122, frescoed by Ambrogio Lorenzetti or his school, now houses two museums. The **Museo d'Arte Sacra** contains good early Sienese works; don't miss the *Madonna* by Segna di Bonaventura, a 1410 *Annunciation* carved in wood by Francesco di Valdambrino, and Ambrogio Lorenzetti's *St. Michael* altarpiece. The Etruscan collections were gleaned from tombs discovered in the area and include a couple of nicely painted 3rd- to 5th-century B.C. vases, funerary urns, and the standard pile of pottery bits. The palazzo is open Tuesday through Sunday from 10am to 1pm and 3 to 7pm. Admission is 4.13€ ($4.75) adults, 2.58€ ($2.95) for students and seniors over 65 (yes, the prices are odd, but very precise).

At the **Museo Cassioli,** Via Mameli 36, with a collection of late-19th- and early-20th-century art by a local artist and his son (open by request at the number above). A block and a half up the street, at Corso Matteotti 80, is the **Antica Farmacia Francini Naldi,** a 19th-century pharmacy where you can view the **Roman mosaic floor** in the basement if you ask politely. At the opposite end of the block stands the Romanesque and Gothic **Collegiata,** built of travertine between the 10th and 13th centuries. The interior has, unusually, three apses and a 15th-century Sienese-school crucifix over the altar.

Asciano is surrounded by *biancane,* land formations where erosion has left emerald lawns like toupees atop knobby white hills. These blend to the south with the *crete senese,* a similarly eerie landscape of eroded clay and Jura limestone hillsides with farmhouses perched atop deep washed-out gullies and cypress crowded along sheer ridges. In the center of these weird badlands, accessible by a couple of side roads out of Asciano, the abbey of **Monte Oliveto Maggiore** ☆ (© **0577-707-611** or 0577-707-017; www.ftbcc.it/monteoliveto) is hidden in its own womb of cypress.

Founded in 1313 by a group of wealthy Sienese businessmen who wanted to retire to a contemplative spiritual life, the redbrick monastic complex was built by the early 15th century. The Olivetans were an order trying to restore some of the original simplicity and charity of the Benedictine rule, and the monks cared for victims during the 1340s Black Death outbreak. What draws most casual visitors today is the 36-scene **fresco cycle** by Luca Signorelli and Sodoma, one of the masterpieces of High Renaissance narrative painting and Sodoma's greatest work. When you arrive, pass under the gate tower with its small cafe and walk through the cool woods for about 5 minutes to the bulky brick of the complex. The entrance to the monastery is around to the right, but first pop into the **church** to see some gorgeous choir stalls inlaid by Giovanni da Verona (1505). A doorway, not always open, leads into the *chiostro grande* ☆☆ and puts you right at the frescoes' start. Otherwise, leave the church by the front and enter the Great Cloister through the doorway to your left.

Signorelli started the job of illustrating the *Life of St. Benedict* here in 1497. He finished nine of the scenes before skipping town the next year to work on Orvieto's Duomo. Antonio Bazzi arrived in 1505 and finished the cycle by 1508 in his own inimitable style. Bazzi was known as "Il Sodoma," a derogatory nickname that Vasari suggests was due to Bazzi's predilection for young men. Sodoma was married at least three times, however, and may have had in the neighborhood of 30 children. On the third, or west wall, are the Signorellis. (Scene 20, *Benedict Sending Mauro to France and Placido to Sicily,* is an interlude by Il Riccio.) Scenes 21 to 28, starting with *Fiorenzo's Death,* are by Signorelli (his last work, no. 29, was destroyed when a door was installed). Sodoma did most of the rest of the painting in this part of the monastery, including the grotesques and monotone details on the pilasters between the scenes and two fine separate frescoes: a small *Christ at the Column* and *St. Benedict Confers the Rule on the Olivetans,* both in the passage leading from the church. Monte Oliveto is open daily from 9:15am to noon and 3:15 to 5:45pm (until 5pm from the last Sun in Oct to the last Sun in Mar). Admission is free.

The SS451 leads 9km (6 miles) to the Via Cassia SS2 and **Buonconvento** (tourist info at the museum). Hidden within a ring of industrial suburbs is Buonconvento's medieval core and an excellent small museum of Sienese-school art, the **Museo d'Arte Sacra,** Via Soccini 18 (© **0577-807-181**), with works by Duccio,

> ## *Tips* Val d'Orcia Website
>
> Several of the towns in the Val d'Orcia, including Montalcino, Pienza, and San Quirico d'Orcia, have banded together online at **www.terradivaldorcia. it/Html_eng/SQuirico_eng.htm**.

Sano di Pietro, Andrea di Bartolo, and Matteo di Giovanni. It's open Easter through October Tuesday through Sunday from 10:30am to 1pm and 3 to 7pm, November through Easter Saturday and Sunday from 10:30am to 1pm and 3 to 5pm. Admission is 3.10€ ($3.60). Before leaving town, drop by the 14th-century **Santi Pietro e Paolo,** where you'll see a pair of *Madonna and Child* paintings, one with saints by Pietro di Francesco Orioli and one without by Matteo di Giovanni. Just south of Buonconvento on the right is the turnoff for Montalcino.

1 Montalcino: Home of the Mighty Brunello

42km (25 miles) S of Siena; 112km (67 miles) S of Florence; 190km (118 miles) NW of Rome

Montalcino presents a mighty image on the approach from the valley—a walled town set very high on a tall hill with the spires of medieval buildings sprouting from the middle and a glowering fortress at one end. Up close, the town becomes a much smaller, meeker place, but the precipitous medieval alleyways and stone buildings make it a day-trip delight, and the views of the valleys from which you just ascended are magnificent from this height.

Paleolithic tribes and the Etruscans set up camp here, but it wasn't until the Roman era that a permanent settlement formed. By the Middle Ages, Montalcino was a bustling town and a defensive center for the surrounding farming community. Although it divided itself into four minuscule neighborhood *contrade* after the Sienese model, Montalcino was initially allied to Florence and at odds with its northerly neighbor Siena. After several skirmishes, though, the Sienese took over Montalcino in the 13th century. By 1462, the town had grown large enough to be declared a city, and in 1555 its now-cozy relations with Siena led it to harbor the 700 Sienese families who refused to submit to the Medici when Florence defeated Siena. The exiles set up the defiant "Republic of Siena at Montalcino," which lasted 4 years until the Medici grand dukes finally laid their hands on both the Sienese and Montalcino through treaty. Montalcino's loyalty is honored to this day—their standard-bearer rides in pride of place at the front of Siena's annual pre-Palio parade.

Montalcino's Medici-induced slide into obscurity began to turn around in the 1960s, when the world discovered that the sangiovese grosso grapes—known as "Brunello" to the locals, who had been quietly experimenting with them for about a century—made one of the finest red wines in all Italy. Today, with an annual production of more than 3.5 million bottles of **Brunello di Montalcino**—and 3 million of its lighter-weight cousin Rosso di Montalcino—Montalcino has become a rather well-to-do town. Also, don't miss the white dessert wine called Moscadello or the fine honey.

ESSENTIALS

GETTING THERE   By Train   The bus is better, as few trains on the Siena–Grosseto line stop at either Torrenieri or Sant'Angelo (both about 10km/6 miles away), from which there are a few buses to connect you with Montalcino.

Sampling the Vino

Brunello di Montalcino exudes the smell of mossy, damp earth and musky berries. It tastes of dark, sweet fruits and dry vanilla. It's also the backbone of Montalcino's economy. As the deep ruby liquid mellows to garnet, the wine takes on its characteristic complex and slightly tannic aspect. Brunello is one of Italy's mightiest reds, a brawny wine that can tackle the rarest *bistecca alla fiorentina*. It's also the perfect accompaniment to game, pungent mushroom sauces, and aged cheeses.

Though Montalcino has produced wine for centuries, its flagship Brunello is a recent development, born out of late-19th-century sangiovese experiments to concentrate the grapes through very strict cultivation methods. By the 1960s, Brunello was becoming known as one of Italy's finest reds, and it has found its way to discriminating cellars around the world—Queen Elizabeth II is fond of a quaff, and President Reagan toasted his 1980 inauguration with a Brunello. Most Brunellos are drinkable after about 4 to 5 years in the bottle, and the complex ones are best after 10 years or so (few last beyond 30). The best recent vintages are '85, '88, '90, and especially '95 and '97 (but steer clear of the '89 and '92); Brunellos from '91, '93, or '94 aren't bad either, and bottles of '98, '99, and even 2001 look as if they'll all be right up there with the near-tops (once they're finished aging and released on the market). Montalcino's **wine consortium** (© **0577-848-246;** www.consorziobrunellodimontalcino.it) is inside the Palazzo Comunale at Costa del Municipio 1, and staff members are happy to answer your questions and provide you with information on area *vini*.

In town, the best informal introduction to the deep-red liquid is a few hours spent at the **Enoteca La Fortezza** (© **0577-849-211;** www.enotecalafortezza.it) inside the fortress. The stone-and-brick vaults are filled with excellent wines and grappa, as well as prosciutto, salami, pecorino cheese, biscotti, and Montalcino's famous honey. The enoteca came under new management in 2003, but rest assured: The new staff is as adept as the old one at helping you and the wine get better acquainted, and glasses start at 1.50€ ($1.75). The Brunello is 3.50€ ($4.05). The Enoteca is open the same hours as the fortress (see below).

On the town's main square, the 19th-century cafe **Fiaschetteria Italiana,** Piazza del Popolo 6 (© **0577-849-043**), offers more imbibing pleasure, open Friday through Wednesday from 7:30am to midnight. A glass of wine can range anywhere from 4€ to 12€ ($4.60–$14).

By Car   Montalcino is about 8km (5 miles) off the SS2 Via Cassia running between Siena and Rome. There is a small parking lot next to the fortress just inside the walls. If it's full, there's some parking just outside the walls.

By Bus   There are vaguely hourly Tra-in buses from Siena (1 hr.); a few require a change at **Buonconvento.** SITA (© **06/4173-0083** in Rome; www.sita-on-line.it)

If you prefer to go right to the source, the following Brunello wine estates welcome visitors. **Poggio Antico** (© **0577-848-044**; fax 0577-846-563; www.poggioantico.com) is 4km (2 miles) south of town along the Grosetto road (right-hand road at the fork). Its Brunellos, especially the *riserve*, are consistently voted among the top 100 wines in the world by leading oenological magazines—and they often hold the number-one spot among Brunello wines. Their elegant and velvety elixir deserves to be at least one of the bottles you bring home. *Cantina* visits should be reserved at least a day in advance (more in summer), but the direct-sales store is open daily to drop-ins from 8am to 5pm. Poggio Antico also has an excellent restaurant (p. 325).

Banfi (© **0577-816-001** or 0577-840-111; www.castellobanfi.com) above Sant'Angelo Scalo, 10km (6 miles) south of town (right-hand road at the fork), is part of an American-owned exporting empire, an enormous ultramodern vineyard with a massive *cantine*. The *riserva* wines are precisely balanced Brunellos. Banfi also makes Moscadello and various non-Montalcino wines and runs a small museum (2.50€/$2.90 admission) on the history of glass and wine in its medieval castle. This place has a highly developed commercial end. The huge *enoteca* sells books, ceramics, packaged local foods, and all the Banfi wines. This is also where you go for tastings; your first glass is free, but after that prices range from 2€ to 6€ ($2.30–$6.90) per glass. The enoteca and museum are open daily from 10am to 7pm (until 6pm Oct–Mar). Call ahead for an appointment (best at least a week in advance) to take a free guided tour of the cellars at 4pm Monday through Friday. They also run an *osteria* for light snacks and a *ristorante* for pricey full meals with multiple wine tastings.

Fattoria dei Barbi (© **0577-841-111**; fax 0577-841-112; www.fattoria deibarbi.it), 5km (3 miles) south of town on the road to Castelnuovo (middle road at the fork), makes a mean Brunello di Montalcino *riserva*, Vigna del Fiore. The *cantina* also sells Moscadello and vin santo and is open Monday through Friday from 10am to 1pm and 2:30 to 6pm, Saturday and Sunday from 2:30 to 6pm. The slightly refined *taverna* (© **0577-841-200**) serves good traditional meals off a seasonally changing menu using their own farm products (olive oil, cheeses, and, of course, wine) at a middlin' price, open Thursday through Tuesday from 12:30 to 2:30pm and 7:30 to 9:30pm. Free *cantina* tours and wine tastings are given Monday through Friday hourly at 11am, noon and 3, 4, and 5pm. You can buy their delicious cheeses weekdays from 9am to noon and 1:30 to 5pm (closed 4pm Fri).

makes two runs daily from Rome. The **bus terminus** in Montalcino is Piazza Cavour; buy your tickets at Bar Prato on the piazza.

VISITOR INFORMATION   The **tourist office** (© and fax **0577-849-331**) is across from the entrance to the Palazzo Comunale at Via Costa Municipio 8. It's open Tuesday through Sunday from 10am to 1pm and 2 to 6pm.

FESTIVALS   Celebrating the opening of hunting season is the **Torneo della Apertura della Caccia,** held on the second Sunday in August. The events, dating from the 14th century, include archery competitions and lots of food as everybody struts in medieval costume. The residents dust off those outfits again for a similar but much larger festival called the **Sagra del Tordo** ⚘, held the last weekend in October. It kicks off at noon on Saturday with an archery competition pitting Montalcino's four *contrade* against one another. Parades, pageantry, and plenty of food follow for the next 2 days. The *festa* honors the lowly thrush, hundreds of which meet their maker on huge spits over open fires during the weekend. The fowl is accompanied by plates piled high with *pici* pasta and Brunello to wash it all down. Friday is **market** day on Viale della Libertà.

STROLLING THROUGH MONTALCINO

The dominant feature of Montalcino's skyline is the 14th-century Sienese **fortress** ⚘⚘, expanded in 1571 by Duke Cosimo I. The inside is now a pretty little park; duck through the archway into a small garden planted with ilex trees on a plateau with a view of the valley. Inside the old keep is the **Enoteca La Fortezza** wine shop (© **0577-849-211;** www.enotecalafortezza.it; see "Sampling the Vino," above), where you can buy tickets to climb up onto the ramparts for panoramic views of the Val d'Orcia and Vallombrone. In one of the castle rooms, the last battle standard of the Sienese Republic is preserved. April through October, the fortress is open daily from 9am to 8pm; November through March, hours are Tuesday through Sunday from 9am to 6pm. Admission is 3.50€ ($4.05) adults and 1.50€ ($1.75) children under 12. A 6€ ($6.90) cumulative ticket also gets you into the Museo Civico e Diocesano, but you must buy it at the museum (see below).

Walk down Via dell'Oca and turn left on Via Panfilo to **Piazza Garibaldi,** with the small 11th-century church of **Sant'Egidio.** Inside is a frescoed triptych by Francesco Cozza and a *Madonna and Saints* by Luca di Tommé.

Out the other end of the piazza, Costa del Municipio leads past the entrance to the **Palazzo Comunale** (1292), which houses a small display on the history of Brunello and other Montalcino wines and the headquarters of the wine consortium. The elongated front of the palazzo on Piazza del Popolo, sporting the mayoral coat of arms of past *podestà*, looks far too narrow to stand. It's nothing more than a slender clock tower with a loggia off the left side. On the long piazza is a 14th- to 15th-century **loggia** and the 19th-century cafe **Fiaschetteria Italiana** ⚘ (see "Sampling the Vino," above), focal point of the evening *passeggiata* up Via Mazzini.

A stepped street leads uphill from Piazza del Popolo to the 14th-century church of **Sant'Agostino,** rarely open these days, but which has lots of frescoes covering the walls, including the *Life of St. Augustine* by Bartolo di Fredi in the choir.

Just to the right of the church, in its former convent, is the **Museo Civico e Diocesano** (© **0577-846-014**) a good little grouping of 12th- to 16th-century Sienese paintings and sculpture. The most important works are some 12th-century illuminated bibles; *Madonna and Child* paintings by Luca di Tommé, Simone Martini, Vecchietta, and Sano di Pietro; and several good Bartolo di Fredi works. There are also 15th-century glazed terra cottas by Andrea della Robbia and a passel of 14th- and 15th-century polychrome wood statues in excellent repair, including some by Francesco di Valdambrino and Domenico Cafaggi. It's open Tuesday through Sunday: January through March from 10am to 1pm and 2 to 5:40pm and April through December from 10am to 5:50pm (might close 1–2pm if staffing is short). Admission is 4.50€ ($5.20) adults and 3€ ($3.45) under 12; or you can get a 6€ ($6.90) cumulative ticket that also gets you into the fortress (see above).

A ROMANESQUE ABBEY NEAR MONTALCINO

In a pocket-size vale bounded by low green hills, the Cistercian abbey of **Sant'Antimo** *★★★* (© 0577-835-659; www.antimo.it) rises amid olive groves. Its church is one of the most astoundingly intact Romanesque countryside temples left in Tuscany, but its monastery is mostly ruins. Since 1992, a handful of French monks have inhabited what's left, and the church interior echoes with their haunting Gregorian chant throughout the day. The first stone was supposedly laid on the order of Charlemagne in A.D. 781, but the current structure dates from 1118. Its amalgamated Lombard-French architecture has produced a building of singular beauty, with strong simple lines of pale yellow and white stone. The fabric of the walls is studded with recycled materials, some inscribed and many with fantastic medieval (and even a few Roman) reliefs. A cypress is challenging the 30m (100-ft.) bell tower to a height contest. One side of the campanile supports a medieval relief of the *Madonna and Child,* and the carvings of animals and geometric designs around the doors are worth study. Before going inside, walk around to the back; at the base of the apse is a small, round window through which you can glimpse a bit of the 9th-century crypt underneath, part of the original church.

The honey-colored travertine interior of the church, with its second-level women's gallery adapted from Byzantine models, is filled even on cloudy days with a warm, diffuse light. Two Lombard lions, now toothless with age, once flanked the entrance but have been moved inside. Several of the column capitals have intricate alabaster carvings. One on the right aisle tells the story of *Daniel in the Lion's Den,* and, like the other alabaster capitals and column bases here, glows as if lit from within when sunlight streams into the church. You can descend to the cramped crypt with a *Pietà* fresco and spend hours admiring the carvings—a plethora of eagles and evangelists, sheep and medieval Christs—throughout the church. Behind the high altar and its 13th-century wooden crucifix is an unusual three-apsed ambulatory that gets plenty of sun—your best bet for seeing that luminous effect on the alabaster column bases and capitals. Ask the guy at the postcard desk *"Posso vedere la sagrestia per piacere?"* (*poh*-so ved-*air*-ay la sah-gres-*tee*-yah pair pee-ah-*chair*-ay) for a peek into the sacristy and its cartoonish 15th-century frescoes by Giovanni di Asciano on the *Life of St. Benedict,* interesting mainly for their earthy details and the animal extras that often seem wonderfully oblivious to the holy events happening around them. (One scene features a blatantly amorous pig couple.) Sant'Antimo is open to visitors Monday through Saturday from 10:30am to 12:30pm and 3 to 6:30pm, Sunday from 9:15 to 10:30am and 3 to 6pm. Admission is free.

WHERE TO STAY

Hotel dei Capitani *★*   In 1996, Letizia and Roberto Fioravanti opened Montalcino's first new hotel in years, offering friendly service at a comfortable inn of modest refinement. The building probably served the Sienese army as a refuge from the Florentines during their incessant wars in the Middle Ages. The halls are carpeted, the staircase is travertine, and the rooms are mainly rustic in style, with wood-beamed ceilings and terra-cotta floors. Most are furnished with the wares of the artisan wood workshops of Arezzo. The four mini-apartments, with lofted master bedrooms and a pair of futon chairs in the living space, are great for families. A drop-dead view of the Val d'Orcia and Val d'Arbia is visible from about half the rooms, the breakfast space, and the gravel-covered terrace with a tiny pool out back. The Capitani is located in the heart of Montalcino's pedestrianized zone, making for a quiet stay.

Via Lapini 6 (down the hill from Piazza Cavour), 53024 Montalcino (SI). © **0577-847-227.** Fax 0577-847-239. www.deicapitani.it. 29 units. 103€ ($118) double; 134€ ($154) triple; 165€ ($190) miniapartment. Rates include continental breakfast. AE, DC, MC, V. Parking in small lot next door or public lots nearby. Closed Jan–Feb. **Amenities:** Outdoor pool (open May–Sept, weather permitting); bike rental arrangements; concierge; tour desk; limited room service (breakfast and bar); nonsmoking rooms. *In room:* A/C, TV, minibar, hair dryer, safe.

Hotel II Giglio ⭐ *Value*   Several years ago, when this hotel in the center of town was taken over by a new family, the tired old pensione was transformed into a board-rated three-star hotel—serious competition for the youngster Hotel dei Capitani (see above). Now, after an extensive renovation in 2002, it sports a similar rustic theme (beamed ceilings and tiled floors) in slightly smaller rooms with very compact bathrooms, but adds touches of leafy flowers and other grotesques painted on the high reaches of the walls, plus cast-iron bed frames surrounded by functional furniture. The best part is the view (from eight of the rooms) of the cliff-clinging houses of Montalcino to your left and the rumpled patchwork of green valleys stretching out below. Il Giglio has a pair of slightly larger rooms, each with a futon chair, good for families. The family also runs a Tuscan trattoria. If they run out of room, the owners will send you to their five rental rooms or one efficiency apartment in the *"dependence"* on a medieval street around the corner. Some of these have painted stuccoed ceilings, but there are no phones (hence the lower price; the apartment with kitchenette costs a bit more, depending on how many people occupy it).

Via Soccorso Saloni 5, 53024 Montalcino (SI). © and fax **0577-848-167.** www.gigliohotel.com. 17 units. 75€ ($86) double in main hotel, 80€ ($92) double with terrace; 58€ ($67) double in the *dependence.* Breakfast 8€ ($9.20). AE, MC, V. Parking in public lots (Fortezza). Closed Jan 7–28. **Amenities:** Restaurant; concierge; tour desk; limited room service; babysitting; laundry service. *In room:* TV, kitchenette (only in *dependence* apt.), minibar, hair dryer.

WHERE TO DINE

Pick up excellent pastries at **Mariuccia** ⭐, Piazza del Popolo 29 (© **0577-849-319**), where since 1935 they've turned out homemade *torrone, panforte,* Sienese cookies, and the formidable *cioccolatoni di Mariucia* (giant chocolate truffles filled variously with cream, caramel, coffee, grappa, or walnut cream). The *bacio di Montalcino* is best described as a semi-frozen "death, burial, and several weeks of mourning" by chocolate.

La Fortezza del Brunello ⭐ *Finds* INVENTIVE TUSCAN/ITALIAN   Marco Sasseti and his Scottish wife, Laura Gray, run this gastronomic retreat on the main square of a perfect little untouristed hill town a few kilometers south of Montalcino. It's a kind of subtly refined medieval fantasy, with cast-iron sconces, chandeliers, and grates; stone and brick walls; and split-level curtains finished off with mini crenellations. The ingredients are Italian, and the touch Tuscan, but the dishes don't always stick to tradition. The *cestino di formaggio* appetizer is a cheese pastry bowl filled with shredded lettuce and ostrich carpaccio. My favorite primo is the flavorful risotto made with taleggio cheese and zucchini flowers. Secondi tend to be heavy, such as a *filetto di bue al Brunello* (ox filet cooked in Brunello), or *chinghiale* (wild boar) cooked in wine with polenta, but there's always an at-the-whim-of-the-chef vegetarian option. They also run the piazza's relaxed *enoteca* wine bar if you don't want a full meal, and have just finished constructing an out-door deck with shade umbrellas for enjoying a light lunch alfresco.

Costa Castellare 1–3, Sant'Angelo in Colle (a hill town south of Montalcino). ⓒ **0577-844-012** or 0577-844-175. www.lafortezzadelbrunello.com. Reservations highly recommended. Primi 9€–10€ ($10–$12); secondi 17€–20€ ($20–$23). AE, DC, MC, V. Thurs–Tues 12:30–2pm and 7:30–9:30pm. Closed last 2 weeks of Nov and throughout Jan.

Ristorante di Poggio Antico ★★ FINE TUSCAN   The most refined din-ing around Montalcino is offered in these converted stalls surrounded by the vineyards of an award-winning wine estate. Huge windows fill it with light, and designer halogen lamps pop out from between the wood beams of the ceiling. Bouquets of fresh wildflowers sit on each table, the staff is informative, and the tiny flavored rolls are freshly baked. The best deal is the menù degustazione, small samplings of the restaurant's specialties, including a ravioli stuffed with wild boar and a selection of desserts. The *parfait di fegatini in salsa di moscadello* (mousse of chicken livers prepared as foie gras in a sweet sauce of reduced Moscadello wine) is excellent, and the *ravioli alle erbette* (ricotta-and-herb ravi-oli in butter sauce with grated black truffles) are fine as well. For a second course, try the *piccione disossato con vin santo* (deboned pigeon with a sweet liqueur) or the *tagliata alle erbette* (thick short strips of prime beef).

Loc. i Poggi (just south of town). ⓒ **0577-849-200.** Reservations highly recommended. Primi 10€–25€ ($12–$29); secondi 20€–36€ ($23–$41); menù degustazione without wine 35€–46€ ($40–$53). MC, V. Apr–Oct Tues–Sat 12:30–2:30pm and 7:30–9:30pm; Sun 12:30–2pm. Closed Sun in winter. Closed Jan 8–Feb 4. Follow the Grosetto road 3.6km (2¼ miles) south of Montalcino to the turnoff at the signpost on the right.

Trattoria Sciame SOUTHERN TUSCAN   You'll be lucky to wrest one of the seven tables (crammed into Sciame's small, modern dining room) away from the devoted locals who fill it with clamorous chatter almost every night. The food here is firmly *cucina casalinga*. You needn't decide on an appetizer because they're gathered together in the *antipastone misto*. Top honors go to both the *pinci al cinghiale* (fat spaghetti in a sauce of tomatoes and wild boar) and the *zuppa di fagioli* (a bean-and-cabbage soup poured over bread, with a red onion to weepingly slice over it). Afterward try a *pollo arrosto* (roast chicken or guinea hen) or the *scaloppina agli asparagi* (veal scallop with wild asparagus). For dessert, order the *cantucci e ossi di morti con moscadello* (almond cookies and brit-tle, hollow "bones of the dead" cookies with sweet white dessert wine).

Via Ricasoli 9 (a block from the fortress). ⓒ **0577-848-017.** Reservations strongly recommended. Primi 5.50€–8€ ($6.30–$9.20); secondi 5.50€–11€ ($6.30–$13). AE, DC, MC, V. Wed–Mon noon–2:30pm and 7–9:30pm. Closed Feb and last week of July.

EN ROUTE TO PIENZA

The Via Cassia SS2 meets the SS146 toward Pienza at **San Quírico d'Orcia;** the tourist office is at Via Dante Alighieri 33 (ⓒ **0577-897-211**), open April through October (and Dec 19–Jan 6) daily from 10am to 1pm and 3:30 to 7pm. This farming village with its 12th-century Romanesque **Collegiata** ★ makes a good half-hour diversion. The travertine church has three elaborate medieval portals. The front entrance is the oldest and most intricate, a Lom-bard-style affair with animal heads as capitals, a receding stack of carved arches, friezes of dueling fantasy animals, and columns made of four slender poles knot-ted in the middle. To the right side is the second portal, perhaps by Giovanni Pisano, with telamon columns posing atop lions' backs. Another kneeling tela-mon supports a nearby window arch. The smaller, final portal dates to 1298. Inside is a Sano di Pietro polyptych (any coin in the box will light it up) and a set of 15th-century intarsia choir stalls by Antonio Barili that were originally set up in a chapel of Siena's Duomo. Down the block in the main square is the entrance to the **Horti Leonini,** a Renaissance Italianate garden (1580) with geometric box-hedge designs and shady holm oaks, originally a resting spot for holy pilgrims on the Francigena road from France to Rome. It's open daily from sunrise to sunset.

Five kilometers (3 miles) south on SS2 is **Bagno Vignoni** ☆, little more than a group of houses—a few of them fine spa hotels—surrounding one of the most memorable piazze in Tuscany. The Medici harnessed the naturally hot sulfur springs percolating from the ground by building a giant outdoor pool that fills the main square, lined with stone walls and finished with a pretty loggia at one end. Even St. Catherine of Siena, when not performing religious and bureaucratic miracles, relaxed here with a sulfur cure. Alas, swimming is no longer allowed on the main square, but there's a modern pool below. To see the springs in their more natural state, take the second turnoff on the curving road into town and pull over when you see the tiny sulfurous mountain on your right. The waters bubble out here in dozens of tiny rivulets, gathering in a pool at the bottom, and there's a fairy-tale view, especially on misty days, of the Aldobrandeschi **Rocca d'Orcia.**

Eighteen kilometers (11 miles) farther down the SS2, in a land filled with dramatically eroded swathes of *crete,* **Radicófani** glowers from atop its basalt outcropping; the tourist office is at Renato Magi 25 (© **0578-55-684** or 0578-55-905; open July–Aug daily 9:30am–1pm and 3:30–7:30pm; Sept–June Sun only, same hours). The remains of the **Rocca fortress** (© **0578-55-867**) are surrounded by a medieval warren of streets and houses with outdoor stairs in stony gray basalt; all were seriously damaged by explosions and earthquakes in the 18th century. The castle was built by Hadrian IV, the only English pope, but is most famous as the base of operations of the "gentle outlaw" Ghino di Tacco, immortalized by both Dante in his *Inferno* (*Purgatorio,* Canto VI) and Boccaccio in the *Decameron* (day 10, tale 2). Ghino was something of a Robin Hood figure, robbing from the rich to give to the poor—and taking a hefty share himself. It's open November through March Saturday and Sunday from 10am to 5pm, April through October daily from 10am to 7pm (until midnight July–Aug). Admission is 3€ ($3.45).

There are some **della Robbia terra cottas** in Radicófani's churches of San Pietro and Sant'Agata, and the views from Radicófani of the surrounding rugged farmscape can be especially evocative when there's a morning mist melting shadows into soft relief. The locals call the region the Mare di Sassi ("Seas of Stones")—an assessment with which Dickens, Montaigne, and other grand tourists heartily agreed. Those intrepid early travelers all stayed at the **Palazzo la Posta,** a hotel converted from Grand Duke Ferdinando I's hunting lodge along the road south out of town down to Via Cassia. The 1584 structure was designed by Buontalenti, but these days it sadly crumbles by the roadside across from a 1603 **Medici fountain.**

2 Pienza: The Ideal Renaissance City

24km (15 miles) E of Montalcino; 55km (33 miles) SE of Siena; 125km (75 miles) S of Florence; 177km (110 miles) NW of Rome

In the midst of the rolling farmland of Tuscany's Val d'Orcia, on a tiny bump of a hill, the village of Pienza sits as a testament to one man's ambition and ego. At the height of the 15th-century Renaissance, humanist Pope Pius II, with the help of architect Bernardo Rossellino, converted the tiny village in which he had been born into the ideal Renaissance city. The "city" began and ended with the new central square and its buildings—the plan to cover the surrounding area with a grid of streets never materialized. The village of Pienza, however, retains its remarkable city-size piazza, one of the grandest achievements of Renaissance architecture and the only intact example of a city-planning scheme from the era. Director Franco Zeffirelli was so taken by the village's look he dethroned Verona as the city of the Montagues and Capulets and filmed his *Romeo and Juliet* in Pienza. Pienza was also used in the Oscar-winning epic *The English Patient*.

But for all Pius's dreams, Pienza never became more than a village. Today, its 2,500 inhabitants put up with the stream of day-trippers with good humor, lots of craft stands, and a surfeit of health-food stores. The main drag, **Corso Rossellino,** goes in one end of town and out the other in less than 2 minutes at a stroll. There are a handful of spacious side streets within Pienza's proud little walls, and modest new developments surround the burg on three sides (the 4th is saved for a view). Pienza will take no more than half a day in your schedule, time enough to admire the palaces, Sienese art collection, and Duomo at the town's perfect core; nibble on the famous goat cheeses and honey; and take a short walk to the odd, isolated medieval churches in the countryside outside the walls.

ESSENTIALS

GETTING THERE   By Train   There's no convenient train station. You can take the main **Rome-Florence** line to Chiusi/Chianciano Terme, about 30km (19 miles) away, and from there an LFI bus to Montepulciano, where you can change for another bus to Pienza.

By Car   Pienza is on the SS146 between San Quírico d'Orcia and Chiusi. From Montalcino, take the road toward Torrenieri and the SS2; take the SS2 south 7km (4 miles) to San Quírico d'Orcia, where the SS146 toward Chianciano/Chiusi runs for 10km (6 miles) to Pienza. From Siena, take the SS2 south to the SS146 (or the SS148 south through Asciano and Monte Oliveto Maggiore). You can park along the streets surrounding the city walls.

By Bus   Tra-in buses run from **Siena** (five daily; 80 min.) and **Montepulciano** (10 daily; 20 min.) In Pienza, buy tickets at the little Edicola Libreria at Piazza Dante 8.

VISITOR INFORMATION   The **tourist office** is under the portico of the Palazzo Pubblico on Piazza Pio II, Corso Rossellino 59 (*©* and fax **0578-749-071;** open daily 9:30am–1pm and 3–6:30pm). You can also find more about the city online at **www.pienza.info**.

FESTIVALS & MARKETS   On the first Sunday in September, Pienza celebrates its peerless pecorino goat cheese in the **Fiera di Cacio** with a low-key medieval festival. It also tries to keep current by sponsoring **modern art exhibits** April through October. **Market** day is Friday.

PONTIFICAL EGOMANIA

When local boy Enea Silvio Piccolomini was elevated from cardinal to Pope Pius II in 1458, he decided to play God with his hometown of Corsignano and rebuild the village based on High Renaissance ideals. The man he hired for the job was Bernardo Rossellino, a protégé of Florentine architect Leon Battista Alberti. Rossellino leveled the old center of town and built in its place **Piazza Pio II** ⭐⭐, a three-dimensional realization of the "Ideal City" paintings by artists like Raphael and Piero della Francesca.

The square is flanked by the cathedral and three palaces: one for the government, one for the bishop, and one (of course) for Pius II. The pope liked the result so much he felt the village needed a new name for its new look, and he modestly decided to rename it after himself: Pienza ("Pio's Town"). As with modern big productions, Rossellino's civic face-lift came in both late and way over budget. (He fudged the account books so Pius wouldn't realize how deep the architect was dipping into the papal purse for funding.) Pius, aware of the duplicity but still immensely pleased with his new burg, reportedly reduced Rossellino to tears by saying, "You did well, Bernardo, in lying to us about the expense. . . . Your deceit has built these glorious structures, which are praised by all except the few consumed with envy." When the pope went south to try to drum up support for a Crusade to the Holy Land, he left a papal bull that said, in refined Latin, "Don't touch anything till I get back." He died in 1464, trying to raise his army in Ancona, and Pienza dutifully kept the cathedral and palaces exactly as Pius II left them in the 15th century—the only Renaissance town center in Italy to survive the centuries perfectly intact.

Pius II liked the German churches he'd seen in his travels, so he had Rossellino grace one side of the piazza with a syncretic **Duomo** 🏛🏛 whose Renaissance facade hides a Gothic interior. The gigantic coat of arms gloating above the rose window is that of Pius II's Piccolomini family. Not above letting everyone know who was financing all this, Pius II had the family *cinque lune* (five moons) device repeated more than 400 times throughout the church. The apse is set right on the cliff's edge so that sunlight can stream through its tall Gothic windows unencumbered by surrounding buildings, making this by far the best-lit church in Italy. Alas, the site has proved none too stable, and dangerous cracks have appeared in the apse fabric. With no good way yet found to shore up the structure, the altar end of the church threatens to slide down the slope without warning.

The **five altarpieces** inside were painted specifically for the cathedral by Sienese masters (1461–63), and they make a good study of how the mid-15th-century artists worked a theme: Four of the five paintings are *Madonna and Child with Saints* (the other's an *Assumption*). First, on your right, is Giovanni di Paolo's take, where angels cluster around Mary to coo at the baby. A young Matteo di Giovanni rendered the scene next, his Mary accompanied by Saints Catherine of Siena, Matthew, Bartholomew, and Lucia (the last carrying an awful lot of her martyrs' eyeballs on a plate). The following chapel has a marble **tabernacle** by Bernardo Rossellino (there's a bit of St. Andrew's head inside), and after the choir stalls comes Vecchietta's *Annunciation,* in which it takes quite a number of angels to boost Mary up to Heaven. The Duomo is open daily from 7am to 1pm and 2:30 to 7pm. Admission is free.

Coming out of the Duomo, you'll see the travertine portico of the **Palazzo Comunale,** also by Rossellino and another odd hybrid—this time Renaissance architecture masquerading as a medieval Tuscan town hall. To your right is the **Palazzo Vescovile,** built by Cardinal Roderigo Borgia, who later became Pope Alexander VI. It's the new home of the **Museo Diocesano** (✆ **0578-749-905**), entered at Corso Rossellino 30, which collects treasures of Sienese art from the churches of Pienza and small towns in the area. One of its most important works is the early-14th-century Cape of Pius II, a silk papal garment embroidered with gold, saintly portraits, and colorful scenes from the Life of the Virgin. The 14th-century school of Bartolo di Fredi produced a portable triptych that reads like a comic book, and the master himself is responsible for the *Madonna della Misericordia* (1364), in which Mary protects a kaleidoscope of tiny saints under her shawl. Il Vecchietta's altarpiece of the *Madonna and Child with Saints, Annunciation* lunette, and predella show off the peculiar grace and intent perspective of his flowing lines. From March 15 to November 1, the museum is open Wednesday through Monday from 10am to 1pm and 3 to 6:30pm; November through mid-March, it's open weekends only from 10am to 1pm and 3 to 6pm. Admission is 4.10€ ($4.70) adults and 2.60€ ($3) ages 6 to 12.

Across the piazza, past Rossellino's Renaissance well, is the architect's finest palace (Pius II's Pienza digs). The **Palazzo Piccolomini** ★★ (© **0578-748-503**) was inspired by Alberti's Palazzo Rucellai in Florence, but Rossellino added an Italianate hanging garden out the left side of the inner courtyard. Pius particularly liked his small patch of box hedges backed by a triple-decker loggia. It's perched on the edge of Pienza's tiny bluff and offers postcard views across the rolling cultivated hills of the wide Val d'Orcia to Monte Amiata. Half-hourly tours take you through the pope's private apartments and out on the loggia to see the gardens Tuesday through Sunday from 10am to 12:30pm and 3 to 6pm (last tour leaves 5:30pm). Admission is 3€ ($3.45) adults and 2€ ($2.30) students. Members of the Piccolomini family lived here until the 1960s but kept the Renaissance look in the pope's bedroom, the library, and a heavily armed great hall.

SHOPPING FOR WINE & CHEESE

Even though it's far tinier than neighboring hill towns, Pienza has about the same number of wine shops. The main difference is that these stores aren't tied to a single estate or producer (in Montalcino and Montepulciano, most *enoteche* are thinly disguised branches of nearby vineyards). Here you can often get a more well-rounded tasting experience, plus less biased advice.

These shops—indeed, any food store in town—usually double as outlets for other regional specialties, including the king of all sheep cheeses, Pienza's own **pecorino** ★ (or *cacio*). You can get it *fresco* (fresh), *semistagionato* (partially aged), or *stagionato* (aged and suitable for grating, though it really needs a few extra years for that). Many pecorini are also dusted with ground materials to keep them soft and alter the taste slightly. Most popular are *cenerato* or *sotto cenere* (an ash coating that's mainly a softening technique), *peperocinato* (hot peppers), and *tartufato* (truffles). A few producers even mix ingredients directly into the cheese (*tartufi* are a favorite), but others claim this mars the purity of the pecorino. Luckily, you can judge for yourself, as pecorino tasting is even more popular here than wine tasting. Two of the best places are **La Bottega del Cacio,** Corso Rossellino 66 (© **0578-748-713**), and the tiny **La Bottega del Naturista,** Corso Rossellino 16 (© **0578-748-760**).

On Corso Rossellino you'll find several ceramics stores and the showroom for **Biagiotti Fratelli** (© **0578-748-666**), a family of artisans who specialize in *ferro battuto* (cast iron). Its workshop and foundry is on SS146 on the way to Montepulciano. **Calzoleria Pientina,** down a side street at Via Gozzante 22 (© **0578-749-040** or 0578-748-195), handcrafts leather shoes to measure as well as bags and purses.

WHERE TO STAY

Dal Falco (© **0578-749-856** or 0578-748-551; www.nautilus-mp.com/tuscany/affitti/falco) recommended as a restaurant below, also rents six simple **rooms** upstairs, all with bathrooms and TVs (but no phones), for 62€ ($71) for a double or 78€ ($90) for the room with four beds, perfect for a family.

Castello di Ripa d'Orcia 𝒦𝒦   This oasis of tranquillity in the countryside occupies an early medieval castle mentioned as far back as 1218. The Piccolomini family—who've owned it since 1484—transformed several of the buildings into a hotel in 1988. The fairy tale views sweep across forested hillsides (protected as a nature preserve) capped with other medieval castles, and the 10-minute dirt road that winds its way out here only enhances the feeling of solitude and a quiet retreat. In fact, they stress relaxation: The rooms, which require at least a 2-night stay, have phones, but no TVs or other worldly temptations. The rooms are enormous country affairs, with antique furnishings and very comfy beds surrounded by thick stone walls and heavily beamed ceilings. There's a reading room with a fireplace and chessboard in the former granary, a quite good restaurant below the rooms (closed Mon), and, they have installed an *enoteca* in the old cantina. The office will provide you with a map for hikes to sights in the surrounding area. Check-in is only from 2:30 to 5pm; call to arrange arrival at any other time.

Loc. Ripa d'Orcia (signposted from San Quírico), 53023 San Quírico d'Orcia (SI). ℭ **0577-897-376.** Fax 0577-898-038. www.castelloripadorcia.com. 6 units, 8 apts (sleep 2–4). 99€–130€ ($114–$150) double (2-night min.); 490€–575€ ($564–$661) per week apt for 2; 649€–750€ ($746–$863) per week apt for 4. Rates for units (not apts) include breakfast. MC, V. Free parking. Closed Nov to mid-Mar. **Amenities:** Restaurant (closed Mon, dinner only); bike rental; concierge; nonsmoking rooms. *In room:* Kitchenette in apts, minibar, hair dryer, safe in some apts.

Hotel Il Chiostro di Pienza 𝒦   Even though this hotel in a 15th-century Franciscan convent faces no competition within Pienza's walls, the young staff still strives to maintain a high level of comfort with a keen attention to detail. The interior atmosphere—frescoes on a few walls, the enlarging of old monks' cells to make larger rooms—owes much to the building's 19th-century incarnation as a seminary, but most of the rooms feature modern touches like glass-topped tables and fabrics in bright colors. A few rooms in a recently opened wing have a more antique charm, with simple peasant-style furniture made of old wood. The garden outside the breakfast room/restaurant (which offers fine Tuscan food) has sweeping views of the Val d'Orcia and tables for breakfast and bar service in summer. During the high season, light lunches are served under the arcades of the convent's cloister for those just passing through town.

Corso Rossellino 26, 53026, Pienza (SI). ℭ **0578-748-400.** Fax 0578-748-440. www.relaisilchiostrodi pienza.com. 37 units. 180€ ($207) double; 220€ ($253) suite. Rates include breakfast. AE, DC, MC, V. Free parking. Closed Jan 5–Mar 15. **Amenities:** Restaurant; outdoor pool; concierge; tour desk; limited room service; massage; babysitting; laundry service; dry cleaning. *In room:* TV, minibar, hair dryer, safe.

WHERE TO DINE

The restaurant at **Il Chiostro di Pienza** (see above) serves fine Tuscan food.

Dal Falco TUSCAN HOME COOKING   In a modern building off the large piazza just outside Pienza's main gate, Dal Falco offers good cheap meals and good cheap rooms. You know this is a true local trattoria because there's a TV in the corner that's usually locked into a soccer match. *Pici* take the place of honor among the primi, and those made *all'aglione* have just the right amount of hot pepper in the tomato sauce. Grilled meats are the specialty secondo, and you can go for an *arrosto misto alle brace* or *pecorino alle brace* (grilling it sweetens the thick slab of sheep's cheese sandwiched between two slices of prosciutto). The house red is highly recommended.

Piazza Dante Alighieri 7, 53026, Pienza (SI). ℭ and fax **0578-749-856** or 0578-748-551. Reservations recommended. Primi 4.50€–8€ ($5.20–$9.20); secondi 5.50€–13€ ($6.30–$15); fixed-price menu without wine 18€ ($21); fixed-price menu with wine 21€–24€ ($24–$27). AE, DC, MC, V. Sat–Thurs noon–3pm and 7–10pm. Closed 10 days in Nov, 10 in July, and 10 in Feb.

Trattoria Latte di Luna ⚤ *Kids* SOUTHERN TUSCAN   Opened in 1994, this friendly, easy-going trattoria has quickly captured a following of everyone from English art students to local *carabinieri*. To enter, thread through the wedge of outdoor tables and past the cage of Willy, a merlin who squawks "Ciao" and "Come stai?" at each passerby. Inside, brick and yellow stucco are the backdrop for your *pici all'aglione* (with spicy tomato-and-garlic sauce) or *zuppa di pane* (a local variant on *ribollita*, with more cabbage and no extra day of cooking, so the bread is still in slices). You can follow this up with *vitello girello* (thin slices of veal, with or without mushrooms) or the specialty, *maiellino arrosto* (roast suckling pig). For dessert, the restaurant makes its own *semifreddi* flavored with seasonal ingredients.

Via San Carlo 2–4 (at Porta al Ciglio end of Corso Rossellino). © **0578-748-606**. Reservations recommended. Primi 5.50€–9.50€ ($6.30–$11); secondi 5.50€–13€ ($6.30–$15). MC, V. Wed–Mon 12:20–2:20pm and 7:30–9:20pm. Closed Feb–Mar 15 and July.

3 Montepulciano & Its Noble Wine

13km (8 miles) E of Pienza; 67km (40 miles) SE of Siena; 124km (74 miles) SE of Florence; 186km (115 miles) N of Rome

The biggest and highest of southern Tuscany's hill towns, steeply graded Montepulciano, with its medieval alleyways and plethora of Renaissance palaces and churches, has just enough city feel and tourist infrastructure to make it one of the best bases for visiting the region. The fields around the town produce a violet-scented, orange-speckled ruby wine called **Vino Nobile di Montepulciano.** This area has been known since at least the 8th century for its superior wine, and in the 17th century, when Francesco Redi wrote his vino-praising poem, *Bacchus in Tuscany,* he described the Noble Wine of Montepulciano as "The King of all wines." Vino Nobile is known as Tuscany's number-two red because it's slightly less beefy than Montalcino's Brunello. But for my money, its high quality and more mellow character make it a better all-around wine, good to age and save for special occasions but also to toss back with dinner or on a picnic.

The locals call themselves Poliziani after the Roman name for the town, and Poliziano is also the name the local classical scholar/humanist Angelo Ambrogini took when he went to Florence to hold discourses with Lorenzo de' Medici, tutor Lorenzo's sons, and write some of the most finely crafted Renaissance poetry of the era—some say his *Stanze per la Giostra* inspired Botticelli's mythological paintings, like the *Birth of Venus* and *Allegory of Spring.*

ESSENTIALS

GETTING THERE   By Train   Use the Chiusi/Chianciano Terme station, whether you're on one of the 30 daily trains on the main **Rome–Florence** line (1 hr. 45 min.–2 hr. 45 min. from Florence) or the 16 trains on the secondary **Siena** line (1 hr. 15 min.). On the Siena line, don't get off at the stop called Montepulciano Staz. It's about as far from Montepulciano as the Chiusi stop, but local LFI buses to Montepulciano are coordinated with the trains only at the Chiusi station.

By Car   From Siena, the quicker, more scenic route is south on the SS2 to San Quírico d'Orcia, where you get SS146 through Pienza to Montepulciano. From Florence, take the A1 south to the Chianciano Terme exit, and then take SS146 (direction Chianciano) for 18km (11 miles).

By Bus   Five to eight **Tra-in** buses (✆ **0577-204-111;** www.trainspa.it) run three to five times daily from Siena (1½ hr.) through Pienza (20 min.). **LFI** (✆ **0578-31-174**) buses run hourly from Chiusi (50 min.) through Chianciano Terme (25 min.), and twice daily from Florence to Bettole, where you transfer for the bus to Montepulciano (2 hr. total). There are three direct buses daily from Florence run by **Ferroviaria** lines (no phone).

In Montepulciano, buy **Tra-in** and **Ferroviaria tickets** at Caffè Tubino, in the little parking lot just below Porta al Prato; get **LFI tickets** from the *tabacchi*/bar at Via Gracchiano del Corso 36–38.

VISITOR INFORMATION   Montepulciano's **tourist office** is tacked onto the right side of Sant'Agostino at Via Gracchiano nel Corso 59a (✆ **0578-757-341;** www.comune.montepulciano.siena.it or www.prolocomontepulciano.it.) It's open daily from 9:30am to 12:30pm and 3 to 6pm (until 8pm in summer); closed Sunday afternoons, but not for *riposo* in Aug.

FESTIVALS & MARKETS   Poliziani in general are still adept wordsmiths and poets. The tradition of popular theater, which had its roots in extemporaneous performances on threshing-room floors, is carried on by a company of locals who write lyric plays on themes of religion, local legends, and chivalric romances. During the annual **Bruscello,** the townspeople perform their homespun musicals out on the piazze on the days surrounding August 15 (Assumption Day).

Poliziani also used to gallop horses pell-mell through the streets in an annual palio, but for safety reasons this has been reduced in modern times to the **Bravio delle Botti** ★★. In this only slightly less perilous race, the locals don 14th-century costumes as teams from the traditional *contrade* neighborhoods roll barrels weighing more than 175 pounds toward the finish line. (Oh, yeah: It's uphill.) To witness the hernias and join in the pageantry before the race and the feast after, drop by town on the last Sunday in August.

This display of brute strength follows a few weeks of classic and modern music, dance, theater, and art in the **Cantiere Internazionale d'Arte.** Never ones to let everyone else do all the work, the Poliziani again turn up as key players in the festival, performing alongside the hundreds of international artists who attend. It starts in late July and lasts until mid-August.

Montepulciano's **market** day is Thursday.

A STROLL THROUGH MONTEPULCIANO

Outside the city walls below Porta al Prato squats the church of **Sant' Agnese,** with a striped 1935 facade surrounding a 14th-century portal. Inside, the first chapel on the right (hit the free light switch) has a frescoed *Madonna* by Simone Martini. Ring at the door to the right of the altar for access to the pretty cloister. Die-hards can make the 1.6km (1-mile) trek down Viale Calamandrei to **Santa Maria delle Grazie,** with *Mary of the Graces* and *Annunciation* figures by Giovanni della Robbia on the second altar and a rare late-16th-century organ with cypress wood pipes to which musicians from all over the world travel to play.

You'll see architecture by Antonio Sangallo the Elder before you even get inside the walls. **Porta al Prato** was reconstructed in the 1500s on his designs, and the Medici balls above the gate hint at Montepulciano's long association with Florence. One block up Via Gracchino nel Corso, a Florentine Marzocco lion reigns from atop a **column.** (It's a copy of a 1511 original, now in the museum.) To the right (no. 91) is the massive **Palazzo Avignonesi,** with grinning lions' heads, and across the street is the **Palazzo Tarugi** (no. 82). Both are by Vignola, the late Renaissance architect who designed Rome's Villa Giulia. A

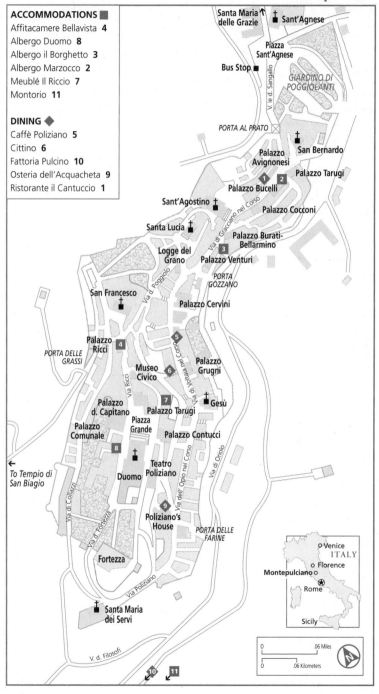

Montepulciano

ACCOMMODATIONS ■
Affitacamere Bellavista **4**
Albergo Duomo **8**
Albergo il Borghetto **3**
Albergo Marzocco **2**
Meublé Il Riccio **7**
Montorio **11**

DINING ◆
Caffè Poliziano **5**
Cittino **6**
Fattoria Pulcino **10**
Osteria dell'Acquacheta **9**
Ristorante il Cantuccio **1**

Santa Maria delle Grazie
✝ Sant'Agnese
Piazza Sant'Agnese
Bus Stop ■
Via d. Sangallo
GIARDINO DI POGGIOLANTI
PORTA AL PRATO
✝ San Bernardo
Palazzo Avignonesi
Palazzo Tarugi
❶ ❷
Palazzo Bucelli
Sant'Agostino ✝
Via di Gracciano nel Corso
Palazzo Cocconi
Santa Lucia ✝
Palazzo Burati-Bellarmino
Logge del Grano
❸
Palazzo Venturi
PORTA GOZZANO
Via d. Poggiolo
San Francesco ✝
Palazzo Cervini
Palazzo Ricci ❹
PORTA DELLE GRASSI
❺
Via Ricci
Museo Civico ❻
Palazzo Grugni
Via di Voltaia nel Corso
❼
✝ Gesù
Palazzo d. Capitano
Palazzo Tarugi
Piazza Grande
Palazzo Comunale
Palazzo Contucci
❽ ✝
Via dell' Opio nel Corso
Via di Oriolo
Teatro Poliziano
To Tempio di San Biagio ←
Duomo
Via di Collazzi
❾
Poliziano's House
PORTA DELLE FARINE
Via d. Fortezza
Fortezza
Via Poliziano
✝ Santa Maria dei Servi
V. d. Filosofi
❿ 11

0 .06 Miles
0 .06 Kilometers

Venice
ITALY
Florence
Montepulciano
Rome
Sicily

Underground Tunnels & Noble Wine

The local wine consortium, the **Consorzio del Vino Nobile di Montepulciano** (www.consorziovinonobile.it and www.vinonobiledi montepulciano.it), has recently ramped up its visitor's program, and has just installed a **showroom and tasting center** in the Palazzo del Capitano on Piazza Grande where you can sample the wares of every single member (which means most Vino Nobile vineyards) Monday through Friday from 11am to 1pm and 4 to 7pm, Saturday from 11am to 3pm. There are also plans underway to convert more of the palazzo into a wine museum. However, many folks still like to visit the cellars of individual producers.

Montepulciano has more *enoteche* and *cantine* (wine cellars) than you can shake a wine bottle at, most offering the chance to sample local products: pecorino cheese, salami, honey, olive oil, and, of course, Vino Nobile di Montepulciano. Many shops also let you descend into their *cantine,* often a linked maze of basements, underground tunnels that once connected the palaces, and older grottoes carved into the tufa of the mountain. Calling the grottoes "Etruscan tombs," as the signs in the stores proclaim, may not be far from the truth—the earliest foundations of a city on this site are still contested.

The *cantine* with the most attention-grabbing tunnels include the second of Montepulciano's two **Pulcino** wine shops, at Via Gracciano nel Corso 80 (*℃* **0578-757-948;** www.pulcino.com), which boasts a grab bag of "attractions" in its lengthy cellars, from a wishing well and an Etruscan tomb to a collection of iron implements found here—medieval weapons, household tools, and even a chastity belt. The **Gattavecchi** *cantine* (*℃* **0578-757-110;** www.gattavecchi.it) burrow under Santa Maria dei Servi (see below), with moldy tunnels and a staircase leading down to an even moldier chapel-like structure carved into the rock—no one knows when it dates from or what it was, but it's intriguingly and suggestively located directly below the altar end of the church. At Piazza Grande, the **Contucci** winery (*℃* **0578-757-006;** www.contucci.it) occupies the 13th-century cellars of the Palazzo Contucci. Down at the opposite end of town, the classy showrooms of the **Avignonesi** wine empire reside at Via Gracchiano nel Corso 91 (*℃* **0578-757-872;** www.avignonesi.it).

bit higher up on the left is the **Palazzo Cocconi** (no. 70) by Sangallo; the top floor looks out of place because it was added in the 1890s. In lieu of an Etruscan museum, Montepulciano has the **Palazzo Bucelli** (no. 73), the sort of place that makes archaeologists grit their teeth—the lower level of the facade is embedded with a patchwork of dozens of Etruscan reliefs and funerary urns. Most probably came from the Chiusi area, and they represent the collection of 18th-century antiquarian scholar and former resident Pietro Bucelli.

Next on the right is **Sant'Agostino** *✿*, with a facade by Michelozzo in a style mixing late Gothic with early Renaissance. The first altar on the right has a *Resurrection of Lazarus* by Alessandro Allori. Over the high altar is a wooden crucifix by Donatello, and, behind it, the entrance to the choir of an older church on this spot, with frescoes and an Antonio del Pollaiolo crucifix. On the right as you leave is a painted *Crucifixion* by Leonardo da Vinci's protégé Lorenzo di Credi. On Piazza Michelozzo in front of the church stands the **Torre di Pulcinella,** a short clock tower capped with a life-size Pulcinella, the black-and-white clown from Naples, who strikes the hours. It was left by a philandering Neapolitan bishop who was exiled here for his dalliances. At the next corner on the left is the **Palazzo Burati-Bellarmino** (no. 28), where the door is kept open so you can admire the Frederico Zuccari frescoes on the ceiling inside.

The road now rises steeply to Piazza delle Erbe and the **Logge del Grano,** a palazzo designed in the 15th century by Vignola with an arcaded porch and the Medici balls prominent above the entrance. The main road (it takes a left here) now becomes Via del Voltaia nel Corso, passing the grandiose **Palazzo Cervini** (no. 21) on the left, probably designed by Antonio Sangallo the Younger (Sangallo the Elder's nephew) for Cardinal Marcello Cervini just before he was elevated to the papacy. One of the shortest-lived pontiffs, Pope Marcellus II died 21 days into office. Climbing farther, you'll pass the elegant 19th-century **Caffè Poliziano** (, which serves snacks and pastries. Next comes the rough facade of the baroque **Chiesa del Gesù** (the little *trompe l'oeil* cupola on the dome inside is courtesy of Andrea Pozzo) and, much farther on—the street's name is now Via del Poliziano—the **house where Poliziano was born** stands at no. 5. A scholar, writer, and philosopher, Angelo Ambrogini (called Poliziano after the Latin name of his hometown) had an enormous impact on the Florentine humanist movement as a friend of Lorenzo de' Medici and tutor to his children. Just before his house, Via delle Farine leads left to **Porta delle Farine,** an excellent and intact example of a 13th-century Sienese double gate.

The main road now passes out of the city walls, wrapping around the **Medici fortress** (now a school) and passing the seldom-open **Santa Maria dei Servi,** with another late-17th-century interior by Andrea Pozzo and a *Madonna and Child* by the Duccio school (3rd altar on left).

Back inside the walls, you come to Montepulciano's historic and civic heart, **Piazza Grande.** On the left is the **Palazzo Comunale** (, designed by Michelozzo as a late-14th-century variation in travertine on Florence's Palazzo Vecchio. Monday through Saturday from 8am to 1pm, you can wander through dingy civic offices and past overflowing file cabinets to climb the tower for a great view of the surrounding countryside. (It's free; watch your head.) Back on terra firma, to your left is the **Palazzo Tarugi,** with an arcaded loggia on the corner facing a **well** topped by the Medici arms flanked by two Florentine lions and two Poliziani griffins. Both palace and well are the design of Antonio Sangallo the Elder, as is the **Palazzo Contucci** across from the Palazzo Comunale.

The last side of Piazza Grande is taken up by the rambling brick nonfacade of the **Duomo** (, a somewhat embarrassing reminder to Poliziani that, after building so many palaces and fitting so many of them with travertine, the city ran out of money to finish the ambitious plans for rebuilding the cathedral and had to leave it faceless. To the left of the church, the suspiciously 1950s-looking bell tower is actually the oldest thing on the piazza, dating from the 14th century and the cathedral of Santa Maria that once stood here. Inside, the Duomo makes up for its plain facade with two important works. The first takes some explaining because it's scattered in pieces around the church. Between 1427 and 1436, Michelozzo carved a monumental tomb for Bartolomeo Aragazzi, secretary to Pope Martin V. In the 18th century it was disassembled and the pieces lost until they were discovered under the altar of the Duomo in 1815. Two of the figures were stolen and eventually found their way to London, but the rest remain here. Because no indication of what the monument originally looked like exists and the supporting architecture is gone, the various figures are distributed throughout the church. They start with a reclining statue of the deceased to the right of the central entrance door (he's the one with the hood) and two bas-reliefs on the first two columns on either side of the nave. The Greco-Roman-influenced statues flanking the high altar and the *putti* frieze above it, along with a statue in a niche to the right of the altar, are the other main pieces of the monument.

The gold-heavy triptych on the high altar is by Taddeo di Bartoldo (1401) and depicts the *Assumption of the Virgin with Saints* topped by *Annunciation* and *Crowning of the Virgin* pinnacles, and is banded with a *Passion* cycle in the predella. Bartoldo was one of the masters of late-14th-century Sienese art, and this is one of his greatest works. (I particularly like the predella panel where one child is shimmying up a tree to get a better view of Christ entering Jerusalem.) On a pilaster to the right of the altar is a *schiacciato* bas-relief tabernacle by Vecchietta. Also inside the Duomo, as you walk out on the right, is an almond-eyed *Madonna and Child* (1418) by Sano di Pietro, located on the pilaster between the first two chapels. In the last chapel stands a 14th-century baptismal font with bas-relief and caryatid figures and, on the wall, a della Robbia altar surrounding a gilded marble bas-relief of the *Madonna and Child* by Benedetto di Maiano.

Continue down Via Ricci to the intersection with Via del Paolino, where you can cut back to the left on Via de' Grassi. Head outside the city walls and you'll be on the road toward Antonio da Sangallo the Elder's **Tempio di San Biagio** ✸✸ (1518–34), one of the true masterpieces of High Renaissance architecture. It became fashionable in the High Renaissance to build a church, usually on a Greek cross plan, just outside a city so that the classically inspired architecture would be unimpaired and uninhibited by surrounding buildings and the church could be appreciated from all angles. Todi and Prato each have their own version, but Montepulciano's is the best of the lot, a pagan temple built entirely of travertine, dedicated to the gods of mathematical and architectural purity and only nominally to any saint. Two bell towers were to have been fitted into the corners at the front, but the right one reached only 4.5m (15 ft.). The interior, while as peaceful and elegantly restrained as the overall structure, has nothing to hold you. Sangallo also designed the companion canon's house nearby, which was built after his death.

WHERE TO STAY

If the hotels below are full, try the **Albergo il Borghetto,** Borgo Buio 7, off Piazza Michelozzo (© **0578-757-535;** fax 0578-757-534; www.ilBorghetto.it), where doubles cost 105€ ($121). You might get a view and a grand antique armoire, and you'll certainly get a family-style reception as well as access to the cozy salons in the *cantina* and the tiny garden on the warrior's walk atop the medieval city walls. All rooms have private bathroom, phone, and dataport, and most have satellite TV. They also rent out two suites next door for four 152€ ($175), perfect for families. One daughter is even a professional guide if you want to organize a small tour.

Certainly don't overlook the three doubles Marcella rents for 40€ ($46) over her restaurant **Cittino** (© **0578-757-335;** see "Where to Dine," below); stay if only to get great food without leaving the building. In a pinch, you can fall back on the **Affitacamere Bellavista,** Via Ricci 25 (© **0578-716-341** or 347-823-2314 or 338-229-1964; fax 0578-716-341; www.cretedisiena.com/Camerebellavista;

49€–60€/$56–$69 double). Don't accept no. 5, the only room without a view, but do try for no. 6, which has a small terrace.

Albergo Duomo ✪ Although it's more expensive than the Albergo Marzocco (see below), for my money this family-run place is the better hotel. The very firm beds have thick floral-print quilts and pleasingly simple cast-iron frames, and the furniture, while mostly unobtrusively modern, includes a few writing tables and fat armoires made of old wood. There's a sitting area with a fireplace at one end of the breakfast room and a cozy TV room that opens onto a small terra cotta–tiled courtyard where you can take your coffee and rolls in the morning.

Via San Donato 14 (next to the Duomo), 53045 Montepulciano (SI). ℂ and fax **0578-757-473**. www.albergo duomo.it. 13 units. 100€ ($115) double; 124€ ($143) triple. Breakfast included. MC, V. **Amenities:** Non-smoking rooms. *In room:* TV, dataport.

Albergo Marzocco ✪ The largest hotel inside the walls is just a block up from Porta al Prato on the piazza sporting the establishment's namesake Florentine lion. The rooms are spacious enough, if not overly special, and have a few antiques in 18th-century Venetian style alongside some modern pieces. Several accommodations have large terraces over a side piazza; others look over the Marzocco sitting atop his column out front. A limited renovation in 2002 spiffed up some guest rooms and baths. The somewhat dusty sitting rooms give the hotel the feel of a Victorian-era *pensione,* though the pool table makes a rather strange contrast.

Piazza Savonarola 18 (on Via Grachiano nel Corso), 53045 Montepulciano (SI). ℂ **0578-757-262**. Fax 0578-757-530. www.cretedisiena.com/albergoilmarzocco. 16 units. 90€ ($104) double; 120€ ($138) triple. Rates include breakfast. AE, DC, MC, V. Free parking. Closed Jan 20–Feb 10. **Amenities:** Limited room service. *In room:* TV, hair dryer.

Meublé Il Riccio *(Finds)* This hotel's name comes from the *ricci* (hedgehogs) that were carved on the wooden supports once adorning the outside of this 13th-century house. They now decorate the rooms. The mosaics in the small colonnaded entrance courtyard come from the school founded by the hotel proprietor's father. Upstairs are comfortable rooms with functionally modern furniture and whitewashed walls. Guests share the pretty sitting room, with floral-print couches, and a rooftop terrace where the views stretch over the Valdichiana and even get in the top of the Palazzo Comunale's tower. In 2002, they expanded into the floor below with a large new reception area and breakfast room. It's a two-story walk-up with no elevator.

Via Talosa 21 (a few steps off Piazza Grande), 53045 Montepulciano (SI). ℂ and fax **0578-757-713**. www. ilriccio.net. 6 units. 80€ ($92) double; 96€ ($110) triple. Breakfast 8€ ($9.20). AE, DC, MC, V. Free parking (with permit for lot). Closed June 1–15 and Nov 1–15. **Amenities:** Laundry service; nonsmoking rooms. *In room:* A/C, TV, hair dryer, safe.

Montorio ✪✪ Founded on a lark by two sisters in 2000, these five spacious mini-apartments perch atop a hill overlooking the Tempio di San Biagio and the Sienese countryside just outside Montepulciano's walls. All save the smallest of the sumptuously homey accommodations combine the best of countryside tradition (beamed ceilings, terra-cotta floors, sturdy furnishings made of old wood) with modern amenities such as full kitchens, complimentary wine upon arrival (everything in the stocked mini-fridges is free as well), and separate sitting rooms and bedrooms; the smallest unit is more like a suite with a kitchenette. They've also completed renovations on the **Villa Poggiano** (ℂ **0578-758-292**; www.villa poggiano.com), cloaked in quiet, with views of sheep-dotted hillsides 1.5km (¾ mile) along the road to Pienza. It now boasts 10 enormous, two-room suites, inheriting the wildly dramatic and elegant touches of its 1930s owner, including marble floors and walls, nonfunctioning fireplaces, and a (functioning) swimming pool in geometric travertine. Either property makes a perfect base for exploring southern Tuscany. The only drawbacks: Montorio is a stiff 20-minute walk uphill into town, and no children under 10 are allowed.

Strada per Piezna 2, 53045 Montepulciano (SI). ℂ 0578-717-442. Fax 0578-715-456. www.montorio.com. 135€–230€ ($155–$265) depending on size, plus 52€ ($60) for each additional person (up to 4). Breakfast included. AE, DC, MC, V. Free parking. **Amenities:** Bike rental; concierge; tour desk; limited room service; massage; laundry service; dry cleaning. *In room:* TV, dataport, minibar, coffeemaker, hair dryer, safe.

WHERE TO DINE

To accompany their celebrated Vino Nobile, the Poliziani concentrate their culinary energies on grilled and roasted meats (beef, duck, and pork) and handmade pasta: gnocchi, tagliatelle, and especially *pici* (fat, chewy spaghetti rolled out between the palms so they're wonderfully irregular and hold the ragù or *piccante* tomato sauce well).

Besides the restaurants below, Montepulciano has a couple of good *osterie* that double as bars and stay open past midnight. One of the three proprietors of the **Osteria dell'Acquacheta,** Via Teatro 22 (ℂ **0578-758-443** or 0578-717-086) is in the cheese-making business, and a selection of his pecorino creations makes a good main course. Come early to try items like the fresh ricotta with honey before they run out. A full meal will run you about 25€ ($29). It's open Wednesday through Monday from 12:30 to 2:30pm (or so) and 7:30 to 10:30pm (or later, if things are hopping).

Cittino 🟡 *Value* POLIZIANA   Despite the dozen set tables, Cittino makes you feel as though you stumbled by accident into someone's living room and were invited to stay for dinner. The owner, Marcella, is an auxiliary *mamma* to anyone who walks in. She makes all her pasta by hand and will basically decide what you want to eat (she's usually right) and bustle off to her kitchen to prepare it fresh. Choosing to recommend her *pici* over her gnocchi or tagliatelle would be like singling out a favorite child, and a more flavorful rosemary-laden pork steak is hard to find. The bill will often seem suspiciously less than the sum of its parts.

If you find yourself too stuffed to move after the meal, Marcella rents three plain yet comfortable rooms upstairs for 40€ ($46)—one of which, with a double and a bunk bed, is perfect for families on a budget.

Vicolo della Via Nuova 2 (off Via Voltaia nel Corso). ℂ **0578-757-335.** Primi 6€–7€ ($6.90–$8.05); secondi 6€–9€ ($6.90–$10); fixed-price menu 16€ ($18). No credit cards. Thurs–Tues noon–3pm and 7–11pm. Closed June.

Fattoria Pulcino 🟡 TUSCAN   You run into a gauntlet of farm products at this 16th-century farmhouse just outside town before arriving at the giant dining room with long communal tables set with stainless steel platters (you can also dine outside on the terrace). Go for Poliziani dishes, such as *pici di Montepulciano* (in a ragù) or *ribollita,* followed by a steak or other grilled meat. For dessert, make sure you try the owner's own fruitcake sweetened with honey—*panella alla Gabriella*—supposedly based on a Franciscan recipe. (This was once a monastery.) Accompany it with one of the estate's Ercolani label Vino Nobile wines.

Via SS146 per Chianciano 35 (3km/2 miles SW of town). ℂ **0578-758-711.** www.pulcino.com. Primi 6€–8€ ($6.90–$9.20); secondi 10€–20€ ($12–$23); fixed-price menu 12€ ($14). AE, DC, MC, V. Easter–Dec daily noon–11pm; winter daily noon–3pm (reserve ahead and they'll open for dinner too), Sat–Sun 7–10pm. Bus: LFI from outside Porta al Prato toward Chianciano.

Ristorante il Cantuccio TUSCAN/POLIZIANA   In a long room divided by a double brick arch with a roaring fire at one end in winter, locals come to get

A Famous Spa Town En Route to Chiusi

Take the SS146 about 7km (4 miles) southeast out of Montepulciano to **Chianciano Terme** (© 0578-682-923; www.termechianciano.it), one of Tuscany's most famous spas. You drink the thermal mineral waters of the **Acqua Santa,** Piazza Martiri Perugini (© 0578-68-411) to clean out your liver (open daily 8am–2pm; Mar 16–Nov 15 also 4–6pm) and those of **Acqua Sillene,** Piazza Marconi (© 0578-68-551) to tidy the gastrointestinal tract (open year-round daily 8am–6pm). The springs of **Acqua Fucoli,** Viale G. Baccelli (© 0578-68-430), are used for thermal baths and to make mud packs for aching muscles and joints (open Apr 16–Oct 16). **Chianciano Terme** (the old town) and **Chianciano Bagni** (the spa) are of the same *comune* but really separate communities, about 1.6 kilometers (1 mile) apart, connected only by an umbilical cord of hotels called Viale Libertà.

The old town is compact and full of cars (with no pedestrian zones as in more popular hill towns), but it's still pretty. The **Museo della Collegiata,** Piazzolina dei Soldati (© 0578-30-378; open Tues–Sat 10am–12:30pm and 3–6:30pm; Nov–Mar open only on request), has some good Florentine and Sienese art from the 13th to the 18th century. Admission is 1.55€ ($1.80); ring the bell for the custodian.

There are many hotels in town, so the **tourist office,** Piazza Italia 67 (© 0578-671-122; fax 0578-63-277; www.chianciano.turismo.toscana.it), will be able to find something to suit you, but you'd do well at the **Grand Hotel Ambasciatori,** Viale della Libertà 512 (© and fax **0578-64-371;** www.barbettihotels.it). It offers all the amenities, a rooftop pool, and a small gym, and doubles cost 95€ ($109).

About 5km (3 miles) south of Chianciano on a side road is **La Foce** (no admittance), the house where American Iris Origo and her Italian husband aided and hid partisans fighting against the German occupation of Italy during World War II. A scholar and biographer, Origo penned the famous biography of 13th-century businessman Francesco Datini titled *The Merchant of Prato,* and she also recorded her war experiences at this villa in the well-regarded *War in the Val d'Orcia.* From the road you get a good view of the eroded biancane and a famously scenic Etruscan road winding its way back and forth up the next hill (you'll recognize it instantly from all the postcards). Many an amateur watercolorist, including Prince Charles, has taken a stab at capturing the scene on paper.

the closest thing to fine dining in town. Start with the excellent mixed antipasto of various sliced salamis and assorted *crostini.* If you choose *la bruschetta contadina* (two slabs of toasted bread loaded with prosciutto, tomatoes, cheese, and arugula) over the *tagliatelle al sugo di anatra* (in duck ragù) to start, you can have the fowl as your secondo in the *anatra con le* (covered with cooked-down onions). The grilled sausage or steak is also good, accompanied by roast potatoes or *fagioli all'olio* (Tuscan beans). *Torta alla ricotta,* the pielike forerunner of cheesecake, rounds out a meal nicely.

Via delle Cantine 1–2 (off Via Gracciano nel Corso). ℂ **0578-757-870.** www.opificidigitali.it/romano. Reservations recommended. Primi 5.20€–9.40€ ($6–$11); secondi 7.30€–23.80€ ($8.40–$27). AE, DC, MC, V. Tues–Sun 12:30–2:30pm and 7:30–10pm. Closed 2 weeks early Nov, 2 weeks June or July.

4 Chiusi: In the Footsteps of the Etruscans

21km (13 miles) SE of Montepulciano; 89km (55 miles) SE of Siena; 151km (94 miles) SE of Florence; 165km (102 miles) N of Rome

One of southern Tuscany's smaller hilltop cities, Chiusi doesn't transport you to the Middle Ages or wow you with the Renaissance. You come to Chiusi for one thing: Etruscans.

Alternately spelled *Camars* or *Clevsins,* the Etruscan center here was of considerable importance in the 7th and 6th centuries B.C. One of the more powerful among the Etruscan 12-city confederation, it was ruled in the late 500s B.C. by the *lucumo* (king) Lars Porsena, who was famous for attacking Rome from 507 to 506 B.C. Like Cortona just up the Valdichiana (see chapter 9 for more information), the lowlands around Chiusi are a treasure trove of tombs. Most of the archaeologically important ones are closed for preservation, but you may visit a few with a guide. And the less famous ones are open to anyone armed with a good map, a few oranges in their pocket, and half a day to explore the valley on their own. Chiusi's excellent restaurants await you after a hard day's tomb hunting.

ESSENTIALS

GETTING THERE   By Train   The Chiusi/Chianciano Terme station (ℂ **0578-20-074**) is a major stop on the main **Rome-Florence** line (which passes through Arezzo) and is also the terminus of a secondary line that originates in **Siena** (about 12 trains daily). A bus will carry you up to the *centro storico.*

By Car   From Montepulciano, follow the SS146. From **Florence,** take the A1 to the Chiusi exit. From **Siena,** take the SS326 toward Sinalunga to the A1 south to the Chiusi exit. You can **park** off Via Pietriccia and Via dei Longobardi.

By Bus   Because Chiusi has one of the main train stations in the region, most towns run several LFI buses here daily. There are 16 daily from Montepulciano (45 min.) that stop in Chianciano Terme (25 min.) along the way. Ask to get off at the *centro storico* or you'll end up in the meatpacking town of Chiusi Scalo down below.

VISITOR INFORMATION   The **information office** is at Piazza Duomo 1 (ℂ and fax **0578-227-667**), open Monday through Saturday from 9:30am to 12:30pm and 3 to 5pm (sometimes to 7pm in summer) and Sunday from 9am to 12:30pm (the office itself admits these hours are more indicative, not precise; they might open at 10am or close at noon).

SPECIAL EVENTS   Chiusi has no festivals of particular note, although locals do drive their Fiats to the lake on July 2 to have the **cars blessed** in the name of the city's St. Mustiola and to watch fireworks. From mid-July to August, a series of outdoor concerts, films, and theater productions are staged for **Summer Under the Stars.** The local restaurants get involved with **neighborhood feast days** on May 5, May 26, and June 29 and 30. Also in May are a **costumed procession** (on the 17th) and a **classic car race** (on the 2nd). **Market** day is Tuesday.

ON THE TRAIL OF THE ETRUSCANS

Although a huge portion of Chiusi's rich archaeological patrimony was carried off by early archaeologists to museums in Orvieto and elsewhere, the city's **Museo**

Archeologico Nazionale Etrusco 👁👁, in Via Porsenna (© **0578-20-177**), has no mean share of what's left. The collections inside this neoclassical building are in eternal rearrangement. There are plenty of the famous rectangular Etruscan funerary urns, in which the deceased's ashes were kept in a box topped by a lid carved with the man or woman's reclining likeness. Keep on the lookout for find no. 407, featuring a winged version of the split-tailed siren—the mythological symbol of sex and fertility, which pops up as late as the Middle Ages on Christian buildings like Pienza's Pieve. One of the museum's greatest treasures is a set of **painted urns** dating back to the 2nd century B.C. on which the polychrome decorations are still marvelously intact.

Another Etruscan funerary vehicle on display is the anthropomorphic canopic jar, made of terra cotta and sometimes bronze with a carved human head for a lid and handles like arms. Occasionally an entire statue would top off the affair, as in the 7th-century B.C. example here. The deceased, perched on the lid, is apparently orating, surrounded by stylized griffins whose heads are raised high, crying out. Aside from the prehistoric and Villanovan bits, the imported Attic black- and red-figure vases, and some ebony-toned 7th- to 6th-century B.C. *bucchero* ceramics, keep your eyes peeled for the marble portrait of Augustus and the 3rd-century A.D. mosaic of a boar hunt. The basement is devoted to depicting local necropoli and their excavations. The museum is open Monday through Saturday from 9am to 2pm and Sunday from 9am to 1pm (it stays open to 8pm July–Sept, and may continue to do so year-round; phone ahead). Admission is 4€ ($4.60) adults, 2€ ($2.30) youth ages 18 to 25, free for children under 18 and people over 65.

A block up from the museum, **Piazza del Duomo** opens off to your left, past a medieval tower converted to Christianity in the 16th century as the bell tower to San Secondiano cathedral. The piazza, with its loggia running down one side, is a small but striking square of light-gray cut stone that matches the facade of the 12th-century **Duomo** at one end. The inside was restored in the late 19th century but retains its recycled columns and capitals pilfered from local Roman buildings. On closer inspection, you'll note those seemingly early medieval "mosaics" covering every inch of the nave and apses are actually made of paint— an 1887 to 1894 opus by Arturo Viligiardi (viewable by coin-op lights).

The entrance to the **Museo della Cattedrale** (© **0578-226-490**) is to the right of the Duomo's doors under the arcade. The first floor has some uninspired paleo-Christian and Lombard remains, but in the gardens are remains of the Etruscan city's walls and a 3rd-century B.C. tower. The museum's main attraction is upstairs, a series of 21 **antiphonals** from the abbey of Monte Oliveto Maggiore that were illuminated by artists like Sano di Pietro and Liberale da Verona in the 15th century. The entire set was stolen in 1972, but miraculously all save one and a few pages of another were recovered. The museum is open daily: from June to October 15 from 9:30am to 12:45pm and 4 to 7pm and from October 16 to May from 9:30am to 12:45pm (Sun also 3:30–6:30pm). Admission is 2€ ($2.30).

Meet at the museum desk for the obligatory guided tour of the **Labirinto di Porsena (Labyrinth of Porsena)** 👁 (© **0578-226-490** for reservations), the tourist board's inventive way to describe a jaunt through a painstakingly excavated portion of the tunnel system carved under the city by the Etruscans. The cathedral museum and gardens in the square above were once the bishop's palace, and the tunnels were used as a refuse dump. They were rediscovered in the 1920s by some kids who decided to start cleaning them out. The good-hearted teenagers kept at their task, eventually becoming a volunteer society of amateur archaeologists, and slowly the tunnels were reopened. A goodly stretch of the *cunicoli* (water sewers) was opened to the public in 1995. The narrow passages were apparently part of a vast plumbing system that once supplied the entire Etruscan city from a huge underground lake (also being archaeologically explored, but not yet public). As a bonus to the tour, the cathedral bell tower sits right on top of this well, and the climb to the top is worth it for the sweeping city and countryside vista. The half-hour tours cost 3€/$3.45 (or 4€/$4.60 combined with Museo); free for those under 10, and leave about every 30 minutes during museum hours.

Of the **Etruscan tombs** 🌟🌟 in the surrounding area, especially to the north and northeast toward the small Lake Chiusi (a remnant of the once widespread Valdichiana marshes), currently only the **Tomba della Pellegrina** (with 4th-c. B.C. sarcophagi and 3rd-c. B.C. cinerary urns still in place) and **Tomba del Leone** (still showing a bit of color on its walls) are open to visitors. For the moment at least, on Tuesday, Thursday, and Saturday, you can also book ahead (space is limited for two visits a day, around 11am and 3:30pm—but those hours aren't fixed) to see the famous painted **Tomba della Scimmia,** though its accessibility is decided year to year. To visit any of them, make an appointment at the archaeological museum (© **0578-20-177**). You must have your own car, in which the custodian accompanies you.

You must also have wheels to visit the 3rd- to 5th-century A.D. **paleo-Christian catacombs** in the same area. Meet the guide at 11am at the cathedral museum's desk (in summer also around 4pm).

Few other sights in town hold much interest, but on a stroll you might pass through the market square of **Piazza XX Settembre,** anchored at one end by the 13th-century **Santa Maria della Morte,** with its tall, flat tower and with a 14th-century loggia along one side. At the square's other end sprouts a **clock tower,** near which is the medieval **San Francesco.** Via Petrarca leads from Via Porsenna to a **panorama** over the Valdichiana from Piazza Olivazzo. The west end of town is a **public park** with a more intimate vista of Chiusi's cultivated slopes.

WHERE TO STAY

If **Albergo La Sfinge** (see below) is full, there are some unobjectionable if utterly bland places around Chiusi Scalo in the valley near the train station.

Albergo La Sfinge   There's only one game in town when it comes to spending the night. Luckily, the family who runs Chiusi's sole inn is as friendly as can be. Most rooms have wrought-iron bedsteads, tiny Tiffany-style bedside lamps, and old-fashioned armoires and desks (a few still have the old yawningly modern units). Some rooms come with tile floors and wood-beamed ceilings, others with a vista over Monte Amiata, and, as you can see below, with any of a combination of amenities. There are also two rooms with a common door that can be made into a family suite. The innkeepers have plans to install air-conditioning in all the guest rooms by the time you read this.

Via Marconi 2 (just off Via Garibaldi), 53043 Chiusi Città (SI). © and fax **0578-20-157**. www.albergola sfinge.com. 15 units. 77€ ($89) double with bathroom; 60€ ($69) double with private, external bathroom. Breakfast 5€ ($5.75). MC, V. Limited free parking or 10€ ($12) in garage. Closed Jan 30–Mar 8. *In room:* A/C in 4 units, TV in 9 units, hair dryer in 5 units.

Hotel La Fattoria 🌟 *(Finds)*   The rooms at this 1850s lakeside farmhouse are fitted out in full country-inn style, with dark wood furniture and floral-patterned fabrics. Most are fairly large, and a few have a view out over the lake. In the large restaurant (closed Mon) you can get *afettati misti* (cold cuts sliced the old-fashioned way, by hand) and fish fresh from the lake. In summer, you can dine on an open lake-view terrace and toast the view with a *torta al limone* (in this case, an American-style lemon meringue pie) for dessert.

Via Lago di Chiusi (5km/3 miles east of Chiusi on the lake), 52043 Chiusi (SI). ℂ 0578-21-407. Fax 0578-20-644. www.la-fattoria.it. 8 units. 83€–93€ ($95–$107) double; 103€ ($118) triple. Half and full pension available. Rates include continental breakfast. AE, DC, MC, V. Free parking. Closed Jan 10–Feb 10. The LFI bus to Lago di Chiusi stops here. **Amenities:** Restaurant; bike rental; children's playground; limited room service. *In room:* A/C, TV, minibar, hair dryer, safe.

WHERE TO DINE

Every Chiusi restaurant excels at both traditional, hearty peasant dishes and putting creative spins on old favorites. Don't forget to consider a countryside lunch at **La Fattoria,** mentioned under hotels, above.

La Solita Zuppa ✿ SOUTHERN TUSCAN   An ex-theater couple runs this excellent restaurant, where the atmosphere is a strange mix of country trattoria and refined *boîte,* with Ella Fitzgerald and Louis Armstrong as the musical accompaniment. When I asked Laura Pacchieri if she had a menu, she responded, "I have me," and proceeded to describe each dish in such succulent detail it was tough to choose (although there is, in fact, a written menu). You'll be served a delicious assortment of warm *crostini* and sliced salamis and an aperitif while you decide between *pici* or *lasagne al cinghiale* (lasagne layered with cheese and wild boar), cooked in a ceramic casserole. Some of "The Same Old Soups" of the restaurant's name include *porri e patate* (potato leek), *fagioli e farro* (bean and emmer), and a peasant *lenti e castagne* (lentils and chestnuts). For secondi, the chef makes a slightly *piccante* (spicy) *abbachio* (lamb) and a mean *maiale alle mele* (suckling pig with apples).

Via Porsenna 21. ℂ **0578-21-006.** www.lasolitazuppa.it. Reservations recommended. Primi 5.70€ ($6.55); secondi 8.30€ ($9.55). AE, DC, MC, V. Wed–Mon 12:30–2:30pm and 7:30–10pm. Closed Jan 15–Mar 10.

Ristorante Zaira ✿✿ SOUTHERN TUSCAN   Regarded as the best restaurant in a city where the competition is tough, Zaira highlights its success by lining the entrance with a gallery of the distinguished guides that recommend it. Try *trota in carpione* (marinated trout) as an appetizer in place of the same old *crostini misti* before passing on to the justifiably famous house specialty, the tasty *pasta del lucumone* (ziti baked with ham and three types of cheese in a ceramic casserole). The *lucumone* is a tough act to follow, but you can try with *coniglio al limone* (rabbit kissed with lemon) or *anatra al vino nobile* (duck cooked in red wine) with *carciofi fritti* (fried artichokes). Ask to visit the rambling wine cellars, which house more than 20,000 bottles.

Via Arunte 12. ℂ **0578-20-260.** www.zaira.com Reservations recommended. Primi 5.50€–8.50€ ($6.30–$9.80); secondi 8.50€–14€ ($9.80–$16). AE, DC, MC, V. Daily noon–2:45pm and 7–10:30pm (closed Mon mid-Jan to June and Oct–Nov). Closed 15 days in Nov.

9

Arezzo &
Northeastern Tuscany

The province of **Arezzo,** bounding Tuscany's northeast corner, is a land of castle-dominated hill towns, misty blue mountains, and the vestiges of Apennine forests. Snowy-white cattle graze in the wide Chiana Valley, while light industry toils at the edges of medieval centers. In the reaches of the mountains lie hermitages of ecologically minded vegetarian monks and **La Verna,** St. Francis's favorite spot to pray, where he became the first human to receive the stigmata.

This is the area where the brawny, humanist Renaissance of Florence meets and melds with the intangible, hazy spirituality of Umbria's green hills. This hybrid is perfectly displayed in the works of the region's two most famous artistic sons, Piero della Francesca and Luca Signorelli, both masters of mathematical proportion and of rarefied moods and landscapes in painting. Piero is the focus of his native **Sansepolcro,** and one of the main draws in **Arezzo,** a low-key city of amiable citizens and modest art treasures. Art-rich **Cortona,** Luca Signorelli's hometown, is an ancient Etruscan hill town that doesn't quite fill up its medieval walls; much of the space is occupied by oversize gardens.

Arezzo province has given us the melodic genius of Guido Monaco, inventor of the musical scale, and the earthy, bold painting of Masaccio, the first artist to master perspective. It brought forth the great poet Petrarch, whose classical studies and humanist philosophy rang in the Renaissance and earned him the moniker "the first modern man," and Giorgio Vasari, architect of the Uffizi, court painter to Cosimo I, and the Western world's first art historian. Vasari brought Petrarch's movement full circle by literally writing the book on the Renaissance. It's no surprise the ultimate Florentine of the Renaissance era, Michelangelo, was born in the forested hills east of Arezzo.

THE CASENTINO: FROM FLORENCE TO AREZZO

The forested mountains of the **Casentino,** the route from Florence to Arezzo closest to the Apennines, have been a hotbed of spirituality for centuries, the corner of Tuscany most like a bit of mystical Umbria. For information on the region, call 🕾 **0575-593-098** or check www.turismo.casentino.toscana.it.

Head east out of Florence, and on the other side of Pontassieve, a right toward Pèlago leads a winding, scenic 24km (15 miles) to **Vallombrosa.** In 1038, the **abbey** here was the site of the foundation of the Vallombrosan order by Giovanni Gualberto, a Florentine moved to the spiritual life when he was confronted with his brother's murderer and found he had a greater desire to pardon him than to seek revenge. The current 15th- to 18th-century incarnation of the monastery doesn't welcome visitors, but it's surrounded by stands of evergreen recalling the verdant forests that impressed Milton enough to include them in *Paradise Lost.*

Another picturesque road leads back up to the SS70, where you can continue 20km (12 miles) to the medieval hill town of **Poppi,** whose **Castello dei Conti Guidi** (© **0575-520-516**) is visible for miles. This castle, started by the architect Lapo in 1274 and finished by his student Arnolfo di Cambio, was the seat of the Guidi counts who ruled the Casentino until 1440, when it came under Florence's realm. Rouse the custodian to visit the frescoed main hall and the Taddeo Gaddi–decorated chapel (1330–40). It's open summer daily from 10am to 7pm, winter Thursday through Sunday only from 9:30am to 1pm and 2:30 to 5:30pm. Admission is 4€ ($4.60).

The rest of diminutive Poppi is fun to explore. Many of the medieval buildings have retained their wooden porticos, and a slightly sleepy village atmosphere prevails. The church of **San Fedele** is home to a 13th-century *Madonna and Child* in the right transept painted by the "Maestro della Maddalena." A few of the town's other churches contain paintings by the local baroque talent Francesco Morandini, universally known as Il Poppi.

A branch road leads 15km (9 miles) north from Poppi into the Tuscan half of the national park of **Monte Falterona, Campigna, e Foreste Casentinesi** (www. parks.it/parco.nazionale.for.casentinesi), one of the last sizable chunks of native forest left in Italy; you can get information at the website above, or in Pratovecchio at Via G. Brocchi 7 (© and fax **0575-559-054;** www.turismo.casentino. toscana.it), open Tuesday through Sunday from 10am to noon and 3 to 5pm (Oct–Mar open Sat–Sun only, and possibly Fri). Among the beech and silver fir trees are the sylvan religious complexes of **Camáldoli.** The hermitage was founded in 1012 under a rigorous rule of purity and meditation. Such a rarefied spot so near Florence and Arezzo immediately attracted a number of meditative hacks who just wanted a few weeks' worth of monkish life. Because this threatened to disrupt the contemplative routine of the hermitage, in 1046 the founder, St. Romualdo, wisely decided to build a **Monastero di Camáldoli** about 20km (12 miles) down the road for the dabblers to use. This is now home to the pharmacy, where you can buy the monks' herbal remedies and poultices. Although the monks in the hermitage no longer live as hermits but as monastics, they're still strict about their purity. Vegetarians who eat only what they can grow, members of the order help replenish the forest slowly by planting 5,000 trees yearly, and they don't allow women past the gate into the hermitage proper. (You're not missing much; it's like a miniaturized subdivision of monks' cottages surrounded by tall pines.)

Bibbiena, just 7km (4 miles) down the road from Poppi, has had most of the charm industrialized right out of it; the **tourist office** is at Via Berni 29 (© and fax **0575-593-098;** open Mon–Sat 9am–12:30pm and 3:30–6:30pm, Sun 10am–noon and 3:30–6:30pm; winter Mon–Fri only). However, the church of **San Lorenzo** has some della Robbian terra cottas and **San Ippolito e Donato** has a *Madonna and Child with Saints* triptych by Bicci di Lorenzo.

You can branch off here onto the SS208 and travel 25km (16 miles) to the holy mount of **La Verna** ⚑. Count Orlando Cattani gave this secluded rock outcropping to Francis of Assisi for his new monastic order in 1213. Francis loved to come here to meditate and sleep on the rocks—a vision had informed him the odd rents in the rocky ground were caused by the earthquakes that occurred when Christ was crucified. On his last trip here, the night of September 14, 1224, he was praying alone on the rocks when he was visited by a seraph who left him with a wholly new mark of sanctity—the stigmata of Christ's wounds. Although the wounds in his feet caused him much pain while walking for the remainder of his life, the stigmata confirmed the spirituality of a man already widely believed to be just about the holiest person alive. The small **mud-hut monastery** he founded has grown and is still a pilgrimage site for the devout. Even those with just a passing interest can tour it to see the saint's cell and the spot where the miracle occurred (tours daily 6:30am–9:30pm, until 7:30pm in winter).

In the **main church,** Andrea della Robbia left some of the greatest, most spiritual examples of his glazed terra-cotta works, like an *Ascension* and a beautifully simple *Annunciation.* The door to the chapel built around the rock where St. Francis received the stigmata is marked with a tondo of the *Madonna and Child* by Luca della Robbia; the *Crucifixion* inside is by Andrea. The small **Santa Maria degli Angeli,** begun while the saint was alive, has another Andrea della Robbia *Assumption.* Scramble up to the summit of **La Penna** for spectacular countryside views.

Just below La Verna is the village of Chiusi, which was governed with the hamlet of **Caprese** for 6 months (late 1474 to early 1475) by the assigned *podestà* (mayor) from Florence, an impoverished minor nobleman named Ludovico Buonarroti. This brief term of office was just long enough for Ludovico's second son to be born in the house of the *podestà* at Caprese on March 6, 1474. The baby was christened at the local church of San Giovanni as Michelangelo Buonarroti. Caprese has never forgotten it and has even changed its name to Caprese Michelangelo after the boy grew up to become one of the greatest artists the world has ever known. His birthplace above the town and the nearby small castle have been converted into a small, and not terribly engrossing, museum about Michelangelo's career called the **Museo Michelangiolesco** (© **0575-793-776;** open daily 9:30am–6:30pm, closed Mon in winter). Admission is 3€ ($3.45) adults, 2€ ($2.30) ages 7 to 14, free for children under 7. Later in life, Michelangelo wrote to Giorgio Vasari, "If my brains are any good at all, it's because I was born in the pure air of your Arezzo countryside."

1 Arezzo: Where Life Is Beautiful

85km (53 miles) SE of Florence; 246km (153 miles) N of Rome

Arezzo is a medium-size Tuscan city, an agricultural center clambering up a low hill. It's a town of friendly citizens, artistic masterpieces by Piero della Francesca, and stained-glass marvels by Guillaume de Marcillat. Arretium was an important member of the 12-city Etruscan confederation, and it was famous in Roman times for its mass-produced *corallino* ceramics. The Ghibelline medieval *comune* ran afoul of Florence's Guelfs, and the city's armies were soundly trounced by Florence in the 1289 Battle of Campaldino. (The Florentine forces counted a young Dante Alighieri among the foot soldiers.) More recently, the city's gotten some international face time as the setting for Roberto Benigni's 1999 Oscar-winning film *La Vita è Bella (Life Is Beautiful).*

Arezzo has produced an unusual number of cultural giants. Guido Monaco (or Guido d'Arezzo), born around A.D. 995, invented the modern musical scale and notation. The poet Petrarch (1304–74) helped found the humanist movement that was the basis for the entire cultural Renaissance. Spinello Aretino (1350–1410) was one of the great *trecento* masters of Italian fresco. Pietro Aretino (1492–1566), a gifted poet, was capable of writing the most vituperative, scandal-causing verses. He was an even more gifted blackmailer, adept at appealing to powerful men's purses in order that his select words about them might never reach the general public. Another towering Aretine was Giorgio Vasari (1512–74), a mediocre painter, a much more talented architect, and, with his book *Lives of*

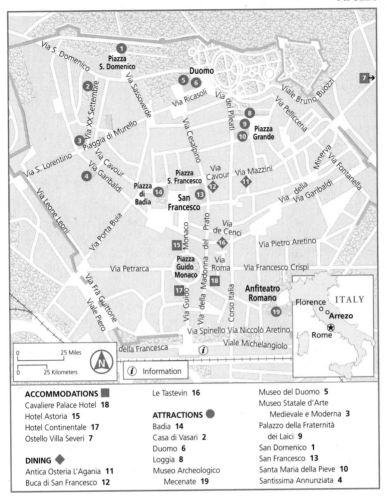

ACCOMMODATIONS ■
Cavaliere Palace Hotel **18**
Hotel Astoria **15**
Hotel Continentale **17**
Ostello Villa Severi **7**

DINING ◆
Antica Osteria L'Agania **11**
Buca di San Francesco **12**

Le Tastevin **16**

ATTRACTIONS ●
Badia **14**
Casa di Vasari **2**
Duomo **6**
Loggia **8**
Museo Archeologico
Mecenate **19**

Museo del Duomo **5**
Museo Statale d'Arte
Medievale e Moderna **3**
Palazzo della Fraternità
dei Laici **9**
San Domenico **1**
San Francesco **13**
Santa Maria della Pieve **10**
Santissima Annunziata **4**

the Artists—a collection of biographies of masters from Cimabue and Giotto through Michelangelo—the unwitting author of the first art history text.

ESSENTIALS
GETTING THERE   By Train   The main line between **Rome** (22 daily; 2–2 hr. 55 min.) and **Florence** (45 daily; 40–90 min.) also passes **Chiusi/Chianciano Terme** (24 daily; 35–70 min.) and **Orvieto** (15 daily; 50–80 min.) on its way to Arezzo. You can transfer at Terontola/Cortona for the dozen daily trains to **Perugia** (2¼ hr. total riding time) and **Assisi** (2 hr. 40 min.). The **train station** (© 0575-20-553) is at Piazza della Repubblica just southwest of the city walls. All hotels are within a few blocks' walk.

By Car   The quickest route from Florence or Rome is the **A1 autostrada.** You can **park,** usually not free, along Via Niccolò Aretino just inside the southwest corner of the walls and Via B. Alberti, behind the train station. There's free parking on Via Pietri and Vai XXV Aprile.

By Bus SITA buses (© 0575-749-818; www.sita-on-line.it) from **Florence** (1 hr. 20 min.–2 hr.) and **LFI** buses (© 0575-324-294) from **Siena** (1½ hr.) let you off in front of the train station.

VISITOR INFORMATION The **APT information office** is at Piazza della Repubblica 28, just outside the train station (© 0575-377-678, or © and fax 0575-20-839; www.apt.arezzo.it; open Mon–Fri 9am–1pm and 3–7pm, Sun 9am–1pm). There's a **provincial APT office** at Piazza Risorgimento 116 (© 0575-23-952 or 0575-23-523; fax 0575-28-042); go up Via Guido Monaco a block and turn right; call for hours. The website **www.cittadiarezzo.com** is also very helpful for planning a visit.

FESTIVALS & MARKETS In the last week of August, Guido Monaco's musical traditions are carried on in a series of choral concerts called the **International Polyphonic Conference.**

On the third Sunday in June and the first Sunday in September, Arezzo pulls out the stops for a full-fledged medieval jousting tournament, the **Giostra del Saracino** , dating from at least the 16th century. After an afternoon of complex flag-tossing and pageantry, mounted, armored riders thunder across dirt-lined Piazza del Duomo with their lances aimed at the effigy of a Saracen warrior. The twist is that when the "knights" strike a blow on his shield, the Saracen swivels and his other arm is carrying a whip. Hitting the shield's bull's-eye is only half the trick—the other is dodging the whip.

On the first Sunday of every month, Piazza del Duomo is filled with more than 600 dealers in one of Italy's leading **antiques fairs** . The dealers specialize in 19th-century furniture and 17th- to 19th-century glass, but items dating from the Renaissance are well represented (as are items from the 1950s and '60s). It draws serious collectors from around the world. In winter, the fair runs from 7:30am to 3pm (in summer as late as 7 or 9pm).

WHAT TO SEE & DO

Arezzo's main square, **Piazza Grande** , is charmingly off-kilter. Since 1200, it has listed alarmingly to one side, creating a slope crowned with a graceful **loggia** designed in 1573 by Giorgio Vasari. Perpendicular to where the shop-filled tunnel-like loggia runs out of the square sits the composite **Palazzo della Fraternità dei Laici.** The Gothic lower half (1377) has a detached Spinello Aretino fresco of the *Pietà* and a Bernardo Rossellino *Madonna della Misericordia* (1434) in bas-relief above the door. The upper loggia was built in 1460, and the clock bell tower added by Vasari in 1552. An extensive renovation of the palazzo was completed in 2002. One palace down to the left is the arcaded apse of Santa Maria della Pieve (see below).

San Francesco One of the greatest fresco cycles by one of the greatest artists of the Renaissance covers the sanctuary of this 14th-century church. Piero della Francesca's ***Legend of the True Cross*** (1448–66) has drawn art-loving pilgrims from around the world for centuries. Piero's work features perfect perspective and hauntingly ethereal, woodenly posed figures that nonetheless convey untold depths of emotion. It fascinates art theorists just as his innovative narrative schemes and figurative style earned him the admiration of his contemporaries. The entire cycle was gorgeously restored from 1985 to 2000 to fix the extensive damage wreaked by 500 years of fires, earthquakes, Napoleonic troops, and creeping dampness in the plaster. You can see them from the ropes at the base of the altar steps, about 10m (33 ft.) away, but it is well worth booking a ticket to get up close.

French master Guillaume de Marcillat painted the **rose window** in 1520, and for a peek at what Piero's assistant Lorentino d'Andrea was capable of, check out the first altar on the right. Here in 1463, Lorentino frescoed a scene of San Bernardino leading the Aretines out of this very church on a good old-fashioned pagan-smashing day trip to destroy the cultish temple of Fons Tecta. Just beyond it is a *Sacred Conversation* by Niccolò Soggi and, in the second chapel, scenes from the *Life of St. Bartholomew* by another of Piero's followers. Spinello Aretino painted the ***Annunciation*** at the end of the right aisle.

A new policy requires visitors to make reservations to view the fresco cycles. Twenty-five people are admitted every 30 minutes, and are required to leave at the end of the time slot. Go online to the website listed below, or to www. ticketeria.it/pierodellafrancesca.htm. Note that you're required pick up your tickets at least a half-hour before your entry time or you risk losing your space on the tour.

Piazza San Francesco. ℂ **0575-20-630**; required reservation for Piero cycle tickets at 0575-24-001, 06-32-810 or www.pierodellafrancesca.it. Admission to church free; Piero cycle 5.03€ ($5.80) including the booking fee. Church daily 8:30–noon and 2:30–6:30pm. Piero cycle by 30-min. guided tour only, leaving on the half-hour Mon–Fri 9am–6pm; Sat 9am–5:30pm (5:45pm in winter); Sun 1–5:30pm. Box office closes 1 hour earlier.

Santa Maria della Pieve ⚜ This 12th-century church is Lombard Romanesque architecture at its most beautiful, with a craggy, eroded **facade** ⚜ of stacked arcades in luminous beige stone. The spaces between the columns of the arcades get narrower at each level, which, along with the setting on a narrow street, only adds to the illusion of great height. The occasional carved column was mixed in; look for the human telamon in the top row. The fat 36m (120-ft.) **bell tower** "of the hundred holes" with its bifore windows is a 1330 addition. If the restoration on the main doorway is finished, you can admire the medieval reliefs lining it. They depict the months of the year, including the two-faced pagan god Janus sitting in for the month of January (named after him).

The arches in the interior are just starting to get plucked to Gothic pointiness, and dozens of windows light the place. On the high altar above the raised crypt is a 1320 **polyptych of the *Madonna and Child with Saints*** ⚜—all wearing gorgeously worked fabrics—by Sienese master Pietro Lorenzetti. In the crypt, with its carved medieval capitals, is a 1326 reliquary bust by Aretine goldsmiths Peter and Paul; inside are the remains of Arezzo's patron saint, St. Donato, a local bishop martyred in the 5th century.

Corso Italia 7. ℂ **0575-22-629**. Free admission. May–Sept daily 8am–7pm; Oct–Apr daily 8am–noon and 3–6pm.

Duomo At the highest point in town, surrounded by the Parco il Prato with its 16th-century Medici fortress ruins, Arezzo's cathedral was slowly agglomerated between 1278 and 1510, though it took until 1859 to raise the neo-Gothic bell tower and until 1935 to finish the simple facade. Among the masterpieces inside, the greatest may be the **stained-glass windows** ⚜ (1519–23) by the undisputed master of the form, the French immigrant Guillaume de Marcillat. This is one of the few complete cycles of his work in Italy that hasn't been destroyed, and it includes the *Pentecost* rose window in the facade; the *Calling of St. Matthew,* the *Baptism of Christ,* the *Expulsion of Merchants from the Temple,* the *Adulteress,* and the *Raising of Lazarus* along the right wall; and *Saints Silvester and Lucy* in the chapel to the left of the apse. De Marcillat, who left France after becoming a Dominican friar (apparently to avoid murder charges), was no mean frescoist either, and painted the first three **ceiling vaults** of the nave.

There are fine Gothic tombs throughout the church, and the city's patron saint, St. Donato, is buried under the beautifully sculpted 14th-century Gothic **high altar.** At the end of the left aisle, on the wall next to the sacristy door, is a scraggly-haired but still magnificent *Mary Magdalene* frescoed by Piero della Francesca (use the switch hidden on the pillar across from the fresco to turn on the light). Sienese sculptors Agostino da Giovanni and Agnolo di Ventura, who worked on the high altar, created the Gothic stone comic book of the **tomb of Bishop Guido Tarlati** in the left aisle. The 14th-century relief panels depict scenes from the life of the warrior bishop with Aretine landscapes in the background. The mammoth 1535 *cantoria* beyond it was Vasari's first go at architecture.

The large **Cappella della Madonna del Conforto (Lady Chapel)** in the left aisle near the church entrance preserves several della Robbia terra cottas, including an *Assumption,* a *Crucifixion,* and a pretty *Madonna and Child* by Andrea, plus a polychrome *Madonna and Child with Saints* attributed to Giovanni. In the small **baptistery** is a **font** bearing Donatello-school *schiacciato* relief panels—the *Baptism of Christ* scene may have been carved by Donatello himself.

Piazza del Duomo. ⓒ **0575-23-991**. Free admission. Daily 7am–12:30pm and 3–6:30pm.

Museo del Duomo   This small but worthy museum is hidden on the back side of Arezzo's Duomo. Inside are three painted wood crucifixes from the 12th and 13th centuries and a terra-cotta *Annunciation* (1434) by Bernardo Rossellino. The annunciation is a popular theme here, and you can see how Spinello Aretino, his teacher Andrea di Nerio, and Spinello's son Parri each handled the scene in fresco. One of the collection's star frescoes is a 15th-century *St. Jerome in the Desert* by Bartolomeo della Gatta, who collaborated with Domenico Pecori on the 1520 *Madonna and Child with Saints Fabian and Sebastian.* The museum also preserves some of hometown boy Giorgio Vasari's better works, a *Preaching of the Baptist* and a *Baptism of Christ* (1549) surrounded by a lyrical, pastoral landscape.

Piazzetta dietro il Duomo (entry sometimes through sacristy in Duomo's left aisle). ⓒ **0575-23-991**. Admission 2.60€ ($3). Thurs–Sat 10am–noon.

San Domenico   The interior of this 1275 church, fronted by a brick-lined piazza planted with lime trees, is very dark, but to the left and right of the altar are fuse boxes where you can switch on the lights. Lots of good 14th-century **fresco fragments** line the walls, and over the high altar is a painted *Crucifix* ⭐ by Cimabue, brilliantly restored and returned to this place of honor in early 2003.

On the entrance wall are frescoes of the *Crucifixion* and the *Life of St. Nicholas of Bari* by Parri di Spinello. On the right wall, under a Gothic canopy, Luca di Tommé painted a very young *Christ with the Doctors of the Church* in the Sienese style. The chapel to the right of the high altar contains a 14th-century stone *Madonna and Child* and a delicate fresco of the *Annunciation* by Spinello Aretino. More frescoes line the church's left wall, and the last one on your right as you leave is a 15th-century *St. Vincent Ferrer.* According to Giorgio Vasari, this is the only known work by his grandfather, Lazzaro Vasari.

Piazza San Domenico. ⓒ **0575-22-906**. Free admission. Nov 3–Mar 22 daily 9am–6:30pm; Mar 23–Nov 2 daily 9am–7pm.

Casa di Vasari (Vasari's House)   Giorgio Vasari bought this house in 1540 and decorated it with rather bland, semi-mannerist paintings with the help of his contemporaries and students. There are works by Il Poppi, Alessandro Allori,

Santi di Tito, and, of course, Giorgio himself. The best of the Vasari pieces are a *Deposition* in the second room and a painting in the first room of **Virtue, Envy, and Fortune** duking it out on the ceiling. It features a nifty optical trick: The figure that appears to be on top changes as you view it from different perspectives.

Via XX Settembre 55. (✆ **0575-409-040**. Admission 4.90€ ($5.65), 2.90€ ($3.35) ages 18–25, free under 18. Wed–Sat and Mon 9am–7pm; Sun 9am–1pm.

Museo Statale d'Arte Medievale e Moderna   Every epoch of Aretine and imported artistry from the Middle Ages to the Macchiaioli is represented in the moderately large, moderately interesting collections here. A room off the ground-floor courtyard has **medieval sculptures** ranging from 11th-century capitals to 14th-century *Madonna*s rescued from various town gates and defunct churches. On the first floor are a Byzantine-style 13th-century painting of *St. Francis* by Margaritone d'Arezzo and an early-Sienese-school *Madonna* embedded with baubles. The 15th-century frescoes of Spinello Aretino's pupil Giovanni d'Agnolo di Balduccio dominate room 2. The master weighs in in the next room with a *Trinità,* accompanied by his son Parri's **Sconfitta di Massenzio,** a battle scene discovered in the Badia during World War II cleanup. Historic tournament armor is preserved in room 5 in the form of loads of 17th-century weapons of death. There are two paintings by Bartolomeo della Gatta here of **St. Roch**—one shows a medieval Arezzo in the background but doesn't reveal that the city is in the throes of the Black Death. This work was part of an offering to the saint begging him to intercede to stop the disease.

An ancient pottery center, Arezzo is always ready to appreciate art from outside masters. Its museum has a fine collection of 14th- to 18th-century **majolica ceramic** works from Faenza, Gubbio (including one precious plate by the famous Mastro Giorgio), and Deruta, along with some Andrea della Robbia terra cottas. The first-floor collections contain mannerist and baroque canvases by Il Poppi, Empoli, and Salimbeni, plus several by Vasari—the best is his large, crowded 1548 **Supper for the Marriage of Esther.** The second floor has a gathering of small Macchiaioli paintings and a pair of Luca Signorelli **Madonna with Child** paintings (1518–22) but sputters out into insipid baroque pieces.

Via San Lorentino 8. (✆ **0575-409-050**. Admission 4.90€ ($5.65) adults, 2.90€ ($3.65) ages 18–25, free for children under 18 and seniors over 68. Tues–Sun 9am–6pm.

Santissima Annunziata   The main attractions of this 14th-century church's Renaissance interior—designed by Bartolomeo della Gatta and Giuliano and Antonio da Sangallo the Elder—are a series of **stained-glass windows** by Guillaume de Marcillat. Just inside to the right is what may be his masterpiece, the **Marriage of the Virgin.** Behind the high altar is an *Assumption,* and saints are depicted in windows along the aisles. The church retains some good baroque works, as well as Niccolò Soggi's restored 1522 **Nativity** to the left of the high altar, and, on the first altar on the left, a painting of the *Deposition* that an 18-year-old Giorgio Vasari painted based on a Rosso Fiorentino cartoon.

Via Garibaldi 185. (✆ **0575-26-774**. Free admission. Daily 7:30am–12:30pm and 3:30–7pm.

Badia   In 1565, Giorgio Vasari performed a High Renaissance architectural overhaul on this 13th-century church. He did such a good job that in 1865, church officials hijacked what Vasari had intended to be his and his family's tomb, installed in the Pieve di Santa Maria, and reassembled it here in the Badia as the church's **high altar.** Vasari's paintings adorning the altar include a 1551

Calling of St. Peter in cotton-candy pastels and a watery classical background. On the inside entrance wall of the church is a 1476 fresco by Bartolomeo della Gatta, who painted a remarkably lifelike face on *St. Lawrence* in a *trompe l'oeil* niche. Past the third altar on the right is a 1320 **crucifix** by Segna di Bonaventura. Above the transept is the restored *trompe l'oeil* **dome** painted on canvas (1702) by the baroque master of perspective illusion, Andrea Pozzo. There actually is a dome there, but it's a shallow one—Pozzo was hired to make it look mightier. The best effect isn't from directly underneath but from the little bronze marker in the aisle near the front of the pews.

Piazza di Badia. © 0575-356-612. Free admission. Mon–Sat 8am–noon and 4–7pm, Sun 7:15–9:15am and 10:15am–12:30pm.

Museo Archeologico Mecenate   Arezzo has made a small park out of the remains of its **Roman amphitheater** (entered from Via Crispi). Atop one of the amphitheater's curves, a 15th-century convent with a double loggia has been converted into an archaeological museum housing remains from Etruscan and Roman Arretium. After some 6th-century B.C. bronzes and a red-figure amphora from the 5th century B.C., rooms 6 to 8 contain the museum's pride, a collection of the mass-produced *corallino* **pottery** that made Roman Arezzo famous from 50 B.C. to A.D. 70. These waxy brick-red ceramics were decorated with stamped reliefs and depressions, and the tools and styles of various production studios are didactically laid out. Room 8 contains the remnants of the famed Ateius workshop, which at its height had branch ateliers in Pisa and Lyons. Upstairs are some relics from the Chiusi area, including an unusually anthropomorphic 7th-century B.C. urn with human arms and a lid shaped like a human head. Don't miss the highly refined tiny **portrait of a toga-wearing man** incised on gold and silver leaf and protected by a glass disk. This remarkably realistic artistry dates from the early 3rd century A.D.

Via Margaritone 10. © 0575-20-882. Admission 4€ ($4.60) adults, 2€ ($2.30) children. Daily 8:30am–7:30pm.

WHERE TO STAY

Hotels in Arezzo are nothing to write home about, as they cater mainly to businesspeople passing through. A distant third choice after the places listed below is the **Hotel Astoria,** Via Guido Monaco 56 (© **0575-24-361;** fax 0575-24-362). The carpeted institutional doubles, with beds that give all the spinal support of a wet noodle, go for about 62€ ($71) with bathroom or 47€ ($54) without. Actually, the city's most atmospheric inn is the new **Ostello Villa Severi** youth hostel, Via Redi 13 (© and fax **0575-299-047**), a modernized but still pretty 16th-century villa nestled in the countryside a half-hour walk from town (take bus no. 4 from Via Guido Monaco). Beds are 15€ ($17), plus 2.60€ ($3) for breakfast. It's open May through September.

Cavaliere Palace Hotel   A complete 1995 restructuring of the former Hotel Milano left most of this inn sparkling new. New owners overhauled it again in 1999, making it the nicest (but priciest) game in town. The functional furnishings and carpeted floors are pleasantly unassuming and comfy, and you can breakfast on a viewless terrace in summer. The hotel is tucked on a side street off the right of Piazza Guido Monaco, so it's generally quieter than the Continentale.

Via Madonna del Prato 83 (off Via Roma just east of Piazza G. Monaco), 52100 Arezzo. © 0575-26-836. Fax 0575-21-925. www.cavalierehotels.com. 27 units. 135€ ($155) double. Rates include breakfast. AE, DC, MC, V. Parking 15€ ($17) in nearby garage. **Amenities:** Concierge; tour desk; limited room service. *In room:* A/C, TV, dataport, minibar, hair dryer, safe.

Hotel Continentale   In a 1950s building on the south edge of Piazza Guido Monaco, the Continentale offers uninspiring but comfortable modern rooms with built-in white lacquer furniture and floral-print curtains and upholstery. Most accommodations are carpeted, but some have parquet floors. Try to get one away from the main street or piazza, both of which suffer from traffic noise. Rooms whose numbers end in "22" are larger and come with satin quilts, plush easy chairs, curtained archways, and nifty flip-top desks. A recent restoration has added air-conditioning to all the guest rooms. A new breakfast room was also part of the restoration, or you can take breakfast on a large panoramic terrace upstairs in summer.

Piazza Guido Monaco 7 (between the station and San Francesco), 52100 Arezzo. ✆ **0575-20-251.** Fax 0575-350-485. www.hotelcontinentale.com. 73 units. 98€ ($113) double; 132€ ($152) triple. Breakfast 8€ ($9.20). AE, DC, MC, V. Parking 10€ ($12) in nearby garage. **Amenities:** Bike rental; concierge; tour desk; car-rental desk; 24-hr. room service (bar); babysitting; laundry service; Internet access. *In room:* A/C, TV, VCR in 5 units, fax, minibar, hair dryer, safe in some units.

WHERE TO DINE

Antica Osteria L'Agania TUSCAN   This small joint doesn't bother with a wine list; a staff member plunks down a bottle of the eminently quaffable house chianti, and you pay for what you drink. The locals pack into this long, wood-paneled room for delicious, unpretentious food like their grandmas used to make. They come especially for the thick rib-sticking *ribollita,* but you can also mix and match gnocchi, tagliatelle, and creamy polenta with the basic Tuscan sauces (the gnocchi and the ragù make a nice combo). The trattoria proudly offers the lovely "local dishes" foreign visitors rarely order, such as tripe and the very fatty *grifi e polenta* (chunks of veal stomach in polenta). You may find your taste buds more attuned to the *arista* (roast pork) or *polpette fritte con patate* (fried meatballs with roast potatoes).

Via Mazzini 10 (near San Francesco). ✆ 0575-295-381. www.osteriagania.it. Reservations recommended. Primi 4€–7€ ($4.60–$8.05); secondi 4€–7€ ($4.60–$8.05). AE, DC, MC, V. Tues–Sun noon–3pm and 7–10:30pm. Closed 2nd 2 weeks of June.

Buca di San Francesco ⭐ ARETINE   The Buca resides in the frescoed cellar of a 14th-century palazzo and has been run by the same family for over 70 years. Mario de Fillipis likes to keep "the memory of old flavors" in his ancient dishes. Try the respectable *ribollita* or good *bringoli casalinghi con il sugo finto* (homemade spaghetti in chunky tomato sauce). If you're waffling over a secondo, order *la saporita di bonconte,* a plate piled with portions of all the restaurant's specialties—tripe, roasted sausages, baked rabbit, and others—a dish from the days when an army on the march had to make a communal stew out of what each man could muster (it comes with a commemorative plate). They'll keep pouring the vin santo until you run out of *cantucci* or fall off your chair, and they love sending you off with a bag of little goodies. (Tell them *Frommer's* sent you, and they may throw in an original print or collection of de Fillipis's famous bookplates.)

Via San Francesco 1 (next door to San Francesco). ✆ **0575-23-271.** www.bucadisanfrancesco.it. Reservations recommended. Primi 5€–10€ ($5.75–$12); secondi 8.50€–11€ ($9.80–$13). AE, DC, MC, V. Wed–Mon noon–2:30pm; Wed–Sun 7–9:30pm. Closed 2 weeks in July.

Le Tastevin INVENTIVE ARETINE   An odd mix of rooms, one dedicated to old film stars and another done up trattoria style with hammered copper pots and the like, is filled with an odd mix of funk and jazz music and (on weekend nights) owner Giancarlo serenading his guests on the piano. Tastevin serves up Aretine dishes but plenty of more innovative foods, too (the latter take pride of place at Fri-night set-price dinners). The *risatoni a'le Tastevin* is a creamy version with truffles and asparagus, while the very good *penne alla Tastevin* comes in a cream sauce of puréed yellow peppers. Or, you can try a variety of fish dishes or a *bistecca di vitello al pepe verde* (beef cooked in its own juices with whole peppercorns). Be aware, however: If you're not a regular, service can verge on rude.

Via de' Cenci 9 (between Via Maddona del Prato and Corso Italia). ℂ **0575-28-304**. Reservations recommended. Primi 5€–7€ ($5.75–$8.05); secondi 8€–11€ ($9.20–$13). AE, DC, MC, V. Tues–Sun 12:30–3pm and 7–10pm.

EN ROUTE TO SANSEPOLCRO

Twenty-five kilometers (16 miles) from Arezzo on the SS73 toward Sansepolcro is the turnoff onto SS221 to **Monterchi** (www.monterchi.it). This is home of Piero della Francesca's ***Madonna del Parto*** 🏛🏛, which you can see in a museum built specially for it at Via della Reglia 1 (ℂ **0575-70-713** or 0575-70-710). This psychologically probing fresco depicts the Virgin Mary 9 months pregnant with Jesus, shown to us by a pair of angels who hold back the intricately embroidered flaps of a tent. It's one of the earliest depictions of a pregnant Madonna, a subject exceedingly rare in Italian art (one in Prato predates it slightly). Mary here is heavy with child, with one eyelid drooping and a hand on her swollen belly. She emanates a solemnity that's at once human yet regal, reflecting the grave import of becoming the mother of the Savior.

The *Madonna del Parto* has come far. It started as a lowly chapel decoration for a church in the local cemetery. Much of the church was demolished in 1785, but the chapel and fresco remained and became the focus of pilgrimages by both art historians and pregnant women praying for an easy birth. It was moved a few years ago after extensive renovation to its current high-tech command bunker, though the sterile museum environment has robbed the work of some of its mysticism and charm. Monterchi was the birthplace of Piero's mother, and some believe she was buried in the cemetery and the fresco was painted as a memorial. It's open Tuesday through Sunday from 9am to 1pm and 2 to 7pm (until 6pm Oct–Mar). Admission is 3.10€ ($3.55) adults and 1.81€ ($2.10) students; children under 14 are free. If you're planning to visit Sansepolcro, the best way to get here is by bus. It's a 30-minute ride; there are six runs on weekdays and two on Sundays (see below for details).

2 Sansepolcro: Artistic Treasures Off the Beaten Path

37km (23 miles) NE of Arezzo; 15km (9 miles) N of Città di Castello; 122km (76 miles) E of Florence; 240km (149 miles) N of Rome

The medieval walled town of Sansepolcro is far off the tourist path for anyone not enamored with the art of **Piero della Francesca.** It's the birthplace of painters Raffaellino del Colle (1490–1566) and Santi di Tito (1538–1603) and of the Buitoni pasta empire. The small village founded here around A.D. 1000 was so proud of the bits of the Holy Sepulcher a couple of pilgrims brought back that the town was named Borgo San Sepolcro. Chances are, if they'd held off on the christening a few hundred years, the place would now be called Borgo Piero della Francesca, after the monumentally important painter who was born here around 1420.

One of the leading lights of the early Renaissance, Piero took the perspective obsession of Florentine masters Masaccio and Paolo Uccello and mixed it with the ethereal posed beauty of the Umbrian school to create a haunting style all his own. Piero's figures are at the same time hyper-posed masses of precision Euclidean geometry and vehicles for a profound expressive naturalism and astute psychological studies. His backgrounds, even those of the countryside, are masterpieces of architectural volume. His painting has so fascinated the modern world that the connect-the-dots loop of cities preserving his works has become known as the **Piero della Francesca Trail,** a pilgrimage route of sorts for art lovers. When Piero's eyesight began to fail later in life, he wrote two treatises, *On the Five Regular Bodies* and *On Perspective in Painting,* which together set the rules for his universe of perspective and logic, broke down the human body into a geometric machine of perfect proportions, and became required reading for almost every Renaissance artist. He died near his hometown in 1492.

Piero is somewhere between a cultural hero and a patron saint here. Every Sansepolcran seems to be a Piero expert. The tourist-office lady argues stridently that Piero's is the first pregnant Madonna. The Fiorentino owner can give a ready discourse on the man and his art. And there's a tired office worker who climbs the steps to the glass window of the museum's Piero room every evening—he just pauses and peers through the glass at the Piero della Francesca masterpieces inside for a few moments before walking back down the stairs and heading home.

ESSENTIALS

GETTING THERE   By Train   Unless you're coming from Umbria, the train is out. Sansepolcro anchors one end of the private FCU train line, with about twenty trains daily from **Perugia** (80 min.–2 hr.). Seven trains a day run from **Rome** to Terni, where you can switch to this FCU line (3½ hr. total if you hit the layover right). The station (© **0575-742-094**) is just outside the city walls at Piazza Battisti.

By Car   Sansepolcro lies where the SS73 from Arezzo intersects with the SS3bis from Perugia. You can park outside Porta Fiorentina along Viale Vittorio Veneto to the east, or north outside Porta del Castello.

By Bus   CAT buses (© **0575-736-083** or 0575-85-211) arrive and leave at the traffic circle off Via G. Marconi (at the west end of Via Aggiunti). Buses serve **Arezzo** (1 hr.), **Florence** (1½ hr.), **Monterchi** (25 min.), and **Caprese Michelangelo** (40–75 min.). Buy tickets at the Bar Autostazione on the piazza.

VISITOR INFORMATION   The helpful **tourist office** is inside the Palazzo Pretorio at Piazza Garibaldi 2 (© and fax **0575-740-536;** www.sansepolcro.net; open daily 9:30am–1pm and 3:30–6:30pm).

FESTIVALS & MARKETS   On the second Sunday in September, the **Palio della Balestra** allows Sansepolcro a crossbow rematch with its traditional rivals from Gubbio. This medieval test of archery skill is highlighted with a display from Sansepolcro's famous *sbandieratori* (flag tossers). They perform their medieval act of juggling colorful banners dressed in Renaissance costumes lifted straight from Piero paintings. Call © **0575-75-827** or visit www.balestrierisansepolcro.it for more info. A huge **market** is held after the fourth Sunday of Lent, and August 16 is a more low-key local festival in honor of **San Rocco.**

ENJOYING SANSEPOLCRO'S ARTISTIC LEGACY

Sansepolcro's only outstanding sight is the Museo Civico (see below), housed in a 15th-century building that was once the **Palazzo Comunale.** An outdoor staircase runs to the former main entrance, now a glassed-in doorway where you can see into one of the museum's main halls. There you can gaze on Piero della Francesca's masterpieces at any time of day or night—Sansepolcro's singularly unselfish way of opening its artistic patrimony to everyone, regardless of whether they buy a ticket to the museum. One local, nodding approvingly, called the arrangement "highly advanced."

The palace is connected by a bridge to a perpendicular building, the 14th-century **Palazzo Pretorio,** embedded with two orderly rows of della Robbian terra-cotta coats of arms left by previous mayors. Both palaces were heavily restructured in the 19th century. If you pass under their connecting bridge and cross the street, you'll be on a small piazza flanked on the right by **San Francesco** and the left by **Santa Maria delle Grazie.** The former has some baroque can-vases and a 1304 Gothic sandstone altar carved with reliefs; the latter is fronted by a 1518 double loggia and preserves a small *Madonna in Prayer* by Raffaellino del Colle and a wood ceiling carved by Alberto Alberti.

Back under the bridge connecting the palazzi, you'll see the huge portico of the late-16th-century **Palazzo della Laudi** across from them. Next door is Sansepolcro's **Duomo,** with a Romanesque-Gothic interior. On the right wall is a fresco of the *Madonna with Saints Thomas Becket and Catherine of Alexan-dria* (of whom only the iconographic wheel remains) painted by a Rimini-school artist in 1383. Just past it is Santi di Tito's baroque *Incredulity of St. Thomas* (1575), followed by a faded Bartolomeo della Gatta fresco of the *Cru-cifixion.* Behind the high altar is Niccolò di Segna's polyptych, whose "Resur-rection of Christ" scene heavily influenced Piero della Francesca's famous version now in the Museo Civico. To the altar's left is a 10th-century wood *Volto Santo* crucifixion. Between the first two altars on the left wall is an *Ascen-sion* by Umbrian master Perugino, restored in 1997, as well as a *Resurrection* by Raffellino del Colle.

Just below the Duomo is Sansepolcro's main square, **Piazza Torre di Berta,** named after a tower demolished in World War II. Off its right side runs the main shopping street and *passeggiata* drag, **Via XX Settembre.** Three blocks down is the intersection with Via L. Pacioli, which leads all the way to the south-ern city walls at Via Santa Croce and the deconsecrated church of **San Lorenzo.** Only die-hard Rosso Fiorentino fans need bother hiking down, as there's no guarantee you'll find anyone in the lace-making school or Choral Society head-quarters next door to let you inside to see Rosso's darkened *Deposition.*

Museo Civico ⊛⊛   Though most famous for its remarkable Piero della Francesca works, Sansepolcro's museum also has paintings by native baroque masters Santi di Tito and Raffaellino del Colle and a piece by Luca Signorelli. First, though, a staircase off the entrance leads down to a small didactic collec-tion of **prehistoric remains** (stone tools and bits of ceramics) as well as a room of churchly vestments and reliquary busts alongside a courtly **13th-century stone frieze** of knights and monsters.

Room 1 sports a 19th-century terra-cotta bust of Piero della Francesca. Among the 17th-century works in room 2 is a late mannerist *Crucifixion* painted by il Passignano or someone in his circle. Stairs lead up to a pair of rooms hous-ing detached 15th-century frescoes by unknown local artists, some with their *sinopie* (preliminary sketches).

Room 3 houses Piero's ***Madonna della Misericordia*** ⊛ (1445–62), reassem-bled without its frame. The Mary of Mercy spreads her cloak around kneeling donors (the one to the left of her, looking up, is believed by some to be a self-portrait by Piero), while a sleepy-eyed St. John the Baptist and other saints look on. The central panel and Sts. John and Sebastian are certainly from Piero's brush, as is the Crucifixion above and the Angel and Virgin Annunciate panels flanking it. The rest were probably worked on by assistants or a miniaturist.

Room 4 starts with two detached frescoes by Piero, one **San Ludovico da Tolosa** (1460, and attributed by some to Piero's student Lorentino), and a famous partial fresco of **San Giuliano** ✿ (1455–58) discovered in the 1950s under the whitewash of Sant'Agostino (later Santa Chiara) Church.

At the end of the room is one of Piero's indisputable masterpieces, the **Resurrection of Christ** ✿✿✿. Painted in 1463 for another room in this palace and moved here in 1480, this work made Piero's modern reputation—art historians began paying attention to it and Piero in general after 1925, when Aldous Huxley dubbed it the "best picture in the world." The fresco-and-tempera work displays a resounding naturalness in its perfect perspective and the almost uncanny modeling of the figures and faces. At the same time it's imbued with an eerie spirituality, or rather supernaturalness, in the deadpan gaze of the risen Christ—here, truly a god in human form—and in the soldiers who look less asleep than under a magic spell of suspended animation. Piero lets the power of his art speak through his incomparable technique, leaving the religious symbolism to be relayed simply through the background: As the Savior rises from the dead, the trees and the land come back to life around him from left to right. The second sleeping soldier on the left in the brown armor is thought to be a self-portrait of Piero. This fresco may be one of the few pieces of art that actually did save its city from destruction. In 1944 a British commanding officer had orders to bomb Nazi troops occupying the city. The officer, having read Huxley's words, held off the attack until the Germans withdrew on their own.

Room 5 has a 16th-century Umbrian-school *Assumption* and a processional banner painted in 1505 by Luca Signorelli with the **Crucifixion** (with a beautiful group of mourning Marys) on one side and a *St. Anthony Abbot and San Egidio* on the other. Matteo di Giovanni's 1440 cathedral altarpiece is missing the central *Baptism of Christ* panel by Piero (it's in London's National Gallery), but the *St. Peter* and *St. Paul* are worth a study, and (in an innovative touch) a slide projector fills in the missing gap with a blurry reproduction. Room 6 has two paintings by Raffaellino del Colle, a huge 1526 *Assumption and Coronation of the Virgin* and a detached fresco of *St. Leo I* (1520–30), as well as a *Martyrdom of St. Quentin* (1518) by quintessential mannerist master Pontormo. The last few rooms are filled with mannerist and baroque canvases, including five by Santi di Tito.

Via Aggiunti 65 (back side of the former Palazzo Comunale on Piazza Garibaldi). ✆ **0575-732-218.** Admission 6.20€ ($7.15) adults, 4.50€ ($5.20) seniors over 65, 3€ ($3.45) ages 10–16. June–Sept daily 9am–1:30pm and 2:30–7:30pm; Oct–May daily 9:30am–1pm and 2:30–6pm.

WHERE TO STAY

Besides the following, **Da Ventura** restaurant (see below) also rents basic rooms.

Hotel Fiorentino   Since 1807, Piero pilgrims and other Sansepolcro visitors have been stopping at this inn. The rooms are nothing special—tiled floors with a throw rug or two, a random assortment of furniture and Piero posters, and many shower heads without a curtain—but the Fiorentino is central, clean, friendly, and very well priced. And you never have to leave the building for the best restaurant in town (see Ristorante Fiorentino, below). The accommodations on the third floor are a bit smaller but more pleasant, with nice parquet floors, views over the rooftops (some to the mountains beyond), and country-style quilts. There's also a small terrace where you can breakfast in nice weather. A recent renovation has added bathrooms to all the rooms.

Via L. Pacioli 60 (on the corner of Via XX Settembre), 52037 Sansepolcro (AR). © **0575-740-350.** Fax 0575-740-370. www.albergofiorentino.com. 21 units. 70€ ($81) double; 90€ ($104) triple; 100€ ($115) quad. Breakfast 2€ ($2.30). MC, V. Parking 9€ ($10) in garage. **Amenities:** Best restaurant in town; limited room service (breakfast). *In room:* TV.

Hotel La Balestra   Past a shopping complex in a modern building on the major road running along the north side of town, La Balestra provides more solid comfort than the Fiorentino (above). If you want large, carpeted rooms with built-in furniture and all the trimmings—and don't mind the total lack of charm and 10-minute hike to the Pieros at the Museo Civico—this is the place for you. Ask for a room off the front, as there's traffic all night. Rooms were redone and prettied up in 2002. The moderately priced restaurant offers Tuscan dishes (the ricotta-stuffed cannelloni are good) and a decent wine list, and you can eat on a shaded veranda in summer. Half- and full-pension options are also available (add 16€/$18 per person for half pension, 26€/$30 per person for full pension). The hoteliers have plans to open **Villa del Trebbio,** a villa with apartments and a swimming pool 2km (1 mile) outside of town, in June 2004.

Via Montefeltro 29 (northeast of the city walls), 52037 Sansepolcro (AR). © **0575-735-151.** Fax 0575-740-282. www.labalestra.it. 52 units. 80€ ($92) double; 92€ ($105) triple. Rates include breakfast. AE, DC, MC, V. Free parking. **Amenities:** Restaurant; concierge; tour desk; limited room service; laundry service; dry cleaning; nonsmoking rooms. *In room:* A/C, TV, minibar, hair dryer, safe.

WHERE TO DINE

Da Ventura ⭐ TUSCAN   Service at this unpretentious trattoria, in its third generation of Tofanelli family management, is truly "by the cart." Under rough-hewn wood ceilings and arches made of wine bottles, you can mix and match your own antipasto with selections from a wheeled cart. Another cart bears fresh homemade tagliatelle so you can choose the sauce of your choice to top it. (The ragù is a tasty bet.) The *bistecca di vitello* (thick veal steak) or *maiellino in porchetta* (roast suckling pig) are also accompanied by a gurney of *contorni* so that you can sample several side dishes. Of course, it's all capped off with a cart of homemade desserts. Upstairs are seven very plain rooms with bathrooms that rent for 47€ ($54) per double.

Via Aggiunti 30 (a few blocks west of the Museo Civico on the other side of the walls). © and fax **0575-742-560.** Reservations recommended. Primi 7€–15€ ($8.05–$17); secondi 8.50€–15€ ($9.80–$17). AE, DC, MC, V. Tues–Sat 12:30–2:30pm and 7:30–9:30pm, Sun 12:30–2:30pm. Closed Jan 1–10 and Aug 1–20.

Ristorante Fiorentino ⭐⭐ TUSCAN   This very traditional 190-year-old place with coffered wood ceilings has a mélange of trattoria artifacts crowding the walls and a genial owner, Alessio, who'd rather recite what the kitchen is most proud of that night than break out an impersonal menu. Everything is fresh, the pasta is made by hand, and though the kitchen sticks to antique recipes, it does trim meats lean, and they won't look askance if you order a *porzione ridotto* (small portion). The *cappelli d'Alpino con pasta verde* (ricotta and veggies stuffed into spinach ravioli) is the primo to order, but you may also enjoy the *pappardelle al sugo di lepre* (noodles with hare sauce). Afterward, try the *coniglio arrosto* (slices of roast rabbit filled with herbed bread stuffing) or the *involtini di vitello* (veal rolled around artichokes or zucchini and cooked in its own juices).

Via L. Pacioli 60. (**(C)** **0575-742-033**. Reservations recommended. Primi 5€–7€ ($5.75–$8.05); secondi 9€–13€ ($10–$15). DC, MC, V. Thurs–Tues 12:30–3pm and 7:30–10:30pm. Closed Jan 20–30 and last 2 weeks of July.

EN ROUTE TO CORTONA

From Sansepolcro, it's a 15km (9-mile) jaunt across the border to **Umbria** (see chapters 10 and 11 for more information). If you haven't finished with Tuscany, you can head back toward Arezzo, turning south on the SS71 to go down the wide **Chiana Valley (Valdichiana),** famous for its snowy-white cattle that make such excellent *bistecca fiorentina,* toward Cortona.

Along the way, you'll pass **Castiglion Fiorentino,** a fortified medieval town dominated by a pronglike tower, the **Torre del Cassero.** The tourist info office is at Corso Italia 111 (**(C)** **0575-658-278;** fax 0575-659-457). It's open Tuesday through Sunday from 10:30am to 12:30pm and 4:30 to 7:30pm but may keep shorter hours in winter. The center of town is **Piazza del Municipio,** bordered by a 16th-century loggia supposedly by Giorgio Vasari. Just above this is the deconsecrated church of Sant'Angelo, now the entrance to the **Pinacoteca Comunale,** Piazza del Municipio 12 (**(C)** **0575-657-466**). Its well-labeled collections include some medieval gilded copper crosses, a Taddeo Gaddi *Madonna and Child,* and an odd Bartolomeo della Gatta *St. Francis Receiving the Stigmata.* (Tradition holds the other friars nearby weren't awake when Francis was visited by the seraph, but here one clearly is.) There's a good view from a tower here. The museum is open Tuesday through Friday from 10am to 12:30pm and 4 to 6:30pm (until 7pm Sat–Sun). Admission is 3€ ($3.45) adults and 2€ ($2.30) children, or 5€ ($5.75) if you want to tack on a visit next door to the **Palazzo Pretorio** and its tiny museum of Etruscan remains found in the area. Also worth calling on is the **Collegiata,** 300m (990 ft.) away on Piazza San Giuliano, with a *Madonna Enthroned with Saints* by Bartolomeo della Gatta on the third altar on the right, Lorenzo di Credi's *Adoration of the Child* in a chapel to the right of the high altar, and a huge *Maestà* by Segna di Bonaventura in the left transept. The **Pieve** next door (ask the Collegiata sacristan to unlock it) preserves a *Deposition* by Signorelli's school. On the edge of town is the High Renaissance templelike church of **Madonna della Consolazione,** an octagonal structure built in the 16th century.

A bit farther south along the SS71, you'll see the 13th-century walls of **Montecchio Vesponi** off to the left. The Florentines gave this castle to the English *condottiere* John Hawkwood (the gentleman in Paolo Uccello's equestrian painting in Florence's Duomo), who had fought battles for them.

3 Cortona: "City of Art"

34km (22 miles) S of Arezzo; 105km (63 miles) SE of Florence; 194km (120 miles) N of Rome

Cortona sits implacably on a green mountainside above terraced olive groves, stony yet inviting. It's a steep medieval city where cut-stone staircases take the place of many streets, and views over the wide Chiana Valley stretch south to Umbria's Lake Trasimeno. Cortona proclaims itself a "City of Art," and having spawned (among others) the great pre-Michelangelo painter Luca Signorelli and the early-17th-century painter/architect Pietro da Cortona, it has a pretty strong claim. (Witness the very respectable church embellishments and the particularly rich collection of the tiny Museo Diocesano.)

The city's roots are deep and long. It claims to be no less than "the mother of Troy and grandmother of Rome," and legendarily had its start when Dardanus (who'd later go to Turkey and found Troy) dropped his helmet *(corythos)* during a battle—not an overly auspicious beginning for the town he founded here and named Corito. Cortona was already a thriving city by the 4th century B.C., when it was one of 12 cities that formed the Etruscan confederation. New finds at Melone II, one of the several Etruscan tombs dotting the hillside and valley below the town, suggest it may have been an even more important center than previously believed.

Even though it was long in a fairly undervisited corner of Tuscany, Cortona never succumbed to the all-too-common fate of becoming a dusty abandoned backwater. It retained a good bit of *passeggiata* action most evenings on the **Rugapiana** ("flat street," a nickname for Via Nazionale, the only road in town that even comes close to fitting that description), and in summer the city hosts a modest outdoor film festival in the Parterre Gardens behind San Domenico. Its art treasures ensure a steady stream of tourists, and the 140 University of Georgia students who descend every summer to study art help keep it on its toes—and make it the only place in Italy where you'll find wrinkled old olive farmers wearing "Go Dawgs!" sweatshirts.

However, the huge popularity of Frances Mayes' book *Under the Tuscan Sun,* about buying and renovating a villa just outside town, has hurled Cortona from relative obscurity to the forefront of Tuscany tourism, just behind Florence, Siena, Pisa, and the Chianti. Expect more crowds than you'd, er, expect for a town this size, especially in summer.

ESSENTIALS

GETTING THERE   By Train   Cortona doesn't have its own station, but two stops on the main **Rome-Arezzo** line serve it. The nearer one, Camucia/ Cortona (© **0575-603-018**), is just 5km (3 miles) from town, but only local trains stop here. More trains stop at Terontola/Cortona (© **0575-67-034**) station, 11 kilometers (7 miles) from town. It's about a 25-minute ride from **Arezzo** (26 daily), 1 hour (2 hr. on the slow line) from **Florence** (24 daily), and 2 hours from **Rome** (15 daily). To save time, you can buy tickets at Cortona's tourist office.

From both stations, LFI buses leave about every 30 minutes for Cortona. At Camucia you can buy tickets at the bar outside the station or, if it's closed, the *tabacchi* up the street near the next bus stop.

By Car   From Arezzo, take the SS71 and turn off for Cortona at Il Sodo (especially for Il Falconiere hotel) or Camucia. From Florence or Rome, take the A1 to the Valdichiana exit and follow the SS326 (direction: Perugia) until the Cortona exit at Appallo. This same highway originates in Siena. There is some parking in town, but your best bet is the free lot outside Porta Santa Maria.

By Bus   LFI bus lines run from **Arezzo** (more than 20 daily; 35–60 min.), **Montepulciano** (one early afternoon run on school days; 1½ hr.), and several other, smaller places in the area.

VISITOR INFORMATION   The **APT office** is at Via Nazionale 42 (© **0575-630-353;** fax 0575-630-656). May through September, it's open Monday through Saturday from 9am to 1pm and 3 to 7pm and Sunday from 9am to 1pm and 3:30 to 6:30pm; October through April, hours are Monday through Friday from 9am to 1pm and 3 to 6pm and Saturday from 9am to 1pm.

FESTIVALS & MARKETS   On a Sunday in late May, the town turns out in late-14th-century costume for crossbow competitions in the annual **Giostro**

Cortona

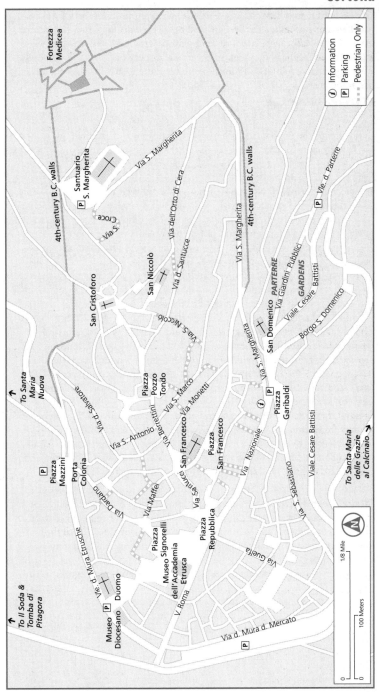

Legend:
- (i) Information
- P Parking
- ⋮⋮⋮ Pedestrian Only

Fortezza Medicea

4th-century B.C. walls

Santuario S. Margherita

Via S. Margherita

Via dell'Orto di Cera

Via S. Croce

San Niccolò

Via d. Santucce

San Cristoforo

Via S. Niccolò

4th-century B.C. walls

Via S. Margherita

Via S. Margherita

San Domenico

PARTERRE

Via Giardini Pubblici

Viale Cesare Battisti

GARDENS

Borgo S. Domenico

Vle. d. Parterre

To Santa Maria Nuova

Via d. Salvatore

Piazza Pozzo Tondo

Via S. Antonio

Via Berrettini

Via S. Marco

Via Monetti

San Francesco

Piazza San Francesco

(i)

P Piazza Garibaldi

Via Nazionale

Piazza Mazzini

Porta Colonia

Via Dardano

Via Maffei

Via Santucci

Piazza Repubblica

Via S. Sebastiano

Viale Cesare Battisti

To Il Soda & Tomba di Pitagora

Museo Diocesano

P Duomo

Piazza Signorelli

Museo dell'Accademia Etrusca

V. Roma

Vle. d. Mura Etrusche

Via Guelfa

To Santa Maria delle Grazie al Calcinaio

Via d. Mura d. Mercato

P

0 — 1/8 Mile
0 — 100 Meters

dell'Archiado. At the end of July, Cortona takes part in the **Umbria Jazz festival** (Umbria's just across the border), and a well-regarded **antiques fair** is held in late August/early September (© **0575-630-610** for info). From August 14 to 15, Cortona celebrates the mighty Chiana Valley beefsteak with a **Sagra della Bistecca,** holding a huge communal barbecue in the Parterre Gardens. **Market** day is Saturday.

RENAISSANCE ART & ETRUSCAN REMAINS

Cortona has an embarrassment of art riches for a town of its size. When you've finished with the main sights below, you might want to visit other attractions like **San Domenico,** near Piazza Garibaldi (the 1st square in town you come to by car or bus), with its faded *Fra' Angelico* under glass above the door and Luca Signorelli's *Madonna and Saints* (1515) to the left of the altar. The 15th-century altarpiece by Lorenzo di Niccolò Gerini is a cross between a Gothic composition and a classic early Renaissance style, plus—unlike many large altarpieces across Italy that have been broken up over the ages—it's completely intact, pinnacles, predella, and all. There's a pleasant **public park** behind the church.

On Piazza San Francesco, **San Francesco,** the second Franciscan church ever built and the burial place of the saint's main disciple, Brother Elias, has been undergoing extensive renovations for quite some time, and Pietro da Cortona's last work, an *Annunciation* in the third chapel, has been removed for safekeeping. Luca Signorelli also may be buried in the church's crypt.

San Niccolò, high in town off Via Berrettini, is a small 15th-century church with a quiet cypress-framed gravel courtyard. Inside, you'll find a detached *Madonna and Saints* fresco (left wall) and a two-sided altarpiece, both by Luca Signorelli. To get into the church, ring for the custodian around to the left; once inside, point to the *Deposition of Christ* altarpiece and ask, *"Posso vedere l'altro lato?"* (*poh*-so veh-*dair*-ay *lahl*-trow *lah*-toe?) so you can see the *Madonna and Child* on the flip side.

Most of the Etruscan city is hidden in basements, but you can see part of the original **4th-century B.C. walls** at the base of Porta Colonia's outer side. From here, take the path outside the walls down to the centrally planned 16th-century church of **Santa Maria Nuova,** in which Giorgio Vasari and Christofanello both had a hand. (Works by Alessandro Allori and Empoli are inside.)

Museo dell'Accademia Etrusca ✦   Cortona was one of the 12 cities of the Etruscan confederation, and the proliferation of artifacts discovered in the area led to the founding of an Etruscan Academy in 1727. The collections are now housed in the Palazzo Casali, a 13th-century mansion built for the city's governors; the building's side is embedded with centuries' worth of gubernatorial coats of arms.

The first room contains numerous small **bronze devotional figures** of Etruscan and Roman origin covering a period from the 6th to the 1st century B.C., along with some 15th-century **northern Italian ivories** and a remarkably intact 4th- or 5th-century A.D. paleo-Christian glass chalice. The pride of the museum's collection is an **Etruscan oil lamp chandelier** from the late 4th century B.C. decorated with human heads, allegorical figures, and a few virile Pans playing their pipes, all surrounding a leering Gorgon's head on the bottom. On the walls hang **paintings** spanning the Renaissance and baroque periods, with works by Luca as well as Francesco Signorelli, Pinturicchio, Pietro da Cortona, Empoli, and Cristofano Allori. The one painting set apart is the famous *Musa*

Polimnia, an encaustic (pigmented wax on wood) portrait that has of late been accused of being an 18th-century fake rather than a 1st-century A.D. Roman original.

The small **Egyptian collection** includes some brightly colored wood sarcophagi and a rare wooden model of a funerary boat. In the jumble of Etruscan remains and post-16th-century fine and decorative arts filling the next few rooms, don't miss the 19th-century **Cantonese chessboard** or the elaborately rococo glazed ceramic *Tempietto Ginori* (1756), dripping with fanciful allegorical figures and studded with portrait medallions. There's also a 12th- or 13th-century Tuscan mosaic of a *Madonna* with oversized hands praying. Its psychedelic coloring makes it look almost like a modern work; keep this in mind when you see actual 20th-century mosaics around town (especially the Passion stations on the steep Via Santa Margherita) done by **Gino Severini.** Severini (1883–1966) was Cortona's most recent artistic master, and the last room on this floor is devoted to his works. Severini's goal apparently was to paint at least one piece in every major artistic style and movement from the first half of this century, though he was ostensibly a die-hard Futurist.

Upstairs is an exhibition of the ongoing excavations of the **Melone II** tomb and its altar, a remarkable Etruscan find first uncovered in 1990 (see below). The more portable pieces from the dig have been removed here for safekeeping, and there's also a plaster cast of one of the sphinxes from the altar.

Piazza Signorelli 9. (✆ **0575-630-415** or 0575-637-235. www.accademia-etrusca.org/museo. Admission 4.20€ ($4.83) adults, 2.50€ ($2.90) children. Tues–Sun 10am–7pm (until 5pm Nov–Mar).

Duomo   The Duomo's High Renaissance barrel-vaulted interior from the 16th century contains many mediocre 17th-century works and decorations alongside good pieces. You'll see Raffaello Vanni's *Transfiguration,* with a rather effeminate Christ (2nd altar on the right), and Lorenzo Berrettini's *Death of St. Joseph* (4th altar), a touching scene where a frightened, dying Joseph turns to Jesus and grasps his son's hand for reassurance. Behind the high altar, in the choir (hit the free light switch), is a collection of 16th- and early-17th-century paintings. In the middle of the right wall is Andrea Commodi's richly detailed *Consecration of the Basilica of San Salvatore.* The back wall has a thematic link from right to left, starting with Luca Signorelli's badly deteriorated *Crucifixion,* then Francesco Signorelli's *Incredulity of St. Thomas,* who pokes his finger suspiciously into the risen Christ's wound. Thomas doubts again in Alessandro Allori's *Madonna of the Holy Girdle.* The only work of note on the choir's left wall is Andrea del Sarto's *Assumption.* As you leave the church, pause at the third altar on your right to see local baroquie Pietro (Berrettini) da Cortona's *Adoration of the Shepherds.*

Piazza del Duomo (at the end of Via Casali). No phone. Free admission. Summer daily 7:30am–1pm and 3:30–6:30pm; winter daily 8am–12:30pm and 3–5:30pm (hours not set in stone).

⌒ **Finds Cortona Ceramics**

Giulio Lucarini, Via Nazionale 54 (✆ **0575-604-405**), makes terra-cotta ceramics in traditional Cortonese patterns of green and dark yellow on off-white. **Il Cocciaio,** Via Nazionale 69 and Via Benedetti 24 (✆ **0575-601-246**), carries more pattern varieties, including lots of old-fashioned blue-on-white designs.

Museo Diocesano ⊛   Across from the Duomo in the deconsecrated church of the Gesù is a little museum where almost every work is a masterpiece. Just inside the door on the right is a **Roman sarcophagus** from the late 2nd century A.D., made of Apuan marble and carved with a battle scene full of action. The work so impressed Donatello that he rushed home to describe it to his buddy Filippo Brunelleschi, whereupon the architect scurried off to Cortona to sketch the object.

Head next into the former nave of the old church, with its 1536 carved and painted wood **ceiling** by a local maestro called Mezzanotte ("Midnight"). There you'll see a crucified *Christ* (1320) gushing blood, by a young Pietro Lorenzetti; a *Madonna and Child with Saints* (1435) by Sassetta (another possible Cortonan) in which Mary looks with surprising tenderness (for early-15th-c. art) at her baby; and a late-15th-century marble baptismal font. In Bartolomeo della Gatta's *Assumption* (1475), Mary, surrounded by a host of heavenly musicians and russet cherubim, dangles her girdle almost suggestively to the incredulous Thomas below. (The other saints are looking very pious; see "Prato & the Virgin Mary's Girdle" in chapter 6 for the story.)

The room's true treasures are the Fra' Angelicos. The polyptych *Madonna Enthroned with Four Saints* (1437), in bright primaries, stands out against the gold-leaf background. Over the altar is the theme at which Angelico was the master, an *Annunciation* (1436). The delicate feathers on Gabriel's wings and carpet of wildflowers show Angelico's command of minute detail, and the composition demonstrates his deep understanding of meaning in the Bible stories he illustrated so well. In the background is the finale of Man's fall from grace, the expulsion of Adam and Eve from Eden; the theme is brought full circle in the foreground's Annunciation of the birth of Christ, the beginning of Man's salvation. The room behind the altar has a Pietro Lorenzetti *Madonna and Child* and a damaged 13th-century *St. Margaret of Cortona* by the Aretine school.

The large room off the entrance gives you a chance to appreciate how skilled the master was in comparison to his workshop, his school (painters who imitated him), or even his nephew. Luca Signorelli himself painted the *Deposition* (1502), with the crucifixion, the resurrection, and a surreal city by a lake all in the background, and in the foreground a swooning Mary, a well-modeled Christ, and a saint pocketing a crucifixion nail and the crown of thorns—presumably destined for numerous Italian reliquaries. Vasari tells us the face of Christ is actually a portrait of Luca's son, who died during the 1502 plague. Luca also signed the *Communion of the Apostles* (1512), painted with a very strong sense of perspective and liberal use of bright primaries and illusionistic marble floor panels (notice Judas in the foreground—ashamed of his imminent betrayal, he can't swallow the Host and instead hides it in his purse as he turns away). The other paintings in the room are by Luca's workshop or the school that followed him.

Piazza del Duomo 1. ⓒ **0575-62-830**. Admission 5€ ($5.75) adult, 1€ ($1.15) ages 8–12. Apr–Sept Tues– Sun 9:30am–1pm and 3:30–7pm; Oct Tues–Sun 10am–1pm and 3:30–6pm; Nov–Mar Tues–Sun 10am–1pm and 3–5pm.

SIGHTS OUTSIDE THE WALLS

Just below the city walls, on the hillside carpeted with olive trees, sits Cortona's tribute to High Renaissance architecture: **Santa Maria delle Grazie al Calcinaio** ⊛. It was built between 1485 and 1513 and is the masterpiece (and only definitely attributable work) of Francesco di Giorgio Martini. He designed it on a Latin cross plan to mark the spot where a worker in a lime kiln *(calcinaio)* saw a miraculous image of the Virgin appear on the rock wall. The harmonious Brunelleschian interior has a rose window in stained glass by the French master of that art, Guillame de Marcillat, as well as a late-16th-century *Madonna and Saints* by Florentine artist Alessandro Allori in the right transept.

Continuing down the hill, you'll come upon a turnoff to the right for the **Ippogea** or **Tomba di Pitagora,** a 3rd- or 2nd-century B.C. Etruscan tomb. It's on a circular plan with a vaulted roof that a 19th-century "restoration" left bare of its probable earth covering (but surrounded with solemn cypresses). The tomb's name comes from someone who didn't do his homework and confused Cortona with Crotone, Calabria, the home of Greek mathematician Pythagoras. Giorgio Vasari confused matters further in the 16th century when he decided to rename it the Tomb of Archimedes, for no apparent reason. The buzzer for the custodian is hidden behind the ivy at the gate.

For more Etruscan heritage, continue down to the SS71 crossroads and the hamlet known as Il Sodo. To the left of the stream, a road leads to a group of houses around the **Ippogeo Melone I del Sodo ("First Big Melon")** ✦; to get inside, book an appointment ahead of time at ℂ **0575-630-415** or 0575-612-778. The passage and chambers inside this 6th-century B.C. Etruscan tomb are in excellent condition, due in no small part to the fact that the bits that were missing were replaced by brick guesswork after it was discovered in 1909. The walls are made of tufa from Orvieto (how the rock got all the way here is anybody's guess), and there's an Etruscan inscription (read right to left) above a small passage between two of the burial chambers. The inscription explains this side door: The chambers were the final resting places of a husband and wife; the passage was there in case they felt like visiting each other during eternity.

To the right of the stream, a set of tire ruts leads past a ceramics plant to the **Melone II il Sodo ("Second Big Melon")** ✦✦, an Etruscan tumulus tomb dating back at least to the late 7th century B.C. Long in the shadow of its partner across the way, the tomb catapulted to the fore of Etruscan archaeological interest after the chance discovery in the early 1990s of a 6th-century B.C. altar sticking out of one side of the circular tumulus. The feature, previously unknown on any Etruscan tomb, led to a flurry of interpretations (one surely significant fact is that the altar is perfectly aligned with Cortona). An ongoing dig has unearthed more bits from the altar, which is reached by a monumental stairway flanked by two sphinxes biting the heads off warriors who are simultaneously stabbing the animals in the side, thought to represent the battle between life and death. The digs have also revealed a second passage tomb into the hillside and at least 17 more tombs in the ground around the tumulus. Some of these predate the altar, but most are from the Hellenistic and Roman eras, all the way to the 1st century A.D. (In fact, many were lined with stones pirated from the altar,

---

Take a Hike

Link all the sights listed here outside the walls for a good long half-day's hike. It's roughly 4km (2.5 miles) of winding road through olive groves from Cortona all the way down to the Etruscan tombs at Sodo. In front of **Melone I** (see below) is a teensy minimart where you can stock up on provisions; the kindly owners will make you a *panino* or share some local pastries.

which implies that the altar must've lost some of its religious importance by the 2nd c. B.C.) To visit this dig-in-progress you need to reserve ahead at © **0575-612-565;** although it's temporarily closed to visitors, you can still get a decent look at the altar from the fence.

WHERE TO STAY

Aside from the two top places below, you can find comfortable rooms with board-rated three-star amenities near the main piazza at the **Albergo Italia** ⋆, Via Ghibellina 5 (© **0575-630-254** or 0575-630-264; fax 0575-605-763; closed Nov 20–Dec 7), for 85€ to 97€ ($98–$112) per double depending on the size of the room and its view. For standard yet comfortable rooms—some with a great view—in a modern hotel, the **Hotel San Luca,** Piazza Garibaldi 1 (© **0575-630-460;** fax 0575-630-105; www.sanlucacortona.com), is your best bet. The staff is very friendly, and doubles run 100€ ($115) with breakfast. The attached restaurant, Tonino, has an elegant atmosphere at elegant prices and a wonderful valley vista.

Hotel San Michele ⋆⋆   This 11th-century palace is done in High Renaissance Brunelleschian style with off-white plaster walls and vaulted ceilings accented by arches in gray *pietra serena*. It's the nicest place to stay in the center of town. The antiques and wood-beamed ceilings in the accommodations maintain the Renaissance effect. None of the rooms is overly spacious, but that just renders ones like no. 250 in the tower more cozily romantic (and it has great views to boot). The breakfast spread is generous, with fruit and ham, and there are two bar lounges, one of them frescoed, to relax in after dinner at Ristorante Preludio next door (under separate management; see below). Five more large suites, some with terrace, were completed in 2002.

Fifty meters (150 ft.) from the hotel is a *dipendence* annex with 10 modest-size rooms of wood-beamed ceilings, wrought-iron bed frames, and the same amenities for 100€ ($115). They also run the **Residence San Pietro** (same phone; www.borgosanpietro.com) 4km (2.5 miles) outside town, with 13 apartments each with kitchenette. These rent by the week at 545€ to 1,090€ ($627–$1254) for two, 646€ to 1,262€ ($743–$1,451) for four, depending on the season. It stays open year-round (add 13€/$15 per day for heat in winter).

Via Guelfa 15 (just off Piazza della Repubblica), 52044 Cortona (AR). © 0575-604-348. Fax 0575-630-147. www.hotelsanmichele.net. 42 units. 134€ ($154) standard double; 150€ ($173) superior double; 170€ ($196) triple; 190€ ($219) quad; 165€ ($190) junior suite, 200€ ($230) suite. Rates include buffet breakfast. AE, DC, MC, V. Parking 11€ ($13) in garage. Closed Jan 6–Mar 6. **Amenities:** Bike rental; concierge; tour desk; car-rental desk; limited room service; babysitting; laundry service; dry cleaning; nonsmoking units. *In room:* A/C, TV, minibar, hair dryer.

Relais Il Falconiere ⋆⋆⋆   Riccardo and Silvia Baracchi have turned a series of 17th-century buildings into a countryside idyll overlooking their own olive grove to the Valdichiana. The rooms are scattered between the main villa, two flanking the little chapel, and seven very large rooms and mini-suites in a series

---

A Vino Break

The **Enoteria,** Via Nazionale 18 (no phone), offers wine tasting accompanied by snacks made from local food products. In addition to wine, it sells honey, preserves, cured meats, cookies, dried spices, olive oils, sauces, and dried pici.

of stone buildings a bit removed from the rest of the complex for some privacy. Each accommodation is different, many with worn terra cotta–tiled floors, cast-iron canopied bed frames, hand-woven linens, antique-style furnishings, timbered ceilings, hydromassage baths, and frescoes on some of the walls. The property is landscaped with gardens, olive groves, grapevines, a chapel, and two pools. Quiet rules supreme. The old *limonaia* (lemon house) has been converted into one of the best restaurants in the area, recommended below.

Loc. San Martino in Bocena 370 (3km/2 miles north of Cortona), 52044, Cortona (AR). © **0575-612-616** or 0575-612-679. Fax 0575-612-927. www.ilfalconiere.com. 19 units. 240€–300€ ($276–$345) double; 400€ ($460) jr. suite; 550€ ($633) suite. Rates include breakfast. AE, DC, MC, V. Free parking. Follow directions to Cortona listed above and turn to head up toward the city at Il Sodo intersection of the SS71; the main road to town immediately curves up to the right, but follow instead the small road veering left (a blue sign reads SAN MARTINO IN BOCENA). **Amenities:** Excellent restaurant (recommended separately below); 2 pools; free bikes; concierge; limited room service; babysitting; laundry service; dry cleaning. *In room:* A/C, TV, dataport, minibar, hair dryer, safe.

WHERE TO DINE

Cortona specializes in no food outside of the standard Tuscan realm, but the city's restaurants do home-cooked meals rather well, especially at any one of the trattorie on Via Dardano. Besides **Trattoria Dardano,** reviewed below, you can also try **Trattoria Toscana,** no. 12, near Piazza Signorelli (© **0575-604-192**), or **Trattoria Etrusca,** no. 37, near Porta Colonia (© **0575-630-556**).

The local **white wine,** Vergine di Valdichiana, is highly recommended, but most local red table rotgut is overly sweet and harsh.

Relais Il Falconiere ✦✦✦ *Finds* REFINED TUSCAN   The old *limonaia* of this 17th-century estate, highly recommended as a hotel above, was converted in 1989 into one of the best restaurants in the area (and renovated in 2003), and is recommended even if you don't stay here. It serves refined Tuscan food (the chef is a master at balancing disparate flavors) in an elegant setting with classical music in the background and has an excellent wine list. Even simple dishes like *crostini* get an extra touch—duck pâté has slivers of roast duck on top— while more complex ones include a broccoli soufflé topped with grated black Norcia truffles. As many ingredients as possible come from the hotel's garden, and the olive oil is from the grove that extends down the hillside below. In warm weather, you can dine on the terrace with an ancient stone fountain at one end and views of the wide Valdichiana.

Loc. San Martino in Bocena 370 (3km/2 miles north of Cortona). © **0575-612-679.** www.ilfalconiere.com. Reservations highly recommended. Primi 15€–20€ ($17–$23); secondi 18€–25€ ($21–$29). Tasting menus 60€–65€ ($69–$75). AE, MC, V. Daily 1–2pm and 8–10pm (closed Mon–Tues afternoon Jan–Feb). Closed several days in Jan.

Ristorante La Loggetta TUSCAN/ITALIAN   Piazza della Repubblica is your dining backdrop if you come in warm weather and plunk down the extra charge for one of the alfresco tables under this restaurant's namesake little loggia, overlooking the main square. If you choose to sit indoors, you'll be in 16th-century stone-and-brick wine cellars. The *verdure grigliate* (grilled vegetable slices under oil) as an antipasto will make you feel healthy even if you order the succulent *bistecca fiorentina* as a secondo (it goes excellently with roast potatoes). In between, consider the *risotto zucchini e scampi* or the ravioli *gnudi alla fonduta di tartufo,* "naked ravioli," just the ricotta and spinach stuffing, which is good even if the fondue sauce masks the delicate flavor of the truffles. The new owners, bucking Italian trends, have actually lowered prices a bit.

Piazza di Pescherio 3 (above Piazza della Repubblica). © **0575-630-575.** Reservations recommended. Primi 4.20€–8€ ($4.85–$9.20); secondi 7€–15€ ($8.05–$17). AE, DC, MC, V. Tues–Sun 12:30–2:30pm and 7:30–10:30pm. Closed Jan.

Ristorante Preludio 🎔🎔 INVENTIVE TUSCAN   In a town otherwise steeped in tradition, Preludio draws crowds for its unique nouvelle twist on Tuscan cooking. The white walls, high ceilings, and gray stone accents give the restaurant a Renaissance look, even though the lunette frescoes are modern. The *bruschette miste* (toasted bread sliced and topped with tomatoes, liver pâté, or cheese and arugula) makes a tasty start, followed by *ravioli di caciotta ai pomodorini* (homemade ravioli stuffed with fresh sheep's cheese and spinach and topped with barely cooked tomatoes and garlic). The *carpaccio alla rucola* is a classic secondo, but even better is the *petto d'anatra ai quattro pepi* (rich, delicate slices of duck served in a sauce laden with four types of softened peppercorn). One piece of advice: Order bottled wine rather than the limp house red.

Via Guelfa 11 (next to the Hotel San Michele). © **0575-630-104.** www.ilpreludio.net. Reservations recommended. Primi 7€–9€ ($8.05–$10); secondi 12€–18€ ($14–$21). AE, DC, MC, V. June–Oct Tues–Sun 12:30–3:30pm and 7:30–10pm; early Nov and Dec–May Tues–Sun 7:30–10pm, Sun noon–2pm. Closed Nov 15–Dec 15.

Trattoria Dardano 🎔 *Value* TUSCAN HOME COOKING   Of the several good *casalinga* (home cooking) trattorie along this street, this one merits singling out if only for its heavenly tiramisù, made the old-fashioned way. Before dessert, though, you may want to dip your spoon into the thick *ribollita*—Cortonans ask for hot pepper to sprinkle over it, but you can just drizzle on olive oil if that's more your style. When it comes to secondi, Dardano specializes in roasts: Try *pollo* (chicken), *anatra* (duck) or *faraona* (guinea hen)—or go for a modest splurge with a *bistecca alla fiorentina* (this being the valley whence comes Tuscany's best beef).

Via Dardano 24. © **0575-601-944.** Primi 4.50€–6.50€; secondi 4.50€–8€ ($4.20–$9.20); fixed-price menu without wine 13€ ($15). No credit cards. Thurs–Tues noon–2:45pm and 7pm–10pm. Closed Jan–Feb.

Trattoria La Grotta INVENTIVE TUSCAN   In nice weather, you can eat outside in the tiny dead-end piazzetta just off Piazza della Repubblica. When winter hits, the service moves into the "grotto," a series of stone- and brick-walled rooms that have a medieval air. A rich, creamy first course is the *gnocchi di ricotta e spinaci,* soft crumbly spheres of fresh ricotta and minced spinach in tomato sauce. For a secondo, order one of the grilled meats, such as *agnello* (lamb) or *salsicce* (sausage), which go well with a plate of *fagioli bianchi* (Tuscan white beans) on the side. There is usually a fair number of Americans here; La Grotta is popular with visiting students from Georgia.

Piazza Baldelli 3 (just off Piazza della Repubblica). © **0575-630-271.** Reservations recommended. Primi 5.50€–9€ ($6.30–$10); secondi 5.50€–16€ ($6.30–$18). AE, DC, MC, V. Wed–Mon noon–2:30pm and 7–10pm. Closed Jan 7–mid Feb and first week of July.

4 The Western Valdichiana: Exploring the Chiana Valley

The wide Valdichiana (Chiana Valley) has been an agricultural area since at least the 3rd century B.C., when Hannibal fed and provisioned his entire army here, elephants and all, before marching off to defeat the Roman legions at Lake Trasimeno. From the fall of the Roman Empire until the era of the Tuscan grand dukes, the untended valley reverted to boggy marshland, leaving only the craggy cities on either side. On the eastern fringe they included **Castiglion Fiorentino** and **Cortona.** The western side of the valley borders Siena's province and is dominated by **Monte San Savino, Lucigiano,** and **Sinalunga.**

EXPLORING THE REGION BY TRAIN   Train service from Arezzo to Sinalunga—stopping at Monte San Savino and, albeit a bit far away, Lucignano— is operated by the private firm **LFI,** not FS (the state railway). For LFI info, call ℂ **0575-22-663** in Arezzo.

WHAT TO SEE & DO IN THE VALLEY

MONTE SAN SAVINO   Monte San Savino is 43km (27 miles) from Arezzo on the SS73; tourist info consists of pamphlets left in the foyer of the **town library** at Piazza Gamurrini 3 (ℂ **0575-843-098;** www.promontesansavino.it). It was a Roman city partly demolished in 1325 by the Aretines. The scenic walled hill town retains some medieval and Renaissance structures that make it worth stopping over. Its ceramic and majolica trade, famous for centuries and still going strong in little shops throughout town, produced ceramist Andrea Contucci (1460–1529), who eventually took up sculpture as well and became known as Andrea Sansovino, master Renaissance carver.

You can see two of Andrea Sansovino's ceramic pieces in the church of **Santa Chiara;** his altarpiece of the *Madonna and Child with Saints* was probably glazed by Andrea or Giovanni della Robbia, and the unglazed *Saints Lorenzo, Roch, and Sebastian* was one of his earliest masterpieces. Next door in the 14th-century **Cassero,** site of the summertime tourist office, is a small ceramics museum open by appointment (ℂ **0575-844-845**). Admission is 2€ ($2.30), and they'll open the doors Tuesday through Sunday from 9:30am to 12:30pm and 4 to 7pm.

Corso Sangallo leads from here past the 1515 **Palazzo di Monte** on the right, built by Antonio da Sangallo the Elder, who collaborated with Sansovino on the weather-beaten but harmonious **Loggia dei Mercanti** across the street (1518–20). The **Pieve** farther along the street on the right, built in 1100 but remodeled in the 18th century, contains some early Sansovino works, including a sarcophagus (1498) just inside the main door. The **Palazzo Pretorio** beyond on the right is a 14th-century Perugian structure, while on Piazza di Monte is the disintegrating Sansovino door on **Sant'Agostino.** Andrea Sansovino designed the double loggia against the inside front wall of this church, as well as the cloister (1528), entered from a door to the left of the facade on the piazza outside. The artist's simple tomb slab was discovered in 1969 under the pulpit. Giorgio Vasari did the altarpiece of the *Assumption* in 1539.

LUCIGNANO   A byroad leads 8km (5 miles) south to the tiny elliptical burg of Lucignano (www.comune.lucignano.ar.it), a popular aerial photo on posters in area tourist offices. The focuses of the town's four concentric ellipses are the **Collegiata,** with its pretty oval staircase, and the **Palazzo Comunale,** with its small museum (ℂ **0575-836-128** or 0575-838-001). The collections include two Signorelli works, 15th-century frescoes, a triptych by Bartolo di Fredi, and a beautifully crafted gold reliquary more than 2.4m (8 ft.) high called the *Tree of Lucignano* (1350–1471). The museum is open Tuesday and Thursday through Sunday from 10am to 1pm and 2:30 to 6pm. Admission is 3€ ($3.45) adults, 2€ ($2.30) seniors over 60.

SINALUNGA   Although technically in Siena's province and not Arezzo's, the industrial center of Sinalunga is a Valdichiana town 8km (5 miles) south of

Lucignano. The **tourist office** is at Piazza della Repubblica 8 (© **0577-636-045;** www.sinalunga.it/info), open from May to October 14 Monday through Saturday from 9am to noon and 4 to 7pm, October 15 through April Tuesday through Saturday from 9am to noon. The **Collegiata** has a *Madonna and Child* by Sodoma in the left transept. The Franciscan convent **San Bernardino** on the edge of town still preserves its *Annunciation* (1470) by Benedetto di Giovanni, but Sano di Pietro's *Madonna and Child* was stolen in 1971 and replaced with a photograph. Sinalunga is near Montepulciano and the hill towns of southern Tuscany (see chapter 8 for more information).

WHERE TO STAY & DINE

Castello di Gargonza ⋆⋆ Nestled among the trees of the forested mountains west of the Valdichiana, Gargonza is a 13th-century walled hamlet complete with a fairy-tale, crenellated castle tower. Count Riccardo Guicciardini, whose family has owned the property for 300 years, decided to save the abandoned village from decay in the 1960s by converting it in its entirety into a guest "residence." It's not a hotel, so don't come expecting hotel amenities, just a wonderfully evocative and isolated retreat. Now the former peasant houses contain self-catering apartments, complete with kitchenettes and working fireplaces, and the *foresteria* has basic doubles with tile and wood beamed ceilings and lazy-springed beds. After a flirtation with 20th-century designer furniture, the complex is being refitted with simple late-17th-century pieces. The old olive-press building has been converted into a common space, with sitting/TV rooms, a bar/breakfast room, and access to the gardens. There's also a pool surrounded by wild rosemary and plenty of wooded park. The Tuscan restaurant is so good, you needn't venture out for your meals.

Loc. Gargonza (8km/5 miles west of Monte San Savino), 52048 Monte San Savino (AR). © **0575-847-021.** Fax 0575-847-054. www.gargonza.it. 7 units, 25 apts. 101€–110€ ($116–$127) double; 122€–134€ ($140–$154) triple; 147€–276€ ($169–$317) suite (actually they put you in one of the smaller apts and call it "suite" for short stays); 672€–847€ ($773–$974) 2-person apt per week; 819€–1,715€ ($942–$1,972) 4-person apt per week. Double, triple, and suite rates include breakfast; extra charge for maid service and breakfast with apts. AE, DC, MC, V. Free parking. Closed 2 weeks in mid-Nov, 2 weeks in Jan. Take the A1 to exit 27 (MONTE S. SAVINO), then the SS73 11km (7 miles) to the turnoff for Gargonza. **Amenities:** Restaurant; outdoor pool; bike rental; concierge; tour desk; car-rental desk; babysitting. *In room:* Dataport, kitchenette in apts, minibar, hair dryer.

Locanda dell'Amorosa ⋆⋆⋆ This 14th-century Amorosa farming estate has been preserved as a hotel complex with a luxury-class restaurant. A cypress-lined lane leads to the large central piazza bounded by double loggiaed brick buildings and a tiny chapel with a well at the center—all immaculately maintained and feeling a bit like a posh Spanish hacienda. The accommodations are comfortably fitted out with a mélange of period pieces under beamed ceilings, and the suites have working fireplaces—there's even a two-story deluxe suite on the back with gorgeous vistas over the vineyards. The rooms were an afterthought to the restaurant. When it opened in former cattle stalls in the 1970s, the idea was to bring the products of the farm directly to the public in refined Tuscan cuisine. The chef excels at fish dishes (rare this far inland) as well as homemade pastas and beef, but be warned: A full meal can cost well over 60€ ($69). There's also a (relatively) cheaper *enoteca* where you can sample a full range of wines from Siena province accompanied by regional dishes.

Loc. Amorosa (1.5km/1 mile south of Sinalunga), 53048 Sinalunga (SI). ℂ **0577-677-211.** Fax 0577-632-001. www.amorosa.it. 20 units. 234€ double ($269); 280€ ($322) superior double; 325€ ($374) deluxe double; 365€ ($420) suite. Rates include breakfast. AE, DC, MC, V. Free parking. Closed mid-Jan to early Mar. Take the A1 to the Valdichiana exit, follow the signs to Sinalunga and then the signs to Chiusi/Chianciano; the hotel is off the SS326 (Sinalunga–Torrita di Siena Rd.). **Amenities:** Excellent refined restaurant and simpler taverna; outdoor pool (June–Sept); bike rental; concierge; tour desk; car-rental desk; limited room service; babysitting; laundry service; dry cleaner; Internet terminal with printer. *In room:* A/C, TV, VCR, minibar, hair dryer, safe.

10

Perugia, Assisi & Northern Umbria

Northern Umbria is the mind and soul of the region. The morning mists rolling over the hills of this "green heart of Italy" imbue the place with a sort of magic, an ethereal spirituality that shines from the paintings of Perugino and that has, in the past, coalesced into saints such as Francis and Clare.

The capital city, **Perugia,** is the birthplace of the Umbrian style of painting, which took form during the Renaissance in the work of Perugino and his students Pinturicchio and Raphael. Perugia gets hep each fall with one of Europe's greatest jazz festivals and spends the rest of its time selling Baci chocolates to the world. Nearby **Assisi** was home to St. Francis, Italy's patron saint and favorite mystic. The

basilica raised to honor St. Francis was decorated by the greatest artists of the early Renaissance: Cimabue, Simone Martini, Pietro Lorenzetti, and Giotto.

Northern Umbria was the stronghold of the ancient Umbri tribes, neighbors to the Etruscans and even more mysterious. Their strange half-forgotten culture continues to manifest itself in colorful pagan festivals such as the Corso dei Ceri in the stony northern border town of **Gubbio.** Umbria continues in many ways to be a green heart of silence, a landscape of contemplation, and a historic core of overgrown villages surrounded by wild corners of the Apennines where wolves still roam and roads don't go.

1 Perugia: Capital of Umbria & Quaint Hill Town

164km (102 miles) SE of Florence; 176km (109 miles) N of Rome

Perugia is a capital city in a medieval hill town's clothing—a town of Gothic palaces and jazz cafes, where ancient alleys of stone drop precipitously off a 19th-century shopping promenade. It produced and trained some of Umbria's finest artists, including Gentile da Fabriano and Perugino (born Pietro Vannucci in nearby Città della Pieve), from whose workshop emerged Pinturicchio, Lo Spagna, and Raphael. It's a respected university city whose student population ensures a lively cultural calendar. After a long and bloody history, Perugia seems to have settled well into its role as capital of Umbria.

Perugia was one of the 12 cities of the Etruscan confederation, and though it submitted to general Roman authority in 310 B.C., it remained a fractious place, always allying itself with a different Roman faction. It chose the losing side in Octavian's war with Marc Antony, and when the future emperor defeated Marc Antony's brother here in 40 B.C., a panicked Perugian noble set fire to his house in a suicide attempt. The flames spread quickly, and most of Perugia burned to the ground. Soon after, Octavian, now Emperor Augustus, rebuilt the city as

Perugia

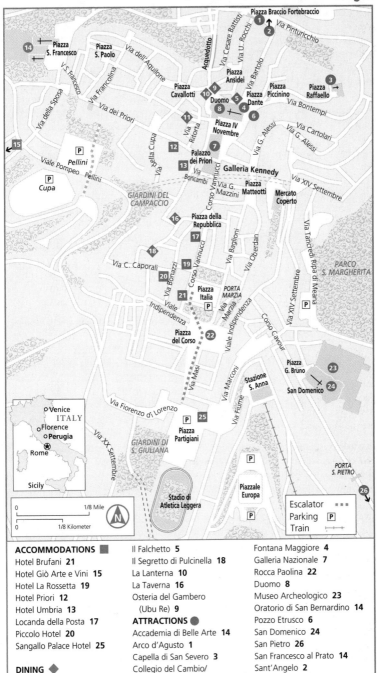

Escalator ··· ·
Parking P
Train ⊦⊦⊦⊦

Augusta Perusia. Throughout the Dark Ages, Perugia held its own against the likes of Totila the Goth, but it became subject to the Lombard Duchy of Spoleto in the later 6th century.

By the Middle Ages, Perugia was a thriving trade center and had begun exhibiting the bellicose tendencies, vicious temper, violent infighting, and penchant for poisons that would earn it such a sunny reputation among contemporary chroniclers. When not out bashing neighboring towns into submission, Perugia's men would put on minimal padding and play one of their favorite games, the *Battaglia dei Sassi* (War of Stones), which consisted of pelting one another with hefty rocks until at least a few dozen people were dead.

What they did to others didn't even come close to the nastiness that went on among Perugini themselves. The Oddi and Baglioni were just two of the noble families who waged secret vendettas and vied with the middle-class burghers for absolute power. Burgher Biordo Michelotti, egged on by the pope, managed to seize power in 1393 by murdering a few rivals from the Baglioni family. Five years later, his despotic rule ended with a knife in the back. A period of relative calm came in 1416 with the stewardship of Braccio Fortebraccio ("Arm Strongarm"), under whose wise and stable rule the city's small empire expanded over the Marches region. In the end, he was done in by a fellow Perugian while he was besieging L'Aquila in 1424. And then there were the Baglioni.

When their rivals, the Oddi, were run out of town in 1488, the field was more or less clear for the Baglioni to reign in all their horrible glory. The family turned assassination, treachery, and incest into gruesome art forms. When not poisoning their outside rivals, they killed siblings on their wedding nights, kept pet lions, tore human hearts out of chests for lunch, and married their sisters. In a conspiracy so tangled it's almost comic in its ghastliness, the bulk of the family massacred one another on a single day in August 1500.

The last of the surviving Baglioni, Rodolfo, tried to assassinate a papal legate in response to his uncle's murder at the hands of the pontiff. All that did was anger Pope Paul III, who upped the salt tax a year after promising otherwise. The rebellion Paul was trying to provoke ensued, giving the pope the excuse he needed to subdue the city. Papal forces quickly quashed the city's defenses and leveled the Baglioni's old neighborhood. After riding triumphantly into town, the pope had all Perugia's nuns line up to kiss his feet, an experience he reported left him "very greatly edified."

The enormous Rocca Paolina fortress he built to keep an eye on the city quelled most rebellious grumblings for a few hundred years, during which time the Perugini slowly mellowed, save for the uprising in 1859. The pope sent his Swiss Lancers to halt the rebellion, a task they accomplished by pillaging the shops, torching the houses, and murdering citizens in the streets. Within a year, though, Italian unification hit town. King Vittorio Emanuele prudently sent a contingent of troops to protect the Swiss guards as they hastily retreated from a Perugia finally free from papal control.

Since then, Perugia has thrown its energies into becoming the most cosmopolitan medieval city in the world. It's home to one of Italy's largest state universities as well as the Università per Stranieri, the country's most prestigious school teaching Italian language and culture to foreigners. Local industry's biggest name is Perugina, purveyor of Italy's finest chocolates, and the city stages an urbane and stylish *passeggiata* stroll every evening and one of Europe's most celebrated jazz festivals every summer.

ESSENTIALS

GETTING THERE   By Train   Coming from **Rome,** there are five direct trains (2¼ hr.), and about six more that require a transfer at Foligno. From **Florence,** take one of the dozen daily trains to Terontola/Cortona (1½ hr.) that meet up with a connecting train to Perugia (35–50 min.). From **Assisi,** there are some 24 trains daily (20 min.). These lines are part of the FS state-run railway system and stop at the Fontiveggie station on Piazza Vittorio Veneto (✆ **147-888-088**), a 15-minute ride on bus no. 26, 27, 29, or 32 to 36 from Piazza Italia in the center of Perugia.

Perugia also sits on the privately run FCU train line that serves Umbria. From 10 to 12 trains run daily from **Sansepolcro** (1¼ hr.), and 14 run north from Terni through **Todi** (35–45 min.). These trains pull first into the outlying Ponte San Giovanni Station (✆ **075-393-615**), then chug 8 minutes up a capillary line to the Santa Anna Station (✆ **075-572-3947**) in town, under the curve of Viale Roma under the Piazza Italia end of town. All outgoing trains depart first from Santa Anna Station.

By Car   From **Florence,** take the A1 south to the Valdichiana exit and the SS75bis to Perugia. The SS326 also leads to this interchange from Siena. From **Rome,** exit the A1 north at Orte to take the SS204 to the SS3bis north. The SS3 and SS3bis cross at Perugia to connect with northern and southern Umbria. The center is closed to traffic, though you may drop off your baggage at your hotel.

Parking (✆ **075-573-2506**) is fairly abundant, with the most convenient being the underground pay lot at Piazza Partigiani, at .80€ (90¢) for the first hour and 1.05€ ($1.20) each subsequent hour; or you can *pay when you first arrive* at the special "tourist rate": 7.75€ ($8.90) per day for the first 2 days, then 5.20€ ($6) per each additional day (you get a temporary parking pass ticket that lets you come and go as you please). The lot is south of the city, but there's an underground escalator through the buried medieval city up to Piazza Italia. Two other pay lots are under the Mercato Coperto (elevator up to Piazza Matteotti) and at Pellini (escalator up to Via dei Priori). Below the latter is free parking on Piazza della Cupa, with an escalator up to Pellini. For more information about parking in Perugia (and other Umbrian cities), visit **www.sipaonline.it**.

By Bus   Only one daily SITA bus makes the 1-hour, 45-minute trip from **Florence,** and you must reserve a seat (✆ **055-214-721;** www.sita-on-line.it). SULGA lines (✆ **075-500-9641;** www.sulga.it) also has one bus daily from **Florence,** and four or five a day from **Rome** (2½ hr.). APM (✆ **075-573-1707**) buses connect Perugia with **Assisi** (six daily; 50 min.), **Gubbio** (eight daily; 1 hr. 10 min.), **Todi** (six daily; 1¼ hr.), and **Chiusi** (five daily; 1 hr. 25 min.). APM (✆ **800-512-141** or 075-506-781; www.apmperugia.it) runs two buses daily from **Spoleto** (1 hr. 25 min.), 7 from **Assisi** (50 min.) 10 from **Gubbio** (1 hr. 10 min.), 8 from **Todi** (1 hr. 15 min.), and 4 from **Chiusi** (90 min.; none on Sun). There are about half as many runs by all bus lines on Sunday. The **bus depot** in Perugia is Piazza Partigiani, an escalator ride below Piazza Italia. The stand there sells tickets for all lines.

VISITOR INFORMATION   The **tourist office** is to the right of the stairs of the Palazzo dei Priori on Piazza IV Novembre (✆ **075-573-6458;** fax 075-573-9386; www.umbria2000.it or www.umbria-turismo.it). It's open Monday through Saturday from 8:30am to 1:30pm and 3:30 to 6:30pm, and Sunday from 9am to 1pm. The **provincial APT office** is at Via Mazzini 6 (✆ **075-572-8937** or 075-572-9842; fax 075-573-9386). You can also pick up a copy of *Viva Perugia* (.50€/60¢) to find out what's going on around town.

FESTIVALS & MARKETS   Perugia is something of a musical nucleus for central Italy. The fun starts with the rather tame **Rockin' Umbria** festival at the end of June. For information, contact ARCI-Perugia, Via della Viola 1 (℃ **075-573-1074;** fax 075-573-0616). It's followed by one of Europe's most important jazz festivals, **Umbria Jazz** 𝒜𝒜, which usually runs for 2 weeks in mid-July. Established in 1973, it draws top international names to town for concerts, and instructors from Boston's prestigious Berklee School of Music hold seminars and workshops. It's so popular that a smaller version, **Umbria Jazz Winter,** takes place from December 29 to January 5 in nearby Orvieto. It includes a traditional New Year's Eve banquet and all-night jazz parties. For information, contact the Associazione Umbria Jazz–Perugia, Piazza Danti 28, Casella Postale 228 (℃ **075-573-2432;** fax 075-572-2656; www.umbriajazz.com).

During the second and third weeks of September, Perugini celebrate music of a different sort in the **Sagra Musicale Umbra,** an international festival of sacred music that has, since 1937, become one of the top musical events of its kind in Italy. For more information, contact the Associazione Sagra Musical Umbra-Perugia, Via Podianai 11 (℃ **075-572-1374;** fax 075-572-7614; www.sagra musicaleumbra.com). The summer-long gig is rounded out the last week of September with **Perugia Classico,** a classical music festival that includes an antique-instrument market, concerts, shows, musical workshops, and chamber-music performances throughout town. Contact the Comitatio Promotore Perugia Classico, c/o Comune di Perugia, Ripartizione XVI Economia e Lavoro, Via Eburnea 9 (℃ **075-577-2253;** fax 075-572-4252; www.perugiaclassico.it).

On July 29 and 30, the cathedral shows off the **marriage ring of the Virgin** that 15th-century Perugini swiped from rival Chiusi. You might drop by town the last week of October for the **antiques market** held in the Rocca Paolina. From November 1 to 5, the town holds secular celebrations for the **Fiera dei Morti** in honor of All Saints' Day. (Contact the *comune* at ℃ **075-577-3898.**)

Market days are Tuesday and Saturday on Via Ercolane and Saturday at Pian di Massiano. There's also a daily covered market off Piazza Matteotti.

SEEING THE SIGHTS

Perugia's public living room is **Corso Vannucci** 𝒜, a wide promenade that's the stage for one of Italy's most lively and decorous evening *passeggiate.* People saunter up and down the Corso at twilight to see and be seen, to pause in the cafes for an espresso, and to discuss politics and soccer scores. One end of Corso Vannucci is anchored by the 19th-century **Piazza Italia** (see "Perugia's Medieval Pompeii," below), while along one side of the other end undulates a huge solid mass of crenellated travertine called the **Palazzo dei Priori.**

Calling All Chocoholics!

The weeklong **Eurochocolate Festival** is held annually from mid- to late October in Perugia. Pick up a list of hour-by-hour festivities held throughout town, staged by chocolate manufacturers from all over the world. You can witness a chocolate-carving contest, when the scraps of 1,000-kilo blocks are yours for the sampling, and entire multiple-course menus are created around the chocolate theme. Half-day lessons from visiting chefs are also available. For details, contact the **Eurochocolate Organization,** Via D'Andreotto 19, 06124 Perugia (℃ **075-573-2670;** fax 075-573-1100; www. eurochocolate.perugia.it).

One of the largest town halls in Italy, this palazzo was started in the 1290s and expanded in 1443. Inside are the Collegio del Cambio and the Galleria Nazionale (see below). The far end of the building has the oldest **facade,** with an off-center main portal from which spills a fan of steps. At their top are a small terrace and the palazzo's first entranceway, flanked by bronze copies of the Perugian griffin and the Guelf lion. (The originals are inside.) Through the door is the **Sala dei Notari,** a long rectangular room supported by eight large arches, formerly a citizens' assembly chamber and now used for public lectures and concerts. Matteo Tassi repainted much of it in 1860 with the coats of arms of Perugia's *podestà* (mayors) from 1297 to 1424, but in the spandrels of the arches remain the Old Testament and mythological scenes painted in 1297 by a follower of the Roman master Pietro Cavallini. The building is open Tuesday through Sunday (and Mon June–Sept) from 9am to 1pm and 3 to 7pm.

This end of the palazzo borders Perugia's superb main square, **Piazza IV Novembre,** the turnstile for the evening *passeggiata*—strollers swing around here to start back up Corso Vannucci in the other direction. The centerpiece of the piazza is the **Fontana Maggiore** ✦✦, one of Italy's prettiest public fountains. It was designed by local monk Fra' Bevignate in 1278, and the two stacked basins are set with panels and figures carved by Gothic master sculptors Nicola Pisano and his son Giovanni. These panels were designed to highlight the glories of Perugia's past and character and are filled with references to everyday life—a man roasting a chicken, a woman picking figs, and a love-stricken knight galloping after his lady fair and clutching a bunch of roses. The fountain emerged spectacularly in 1999 after years of restoration, gleaming white as new.

Via delle Volte twists off the back corner of the piazza, under a high flying arch, and spills into **Piazza Cavallotti,** under which excavations of a Roman-era road and the foundations of some houses are sometimes open in summer. (To ensure a visit, reserve a few days in advance by calling ✆ **075-572-7141.**)

Collegio del Cambio ✦✦   The meeting rooms of Perugia's Exchange Guild make up one of the best-preserved "office suites" of the Renaissance. Perugino was hired in 1498 to fresco one of the rooms with a **style and scenery** illustrating the humanist marriage of Christianity and classicism. It's perhaps his masterpiece in the medium, replete with a studied naturalism and precise portraiture, and a virtual catwalk of late-15th-century fashion. He finished by 1500 with the help of his students, probably including a 17-year-old Raphael, to whom art historians attribute the figure of Fortitude seated on a cloud in the second bay of the left wall and whose young mug may have served Perugino as the model for the prophet Daniel on the right wall. Perugino frescoed a superlative self-portrait on the pilaster of the left wall, looking sternly out of violet eyes set in a chubby, double-chinned face topped by a red cap. Perugino's less talented student Giannicola di Paolo frescoed the second room from 1509 to 1529 with a St. John the Baptist theme.

A few doors down at no. 15 is the **Collegio della Mercanzia** ✦ (✆ **075-573-0366**), home to the 13th-century Merchants' Guild since 1390—the guild still operates as a charitable institution out of the palazzo. In the 15th century, the walls and ceilings were swathed in remarkable woodwork carved and inlaid by anonymous craftsmen, probably northern European. It's open the same hours as the Collegio del Cambio, but it closes at 1pm instead of 12:30pm.

Palazzo dei Priori, Corso Vannucci 25. ✆ **075-572-8599**. Admission to either 2.60€ ($3) adults, 1.60€ ($1.85) seniors over 65, free for children under 12. Combined ticket for both 3.10€ ($3.55) adults, 2.10€ ($2.40) seniors over 65. Dec 20–Jan 6 Tues–Sat 9am–12:30pm and 2:30–5:30pm, Sun 9am–1pm; Mar 1–Oct 31 Mon–Sat

9am–12:30pm and 2:30–5:30pm, Sun 9am–1pm; Nov 1–Dec 19 and Jan 7–Feb 28 Tues–Sat 8am–2pm, Sun 9am–12:30pm.

Galleria Nazionale ✮✮✮ One of central Italy's top museums, Perugia's National Gallery houses the largest and finest collection of Umbrian art in the world, including plenty of Perugino paintings. The gallery begins on the second floor, but on your way upstairs pause at the first floor to peek into the glass window in the door of the **Sala del Consiglio Comunale.** You'll see the original bronze griffin and lion from the palazzo's old entrance on Piazza IV Novembre. Recent studies suggest the griffin may actually be an ancient Etruscan sculpture, to which new wings were added when the lion was cast in 1281.

Room 1 currently houses 16th- to 18th-century works, including Caravaggiesque paintings by the likes of Orazio Gentilleschi and Valentin de Boulogne, as well as a baroque *Nativity of the Virgin* (1643) by Pietro da Cortona.

Rooms 2 and 3 show the development of 13th-century Perugian painting. It was heavily influenced by the artists working on Assisi's Basilica di San Francesco and therefore torn between the local traditional eastern influences and the classicism of the new Florentine masters, Cimabue and Giotto. The artist called the Maestro del Trittico di Perugia represents the former styling, though he did indulge in a highly creative take on Byzantine motifs in the *Madonna and Child* on the shutters of the tabernacle here. The Maestro di San Francesco and especially the Maestro di Farneto are much more firmly rooted in the Giottesque school of late medieval art that was beginning to form into the Renaissance.

Room 4 is full of 14th-century painting and sculpture, with the Sienese influence represented by works from the early master Duccio di Boninsegna—a 1304 *Madonna and Child* featuring six tiny angels and a similar 1330s scene by his follower Meo di Guido da Siena. On the left wall is a tiny parchment painting of the *Madonna and Child with the Crucifixion* by Puccio Capanna, one of the most modern and skilled of Giotto's followers. On the far wall is the museum's greatest masterpiece, Piero della Francesca's ***Polyptych of Sant'Antonio*** ✮✮✮. The master from Sansepolcro probably painted this large altarpiece in the mid-1460s, with a Madonna enthroned in a classical niche surrounded by solid-bodied saints. The most arresting portion, though, is the pinnacle's *Annunciation* scene, worked with a delicacy and sense of perspective unheard of at the time. The scene is all the more engrossing for the illusory hole punched straight through the center of it by a receding arched colonnade that puts a gulf between the angel Gabriel and Mary.

Rooms 5 to 8 are devoted to early-15th-century altarpieces from the brushes of Taddeo di Bartolo, Bartolo di Fredi, Ottaviano Nelli, Lucca di Tommè, Giovanni Boccati, and Bicci di Lorenzo. Among them, in room 6, is Gentile da Fabriano's tiny gemlike ***Madonna and Child*** ✮ (1405), an International Gothic masterpiece. Gentile used layers of transparent paints, plenty of gold, and a sure, delicate hand to produce this unique work.

Rooms 9 and 10 house large canvases by Benedetto Bonfigli, a fairly talented painter of the Perugian Renaissance. These works inspired H. V. Morton to dub the museum a "haunt of exquisite musical angels," and their cityscapes and background buildings offer us a glimpse of Perugia in the 1400s. **Room 11**— alongside a Perugino *Adoration of the Magi* (1523) and a few Agostino di Duccio *Madonna*s—has eight panels depicting the *Miracles of St. Bernardino of Siena.* They were painted in a 1473 workshop in the limpid, colorful Umbrian style soon to be popularized by Perugino; he and Francesco di Giorgio Martini are two of the artists to whom the panels have been tentatively attributed.

Perugia's Medieval Pompeii

To cow the insurgent Perugini into submission after he put down their rebellion against his salt tax, Pope Paul III demolished more than one quarter of the city in 1530, pointedly including the palaces of the fractious former leaders, the Baglioni family. He then ordered Antonio da Sangallo the Younger to build him a fortress, the **Rocca Paolina** ✱, in the gaping empty space. By 1543, the massive bastion was complete, and it helped uphold papal domination over Perugia for more than 300 years. At the Italian unification in 1860, when Perugia was finally freed from the pope's yoke, workers came to dismantle the fortress. They found themselves outnumbered, however, as almost every man, woman, and child in the city descended with grim faces on the hated *rocca* and began to tear it apart stone by stone with pickaxes, shovels, and their bare hands.

Sangallo didn't merely raze all the buildings, however. The land sloped away from Perugia's ridge here in all three directions, so to make a flat plain on which to build the fortress; he leveled the field, using the houses, towers, and churches in the area as supports for the *rocca,* aided by brick pillars and vaults. In the process, a whole neighborhood of the medieval town was preserved, intact but eerily silent and still, buried beneath the newer streets above. The vaults of the *rocca* now serve as a **public exhibition space,** and stretches of the subterranean streets are interspersed with the escalators that connect Piazza Italia, which partially takes up the space the dismantled fortress left, with the parking lots below. An underground "Via Baglioni" leads through a section of this almost-forgotten city, with dozens of houses and churches abandoned for hundreds of years. The mid-20th-century travel writer H. V. Morton called it a **medieval Pompeii** and imagined its narrow alleys and ruinous buildings inhabited by covens of witches brewing Perugia's notorious poisons. You can clamber through doorless entrances, climb the remains of stairways, walk through empty rooms, and wander at will through the maze of mute walls. Bring a flashlight.

Sangallo also couldn't bring himself to destroy the Etruscan **Porta Marzia (Mars Gate)** to the city. He quietly had workers take it apart and reassemble it as a doorway to the fortress's outer wall, where Via Baglioni now reemerges into the sunlight onto Via Marzia. The worn, dark stone heads probing out from around the arch are said to be those of Etruscan gods.

You can enter the underground city daily from 8am to 7pm (no admission fee) from the escalators at the Prefettura on Piazza Italia, through the Porta Marzia on Via Marzia, or by riding the escalators up from Piazza Partigiani.

After a hall of 17th- and 18th-century **majolica** from Deruta and the Abruzzi and a chapel frescoed by Benedetto Bonfigli comes **Room 15,** which contains what many visitors come here for: the 15th- and 16th-century art starring large **altarpieces by Perugino** ✱. The *Adoration of the Magi* (1475) is an early Perugino work, painted when he was just 25 and still had a heavy Florentine influence. He may have been assisted on the 1505 *Monteripido Altarpiece* background by his young pupil Raphael. His later works here, especially the 1517 *Transfiguration,* show how he eventually developed a more transparent, spatially spare style with delicate landscapes and crafted pastel figures.

Palazzo dei Priori, Corso Vannucci 19. ℂ **075-574-1247** or 075-57-411. Admission 6.50€ ($7.50) adults, 3.25€ ($3.75) ages 8–25 and seniors over 65. Mon–Fri 8:30am–7:30pm; Sun 9am–1pm. Closed first Mon of every month.

Duomo For a major Italian city and provincial capital, Perugia has a pretty disappointing cathedral. First raised in the early 14th century on the Gothic model of the German hall churches, it didn't take its present form until the 16th century. Unsure whether the front on Piazza Danti or the flank facing Piazza IV Novembre should be the facade, Perugians slapped a bit of desultory decoration on both. On the Piazza IV Novembre side is a **statue of Pope Julius III** giving benediction.

The **interior** is a bit gaudy (those columns are painted, not real marble), but there is a handful of good paintings. The first chapel on the left aisle is the **Cappella del Santo Anello,** where a gilded box protected by 15 locks supposedly holds the wedding ring of the Virgin Mary, stolen from Chiusi in 1473. Church officials solemnly take out the ring—set with a pale gray agate whose color they swear changes, mood-ring style, to reveal the character of the person wearing it—to show the crowds on July 29 and 30.

In the **Cappella di San Bernardino** (1st on the right aisle) is baroque painter Frederico Barocchio's finest work, a tumultuous *Descent from the Cross* painted in 1567. Against the third pillar of the right aisle is the *Madonna della Grazie,* whose hallowed status is given away by dozens of ex-votos and burning candles surrounding it. It's attributed to Perugino's early-16th-century student Gianicola di Paolo. Just beyond it on the right aisle, in the **Cappella del Sacramento,** Luca Signorelli's 1484 *Madonna* altarpiece is provisionally installed.

Piazza IV Novembre/Piazza Danti. ℂ **075-572-3832.** Daily 8am–noon and 4pm–sunset.

Pozzo Etrusco (Etruscan Well) When the 3rd-century B.C. Etruscans needed water, they sank a 5.4m- (18-ft.) wide shaft more than 34.5m (115 ft.) into the pebbly soil under Perugia. To support the cover over the well, they built two massive trusses of travertine that have stood the test of more than 2,000 years. You can climb down past the dripping walls to a bridge across the bottom.

Piazza Danti 18 (at the end of the tunnel). ℂ **075-573-3669.** Admission 2.50€ ($2.90) adults, 2€ ($2.30) seniors over 65, 1€ ($1.15) ages 7–14, free for children under 7; includes admission to San Severo (see below), valid 1 week. MC, V (at Pozzo Etrusco only). Apr–Oct Wed–Mon 10am–1:30pm and 2:30–6:30pm; Nov–Mar Wed–Mon 10am–1:30pm and 2:30–7pm.

Capella di San Severo Before he set off for Florence and Rome, a young Perugino protégé named Raphael Sanzio made his first attempt at fresco in this chapel in 1505. Though damaged, the upper half of this work, with the *Holy Trinity* surrounded by saints seated on clouds, shows the germ of Raphael's budding genius and his eye for composition and naturalism. By 1521, Raphael had died young, and his now-septuagenarian teacher, Perugino—just 2 years from the grave himself, with his talent fading—finished the scene with six posed saints along the bottom. The rest of the church, which was built in the 11th century by Camaldulensian monks on the site of an old pagan temple, is usually closed.

Piazza Raffaello. ℂ **075-573-3864.** For admission and hours, see Pozzo Etrusco, above.

San Bernardino and San Francesco   On your way down Via dei Priori, you'll pass the alley **Via della Gabbia** behind the Palazzo dei Priori, where in the bad old days the Perugian council members would leave people who didn't see eye to eye with them locked in a cage until the dissidents starved. The long spikes left on some of the walls are where the heads of convicted criminals were impaled. As Via dei Priori continues down even more steeply, you'll see the stone **Torre degli Sciri,** the last of Perugia's medieval towers.

The grassy lawn at the hill's bottom, a lounging spot for university students on sunny days, is bordered by two of the finest church facades in Perugia. On the left is the small **Oratorio di San Bernardino,** whose facade is layered with bas-reliefs and sculptures of saints and angel musicians (1457–61, beautifully restored in the 1990s) by Florentine sculptor Agostino di Duccio in his unique, vaguely Asiatic style. Inside is a 1464 processional banner by Benedetto Bonfigli and a carved 4th-century paleo-Christian sarcophagus serving as the altar. The oratory's lumbering big brother next door is **San Francesco al Prato,** with an unusual, vaguely Moorish geometric facade. The unstable ground under it began to shift almost as soon as the structure was raised in the 13th century. The altar end has since lost its roof, and the interior has been closed. It's being restored to serve as a public space for concerts and exhibits.

Between the two churches is the entrance to the **Accademia di Belle Arte,** Piazza San Francesco 5 (© **075-572-6562**), an odd assemblage of turn-of-the-20th-century plaster statues reproducing Italy's great sculptures, from classical through Michelangelo to neoclassical. The museum was closed in 2001 for "rearrangement," and at press time there was no word yet on when it may reopen.

Piazza San Francesco (at the bottom of Via dei Priori). Free admission. Daily 8am–12:30pm and 3–6pm.

Arco d'Agusto and Sant'Angelo   At the end of Via U. Rocchi (behind the Duomo) is the **Arco d'Agusto (Arco Etrusco).** In the 3rd century B.C., the Etruscans laid the massive stones of the base. Augustus Caesar engraved it with "Augusta Perusia" after he rebuilt the city. And in the 16th century, the left-hand tower was capped off with a Renaissance loggia.

Via G. Garibaldi leads from the piazza to the oldest church in Umbria, **Sant'Angelo** ✿. At the end of a quiet cypress-lined lawn, this venerable church was built in the 5th century, perhaps into the remains of a pagan temple. It retained the circular ground plan of its Roman predecessor, which may also have contributed the inner ring of columns inside. It's a peaceful church, with few visitors and only some 14th-century frescoes inside.

Free admission. Sant'Angelo open daily 8am–noon and 4pm–sunset.

Museo Archeologico (Archaeology Museum)   Among the cluttered collections here, you'll find a 2nd-century A.D. well head carved with a frieze of Greeks battling Amazons; several 1st-century A.D. portrait busts of Roman bigwigs such as Augustus, Claudius, Germanicus, and Agrippina; a 6th-century B.C. Etruscan sphinx discovered near Cetona; and plenty of Etruscan funerary urns sculpted with intricate relief scenes. Among the collection's prizes are a signed terra-cotta statue of Heracles, a large bronze shield from a 2nd-century B.C. tomb, and a travertine cippus known as the *Inscription of Perugia.* It's the longest document yet discovered written in the Etruscan language—apparently by lawyers. (It seems to resolve a property dispute.)

Inside **San Domenico church** is Italy's second-largest stained-glass window (Milan's Duomo beats it), assembled in the 15th century, and a Gothic monument of Benedict XI, carved in the early 14th century.

Piazza G. Bruno 10 (in the cloisters of San Domenico). © **075-572-7141.** www.archeopg.arti.beniculturali.it. Admission 2€ ($2.30) adults, 1€ ($1.15) ages 18–25 and seniors over 65. Mon–Sat 8:30am–7:30pm; Sun 9am–1pm.

San Pietro ✦ This Benedictine monastery at Perugia's edge, its pointed **Gothic tower** a city landmark, was founded in the late 900s. Inside the first courtyard is the Romanesque entrance to the monastery's San Pietro church. The church's old **facade** was uncovered in the 1980s, revealing 14th-century Giottesque **frescoes** between the arches—the enthroned three-headed woman on the right may represent the Holy Trinity. The 16th-century **interior** is supported by ancient granite and marble columns (pilfered from a pagan temple) and is heavily decorated—wallpapered with 16th-and 17th-century canvases, frescoed with grotesques, and filled with Renaissance and baroque paintings. The first altarpiece on the right is a colorful 16th-century *Madonna with Saints* by Eusebio da San Giorgio. Toward the end of the right aisle is the door to the sacristy (track down a monk to open it), which contains five **small Perugino paintings of saints** that were stolen in 1916 but found their way back here by 1993. Also here are two small Caravaggiesque works: The *Santa Francesca Romana with an Angel* is attributed by some to Caravaggio himself, and the *Christ at the Column* copperplate sketch is a copy, perhaps of a lost Caravaggio original.

Ask the sacristan also to light up the choir so you can see the incredible **wooden choir stalls** ✦, some of the finest examples of wood intarsia in all Italy, produced in 1526 by a workshop under the direction of Bernardino Antinibi and Stefano Zambelli. In 1536, Stefano's brother Fra' Damiano inlaid the masterpiece door at the back, whose panels could hold their own against any painting of the Renaissance.

At the altar end of the left aisle are a strikingly medieval Pietà scene painted by Fiorenzo di Lorenzo in 1469 and paintings of *St. Peter* and *St. Paul* attributed to Il Guercino. The **Cappella Vibi** houses a gilded marble tabernacle by Mino da Fiesole, and in the **Cappella Ranieri** next door hangs Guido Reni's *Christ in the Garden.* Continuing down the left aisle, before the third altar, is another Eusebio da San Giorgio painting, this one of the *Adoration of the Magi* (1508). Between the second and first altars is a late *Pietà* by Perugino.

Down Corso Cavour, out Porta San Pietro, and to the end of Borgo XX Giugno. © **075-30-482.** Free admission. Daily 8am–noon and 4pm–sunset.

WHERE TO STAY

Most Perugian hotels are flexible about rates, which dive 40% to 50% below posted prices in the off season, so it always pays to ask. Reserve well in advance if you plan to visit during the booked-solid Umbria Jazz season.

Promhotel Umbria is a local travel agency that can book you into one of more than 80 hotels in Perugia and throughout Umbria (© **0678-62-033** toll-free in Italy, or 075-500-2788; fax 075-500-2789; promhotelumbia@krenet.it).

VERY EXPENSIVE

Hotel Brufani ✦ Where the bastions of the papal Rocca Paolina once glowered now rises Perugia's bastion of luxury, built in 1883 by a Grand Tour guide as an inn for his English clients. It offers standardized comforts and (from most rooms) spectacular views—some over the valley, stretching south all the way to Monte

Amiata, others toward Assisi. Most accommodations are done in a modernized classic style—or, in the newer ones, a gilded 18th-century decor to match the original marble statues in the public areas—all with fresh carpets and wall fabrics, heavy curtains, and sparkling bathrooms with marble sinks; some have Jacuzzi tubs. The spacious two-room suites feature plush red tassled sofas and double sinks in the large bathrooms. Many rooms were refurbished in 2000 and 2001, when they seamlessly reincorporated their old sister hotel Bellavista, which occupied a wing of the building until 1999. The first-floor rooms are older and grander—a few even have high frescoed ceilings and the original furnishings. The public areas include grand salons of chandeliers, intricately inlaid wood floors, high coffered and stuccoed ceilings, and terraces opening to cliff-hanging views over the valley. A new pool and exercise room have now been installed.

Piazza Italia 12, 06100 Perugia. (C) **075-573-2541.** Fax 075-572-0210. www.sinahotels.com. 94 units. 337€ ($388) double; 465€ ($535) junior suite; 699€ ($804) suite. Breakfast 23€ ($26). AE, DC, MC, V. Parking 31€ ($36) in private garage. **Amenities:** Umbrian fare in intimate Collins restaurant/American bar (tables on the piazza in summer); indoor pool; small exercise room; concierge; tour desk; car-rental desk; business center; 24-hr. room service; in-room massage; babysitting; laundry service; same-day dry cleaning; nonsmoking rooms. *In room:* A/C, TV, VCR and fax in suites, dataport, minibar, hair dryer, safe.

MODERATE

Hotel Giò Arte e Vini ✦   This operation may be commercial to the core, but it's one of the most felicitous concentrations of capitalism around. It's on the outskirts of town, inhabiting an ugly 1960s brick architectural mistake, but the rooms on the back face a small tree-shaded valley, the only oasis of green on Perugia's developed slopes. The rooms are comfortable, large, and well furnished. A contemporary artist and a wine label are paired in each room: The glass-topped desks contain tiny *enoteche,* the art hangs on the wall, and you're welcome to buy either. The restaurant serves Umbrian recipes tweaked to fine cuisine levels and accompanied by bottomless wine tasting. The attached *enoteca/gastronomia* stocks almost 800 labels of wine and regional products, from Italy and around the world.

Via Ruggero d'Andreotto 19, 06124 Perugia. (C) and fax **075-573-1100.** www.hotelgio.it. 130 units. 120€ ($138) double or junior suite. Half pension available. Rates include breakfast. AE, DC, MC, V. Free parking. Bus: 6 or 7. By car, the E45 passes just below the hotel. **Amenities:** Restaurant; concierge; small business center; limited room service; babysitting; laundry service; dry cleaning; nonsmoking rooms. *In room:* A/C, TV, dataport, minibar, hair dryer.

Hotel La Rosetta ✦   This 19th-century medieval-styled palazzo, anchoring the Piazza Italia end of Corso Vannucci with its cute faux-Romanesque brick entry courtyard, has been a hotel since 1922. The accommodations range from cramped to palatial, but a renovation has refined them all. A few rooms open onto the Corso (great people-watching but rather noisy). Those on the first floor occupy the palazzo's old *piano nobile,* so they come with high vaulted ceilings, the occasional chandeliers, and some with stunning frescoes from the 1800s or 1920s. Choosing such "superior" doubles lends your stay more antique character, but bumps you well into the Expensive category. At these prices, one wishes all the bathrooms came with shower curtains (and fuzzy towels, for that matter).

Piazza Italia 19, 06121 Perugia. (C) and fax **075-572-0841.** www.perugiaonline.com/larosetta. 90 units. 117.50€–156€ ($135–$179) standard double; 156€–168€ ($179–$193) superior double; 157€–196€ ($181–$225) standard triple. Ask for discounts for longer stays. Rates include breakfast. AE, DC, MC, V. Free parking in nearby piazza. **Amenities:** Restaurant; concierge; tour desk; car-rental desk; limited room service; babysitting; laundry service; nonsmoking rooms. *In room:* A/C, TV, dataport, minibar, hair dryer, safe.

Locanda della Posta 𝒜𝒜   The Posta is in the heart of the action on Corso Vannucci, a few palaces down from the National Gallery and in the midst of the *passeggiata*. Although pricey and rather characterless, it offers comfort as solid as the Brufani (above) at a better rate. The Posta was the only hotel in Perugia when it opened in the late 1700s and has entertained Goethe, Frederick III of Prussia, and Hans Christian Andersen. The small breakfast room retains its frescoed ceiling, yet most of the property was redecorated in the early 1990s in mainly dark, muted colors; only a few canvases on corridor walls remain of the 18th-century decor. The sizable accommodations' look now includes padded fabric-lined walls, matching Art Nouveau floral prints on the quilts and chair upholstery, and modern wood furniture.

Corso Vannucci 97, 06121 Perugia. © **075-572-8925.** Fax 075-573-2562. www.venere.it/perugia/locanda_della_posta. 39 units. 170€ ($196) double; 201€ ($231) suite. Rates include breakfast. AE, DC, MC, V. Parking 20€ ($23) in garage or free in front of Brufani nearby. **Amenities:** Concierge; tour desk; limited room service; laundry service; same-day dry cleaning. *In room:* A/C, TV, dataport, minibar, hair dryer, safe.

Sangallo Palace Hotel   Ranking just under Hotel Brufani, this palace just below the historic center—it sits atop the Partigiani garage, so it's just a 10-minute walk and few escalator rides from Corso Vannucci—is modern, elegant, and preferred by business types in town for conferences. Over each bed is a framed reproduction of a Perugino or Pinturicchio. The medium-size to spacious guest rooms come with amenities like private safes, interactive television, wide beds with firm mattresses, and often open onto panoramic countryside views. Many of the tiled bathrooms have techno-Jacuzzi tubs. Il Sangallo restaurant is justifiably praised for its Umbrian and national cuisine, with much of the produce coming from the Umbrian countryside; the cellar is well stocked in regional wines. In summer, breakfast is served on the (noisy) terrace.

Via Masi 9, 06121 Perugia. © **075-573-0202.** Fax 075-573-0068. www.sangallo.it. 93 units. 125€–168€ ($144–$193) double; 155€–190€ ($178–$219) suite. Rates include breakfast. AE, DC, MC, V. Free parking or 11€ ($13) valet parking. **Amenities:** Restaurant; small (but technologically advanced) indoor heated pool; tennis courts (1km away); small exercise room; Jacuzzi; small children's center; concierge; tour desk; car-rental desk; courtesy car; business center; 24-hr. room service; in-room massage; babysitting; laundry service; same-day dry cleaning; nonsmoking rooms. *In room:* A/C, TV w/Internet access, VCR in suites, fax, dataport, minibar, hair dryer, safe.

INEXPENSIVE

Travelers watching their purse strings might want to forgo the more expensive choices above for two quiet hotels in the medieval streets east of Corso Vannucci. The **Piccolo Hotel,** Via L. Bonazzi 25 (© **075-572-2987**), is a surprisingly pleasant place on a street parallel to the Corso with 12 very simple but clean double rooms going for around 35€ to 40€ ($40–$46) without bathroom or 43€ to 48€ ($49–$55) with bathroom (no credit cards). The 75€ ($86) doubles at **Hotel Umbria,** Via Boncambi 37 (© and fax **075-572-1203;** www.hotelumbria.com), are considerably more of a climb back up to Corso Vannucci, but all 18 rooms have bathrooms and TVs, and modular furnishings. For info about the city's **youth hostel,** call © **075-572-2880.**

Hotel Priori 𝒜𝒜 *Value*   The best of Perugia's budget lodgings is just 60m (200 ft.) down the hill through the central arch of Palazzo dei Priori. Plants liven up the halls, and though the huge, sunny terrace surrounded by the buildings and roofs of old Perugia doesn't have a vista, it's great for breakfast alfresco in warm weather. Many savvy younger travelers and Italian families stay in the whitewashed, tile-floored rooms. The fine dark wood furniture was handmade by a local craftsman. The six newer rooms, just off the reception, have 17th-century detailing and air-conditioning.

Via Vermiglioli 3 (at Via dei Priori), 06123 Perugia. ℂ **075-572-3378.** Fax 075-572-3213. www.perugia. com/hotelpriori. 57 units. 45€–60€ ($52–$69) single; 60€–85€ ($69–$98) double; 100€–135€ ($115–$155) suite. Ask about discounts during slow periods. Rates include breakfast. MC, V. Parking 10€–15€ ($12–$17) in garage. **Amenities:** Concierge; tour desk; car-rental desk; limited room service (breakfast); babysitting; laundry service; dry cleaning. *In room:* A/C in the 6 newest units, TV in 20 units (for 5€/$5.75 extra), hair dryer on request.

WHERE TO DINE

Dining in Perugia is polarized: There are several worthy fine restaurants and plenty of cheap *pizzerie* supported by the vast student population, but very few *trattorie* in between. The local cuisine includes a secondo called ***torello alla Perugina*** (veal scallops served under liver pâté) that deserves sampling. Of the *pizzerie*, the best is **Il Segretto di Pulcinella,** Via Large 8, off Via Bonazzi (ℂ **075-573-6284**). Pizzas are 4€ to 7€ ($4.60–$8.05). It's open Tuesday through Sunday from 12:10 to 2:30pm and 8:30pm to midnight.

EXPENSIVE

Il Falchetto ✸✸ PERUGINA   Il Falchetto is one of Perugia's best and most popular dining spots. Try to sit in the more atmospheric back room, with its 14th-century stone walls and ceiling, or out on the piazza if it's summer—during Umbria Jazz; it's like having free seats to the concerts on Piazza IV Novembre. The dish to order is *falchetti verdi,* a personal-size casserole of rich, filling spinach and ricotta gnocchi baked with tomato sauce and cheeses. Or, sample the *umbrichelli alla casalinga* (homemade fat spaghetti in spicy tomato sauce). Then try a *tris della casa,* made up of three regional specialty secondi that might include *torello alla Perugina, filetino di vitello* (very thick, tender milk-fed veal served with porcini, truffle, and wood mushrooms), or an *agnello* rope twist of grilled lamb.

Via Bartolo 20 (2 steps north of the Duomo). ℂ **075-573-1775.** www.ilfalchetto.it. Reservations recommended. Primi 5.50€–15€ ($6.30–$17); secondi 8.50€–13€ ($9.80–$15). AE, DC, MC, V. Tues–Sun 12:30–2:30pm and 7:30–10:30pm. Closed Jan.

MODERATE

Il Cantinone UMBRIAN   On a side street just a few yards off Piazza IV Novembre, this low-key restaurant is set in a medieval mélange of vaulted ceilings and stone walls. The wall art is of questionable merit, but the food is of unmistakable quality. Both the ravioli (covered in spinachy cream sauce) and the *gnocchi al pomodoro* (potato dumplings in tomato sauce) are made from scratch, and the *grigliata mista* (mixed grilled meats) and *torello alla Perugina* (veal smothered in chicken liver pâté) are good secondi. Il Cantinone is one of the better, cheaper choices in town for those who don't mind the occasional outbreak of Village People music on the radio.

Via Ritorta 4–8 (near the Duomo). ℂ **075-573-4430.** Reservations recommended. Primi 6€–8€ ($6.90–$9.20); secondi 7€–14€ ($8.05–$16); pizze 4.40€–6.50€ ($5.05–$7.50). AE, DC, MC, V. Wed–Mon 12:30–2:30pm and 7:30–11pm. Closed Dec 22–Jan 5.

La Lanterna ✸ CREATIVE UMBRIAN   A series of brick-vaulted rooms descends under a medieval palazzo past an open kitchen from which emerge billows of steam and the slightly adventurous creations of the cooking staff. One filling antipasto is the *insalata di radicchio, caciotta, noci, e tartufo,* a strange but palate-pleasing salad of bitter lettuce, pecorino cheese, nuts, truffle shavings, and corn. Continue with the light and delicious *ravioli all'arancia e petali di rosa* (cheese ravioli in cream sauce flavored with mandarin orange slices and rose petals) or *agnolotti alla Norcina* (a typical Umbrian dish of small meat ravioli under a sauce of cream, sausage, and black truffle). The *arrosto misto* is a particularly good grab bag of roast rabbit, guinea hen, lamb, and other meats, while the *filetto balsamico* (filet of veal cooked in balsamic vinegar) might appeal to more delicate palates.

Via U. Rocchi 6 (behind the Duomo). © **075-572-6397**. Reservations recommended. Primi 6€–10€ ($6.90–$12); secondi 7€–16€ ($8.05–$18). AE, DC, MC, V. Fri–Wed 12:30–2:30pm and 7:30–10:45pm (daily in summer).

La Taverna CREATIVE UMBRIAN   One of the more refined restaurants in town, candlelit La Taverna is removed from the hubbub (but still central; just follow the signs). Soft music fills the brick barrel-vaulted ceilings under which couples meet romantically and families celebrate special occasions. There's a trio of recommended first courses: *zuppa di fave e carciofi* (purée of fava beans with artichoke hearts), *tagliatelle al ragout di anatra* (noodles in duck ragù), and ravioli, stuffed with always-changing and oddly appetizing combinations. The chef gets most creative with the secondi, offering a *stinco do maialino al forno* (the baked piglet's ankle is good, but leave the lyonnaise potatoes alone) and the sweet-sour-salty experience of *baccalà con prugne, uvetta, a pinoli* (salt cod cooked with prunes, raisins, and pine nuts). La Taverna is justly renowned for its excellent dessert cart.

Via delle Streghe 8 (near Corso Vannucci's Piazza Repubblica). © **075-572-4128**. Reservations recommended. Primi 5€–12€ ($5.75–$14); secondi 9€–16€ ($10–$18). AE, DC, MC, V. Tues–Sun 12:30–2:30pm and 7:30–11:30pm.

Osteria del Gambero (Ubu Re) ★★ CREATIVE UMBRIAN/SEAFOOD
Ubu Re feels a bit like a private club, with modern art prints, soft jazz, and soft sconce lighting. Though most Italian and international guides haven't yet acknowledged it, this upstart—opened a dozen years ago in a town where most restaurants have decades of pedigree—has become the best restaurant in Perugia, and it's pretty cheap to boot. Perhaps it'll get more notice now that it's moved from the second floor down to street level and in a more prominent location. The unique breads, pasta, and desserts are made on-site, and whatever else you do, be sure to order the *mousse tepida di piccione* (pigeon soufflé in black truffle sauce). They offer a "typical cuisine" fixed-price menu, a fish menu, and (in season) a show-stealing *degustazione* (tasting) menu of dishes prepared with Norcia's black truffles—perhaps the cheapest way in town to taste how Umbria's elusive and most prized tuber goes with each course. The wine list represents the entire Italian peninsula well, but is a bit weighty on price.

Via Baldeschi 8/a (behind the Duomo). © **075-573-5461**. Reservations recommended. Primi 7€–8€ ($8.05–$9.20); secondi 9€–11€ ($10–$13); fixed-priced menus 24€/$27 (32€/$37 if you want to accompany each of the 4 courses with a glass of a different wine). MC, V. Tues–Sun 12:30–2:30pm and 7:30–11:30pm. Closed 2 weeks in Jan, 2 weeks in July.

NEAR PERUGIA: ETRUSCAN TOMBS, WINE, CERAMICS & MORE

About 5km (3 miles) south of Perugia, on the road to Foligno but still in Perugia's suburbs, you'll see the **Ipogeo dei Volumni** ★ (© **075-393-329;** www. archeopg.arti.beniculturali.it; open Sept–June daily 9am–1pm and 3:30–6:30pm; July–Aug daily 9am–12:30pm and 4:30–7pm), a tomb of the late Etruscan era that was used from the mid–2nd century to the mid–1st century

B.C., the era of ascending Roman authority. This is one of the finest Etruscan tombs in Italy, built like a house underground and still set with its cinerary urns. The ashes of Arunte Volumni, the father of the clan buried here, rest in the central travertine urn carved with his effigy, reclining in true Etruscan style. His daughter's effigy, however, shows a seated lady after the Roman fashion, an indication of the increasing influence of the Latin conquerors on local customs. Unlike other tombs of this style, it's decorated with carved reliefs— Medusa heads, dolphins, and owls—rather than paintings. Admission is 2€ ($2.30). If your group is larger than five, you must reserve ahead through the **Soprintendenza Archeologica per l'Umbria** (© 075-572-7141). You can also take the bus from Perugia's Piazza Garibaldi; it's the one headed for Ponte San Giovanni. (The bus doesn't always stop here, so let the driver know where you're going.)

Torgiano, 15km (9 miles) south of Perugia, is celebrated for its wines, considered the best in Umbria. The top label is the complex red **Rubesco Riserva** 𝒜𝒜, produced by the local estates of the Fondazione Lungarotti (www.lungarotti.it), whose vintages were formulated by contemporary wine guru Giorgio Lungarotti. Although he used modern techniques and experimental methods to concoct his excellent reds and vin santo, Lungarotti was also in touch with the region's oenological roots and founded a **Museo del Vino (Wine Museum),** set up in the Palazzo Baglioni at Corso Vittorio Emanuele 11 (© 075-988-0200). It's one of the best didactic collections of its kind, fascinating even for those mildly interested in viticulture, and most of the explanatory signs are translated into English. Admission is 4€ adults and 2.50€ ($2.90) children under 6. It's open daily from 9am to 1pm and 3 to 6pm (until 7pm in summer). The nearby hotel/restaurant complex **Tre Vaselle** 𝒜 (© 075-988-0447; fax 075-988-0214; www.3vaselle.it) also belongs to the wine estate and serves exquisite Tuscan fare in a refined dining room (pricey, but worth it). It also offers upscale guest rooms rambling through several 17th-century buildings; doubles go for 185€ to 210€ ($213–$242), suites for 250€ ($288). The hotel has an indoor and outdoor pool and a large conference center.

Another 5km (3 miles) down the road is a ceramic production center that has been one of Italy's most famous since the 14th century, the crafts town of **Deruta** 𝒜𝒜. The town has, for some reason, closed down its tourist office (which used to be located at Piazza dei Consoli 4), and locals don't seem sure it they'll bother opening one back up again. The private websites **www.deruta info.it** and **www.comune.deruta.pg.it** have some good local info on them.

Large modern factories now crank out huge numbers of assembly-line plates, bowls, and vases in traditional colors and patterns, and that is what's hawked behind the plate-glass windows of the large showrooms forming a phalanx along the new town's main drag below the highway. The merchandise is usually pretty good quality, but if you explore the back roads in the old town, you can find true artisans hand-painting ceramics they've tossed on foot-powered wheels. My favorites are the traditionalists **Deruta Placens,** with shops at Via B. Michelotti 25 (© 075-972-277) and Via Umberto I 16 (© 075-972-4027); and **Miriam,** where at Marcella Favaroni's Via Umberto I 15 shop (© 075-971-1452) she paints vividly colorful and intricate patterns at half the prices most shops charge. Her husband's shop at Piazza dei Consoli 26 (© 075-971-1210) carries more traditional pieces and quality Renaissance reproductions. To get a sense of the evolution of ceramics, visit the **Museo Regionale della Ceramica (Regional**

Museum of Ceramics), Largo San Francesco (© **075-971-1000**), which houses a precious collection of Deruta ceramics of various periods from the Middle Ages to the 1930s. April through September, it's open daily from 10:30am to 1pm and 3 to 6pm; October through March, hours are Wednesday through Monday 10:30am to 1pm and 3:30 to 7pm (check for shorter hours off season). Admission is 3€ ($3.45).

2 Assisi: An Artistic Pilgrimage

27km (17 miles) E of Perugia; 190km (118 miles) SE of Florence; 175km (109 miles) N of Rome

Assisi should be a perfect Umbrian hill town. It's a tiered, overgrown village of pink and pale-gray stone drawn out along a mountainside and surrounded by a valley patchwork of fields and olive groves. It boasts Roman roots, a glowering castle and twisting alleyways from the Middle Ages, and some of Italy's finest early Renaissance art—all backed by the brilliant green slope of sacred Mt. Subasio. But this city with a population of less than 3,000 (and shrinking) saw, at the end of the 20th century, an average of 4 to 5 million visitors every year. This constant flood of travelers has polished the usual hill-town charm right off Assisi. Countless pilgrims, art lovers, and just plain curious travelers over the last 700 years have imparted to the town a thick tourist shellac it often can't quite shake even in its quietest, least visited corners. It's no accident the University of Perugia's "tourism studies" program is based here.

All this aside, Assisi is still one of Italy's top sights, ranking with the Colosseum, Pompeii, and Venice's canals. It preserves the remarkably intact portico of a Roman temple on its main square, one of the better-preserved Albornoz Roccas with sweeping views, and a two-story basilica hulking at one end of town that's a festival of frescoes. The basilica showcases the talents of the greatest geniuses of the early Renaissance, both Sienese (Pietro Lorenzetti and Simone Martini) and Florentine (Cimabue and the incomparable Giotto).

In the late Middle Ages, Assisi witnessed the birth and lives of saints Clare and Francis. Francis is Italy's patron saint, founder of one of the world's largest monastic orders, and generally considered just about the holiest person to walk the earth since Jesus. The town is choked with visitors from Easter to June, and you sometimes can't move in the basilica on religious holiday weekends. The tourism support network, though, is in full force only when the crowds are in town, so while Assisi is packed beyond the limits in high season (book well in advance), you'll find it a ghost town January through March; about three quarters of the hotels, restaurants, and museums close.

Earthquakes in 1997 rocked the heart of Umbria. In Assisi, Santa Chiara church and the Duomo were both damaged, but the Basilica di San Francesco was the worst hit. Part of the ceiling in the upper church collapsed, killing four people, destroying frescoes by Cimabue and his followers, and damaging Giotto's *Life of St. Francis* frescoes. Knowing the Papal Jubilee celebrations would begin at Christmas 1999, the Pope pulled some strings (luckily, the basilica is the only sovereign land belonging to the Vatican outside Rome's Vatican City) and restoration sped along at a remarkable pace. The lower church reopened within weeks, and the upper church and its frescoes by early 2000. While full restoration of the entire structure may take a few more years to complete, the most important bits are already open again.

The rest of Assisi wasn't so lucky, and it was years before many of the churches and museums in town were able to open their doors once again—though I'm

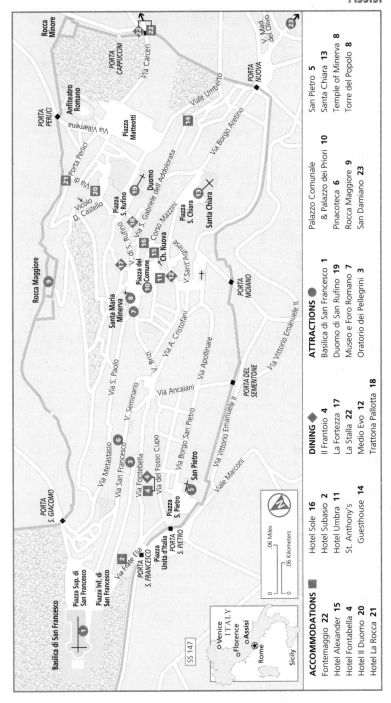

Assisi

ACCOMMODATIONS
Fontemaggio **22**
Hotel Alexander **15**
Hotel Fontabella **4**
Hotel Il Duomo **20**
Hotel La Rocca **21**
Hotel Sole **16**
Hotel Subasio **2**
Hotel Umbra **11**
St. Anthony's Guesthouse **14**

DINING ◆
Il Frantoio **4**
La Fortezza **17**
La Stalla **22**
Medio Evo **12**
Trattoria Pallotta **18**

ATTRACTIONS ●
Basilica di San Francesco **1**
Duomo di San Rufino **19**
Museo e Foro Romano **7**
Oratorio dei Pellegrini **3**
Palazzo Comunale & Palazzo dei Priori **10**
Pinacoteca **6**
Rocca Maggiore **9**
San Damiano **23**
San Pietro **5**
Santa Chiara **13**
Temple of Minerva **8**
Torre del Popolo **8**

happy to report that everything mentioned below has reopened, virtually all with set hours. However, many streets in town remain dense tunnels of wood supports desperately shoring up the medieval buildings on either side to keep them from falling in on each other. Doorways and arches have been filled in with temporary struts, and the Palazzo Comunale on the main square has only recently come out from under wraps. Hundreds of residents who had been living in "temporary" shipping containers outside town only got to move back home in 2001. It'll be a long time until Assisi recovers fully. Realize that all the sightseeing information below is subject to change as repairs are continued to be made to the city; call the tourist office (which itself has moved around quite a bit) for the latest details before you visit.

ESSENTIALS

GETTING THERE   By Train   From **Perugia,** there are about 20 trains daily (25–30 min.). From **Florence,** there are 11 daily Rome-bound trains, from which you transfer at Terontola/Cortona for Assisi (2–3 hr., often with long layovers). Coming from **Rome,** nine daily trains make the connection through Foligno (2–3 hr. total). The **station** (© 075-804-0272) is in the modern valley town of Santa Maria degli Angeli, about 5km (3 miles) from Assisi, with bus connections to Assisi every 20 minutes, or you can take a **taxi** for about 10€ to 13€ ($12–$15).

By Car   Assisi is only 27km (17 miles) from Perugia, but you have to take several roads (most are well signposted). Head south of town to the SS3, which you take in the direction of Umbertide. Get off the SS3 after 3.5 kilometers (2¼ miles) onto the SS75 toward Foligno. After 9 kilometers (6 miles), you'll come to the exit for Assisi at Santa Maria degli Angeli, its modern suburb. It's another 5 kilometers (3 miles) up to town. Assisi is almost entirely closed to traffic except hotel luggage drop-offs and pickups.

You can **park** (© 075-813-707) in the huge lot under Piazza Matteotti ("Parcheggio C") on the town's eastern edge; on Piazza Unità d'Italia outside Porta San Pietro ("Parcheggio A"), the smallest but nearest to the Basilica di San Francesco; or outside the walls' southeastern corner at Porta Moianbo and Porta Nuova ("Parcheggio B," with an elevator up into town). These are all pay-by-the-hour lots that fill up quickly in summer. Rates are 1.15€ ($1.30) per hour, but if you're staying in an Assisi hotel they'll give you an **Assisicard** that lets you park for 24 hours for 11€ ($12). The card also gets you small discounts in shops and some restaurants around town.

For the best **free parking,** drive to the north side of town, up along the ridge above the city, where there's plenty of space in the lot near the cemetery off Viale Albornoz behind the walls; even better are the spaces lining Via della Rocca just inside the walls near the Rocca (enter through Porta Perlici off Viale Albornoz and take the 1st right within the walls). To test your luck, drive all the way to the end of Viale Albornoz where it enters town through Porta San Giacomo; outside this gate are a few free spaces just a 2-minute stroll from San Francesco.

By Bus   Eight **APM** buses (© 800-512-141 or 075-506-781; www.apm perugia.it) run seven times daily between **Perugia** and Assisi's Piazza Matteotti. Most also pass by the lower half of Piazza San Pietro (at the bottom of the big traffic curve) at the other end of town. They also run about five buses from **Gubbio. Sulga** (© 075-500-9641; www.sulga.it) runs two buses daily from

Rome's Tiburtina station, and one daily from Piazza Adua in **Florence.** In Assisi, buy tickets in any *tabacchi* or at the tourist office.

VISITOR INFORMATION   The **tourist office** (© **075-812-534** or 075-812-450; fax 075-813-727; www.umbria2000.it) is on Piazza del Comune. It's open summer daily from 8am to 6:30pm, winter Monday through Saturday from 8am to 2pm and 3:30 to 6:30pm, Sunday from 9am to 1pm. The private websites **www.assisionline.com** and **www.assisiweb.com** also have good info.

FESTIVALS & MARKETS   In the city of St. Francis, all **church holidays** are pilgrim-ridden, solemn religious rites. Processions and church ceremonies—occasionally mixed with some livelier restaurant feasts—are celebrated throughout Easter Week and on Corpus Domini (early June), Festa del Voto (June 22), Festa del Perdono (Aug 1 and 2), Festa di San Rufino (Aug 11), Festa di Santa Chiara (Aug 12), Ascension Day (around Aug 15), Festa di San Francesco (Oct 3 and 4), and Christmas Eve and Day (Dec 24 and 25).

But for the **Calendimaggio** ★★ spring celebration, the first weekend (starting Thurs) after May 1, Assisi goes totally pagan. The town divides itself into "upper" and "lower" factions that date to the 1300s. The festivities, with processions, medieval contests of strength and skill, and late-night partying—all in 14th-century costume, of course—go back much further to the pre-Roman rites of spring. The winner of the contests gets to have the fair damsel of his choice declared Lady Spring. The whole shebang ends with a singing duel on the main piazza. Call © **075-812-534** for info.

In May, there's an **antiques market.** The regular **weekly market** is Saturday along Via Alessi and Via San Gabriele dell'Addolorata.

SEEING THE BASILICA

In the unofficial Italian hierarchy of the divine, first and foremost, without a doubt, comes la Madonna, the Virgin Mary. Then come Jesus, St. Francis, and a local patron saint or two before you get to God. In Assisi, even the Madonna is demoted to let San Francesco reign supreme.

Basilica di San Francesco ★★★   Francis's story is told below, with the handy visual aid of Giotto's fresco cycle in the upper church. But suffice it to say that Assisi's grandiose, gorgeously embellished Basilica di San Francesco is an incongruous memorial to a man who preached and lived an utterly simple life—one of poverty, abstinence, and renunciation of worldly goods in search of greater spirituality. The basilica's implacable bulk rises like a force of nature from the rock of the mountainside, and the first sight of it as you approach the town from the valley is stupefying.

The person responsible for this edifice was one of Francis's right-hand men, the Cortonan disciple Brother Elia. For all his spiritual devotion, Elia remained much more worldly than Francis. In fact, it was probably Elia's tireless marketing and promotion of the Franciscan order, coupled with papal encouragement

---

Tips **Dress Appropriately**

San Francesco and Santa Chiara, like many other churches throughout Italy, has a strict **dress code:** Entrance to the basilica is *forbidden* to those wearing shorts or miniskirts or showing bare shoulders. You also must remain silent and cannot take photographs in the Upper Church of San Francesco.

(which had political motivations of its own), that ensured the longevity of the Francescani. With the basilica he built in 1230 to house Francis's recently sanctified bones, Elia was basically sending a public-relations message: Here was a man so holy he needed not just one but two churches, stacked on top of each other, to honor him. The bi-level basilica enjoys an odd marriage of form and function as one of the world's focal points of both high art and intense spirituality. It moves the devout to tears and art lovers to fits of near-religious ecstasy.

THE LOWER CHURCH   Entered through a Gothic portal under a Renaissance porch on Piazza Inferiore di San Francesco (the lower of the two squares abutting the church), the basilica's bottom half is a low-ceilinged, extremely dim cryptlike church. It's full of masterpieces of the early Sienese school of painting, but they're poorly lit, mainly by beautiful but unfortunately not very transparent stained-glass windows, many of which are as old as the church itself.

There's a 1422 fresco of the *Madonna Enthroned with Saints* by Eugubian master Ottaviano Nelli just past the tiny decorated chapel on the left as you enter, plus some fine Gothic tombs along the right wall. At the opposite end of this hall, past the nave, is the **Cappella di Santa Caterina** (usually closed), frescoed by Andrea de' Bartoli with scenes from the *Life of St. Catherine* (1367). The nave was the first part of the church to be frescoed, with the *Passion* on the right wall and *Life of St. Francis* on the left—all of them damaged when the side chapels were built and all painted by the mysterious but talented master named, because of this job, the Maestro di San Francesco. The first chapel off the nave on the right was decorated in 1574 by Dono Doni with the *Life of St. Stephen.*

Across the nave, the first chapel on the left is the **Cappella di San Martino** ⭐⭐, frescoed with that saint's life by the Sienese genius Simone Martini (1312–15). Martini amply displays both his penchant for boldly patterned fabrics—not unusual in an artist from a textile center—and his mastery of the medieval forms and themes of late Gothic Sienese painting. The scene on the right wall, *St. Martin Is Knighted by Emperor Julian,* sums up the chivalric medieval ideal perfectly: the ceremony of a king strapping on a knight's sword and a squire slipping on his spurs; the noble sports of the hunt and falconry; and the love of good music and singing of the bel canto. The portrait of Julian, by the way, is probably accurate; Martini based it on the official profiles stamped on Roman coins from the emperor's era.

Halfway up the nave on either side are stairs descending to the **crypt** containing the venerated stone coffin of St. Francis surrounded by the graves of four of his followers. This crypt was lost until the 19th century, sealed up by canny Brother Elia to keep rival Perugians from stealing the saintly remains. Up in the nave again, beyond the stairs on the left wall, is a *cantoria* tricked out with cosmatesque colored marbles. Above it is a niche with the remains of a *Coronation of the Virgin* (1337) and other frescoes by Giotto's talented disciple Puccio Capanna.

Across the nave again, the middle chapel on the right side has 17th-century decorations, but the **Cappella della Maddalena** ⭐ next door, the last chapel on the right, was frescoed with the *Life of St. Mary Magdalene* by Giotto and his assistants (1303–09). For two of the more dramatic scenes—the *Raising of Lazarus,* where bystanders dramatically cover their noses at the stench of Lazarus's rotting flesh, and a *Noli Mi Tangere* where Christ appears almost to hitch up his robes as he scurries from the Magdalene's touch—Giotto borrowed the compositions from the same scenes he'd recently finished in his fresco cycle for Padua's Scrovegni Chapel.

In the **left transept's barrel vault** and on its walls, early Sienese master Pietro Lorenzetti left one of his masterpieces. A 1320 cycle of *Christ's Passion* ends with a huge and colorful, but sadly damaged, ***Crucifixion*** ★★, and on the wall is a touching and dynamic *Deposition,* featuring a gaunt Christ and whimpering Marys.

The **barrel vault of the right transept** ★ was originally frescoed in 1280 by Giotto's master, Cimabue, but only his *Madonna Enthroned with Four Angels and St. Francis* survives, containing what has become the most popular portrait of the saint. This panel sticks out like a sore thumb amid the early-14th-century frescoes on the *Childhood of Christ* painted by Giotto's assistants under his direction—though the master himself apparently took his brush to the *Crucifixion* scene. Beneath the Cimabue fresco is the tomb of five of Francis's original followers, above which Pietro Lorenzetti frescoed their portraits. To the left of the door and on the end wall are half-length figures of the *Madonna* and seven saints (including St. Clare) by Simone Martini.

Giotto's assistants also frescoed the large **Cappella di San Nicola** beyond the transept's end according to the master's plans. (Giotto may have dabbled directly in the triptych of the *Madonna and Child with Saints Nicholas and Francis.*) One of Francis's famous brown habits is sometimes displayed here.

A doorway in the right transept opens onto the **chapter house,** housing a 1340 *Crucifixion* by Puccio Capanna and a horde of Franciscan relics. These include a patchwork moth-eaten tunic, shirts and slippers, one of only two surviving letters signed by the saint, the rock on which his head rested in his coffin, a staff presented to him by the Sultan of Egypt (after Francis proved his holiness, or at least impressed the Sultan, by walking over hot coals), and the "Rule of the Franciscans" sent to Francis by Pope Honorius II in 1223.

Stairs lead up from the lower church's two transepts to the upper level of a 15th-century **cloister.** More stairs lead from here to the **upper church,** but you may want to take a minute to zip through the **gift shop** and the **treasury** (closed at press time). Its best works are a 15th-century altar frontal, a Flemish tapestry of *St. Francis,* and a 1290 silver chalice with an enameled portrait of Pope Nicholas IV. Beyond the treasury is the **Mason Perkins Collection** of paintings by Lorenzo Monaco, Taddeo di Bartolo, Pietro Lorenzetti, and Pier Francesco Fiorentino, among others (closed at press time).

THE UPPER CHURCH   The tall, light-filled Gothic interior of the upper church is a striking contrast to its downstairs neighbor. Though its best to start with the lower church (so you can view the art chronologically) you could also enter the upper one through the plain medieval facade with its double portal (common in pilgrimage churches) and large rose window behind a small grassy park called Piazza Superiore di San Francesco. However, I'll assume you're coming up from the lower church and begin with the oldest frescoes in the upper church, those in the **transept.** The **choir** is lined with early-16th-century inlaid stalls, including a papal throne—the only one outside the Vatican. Above them are large frescoed scenes whose weird photo-negative quality is the result of oxidation in the pigments. As with most of the frescoes in this church, no one can agree on the attribution of these works. Some hold the Vasari opinion that Cimabue did them all (with the help of assistants) in 1277; others allow him only the masterful and dramatic composition of the *Crucifixion* ★ and pin the others on his Roman assistants (Jacopo Torriti, Rustici, and possibly Pietro Cavallini).

By 1288, the artist or artists had moved on to the upper register of the nave, filling the top half of the left wall (standing at the altar and facing the main entrance) with stories from the Old Testament and the upper-right wall with scenes from the New Testament. Among Cimabue's assistants working here was a young Giotto, who's now given credit for the two red-heavy scenes in the second bay of the left wall depicting *Isaac Blessing Jacob* and *Esau Before Isaac.*

The lower register of the nave, with 28 scenes of the ***Life of St. Francis*** ⭐⭐⭐, is what most art aficionados have traveled here to see: the frescoes of Giotto (see "The Genius of Giotto," below). These frescoes were fully restored in 2002, 5 years after the earthquake that shattered them. Again, there were probably assistants at work here, and there's strong evidence that one pupil, the anonymous Maestro di Santa Cecilia, finished the final four compositionally crowded scenes and may have touched up the first. But most of the attempts to find some additional unknown master can be written off as mere iconoclasm—everyone from Giotto's contemporaries to Vasari to many modern-day art historians accepts Giotto as the primary author of the cycle.

Francesco (Francis), the son of a wealthy local cloth merchant and his Provençal wife, spent much of his youth carousing, drinking, gambling, and going off to wars with his buddies—he even spent a year stewing in Perugia's dungeons as a prisoner of war. Restless and bored, the youth began to suspect there was more to life. The frescoes pick up the story (at the transept end of the right aisle) as Francesco's initial glimmers of saintliness begin to appear. The first few frescoes illustrate the traditional background for the saint's beginnings (I've described only the most important ones here): (1) Francis is honored by a simple man, who lays his cloak in the mud for the future saint to walk on—you can tell it's Assisi because of the Temple of Minerva in the background. (2) Francis gives his mantle to a poor man (typical first sign of saintliness). (3) Francis, while praying in front of a crucifix (now in Santa Chiara) in the ruins of the church of San Damiano, hears the cross speak to him. It charges him to "go and repair my house, which as you can see is falling into ruin." The church is obviously falling apart, and Francis went on to take the command both literally, fixing the place up, and figuratively, reforming the spirituality of his fellow man. (4) Francis renounces his father's inheritance, taking off all his clothes and returning them to Dad. (5) Pope Innocent III dreams the Lateran basilica, cathedral of Rome, is on the verge of collapse when a poor little man (Francis) arrives to shore it up with his own shoulders. Finally (6), Francis and his small band of followers journey to Rome, where the pope, for political reasons, approves the Franciscan rule of poverty, chastity, and obedience and gives the pilgrims papal approval to wear monastic tonsures and preach in public.

The rest of the frescoes focus primarily on the miracles of Francis, including the exorcism of some demons from the pastel buildings of a medieval Arezzo. In a later scene, Francis creates the first Christmas crèche—Francis's humble, earthy views show here, as he ensures the farm animals and faux rustic setting become an integral part of the Nativity. On the entrance wall is perhaps the most famous and charming of the scenes, where Francis preaches to the birds. Francis taught that, because God was present in all life, everything from the animals to the trees to the smallest bird is worthy of love and respect. Francis was quite the talented poet as well, and his flower-child attitude shows through his most famous composition, a beautifully simple poem and prayer to the elements called "Canticle of the Creatures," or "Brother Sun, Sister Moon" (you'll see copies of it everywhere around town). Also don't miss the scene on the right wall where Francis,

The Genius of Giotto

Short in stature, ugly of countenance, merry in wit, and one of the single greatest artistic talents in Western history, **Giotto di Bondone** (1266–1337) was born a shepherd boy. According to Giorgio Vasari, the renowned artist Cimabue discovered Giotto one day sitting by his herd, scratching a sketch of one of the sheep with a pointed rock on a stone slab. Cimabue took the lad under his wing and into his studio, and it wasn't long before the student's mastery eclipsed that of his teacher. As Dante wrote, "Cimabue thought to lord it over painting's field / And now his fame is obscured and the cry is Giotto."

Other artists, including Cimabue, had begun to introduce elements of naturalism to the rigid, highly stylized Byzantine tradition that had governed European painting since the Middle Ages. But, Giotto exploded convention and plunged painting into a Gothic humanism that quickly developed into the Renaissance.

Giotto did more than just paint pretty pictures. He filled his art with the symbolism of a philosophy and a decisive stamp of realism, of painting from nature for the mind. Boccaccio, in one of his Decameron tales just 10 years after Giotto's death, wrote of Giotto's painting as "that art which had been buried for centuries by the errors of some who painted more to please the eyes of the ignorant than the intellect of the wise." The poet went so far as to call him "the best painter in the world." True, Giotto didn't have a good grasp of single-point perspective or a sense of photographic realism—but to be fair, neither concept had been invented. What Giotto did was portray his biblical characters in a manner unlike any seen before.

The figures in his paintings have bulk under their clothes, they have weight, they're expressive, and they have distinct faces with unique personalities—they are, in a word, individuals. Instead of expressionless medieval Madonnas with tiers of identical angels arranged stiffly around her as if posing, Giotto's scenes are natural, almost like glimpses of private moments—the people laugh, sleep, fidget, preach, move, cry, and even sit with their backs turned.

Whether he was helped extensively or merely moderately by assistants in the painting of Assisi's upper church of San Francesco is in some ways irrelevant, because it was Giotto's vision and influence that humanized the frescoes and allowed reality to slip into the paintings. Giotto shows us the crisscross of lumber on the backs of altar crucifixes, friars singing heartily at a Christmas service, and monkish faces wrinkled in painful sorrow at the death of Francis. There are no stylized wails of anguish here, but rather real, heartfelt tears that well up from inside the friars, creating a moment almost too private to view.

praying on Mt. Verna in 1224, is visited by a heavenly seraph who imparts to him a singular honor, the stigmata of Christ's wounds. Although later saints were also blessed with the stigmata, Francis was the first, and the miracle pretty much cinched his sainthood. After a life spent traveling as far as Spain, Morocco,

Egypt, and Palestine to preach simplicity and a return to kindness and the basics, Francis died near his hometown in 1226. Within 2 years, he was made a saint, and in 1939 he was proclaimed the official patron saint of Italy.

Piazza Superiore di San Francesco/Piazza Inferiore di San Francesco. ℭ **075-819-001.** www.sanfrancesco assisi.org. Free admission. Lower church daily 6 am–7pm; upper church daily 8:30am–7pm (until 6pm in winter). Treasury and Perkins Collection Easter–Oct Mon–Sat 9:30am–7pm. You may visit church for Mass on Sun morning (before 2pm), but purely touristic visits at this time are frowned on.

EXPLORING THE REST OF ASSISI

The main square in town is **Piazza del Comune.** The medieval edition of what may have been the old Roman forum (see below) is most famous for the six gleaming white Corinthian columns and tympanum of the **Temple of Minerva** ⚑, a 1st-century B.C. Roman temple the Assisians sensibly recycled into a church with a thoroughly uninteresting baroque interior. This was the first object in all Italy that Goethe—traveling the peninsula for the sole purpose of communing with the ruins of ancient Rome—showed anything but contempt for in his *Italian Journey:* "[L]o and behold!—there it stood . . . so perfect in design . . . one could never tire of looking at the facade. . . . I cannot describe the sensations which this work aroused in me, but I know they are going to bear fruit forever." He didn't give the frescoes in San Francesco the time of day.

Next door to the temple is the tall 13th-century **Torre del Popolo,** with the coeval mayor's palace next to that. Across the piazza are the Gothic piles of the **Palazzo Comunale** and connected **Palazzo dei Priori.**

San Pietro   This pretty and sober little church downhill from the Basilica di San Francesco was consecrated in 1253, but the simple rectangular facade with its three large spoked windows wasn't finished until 1268. The piazza is used by local boys as an impromptu soccer field, and there's a view over the valley from the square's edge. A relief of ivy patterns running around the central portal ends in two weather-beaten Lombard lions that guard the main door. The interior is spare, of interest mainly for its strange pre-Gothic pointed ceiling vaults and the odd dome, a concentric cone of bricks in the Arab-Norman style.

Piazza San Pietro. No phone. Free admission. Currently still closed (normally daily 7am–noon and 2pm–sunset).

Oratorio dei Pellegrini ⚑   The white-robed sisters are nearly always kneeling inside praying, so you'll most likely only be able to poke your head through the heavy curtains and peer through the glass doors for a respectfully quick glance at the 15th-century frescoes inside. Matteo di Gualdo, who was responsible for the painting on the outside wall, frescoed the scenes on the altar wall, and one Pierantonio Mezzastris took care of the ceiling and side walls in 1477, with miracle scenes of *St. Anthony Abbot* on the left and *St. James* on the right. The three saints frescoed on the entrance wall were once attributed to a young Perugino, but these days it seems more likely that L'Ingengno did them.

Via San Francesco 11. No phone. Free admission. Daily 9am–noon and 3–6pm, except when nuns are praying. **Note:** The Oratorio closed for longer than most places following the quake, and it now keeps very sporadic hours, which means it's usually closed; still, it's well worth popping by every time you happen to be passing just in case the doors are open.

Museo e Foro Romano ⚑   The piles of ancient **Roman artifacts** stacked against the walls here aren't quite the bother of matching them with the detailed list you're handed at the door. But keep on the lookout for the 1st-century A.D. stele on the right wall, with symbols of the deceased's civic scribely duties (a scroll and codex), and the fresco remnants around to the left. A corridor leads under Piazza del Comune to Assisi's old **Roman Forum**—or at least a central religious square—now some 3.9m (13 ft.) below ground level. The plain stone rectangular slab in the middle was probably used as an altar for votive statues. To its left is the base of the stairs leading up to the **Temple of Minerva,** which is still in good shape on the piazza above. Farther along the corridor, ongoing excavations have revealed the bases of some **Roman buildings,** probably shops.

Via Portica (on the edge of Piazza del Comune). (✆ **075-813-053.** www.sistemamuseo.it. Admission 2.50€ ($2.90) adults; 2€ ($2.30) students, children under 18, and seniors over 65. Mar 16–Oct 15 daily 10am–1pm and 4–6pm; Oct 16–Mar 15 daily 10am–1pm and 2–5pm.

Pinacoteca   The town's picture gallery is nothing overly special, existing mainly to preserve the faded remains of frescoes from street tabernacles. The collection includes some 13th-century knights on horseback detached from the Palazzo del Capitano del Popolo, and a *Crucifix* by the Maestro Espressionista di Santa Chiara. Pace di Bartolo also did some nice works here, including a *Madonna and Child with Angels,* on whose backside Giotto's student Puccio Capanna painted *St. Francis and Child.* Of later works, there's a *Madonna della Misericordia* with St. Biagio by L'Alunno and a Dono Doni *Annunciation.*

Via San Francesco 10. (✆ **075-812-0333.** www.sistemamuseo.it. Admission 2.20€ ($2.50) adults, 1.50€ ($1.75) children under 18 and seniors over 65. Mar 16–June 30 and Sept 1–Oct 15 daily 10am–1pm and 2–6pm; July 1–Aug 31 daily 10am–1pm and 2:30–7pm; Oct 16–Mar 15 daily 10am–1pm and 2–5pm. Closed Jan 1, Dec 25.

Santa Chiara ⊛   The resting place of St. Clare's bones and Francis's miraculous crucifix is fronted by a lively terracelike piazza with views over the valley and some shade trees. The 1260 church is early Gothic. The **facade,** done in strong bands of Assisian pink and white, is set with a giant wagon wheel of a rose window and stabilized by the unwieldy wings of two cumbersome flying buttresses.

The vast **interior** is dark and perennially crowded with people filing down into the neo-Gothic **crypt** to see the original stone tomb of St. Clare. Born to a local minor noble family in 1193, Chiara (anglicized to Clare) was a friend of Francis who followed the mystic's example against her parents' wishes. In 1211, she abandoned her parental household and ran off to meet Francis, who clothed her in sackcloth after his own fashion and hacked off her hair, signaling Clare's renunciation of earthly goods and the beginning of her quest for spiritual enlightenment. This path she pursued with a vengeance, adopting the rule of St. Benedict tempered with Francis's preaching of poverty. She soon gathered a large enough female following at San Damiano that Francis urged her to set up a convent there, and she became abbess. (The order she founded, the Poor Clares, didn't move into town until after her death.)

Chiara's miracles accumulated as Francis's did, and she became adept at using the Eucharist (the communion wafer) to ward off Assisi invaders as diverse as the Saracens (1240) and local thug Vitale d'Aversa (1241). Bedridden and less than a year from death, on Christmas Eve 1252 Clare was upset that her illness was keeping her from the Franciscans' singing of Mass in the new basilica of St. Francis in town. Suddenly, she was blessed with a vision of the Mass, both hearing and seeing it miraculously from several miles away. In 1958, the pope latched on to the audiovisual aspect of the miracle and granted Clare the rather dubious honor of becoming the patron saint of television.

Off the right wall of the church built to house her tomb is the **Oratorio del Crocifisso,** preserving the venerated 12th-century crucifix that spoke to St. Francis at San Damiano and set him on his holy path. Against this oratory's back wall are some holy relics, including tunics worn by Francis and Clare, a shirt she embroidered, and some of the hair Francis sheared from her head. The chapel divided from this one by glass walls is the **Cappella del Sacramento,** with frescos by Pace di Bartolo and a triptych of the *Madonna and Saints* by Puccio Capanna. Of the frescoes that covered the interior of the church until the 17th century, only some colorfully intense 13th-century ones by an anonymous follower of Giotto remain, up in the transept.

Piazza Santa Chiara. *C* **075-812-282.** Free admission. Daily 7am–noon and 2pm–sunset.

Duomo di San Rufino   Assisi's cathedral is off a quiet walled **piazza** that receives some historians' votes as the true site of Roman Assisi's forum. The first church on this spot may have been raised as early as the 5th century. In 1028, the town's bishop witnessed an unrecorded miraculous event and had the old church torn down and a Romanesque one built to replace it, accompanied by a fat bell tower built over a Roman cistern. In 1134, however, another bishop had an even greater miraculous vision, and the poor church was flattened to make way for the present structure, saving only the bell tower. Alas, in the more than 100 years it took to build the church, the Romanesque styling of the lower two-thirds of the **facade**—including highly decorative friezes, Lombard lions and griffins at the doors, stone-spoked rose windows, and a classical dividing arcade of thin columns—gave way to Gothic fashion. The top third was finished with a jarring pointed blind arch set in the tympanum.

The **interior** was remodeled in 1571 following structural damage and deserves your attention only if you're interested in the **font** in which St. Francis, St. Clare, and Emperor Frederick II were baptized (to the right as you enter). At the altar are two canvases by Dono Doni—a *Deposition* on the right and *Crucifixion* on the left. A door at the end of the left aisle leads to the **Museo della Cattedrale** (*C* **075-812-712** or if no answer 347-874-0224), which preserves detached frescoes by Puccio Capanna, more works by Dono Doni, and triptychs by L'Alunno and Matteo da Gualdo. The museum is in the process of expanding and will by late 2004 display even more works along with a small archaeological collection. You can enter the **crypt** from the door to the right of the facade; its rough vaulting and Ionic columns are, along with the bell tower, the only surviving bits of the 11th-century cathedral.

Piazza San Rufino. *C* **075-812-283.** www.assisimuseocattedrale.com. Free admission to the church; crypt and Museo della Cattedrale, 3€ ($3.45) adults, 2.50€ ($2.90) ages 12–18 and seniors over 60. Church, daily 7am–noon and 2pm–sunset. Crypt and Museo Capitolare, Thurs–Tues: Mar 16–Oct 15 daily 10am–1 and 3–6pm (Aug 10am–6pm); Oct 16–Mar 15 10am–1pm and 2:30–5:30pm.

Rocca Maggiore 🟊🟊   The bleached yellow bones of this fortress glower high above the city, a reminder of the hated Cardinal Albornoz, who built the 14th-century version we see today to establish papal authority over Assisi. A young Frederick II, future Emperor of Swabia, spent his earliest childhood within the walls of the short-lived 12th-century fortress that stood here, on an Umbri burial site. Beyond the circular rampart added in the 16th century by Pope Paul III, you can enter the outer walls to visit the recently restored keep and soldiers' quarters. A very long corridor lit by repeating arrow slits leads to a polygonal watchtower, with a panoramic view, that's not lit at all. The warning sign at the corridor's base is no joke—a spiral staircase in the pitch dark can be quite a challenge for those who don't come equipped with a flashlight. From the top of the keep is a view down the walls to the tower of the smaller **Rocchiola (Rocca Minore)** at the northeast corner of the city's defenses. As we went to press, the rocca was still undergoing an extensive restoration, and only part of the fortress was open to the public.

Piazzale delle Liberta Comunali, at the top of town, at the ends of Via della Rocca, Via del Colle, and the stepped Vicolo San Lorenzo off Via Porta Perlici. © 075-815-292. www.sistemamuseo.it. Admission 1.70€ ($2) adults, 1€ ($1.15) students, children under 18, and seniors over 65. Daily 10am–sunset.

EXPLORING OUTSIDE THE WALLS

Ereme delle Carceri and Monte Subasio ✦   A signposted lane leads left from Porta Cappuccini onto the oak- and ilex-covered slopes of **Mt. Subasio,** where nestled among the trees is the peacefully isolated hermitage built on the site where St. Francis often withdrew to meditate and pray with his followers. The monks living here will show you around—they live on alms alone, so a nice tip of a few thousand lire is appreciated. You'll see the rocky bed where Francis slept, a few worn frescoes, the site where Francis caused water to gush from the rocks, the crevice where he tossed a pesky demon back down to hell, and the ancient ilex tree, now on iron crutches, where the saint preached his sermons to the birds.

The hermitage also makes a good starting point for **walks in the woods.** Monte Subasio is a protected regional park, and there are plenty of marked trails to follow. (Maps are available in town.)

Via Eremo delle Carceri (4km/2.5 miles from Porta Cappuccini). © 075-812-301. Free admission. Ermeo delle Carceri, daily 6:30am–7pm. Walk or take taxi from Piazza Santa Chiara.

San Damiano   San Damiano is where it all began, a dilapidated old church that in 1205 housed a 12th-century painted crucifix before which young and restless Francesco was praying one day when the Christ on it spoke to him. Francis first acted on its "rebuild my church" injunction in literal terms: He decided Jesus wanted him to shore up this decaying building, and reconstructed the church stone by stone. The church later became a favorite retreat for Francis and his followers. St. Clare founded her order of the Poor Clares here, lived out her life as its abbess, and passed away within these walls. The pretty little church is still, in a city filled with garish and monumental memorials to the saint, a pleasingly simple and rudimentary place, with rustic wooden choir stalls and a few simple frescoes on the walls. The monastery, with its quiet 15th-century cloister, is also usually open to visitors.

Via San Damiano (1.5km/1 mile from Porta Nuova). © 075-812-273. Free admission. Daily 10am–12:30pm and 2–6pm.

WHERE TO STAY

Book ahead, book ahead, book ahead. Never show up in Assisi, especially from Easter to fall, without a reservation. If you do, you'll spend half your morning at the tourist office calling hotels, only to find yourself stuck overnight in one of the hideous large constructions 5 miles away in Santa Maria degli Angeli. If you plan to visit at Easter or the first weekend in May, book at least 6 months in advance. Behind only Rome and Bethlehem (tellingly, Assisi's sister city) as a Christian pilgrimage site, Assisi fills up for any religious holiday. On the bright side, it has more guest beds per square foot than any other town in Umbria. The official central booking office is **Consorzio Alberghi ed Operatori Turistiche,** Via A. Cristofani 22a (© **075-816-566;** fax 075-812-315).

Besides the larger, more standard hotels, dozens of smaller board-rated one- and two-star outfits offer 6 to 10 rooms each. Additionally, families often have a few rooms to rent (*affitacamere;* ask at the tourist office), and many of the religious orders in town will let you play at being a nun or a monk for a few nights at a very low price (usually with many rules about curfew, noise, and bunkmates).

Of the simpler hotels, the **Hotel Il Duomo,** Vicolo San Lorenzo 2 (✆ **075-812-742;** fax 075-812-803), above the cathedral, offers the basics without amenities. The large accommodations with cast-iron bed frames and small modern bathrooms go for 40€ to 42€ ($46–$48) double; breakfast is 4€ ($4.60) per person. The hotel is usually closed the last half of February. They have another, ever-so-slightly ritzier hotel called the **San Ruffino** just around the corner on the main street at Via Porta Perlici 7 (✆ **075-812-803**), where doubles go for 47€ to 50€ ($54–$58), plus 4.50€ ($5.20) per person for breakfast.

The same family runs **Hotel La Rocca,** Via Porta Perlici 27 (✆ and fax **075-812-284;** www.hotelarocca.it), in the dizzying heights of town on the road to the castle. It has functional modern furniture and few amenities in 27 well-maintained tile-floored rooms (16 with bathroom), some of which have balconies and views over town. Doubles run around 43€ ($49). The hotel shuts down for the last 2 weeks of January.

For a stay with a religious order, try **St. Anthony's Guesthouse,** Via G. Alessi 10 (✆ **075-812-542;** fax 075-813-723; atoneassisi@tiscalinet.it), run by the Franciscan Sisters of Atonement, an American order of nuns. They offer 20 comfortable hotel-like rooms with bathroom (some have views) from 50€ ($58) double with breakfast. They're open for business March through October, have a minimum stay of 2 nights, and usually require a deposit by mail.

At **Fontemaggio,** hidden in the woods about 1.6 kilometers (1 mile) east of town at Via Eremo delle Carceri 8 (✆ **075-813-636;** fax 075-813-749), are a campground, a hostel, bungalows, and a hotel complex with one of the best countryside restaurants in Umbria (La Stalla; see p. 402). The campground has 950 sites and costs 5€ ($5.75) per person, plus 4.20€ ($4.85) per tent, plus 2.50€ ($2.90) per car. The hostel has around 100 bunks, some in rooms of just four, costing 18.50€ ($21) per person. The eight bungalows sleeping four cost 50€ to 70€ ($58–$81); those sleeping six to seven run 140€ ($161). There are 17 rooms in the hotel portion, with bathroom, phone, and views of the valley, costing 52€ ($59) per double with breakfast.

Hotel Alexander

Though now owned by a hotel just around the corner, the Alexander still feels a bit as if you're visiting your Umbrian parents' house for the weekend. The good-size accommodations in this medieval building across the street from where St. Francis was born are carpeted and scattered with rugs and Savonarola chairs for atmosphere. They have clean white walls, comfy beds, and fairly new bathrooms. Most of the rooms have multiple beds, which together with the homelike atmosphere makes the place great for families. The separately owned Pizzeria Otello underneath will even make pizza to go, so you can bring it back and really feel at home.

Piazza Chiesa Nuova 6 (just down from Piazza del Comune), 06081 Assisi (PG). ✆ **075-816-190** or 075-812-237 (its parent Hotel Prori). Fax 075-816-804. www.assisi-hotel.com. 8 units. 60€–100€ ($69–$115) double; discounts in low season. Rates include breakfast (taken in Hotel Priori, around the corner at Corso Mazzini 15). MC, V. Parking 8€–11€ ($9.20–$13) in garage. **Amenities** (all via the Hotel Priori): Concierge; tour desk; car-rental desk; courtesy car; limited room service (breakfast); in-room massage; babysitting; laundry service; dry cleaning. *In room:* TV.

Hotel Fontebella ✦ Kids

The spacious rooms in this 17th-century Illuminati family palazzo are fitted with contemporary furnishings done in a repro-Renaissance style in rich yellow and gold and green fabrics. The rooms without wood

floors have knobby carpets, and the proprietors jokingly refer to the smallish singles as their "Franciscan cells." The suites are bi-level, lofted affairs good for families, and there are a few attractive little rooms with wood-beamed ceilings in a
small annex across the back alley from the main building. The hoteliers plan to
add an outdoor swimming pool in 2004.

Via Fontebella 25 (between the basilica and Piazza del Comune), 06081 Assisi (PG). 𝄢 **075-812-883**. Fax
075-812-941. www.fontebella.com. 46 units. 99€ ($114) "classic" double; 140€ ($161) "quality" double;
195€ ($224) "superior" double; 230€ ($265) suite. Rates include continental breakfast. AE, DC, MC, V. Free
parking in front. **Amenities:** Restaurant (Il Frantoio, recommended below); concierge; car-rental desk; business center; 24-hr. room service (bar); laundry service; dry cleaning; nonsmoking rooms. *In room:* A/C, TV,
dataport, minibar, hair dryer, safe.

Hotel Sole   The Sole, divided between two buildings on a main road in town,
has nondescript rooms—all a bit worn around the edges from the occasional student stampede brought by study-abroad programs—but the price is good and
the location central. There's a smattering of antique-style bed frames and furniture on the tiled flooring, but most of the decor (in painted yellow metal or light
wood) is functionally modern. The beds are lumpy and spread with tatty tan
chenille bedspreads. The bathrooms are aging but in good shape. Although the
rooms in the annex are serviced by an elevator, they don't have the odd 15th-
century palazzo elements sometimes found in the main building. The magnificently stone-vaulted restaurant (closed in winter) serves tasty Umbrian fare.

Corso Mazzini 35 (between Piazza del Comune and Santa Chiara), 06081 Assisi (PG). 𝄢 **075-812-373**. Fax
075-813-706. www.assisihotelsole.com. 37 units, 35 with bathroom. 62€ ($71) double; 83€ ($95) triple. Pension plan available: add 19€ ($22) per person half pension, 29€ ($33) for full pension. Breakfast 6€ ($6.90).
AE, DC, MC. V. Parking 11€ ($12) in nearby lot. **Amenities:** Restaurant; concierge; tour desk; car-rental desk;
limited room service (breakfast and bar); babysitting. *In room:* A/C on request (for 10€/$12 extra per day),
TV, hair dryer some units, safe.

Hotel Subasio 𝄼   If you came to town for Giotto's frescoes, you can do no
better than this hotel, which opened next to the basilica in 1860. Accommodations in this former 16th-century palazzo vary widely in color scheme, decor,
size, and appointments. The only real consistencies are the owners' pleasing tendency to fill each room with antiques and the fact that rooms overlooking the
valley or the facade of San Francesco are larger, better furnished, and all-around
nicer—insist on one. Bathrooms were recently overhauled. The Umbrian restaurant is partly installed in a 13th-century vaulted cellar. For tradition (Bette
Davis, Alec Guinness, and the king of Bulgaria all lodged here) and the location
just 100 paces from the basilica, the Subasio's a prime choice.

Via Frate Elia 2 (the bottom side of the lower Piazza di San Francesco), 06082 Assisi (PG). 𝄢 **075-812-206**.
Fax 075-816-691. hotelsubasio@interbusiness.it. 62 units. 181€ ($208) double; 207€ ($238) triple; 233€
($268) junior suite. Pension plan available. Rates include breakfast. AE, DC, MC, V. Parking 11€ ($12) in
nearby lot. **Amenities:** Restaurant; concierge; tour desk; car-rental desk; 24-hr. room service (bar); in-room
massage; babysitting; laundry service. *In room:* A/C, TV, minibar, hair dryer.

Hotel Umbra 𝄼𝄼   The odd, stone, pointed Gothic arch and a few other
architectural elements remain from the collection of 13th-century houses from
which the Umbra was converted. The carpets in the large-ish whitewashed
rooms support agreeable old furniture like 19th-century dressers, 18th-century
desks, and 17th-century armoires. Many rooms have views over the rooftops and
valley, some have balconies, and the hotel is tucked with little hidden panoramic
terraces. The bathrooms are sheathed in marble or feature brass fixtures. Ask to
see the basement kitchen and laundry rooms, where the town's Roman walls
make up part of the foundations. The restaurant is well regarded for its Umbrian

food and makes use not only of the standard black truffles but also of Gubbio's rare white variety when in season. In summer, the tables are moved out onto a terrace for lamplit dinners in a pretty vine-shaded garden. Half-pension is available for an additional 23€ ($26) per person.

Via dei Archi 6 (15 paces off the west end of Piazza del Comune), 06081 Assisi (PG). ① **075-812-240.** Fax 075-813-653. www.hotelumbra.it. 25 units. 98€ ($113) standard double; 116€ ($133) superior double. Rates include breakfast. AE, DC, MC, V. Parking 11€ ($13) in garage. Closed mid-Jan to Easter. **Amenities:** Restaurant; bike rental; concierge; tour desk; car-rental desk; limited room service (breakfast and bar); babysitting; laundry service; dry cleaning. *In room:* A/C, TV, minibar, hair dryer.

WHERE TO DINE

Several of Assisi's restaurants serve a local flatbread called ***torta al testa,*** usually split and stuffed with cheeses, sausages, and vegetables (spinach is popular). The breads make good snacks and appetizers, and are best at La Stalla.

Il Frantoio UMBRIAN   The restaurant occupies a 17th-century olive-press building with modernized interiors, a lovely garden terrace, and a stony medieval room below the Hotel Fontebella. Staff members wisely suggest you begin with a *frittatina in salsa di tartufo* (a thin omelet spread with truffle pâté). The chef's specialty first course includes *tortelloni frantoio* (ricotta-and-spinach-filled pasta in a sauce of creamlike mascarpone cheese, sausage, and sage) and *stringozzi paesani* (homemade thick spaghetti with tomatoes, artichokes, and a pinch of hot pepper). Secondi run the gamut from Umbrian standards such as *grigliata di carne miste* (various grilled meats) to *chateaubriand* to *fesa di tacchino ai formaggi* (a huge turkey breast in cheese sauce). The wine list is a book, the wine steward the president of an Italian sommelier association.

Vicolo Illuminati (can enter at Via Fontebella 25). ① **075-812-977.** Reservations recommended. Primi 8.50€–13€ ($9.80–$15); secondi 12€–19€ ($13–$22). AE, DC, MC, V. Tues–Sun noon–2:30pm and 7–9:30pm.

La Fortezza 🏵🏵 UMBRIAN/CREATIVE   This is one of Assisi's great hidden pleasures. Since 1960, the Chiocchetti family has offered refined *ristorante* service and often inspired cuisine at trattoria prices, and all just a few steps above the main piazza. The *cannelloni all'Assisiana* are scrumptious (fresh pasta sheets wrapped around a ragù made with yearling veal, all baked under parmigiana), as is the *gnocchi alla Fortezza* (homemade gnocchi tossed with a garden of chopped vegetables: tomatoes, mushrooms, zucchini, peas, onions, and more). For a secondo, try the *coniglio in salsa di mele* (rabbit in a sort of curry of white wine, saffron, and apples). The wine list is short but the selection good; they even have half-bottles of Umbria's top-rank Lungarotti vintages at wine-shop, not restaurant, prices. The whole family works hard, in the kitchen and the stone-walled dining room, and if you take a liking to them, you can stay over in their seven simple but pleasant rooms upstairs for 52€ to 65€ ($60–$75).

Vicolo della Fortezza/Piazza del Comune (up the stairs near the Via San Rufino end). ① **075-812-418.** Reservations recommended. Primi 5€–8.50€ ($5.75–$9.80); secondi 7€–11€ ($8.05–$13); fixed-price menu without wine 17€–22€ ($20–$25). MC, V. Fri–Wed 12:30–2:30 pm and 7:30–9:30pm. Closed Feb and 1 week in July.

La Stalla 🏵🏵🏵 RUSTIC UMBRIAN   Now this is what a countryside trattoria is all about. It's a series of former livestock stalls made of stone walls and low-beamed ceilings thoroughly blackened by and still filled with smoke. The smoke rises tantalizingly from the open wood-fire grill and will have your mouth watering long before you secure a seat at one of the wobbly long communal tables. It's noisy, it's chaotic, it's not for the fainthearted, and it offers what just may be one of your most memorable Umbrian meals, especially if you squeeze in with the traditional Sunday lunch crowds. Start with the *assaggini di torta al testo,* small samplers of Assisian flatbread split and stuffed with prosciutto and cheese or spinach and sausage. Next up: the *trittico,* a scooped-out wooden platter laden with a trio of the house specialty primi, usually *strangozzi, gnocchi* (both in tomato sauce), and *bigoli* (a ricotta-and-spinach log dusted with Parmesan). For secondi, you have a wide range of choices: *bistecca di vitello* (grilled veal), *spiedino di cacciagione* (grilled game), or *spiedino di maiale* (grilled pork). Their *salsicce* (sausages) are out of this world. The conversation, generous imbibing, and general good mood can carry on for hours after official closing time.

Via Ermeo delle Carceri 8 (1.6km/1 mile east of town). *C* **075-812-317.** Reservations strongly recommended (but not always accepted). Primi 3.50€–4.50€ ($4.05–$5.20); secondi 2.50€–6.50€ ($2.90–$7.50). No credit cards. Tues–Sun 12:15–2:30pm and 7:15–10pm. Head out Porta Cappuccini; the turnoff is about 1km/half-mile along on the right (follow the signs for the Fontemaggio campground/hostel complex).

Medio Evo *⚜* UMBRIAN/ITALIAN   Down a steep S-curve from the center of town, Medio Evo offers well-spaced tables set with flowers beneath magnificent stone-vaulted ceilings that truly deserve the title of medieval. For antipasto, treat yourself to simple but exquisite aged prosciutto di Parma. There are concessions to local ingredients in dishes like *conchiglie alla Norcina* (shell pasta with black truffles and sausage) but also creations that smack of northern Europe, such as *pennette alla moscavita* (with salmon, vodka, and tomatoes). For your secondo, the Valdichiana beefsteak reigns supreme, and you can order it *alla fiorentina* (grilled with a bit of olive oil and pepper), as an *entrecôte "Madagascar"* with green peppers, or as a flambéed filet *alla moda dello chef.* Pork, mutton, and veal are available for lighter appetites, or try the superb *fritto misto* with fried meats and vegetables, cheese, olives, and salami.

Via dell'Arco dei Priori 4B (a dogleg down from Piazza del Comune). *C* **075-813-068.** Reservations strongly recommended. Primi 8€–18€ ($9.20–$21); secondi 10€–16€ ($12–$18). AE, DC, MC, V. Thurs–Tues noon–2:30pm and 7:30–10pm. Closed July 1–20.

Trattoria Pallotta UMBRIAN   Pallotta's pair of brightly lit stone-and-plaster rooms sees its share of tourists siphoned off from the nearby Piazza del Comune, but it hasn't wavered from serving good Umbrian food at fair prices. The *antipasto misto* is a meal in itself, with Assisi's *torta al testo, crostini,* sliced meats, and more. The *strangozzi alla Pallotta* are served with a pesto of olives, mushrooms, and some peperoncino for kick, and the *ravioloni al burro e salvia* come in a light butter-and-sage sauce. Move on to the *coniglio alla cacciatore* (rabbit in tomato sauce with a side of plain *torta al testo*) or the *pollo arrosto* (roast chicken). Although the *menù turistico* includes wine, the tasting menu offers better food choices.

Via S. Rufino 4 (just through the Palazzo del Comune's large main arch on Piazza del Comune). *C* **075-812-649.** www.pallottaassisi.it. Reservations recommended. Primi 5€–15€ ($5.75–$17); secondi 5€–15€ ($5.75–$17); menù turistico with wine 15€ ($17); tasting menu without wine 24€ ($27). AE, MC, V. Wed–Mon noon–2:30pm and 7:15–9:30pm. Closed 1 week in late Feb.

3 Gubbio: Town of Festivals

39km (24 miles) NE of Perugia; 170km (105 miles) SE of Florence; 200km (124 miles) N of Rome

Gubbio looks every inch the no-nonsense town, a central Italian city of distilled medieval fundamentals. Sharp-edged fortresslike buildings of light stone line long roads that are stacked up the base of the monumental tree-covered pyramid of a mountain. Gubbio is proud of its patron saint, medieval palaces, and home-spun school of painting. And its hill-town cocoon of Gothic silence occasionally bursts open with the spectacular color and noise of some of the region's most deeply ingrained traditional festivals.

With the romantic ruins of its Roman theater just below the panoramic terrace of its main piazza, Gubbio appears no more than a compact center unimposingly guarding a wide valley filled with farmland. But make your way up the slopes of its overgrown hill, past the temple of the city's patron saint, St. Ubaldo, to the scanty remains of its medieval mountaintop fortress, and you'll see what gives Gubbio its windswept border-town feeling. It's at the edge of a sea of mountains, wood-covered snow-capped Apennines that flow back for dozens of miles, a wild landscape on the cusp of nowhere that seems to have no business being associated with a quaint central Italian hill town.

To many, Gubbio looks as if it slipped off its mountain to settle at the foot, but the city has in fact slowly crept up the hillside. Prehistoric peoples may have lived on the lower slopes of Mts. Ingino and Foce next door—in fact, traces of both Neanderthals and early Homo sapiens have been found around here, proving that Gubbio has been prime hominid real estate for well over 30,000 years. But the Umbri tribes that established their city in the 3rd century B.C. probably lived on the valley floor, with their backs against the mountainside. They allied themselves with the Etruscans, then with the encroaching Romans, and, as the Roman municipium Iguvium, lived wholly on the valley floor.

It was a modestly prosperous city during Roman times, but the fact that the Roman Via Flaminia skipped it helped keep Gubbio out of the limelight and free from complete absorption into the empire. In effect, Iguvium managed to remain an autonomous city of the Umbri while many of its Etruscan neighbors were subjected and Latinized in more fundamental ways into Roman towns.

The Eugubium of the Dark Ages suffered its share of Gothic sacking, but by the 11th century it emerged as a bustling trade center. The smooth talking of its incorruptible and wise bishop Ubaldo saved the town from Barbarossa in 1155, and after dutifully sanctifying the man soon after his death, the medieval city went about building walls and attacking its neighbors in grand Umbrian style.

Though a worthy antagonist to warlike Perugia down the road, Gubbio never neglected its spiritual side. It welcomed St. Francis, and later his monastic cult, and became particularly beholden to the saintly Assisian after one visit. Francis, on hearing of the problem the Eugubians were having with a voracious wolf, went out into the woods and had a serious tête-à-tête with the offending lupine. Francis returned to town with the giant black wolf trotting at his heels and, in front of the townsfolk, made a pact with the wolf that it would no longer attack the local sheep and men if the town would feed it regularly; the deal was sealed with a paw-shake.

In the early 14th century, riding high, Gubbio built its monumental center and the best of its palaces. In 1387, however, began the long, boring, but basically benevolent reign of the Urbino counts of Monteferalto. During this time, Gubbio became widely known for the high-quality glazed ceramics and majolica that came out of its workshops, especially that of Maestro Giorgio Andreoli (ca. 1465–1552), an innovator and one of the world's greatest masters of the craft. After the Monteferalto line petered out in the early 16th century, the city found itself under the stifling rule of the Papal States. It reemerged at Italian unification in the 1860s.

Gubbio

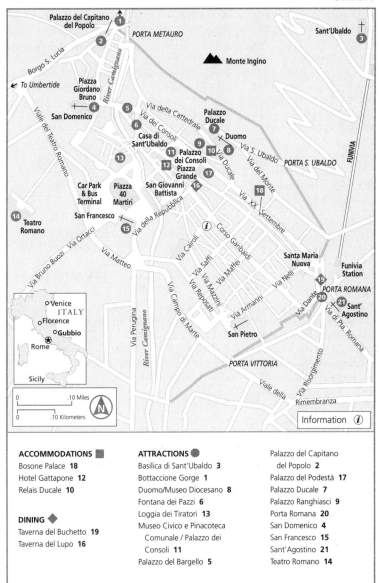

ACCOMMODATIONS

Bosone Palace **18**
Hotel Gattapone **12**
Relais Ducale **10**

DINING

Taverna del Buchetto **19**
Taverna del Lupo **16**

ATTRACTIONS

Basilica di Sant'Ubaldo **3**
Bottaccione Gorge **1**
Duomo/Museo Diocesano **8**
Fontana dei Pazzi **6**
Loggia dei Tiratori **13**
Museo Civico e Pinacoteca
 Comunale / Palazzo dei
 Consoli **11**
Palazzo del Bargello **5**

Palazzo del Capitano
 del Popolo **2**
Palazzo del Podestà **17**
Palazzo Ducale **7**
Palazzo Ranghiasci **9**
Porta Romana **20**
San Domenico **4**
San Francesco **15**
Sant'Agostino **21**
Teatro Romano **14**

ESSENTIALS

GETTING THERE   By Train   The closest **station** is at Fossato di Vico
(℃ **075-919-230**), 19km (12 miles) away on the Rome–Anacona line. Ten trains
run daily from **Rome** (2¼ hr.), and nine daily from **Spoleto** (40–60 min.). Nine
daily buses (six on Sun) connect the train station with Gubbio (30 min.).

By Car   The SS298 leads north from Perugia through rugged scenery. The
most convenient **parking** lot (pay) is off Piazza 40 Martiri. There's also free

parking off Via del Teatro Romano on the south edge of town and at the base station for the *funivia,* outside the east walls.

By Bus   **ASP** (© **075-922-0918**) has 11 buses Monday through Saturday (four on Sun) from **Perugia**'s Piazza Partigiani (1 hr. 10 min.). ASP also runs a daily 8:10am bus from **Assisi**'s Piazza Matteotti to Gubbio (50 min.).

If you're coming from the north, you'll probably have to change in **Umbertide,** from which there are three daily ASP runs to Gubbio (45 min.). From **Florence,** take the daily 5pm **SULGA** bus (© **075-500-9641;** www.sulga.it) to Perugia, where in 40 to 70 minutes (no connection on Sun) there's an ASP connection to Gubbio. The total traveling time is 3 hours. Monday through Saturday, there's a 4pm SULGA bus from **Rome**'s Tiburtina station (3 hr. 20 min.).

Buses to Gubbio arrive at and leave from Piazza 40 Martiri. **Tickets** are available at the newsstand on the piazza or at Easy Gubbio.

VISITOR INFORMATION   The **tourist office** is at Piazza Oderisi 6, a wide spot on Corso Garibaldi (© **075-922-0693** or 075-922-0790; fax 075-927-3409; www.umbria2000.it, www.global-umbria200.it, or www.comune.gubbio.pg.it). It's open Monday through Friday from 8:30am to 1:45pm and 3:30 to 6:30pm, Saturday from 9am to 1pm and 3:30 to 6:30pm, and Sunday from 9:30am to 12:30pm and 3:30 to 6:30pm; October through March, afternoon hours are 3 to 6pm. The website **www.easygubbio.it** also has lots of good info.

FESTIVALS & MARKETS   Gubbio is a festival sort of town. The biggest annual bash, the pagan **Corso dei Ceri** 🎉🎉🎉 on May 15, is one of Italy's top five traditional festivals. At 10:30am, a dense crowd packs into Piazza Grande to watch the solemn and inscrutable ceremonies atop the steps of the Palazzo dei Consoli. They involve the mayor, the bishop, three teams of burly young men in colorful silk shirts, and the keys to the city. Suddenly the teams go inside the palace and come charging out with three giant wooden battering ram–like objects called *ceri,* or "candles"—possibly after Ceres, the goddess of the harvest, in whose honor this race may once have been run.

With the 15-foot-long candles lined up against the panoramic edge of the square, the teams slip into one end of each a pair of perpendicular poles and attach small statues of St. George, St. Anthony, or the city's patron St. Ubaldo to the other end of each candle. Then each team captain climbs up the poles of his candle and is handed a giant painted ceramic vase full of water. At 11:30am, men hanging directly onto the bell tower's largest bell use their body weight to start it swinging and ringing—the signal to raise the candles. The three captains give a shout, and as their teams leverage the *ceri* (candles) upright, the captains heave the water-filled jugs as far as they can into the crowd. The mass of people parts briefly to let the vases fall and shatter, then descends on the shards in a mad frenzy to acquire a piece—it signifies good crops and good luck for the next year. The candles, now upright, each topped by a saint, and shouldered by the teams, are run three times around the piazza, and then taken off on a long prescribed route through the city streets.

At 2pm, the teams leave the candles on Via Savelli della Posta and return to the Palazzo dei Consoli, where they sit down to an enormous seafood banquet in the medieval hall. At 4:30pm, there's a solemn religious procession of the relics of St. Ubaldo and the *ceri* as they're carried to Via Dante. At 6pm, the real race begins. The teams grab their candles and make another frenetic run through town. With candles swaying and people cheering, they race again around Piazza Grande and then hightail it up to the gate to the mountain road. After a brief pause, the teams pick up their candles and, perhaps the most stupefying part of the whole day, begin running like the devil straight up the mountainside. It's more than 300m (1,000 ft.) of vertical elevation along a switchbacked road, but they reach the finish line at the mountainside basilica of Sant'Ubaldo in under 6 minutes. The first one inside the front doors tries to shut them before the losers get there. But, and this is the best part, the whole race is fixed. St. Ubaldo always wins. The real contest is to see how many times the runners let their candle fall; those that touch ground the fewest times are the real winners of the day.

The last Sunday in May marks part one of the annual face-off between the archers of Gubbio and those of rival Sansepolcro in the **Palio della Balestra** . At 5:30pm, before the main crossbow competition begins, *sbandieratori* come out to practice their mesmerizing flag-tossing. The accuracy and skill of both Eugubian and Sansepolcran marksmen are legendary, and the city that doesn't win the palio prize banner has a chance in September at the rematch in Sansepolcro. At 7pm, there's a procession through the streets, which are lined with people in colorful medieval costumes.

The **Gubbio Festival** brings performers of international status to town for 3 weeks of mainly classical instrumental music in late July. Also during this period, the city sponsors **classical music concerts** in the grassy ruins of the **Roman theater.** During the **Torneo dei Quartieri** on August 14, the city's crossbow sharp-shooters duke it out, and there's flag-tossing and a historic procession—a warm-up for the competition against Sansepolcro 3 weeks later. Gubbio shows off its revered albino tuber at the **White Truffle and Agricultural Fair** from October 29 to November 2.

The *Guinness Book of World Records* votes are in: Gubbio is officially home to the **World's Largest Christmas Tree,** formed by more than 800 lights zigzagging up Gubbio's mountainside to a star at the top. Every December 7, the town's forces of good taste fail to keep someone from throwing the switch on this monstrosity, and it's left on until January 10.

On the last Sunday of every month, there's an **antiques market** on Piazza 40 Martiri, where the regular **weekly market** is also held on Tuesday.

EXPLORING THE TOWN

San Francesco   One of the earliest churches built in honor of St. Francis, this bulky structure with three Gothic apses and an octagonal bell tower was raised in the mid–13th century, but probably not on the designs of Perugian Fra' Bevignate, as was once thought. Inside, all three apses were painted with high-quality frescoes by the Eugubian school. (There's a free light switch behind the speaker next to the confessional on the left aisle to illuminate the chapels.)

The chapel to the right of the main apse was frescoed in the 14th century on two levels with the *Life of St. Francis* in the upper half and a gaggle of saints in the lower. The main apse has some ceiling-scraping, 13th-century frescoes of *Christ Enthroned with Saints,* while the chapel to the left contains a deteriorating but well-painted cycle on the *Life of the Virgin* by Gubbio's early-15th-century master Ottaviano Nelli. Some fine 17th-century altarpieces line the right aisle, and a 16th-century *Crucifixion* by Benedetto Nelli hides in the sacristy. A cloister behind the apse (enter around the back at Piazza 40 Martiri no. 4) preserves a 14th-century *Crucifixion* fresco and pieces of a 3rd-century A.D. Roman floor mosaic that still show some color.

Across **Piazza 40 Martiri,** named after the 40 citizens who were shot by Nazis in 1944 for aiding the partisan movement, is the squared-off, second-story brick arcade of the **Loggia dei Tiratori.** Built in 1603 as a space where local textile workers could dye wool and stretch it to dry, the loggia is the best surviving example of these structures, which were once widespread throughout the peninsula.

Piazza 40 Martiri. No phone. Free admission. Daily 7:30am–noon and 4–7pm.

Museo Civico e Pinacoteca Comunale (Palazzo dei Consoli and Museum) ☆☆

Gubbio's main square is the brick-paved terrace of **Piazza Grande,** a medievally minimalist space bounded along one long side by the orange neoclassical **Palazzo Ranghiasci** but open on the other to a panoramic sweep over the lower part of town and across the wide valley beyond. On the southeast end sits the **Palazzo del Podestà,** suffering from the curse of a few too many architectural rearrangements that've left it looking entirely unfinished. Facing it across the piazza is Gubbio's imposing **Palazzo dei Consoli,** whose square Guelf crenellations and off-center 91m (303-ft.) bell tower dominate Gubbio from afar. The tongue of a staircase sprouting from the raised central door to the piazza below adds a touch of delicate grace to the Gothic solidity. Eugubian master architect Gattapone designed the palazzo in 1332.

Inside the vast and poorly lit barrel vault of the main hall, used for public assemblies of the medieval commune, is the town's **archaeological museum,** with the largest collection of Roman materials in Umbria. There are dozens of broken statues, stretches of cornice, and other architectural fragments, inscriptions, sarcophagi, and amphorae, all leaning against the walls as if someone just set them down temporarily—it's been this way for decades.

At the base of the staircase are a few rooms with small found objects like coins and metal implements and, in a back room, the seven **Eugubian Tables** ☆. These bronze tablets preserve the most extensive example of the Umbrian language. (The Umbri apparently had no alphabet of their own, so they used first Etruscan and later Latin characters and adapted them to spell Umbrian words phonetically.) The tablets were inscribed from 200 to 70 B.C. and tell a bit about Gubbio's ancient territory and enemies but mainly detail the finer points of religious divination—they're priestly textbooks to help find the will of the gods through animal sacrifice and watching the flight patterns of birds. These are the single most detailed set of religious instructions and explanations that survive from any antique culture and are of incalculable value for the insights they offer into the religious and social life of the ancient world. A local farmer turned up the tablets while he was plowing his fields in 1444, and the city convinced him to sell them for two years' worth of grazing rights.

Upstairs is a small **majolica collection,** including a plate painted by Maestro Giorgio (1527) depicting the *Fall of Phaeton.* (Gubbio, which had no pieces by its own master artisan, bought it at Sotheby's in 1992.) Through a narrow "secret corridor" with slivers of cityscape out the window slits, another stair leads up to the small **pinacoteca** gallery of paintings, mainly 13th- to 16th-century Eugubian works. None of the pictures is overly spectacular, but there is a two-sided gonfalon banner (1503) painted in Perugino's style by Sinblado Ibi; a damaged Rutilio Manetti *Flight into Egypt* (1634); a *Madonna and Child* by Sassoferrato; and a 1563 *Pentecost* and odd 1570 *Genealogical Tree of the Madonna,* both attributed to Benedetto Nucci. There's also access to an outdoor **loggia** with views across town. In the **basement** (currently reached by a separate entrance on the palazzo's back side) is a small archaeological collection.

Piazza Grande. ☎ 075-927-4298. Admission 5€ ($5.75) adults, 2.50€ ($2.90) ages 7–25, free for children under 7 and seniors over 60. Apr–Sept daily 10am–1pm and 3–6pm; Oct–Mar daily 10am–1pm and 2–5pm.

Lunacy & Death, Eugubian Style

Via dei Consoli runs downhill out of the west end of Piazza Grande past medieval palazzi to Largo del Bargello and its Gothic **Palazzo del Bargello** (1302), the city's first medieval town hall. At the tiny square's center is the **Fontana dei Pazzi (Fountain of the Crazies):** You can become a certified Eugubian lunatic if you run around the fountain three times—sticklers will also need to draft three locals to splash water on them as they run. You may pick up your *patente da matto* ("certificate of madness") from any of the surrounding shops.

Speaking of odd habits, in the palaces along these streets you'll notice many bricked-up openings that look caught between being a door and being a window. Usually near the main entrance but a few feet above ground, these are known as **porte della morte** ("doors of the dead"). Tradition holds they were used strictly to convey corpses on their final journey out of the house. Whether this was indeed one of the purposes of these doorways—which show up across northern Umbria and nearby Tuscan towns such as Cortona, as well as in the south of France—is unknown. But the fact that behind them is usually a narrow stair leading directly up to the first floor (American 2nd floor) suggests the doors more likely served in times of defense, when the main portal was blocked off.

Duomo   On your way up Via Ducale toward the cathedral, peek through the grate over the basement storeroom of the Palazzo dei Canonici, where sits a rather large **15th-century wine barrel,** boggling the mind with its 19,760-liter capacity.

The interior of the 13th-century **cathedral** is striking for its "wagon vaulting," a receding series of pointed arches defining the graceful bulk and space of the single central nave. Most of the art on the nave altars is by local talent, including multiple works by Virgilio Nucci, Benedetto Nucci, Sinibaldo Ibi, and Antonio Gherardi. In the fourth niche on the right is a *Pietà* by Dono Doni, who also painted the *Way to Calvary* in the seventh niche. In between the two, the fifth chapel on the right is a florid baroque contraption (1644–72). The fine stained glass in the presbytery is a 1913 opus, and don't miss the *Nativity* in the left aisle's sixth niche, a work by a follower of Pinturicchio (perhaps Eusubio di San Giorgio).

The restored Palazzo dei Canonici next door now contains a small **Museo Diocesano,** with paintings by Sassoferrato and Il Pomarancio; admission costs 4.50€ ($5.20) for adults, 2.60€ ($3) for children. Its website www.museo gubbio.it was still "under construction" at press time.

Via Ducale and Via della Cattedrale. ✆ 075-922-0904. Free admission. Daily 10am–1pm and 3–7pm.

Palazzo Ducale   While Renaissance-era Gubbio was under the fairly benevolent ducal rule of nearby Urbino, Duke Frederico di Montefeltro commissioned Francesco di Giorgio Martini to build him this palace in the 1470s. Although the sumptuous decorations have mostly been stripped away—the entire studio of *intarsia* wood paneling was moved to New York's Metropolitan Museum of

Art—a few furnishings, painted ceilings, and simple terra-cotta flooring survive. The ground-floor rooms are hung with **long-term exhibits.**

You enter through a Renaissance courtyard of red brick accented in gray *pietra serena.* Past the ticket booth, a spiral stair leads down to **excavations** of the structures that stood on this site as long ago as the 10th century, along with countless ceramic shards. The old outdoor support vaulting for the Palazzo Comunale that once stood on this site can be entered to the left of the palace off Via Ducale. A gate leads into the palace's **hanging gardens,** open in summer. There's bar service and views over medieval Gubbio to the valley floor.

Via Ducale and Via della Cattedrale. ① **075-927-5872.** Admission 2€ ($2.30) adults, 1€ ($1.15) ages 18–25, free for children under 18 and seniors over 60. Thurs–Thurs 8:30am–7pm. Ticket office closes 30 min. before museum.

Palazzo del Capitano del Popolo   This 13th-century palazzo was restored by its occupant, a kind of modern-day shaman and one of Gubbio's more eccentric characters. He's assembled a collection of medieval torture instruments but uses them merely as a draw for visitors so he can show off his homemade charts. These, he claims, prove the sky quadrants drawn by the ancient Umbri soothsayers and codified in the Eugubian Tables (housed in the Palazzo dei Consoli) were focused on this spot. Stop by only if you're interested in rusty chastity belts, backbreaking racks, and other torture devices.

The neighborhood here around the city's **Porta Metauro** is picturesque, a snarl of narrow alleyways that occasionally spring onto a bridge to cross the Camignano stream. Via T. Gabrielli leads across the stream and onto a path that runs uphill, skirting the city's north walls—and a soon-to-open, mountainside public park. (The entrance will be along here.) For now, the road eventually leads to the Duomo.

Via Capitano del Popolo at Via Gabrielli. ① **075-922-0224.** Admission 3€ ($3.45) adults, 1€ ($1.15) children. Daily 10am–8pm.

Teatro Romano ☆   South of the city walls toward the west end of town, in an overgrown grassy park where Eugubians walk their dogs, the remains of a large Roman theater sprout weeds. Although mined during the Middle Ages for its limestone blocks, the theater's *cavea* has been restored, and several arches that once ringed the back remain. Normally closed to visitors, the theater is used in summer for classical music performances under the stars, with the illuminated buildings of medieval Gubbio as a backdrop. On the gravel of the parking lot between the theater and the main road, old men gather to play *bocce* ball in the late afternoon.

Off Via del Teatro Romano.

Porta Romana   The 13th-century Porta Romana is the only survivor of the six identical defensive towers that guarded Gubbio's entrances. Its private owners are serious history buffs who have restored the gate tower and set up an eclectic, but worthy, museum inside. The museum's most valuable installation is a collection of more than 250 majolica pieces spanning local production from 1500 to 1950. In the central display case are two Maestro Giorgio plates signed and dated 1530, another one attributed to him, and eight pieces by his son and workshop. (The city itself owns only one of Maestro Giorgio's works.)

The old guard tower above is equipped with lances, crossbows, axes, and a 19th-century suit of armor. The owners are inordinately proud of their chastity belt collection, and preserve an odd crossbowlike sling with which nobles once stoned birds. The gaping hole in the floor was defensive, used to pour boiling water down on attackers—hot oil, Hollywood siege scenes notwithstanding, was much too expensive to waste in this manner.

Porta Romana (Via Dante 24). (© **075-922-1199.** www.museoportaromana.supereva.it. Admission 2.60€ ($3) adults, 1.50€ ($1.75) ages 8–16. Daily 9am–1pm and 3:30–7:30pm (until 8pm in summer).

Sant'Agostino ✿   The entire interior of this 13th-century church was once covered with frescoes. Remaining today is the exquisitely detailed and colored **cycle of the** *Life of St. Augustine* covering the walls and vaulting in the apse, and a *Last Judgment* on the arch outside it. The work was carried out by Eugubian master Ottaviano Nelli and his assistants in the 1420s. (If you ring the *parocchio* bell at the door to the left of the apse, a friendly priest from Chestnut Hill, Pennsylvania [or a colleague], will come out to flip on the lights so you can see better.) Nelli's brush also whipped up the *St. Ubaldo and Two Saints* fresco on the fifth altar of the right aisle, while Felice Damiani took care of *St. Ambrogio Baptizing St. Augustine* at the third altar.

Just outside Porta Romana. Free admission. Daily 7:30am–noon and 4–7pm.

San Domenico   Via dei Priori crosses the river into Piazza G. Bruno and the 14th-century church of San Domenico. The interior was remodeled in 1765, but some 15th-century frescoes remain in the first two chapels on the right and the first on the left. Piles of books were left lying around in wood intarsia on the 16th-century lectern in the choir. The left aisle has a run of good baroque works, including Giovanni Baglione's early-17th-century *Mary Magdalene* in the sixth chapel, *St. Vincent Ferrer* in the fifth chapel by Ottaviano Nelli's follower Tomasso, and a *Madonna and Child* fresco (1546) attributed to Raffaellino del Colle in the fourth chapel.

Piazza G. Bruno. No phone. Free admission. Daily 7:30am–noon and 4–7pm.

EXPLORING IN THE MOUNTAINS
BOTTACCIONE GORGE   Out the Porta Metauro, the road toward Scheggia winds above the Camignano stream in the **Bottaccione Gorge** between Mounts Ingino on the right and Foce on the left, a steep and rocky landscape spotted with ilex trees. The 390m (1,300 ft.) of folded geologic strata here recorded a 50-million-year slice of time, including the evidence that led to the popular theory that a huge asteroid impact caused the extinction of the dinosaurs. (American scientists found radioactive minerals, uncommon on Earth but not in asteroids, in the geological layer here corresponding to 65 million B.C.)

On Mt. Foce, off a path reached by backtracking down Via del Fosso from Porta Metauro, are the remains of prehistoric **Cyclopean walls** and the 13th-century **Hermitage of Sant'Ambrogio,** with some frescoes inside and a 14th-century aqueduct nearby.

MONTE INGINO   Outside Porta Romana, a left up Via San Gerolamo leads to the base of the *funivia,* a ski lift contraption that dangles you in a little blue cage as you ride up the side of Mt. Ingino (see below for hours and cost; you can also walk up steep Via San Ubaldo from behind the Duomo, a vertical elevation of 300m/1,000 ft.). It lets you off just below the **Basilica di Sant'Ubaldo.** The current structure is a 16th-century incarnation over whose high altar the withered corpse of the local patron saint, Ubaldo, is preserved in a glass casket. Stored in the aisle are the three giant wooden *ceri* used during the annual Corso dei Ceri (see "Festivals & Markets," earlier in this section).

You can take a path leading from the sanctuary farther up the mountainside to the traces of the 12th-century *rocca* fortress, sitting on the pinnacle of the 900m (3,000-ft.) mountain. The virtually unspoiled wide Saonda Valley lies beyond Gubbio, but even more spectacular is the **panorama** 🏔🏔 that opens up east across the surprisingly wild Apennine Mountains and the snowy peaks of Monte Cucco National Park at the Marches' border in the distance. A few trails run off here if you want to do some backwoods exploring.

The *funivia* (© **075-927-3881**) lift runs daily, but with excruciatingly complicated hours: November through February from 10am to 1:15pm and 2:30 to 5pm; March from 10am to 1:15pm and 2:30 to 5:30pm (Sun 9:30am–1:15pm and 2:30–6pm); April through May from 10am to 1:15pm and 2:30 to 6:30pm (Sun 9:30am–1:15pm and 2:30–7pm); June from 8:30am to 1:15pm and 2:30 to 7pm (Sun 9am–7:30pm); July through August from 8:30am to 7:30pm (to 8pm Sun); September from 9:30am to 7pm (Sun 9am–7:30pm); and October from 10am to 1:15pm and 2:30 to 5:30pm. Round-trip tickets are 5€ ($5.75) adults, 4€ ($4.60) ages 4 to 13; one-way tickets are 4€ ($4.60) adults, 3€ ($3.45) children.

WHERE TO STAY

The **Hotel Gattapone,** Via Ansidei 6 (© **075-927-2489;** fax 075-927-2417; www.mencarelligroup.com), is a solid, centrally located medium-range choice that was completely gutted and overhauled in 1999. Doubles go for 83€ to 99€ ($95–$114).

Bosone Palace 🏔🏔   The Bosone was built for the Raffaelli family in the 14th century and counted Dante among its first guests. (He stayed here after getting booted out of Florence on trumped-up embezzlement charges.) Splurge and book one of the Renaissance suites, with ceilings stuccoed and gorgeously frescoed in the 17th century, even though the furnishings are imitation era pieces. (Try for no. 212, which has the larger bathroom and frescoes in both rooms.) Even if you opt for the standard doubles, you aren't sacrificing. The spacious carpeted or wood-floored rooms are decorated with a studied simplicity the Brunelleschian Renaissance would've appreciated. The breakfast room sports 18th-century grotesques and stuccoes. The hotel's official restaurant isn't the recommendable Bosone Garden underneath, but the Taverna del Lupo (see "Where to Dine," below) a few blocks downhill.

Via XX Settembre 22 (near Piazza Grande), 06024 Gubbio (PG). © **075-922-0688.** Fax 075-922-0552. www. mencarelligroup.com. 30 units. 103€ ($118) double; 145€ ($167) 4-person junior suite; 181€ ($208) 4-person Renaissance suite. Rates include breakfast. AE, DC, MC, V. Free parking nearby. **Amenities:** Concierge; tour desk; car-rental desk (ask at least a day in advance, as it has to be brought from Perugia); courtesy car; 24-hr. room service; laundry service; dry cleaning. *In room:* TV, minibar, hair dryer.

Relais Ducale 🏔🏔   You simply can't get more central than Gubbio's (and the Mencarelli family's) newest hotel. In 1998, the former medieval and Renaissance guest quarters of Duke Montefeltro's palace returned to their original purpose—with all the modern amenities added, of course. The largish rooms are outfitted with antiques, and the bathrooms with heated towel racks and Jacuzzis (in some). The mansard rooms with their sloping ceilings are a bit cheaper, but I'd spring for a room on the upper floors of the Foresteria with a panorama over the jumble of rooftops and Piazza Grande to the stitched-together fields of the green valley beyond. But even Foresteria rooms on the first and second floors are memorable—a pair inhabits long barrel-vaulted rooms of rough ancient stone. The Caffè Ducale attached to the hotel opens directly onto the center of Piazza

Grande, and on summer mornings guests can breakfast on the square. You can even take summer dinners by candlelight on a small hanging garden—or opt for a half-pension deal at the Taverna del Lupo (recommended below).

Via Galeotti 19/Viale Ducale 2 (can also enter from the cafe in the center of Piazza Grande), Gubbio. ℭ 075-922-0157. Fax 075-922-0159. www.mencarelligroup.com. 32 units. 130€–190€ ($150–$219) double; 199€–230€ ($229–$265) junior suite. Rates include breakfast. AE, DC, MC, V. Parking free in public lots nearby. **Amenities:** Restaurants (family owns 3 nearby, including Taverna del Lupo, recommended below, for which pension plans are available); access to nearby gym; bike rental; concierge; tour desk; car-rental desk; courtesy car; secretarial services; limited room service; in-room massage; babysitting; laundry service; dry cleaning; nonsmoking rooms. *In room:* A/C, TV, VCR on request, minibar, hair dryer, safe.

WHERE TO DINE

Taverna del Buchetto UMBRIAN/ITALIAN   This is a crowded local joint, with rough-hewn low wood-beamed ceilings and stuccoed walls. It fills the 13th-century granary where guards from the neighboring Porta Romana gatehouse once stored the tolls paid in the only currency peasant merchants could muster: grain and chickens. The food today is less basic but remains simple peasant fare: *crespelle al buchetto* (a thick sheet of pasta wrapped up with ricotta and spinach and baked with tomatoes and mozzarella) or vegetable *minestrone*. They also make wood-oven pizzas. Though there's a sizable official list of secondi, the staff would much rather bring you local grilled meats like *agnello alla scottaditto* (mutton thrown on the grill with rosemary sprigs and olive oil) and *fegatino di maiale* (grilled pork livers). The desserts are homemade, and the hearty laughter of the young owner Fabrizio and his cronies competes with the TV to add noise to the general convivial chaos.

Via Dante 30 (at Porta Romana). ℭ **075-927-7034.** Reservations recommended. Primi 7€–9€ ($8.05–$10); secondi 8€–11€ ($9.20–$13); pizza 3.50€–9€ ($4.05–$10); set-price menus without wine 14€–18€ ($16–$21). AE, DC, MC, V. Tues–Sun noon–3pm and 7–11pm. Closed 2 weeks in Feb.

Taverna del Lupo ✸ UMBRIAN/EUGUBINA   Each of the five tunnels of vaulted stonework that make up this 30-year-old Eugubian culinary landmark feels like a little medieval trattoria. This is where Rodolfo Mencarelli launched in 1968 what has become a small Umbrian hospitality empire—it includes the hotels Bosone, Relais Ducale, and Gattapone (see "Where to Stay," above). Begin with the *delizie tipiche Umbre,* "typical Umbrian delicacies" that may include a *rosa di arista* (a cold salad of roast pork topped with thinly sliced pears and pecorino cheese). The *frittatina gentile con lamelle di tartufo* (cheese omelet under a shower of white truffle flakes) is excellent, as is the *sfogliatina del Lupo con tartufo* (a light lasagne made with cheese, bits of ham and mushrooms, tiny cubes of tomato, and white truffle shavings). To stay with the precious white mushroom, you can order as a secondo the *scallopina affogato di tartufo* (a tender veal scallop "drowning" in truffles) or the simple and juicy *agnellino* (charcoal-grilled Umbrian lamb). The ever-changing desserts are inventive and delectable.

Via Ansidei 21 (on the corner of Via Repubblica, a few blocks uphill from Piazza 40 Martiri). ℭ **075-927-4368.** Reservations strongly recommended. Primi and secondi 7€–18€ ($8.05–$21); tasting menus without wine 18€–46€ ($21–$53). AE, DC, MC, V. Tues–Sun 12:15–3pm and 7pm–midnight.

11

Spoleto & Southern Umbria

Umbria's southerly reaches border on Lazio, the province of Rome. The flat plains of the Tiber and other rivers are interrupted only by the green swath of long-sacred mountains (national parkland today) to the east and outcroppings of volcanic tufa to the west, atop which are perched towns that were already ancient when Rome was founded. Within an hour's drive of Rome's outskirts, **southern Umbria** boasts a heritage deeper, more complex, and more jumbled than its Latin neighbor, having served for millennia as a buffer zone between Rome and its expansion up to central Europe—and the barbarians' later push south to conquer Rome. The popular culture and architectural legacy of this region draws threads from its many epochs, from the Stone Age through early Umbri settlers, powerful Etruscan colonists, haughty Roman conquerors, iron-fisted Lombard dukes, and centuries of politically active scheming popes who used Spoleto and Orvieto as homes away from the Vatican.

Orvieto tempts with brilliant Signorelli frescoes and cool white wine, while **Todi** offers the stoniest medieval town within Rome's reach. **Spoleto** plays down its Roman theater, medieval remains, and Renaissance art to promote instead its urbane attitude—exemplified by the annual **Spoleto Festival,** one of Europe's most important and anticipated carnivals of contemporary music, art, dance, and theater.

1 Spoleto & the Spoleto Festival

63km (39 miles) SE of Perugia; 212km (131 miles) SE of Florence; 126km (78 miles) N of Rome

Spoleto is a split-level town, a sleepy repository of Roman ruins and medieval buildings terraced from the valley floor up a high hill backed by the deep-green forested slopes of a sacred mountain. It springs dramatically to life toward the end of June when the festival hits town. Dreamed up in 1958 by the Italian-American composer Gian Carlo Menotti, the Spoleto Festival (formerly known as the Festival dei Due Mondi/Festival of Two Worlds) brings heavy-duty culture to Spoleto in the form of music, dance, and theater showcased by premier Italian and international performers. The celebration of modern works, both conservative and experimental, draws thousands of visitors annually.

Although it often seems to revolve around it, Spoleto doesn't begin and end with the festival. A forgotten small city in the 1950s when Menotti chose it as the festival site, Spoleto started out as a Bronze Age Umbri settlement. And as a Roman town in the 3rd century B.C., it repulsed the fierce invader Hannibal. Strategically situated on the ancient Via Flaminia from Rome to the late imperial capital of Ravenna, Spoleto became the stronghold of many powers during the Dark Ages. The Lombards made it the capital of their empire in the 8th century A.D., and the duke they installed here governed all Umbria and much of the

Spoleto

rest of central Italy. At the turn of the 12th century, Spoleto fell into papal hands, and its twilight began.

In the 12th century, Spoleto was the birthplace of Alberto Sotio, the earliest known Umbrian painter, and Lo Spagna, a pupil of Perugino. But the city's main nonmusical treasures are Roman and medieval. Though nothing other than the Duomo, containing Filippo Lippi's last fresco cycle, and the graceful Ponte delle Torri really stands out, the town as a whole makes for a good day's diversion.

ESSENTIALS

GETTING THERE   By Train   Spoleto is a main station on the Rome–Ancona line, and all 16 daily trains from **Rome** stop here (about 1½ hr.). From **Perugia,** take one of the 20 daily trains to Foligno (25 min.) to transfer to this line for the final 20-minute leg. The C bus heads from the **station** (✆ **0743-48-516;** the huge sculpture out front is a 1962 work by American artist Alexander Calder) up to Piazza Libertà in the upper town. (Bus D stops at Piazza Garibaldi in the lower town.) Ask the driver if the bus is going toward the *centro storico.*

By Car   Spoleto is literally on the SS3 (the road tunnels under the city), the old Roman Via Flaminia running north from Rome and connecting in Foligno with the SS75 from Perugia. Parking in the old town is free only along Via Don Bonilli next to the soccer stadium and off Viale dei Cappuccini. (Turn left off the SS3 onto Viale G. Matteotti, then left again.) There's also a parking lot off

Piazza della Vittoria on the north end of lower Spoleto. Parking in the metered *"zona blu"* spaces in the center generally costs .60€ (70¢) an hour.

By Bus   Spoleto's bus company, SIT (© 0743-212-211; www.sitbus.com), runs buses into Piazza della Vittoria (connected to Piazza Garibaldi) from **Perugia** (two afternoon runs, weekdays only; 1 hr.) and **Rome** (an early morning and mid-afternoon run to Terni, where you can switch to many Spoleto-bound coaches; 2½ hr. total). If you can reach Foligno by other means, there are lots of buses from there.

VISITOR INFORMATION   The large **information center** at Piazza della Libertà 7 (© 0743-220-773 for hotels and such, 0743-238-920 for sightseeing and events; fax 0743-46-241; www.umbria2000.it) hands out scads of info and an excellent, if oversized, map. It's open daily from 10am to 1pm and 2 to 7pm.

FESTIVALS & MARKETS   Spoleto's be-all and end-all annual event bridges the end of June and early July. The **Spoleto Festival** ✦✦ (www.spoletofestival.it) is 3 weeks of world-class drama, music, and dance held in evocative spaces like an open-air restored Roman theater and the pretty piazza fronting the Duomo. For details, see the "Calendar of Events" in chapter 2. The festival's cultural beacon keeps the arts alive here for part of the rest of the year. A secondary **"Spoleto-estate"** season of music, art, and theater runs from just after the festival ends through September. (Contact the tourist office for info.) The **"A. Belli" opera and experimental musical theater** season runs from late August to October (© 0743-221-645; fax 0743-222-930; www.tls-belli.it). May and June are full of organ concerts in local churches, and the **theater season** runs November through March. (Call the Communal Cultural Office at © 0743-218-202 for details.) The **weekly market** is held Fridays on Piazza del Mercato and Piazza Garibaldi.

EXPLORING SPOLETO

The Duomo and the Ponte delle Torri are Spoleto's only real attention-grabbers, so if you're pressed for time, skip the lower town (most of which was rebuilt after extensive bombing during World War II) and head straight up to Piazza della Libertà to see the highlights of upper Spoleto.

THE LOWER TOWN   On the east side of the SS3, a 15-minute hike northeast of Piazza Garibaldi and separated from the real world by a cemetery, **San Salvatore** ✦ gathers dust (© 0743-49-606). It's one of Italy's oldest churches, built in the late 4th or early 5th century A.D. The simple facade shows Oriental influences and the remains of what must once have been spectacularly carved doorways. Much of the musty interior incorporates scavenged materials taken from Roman temples, including Corinthian columns and a presbytery fitted together in a complicated late classical architectural fantasy. The patches of frescoes date from the 13th to 18th centuries. It's open daily from 7am to 5pm (until 7pm May–Aug), and admission is free.

The thoroughly unattractive bus depot and gathering spot called Piazza Garibaldi flows seamlessly into **Piazza della Vittoria,** under which you can glimpse portions of two massive travertine arches that belonged to the old Roman **Ponte Sanguinaria.** (The stairs down are cordoned off by a low fence with a gate that is open erratic hours.) The 1st-century B.C. bridge, which once helped Via Flaminia cross the tiny Tessino torrent, was named for the human blood that stained the river red during particularly enthusiastic evenings at the amphitheater upstream (see below).

At the end of the piazza is the 11th-century Romanesque **San Gregorio** (✆ **0743-44-140**), which replaced an earlier oratory here in a cemetery of Christian martyrs. (You'll see bits from the 700s incorporated into the structure.) The church's namesake saint was killed in a spectacle at the nearby amphitheater in A.D. 304, as were a supposed 10,000 lesser-known martyrs whose bones symbolically reside beneath the altar. The bell tower is a cobbled-together affair with a base dating from at least the paleo-Christian period and upper reaches refined in the 1500s. Passing under the portico (a 16th-c. addition), you'll see how a 1950s restoration carefully returned the interior to its medieval state, removing most baroque additions to reveal the Romanesque architecture and 14th-century frescoes by local artists. The presbytery, full of architectural *spoglio* (salvage) from differing epochs—a 6th-century Byzantine capital here, some medieval cosmatesque pavement there—is raised above an antique crypt of slender mismatched columns. It opens daily from 8am to noon and 4 to 6pm, and admission is free.

The quickest route to the upper town is up the arrow-straight, shop-lined *passeggiata* drag, **Corso Garibaldi,** which becomes the steeply curving medieval **Via di Porta Fuga** before ducking under the 13th-century **Porta Fuga** into Piazza Torre dell'Olio.

A diversion off Piazza Garibaldi up Via dell'Anfiteatro gives you a few glimpses of Spoleto's more ancient origins. The long, featureless wall of a former military barracks on the left is broken by a gatehouse. As long as you do it quietly and quickly, you may nip in here and head to the right to see the crumbling arcaded ambulatory in the outer wall of the old **Anfiteatro Romano (Roman Amphitheater).** In its heyday, this 1st-century A.D. arena's ingenious gutter system siphoned so much blood into the Tessino that the river ran red. Totila the Goth turned it into a fortress in 545, and until Cardinal Albornoz ordered Gattapone to sack it for stones to build the *rocca* in 1355, the arcade housed artisan workshops and stores. On Via Santa Cecilia are the best remnants of the **ancient walls,** where 4th-century B.C. master masonry from the Etruscan circuit forms the base for the Roman fortifications and for 15th-century defenses. This road eventually takes you into **Piazza Torre dell'Olio,** with its slender 13th-century defensive tower, and the upper town.

THE UPPER TOWN   Straight up Via Pierleone Leoni from Piazza Torre dell'Olio is the pink- and white-banded 13th-century **San Domenico.** The first altar on the right preserves an early-15th-century fresco of the *Triumph of St. Thomas Aquinas,* with tiny monks, prelates, and scholars discussing the theologian's writings. There are more 15th-century frescoes in the presbytery and transept chapels, plus a painted crucifix from the 1300s above the main altar. The Cappella Benedetti di Montevecchio in the left transept conserves not just any nail from the True Cross but one of those that pierced the Lord's hands. On the left wall is a moving 14th-century fresco of the *Pietà.*

The road uphill doubles back on itself to continue to the tiny **SS. Giovanni e Paolo,** with a bit of 13th-century fresco on the outside. The church was consecrated in 1174, and its interior conserves on the left wall, near a fresco of the *Dance of Salome,* a damaged fresco of the *Martyrdom of Thomas Becket of Canterbury.* The latter was painted by Antonio Sotio just a few years after the saint's death in 1170. Other paintings in the church date from the 12th to 15th centuries. Unfortunately, the charming little church no longer has set hours; you have to get the keys from the Ufficio Culturale del Comune in Via Cerquiglia (call them at ✆ **0743-232-511**).

Spoleto's other main drag, **Corso Giuseppe Mazzini,** leads up to the first of the three main squares, **Piazza della Libertà.** Along the way, contemporary art fans might want to sidestep to the right down Vicolo III and pop into the **Galleria Comunale d'Arte Moderna,** Palazzo Spada (© **0743-45-940** or 0743-46-434). Alexander Calder's models for his 1962 sculpture *Teodelapio* (outside the train station) are here, as is a tiny 1960 Pomodoro sculpture. Admission is 3.10€ ($3.55); it's open Tuesday through Sunday (daily in summer) from 10:30am to 1pm and 3 to 6:30pm.

At the edge of Piazza della Libertà, Via Apollinare leads down to the entrance to the 1st-century A.D. **Teatro Romano** ⭐ (© **0743-223-277**). The theater was partly destroyed and buried over the ages and all but forgotten before 1891, when local archaeologist Giuseppe Sordini began excavating. Extensively restored in the 1950s, it now serves as the most evocative stage for performances during the Spoleto Festival. It retains some of the original spectators' benches as well as a remarkably intact vaulted passageway under the *cavea* behind the seats.

The attached **Museo Archeologico** ⭐ preserves relics from a 7th-century B.C. warrior's tomb and materials recovered from the theater area, including the torso of a young boy and 1st-century A.D. portrait busts of Julius and Augustus Caesar. The final main room contains the *Lex Spoletina.* These two tablets, inscribed after 241 B.C., were set up as markers to protect the lucus ("sacred groves") of the wooded Mounteluco behind the city from woodcutters. In no-nonsense terms, they warn, "These sacred woods, no one may violate. Do not remove or strip away that which belongs to the forest. . . . Whosoever transgresses will offer to Jupiter an ox as placation. If one does it knowingly and with evil intent, to Jupiter he must offer a placating ox plus pay a 300 assi fine." Although modern-day ecologists may not be able to get the ox clause written into the local codes, the tablets do provide one heck of a 2,000-year-old precedent for environmental laws. The theater and museum are open Monday through Saturday from 8:30am to 7:30pm. Admission is 2€ ($2.30) for adults and 1€ ($1.15) for children under 18 and seniors over 65.

Via Arco di Druso passes under the eponymous A.D. 23 **Roman archway.** (The ground level has risen considerably since its construction.) **Piazza del Mercato,** the second main piazza in town and probable site of the old Roman forum, is a bustling spot lined with grocers and fruit vendors' shops. The **Palazzo Comunale** hulks alongside the narrow bi-level Piazza del Municipio. Inside is the **Pinacoteca Comunale** (© **0743-45-040** or 0743-218-270). A guide usually follows you about the sumptuously decorated apartments, inhabited until the 19th century and hung with a collection of paintings spanning the 13th to 18th centuries. There are long-term plans to move the city's painting collections to the restored *rocca* (see below), and during work on the building the entrance to the gallery is sometimes on Via A. Saffi. The museum is open Tuesday through Sunday (daily in summer) from 10:30am to 1pm and 3 to 6:30pm. Admission is 2.07€ ($2.40) adults, 1.55€ ($1.80) those over 60, 1.03€ ($1.20) ages 7–14, free for under 7—or buy a cumulative ticket with the Casa Romana, below, for 4.13€ ($4.75).

Under the Palazzo (a right onto Via Visiale) is the **Casa Romana** (© **0743-2181**), a 1st-century A.D. patrician house that supposedly belonged to Vespasia Polla, the mother of the Emperor Vespasian. The intricate monochromatic patterns in the mosaic floors are well preserved, and you can also see the marble well-cap and the bases of a few carved columns supporting the display cases of smaller excavated materials. Its hours are Tuesday through Sunday (daily in summer) from 10am to 8pm. Admission is 2.07€ ($2.40) adults, 1.55€ ($1.80) those over 60, 1.03€ ($1.20) ages 7–14, free for under 7—or buy a cumulative ticket with the Pinacoteca, above, for 4.13€ ($4.75).

Take another right onto Via A. Saffi to enter (at no. 13 on the left) the court-yard of the **Palazzo Arcivescovado,** built atop the 8th-century palace of the Lombard dukes. The courtyard incorporates the facade of the 12th-century **Sant'Eufemia** ✵ (for admission and hours, see the Museo Diocesano, below). The calm and simple Romanesque stone interior has a second-story *matroneum* (women's gallery), 15th-century frescoes on some of the columns, and a 1200s cosmatesque altar, inherited from the Duomo. The double stairs in the court-yard lead up to the **Museo Diocesano** (© 0743-231-022). Room 1 has a *Madonna and Child with Angels* (1315) and a 15th-century triptych lifted from Sant'Eufemia and attributed to Bartolomeo da Miranda. In room 2 is the Sienese Domenico Beccafumi's 16th-century baroque *Adoration of the Child,* and among the sculptures in room 3 is a 14th-century *Madonna del Cholera.* Room 5 has one of Filippino Lippi's less inspired paintings, a 1485 *Madonna and Child with Sts. Montano and Bartolomeo,* and Neri di Bicci's damaged *Madonna della Neve with Sts. Sebastian and Nicholas.* There's also an exhibit on 18th-century weaving. The church and the museum are open daily from 10am to 12:30pm and 3 to 6pm (2:30–6pm in winter); admission is 3€ ($3.45).

A bit farther along Via Saffi, the low graded steps of Via dell'Arringo flow down to the left into **Piazza del Duomo,** the third and most beautiful main square, with the cathedral backed by the *rocca*-crowned green hill behind it. It makes a fitting stage for the Spoleto Festival finale and, on a more daily basis, a fine soccer field for local children. A 3rd-century A.D. Roman sarcophagus serves as a public fountain at the base of the stairs, and the small octagonal-roofed **Santa Maria della Manna d'Oro** is to the left. (Sometimes the Duomo sac-ristan will unlock it on request.) But the main attraction is the unique facade of the 12th-century **Duomo** ✵✵ (© 0743-44-307), with a 1207 mosaic by Sol-sternus surrounded by eight rose windows. The bell tower was pieced together using stone looted from Roman temples, and the porch is a 1492 addition.

The cathedral was built to replace a church razed by Frederick Barbarossa in 1155, when the emperor destroyed Spoleto for refusing to pay him tribute. The Duomo's interior retains its original pavement, but the rest was baroqued in the 17th century for Pope Urban VII, who's commemorated with a Gian Lorenzo Bernini bust high above the central door inside. The first chapel on the right has a not-quite-finished **fresco** (1497) by a 17-year-old Pinturicchio lit by a light box, which also illuminates the early-16th-century frescoes adorning the chapel next door. The right transept is home to a *Madonna and Child with Saints* (1599) by baroque master Annibale Carracci as well as the empty tomb of Fil-ippo Lippi, designed by his son, Filippino, at the request of Lorenzo de' Medici. According to Giorgio Vasari, Lorenzo couldn't convince the Spoleteans, who "lacked any great marks of distinction and especially the adornment of eminent men," to give the body back to Florence when the irascible painter died just before completing his fresco cycle here. Though technically a monk, Filippo was quite the womanizer, and when he died, rumors ran wild that he'd been poi-soned by the enraged family of a local girl whose honor he had compromised. Filippo's bones mysteriously disappeared a few centuries later, and some say they were removed and scattered by her still-indignant descendants.

Another small coin in a light box will buy you enough time to admire the ***Life of the Virgin*** ✵ fresco cycle covering the apse. Begun by Filippo Lippi in 1467, the frescoes were almost finished by 1469 when the master suddenly died, at the height of his powers. The cycle was finished by his assistants, Fra' Diamante and Pier Matteo d'Amelia. The first scene on the left, the *Annunciation,* is believed to be almost entirely from the master's hand, as is the magnificently colored *Incoronation of the Virgin* in the curving space above, with God taking the place of Jesus and a rainbow of saints and Old Testament figures surrounding Mary's richly patterned gown. The central panel, the *Dormition of the Virgin,* is also mainly from Lippi's brush and contains on the right several portraits by way of signature. Filippo is the man in the black hat, turned toward us and wearing for the last time the white monk's habit that seemed so inappropriate throughout his sensualistic philandering life. Lippi placed portraits of his assistants behind him and that of his 11-year-old son Filippino Lippi, who was already becoming a painting prodigy, in front as a candle-holding angel. The final *Nativity* scene was completed by Filippo's assistants.

As you leave the Duomo, you'll pass the entrance to the **Cappella delle Reliquie (Reliquary Chapel)** on the left aisle, restored in 1993. They include 16th-century intarsia wood cupboards, a 14th-century painted wooden *Madonna and Child,* and a letter written and signed by St. Francis. (Assisi has the only other bona fide signature.) The last altar before the exit has a colorful *Crucifix,* painted and signed in 1187 by Alberto Sotio. The cathedral opens its doors daily from 8am to 12:30pm and 3 to 5:30pm (until 7pm Mar–Oct).

Up Via A. Saffi from the Duomo is the shady car park **Piazza Campello,** with its Oz-like wall fountain, the 1642 **Fontana del Mascherone,** a bit of baroque silliness marking the end of the old Roman aqueduct (see the Ponte delle Torri, below). Also here is the entrance to the **Rocca Albornoziana** ⍟ (✆ **0743-43-707** or 0743-223-055), a well-preserved fortress built from 1359 to 1362 by Gubbio's master architect, Gattapone, for the pope's watchdog, Cardinal Albornoz, who governed this leg of the Papal States. In 1499, it served as home to the beautiful Lucrezia Borgia, sent here by her father, Pope Alexander VI, to get her away from her second husband, Alfonso of Aragon. Various popes later holed up here when visiting Spoleto. It rests atop the site of the oldest prehistoric settlement in Spoleto and was used as a prison until 1982—celebrity inmates included members of the Red Brigades terrorist organization and Mehmet Ali Agca, who tried to assassinate Pope John Paul II in 1981. It's now open to the public as a museum (and space for exhibitions and performances), and eventually will include the city's painting collections and an exhibit on the Lombard and medieval Duchy of Spoleto. Admission is 4.65€ ($5.35) adults, 3.60€ ($4.15) for ages 7 to 14 and seniors over 60. It's open (though these hours may change) from March 15 to June 10 and September 16 to October Monday through Friday from 10am to 1pm and 3 to 7pm, Saturday and Sunday from 10am to 7pm; from June 11 to September 15 daily from 10am to 8pm; from November to March 14 Monday through Friday from 2:30 to 5pm, Saturday and Sunday from 10am to 5pm.

Walk along the right flank of the fortress, Via del Ponte, and around the bend will swing into view the stately **Ponte delle Torri** ⍟⍟. This bridge's nine tall pylons separating graceful, narrow arches span the sheer walls of the valley behind Spoleto, a gorge swimming in the dense green of an ilex forest. The 80m- (264-ft.) high and 228m- (760-ft.) long bridge was most likely raised by Eugubian architect Gattapone in the 13th century, though the two most central pylons contain traces of older masonry, supporting the long-held theory that the bridge was built on a Roman aqueduct. The span received the hard-won praise of Goethe in

1786 (apparently because he thought the whole shebang was Roman) and is named after the 13th-century towers that are crumbling at its opposite end.

You can circle all the way around the *rocca* back into town from here, enjoying fine views of the valley and bridge, but a far more rewarding afternoon can be spent hiking the slopes of **Monteluco** ✿ at the bridge's other end. As the *Lex Spoletina* cippus stones in the Archaeology Museum record, the Romans held these woods sacred, as did the medieval Christians—St. Francis and St. Bernardino were both fond of meditating in the holy greenery. Michelangelo himself came here to unwind from the pressures of Rome's papal court, writing to Vasari in 1556, "I found great pleasure in visiting those hermits in the mountains of poleto . . . indeed peace is not to be found elsewhere than in the woods." The left path at the bridge's end puts you on the road toward the 795m (2,650-ft.) summit, passing the 12th-century **San Giuliano** (someone at the restaurant next door will let you in to see the remains of the 6th-century paleo-Christian church), the small convent St. Francis founded, and the tiny old resort village of **Monteluco.**

The right trail at the tower will take you along a tree-shaded path that eventually branches off toward the ancient **San Pietro** ✿. Its latest reconstruction dates from the 13th century, but the facade incorporates reliefs full of medieval symbolism from its 12th-century Lombard predecessor. The interior, much less interesting since it was subjected to a baroque overhaul in 1699, is occasionally open in the mornings, or you can try to hunt up the custodian, Sig. Pincanelli Evandro (© **0743-44-882**).

WHERE TO STAY

Accommodations are tight during the Spoleto Festival (reserve by Mar), so here are a few places to try in addition to the choices below if you have trouble finding a room. The **Hotel dei Duchi,** Viale G. Matteotti 4 (© **0743-44-541;** fax 0743-44-543; www.hoteldeiduchi.com), has 49 bland rooms in a bland 1959 brick building just south of Piazza Libertà. All the amenities are offered, but the rooms are showing their years, and at 94€ to 124€ ($108–$143) per double, they really should be renovated. Rates go even higher during the Spoleto Festival, when doubles run 170€ ($196).

Cheaper and simpler but for my money more pleasant are the seven spacious doubles above the restaurant (now under separate ownership) **Il Panciolle,** Via del Duomo 3–7 (© and fax **0743-45-677**). They have tile floors, soft beds, relatively new bathrooms, TVs, phones, and minibars, and cost 55€ ($63).

Hotel Aurora ✿   The Aurora is on a quiet courtyard just off Corso Mazzini where it exits Piazza Libertà, with amenities and a level of comfort surprisingly high for its two-star rating and low prices. The modern rooms have been refitted with faux 19th-century cherry-veneer furniture, new beds, and rich, quasi-Renaissance-style fabrics on the cloth headboards, coverlets, and window curtains. The worn carpet is currently being replaced with hardwood flooring. A few rooms have balconies. The hotel is allied with the Apollinare underneath, a restaurant famed for its fine Umbrian cuisine (add 16€/$18 per person for half-board option and 26€/$30 for full-board plan).

Via Apollinare 3 (near Piazza Libertà), 06049 Spoleto (PG). © **0743-220-315.** Fax 0743-221-885. www. hotelauroraspoleto.it. 23 units. 52€–80€ ($60–$92) double. Rates include breakfast. AE, DC, MC, V. Free parking on streets nearby. **Amenities:** Highly recommended restaurant Apollinare (one of the best in town); outdoor pool; concierge; tour desk; car-rental desk; courtesy car; limited room service (breakfast). *In room:* TV, minibar, hair dryer in most units.

Hotel Charleston ★★ (Finds) Many of the rooms in this friendly hotel nestled in a medieval district next to the new modern art museum are quite large and have a 1970s artist's loft feel, with good use of available space and mismatched but tasteful furnishings—though the new owners are replacing most with antique-style pieces. Rough-hewn chestnut-beamed ceilings mirror the wood-plank floors (some are carpeted), and the walls are hung with modern art prints and original works. The firm beds are spread with Black Watch plaid coverlets. If you're feeling particularly hedonistic, you can cough up 10€ ($11) for a trip to the basement sauna, or just cozy up on a cushy sofa before the wintertime fire crackling between the TV and sitting lounges. The room TVs come with VCRs, and the front desk always has a movie or two in English. They also organize all sorts of specialized tours (cooking classes, horseback rides, truffle hunts, and so on).

Piazza Collicola 10 (near San Domenico), 06049 Spoleto (PG). © **0743-220-052.** Fax 0743-221-244. www. hotelcharleston.it. 21 units. 59€–121€ ($68–$139) double; 93€–143€ ($107–$164) triple. Rates include breakfast. AE, DC, MC, V. Parking 8€–10€ ($9.20–$12) in garage. **Amenities:** Sauna; bike rental; concierge; tour desk; car-rental desk; 24-hr. room service (breakfast and bar); massage; babysitting; laundry service; same-day dry cleaning; nonsmoking units; Internet access. *In room:* A/C, TV, VCR in most units (videos 3€/$3.45), dataport, minibar, hair dryer.

Hotel Gattapone ★★★ Spoleto's most stratospheric hotel is a clutch of 17th-century buildings clinging to the cliff behind the *rocca*—isolated and surrounded by nature but still only a 3-minute stroll from the Duomo. It was formerly an artist's home, and its interiors were remodeled to maximize views of the valley and the remarkable 14th-century arched bridge nearby. Most of the wood-floored accommodations have plenty of elbowroom, and while the styling dates from the hotel's birth in the 1960s, it has aged well. The superior rooms have large picture windows, big bathrooms with tubs, and often a dais separating the beds from the sofa-and-desk living area. The standard rooms aren't as large or well appointed but are still worthwhile. The small terrace off the conference room overlooks the full splendor of the bridge, and terraced gardens off the other end of the buildings, where the view, alas, is marred by a highway, are in the works.

Via del Ponte (near the rocca at the top of town), 06049 Spoleto (PG). © **0743-223-447.** Fax 0743-223-448. www.hotelgattapone.it. 15 units. 140€–170€ ($161–$196) standard double; 190€–230€ ($219–$265) superior double. Breakfast included. AE, DC, MC, V. Free parking on road. **Amenities:** Bike rental; concierge; tour desk; car-rental desk; 24-hr. room service; massage; babysitting; laundry service; dry cleaning; nonsmoking rooms. *In room:* A/C, TV, dataport, minibar, hair dryer, safe.

Nuovo Hotel Clitunno ★ Little is left from the time when this 19th-century palazzo was a firehouse. But the Tomassoni family's welcome augments the comfort and warmth of the public area's fireplace, beamed ceilings, and gold-plastered walls. To accommodate disparate tastes, some guest rooms were left in "standard" style, with stylish contemporary furnishings in warm pastel colors, while 10 were refitted in 2001 as *"camere in stile,"* or "old style rooms." Request one and you'll get parquet or terra-cotta floors, antique iron beds and sconces, armoires, and rough-hewn ceiling beams. All have new bathrooms but only 15 of the standard-style rooms offer a handsome view over the Vale Spoletino. The friendly Tomassoni brothers Francesco and Filippo really put themselves out for guests.

Piazza Sordini 6 (just west of Piazza della Libertà), 06049 Spoleto (PG). © **0743-223-340.** Fax 0743-222-663. www.hotelclitunno.com. 45 units. 72€–130€ standard ($83–$150) double; 78€–140€ ($90–$161) *in stile* double. Rates include buffet breakfast. AE, DC, MC, V. Free parking. Closed Feb. Bus from station A, B, C. **Amenities:** Restaurant; nearby tennis court; bike rental; nearby children's playground; concierge; tour desk; car-rental desk; courtesy car; 24-hr. room service (bar); in-room massage; babysitting;

laundry service; same-day dry cleaning; nonsmoking rooms. *In room:* A/C in some units, TV, VCR and minibar on request, hair dryer, safe.

WHERE TO DINE

Enoteca Provinciale *✿* UMBRIAN/SPOLETINA   This wine store cum *osteria* replaces the livestock stalls of a medieval tower with a handful of wooden tables and a radio locked on the Italian pop station. Some regulars drop by just for a sandwich; others swill the day away with dozens of Umbrian wines. *Strengozzi* is handmade spaghetti served *alla Spoletina* (with spicy-hot tomato sauce), *al tartufo,* or in a game-based ragù. The standout soup is *zuppa di farro* (with crushed baby grains enlivened by veggies and meat). The secondi suit all appetites: simple *panini,* delicately flavored *frittata al tartufo* (an omelet for the indulgent in all of us), and daily specials like wild boar cooked in Sagrantino red wine and truffled *agnello* (mutton). Order your wine by the glass so that you can sample a cross section of the best Umbria has to offer, and finish with the local bitter liqueur *amaro di tartufo.*

Via Aurelio Saffi 7. ✆ 0743-220-484. Primi 5€–10€ ($5.75–$12); secondi 6€–13€ ($6.90–$15); wine 1€–6€ ($1.15–$6.90) per glass; menù turistico with wine 15€ ($17). AE, DC, MC, V. Wed–Mon 11am–3pm and 7–11pm (until midnight in summer).

Il Panciolle *✿✿* SPOLETINA   The flagstone terrace out back is scattered with tables in summer, lorded over by a spreading pine, and affords a panorama of rooftops that spills into the valley below. Inside the stone walls, under wood ceilings, you can hear the meat of your secondo sizzling over the large open fire. This former cheap trattoria has lately put its waiters in suits and nearly doubled its prices, but the cooking remains excellent. The *strangozzi alla montanara* is topped with minced veggies and a hint of peperoncini and the *spaghetti al rancetto* is served in a marjoram-scented tomato sauce with pork cheek (like bacon). Put the open fire to good use for your secondo and order *carne alle brace* (grilled meat)—the *spiedino misto* gets you a sampler of sausage, steak, lamb, and beef filet flavored with bay leaves. Vegetarians might enjoy a grill of the smoke-cured cheese *scamorza,* and anyone too stuffed to move afterward can rent one of the fine doubles upstairs (see "Where to Stay," above).

Via del Duomo 3–5. ✆ 0743-45-598. www.ristoranteilpanciollespoleto.com. Reservations recommended. Primi 6.50€–14€ ($7.50–$16); secondi 6.50€–17€ ($7.50–$20). AE, DC, MC, V. Thurs–Tues 12:30–2:30pm and 7:45–10:45pm. Closed Aug 1–12.

Il Tartufo *✿✿✿* FINE UMBRIAN/ITALIAN   Get your appetite and credit card ready for a night at Spoleto's oldest restaurant in the company of Umbria's quasi-divine fungal tuber. The chefs work all seasons of truffle: the coveted white in autumn and early winter and the black *pregiato* the rest of the year. The small dining room is an intimate arrangement of reddish veneer paneling and tables accessorized with pink roses. As Mozart wafts over your table, you can inaugurate the evening with a *terrina di polenta* (slices of truffle-flake polenta in sauce covered with large shavings of truffle). *Strengozzi al tartufo* is the classic truffled pasta primo, or take a *tartufo* break with the strong-flavored *orecchiette alla popla di olive* (tiny handmade pasta shapes served in a sauce of Gorgonzola and crushed olives). The *petto di faraona* is a guinea hen breast stuffed with a mix of potato and truffles. The simplest dish is often exquisite, as is the case with the veal *scaloppa al tartufo.*

Piazza Garibaldi 24. ✆ 0743-40-236. Reservations required. Primi 7.50€–15€ ($8.65–$17); secondi 13€–26€ ($15–$30); set-price regional menu without wine 19€ ($22); set-price traditional menu without wine 30€–35€ ($35–$40). AE, DC, MC, V. Tues–Sat 12:30–3pm and 7–10:30pm; Sun 12:30–3pm. Closed last 2 weeks in July.

Osteria del Matto ⭐⭐ *Finds* UMBRIAN OSTERIA   It might have opened only in December 2000, but this is truly an osteria of the old school, serving simple, solid food and good wines. The stocky, shared wood tables cluster under tall rough beamed ceilings, crude 14th-century brick arches, and goldenrod plaster walls scattered with wine bottle–laden shelves. There's no menu to choose from, just a blackboard telling you what you're going to eat. Various *salumi* hang in the little kitchen area alongside a prosciutto slung in its holder, ready to be carved by hand by the gregarious Filippo Matto (a former butler to Gian Carlo Menotti at his Scottish estate) for your antipasto—a mix of meats, onion frittata wedges, artichokes, and *crostini*. Afterward, there's just a single pasta dish (if you're lucky, the farro stew made with sausage, wine, peperoncini, and soup veggies) followed by the *dolce* of the day—I got a berry marmalade *crostata*.

Vicolo del Mercato 3 (under the big arch on the south side of Piazza del Mercato). ✆ **0743-225-506**. Full meal 14€–16€ ($16–$18) without wine. MC, V. Wed–Mon 11am–3pm and 5pm–2am.

Trattoria del Festival *Kids* UMBRIAN   The cavernous pair of vaulted brick rooms here are large enough to host the festival hordes yet still leave room for die-hard locals who come for the best fixed-priced menus in town. The two more "expensive" of these are the ones to order, because they let you sample a pair of primi (chef's surprise, but one is assured to involve truffles) and include all the incidentals save wine. Start with a foot-long *bruschetta al pomodoro* with a couple of cream-stuffed veal rolls before sinking your fork into the *tagliatelle tartufate* (a particularly successful use of the elusive black mushroom) or the *penne all'erbe* (in a hot-and-spicy tomato sauce laden with chopped herbs). The secondi also tend to be very simple but good. If you don't care for the excellent *frittata al tartufo* (mixed meat fry with truffles), try the *salsicce alle brace* or the *pollo arrosto*.

Via Brignone 8. ✆ **0743-220-993**. www.trattoriadelfestival.com. Reservations recommended. Primi 4.65€–8€ ($5.35–$9.20); secondi 7€–9€ ($8.05–$10); pizza 3.60€–4.40€ ($4.15–$5.05); fixed-price menus without wine 12€–22€ ($14–$25). AE, DC, MC, V. Sat–Thurs 11am–4pm and 6pm–midnight. Closed Feb.

2 Todi: A Taste of the Middle Ages

43km (27 miles) W of Spoleto; 40km (24 miles) S of Perugia; 203km (126 miles) S of Florence; 130km (78 miles) N of Rome

If you had to inflict the word "quaint" on any Italian town, Todi would be a front-runner. It's one of the most enchanting hill towns, a warren of narrow medieval streets twisting and plunging off at every angle, with many alleys whose graceful sets of shallow stairs flow down the center. It's a cobble of mottled grays accented with brick, all surrounding a picture-perfect central square celebrated as one of the finest medieval spaces on the peninsula.

Seemingly frozen in the Middle Ages (modern suburbs aside), Todi actually has much deeper roots. A backwater for the past 500 years or so, it headed its own small Umbrian empire for a while in the early 13th century, and during the long Dark Ages of Lombard rule in central Italy, the *comune* apparently maintained its independence from the Lombard dukes in Spoleto. Todi claims a 2nd-century A.D. martyr to prove it was Christianized early; while only a few bits of the 42 B.C. Roman Tuder survive, traces of the Etruscan border town Tutare are scarcer still. Even the Etruscans were relative newcomers, having conquered the city from an Umbri tribe that probably had displaced the Iron Age squatters who occupied the site in 2700 B.C.

Todi doesn't harbor much great art, with the exception of one jewel of High Renaissance architecture; the wine and cuisine aren't particularly outstanding; and its long heritage is more in the history books than in plain view. People come here mainly just to look; to drink in the vistas from the town's terraces and the medieval character of its alleyways; to nap, picnic, and play in the public gardens; and to sit on the Duomo steps and stare at the Gothic public palaces across the way.

Todi's once-upon-a-time atmosphere hasn't gone unnoticed. It sees it share of film crews, and has gotten press in America as one of the world's eminently livable cities. Property speculators and Italian businessmen have taken advantage of its relative proximity to Rome to buy medieval palazzi, set up housekeeping, and commute to the city. But notwithstanding the disproportionate number of Alfas, Mercedes, and even Range Rovers purring down the constricted medieval streets, Todi remains a showcase hill town, and a refreshing break from a culture-heavy Italian tour.

The best time to visit is in the morning, when churches are likely to be open and you can get a good photograph of Santa Maria della Consolazione with the sun at your back.

ESSENTIALS

GETTING THERE   By Train   Todi is on the private FCU train line (www.fcu.it), not the state-run FS rail routes. There are about a dozen trains daily from **Perugia**'s FCU stations (45 min.). From **Spoleto,** take the train to Terni (22 daily) and transfer to the FCU line (14 per day; about 1 hr. total travel time). There are about eight runs daily from **Rome** to Terni that meet up with an FCU train (about 2 hr. total). At Todi, get off at Ponte Rio (not Ponte Naia) station (© **075-894-2092** or 075-882-092), where a bus will be waiting to take you the 5km (3 miles) up to town. If you're staying at Villa Luisa, tell the driver and he'll let you off at the first stop.

By Car   Todi is off Umbria's central highway, the E45, which branches off the A1 Autostrada heading north from Rome at Orte and continues past Todi to Perugia. The SS79bis makes its winding way between Todi and Orvieto, but the less scenic SS448 is quicker. You can park free in lots just south of the Porta Romana and along the west side of town either below Porta Amerina or behind Santa Maria della Consolazione. Pay parking in the town's center is available in front of the Nicchioni.

By Bus   There are two bus terminals in town. From Piazza della Consolazione, there are four to eight runs daily to and from **Perugia** (40–60 min.); and one early morning run to and early afternoon run from **Orvieto** (2 hr.). From Piazza Jacopone, a bus runs daily to and from **Rome** center and Fiumicino airport (2–2½ hr.), and there's a Friday-only midday tourist run to and from **Orvieto** (2 hr.).

VISITOR INFORMATION   The central **tourist office** is under the arches of the Palazzo del Popolo (© **075-894-2526**). It's open Monday through Saturday 9:30am to 1pm and 3:30 to 7pm, Sunday 10am to 1pm and 3:30 to 7pm (in winter it closes at 6pm, and is not open Sun afternoons). The administrative APT branch has offices at Piazza Umberto I 6 (© **075-894-3395** or 075-894-2686; fax 075-894-2406) and Via Ciuffelli 8 (© **075-894-3867;** fax 075-894-4311).

FESTIVALS & MARKETS   For a decade, the town has put on the classy **Todi Festival,** 10 days at the end of August showcasing theater, music, and ballet, often surprisingly cutting edge. For information, contact **Teatro Comunale,** Via Mazzini (© **075-894-3430** or 075-894-3933). An antiques fair is held around Easter. The weekly **market** is Saturdays at the sports fields south of the center, while an annual **antiques fair** is held in the Palazzo del Vignola the second week of April.

STROLLING THROUGH TODI

Piazza del Popolo 🏛🏛 is not only the center of Todi but also the center of an ideal, a balance of secular and religious buildings in transitional Romanesque-Gothic style that epitomizes the late medieval concept of a self-governing *comune.* On the south end of the piazza squats the brick-crenellated marble bulk of the **Palazzo dei Priori,** started in 1293 and finished in 1339 with the crowning touch of a bronze eagle, Todi's civic symbol. Some lunching Umbri (or Etruscans, depending on which version of the legend you choose) supposedly founded the town after an eagle nicked the picnic blanket out from under them and then dropped it on this hill. (Historically, though, the eagle as city symbol makes its first appearance in 1267.)

The paired Gothic structures running along the piazza's side are the battlemented **Palazzo del Popolo** (1213) and the **Palazzo del Capitano** (1290). They're linked in the middle by a grand medieval staircase onto which you might expect Errol Flynn to come swashbuckling down at any moment. Todi's **Museo/Pinacoteca** (© **075-894-4148**) reopened in 1998 on the Palazzo del Popolo's fourth floor (elevator under the central arches) after a 20-year hiatus. It stars a modest lot of local 16th- and 17th-century pictures, plus an *Incoronation of the Virgin* (1507–11) by Lo Spagna that copies a Ghirlandaio work; Lo Spagna (nickname for the Spanish-born Giovanni di Pietro) seldom bothered coming up with anything original. Also here is a tiny **Etrusco-Roman Museum,** and a 1592 canvas by local painter Sensini in which a gaggle of saints carry a scale model of 16th-century Todi on a plate. It's open Tuesday through Sunday (also Mon in Apr) as follows: April through August 10:30am to 1pm and 2:30 to 6pm; March and September 10:30am to 1pm and 2 to 7pm; and October through February 10:30am to 1pm and 2 to 4:30pm. Admission is 3.50€ ($4.05) adults, 2.50€ ($2.90) ages 15 to 25 and over 60, and 2€ ($2.30) ages 6 to 14.

At the north end of the main piazza rises the **Duomo**'s facade, which ran the stylistic gamut from Romanesque through the Renaissance but still came out blessedly simple in the end. Inside on the entrance wall is a *Last Judgment* frescoed by Ferraù di Faenza in 1596 that owes about 80 percent of its figures and design directly to Michelangelo's *Last Judgment* in Rome's Sistine Chapel. (Ferraù also lifted a few figures directly from Michelangelo's inspiration: Signorelli's version in Orvieto's Duomo.) In the right aisle, under the sprightly thin-columned Gothic arcade added in the 1300s, are a 1507 marble font, what's left of a *Trinity* (1525) by Lo Spagna (here he's cribbing from Masaccio), and an early-16th-century tempera altarpiece by Gianicola di Paolo.

Back across the Piazza del Popolo, go around the right side of Palazzo dei Priori, and a right at Piazza Jacopone will take you to Todi's second major sight. The massive Franciscan shrine of **San Fortunato** ★ was begun in 1291, but finishing touches dragged on to 1459. Rumor has it that the Tuderti, basking in medieval wealth, commissioned Lorenzo Maitani for a sculpture on the facade that would top even his own masterpiece on nearby Orvieto's Duomo. Jealous Orvietan authorities, not to be outdone by rival Todi, decided the most expedient way to prevent this was simply to have the artist killed. Cross the gardens to

Mad Monks & Christmas Carols: Fra' Jacopone

Jacopone (1230–1306) started out in grand Franciscan style, living a fun, sometimes debauched, materialistic life. But when his young wife died in his arms, he had a spiritual crisis. He started going about on all fours like a dog, eating filthy food, and acting like such a nut that the Franciscans didn't at first accept his ecstasies as religious. For quite a while they refused to let him don their robes. He is chiefly remembered for telling off, in verse form, Dante's old nemesis, the reprehensible Pope Boniface VIII (the written jibes got him 5 years in a Roman dungeon). He also wrote catchy late-medieval poetry set to music that became, for all intents and purposes, the world's first Christmas carols.

see the central doorway carvings, testament to the greatness the rest of the facade could have had. It's a late-Gothic tangle of religious, symbolic, and just plain naked figures clambering around vines or standing somberly under teensy carved Gothic canopies. The *Annunciation* statues flanking it are so pretty that several authorities have recently decided they must be Jacopo della Quercia works. Inside, the church is remarkably bright, as Italian churches go, and the whitewashed walls of the chapels sport many bits and pieces of what must once have been spectacular, colorful 14th- and 15th-century frescoes. The best of the surviving fragments are Masolino's 1452 *Madonna and Child with Angels* in the fourth chapel on the right, the damaged Giottesque cycle in the sixth chapel, and the 1340 *Banquet of Herod* in the fifth chapel on the left. The bones of Todi's main Franciscan mystic, Fra' Jacopone (see the box, "Mad Monks & Christmas Carols: Fra' Jacopone"), lie in the crypt.

To the right of the church facade, a little path leads up to the town's public **park,** bordered by a low rambling wall and featuring a large round tower stump—all that remains of Todi's 14th-century **Rocca** fortress. At the other end of this park starts the winding path that wends down to Todi's High Renaissance masterpiece, the **Temple of Santa Maria della Consolazione** ✸✸✸. Like its cousins in Prato and Montepulciano, this 90-year effort of Renaissance architectural theory is a mathematically construed take on a classical temple, a domed structure on a Greek-cross plan. Construction began in 1508 under Cola di Caprarola, who may have had Bramante's help in the design. Before it was finished in 1607, its register of architects included Antonio Sangallo the Younger, Vignola, and Peruzzi, among others. It reposes in quiet, serious massiveness on a small, grassy plot. Although huge, it carries its mass compactly, with all lines curving inward and the domes and rounded transept apses keeping the structure cubically centered. The interior, however, is nothing special.

The walk back into town is along Viale della Consolazione, on the left as you head away from the temple (not the SS79 highway to the right). The road becomes Via **Santa Maria in Camuccia** as it passes the church of that name on the right. Stop in to see the wonderful 12th-century wood statue of the *Madonna and Child* in the third chapel on the left. At Via Roma, take a left, then an immediate right, just before the arch of **Porta Marzia** (a gate in the Etruscan walls, but this version is probably a medieval reconstruction). After the road curves to the left you'll see the best remnants of Roman-era Todi in the form of the **Nicchioni,** four deep travertine niches more than 10m (35 ft.) high that might have once formed the wall of an Augustan basilica. Pragmatic Tuderti recycled these "Big ol' Niches" as foundations for houses in the Middle Ages, and today they form the wall of a parking lot.

WHERE TO STAY

Fonte Cesia 🐦🐦   In 1994, the first hotel in Todi's historic center opened its doors on a successful melding of modern architectural glass and wood elements with a 13th-century palazzo. The public spaces are particularly evocative, with lots of low brick vaulting in the bar, breakfast and dining rooms, and reading and TV lounges. In summer, breakfast is served in a nook of the huge palm-shaded terrace that sits atop the hotel's 17th-century namesake fountain. The standard rooms are carpeted and wallpapered in textured creams, and have command center headboards, pleasantly unassuming dark wood furniture, and matching fabrics on the chairs, bedspreads, and curtains. Each of the suites has a small balcony or terrace and is unique—and worth the splurge, especially when the high-season cost of a double brings the prices close. The "Novecento" has 19th-century antiques, the "Jacopone" Wassily chairs and a claw-foot tub, and the "Venturini" a canopy bed.

Via Lorenzo Leonj 3 (off Piazza S. Jacopo), 06059 Todi (PG). ℭ 075-894-3737. Fax 075-894-4677. www. fontecesia.it. 37 units. 130€–152€ ($150–$175) double; 180€–195€ ($207–$224) suite. Rates include breakfast. 28€ ($32) supplement per person for half pension, 44€ ($51) supplement per person for full pension. AE, DC, MC, V. Free parking. **Amenities:** Restaurant; concierge; car-rental desk; courtesy car; limited room service (during restaurant hours); massage; babysitting; laundry service; dry cleaning. *In room:* A/C, TV, minibar, hair dryer, safe.

Villa Luisa   Although Todi now has a hotel in its center, this remains a favorite (and much cheaper) alternative among the modern inns in the valley. The well-maintained rooms are of a thoroughly uninteresting brand of contemporary standardized comfort, but it's quiet, with a pleasant tree-filled park behind the building. Bathrooms and furnishings were overhauled in 2002, and new construction in 2004 will add a fitness center with sauna and junior suites.

Via A. Cortesi 147 (1km/¹⁄₂ mile outside town), 06059 Todi (PG). ℭ **075-894-8571.** Fax 075-894-8472. www. villaluisa.it. 42 units. 80€–104€ ($92–$120) double; 120€ ($138) triple. Half and full pension available for stays of 3 nights or more. Breakfast included. AE, DC, MC, V. Free parking. If arriving by train, take the bus that meets trains at the station; tell the driver you're staying here and he'll let you off in front. **Amenities:** Restaurant; outdoor pool; bike rental; concierge; tour desk; car-rental desk; courtesy car; limited room service; babysitting; laundry service; dry cleaning. *In room:* A/C, TV, minibar, hair dryer.

WHERE TO DINE

The local Grechetto di Todi white wine accompanies lunch just fine but is otherwise fairly nondescript. Any pasta served here *alla boscaiola* is likely to have a carbonara sauce of egg, cheese, and bacon with asparagus added.

Umbria 🐦🐦🐦 UMBRIAN   Not only does the Umbria have some of the best food in Todi, it also has one of the best views—call ahead in warm weather to reserve a table on the vine-shaded outdoor terrace. In winter you can warm yourself by the huge fireplace and dine in the 15th-century interior under wood-beamed ceilings and wagon-wheel chandeliers. The *spaghetti alla boscaiola* is so scrumptious you almost needn't bother considering the *polenta con fungi e tartufo nero* (truffle shavings and bits of their poorer fungal relatives atop creamy polenta). Enjoy a steak grilled over the open fire, or try the popular *fritto di mozzarella, olive, e carciofi* (fried mozzarella mixed with olives and artichokes) or the tender *anatra stufata con lenticche* (duck cooked, but not covered, with tomatoes and spices served with a side of tiny lentils).

Via S. Bonaventura 13 (through arch between the Palazzi del Popolo and Capitano). © **075-894-2737.** Reservations strongly recommended. Primi 5€–11€ ($5.75–$13); secondi 8€–13€ ($9.20–$15). AE, DC, MC, V. Wed–Mon 12:30–2:30pm and 7:30–10:30pm.

3 Orvieto: Etruscan Ruins & Fine White Wine

45km (27 miles) W of Todi; 87km (54 miles) W of Spoleto; 86km (52 miles) SW of Perugia; 152km (91 miles) S of Florence; 121km (73 miles) N of Rome

The Paglia and Tiber rivers have spent eons washing away most of the volcanic layer of porous tufa that once covered the area around **Orvieto** ✿. But they left a plug of it jutting some 315m (1,050 ft.) above the plain, and its sheer walls are so defensible humans have been scurrying about atop it for thousands of years. The Etruscans probably called the city they inherited from Bronze and Iron Age tribes here Velzna (some scholars render it Volsinii), a major player in the Etruscan confederation of 12 cities and perhaps its religious center.

It was a close enough threat to the Romans that they attacked and leveled it in 265 B.C., driving the Etruscans to settle on the shores of nearby Lake Bolsena. The Romans built a port on the Tiber to ship home a steady supply of the famous wine produced in the area—still much in demand today as Orvieto Classico, one of Italy's finest whites (see "Orvieto's Liquid Gold," p. 433). As a medieval *comune,* the city expanded its empire in all directions until the Black Death decimated the population in the 14th century. Soon after, Orvieto became part of the Papal States and a home away from home to some 32 popes.

The city seems not so much to rise as to grow out of the flat top of its butte. The buildings are made from blocks of the same tufa on which Orvieto rests, giving the disquieting feeling that the town evolved here of its own volition. A taciturn, solemn, almost cold feeling emanates from its stony walls, and the streets nearly always turn at right angles, confounding your senses of direction and navigation. It's as if somehow Orvieto resents the humans who have over-run it. Of course, a goodly dose of wine with lunch can make the whole place seem very friendly indeed, and the stoniness is greatly relieved by the massive Duomo rising head and shoulders above the rest of the town, its glittering mosaic facade visible for miles around.

ESSENTIALS

GETTING THERE   By Train   Fourteen trains on the main **Rome–Florence** line stop at Orvieto daily (1¾ hr. from Florence; 1 hr. 20 min. from Rome). From **Perugia,** take the train to Terontola (16 daily) for this line heading south toward Rome (1¼ hr. total train time). From **Todi,** it's easiest to take the bus (see below) or perhaps a bus to Perugia and train from there (see "Todi: A Taste of the Middle Ages," earlier in this chapter). If you must ride the rails, take the FCU line to Terni, transfer to a Rome-bound train that stops in Orte, and hop on the main line heading north to Orvieto (2 hr. plus layovers).

Orvieto's station is in the boring new town of Orvieto Scalo in the valley. To reach the city, cross the street and take the **funicular** (www.atcterni.it), a mod-ern version of the steep cog railway that ran on hydraulic power in the 19th cen-tury. You can buy a funicular-only ticket for .80€ (90¢) or a combined funicular-and-bus ticket for .90€ ($1.05) that lets you hop on a minibus at the top of the funicular run (Piazza Cahen) and ride into the center of town: The "A" bus heads to Piazza del Duomo and the "B" bus to central Piazza della Repubblica via Piazza XXIX Marzo (it then doubles back to the Duomo). Or you may wish to get the *Carta Unica* cumulative ticket covering the funicular, bus, and museums (see "Exploring the Cathedral & Other Sights," below). From in front of the train station, you could also grab the no. 1 bus that runs to Piazza XXIX Marzo in the city (get two tickets—one for the return trip—at the bar inside the station, as they're hard to come by in town).

By Car If you're coming from **Todi,** the SS448 is the fastest route, but the twisty SS79bis is more scenic; from **Perugia,** shoot down the SS3bis through Deruta to Todi and branch off from there. The SS71 runs here from just east of **Chiusi** in southern Tuscany, and the A1 autostrada between **Florence** and **Rome** has an exit at the valley town Orvieto Scalo.

The most convenient **free parking** is in Orvieto Scalo outside the train station (take the funicular to town; see "By Train," above); at the top of the funicular run on Piazza Cahen (with both free and pay spaces); and, if you can find room, the free lot off Via Roma. There's a new large pay lot (.55€/65¢ per hr.; 6.20€/$7.15 for 24 hr.) at the ex–Campo della Fiera in the valley below the south end of town with elevators to take you up to Orvieto level.

By Bus From **Todi,** there's one bus daily in the early morning (a scenic twisting ride; about 2 hr.). There's one daily to (3:15pm) and from (8am) **Rome's** Tiburtina station (1½ hr.). From other cities, it's best to take the train. For bus information, call ✆ **0763-301-234** or visit the tourist office.

VISITOR INFORMATION The **tourist office** is opposite the Duomo at Piazza Duomo 24 (✆ **0763-341-772;** fax 0763-344-433; www.comune.orvieto.tr.it, www.umbria2000.it, or www.orvienet.it). It's open Monday through Friday from 8:15am to 1:50pm and 4 to 7pm, Saturday from 10am to 1pm and 3:30 to 7pm, and Sunday from 10am to noon and 4 to 6pm.

FESTIVALS & MARKETS Florentines are wimps—they use a little fake bird to set off the cart of fireworks in front of their cathedral at Easter. The Orvietani use the real thing in **La Palombella** ⭐. On Pentecost Sunday, an unlucky white dove is tied to a frame encircled with flares, which slides down a steel cable and, amid much cheering and doubtless a few animal-rights protests, ignites the fireworks and sparklers strapped to a giant Gothic canopy placed outside the Duomo. Assuming the poor thing doesn't have a heart attack, the dove is then given to the couple last married in the Duomo to be cared for until its natural death.

Umbria Jazz moves from Perugia to Orvieto for the winter, celebrating the last 5 days of the year with wine tastings and jazz artists from around the world. Call ✆ **075-573-3363** or visit **www.umbriajazz.com** for info. There are weekly **morning markets** on Thursday and Saturday in Piazza del Popolo.

EXPLORING THE CATHEDRAL & OTHER SIGHTS

The useful *Carta Unica* cumulative ticket for 13€ ($14) adults and 11€ ($12) students and those over 60 gets you into the Duomo's Cappella San Brizio, the Musei Archeologici Faina e Civico, the Torre del Moro, and the Orvieto Underground tour—plus either one funicular plus one bus ride *or* five hours in the ex–Campo della Fiera parking lot. It's available at the tourist office, the above-mentioned sights, and the funicular depots.

Duomo ⭐⭐ Orvieto's most striking sight is, without a doubt, the **facade** of its Duomo. The overall effect—with the sun glinting off the gold of mediocre 17th- to 19th-century mosaics in the pointed arches and intricate Gothic stone detailing everywhere—has led some to call it a precious (or gaudy) gem and others to dub it the world's largest triptych. It is, to say the least, spectacular.

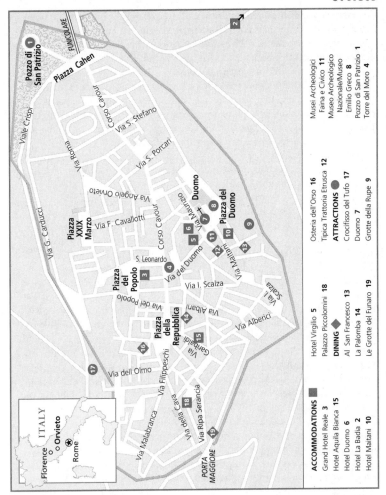

The Duomo was ordered built in 1290 by Pope Nicholas IV to celebrate the miracle that had occurred 27 years earlier at nearby Bolsena. Work was probably begun by Arnolfo di Cambio, but the structure ran through its share of architects over the next few hundred years—including Florentine Andrea Orcagna; a couple of Pisanos; and, most significantly, Sienese Lorenzo Maitani (1310–30). Maitani not only shored up the unsteady structure with his patented buttresses but also left a Gothic stamp on the building, especially the facade. Here he executed, with the help of his son, Vitale, and Niccolò and Meo Nuti, the excellent carved marble **relief panels** ★★ in the lower register (protected by Plexiglas after many vandalism incidents). The scenes on the left are stories from Genesis; God fishes around inside Adam's rib cage with an "I know I left an Eve in here somewhere" look on His face. The far right panels are a Last Judgment preamble for the Signorelli frescoes inside. The most striking is the lower-right panel, a jumble of the wailing faces of the damned and the leering grins of the demonic tormentors dragging them to eternal torture. The anguish and despair are intense, possibly because the damned didn't realize Hell would contain quite so many snakes. The controversial (mainly because they're contemporary) **bronze doors** were cast in 1970 by Sicilian sculptor Emilio Greco. Parts of the facade, including the mosaics, were damaged by the 1997 Umbria earthquakes (see Assisi in chapter 10 for more information).

Save for the 1426 *Madonna* fresco by Gentile Fabriano just inside the doors on the left, there's nothing to grab you in the boldly striped interior until you get to the altar end. The **choir** behind the main altar was frescoed by Ugolino di Prete Ilario in the 14th century, but it's been covered with restoration scaffolding for years. The left transept houses the **Cappella del Corporale** (1357–64), also by Ugolino and his workshop. The left wall depicts various miracles performed by communion wafers throughout the ages, and the right wall pulls out the Sacrament's biggest moment, the Miracle of Bolsena.

In 1263, a young priest who doubted the miracle of transubstantiation—the transformation of the communion wafer and wine into the actual body and blood of Christ—was saying mass at Bolsena, on the shores of a lake a few dozen miles south of Orvieto. As he raised the Host toward the heavens, it began dripping blood onto the *corporale* (cloth covering the altar). The altar cloth instantly became a relic and was rushed to Pope Urban IV, who was cooling his heels in Orvieto in the company of Thomas Aquinas, a visiting professor at the city's theological seminary. They quickly cranked out a papal bull proclaiming the feast day of Corpus Christi. The relic resides in a huge gilded silver case designed in 1339 to mimic the cathedral facade and set with scenes of the Miracle of Bolsena and life of Christ in enameled panels inlaid with silver.

To the right of the high altar is the recently restored **Cappella di San Brizio,** containing one of the Renaissance's greatest **fresco cycles** ✸✸✸. Fra' Angelico started the job in 1447 but finished only two of the vault triangles: Christ as Judge and a gold-backed stack of Prophets. The Orvietan council brought in pinch-hitter Pinturicchio in 1490, but the Perugian painter inexplicably cut out after just five days. It wasn't until 1499 that Cortonan Luca Signorelli strode into town, with the council hailing him Italy's most famous painter and practically throwing at him the contract to finish the paintings. After completing the ceiling vaults to Fra' Angelico's designs, Signorelli went into hyperdrive with his own style on the walls. By 1504, the Duomo had some of the most intense studies ever seen of the naked human body, plus a horrifically realistic and fascinating rendition of the *Last Judgment.* Michelangelo, master of the male nude, who was most impressed, made many sketches of the figures, and found a prime inspiration for his own *Last Judgment* in the Sistine Chapel.

The first fresco on the left wall is *The Preaching of the Antichrist,* a highly unusual subject in Italian art. The Devil-prompted Antichrist discourses in the center, Christians are martyred left and right, soldiers scurry about a huge temple in the background, and the Antichrist and his followers get their angelic comeuppance on the left. The prominent whore in the foreground reaching back to accept money for her services is a bit of painterly revenge—it's a portrait of a girlfriend who had recently dumped Signorelli. On the far left is Signorelli's "signature": two black-robed figures bearing portraits of Signorelli, looking at us, and his skullcapped predecessor Fra' Angelico standing behind.

On the right wall, the first fresco shows the *Resurrection of the Flesh,* in which the dead rise from an eerily flat, gray plane of earth—Signorelli apparently didn't want any background detailing to clutter his magnificently detailed anatomical

Orvieto's Liquid Gold

When the matter of Luca Signorelli's payment came up in his contract to paint the Cappella San Brizio of Orvieto's Duomo, the Cathedral Works Committee decided the best way to compensate the master painter for his work was to pay him 575 ducats, provide him with an apartment, and give him "as much as he wanted of that wine of Orvieto."

The plains and low hills around Orvieto grow the grapes—verdello, grechetto, and Tuscan varietals trebbiano and malvasia—that go into one of Italy's great wines, a pale straw-colored DOC white called simply **Orvieto Classico.** A well-rounded and judiciously juicy white (often with a hint of crushed almonds), it goes great with lunch and has one of the longest documented histories of any wine in Italy. The Etruscans traded it to the farthest reaches of ancient Gaul centuries before the French were competent at winemaking, and the Romans were so fond of the stuff they raised a port on the river nearby in order to slake the Eternal City's thirst by floating amphorae-laden barges down to Rome. One of the myths on the origin of the city's name is even tied to the intoxicating spirit. In the Dark Ages, barbarian invaders looted the town and were triumphantly carrying off chalices stolen from the temples when the gold suddenly melted to a pale liquid in their hands, causing the sackers to run off in fear, shouting, "Aurum vetitum, aurum vetitum!" The "forbidden gold" was, in fact, Orvieto's famous wine, on which the barbarians subsequently became so roaring drunk the Orvietani had no trouble running them out of town.

Orvieto's wine trade is still a cornerstone of the area's economy. Most Orvieto Classico you'll run across is *secco* (dry), but you can also find bottles of the more traditional *abboccato* (semidry/semisweet), *amabile* (medium sweet), and *dolce* (sweet) varieties. The *secco* was created for export to satisfy the general public accustomed to the taste of bad Chardonnay, and the sweeter varieties are treats seldom exported, so try them while you can. You may want to steer clear of big-name labels like Bigi—a perfectly fine wine, but one widely exported abroad—in favor of the smaller producers you can get only here.

To sample a glass (or buy a bottle) with a pastry or *panino,* or to try the quirky, zestier white called Est! Est! Est! that's produced on Lake Bolsena's shores in nearby northern Lazio, drop by the **Cantina Foresi,** Piazza Duomo 2 (© **0763-341-611**). Ask to see the small, moldy cellar carved directly into the tufa. You can also tipple on a visit to one of Orvieto's friendliest shopkeepers at his *enoteca/trattoria* above the Pozzo della Cava excavations (see "Tunnels in the Tufa," p. 436) at **La Bottega del Buon Vino,** Via della Cava 26 (© **0763-342-373;** www. pozzodellacava.it/visita/servizi/bottega.htm). To **visit a vineyard,** pick up a copy of the brochure *Andar per Vigne* at the direct sales/tasting office for the **Barberani** vineyard at Via Maitani 1, bang at the corner with Piazza del Duomo (© **0763-341-532** or 0763-341-820; www. barberani.it); it lists the wineries open to visitors along with the hours of tours and contact numbers.

studies of nudes. The muscular bodies struggling out of the ground seem oblivious to the bright-winged angelic trumpeters standing on the clouds above.

In the arch to the left of the altar, angel musicians summon the lucky ones in the *Calling of the Chosen.* Italian last judgments tend to have infinitely more interesting "damned in Hell" scenes than "blessed in Paradise" ones, and Signorelli's is no exception. His *Crowning of the Chosen* on the left wall, however, is one of the few versions worth pausing over, again mainly because of its studies of nudes. This Chosen is a painterly festival of well-turned calves, modeled thighs, rounded bellies, and firm buttocks.

Then there's how the other half dies. To the right of the altar is *The Entrance to Hell,* filled with Dantean details such as a group of the indolent being led off by a devil bearing a white banner, a man raising his fists to curse God as he sees Charon rowing across the Styx for him, and a would-be escapee downstage whom Minos has captured by the hair and is about to thrash. Two rather militant angels oversee the whole process as if to make sure no one scrambles over the arch to the "Chosen" side. This fresco sets you up for the last and most famous scene: the writhing, twisting, sickly colored mass of bodies, demons, and horror of *The Damned in Hell.* Signorelli didn't pull any punches here. Tightly sinewed parti-colored demons attack and torture the damned while a few of their comrades, menaced by heavily armed angels in full plate mail, toss humans down from the sky. One winged devil is making off with a familiar blonde on his back—the jilted artist's ex-mistress again—but there's also a gray-haired electric-blue devil in the very center of the squirming mass, grasping an ample-bosomed woman and looking out at us from the chaos with a rather sad expression (another self-portrait?).

Piazza del Duomo. ✆ **0763-341-167.** Admission to Cappella San Brizio (✆ **0763-342-477**) by cumulative ticket or 3€ ($3.45) adults, free for children under 10. Tickets available at tourist office across the piazza. Daily 7:30am–12:45pm and 2:30pm–7:15pm (5:15pm Nov–Feb and 6:15 Mar and Oct). (Cappella San Brizio opens 10am but is closed Sun morning).

Musei Archeologici Faina e Civico The core of this Etruscan museum dates from a private collection started in 1864 and contains almost as much material from Chiusi and the Perugia area as it does finds from Orvieto area tombs. The highlights of the museum include a good collection of **Etruscan black *bucchero* ware** from the 6th and the 5th century B.C., and some **Attic black-figure** (6th c. B.C.) and **red-figure** (5th c. B.C.) vases and amphorae that originated in Athenian workshops and were bought by discriminating Etruscan collectors. The museum even has three black-figure **amphorae by Greek master Exekias** (540 B.C.) that were fished out of the Crocifisso del Tufo necropolis (see review below). Of local manufacture is a celebrated group of 4th-century **pots depicting Vanth,** the Etruscan winged goddess of the netherworld, who has snakes wrapped around her arms and carries keys, a torch, or a scroll inscribed with her name.

On the ground floor is the Civic Museum, with Etruscan material from the Cannicella tomb and Temple of Belvedere. These include a famous marble **"Venus"** (530–520 B.C.) of dubious sex appeal, the remarkably realistic **head of a bearded old man** (4th c. B.C.), a well-turned **warrior's torso** (late 5th c. B.C.), and a genuinely frightening **Gorgon's head.** The last room contains an enormous helmeted warrior's head carved in the late 6th century B.C. with some Etruscan script scrawled across it, and a 4th-century B.C. **polychrome sarcophagus** found in nearby Torre San Severo. Its reliefs depict soldiers leading naked prisoners to be garroted and winged women carrying scepters and snakes (Vanth again).

Piazza Duomo 29 (across from the Duomo). © 0763-341-511 or 0763-341-216. www.museofaina.it. Admission by cumulative ticket, or 4.50€ ($5.20) adults, 3.50€ ($4.05) ages 7–12, seniors over 65, and families of 4 or more. MC, V. Apr–Sept Tues–Sun 9:30am–6pm; Oct 1–Mar 30 Tues–Sun 10am–5pm. Closed Mon in Feb and Nov. Bus A.

Museo Archeologico Nazionale Housed in the yellow tufa 13th-century papal palace to the right of the Duomo (walk down the slope toward the picture windows), this collection currently occupies four cavernous medieval rooms. They contain finds from Etruscan tombs in the area dating from the 7th to 4th centuries B.C. Among the treasures are a **soldier's armor** from a 4th-century B.C. burial site at Settecamini and the detached **frescoes** ⚜ (open and lit on request) from his neighbors' tombs. There are also bits of Greek vases and some black *bucchero* ware.

In the part of the palazzo that sticks out into the piazza is the **Museo Emilio Greco** (© **0763-344-605**), dedicated to the sculpture of the sometimes controversial contemporary artist who cast the Duomo's bronze doors. Admission is 2.50€ ($2.90) adults, 1€ ($1.15) ages 18 to 25 and seniors; cumulative tickets with the Pozzo di San Patrizio are 4.50€ ($5.20) and 2.50€ ($2.90) respectively. It's open Tuesday through Sunday from 10:30am to 1pm and 2 to 6:30pm (2–5:30pm in winter).

Piazza Duomo (to the right of the Duomo). © 0763-341-039. www.archeopg.arti.beniculturali.it. Admission 2€ ($2.30), free for children under 12 or seniors over 65. Mon–Sat 9am–8pm (June–Sept until 11pm Sat).

Grotte della Rupe (Etruscan Orvieto Underground) ⚜ The Orvieto *comune* has finally laid its hands on some caves of its own and leads groups down into them to try and explain the network of tunnels honeycombing the tufa subsoil. The visit can be overly didactic and explanatory, but you do get to see an underground medieval olive press (the constant temperature was great for oil making) probably recycled from an Etruscan structure, perhaps a temple. You can also peer down a few claustrophobically narrow Etruscan-era wells, wander around a subterranean quarry for *pozzolano* (a volcanic stone powdered to make cement mix) in use as late as the 19th century, and tour a series of Etruscan pigeon coops (no, seriously) carved out of the cliffside tufa.

Piazza Duomo 24 (tourist info office). © 0763-344-891. www.orvietounderground.it. Admission (by guided tour only) by cumulative ticket, or 5.50€ ($6.30) adults, 4.50€ ($5.20) Pozzo della Cava ticket holders, 3.50€ ($4.05) students and seniors. Tours daily at 11am, 12:15pm, 4pm, and 5:15pm (other times can be arranged). Closed Feb.

Torre del Moro This 45m- (150-ft.) high civic project from the late 13th century was built to keep on eye on Orvietan territory. In the 19th century it served as a main cistern for the city's new aqueduct system, then became the bell-ringing communal timekeeper when a mechanical clock was installed in 1876. You can clamber up for a sweeping view of the city and, on clear days, the countryside as far as Mounts Cetona and Amiata.

At the intersection of Via Duomo and Corso Cavour. © 0763-344-567. Admission by cumulative ticket, or 2.60€ ($3) adults, 1.85€ ($2.10) children. Nov–Feb daily 10:30am–1pm and 2:30–5pm; Mar–Apr and Sept–Oct daily 10am–7pm; May–Aug daily 10am–8pm.

Pozzo di San Patrizio (St. Patrick's Well) ⚜ *Kids* While Emperor Charles V was sacking Rome in 1527, the Medici Pope Clement VII took advantage of a dark night and the disguise of a fruit vendor to sneak out of his besieged Roman fortress and scurry up to Orvieto. Convinced that the emperor would follow him, Clement set about fortifying his position.

Tunnels in the Tufa

The Orvietani have been burrowing into the soft tufa and *pozzolano* stone under their feet for thousands of years. The problem of providing the skyscraping city with water has been tackled since Etruscan times by digging in the ground. The Etruscans hollowed out cisterns to collect rainwater, sank wells to seek out groundwater, and carved public plumbing systems into the rocky foundations of Velzna. The practice was continued by the Romans, the people of the Middle Ages (who also used some defunct wells as rubbish dumps), and even Renaissance Pope Clement VII.

Through the ages, the man-made cavern system has also been used for wine and oil production and storage, artisan workshops, escape tunnels for nobility, and quarries for tufa building blocks and the *pozzolano* dust to cement them with. The official position seems to relegate this peculiar molelike tendency to the past, dating the last tunneling and the closing of the last *pozzolano* mine to the late 19th century. But what everyone appears to ignore are the elevator shafts the city sank through the cliff in 1996 to connect the new parking lots with Orvieto proper—the Orvietani are still tunneling.

Besides the *comune*-run **Grotte della Rupe** caverns (see listing above), many shops and other private buildings sit atop underground excavations—scholars suspect the military base covering a fifth of the city (and closed to visitors) hides some of the finest. Perhaps the best accessible ones are under an *enoteca,* the **Pozzo della Cava,** Via della Cava 28 (© **0763-342-373;** www.pozzodellacava.it), whose personable owner used to invite his customers to poke around his Etruscan tunneled basement gratis. Then the town decided to excavate, discovered an important historic well, set it up as an official tourist sight, and started charging admission. (Sometimes, when no one's looking, the amused shopkeeper still lets you scurry down for free.) The excavations consist of six caves containing, among other things, a few medieval refuse shafts and a kiln from 1300, an Etruscan cistern, and, of course, a well almost 4.5m (15 ft.) in diameter and more than 30m (100 ft.) deep, first used by the Etruscans and later enlarged by Pope Clement VII. It's open in the summer Tuesday through Sunday from 8am to 8pm. Admission is 1.70€ ($1.95) adults and 1.20€ ($1.40) for students, seniors, and holders of tickets to Grotte delle Rupe, Pozzo Patrizio, or the funicular.

Orvieto's main military problem throughout history has been a lack of water. Clement hired Antonio Sangallo the Younger to dig a new well that would ensure an abundant supply in case the pope should have to ride out another siege. Sangallo set about sinking a shaft into the tufa at the lowest end of town. His design was unique: He equipped the well with a pair of wide spiral staircases, lit by 72 internal windows, forming a double helix so that mule-drawn carts could descend on one ramp and come back up the other without colliding.

Although Clement and Charles V reconciled in 1530, the digging continued. Eventually, workers did strike water—almost 10 years later, at which point

Clement was dead and the purpose moot. The shaft was nicknamed St. Patrick's Well when some knucklehead suggested that it vaguely resembled the cave into which the Irish saint was wont to withdraw and pray. What you get for descending the 248 steps is a close-up view of that elusive water, a good echo, and the sheer pleasure of climbing another 248 steps to get out.

In a small park just north of the well are the moss-covered foundation, the staircase, and a few column bases of the so-called **Tempio di Belvedere,** an Etruscan religious building from the early 5th century B.C. It miraculously never had a Roman temple or Christian church grafted onto it, as most temples throughout Tuscany and Umbria did. (Both the Romans and the early Christians recycled holy sites regularly, just changing the name of the honored divinity.)

South of the well, off Piazza Cahen, is a large millstone old men use as a card table. It lies next to a tall gatehouse that, aside from a few of the thicker defensive walls, is all that remains of the 1364 **Albornoz Fortress.** The remnants are laid out as a public **park** with fine views of the valley beyond Orvieto's wall.

Viale San Gallo (near the funicular stop on Piazza Cahen). ℂ 0763-343-768. Admission 3.50€ ($4.05) adults; cumulative ticket with Museo Emilio Greco 4.50€ ($5.20) adults, 2.50€ ($2.90) children. Mar–Sept daily 9:30am–7pm; Oct–Feb daily 10am–6pm.

Crocifisso del Tufo ⟨ This 4th-century B.C. necropolis of houselike stone tombs lies about halfway around the north edge of town off Viale Crispi (leading out of Piazza Cahen). On some tombs you can still see Etruscan script, written from right to left, on the door lintels, but the funerary urns and other relics found inside have long since been carted off to museums. What makes this site unique compared to similar necropoli in Etruria is that Etruscan Velzna, at least for a sizable period, apparently practiced some measure of democracy. None of the tombs is larger or otherwise set apart to denote the status of the occupants; rather, the whole affair is laid out in neat rows of uniform measure, indicating that citizens of differing ranks and occupations were interred side by side.

Viale Crispi. ℂ 0763-343-611. www.archeopg.arti.beniculturali.it. Admission 2€ ($2.30) adults, free for children under 18 and seniors over 60 if they're citizens of EU countries. Apr–Sept Mon–Sat 9am–7pm; Oct–Mar Mon–Sat 8:30am–5:30pm (June–Sept until 11pm Sat). Bus: 1.

SHOPPING
Ceramics shops line Via Duomo. They do cater to tourists, but you can still find some quite lovely pieces. You'll see the **Michelangeli** clan's **wood sculptures,** puppets, and stacked-contour reliefs all over town (the Osteria dell'Orso and Caffè Montanucci, recommended below, are decorated by them). Several Michelangeli showrooms (ℂ **0763-342-660;** www.michelangeli.it) line either side of Via Gualverio Michelangeli. One of the top **antiques shops** in town is **Carlo & Cesare Bianchini,** Via Duomo 37 (ℂ **0763-344-626**), which is filled with gorgeous *pietra dure* tabletops inlaid with semiprecious stones and marbles. But whether antique or made by a local artisan, they don't come cheaply!

WHERE TO STAY
The hotel situation in Orvieto is pretty grim. Most inns are of a consistently bland modern motel style, and the price doesn't come close to justifying the accommodations. The more pleasant choices are profiled below. You might also want to try the **Hotel Aquila Bianca,** Via Garibaldi 13 (ℂ **0763-341-246** or 0763-342-271; fax 0763-342-273; www.argoweb.it/hotel_aquilabianca), a modernized 19th-century palace whose 101€ ($116) doubles are modern and comfortable, with little to displease but little to excite. And the **Hotel Virgilio,**

Piazza Duomo 5–6 (© **0763-341-882;** fax 0763-343-797; www.hotelvirgilio. com), has 13 very basic modern rooms with some of the ugliest lamps I've ever seen, but it's smack on Piazza Duomo. Doubles run 52€ to 85€ ($60–$98), and the hotel is closed from mid-January to mid-February.

Orvieto Promotion, associated with the local travel agency Effe & G Viaggi, Piazza Fracassini 4 (© **0763-344-666;** fax 0763-343-943; effegiviaggi@ effegiviaggi.it), will help with hotel reservations free of charge if the following hotels are full. Specify the category or price range you're interested in.

Grand Hotel Reale 🖈   A very faded beauty, this hotel was Orvieto's most glamorous address in the 1930s. Though it seems that little upkeep has been done since opening day, it remains the only hotel in the center besides the Palazzo Piccolomini (see below) with any character. Most rooms are loaded with 19th- and early-20th-century furniture, and many have gorgeously frescoed ceilings, but the wiring stapled to the walls and the overall wear on everything detracts from the aura. The beds are of the very lazy spring variety and bathrooms are begging for a tune-up. (In many of the most beautiful rooms, ugly modular cube bathrooms have been stuck in the corners.) Don't accept the dreary cheaper rooms—with the antiques and frescoes removed, this place becomes just a very worn *pensione.*

Piazza del Popolo 25, 05018 Orvieto (TR). © and fax **0763-341-247.** 34 units, 31 with bathroom. 55€ ($63) double without bathroom, 88€ ($101) double with bathroom; 140€ ($161) suite with bathroom. Breakfast 8€ ($9.20). MC, V. Free parking nearby. Minibus: B. **Amenities:** Concierge; tour desk; car-rental desk; 24-hr. room service (breakfast and bar); babysitting; laundry service. *In room:* A/C, TV, hair dryer in some units.

Hotel Duomo 🖈🖈   In 1998, the former owner of Tipica Trattoria Etrusca (p. 441) bought this former budget favorite and overhauled it completely into board-rated three-star status. While I kind of miss the old super-cheap flophouse, located just a few steps off the left side of the Duomo's piazza, the new Hotel Duomo still offers an excellent price for the location, with far more comfort and amenities. The rooms—some quite large, others of modest size—now have stylish modern furnishings, beds with firm box springs, original sculpture on the walls, and marble sink tops and heated towel racks (but flat towels) in the new bathrooms. A few rooms overlook the cathedral's striped flank. There's a small garden out front for alfresco breakfasts in summer.

Vicolo di Maurizio 7 (near the Duomo), 05018 Orvieto (TR). © **0763-341-887** or 0763-393-849. Fax 0763-394-973. www.orvietohotelduomo.com. 18 units. 85€–100€ double ($98–$115); 100€–120€ ($115–$138) junior suite; 130€ ($150) triple. Rates include breakfast. AE, DC, MC, V. Parking 10€ ($12) in garage. Minibus: A. **Amenities:** Concierge; courtesy car; 24-hr. room service; babysitting; nonsmoking rooms. *In room:* A/C, TV, dataport, minibar, hair dryer.

Hotel La Badia 🖈🖈   This 12th-century abbey has been a hotel since 1968 and is one of Orvieto's best accommodations, albeit out of the town proper (and the prices have risen alarmingly lately). The harmonious blend of wood and solid tufa-block walls helps the place retain a strong medieval air. The furnishings are a mix of modern and antiques that came from the Badia itself or the houses on its property, including some beautiful inlaid wood pieces. While the decor varies widely, it's singularly tasteful, with amusing touches like TVs fitted into old stone niches. Some rooms are palatial yet others quite cramped; a few are lofted and can sleep families without crowding. The suites are roomy, and those in the outbuilding connected to the church have Jacuzzis and a view of Orvieto up on its rocky perch. Bathrooms on the first floor have been renovated, but the older ones elsewhere throughout La Badia carry their age well. Make sure you duck into the Romanesque church to see the frescoes and gorgeous cosmatesque-style floor.

Tips A Cappuccino Break

On the main drag, **Caffè Montanucci,** Corso Cavour 21–23 (© **0763-341-261**), has since 1913 sold excellent local marmalades, chocolates, and home-made pastries against a backdrop of Michelangeli wood reliefs in an area teeming with locals in the morning and during the evening *passeggiata.* It's open Thursday through Tuesday from 6:30am to midnight and has public computers for Internet access.

The big selling point of **Hescanas,** Piazza del Duomo 31 (© **0763-342-578;** www.hescanas.it), is the outside patio of tables directly across from the cathedral's glittering facade. Its self-serve *bar and tavola calda* inside offer a good variety of *panini,* hot dishes, and packaged gelato.

Though otherwise an unremarkably normal Italian *bar,* tiny **Bar Duomo,** Largo L. Barzini 14 (© **0763-341-623**), is where locals invariably take me for a coffee break. It has a few tables scattered on the cobbles of its wide spot along Via Duomo, and to just about anyone aside from the unknown tourist who stops by, *barrista* Mario usually just glances up and asks "The usual?" as he starts preparing the cappuccino or campari and soda; he already knows what his visitor wants. They make a sinful *cornetto fritto,* fried, sugar-encrusted, cream-stuffed croissant. It's open Tuesday through Sunday from 6am to 9pm.

Loc. La Badia 8 (about 3km/2 miles south of town off the road to Bagnoreggio), 05019 Orvieto (TR). © **0763-301-959.** Fax 0763-305-396. www.labadiahotel.it. 28 units. 172€–228€ ($198–$262) double; 252€–304€ ($290–$350) junior suite; 288€–344€ ($331–$396) suite. Rates include breakfast. AE, MC, V. Free parking. Closed Jan–Feb. **Amenities:** Restaurant; outdoor pool (June–Sept); outdoor tennis court; concierge; limited room service (bar); massage; laundry service. *In room:* A/C, TV, minibar, hair dryer.

Hotel Maitani *(Overrated)*   Just yards down from the front of the Duomo, this was ostensibly the top board-rated four-star hotel in town until the much friend-lier Piccolomini (below) opened up. The public spaces' modern art and a few Victorian chairs and antique dressers in the smallish rooms liven things up a bit, but the relatively high price tag and consistently surly service put me off. Although the location is key, it's still disappointing that, less than a block from the cathedral, only a few rooms are blessed with a sliver view of the facade; the breakfast terrace gets in more.

Via Lorenzo Maitani 5 (½ block from Duomo), 05018 Orvieto (TR). © **0763-342-011.** Fax 0763-342-012. 39 units. 124€ ($143) double; 147€–168€ ($169–$193) suite. Breakfast 10€ ($12). AE, DC, MC, V. Parking 12€ ($14) in garage. Closed Jan 7–31. Minibus: A. **Amenities:** Concierge; tour desk; car-rental desk; 24-hr. room service; in-room massage; laundry service; dry cleaning. *In room:* A/C in suites only, TV, fax, dataport, minibar, hair dryer.

Palazzo Piccolomini ✦✦✦   Converted in 1997 from a 16th-century palazzo, the family-run Piccolomini is the best hotel in town. It's quite a sight nicer (and far, far friendlier) than the Hotel Maitani (see above), and the price is excellent for the level of quality. It retains some palatial grandeur in echoey salons and the remnants of decorative frescoes, but the rooms tend toward the elegantly simple, with missionary-style wood furnishings, compact bathrooms, and modernized comforts (some suites have plush touches like heated towel racks and canopied beds). The ground-floor rooms enjoy high vaulted ceilings, while those on the upper floors often have views across lichen-splayed roof tiles to the countryside.

The basement breakfast room is carved out of the living tufa, and in late 1999 the owners of Le Grotte del Funaro (below) opened a restaurant, La Taverna de' Mercanti, affiliated with the hotel underneath.

Piazza Ranieri 36 (2 blocks down from Piazza della Repubblica), 05018 Orvieto (TR). © 0763-341-743. Fax 0763-391-046. www.hotelpiccolomini.it. 32 units. 116€–138€ ($133–$159) double; 142€–175€ ($163–$201) triple; 205€–227€ suite ($236–$261). AE, DC, MC, V. Breakfast 11€ ($13). Parking 10€ ($12) in main public lot next door. **Amenities:** Restaurant; concierge; tour desk; car-rental desk; courtesy car; 24-hr. room service; in-room massage; babysitting; laundry service; dry cleaning; nonsmoking rooms. *In room:* A/C, TV, VCR on request, dataport, minibar, hair dryer.

WHERE TO DINE

Orvieto's unofficial pasta is *umbrichelli,* simple flour-and-water spaghetti rolled out unevenly by hand and somewhat chewy—similar to the *pici* of southern Tuscany, but not as thick.

If you're in a hurry or on a budget and want to skip the restaurants below, try the cafeteria-style **Al San Francesco,** Via B. Cerretti 10 (© **0763-343-302**), off Via Maitani near the Duomo. It's hard to imagine, but the 450 seats actually fill up during lunch in summer, perhaps because you can get a full meal with wine for 9.60€ to 20€ ($11–$23). The restaurant serves pizzas in the evening and is open daily from noon to 3pm and 7 to 10:30pm (in winter, it closes Sun evenings).

La Palomba ORVIETANA   A giant wooden Pinocchio marks the entrance to this unpretentious place, where sticking to the *"La Casa Consiglia"* ("the house suggests") part of the menu will guarantee a memorable meal of good home cooking. After putting away a plate of warm *crostini misti,* try one of the specialty homemade *umbrichelli* dishes, either *tartufati* (in light butter-and-truffle sauce with fresh truffle grated on top) or *all'arrabbiata* (if it isn't *piccante* enough for you, add peperoncini-spiked olive oil). You can cool your mouth afterward with a simple omelet stuffed with cheeses or order the divine *filetto alla cardinale* (beef filet cooked in cardinal-colored red wine).

Via Cipriano Manente 16 (1st left under the arch at Piazza della Repubblica). © 0763-343-395. Reservations recommended. Primi 4.70€–7.50€ ($5.40–$8.65); secondi 6€–10€ ($6.90–$12). AE, DC, MC, V. Thurs–Tues 12:30–2:15pm and 7:30–10pm. Closed 20 days in July and/or Aug.

Le Grotte del Funaro ✦ UMBRIAN   Dating from at least the 1100s, when the eponymous *funaro* (rope maker) had his workshop here, these grottoes carved into the tufa are filled with delectable smells of Umbrian cooking that draw Italians and tourists alike. The *bruschette miste Umbre* give their Tuscan *crostini* cousins a run for the money, but save room for the *ombrichelli del Funaro* (in a heavy sauce of tomatoes, sausage, artichokes, and mushrooms). For a sampling platter of the best grilled meats, order the *grigliata mista* (suckling pig, lamb, sausage, and yellow peppers) or a fish dish. The wine cellar offers just about every Orvieto Classico, including a good selection of half-bottles. After 10pm, the restaurant transforms into a piano bar; if you're here for lunch, retire outside to digest with the aid of the spectacular view from the terracelike piazza.

Via Ripa Serancia 41 (at the west end of town near Porta Maggiore; well signposted). © 0763-343-276. www.ristoranti-orvieto.it. Reservations recommended. Primi 9€–15€ ($10–$17); secondi 10€–13€ ($12–$15); pizza 5.50€–8.50€ ($6.30–$9.80); fish tasting menu without wine 32€ ($37); minimum 2 people). AE, DC, MC, V. Tues–Sun noon–3pm and 7pm–midnight. Closed 1 week in July.

Osteria dell'Orso ✦✦ UMBRIAN/ABRUZZESE   Chef Gabriele di Giandomenico uses the freshest local ingredients and traditions (mixed with those of his native Abruzzi) to create memorable dishes that change daily, which is why his Neapolitan partner, Ciro Cristiano, prefers to recite them to you in delectable detail rather than break out the printed menu. In the tiny rooms surrounded by Michelangeli wood sculptures—including a remarkably realistic "lacy" curtain— you can sample primilike fresh homemade tagliatelle served perhaps with mushrooms and truffles, with broccoli, or with Neapolitan baby tomatoes, basil, and shredded scamorza cheese. The local specialty secondo is chicken with olives, or you can try Gabriele's *faraona* (game hen) stuffed with truffles.

Via della Misericordia 18–20. (✆ **0763-341-642**. Reservations recommended. Primi 6€–10€ ($6.90–$12); secondi 6€–15€ ($6.90–$17). AE, DC, MC. Wed–Sun 12:30–2:30pm and 7:30–10pm. Closed Feb, July, and Nov.

Tipica Trattoria Etrusca ⭑ ORVIETANA   Squirreled away under a 15th-century palace, this trattoria was a workers' lunch hangout early in the 20th century. The vaulted ceilings are divided by magnificent tufa arches with a massive column at the center and modern art on the walls. Start with *umbrichelli dell'Orvietana* (in a spicy hot tomato sauce mixed with *pancetta*) or the homemade gnocchi. The *coniglio all'Etrusca* (rabbit in a green sauce of herbs and spices) is the house special secondo, but don't rule out the *abbachio a scottaditto* (lamb so piping hot it'll "burn your fingers"). Desserts tend toward antique Orvietan sweets, including fresh ricotta dusted with sugar, cinnamon, and a sweet berry sauce. Ask to see the wine cellars, carved from the living tufa beneath.

Via Lorenzo Maitani 10 (1 block from the Duomo). (✆ **0763-344-016**. Reservations recommended. Primi 4.50€–13.50€ ($5.20–$16); secondi 5.50€–16€ ($6.30–$18); fixed-price menu without wine 20€ ($23). AE, DC, MC, V. Tues–Sun 12–3pm and 7:45–10pm. Closed Jan 7–Feb 7.

Appendix A:
Tuscany & Umbria in Depth

Tuscany is the most famous of Italy's 20 regions—birthplace of the Renaissance, land of Dante's poetry and chianti wine and lovely old towns, and muse to Michelangelo. Umbria is known as the Green Heart of Italy, with the distinction of being the only Italian region that touches neither a sea nor another nation. It's a bit wilder and more mystical than Tuscany, a breeding ground for Sts. Francis and Clare of Assisi and Benedict, founder of Western monasticism.

This appendix covers the basic background and makeup of these regions, with essays on history, culture, art, food, and wine.

1 A Look at the Past

This brief survey of central Italy's long and complex history is oriented toward Tuscany, but Umbria is covered as well. Once we hit the Renaissance, the focus shifts primarily to Florence, which quickly became the leading power and controlled most of Tuscany until the 19th century.

TUSCAN ROOTS: FROM PRE-HISTORY TO THE ETRUSCANS

Although Neanderthals, ancient Homo sapiens, and Paleolithic and Bronze Age humans have left some of their bones and tools lying about and the 9th-century B.C. **Villanovian** Iron Age culture (possibly immigrants from the north) has helped fill museums with pot shards, things really didn't start getting lively in central Italy until the Etruscans rose to power.

The most widely accepted theory is that the **Etruscans** came from modern-day Turkey in Asia Minor—at least, that's what the ancient Romans believed—and arrived in central Italy in late 9th or early 8th century B.C. The fact their language isn't Indo-European but appears similar to some Aegean dialects helps confirm this theory, but there are others who now feel the Etruscans may have risen from native peoples in central Italy, perhaps

Dateline

- **65 Million Years Ago** According to a popular theory based on evidence found at Gubbio, an asteroid strikes the earth, causing a chain reaction that drives the dinosaurs to extinction. The age of mammals begins.
- **1200 B.C.** Umbri tribes start settling in northern Umbria.
- **1000–500 B.C.** Villanovian culture thrives.
- **800–500 B.C.** The Etruscans are a major power in central Italy.
- **600–510 B.C.** The Etruscan Tarquin dynasty rules as kings of Rome.
- **506 B.C.** Lars Porsena, Etruscan king of Chiusi, attacks young Roman Republic and wins.
- **295–265 B.C.** Rome conquers Etruria and allies with Umbria. The Roman Empire spreads throughout central Italy and Latinizes local culture.
- **59 B.C.** Julius Caesar founds Fiorentia, and Florence is born.
- **56 B.C.** The First Triumvirate (Caesar, Pompey, and Crassus) meets in Lucca.
- **ca. 4 B.C.** Jesus is born in Nazareth. Renaissance painters flock there to set up easels.
- **A.D. 313** Roman Emperor Constantine the Great, a convert himself, declares religious freedom for Christians.
- **476** After a long decline, the Roman Empire falls.

a combination of the Villanovians, local tribes, *and* travelers from Asia Minor. Whatever the case, these Etruschi or Tuschi formed the basic cultural/political force in the region that's now named for them, Tuscany.

The Etruscans are a bit of an enigma. Much of what little remains to tell us of them—that which hasn't been corrupted by later Roman influence—consists of tombs and their contents, and it's difficult to reconstruct an entire culture simply by looking at its graveyards. Etruscan society may have been more egalitarian than later Western cultures, or at least women appeared to have more of an active role and a higher status in daily life. Historians say they loved to throw parties, have banquets, go on the hunt, and the like—but that may just be what they chose to celebrate in the few paintings and many carvings they left us. While we can read their language, what script we have goes into little beyond death, divination, and the divine.

What historians are surer of is that Etruscans became enamored with the Attic culture of Greece and adopted many of the Greek gods and myths, as well as many Greek vases, in the 6th century B.C. This era coincided with the height of their considerable power. In fact, from the late 7th century until 510 B.C., Rome was ruled by Etruscan kings of the Tarquin dynasty. Although the Etruscan empire spread south almost to Naples, east to the Adriatic, and west onto Corsica, the heart and core called Etruria covered an area from the Arno east to the Apennines and south to the Tiber, encompassing most of Tuscany, half of Umbria, and northern Lazio.

The Etruscans surrounded their cities with massive defensive walls, were adept bridge builders, and developed sophisticated canal, sewer, and irrigation systems for their cities and fields, draining marshy lands for farming and sinking wells and cisterns and carving

570–774 The Lombard duchies rule over much of Tuscany and Umbria.

774–800s Charlemagne picks up where the Lombards left off.

951 The German emperors and the pope begin to quarrel.

1125 Florence razes neighbor Fiesole to the ground. Florentine expansion begins.

1155 Frederick Barbarossa is crowned emperor of Europe and attempts to take control of part of Italy.

1173 Pisa begins its bell tower. Eleven years later, someone notices the tilt.

1215 Florentine families take sides in the conflict between the emperor (Guelf) and the pope (Ghibelline). Tuscany follows suit.

1250–1600 The Humanist era, when intellectual pursuit of knowledge and study of the classical and Arab worlds take precedence over blind Christian doctrine and superstition and lift Europe out of its medieval stupor.

1284 Genoa trounces Pisa's fleet in the naval Battle of Meloria. A long Pisan decline begins.

1290s Giotto frescoes the *Life of St. Francis* in Assisi. Painting would never be the same.

1300 The Guelfs finally win in Florence and immediately split into the White and the Black factions.

1301 Florence conquers Pistoia.

1302 Dante is exiled from Florence on trumped-up charges. He never returns.

1303–77 The pope moves from Rome to Avignon. Ambassador St. Catherine of Siena is instrumental in returning the papacy to Italy.

1308–21 Dante writes the *Divine Comedy,* which sets the Tuscan dialect as the predecessor of modern Italian.

1310 Siena runs its first Palio race on record.

1348 The Black Death rips through Italy, killing more than half the population. Siena loses more than two thirds of its citizens.

1361 Florence conquers Volterra.

continues

plumbing systems in the rock beneath their cities. (The famous Roman plumbing network was started by the Etruscan kings of Rome.)

Well before this time, around 1200 B.C., Indo-European Italic peoples had wandered into Italy from the north. The Samnites and Latins continued south, but the **Umbri** tribes decided to settle in the Apennines and valleys east of the Tiber, which flows through the middle of modern-day Umbria. Their loosely defined zone of cultural hegemony encompassed what is now northern and eastern Umbria and the Marches over to the sea, as well as corners of Tuscany and Emilia-Romagna. (Modern city descendants include Gubbio and Città di Castello, as well as Assisi and Todi, both of which later became Etruscan and then Roman.) All we really know about the Umbri is they had a highly developed religion based on reading prophecies in animal sacrifices and the flights of birds—Gubbio's famous Eugubian Tables bronze plaques tell us this much. When the Roman influence spread north in the 3rd century B.C., the Umbrian cities for the most part allied themselves to the Latins, were awarded Roman citizenship early, and enjoyed a large degree of autonomy from authorities in Rome. Aside from the usual city rivalries and moderate clashes between expanding empires, the Umbrians appear to have lived more or less amicably with their Etruscan neighbors.

At the close of the 5th century B.C., the Etruscan empire was pushed back from the south by the Greeks and from the north by the Celtic tribes. After expelling the last Etruscan king, Tarquin the Proud, and setting up a republic, Rome in the 3rd century B.C. started nipping at the heels of Etruria itself.

ENTER THE ROMANS: THE FOUNDING OF FLORENCE

In the 3rd century B.C., that Latin city on the Tiber called **Rome** began its

- **1378–1417** The Great Western Schism. Avignon, Rome, *and* Pisa each appoint a pope and the competing pontiffs busy themselves excommunicating one another.
- **1384** Florence conquers Arezzo.
- **1401** Lorenzo Ghiberti wins the competition to cast the baptistery doors in Florence. May the Renaissance begin!
- **1406** Florence conquers Pisa.
- **1434–64** Cosimo il Vecchio consolidates the Medici power over Florence.
- **1439** The Council of Florence takes place, whereby Eastern and Western churches briefly reconcile their ancient differences.
- **1469–92** The rule of Lorenzo de' Medici the Magnificent in Florence. The arts flourish under his patronage.
- **1475** Michelangelo Buonarotti is born in Caprese, near Arezzo.
- **1494** Puritanical Fra' Girolamo Savonarola helps drive the Medici from Florence and takes control of the city.
- **1495** The Bonfire of the Vanities. At Savonarola's urging, Florentines carry material goods seen as decadent, including paintings by Botticelli, Lorenzo di Credi, and others, to Piazza della Signoria and set them on fire.
- **1498** At the pope's urging, Florentines carry Savonarola to Piazza della Signoria and set *him* on fire.
- **1498–1512** The Florentine Republic is free from the Medici.
- **1501–04** Michelangelo carves *David*.
- **1505** For a few months, Leonardo da Vinci, Michelangelo, and Raphael all live and work in Florence at the same time.
- **1527** Charles V sacks Rome. Medici Pope Clement VII escapes to Orvieto, where by papal bull he refuses to annul Henry VIII's marriage to Catherine of Aragon (foundation of the Anglican Church).
- **1530** The Medici firmly takes back power in Florence.
- **1550** Vasari publishes *The Lives of the Artists,* the first art history book.

expansion, and some of the first neighboring peoples to fall were the Etruscans. Some cities, such as Perugia and Arezzo, allied themselves with Rome and were merely absorbed, while others, such as Volterra and Orvieto, were conquered outright. The Romans brought with them the combination of a highly conservative (some say stagnant) culture coupled with a certain degree of adaptability to local religious beliefs and social modes that allowed their empire to stay solvent for so long. As the Romans gained power over the entire peninsula, the removal of political barriers and the construction of roads allowed trade to develop and flow relatively uninhibited.

Many of the old cities flourished, and the general prosperity led to the founding of new cities throughout the region, especially as retirement camps for Roman soldiers. While the Etruscans were keen on building cities on hilltops—both for easy defensibility and to leave more valley land free for farming—the Romans preferred flat ground along rivers, which allowed them to lay out exacting street-plan grids oriented precisely to the points of the compass. They were fanatically single-minded about city planning, rarely wavering from this model.

During the lull of the later Roman Empire, **Christianity** quickly spread throughout much of central Italy—Lucca even claims to have converted in the 1st century A.D. through the efforts of one of St. Peter's own followers, though Pisa tries to one-up its neighbors by claiming a church first built by St. Peter.

GOTHS, LOMBARDS & FRANKS: THE DARK AGES

As the Roman Empire collapsed in the 5th century A.D., Germanic tribes swept down from the north and wreaked mayhem on central Italian cities as group after group fought their way

- 1555–57 Florence conquers Siena.
- 1569 Cosimo I de' Medici becomes the grand duke of Tuscany.
- 1581 The Uffizi opens as a painting gallery.
- 1633 The Inquisition forces Galileo to recant his theory that Earth revolves around the Sun.
- 1737 Gian Gastone, last of the Medici grand dukes, dies.
- 1796–1806 Napoléon sweeps through Italy several times, eventually declaring himself king of Italy.
- 1806 Napoléon gives Lucca to his sister Elisa as a duchy.
- 1814–15 Napoléon is exiled to Elba, which he rules as governor.
- 1824 Lorraine Grand Duke Leopold II starts draining Maremma. The reclamation is finished in 1950 with the defeat of malaria.
- 1848–60 The Risorgimento intellectual movement considers a unified Italy.
- 1860 Tuscany joins the new Kingdom of Italy.
- 1865–70 Florence serves as Italy's capital.
- 1922 Mussolini becomes the Fascist dictator of Italy.
- 1940–45 World War II. Fascist Italy participates as an Axis power.
- 1944 Nazi troops withdraw from Florence, blowing up the Arno bridges. At Hitler's direct order, the Ponte Vecchio is spared.
- 1946 Italy becomes a republic.
- 1946–97 Italy averages a new national government every 9 months (though until 1993, usually merely different arrangements of Christian Democrat Party).
- 1948 Italy's regions are created. Tuscany and Umbria finally get an official dividing line between them.
- 1966 The Arno flood in Florence. Up to 6m (20 ft.) of water and mud destroys or damages countless works of art and literature.
- 1985 Italy's worst winter on record; the frost hits grapevines heavily and comes close to destroying all the olive trees in Tuscany.

continues

down to Rome in a sacking free-for-all, pillaging all the way down and often on the way back north as well. A few tribes decided to engage in a bit of empire-building themselves. The **Ostrogoths** got Ravenna on the Adriatic coast, and when the Byzantine Empire established its base there, it often made attempts to conquer Italy, starting with the first lands it came to: Umbria and Tuscany. The **Goths** swept down in the 6th century A.D., and one of their leaders, **Totila,** conquered Florence in A.D. 552.

Perhaps the strongest force in the Dark Ages were the **Lombards,** who, after settling in the Po Valley in the north of Italy (Milan's region is still called Lombardy), expanded south as well starting in the mid–6th century. They established two major duchies in central Italy, one based at Lucca, which governed most of Tuscany, and the other at Spoleto, which took care of most of Umbria. When their ambitions threatened Rome (now a church stronghold) in the 8th century, the pope invited the Frankish king Pepin the Short to come clear the Lombards out. Under Pepin, and, more important, his son **Charlemagne,** the Lombards were ousted from Tuscany and Umbria.

The Lombard duchy at Lucca was merely replaced by a Frankish margrave, with Tuscany ruled by powerful figures like the **Margrave Matilda.** Charlemagne gave the lands he took from the duchy of Spoleto directly to the pope, but the pontiffs gradually lost control over the region as they busied themselves with other concerns.

With the breakup of Charlemagne's empire in the 9th century, the German emperors started pressing claims over the Italian peninsula. The thorny question of who should wield temporal power, the pope in Rome or the German emperor, embroiled European politics on the larger scale for several centuries. (The effects of this struggle on Tuscany and Umbria

- **1988** Pedestrian zones go into effect in major cities, making historic centers traffic-free (almost).
- **1993** On May 27, a car bomb rips through the west wing of the Uffizi, killing five people and damaging many paintings. Italy's Christian Democratic government, in power since the end of World War II, dissolves in a flurry of scandal. In a chain reaction, far left and right also splinter; more than 16 major parties vie for power in various improbable coalitions.
- **1996** Italy's national government falters again, and Parliament is disbanded. The center-left Olive Tree coalition takes the lion's share of power, with Romano Prodi as prime minister.
- **1997** In Assisi, a series of earthquakes hit the region, and part of the basilica's ceiling collapses, destroying frescoes and damaging Giotto's *Life of St. Francis.*
- **1998** After an unusually long reign, Prodi's coalition dissolves and a new center-left alliance led by Prime Minister Massimo D'Alema eases into power.
- **1999** All Tuscany rejoices when local filmmaker Roberto Benigni, after a victory at Cannes, gathers three Oscars for his Holocaust fable *La Vita è Bella (Life Is Beautiful).*
- **2001** The first cases of BSE (mad cow disease) in Italy are confirmed. Beef consumption plummets over 70%, and the government considers banning such culinary institutions as the famed *bistecca alla fiorentina.* The year ends on a high note as, after more than a decade of desperate measures to keep the Leaning Tower of Pisa from tilting to the point of collapse, the work pays off and the tower reopens to the public. Don't worry—it still leans.
- **2002** On January 2, Italy, along with most of Western Europe, adopts the euro as its currency. On January 2, prices skyrocket.

are discussed under "Guelfs & Ghibellines: A Medieval Mess," below). On the smaller scale, central Italy was plunged into political chaos out of which emerged for the first time the independent city-state republic known as the *comune*.

THE MEDIEVAL *COMUNE:* AN IMPERFECT DEMOCRACY

In the late 11th century, merchants became wealthier and more important to the daily economic life of the small Italian cities, just as the old landed aristocracy was becoming obsolete with the collapse of the feudal system. Many of these merchants were minor gentry who began to get involved in trade and in big business like the textile industry and banking. They organized themselves into **guilds** and gradually became the bourgeoisie oligarchic leaders of the cities. The self-governing *comuni* they established weren't the perfect democracies they've often been made out to be. While many were ruled by popularly elected **councils,** usually only the guild members of the middle class were enfranchised. The majority of city laborers, as well as the rural farmers, remained powerless.

In a tradition first inaugurated by the emperor Frederick Barbarossa, whose empire tenuously extended through the area in the early 13th century, these councils became primarily legislative, while the executive power was placed in the hands of a **podestà**. This sort of governor or mayor was usually brought in from out of town to govern for a set period of time (often a year). It was believed an out-of-towner would be less likely to play favorites with the local powerful families or factions vying for power and could therefore rule more evenhandedly.

As the *comuni* thus stabilized their infrastructures—after dealing with blows like the 1348 Black Death, a plague that swept through Europe and left well over half of central Italy's population dead, they also set about roughing up their neighbors and traditional rivals. Battles were fought both to increase the city-states' trading power and to acquire more towns under their control (or at least secure subservient allies). To this end, instead of raising militia armies, they hired **condottieri,** professional soldiers of fortune who controlled forces of armed mercenaries. These soldiers came from all over and all walks of life.

Many of these trade wars and ancient rivalries were fought between cities that used Europe's big power struggle of the age—the Holy Roman Emperor versus the pope—as an excuse to attack their traditional antagonists. Although in the end the terms *Guelf* and *Ghibelline* meant little to the parties involved (even if they did

■ **2003** Prime Minster Berlusconi, who through private media holdings and his government post controls 98% of Italian television (not to mention the country's largest publishing empire), and who last fall fired his foreign minister and declared he himself would run that office, forces through legislation to protect him from being prosecuted for any crimes while in office—conveniently just as one of the many bribery cases that have been brought against him was about to come to a conclusion.

Looking for Etruscan Remains

If you want to check out some Etruscan remains, head to the following towns: **Volterra** (a museum, a city gate, and walls), **Chiusi** (underground aqueducts to tour and many tombs in the area), **Arezzo** (a museum), **Cortona** (a museum and tombs), **Perugia** (a city gate and a well), and **Orvieto** (tombs, museums, underground tunnels to tour, and a well). There are also major Tuscan finds collected at the archaeological museum in **Florence**.

Guelf or Ghibelline?

Though it's admittedly not the perfect measure, you can sometimes tell which a city was, at least at any given time, by looking at the battlements of the medieval town hall: The **Guelfs** favored squared-off crenellations and the **Ghibellines** swallowtail ones.

Exceptions to this are Siena's **Palazzo Pubblico,** which was built with blocky battlements during the briefly Guelf period of the Council of Nine, and Florence's **Palazzo Vecchio,** which confusingly sports both kinds.

have overriding and longer-term effects on the towns that defined themselves as one or the other), the conflict between these factions comes up constantly in medieval Tuscany and Umbria, so the history behind it bears a brief overview.

GUELFS & GHIBELLINES: A MEDIEVAL MESS

At this time in Europe, two entities competed for absolute power over the continent, the emperor and the pope, who used the argument over who got to appoint parish priests as an excuse to vie for control of Europe. The terms that came to describe Italian supporters of the emperor and Italian supporters of the pope actually stemmed from a German conflict over imperial succession.

In the 12th century, the German throne of the Holy Roman Emperor sat empty. Otto IV's family, the Welf dynasty of Bavaria, fought for it against the lords of Waiblingen, where the house of Swabia ruled under the Hohenstaufen dynasty. The names were corrupted in Italian to **Guelf** and **Ghibelline,** respectively, and when the Hohenstaufens came out winners with Frederick Barbarossa being crowned emperor, the Ghibellines stuck as the supporters of the emperor while the Guelfs became the party that backed the pope.

In Italy, the issue was all about who got to be in charge: the old nobility, who as Ghibellines favored the imperial promise of a return to feudalism and hence their own power, or the Guelf merchant-and-banking middle class, who supported the pope and his free-trade attitudes. While these terms did mean something regarding which faction, nobles or merchants, controlled any one city, they were used mainly to define one city in terms of its opposition to rival cities. So if your rivals were Ghibelline, you'd go Guelf, and if they turned Guelf for some reason, you usually swung around to Ghibelline pretty quickly. Although they all flip-flopped to some degree, Florence (plus Lucca, Arezzo, and Perugia) turned out Guelf, which made rivals Pisa, Pistoia, and Siena Ghibelline.

The Guelf/Ghibelline conflict not only spawned intercity warfare but also sparked intracity strife between rival factions. The most famous intracity conflict occurred in Florence in the 13th century, when powerful warring clans each took up arms and called in alliances, and the city split into Guelf and Ghibelline parties, under which names the parties waged a decades-long struggle over who'd control the city government. In Florence, when the Guelfs finally won in the late 13th century, they further divided into two factions, the **Blacks** (Guelfs) and the **Whites** (Ghibellines, but only because they hated Pope Boniface VIII). When the Blacks came out on top, they exiled the Whites, among whom was a Florentine White Guelf ambassador named Dante who lived the rest of his life in exile, perfecting his poetry.

Florence began to enjoy, at the turn of the 14th century when the Black Guelfs finally came out victorious, a fairly stable republican rule—still of the old assembly system called now the **Signoria,** a ruling council elected from the major guilds.

Florence slowly expanded its power, first allying with Prato, then conquering Pistoia, and by 1406 adding Volterra, Arezzo, and Pisa to the cities under its rule.

As the major guilds accrued more and more power and the top merchants seized control of Florence, the minor guilds and lesser merchants looked to one of the few renegade merchant families sympathetic to their plight. It was an upstart family that, with a bit of luck, had recently risen from virtual anonymity to become one of the most successful banking houses in the city. It was a clan without a particularly distinguished pedigree, a fact that kept them from being fully accepted by the major guild leaders who came from old Florentine families. They called themselves the Medici.

THE RENAISSANCE: CUE THE MEDICI

The Medici came from the hills of the Mugello in the early Middle Ages, quite possibly charcoal burners looking for the good life of the city. The family found moderate success and even had a few members elected to public office in the *comune* government.

At the turn of the 15th century, **Giovanni de' Bicci de' Medici** made the family fortune through a series of shrewd moves establishing the Medici as bankers to the papal curia in Rome. His son, Cosimo de' Medici, called **Cosimo il Vecchio,** orchestrated a number of important alliances and treaties for the Florentine Signoria, gaining him prestige and respect. Though wary enemies like the Albizzi feared Cosimo's growing power—even though he rarely held any official office—and got him imprisoned and then exiled in 1341, he was soon recalled by the Florentine people.

As Cosimo il Vecchio's behind-the-scenes power grew, he made sure to remain almost always a private citizen and businessman, serving the needs and interests of the working and middle class without needlessly angering the big fish in town. While his position also helped him increase his personal fortune, he took care to spend lavishly on the city, building churches, establishing charities, and patronizing artists. He was a humanist leader who believed in the power of the emerging new art forms of the early Renaissance, and he commissioned works from the greatest painters, sculptors, and architects of the day.

Cosimo grew so attached to the sculptor Donatello that, as Cosimo lay dying, he made sure his son, **Piero the Gouty,** promised to care for the also aging artist and to see that he never lacked for work. Cosimo, as a properly modest ruler, was so beloved by the people that they buried him under the inscription *pater patirae* (father of the homeland). Piero's rule was short and relatively undistinguished, quickly superseded by the brilliant career of his son, Lorenzo de' Medici, called **Lorenzo the Magnificent.**

Under the late-15th-century rule of Lorenzo, Florence entered its golden era, during which time it became Europe's cultural and artistic focal point. It was Lorenzo who encouraged the young Michelangelo to sculpt, and he and Medici cousins commissioned paintings from Botticelli and poetry from Poliziano. Lorenzo founded a Platonic academy to further the study of the classical world and was himself an accomplished poet. His political reign was a bit rocky at times; though he continued in his grandfather's manner to be a behind-the-scenes manipulator and adjudicator (and never actually led his city by title), he was a bit more overt about who was actually running the show.

Although Lorenzo fought to maintain the precious balance of power between Italian city-states, in doing so he incurred the wrath of the pope and the Pazzi family, Florentine rivals of the Medici. The young Medici leader's troubles came to a head in the infamous 1478 Pazzi Conspiracy, in which Lorenzo and his brother were attacked during High Mass. The coup failed, and the Pazzi were expelled from the city, which in the end helped solidify Medici power over Florence. Lorenzo, however, was less adept than his grandfather at managing the family bank (losing the papal account had something to do with it, along with well-meaning mismanagement by assistants). His son and successor, **Piero de' Medici,** was almost immediately forced to flee the invading armies of Charles VIII in 1494 (although Charles quickly withdrew from the Italian field).

Into the power vacuum stepped puritanical preacher **Girolamo Savonarola.** This theocrat's apocalyptic visions and book-burning (the original Bonfire of the Vanities) held the public's fancy for about 4 years, until the pope excommunicated the entire city for following him, and the Florentines called it quits, putting the torch to Savonarola as a heretic.

A free republic took Savonarola's place, happily governing itself and commissioning artworks from the likes of Michelangelo and Leonardo da Vinci, and placing Machiavelli in charge of organizing a citizen's militia. In 1512, however, papal armies set another of Lorenzo's sons, the boring young **Giuliano de' Medici,** duke of Nemours, on the vacant Medici throne. Giuliano, and later **Lorenzo de' Medici** (Lorenzo the Magnificent's grandson via the ousted Piero) were merely mouthpieces for the real brains of the family, Giuliano's brother, **Cardinal Giovanni de' Medici,** who in 1513 became **Pope Leo X** and uttered the immortal words "God has given us the papacy, now let us enjoy it."

Pope Leo's successor as leader of the Medici was his natural cousin, **Giulio de' Medici,** illegitimate son of Lorenzo's brother Giuliano. Although blackguards such as Ippolito and **Alessandro de' Medici** held sway in Florence, they really took their orders from Giulio, who from 1523 to 1534 continued to run the family from Rome as **Pope Clement VII.**

Charles V's imperial armies sacked Rome in 1527, sending Clement VII scurrying to Orvieto for safety and giving the Florentines the excuse to boot Alessandro from town and set up a republican government again. In 1530, however, the pope and Charles reconciled and sent a combined army to siege Florence, which hired Michelangelo to design part of the defenses, and eventually Alessandro was reinstated. This time he had an official title: **Duke of Florence.**

After decadently amusing himself as a tyrant in Florence for 7 years, during which time Clement VII died and Alessandro inherited full power, Alessandro was murdered in bed while awaiting what he thought was a secret tryst with a virtuous woman but in reality was a setup by his distant cousin Lorenzaccio de' Medici, who plunged a dagger into the duke's belly and fled to Venice (where he was later assassinated).

The man chosen to take Alessandro's place was a Medici of a different branch, a descendant of Cosimo il Vecchio's brother and the son of the virtuous and valorous warrior, Giovanni delle Bande Nere. All the hidden powers of Florence thought young **Cosimo de' Medici** would be easily controlled when they named him duke of Florence. They were wrong.

Contrary to his immediate Medici predecessors, Cosimo I actually devoted himself to attending to matters of state. He built up a navy, created a seaport for Florence called Livorno, ruled firmly but judiciously (he never was very popular, though), and even conquered age-old rival Siena after a brutal war from 1555 to 1557. His greatest personal moment came in 1569 when his—and through him, Florence's—authority over Tuscany was recognized by the pope, who declared him **Cosimo I, Grand Duke of Tuscany.** Except for the tiny Republic of Lucca, which

The Dignity of the Last Medici Grand Duke

Grand Duke Gian Gastone barely showed his face outside the Pitti Palace—except on one memorable carriage ride through town to prove he was alive, during which he occupied himself by vomiting out the window.

happily trundled along independently until Napoléon gave it to his sister in 1806, the history of Tuscany was now firmly intertwined with that of Florence.

A TUSCAN GRAND DUCHY: THE LONG SNORE

Cosimo's descendants continued to rule Florence and Tuscany in a pretty even, if uneventful, manner. Florence had already begun its long economic decline as a European power. The grand dukes became increasingly pretentious but for the most part harmless. Most did uphold the family intellectual tradition of patronizing the arts (unfortunately, many had a remarkable lack of good taste) and defending the sciences. It was largely due to **Cosimo II's** protection that Pisan scientist **Galileo** wasn't outright executed by the Inquisition for his heretical view that Earth revolved around the sun. The 49-year reign of the bookish if generally genial **Ferdinando II** was marked by nothing so much as a desire not to get involved in any nasty international affairs. The worst were men like the prudish glutton **Cosimo III,** a religious fanatic, money scrimper, and persecutor of Jews.

The last Medici grand duke was **Gian Gastone,** an obese sensualist who spent the few hours he wasn't passed out in a wine-sodden stupor playing with nubile young men in bed. No one mourned his passing in 1737, when the grand dukedom passed to the Austrian **Lorraine** family, married into the Medici line for years. The Lorraines ruled with a much heavier hand and, even worse, a general disregard for traditional Florentine values. The citizens found themselves almost missing the Medici.

Gian Gastone was survived by his sister, **Anna Maria de' Medici,** a devout and dignified lady who, on her 1743 death, willed that the new Lorraine grand dukes would inherit the Medici's vast and mind-bogglingly valuable collection of art, manuscripts, furniture, books, and jewelry. She had only two conditions: None of it could ever be removed from Florence, and it all had to be made available to the public. The works of art filling the Uffizi, the Pitti Palace, and the Bargello are just the beginning of the artistic legacy Anna Maria created for Florence. It was her generosity that helped turn Florence into one of the world's greatest museums and a tourist mecca.

THE RISORGIMENTO: ITALY BECOMES A COUNTRY

The Savoy kings of the northwestern Italian region of Piedmont decided to create a kingdom of Italy in the late 1800s. In 1859, the last Lorraine grand duke, Leopold II, abdicated and in 1860, Florence and Tuscany became part of the newly declared Italian state. From 1865 to 1870, Florence was the capital of Italy, and it enjoyed a frenzied building boom to turn it into such—the medieval walls were torn down and the Jewish ghetto demolished and replaced with the cafe-lined Piazza della Repubblica, and the city quickly gentrified.

The army that was conquering recalcitrant states on the peninsula for **Vittorio Emanuele II,** first king of Italy, was commanded by **Gen. Giuseppe Garibaldi,** who spent much of the end of the war slowly subjugating the papal states—the pope was the last holdout against the new regime. This meant defeating the papal authorities in Umbria, whose armies, however, quickly retreated, leaving cities like

Perugia to cheer on Garibaldi's troops as they freed the region from hundreds of years of papal oppression.

FASCISM: GETTING ROPED INTO WORLD WAR II

The demagogue **Benito Mussolini** came to power after World War I and did much to improve Italy's infrastructure—at least on the surface—and in the process won the respect of many Italians. His Fascist regime accomplished the improbable: drumming up national sentiment in a country where most people, far from normally feeling any sort of patriotism, still looked on the folk in the village 5 miles down the road as foreigners. Then Mussolini got caught up with Hitler's World War II egomania, believing that Italy should have a second empire as great as the ancient Roman one.

Although the Tuscans certainly had their share of collaborators and die-hard Fascists, many Italians never bought into the war or the Axis alliance. Partisan movement was always strong, with resistance fighters holed up, especially in the hills south of Siena. Tuscany became a battlefield as the occupying Nazi troops slowly withdrew across the landscape in the face of American and Allied advancement.

POSTWAR ITALY

Florence was hit with disaster when a massive **flooding of the Arno** in 1966 covered much of the city with up to 6m (20 ft.) of sludge and water, destroying or severely damaging countless thousands of works of art and literature (8,000 paintings in the Uffizi basement alone, and 1.5 million volumes in the National Library). Along with an army of experts and trained restorers, hundreds of volunteers nicknamed "Mud Angels" descended on the city, many of them foreign students, to pitch in and help dig out all the mud and salvage what they could of one of the greatest artistic heritages of any city on earth.

The fortunes of Tuscany and Umbria have in the past 50 years mainly followed those of Italy at large. After the multiple dissolutions of parliament and resignations of prime ministers amid rampant scandal from 1993 to 1996, Romano Prodi and the center-left **Olive Tree coalition** managed to hold power for more than 3 years—a record of sorts in Italy, which since World War II had averaged a new government every 9 months. The Prodi government eased nicely into the similarly left-leaning coalition headed by Prime Minster Massimo D'Alema. But local elections began swinging back to the right of center, and in 2001, media magnate (and the world's 29th richest man) Silvio Berlusconi—briefly prime minister in 1993 but brought down by professional and political scandals—gained control once again of the Italian government as part of a center-right coalition including the neo-Fascist Alleanza Nazionale party and the racist and separatist Lega del Nord.

On a smaller scale, Tuscany and Umbria have seen both sorrow and joy over the past several years. In late 1997, Umbria was rocked by a series of massive earthquakes that destroyed town centers, left thousands homeless, and damaged artistic patrimonies. The most notable victim was Assisi, where many churches and buildings sustained such structural damage they remained closed until 2002 (many private dwellings are still unsafe and stand abandoned). The famed Basilica di San Francesco lost several Cimabue frescoes in a tremor that shook down the painted ceiling of the Upper Church, killing two hapless monks and partially damaging Giotto's renowned frescoes. The Lower Church reopened within weeks, but the major restoration on the Upper Basilica took 2 years (and some of it is still ongoing, though it no longer interferes with tourist visits). Tuscany has also recently enjoyed a unique sort of renaissance in the world of the cinema, led by Prato-area native Roberto Benigni's Oscar-winning *La Vita è Bella (Life Is Beautiful)*, a fable about the Holocaust.

But putting aside glamour and catastrophe, Tuscany and Umbria today thrive on two main sources of economy and livelihood: the land and tourism. Both regions continue to be breadbaskets—and even more, wine casks—in Italy, and most of the citizens are involved in the agricultural industry in some way. Events like the winter of 1985—when the Arno froze, and the lingering frost almost wiped out every last one of central Italy's olive trees—hit the economy so hard they're still recovering. A bad year for the grapes can mean that half of Tuscany takes a major hit.

Mass tourism loves Tuscany. Florence is an essential stop on almost every package tour, and the region is by far Italy's most famous, often the only one foreigners known by name. It's also a precarious economy—witness the drastic decline in tourism dollars in Italy in the wake of the World Trade Center attacks—one that even in peaceful times is dependent on the economies of other countries.

Tourism can have detrimental effects on the vitality of a city as well. Many historic cores, Florence's included, have been all but given over to the tourists, with locals moving to the suburbs or to another city entirely. Part of what drives them out are the increasing restrictions on movement: While it was difficult a decade ago not to cheer as pedestrian-only zones started being erected in Italy's city centers, it does exacerbate an already horrible traffic problem, with parking lots taking over central piazze that were once important communal gathering places. It must be said, though, that much of the dilemma has been created by poor management of the pedestrianizing movement. Umbrian cities have actually been some of the most successful in Italy at the transformation. By creating large parking lots underground and in the valleys below the hilltop cities, and connecting them with town via elevators, escalators, and cog railways, cities like Orvieto, Perugia, and Assisi have actually managed to make themselves blessedly traffic-free without creating too much of a hassle for those with cars.

Luckily, initiatives like those described above have been doing away with traffic difficulties. But the most egregious problem remains the pollution—all those Fiats with no catalytic converters (*still* not required, or fitted, on Italian cars) spewing horrendous amounts of emission and pollutants into the air. In the past, Florence has actually had to issue warnings on certain summer days when, without wind to help carry some of the smog off, they've advised children and the elderly to stay indoors or wear masks to go outside. More visibly, the pollution blackens the historic buildings and outdoor sculpture on which the cities depend for their very survival. So public funds are raised to sandblast the local Duomo every 2 or 4 years, and half the monuments in the country stay wrapped in scaffolding at any given time for cleaning.

2 Art & Architecture 101

FROM CLASSICAL TO ROMANESQUE: THE 8TH CENTURY B.C. TO THE 12TH CENTURY A.D.

ANCIENT ART   The pre-Etruscan **Villanovians** have left us little more than pottery shards, and the Etruscans' neighbors, the Umbri, even less. The prehistoric art remnants of greatest note in Tuscany are the **Lunigiana** cult's statue-stele in Pontrémoli, which is part of Tuscany only on political maps; the culture and the art really belongs to the Ligurian peoples of the nearby coastal province.

The **Etruscans** were prodigious town planners (see "A Look at the Past," earlier in this chapter). In architecture, they used the load-bearing arch, raised rectangular temples approached by steps as the Romans later adopted, and built houses with open atrium courtyards surrounded by colonnaded porticos on the inner face.

Though precious little Etruscan painting survives, the Etruscans were masters of this art form. They painted—in fresco, to boot—scenes rich in the pleasures of everyday life, especially banqueting. What we have most of is their sculpture, which went through an idiosyncratic archaic period (with some Oriental influences), through an Attic period influenced by the art of ancient Greece, and was finally subsumed under the Hellenistic Roman style. They cranked out thousands of votive bronzes—small representations of warriors, washerwomen, and farmers plowing—occasionally producing works of singular expressive beauty, such as Volterra's famed *Shadow of the Evening*.

The Etruscans' most famous forms of sculpture are their **funerary urns,** each of which was capped with a lid carved into a likeness of the deceased, half-reclining as if at an eternal banquet. Most of these have intense expressions and enigmatic smiles that have made them a popular modern image to represent Etruria in general. As Greek culture began to seep in during the 6th century B.C., the cinerary urns under these lids were increasingly carved with reliefs depicting scenes from Greek mythology, often having to do with the movement to the underworld (riding in carts, boats, chariots, and the like).

As **Rome** gained ascendancy in the 3rd century B.C., its conservative and static style of carving, architecture, and painting supplanted the more naturalized and dynamic nature of the Etruscan arts. Keep in mind that Tuscany and Umbria never truly became Roman—Rome's rule just Latinized the adaptable Etruscans and Umbri. The Romans have left us many of their Hellenistic bronze and marble statues, innumerable fragments of decorative friezes and other reliefs, and several theaters and baths in varying stages of decay (at Fiesole, Volterra, Gubbio, and Spoleto). Their most prevalent legacy is perhaps the grid layout that still shows through the street plans of the retirement towns, such as Florence and Lucca, they built for their soldiers.

PALEO-CHRISTIAN ART   The Germanic and later the Frankish invaders who swept down from the north brought with them a meager building and decorative statuary style. Nonetheless, their influence on native primitive modes, as well as late Imperial Roman holdovers like the basilican plan for a church (basilicas started out as Roman law courts), filled the 4th to 11th centuries with what's often referred to as the **Paleo-Christian** style. This period was marked by very simple structures; the few of which survive—including churches in Spoleto, Pienza, and Perugia, and the later and much more unified Sant'Antimo—strike most moderns as hauntingly beautiful and elegant, if architecturally inharmonious. In the north of Tuscany, the architecture quickly developed into the style known as Romanesque (see below).

The sculpted elements of the Paleo-Christian era that are particularly charming—with animal heads, biblical scenes, and fantastically complicated allegories played out in a rough primitive style—are best exemplified in the works of **Guido da Como.** The Paleo-Christians also caught some interior decorative stylings from the nearby empire of Byzantium, especially in the use of glittering gold mosaics. The Byzantines, however, had a much greater influence on Italian painting.

BYZANTINE PAINTING   The political influence of the Byzantine Empire, based in Constantinople, was confined to Italy's northeastern Adriatic coast. But the artistic influence of Byzantium's stylized iconographic tradition in mosaics and panel paintings spread throughout Italy, starting from the Adriatic city of Ravenna in the 5th century.

Byzantine painting is characterized in individual works by gold-leaf backgrounds, stylized gold crosshatching in the blue and red robes of the Madonna, oval faces with large almond eyes and spoonlike depressions at the tops of sloping noses, a flattened look (due to an almost complete lack of perspective or foreshortening), and, above all, conservatism.

Byzantine art had an Oriental decorativeness and severely static rule ensuring the reproduction of icons that wavered little from past models. It kept Italian painting moribund for over 800 years. Painting didn't break out of the conservative funk until the late 13th century, when the International Gothic style finally shook things up (see below).

ROMANESQUE ARCHITECTURE   When Pisa became a major medieval power, it did so as a huge shipping empire, and with this trade came contact with Eastern and Islamic cultures. Pisa poured its 11th-century prosperity into building a new religious core and cathedral, adapting many of the decorative elements from these Eastern contacts. The style that was developed in **Buschetto**'s Duomo and the associated baptistery and bell tower (yes, the one that leans) came to define the Romanesque and quickly spread across northern Tuscany.

The purest, earliest form that arose in Pisa and Lucca—known, sensibly, as the **Pisan-Luccan Romanesque**—was characterized most strikingly by horizontal stripes of marbles on the facades and eventually in some interiors as well (at first they used green and white; later, in Siena, it became black and white; and in Umbria the available local stone made it pink and white). The other key elements were curving semicircular arches; blind arcades of these arches often set with diamond-shaped decorative inlays (or coffered depressions) called lozenges; open galleries supported by thin mismatched columns and often stacked three or four rows high on facades; lots of tiny detail in marble inlay; and often a nave flanked by two colonnaded aisles inside. They also made use of the gold-based mosaics of the Byzantine style, particularly to fill the half-dome of the apse.

The later form of the movement that was adapted in Florence (the Baptistery, San Miniato al Monte, and Badia Fiesolana) and Pistoia (San Giovanni Fuoricivitas and, though later altered, the Duomo) was called the **Florentine Romanesque.** On the surface it was very similar to the Pisan-Lucchese school, but it was practiced along much stricter lines of a geometry gleaned from classical architecture, a predecessor to the mathematically proportional architecture of the Renaissance. Before that could come to pass, however, in the late 12th century a strong northern styling came into vogue called, after its supposed association with the emperors (whether German or Frankish), the Gothic.

INTERNATIONAL GOTHIC: THE 13TH & 14TH CENTURIES

The **Gothic** first started infiltrating Italy as architecture. It was originally imported by French Cistercian monks, who in 1218 created the huge San Galgano abbey church, now roofless (and terribly romantic). Although this French style of the Gothic never caught on, the church was still at the time revolutionary in introducing some of the new forms, which were adopted when **Giovanni Pisano** overhauled Siena's cathedral and Gothicized it.

The preaching orders of monks were responsible for the spread of Gothic architecture. Because it allowed for huge barnlike churches with a single wide nave and few supports, the architecture was convenient for Dominicans and Franciscans who needed to be able to pack throngs of people into the churches to hear their sermons. Almost every major city has at least one of these usually aisleless churches with a rounded apse or squared-off choir behind the altar and a short transept of chapels off either side of it.

The thin-columned windows and lacelike stone tracery the Gothic style used to fill up arch points and the crenellations it strewed across the tops of buildings caught the Tuscan fancy and were incorporated into many palaces, especially in Siena, where the architectural forms otherwise pretty much stayed the same old solid, reliable medieval masonry. Out of this marriage were born the civic palaces of Siena and, more important, Volterra, which served as the model for Florence's own famous Palazzo Vecchio (and similar buildings across the region).

The Palazzo Vecchio's architect was **Arnolfo di Cambio,** the Gothic master of Florence's 1290s building boom. Arnolfo was also responsible for the Franciscan church of Santa Croce and the original plans for the Duomo. The kind of Frankish Gothic building most people associate the term "Gothic," with lots of spires and stony frills, really showed up only in the tiny carved stone jewel of Santa Maria alla Spina along the banks of the Arno in Pisa. **Andrea Orcagna,** who was also a painter, gave us another bit of this sort of Gothic in miniature with his elaborate marble-inlaid tabernacle in Florence's Orsanmichele (the church is also a Gothic structure itself, but an odd one). But Orcagna was really already moving toward the Renaissance when he designed the wide-arched and proportioned space of the Loggia dei Lanzi on Florence's Piazza della Signoria.

The Gothic style was perhaps at its most advanced in sculpture. **Nicola Pisano** probably emigrated from southern Apulia to work in Pisa, where he crowned that city's great Romanesque building project with a Gothic finale in 1260. He created for the baptistery a great pulpit, the panels of which were carved in high relief with a new kind of figurative emotion displayed in the sway of the figures and a degree of activeness in their positioning and apparent movement. By the time Nicola carved the panels on his second pulpit in Siena, along with his son **Giovanni Pisano,** the figures were moving into a radically new sort of interaction, with a multitude of squirming bodies and pronounced stylized curves to add a graceful rhythm and emotion to the characters. Giovanni went on to carve two more pulpits (in Pistoia and back to Pisa for the Duomo) and numerous individual large statues for niches on the facade of Siena's Duomo, on which he was working as an architect, furthering his father's innovations in descriptive storytelling. **Andrea Pisano** (no relation) picked up the thread in Florence when in 1330 he cast the first set of bronze baptistery doors in the now-established Gothic style.

Byzantine tradition kept its hold over painting for quite a while, and the Gothic didn't catch on in this medium until the end of the 13th century. When it did, humanist philosophy was also starting to catch on. Humanism was reviving academic interest in the classical world and its philosophy and architecture, and it was encouraging a closer examination and contemplation of the natural world and everyday life—as opposed to the medieval habit of chaining all intellectual pursuits to theology and religious pondering.

True, in the 1280s Florentine master painter **Cimabue** was beginning to infuse his religious art with more human pathos than Byzantine custom had ever seen, and his Sienese compatriot (some say student) **Duccio** was beginning to adapt a narrative naturalism to his decorative Byzantine style (see "The Sienese School, Part 1," below). But when the Gothic style finally did catch up to painting, it did so with a vengeance and almost overvaulted the Gothic mind-set to land squarely in the Renaissance. When the Gothic style entered the realm of painting, its avatar was Giotto.

THE TRECENTO: SEEDS OF RENAISSANCE PAINTING

In the 1290s, **Giotto di Bondone**—best known as a frescoist who left us masterpiece cycles in Assisi's Basilica di San Francesco, Florence's Santa Croce, and Padua's Cappella Scrovegni—completely broke away from the styling of his teacher, Cimabue, and invented his own method of painting, steeped in the ideas of humanism and grounded in an earthy realism (see "The Genius of Giotto" in chapter 10 for more information). What he did was to give his characters real human faces displaying fundamental emotions; to use light and shadow to mold his figures, giving them bulk under their robes; to employ foreshortened architecture not only to provide a stage-set backdrop but also, and this was key, to give the paintings depth and real space (he let you see through painted windows to heighten the illusion); and to use simple but strong lines of composition and imbue the figures with movement to create dynamic scenes.

The Giottesque school that grew out of his workshop, and later his fame, kept some of the naturalistic elements and realistic foreshortened backdrops, but Giotto's innovations, and especially his spirit, seemed to stagnate at first. Most trecento works remained fundamentally Gothic, especially as practiced by Giotto's pupil and faithful adherent **Taddeo Gaddi,** his son **Agnolo Gaddi,** and **Andrea Orcagna.**

Other artists employed the International Gothic style to ever more decorative refinement (especially in Siena), developing parti-colored palates and simple fluid figures and compositions. Among the Florentines, this is best seen in the works of **Lorenzo Monaco, Masolino,** and (perhaps the most talented of the purely Gothic painters) **Gentile da Fabriano.**

THE SIENESE SCHOOL, PART 1

Siena adapted some of the humanist elements of realism and naturalism into its Gothic painting but left by the wayside the philosophical hang-ups and quest for perfect perspective the Florentine Renaissance soon embarked on. The Sienese school ended up with a distinctive, highly decorative art form rich in colors, patterns, and gold leaf. It was often as expressive as Giotto's work, but this was achieved more through the sinuous lines of its figures and compositional interplay.

Painters like **Duccio di Boninsegna** and **Sano di Pietro** gave the Sienese school a focus in the late 1200s, starting to adapt Gothic elements but still working in a Byzantine tradition, and **Jacopo della Quercia** became a towering figure in Sienese Gothic sculpture. One of the first great painters to come out of Duccio's workshop was **Simone Martini,** who developed a much more refined style of the International Gothic flavor and quickly eclipsed the fame of Duccio with his elegant lines and richly patterned fabrics. Two more of Duccio's students were **Ambrogio** and **Pietro Lorenzetti,** both masters of color and composition who infused their art with the naturalness of common life.

The Black Death of 1348 nipped the emergent Sienese school of painting in the bud. The Lorenzetti brothers perished, and the handful of citizens who lived through the plague were more intent on simple survival than on commissioning artworks, leaving Florence's version of the Renaissance to develop and eventually reign supreme.

THE EARLY RENAISSANCE: THE 15TH CENTURY

Tradition holds that the Renaissance began in 1401 when **Lorenzo Ghiberti** won a competition to cast Florence's new set of baptistery doors. Though confined to Gothic frames, Ghiberti still managed to infuse his figures with an entirely new kind of fluid dynamism and emotional naturalism that earned him accolades when the doors were finished more than 20 years later. (He was immediately commissioned to do another set, which became known as the Gates of Paradise, one of the cornerstone pieces of the early Renaissance.)

One of the men Ghiberti competed against for the first commission was **Filippo Brunelleschi,** who decided to study architecture after he lost the sculpture competition. When he came back from a learning trip to Rome, where he examined the classical construction of the ancients, he was full of groundbreaking ideas. These led to his ingenious red-tiled dome over Florence's Duomo as well as to a new kind of architecture based on the classical orders and mathematical proportions with which he filled Florentine church interiors—all done in smooth white plaster and soft gray stone.

One of his buddies was a sculptor named **Donatello,** who traveled with him to Rome and who on his return cast the first freestanding nude since antiquity (a *David,* now in Florence's Bargello) in an anatomically exacting style of naturalness. Donatello also developed the *schiacciato* technique of carving in very low relief, using the mathematical perspective trick his architect friend Brunelleschi taught him to achieve the illusion of great depth in shallow marble. Another architect friend of Donatello who helped shape Renaissance architecture was **Michelozzo,** Cosimo il Vecchio's favorite builder.

Brunelleschi also passed this concept of perspective along to a young painter named **Masaccio,** who was working with Gothic artist Masolino. Masaccio added it to his experimental bag of tricks, which included using a harsh light to model his figures in light and shadow, bold brushstrokes and foreshortened limbs to imply movement and depth, and an unrelenting realism. He used all of these to create the unprecedented frescoes in Florence's Cappella Brancacci. Part of his secret for creating figures of realistic bulk and volume he learned from studying the sculptures of Donatello and of another friend, **Luca della Robbia,** who besides working on marble and bronze developed a new way to fuse colored enamel to terra cotta and went on to found a popular workshop in the medium he handed down to his nephew, Andrea, and then his son, Giovanni. Masaccio finally got the precision perspective down to a science when painting Santa Maria Novella's *Trinità* (1428), thereby inaugurating the full-blown Renaissance in painting. He died at age 27.

Where Masaccio tried to achieve a new level of clarity and illusionistic reality with his perspective, **Paolo Uccello** became obsessed over experimenting with it, working out the math of perfect perspective and spatial geometry in some paintings and then warping it in others to see how far he could push the tenets for narrative and symbolic ends rather than making his work sheerly representative (at its best in the *Noah* fresco in Santa Maria Novella's Green Cloister). Architect/painter **Leon Battista Alberti** put the icing on the cake when he laid out the new rules of mathematical perspective in the treatise *On Painting.*

Though at first it was secondary to the Florentine school, color continued to be of some importance. This is best exemplified by the still somewhat Gothic **Domenico Veneziano** (Venetian artists always were and would remain supreme colorists), who is most important for teaching **Piero della Francesca,** a Sansepolcro artist whose quiet dramatic style and exploration of the geometry of perspective created crystalline-clear, spacious, haunting paintings with an unfathomable psychology in his figures' expressions.

Lorenzo Monaco imparted what he knew of the Gothic to **Fra' Angelico,** who continued to paint beautiful religious works in the bright colors and intimate detail of a miniaturist or illuminator of bibles. But Angelico's tiny racks of saints are fully Renaissance if you look closely enough; they're well modeled and lifelike, set in a plane of perspective with a strong single light source. **Benozzo Gozzoli** managed to bring to his art the best decorative style of the still-flowering International Gothic and the scientific realism and refined naturalism of the Renaissance.

Fra' Filippo Lippi started a long trend toward tall, thin Madonnas and mischievous angels. His sure lines, realistic depictions, and suffused color palette made him popular and brought into his *bottega* (workshop) apprentices like **Sandro Botticelli,** who would continue to paint exceedingly graceful scenes and flowing drapery that helped make his compositions some of the most fluid of the Renaissance.

The son of Botticelli's teacher became Botticelli's own pupil, and **Filippino Lippi** carried on the workshop's tradition. But Filippino also seemed to add back some of the earthiness seen in the works being turned out by the high-production workshop of **Domenico Ghirlandaio.** Ghirlandaio stayed popular by producing scenes of architectural unity and firmness, figurative grace, and complex coloring—and by adding in plenty of portraits of the commissioner's family members. In 1488, one of the apprentices in his workshop was a young Michelangelo Buonarotti.

That year also saw the death of one of the more innovative sculptor/painters, **Andrea del Verrocchio,** whose quest for hyperrealism and detailing in his carefully created bronzes and marbles and his few surviving exactingly painted panels were to greatly influence a young pupil of his studio, Leonardo da Vinci. The stage was set for new artists, masters on the scale of Giotto and Masaccio, to emerge and define the High Renaissance.

THE SIENESE SCHOOL, PART 2   By the time Siena got back on its feet after the Black Death and began commissioning art again, Sienese artists reverted a bit, hanging on to Byzantine styling or living in the shadow of Florentine ideals, though some of those great fabrics still slipped in. Fifteenth-century notables included **Sassetta,** who strove for more realism and perspective but was often bogged down by his late-Gothic hang-ups, and the gentle **Sano di Pietro,** who cranked out even more Madonna-and-Childs than Raphael. **Domenico di Bartolo,** fond of putting amusing details in his paintings, was largely influenced by Florence's Masaccio, as were the stylized paintings of **Vecchietta** and **Francesco di Giorgio Martini,** whose colorful work also shows the stamp of Botticelli and Martini's penchant for ancient Roman architecture.

THE HIGH RENAISSANCE: THE LATE 15TH TO MID–16TH CENTURY

One of Piero della Francesca's students was **Luca Signorelli,** a Cortonan whose mastery of the male nude in such works as his Cappella San Brizio in Orvieto had a great effect on the painting of Michelangelo. His highly modeled figures of colorful and incisive geometry shared many similarities with the works of the nearby Umbrian school being developed by another of Piero's protégés, **Perugino,** who also studied alongside Leonardo da Vinci in Verrocchio's *bottega* and whose ethereal blues and greens, beautiful landscapes, and limpid lighting would be further refined by his student **Pinturicchio.**

The Best of Michelangelo

Il Gigante, better known as *David,* was the summation of Michelangelo's greatest obsession: the perfect nude male body.

Back in Florence, **Leonardo da Vinci** was developing a highly realistic style in the 1480s. His patented *sfumato* technique revolutionized perspective by softly blurring the lines of figures and creating different planes of distance basically by throwing far-off objects out of focus. Leonardo also studied anatomy with a frightening intensity, drawing exacting models of human and animal bodies in various degrees of dissection just to find out exactly how to paint joints bending and muscles rippling in a realistic manner. He sketched swirls of water flowing and horses rearing, always trying to catch the essential inner motion of the world. In his spare time, he designed scientific inventions (usually on paper) like parachutes, machine guns, water screws, and a few helicopters.

Michelangelo Buonarotti left Ghirlandaio's fresco studio to study sculpture under the tutelage of Donatello's protégé, **Bertoldo,** and by age 23, following his first success in Rome with the *Pietà* in St. Peter's, had established himself as the foremost sculptor of his age with the gargantuan *David.* He's considered by many to be the first artist ever to surpass the ancients in terms of creating muscular bodies that (besides being naturally accurate) were proportioned for the greatest symbolic impact of grace and power. Michelangelo also revolutionized painting with his frescoes on the ceiling of Rome's Sistine Chapel (also evident in Florence's *Doni Tondo,* his only panel painting), where his twisting, muscularly modeled figures, limpid light, bold brush strokes, and revolutionary color palette of oranges, turquoises, yellows, and greens flabbergasted an entire generation of artists and established him as one of the greatest painters of his age. Before his death at the ripe old age of 89 in 1564, he went on to design innovative architecture (the Laurentian Library in Florence and St. Peter's Dome in Rome) and write some pretty good Renaissance sonnets too.

Perugino's star pupil, **Raphael,** melded the clarity and grace he learned from the Umbrian school with the *sfumato* of Leonardo and the sweeping earthy realism of Michelangelo's Sistine Chapel paintings. He created paintings that carried the picture-perfect grace and penetrating emotion to new heights, but his career was cut short with an early death in 1520 at age 37.

Under the influence of these masters, artists began to proliferate in Florence and Rome, where Michelangelo and Raphael worked extensively, and the rest of Italy. Venetians like **Giorgione, Tintoretto,** and the great **Titian** took the Renaissance and melded it to their refined concepts of color to craft their own High Renaissance, examples of which are scattered throughout Tuscany.

In Florence, the era gave rise to Raphael-influenced painters who refined the High Renaissance in a classical mode, including **Agnolo Bronzino,** the Sienese **Sodoma,** and **Andrea del Sarto,** who painted in the highly classical style but also was instrumental in developing the Michelangelo-driven school of Mannerism.

THE MANNERIST EXPERIMENT   Eventually the High Renaissance began to feed off itself, producing vapid works of technical perfection but little substance, perhaps best exemplified by the painting of **Giorgio Vasari.** As Florentine art stagnated, several artists sought ways out of the downward spiral.

Mannerism was the most interesting attempt, a movement within the High Renaissance that found its muse in the extreme torsion of Michelangelo's figures—in sculpture and painting—and his unusual use of oranges, greens, and other nontraditional colors, most especially in the Sistine Chapel ceiling. Other artists took these ideas and ran them to their logical limits, with painters like **Andrea del Sarto, Rosso Fiorentino, Pontormo,** Sienese **Domenico Beccafumi,** and **il Parmigianino** elongating their figures, twisting the bodies in muscularly improbably ways—waifish women with grotesquely long necks and pointy heads ran rampant—and mixing increasingly garish color palettes.

The sculptors fared perhaps better with the idea, producing for the first time statues that needed to be looked at from multiple angles to be fully appreciated, like **Giambologna**'s *Rape of the Sabines* under Florence's Loggia dei Lanzi and the *Fountain of the Moors* at Livorno's harbor by his student, **Pietro Tacca.** Goldsmith/autobiographer **Benvenuto Cellini,** while not strictly a mannerist, did go beyond the pale of the regular High Renaissance with the advanced decorativeness and complexity of his famous *Perseus* bronze, newly restored and in place at Piazza della Signoria's Loggia dei Lanzi.)

Although **Bartolomeo Ammannati** produced mannerist sculptures so overly muscular they look grotesque (Michelangelo denounced his *Neptune* fountain in Florence as a waste of marble), he broke architectural ground with such projects as the extension and massive rustication of Florence's Pitti Palace.

THE BAROQUE: THE MID–16TH TO 18TH CENTURY

The experiments of the mannerists soon gave way to the excesses of the baroque. Architecturally, the baroque era rehashed and reinterpreted yet again the neoclassical forms of the Renaissance, introducing ellipses and more radically complicated geometric lines, curves, and mathematics to replace the right angles and simple arches of traditional buildings. **Bernardo Buontalenti** was the main Tuscan architect of note in the period, and he worked extensively for the Medici, building them villas and sumptuous fanciful gardens. His more accessible works in Florence include the Tribune in the Uffizi, the facade of Santa Trinita, grottoes in the Giardino Boboli, and the Medici Forte di Belvedere. His greatest single achievement, however, was the city of Livorno, a beautiful bit of city planning he performed for the Medici in 1576. However, the best of baroque architecture was raised in Rome on the blueprints of masters Bernini and Borromini.

The baroque artists achieved some success in the field of church facades and altar frames. At their most restrained, they produced facades like those on Florence's Ognissanti and half a dozen churches in Siena, interiors like that of Florence's Santa Maria Maddalena dei Pazzi, and successful chapel ensembles in the cathedrals of Volterra and Siena (the latter one of master **Gian Lorenzo Bernini**'s few works in Tuscany). But mainly they acted more like interior decorators with extremely bad taste—in the era of the Medici grand dukes and other over-rich princelings, the more different types of expensive marbles you could piece together to decorate a chapel, the better. The Medici Cappella dei Principi (Chapel of the Princes) in Florence is the perfect nauseating example.

In painting, the baroque gave birth to genius mainly outside the Tuscan sphere—such as **Caravaggio,** whose *chiaroscuro* style of dark shadows paired with hyperilluminated light areas influenced an entire generation of painters, including Pisan **Orazio Gentileschi** and his more talented daughter, **Artemisia.** **Cristofano Allori** was one of the few notable baroquies to come out of Renaissance Florence. **Pietro da Cortona,** though a Tuscan native, was one of the founders of the more pastel, fluffy Roman baroque style, and has left significant works in his hometown of Cortona and on the Medici's ceilings of the Pitti Palace in Florence.

Painting church ceilings with illusionistic scenes became a hallmark of the baroque, and no one was more adept at making false domes out of flat transept ceilings or monumental, four-story, open-air temples out of one-story church roofs than perspective wizard **Andrea Pozzo.**

Rococo was the baroque gone awry, a world of dripping stuccoes and cotton-candy love scenes on canvas of which you can be thankful very little has survived in Tuscany or Umbria.

FROM THE NEOCLASSICAL TO THE PRESENT

Italy didn't have a major hand in developing many new styles after the baroque, though 19th-century works by Italy's master **neoclassical** sculptor Canova are scattered around Tuscany and Umbria, and Tuscany had one great neoclassical sculptor, **Giovanni Duprè,** born in Siena in 1817. The late 19th century also saw many of the faceless churches clad with fanciful "neo-Gothic" facades designed in admiring imitation of the time period in which the buildings were originally raised, but the prevailing tastes also led the romantic refurbishers to set most of these with glittering Venetian mosaics.

Tuscany had a brief moment in a very localized limelight again from the 1860s to around 1900 when the **Macchiaioli,** a group of artists in Florence and Livorno, junked the old styles and concentrated on exploring the structure of light and color in painting, concerned with the effect of the individual *macchie,* or marks of paint on the canvas. In effect, it was kind of a Tuscan Impressionism.

In the 20th century, little has stood out in the fine arts of Italy. Some individual Tuscan talents are Livorno's **Modigliani,** who garnered fame in France for his innovative oblong portraits; the futurist **Gino Severini** from Cortona; and **Marino Marini,** a Pistoian crafter of stylized bronze horses. In architecture, Tuscany had the privilege of hosting the only major new movement in Italy, its own variant on Art Deco (Art Nouveau in France) called the **Liberty Style.**

As the focus of Western painting and sculpture migrated to countries like France and the United States in the 20th century, Italy turned its artistic energies mainly to the cinema, fashion (Armani, Gucci, Versace, Pucci, and the like)—an industry in which Florence shines—and the manufacture of sleek, fun, and often mind-bogglingly useful industrial design objects like Alessi teakettles, Pavoni coffee machines, Olivetti typewriters, and Ferraris.

THE MODERN CONUNDRUM   Although some towns (like San Gimignano, Spoleto, and Pistoia) actively encourage the development of contemporary art, most Tuscan and Umbrian cities are firmly fixed in, and fixated on, their greatest era. Choosing which artistic epoch to preserve is a tough judgment call to make in a country so steeped in multiple layers of artistic and cultural history, and it's an issue constantly debated across Italy.

Each city chooses differently, motivated by economic tourist pressures, local academic preferences, and deeply instilled senses of pride about certain periods. Florence, for one, is firmly entrenched in the Renaissance and refuses to look forward or backward. Florentines could care less about the Roman ruins lying under their streets, and over the past century have in many churches stripped off baroque and later accretions to return buildings to their "pure" Renaissance (or late Gothic, if there's a Giotto involved) state.

And so, Volterra touts the Etruscan urns in its archaeological museum but not the 15th-century frescoes in San Francesco, and Siena shows you its medieval streets and Gothic palaces but never calls much attention to the baroque church facades. Heaven forbid the much-maligned baroque ever becomes fashionable again or our descendants will detest us for clearing away fanciful baroque altars to reveal the medieval bricks beneath as much as we revile the 18th-century gentlemen who calmly whitewashed over Giotto's frescoes in Santa Croce.

3 A Taste of Tuscany & Umbria

First things first: It was the Tuscans who taught the French how to cook. French cuisine as we know it was founded in the court of Henry II, whose kitchen was staffed by Tuscan cooks imported by his Florentine wife, Catherine de' Medici.

The genius of Tuscan cooking is in its simplicity. Fancy sauces aren't needed to hide the food because Tuscans use pure, strong flavors and the freshest of ingredients. The great dishes are in fact very basic: homemade ribbons of egg pasta in hare sauce, game or free-range domestic animal meats grilled over wood coals, and beans simmered in earthenware pots.

Tuscans and Umbrians alike make only a sparing use of seasonings: salt, pepper, and their library of herbs (basil, rosemary, tarragon, sage, oregano, and the like). The most prominent cooking additives are **wine** and **olive oil.** Tuscan oil is some of the finest in the world, especially that produced around Lucca, and comes in several gradients depending on the level of acidity. The more the olives are bruised before being pressed, the higher the acidity will be, which is why most olive picking is still done by delicate hands and not brutish machines. I don't know why they bother classifying some oils as *vergine, fino vergine,* or *soprafino vergine,* because no self-respecting Italian would use anything but *extra vergine* (extra virgin), some of which is rated DOC and DOCG, just like wine. Olives are harvested and pressed in October, and the oil is best fresh.

Another popular, and expensive, Tuscan and Umbrian garnish is the *tartufo,* or **truffle.** It's a fungal tuber (read: mushroom) that grows inexplicably around the roots of certain trees in certain soils under certain conditions that have for centuries baffled the food industry desperate to farm these lucrative little buggers.

Natural truffles come in both black (rare) and white (exceedingly rare) varieties, and they turn up in only very few areas of the world. Tuscany and Umbria are blessed to have both kinds growing underfoot, the black in many areas, especially Spoleto, and the white around San Miniato in Tuscany and Gubbio in Umbria. Fall is truffle season.

Some of the ingredients in Tuscan cooking may seem suspiciously trendy, but Tuscans have been eating *caprino* goat cheese, sun-dried tomatoes, arugula, and focaccia sandwiches for generations. And Tuscans have a Goldilocks complex whereby they undercook their meat, overcook their vegetables, but make their pasta just right—by which I mean *al dente* ("to the teeth"), softened enough for eating but with a stiff bite to the very core and never, ever soggy.

For a more complete **glossary of menu items and cooking terms,** turn to Appendix B.

THE BASIC ITALIAN MEAL

The basic Italian meal is simple but the dining is long and leisurely, about 2 to 3 hours to finish, the old-fashioned way. Most Italian restaurants will expect you to take something close to a full meal. (It's not a scam to part tourists from their euros, it's just the way Italians eat.) You start with an *antipasto* (appetizer), followed by a *primo piatto* (1st course) of rice or pasta, then a *secondo piatto* (2nd course) of meat or fish. Italians don't usually throw a side dish on the plate with your main dish, so you have to order your *contorno* separately. A *dolce* (dessert) comes much later, and no Italian meal is complete without espresso and a shot of grappa. Below are some of the most typical dishes of Tuscany and Umbria.

ANTIPASTO The classic Tuscan appetizer is an **antipasto misto,** which simply means "mixed." It usually entails *affettati misti* and *crostini misti,* both of which can be ordered alone as well. The former is a plate of sliced cured meats and salami, like *prosciutto* (salt-cured ham), *capocollo* (meaty pork salami), *finocchiata* (capocollo with fennel seeds), and *sopressata* (gelatinous headcheese—better than it sounds). *Crostini* are little rounds of toast spread with various pâtés, the most popular being *di fegatini* (chicken liver flavored with anchovy paste and capers) and *di milza* (spleen), though you'll also often get mushrooms, tomatoes, a cheesy sauce, or (especially in Umbria) a truffle paste.

Another popular appetizer is simple **bruschetta** (in Tuscany often called *fettunta*), a slab of peasant bread toasted on the grill, rubbed with a garlic clove, drizzled with extra-virgin olive oil, and sprinkled with coarse salt—order it *al pomodoro* for a pile of cubed tomatoes and torn basil leaves added on top. In summer, you'll also be offered **panzanella,** a kind of cold salad made of stale bread soaked in cold water and vinegar mixed with diced tomatoes, onions, and basil, all sprinkled with olive oil. A **pinzimonio** is a selection of raw vegetables (celery, fennel, peppers, and the like) with olive oil in which to dip them.

PRIMI Tuscan first courses come in three types. Of the **zuppa** or **minestra** (soup), the top dog is **ribollita,** literally "reboiled," because it's made the day before and reboiled before serving. It's a chunky soup closer to stew than anything else. The prime ingredients are black cabbage, bean purée, and whatever vegetables *Mamma* taught you to add in poured over stale peasant bread. *Zuppa di fagioli* (bean soup) can mean either this or a soupier breadless alternative.

Pasta is the most famous Italian *primo,* and in Tuscany the king is **pappardelle alla lepre** (very wide egg noodles in a strong-flavored sauce of wild hare). From somewhere around Siena and south, every town has its own name for the simple homemade pasta that's basically durum wheat mixed with water and rolled between the hands into chewy fat spaghetti. In Siena province, it's called **pici** or **pinci;** around Orvieto, order **umbrichelli;** and in Assisi or Spoleto, call it **stringozzi** (or some variant thereon). It's usually served in a basic tomato sauce or **alla carrettiera** (a tomato sauce spiked with peperoncini hot peppers).

Other typical pasta dishes are **penne strascicate** (a tomato-and-cream ragù) and **strozzapreti,** "priest stranglers," because clerics would supposedly choke on these rich ricotta-and-spinach dumplings (sometimes called *gnudi*—nude since they're basically ravioli filling without the clothing of a pasta pocket).

Risotto is a thick, sticky rice dish made with boiled-down soup stock, popular in the north of Italy. Tuscans and Umbrians often serve up a few versions, usually *ai funghi* (with mushrooms) or *ai asparagi* (with wild asparagus).

SECONDI Tuscans are unabashed carnivores, and the main course is almost always meat, usually grilled. Italians like their grilled meat as close to raw as rare can get, so if you prefer it a bit more brown, order your bistecca *ben cotta* (well done, which just might get you something close to medium).

The king is the mighty **bistecca alla fiorentina,** traditionally made from thick T-bone steak cut from the sirloin and enveloping the tenderloin of the snow-white muscular cattle raised in the Chiana valley. (During the mad cow disease scare, however, meat on the bone was temporarily banned, forcing cooks to use inferior cuts.) This is grilled over glowing wood coals, then brushed with extra-virgin olive oil and sprinkled with cracked black pepper. So simple, so good. The steaks average 1 to 2 inches thick and weigh about 3 to 4 pounds. Order a powerhouse red wine (this is the time for Brunello) and a plate of *fagioli* (white beans) on the side, and then cancel all meal plans for the next few days.

More everyday *secondi* are **grigliata mista** (mixed grill that may include lamb, sausage, chicken, or steak), **arista** (they usually leave off the *di maiale* because this dish invariably consists of slices of roast pork loin), **fritto misto** (mix of chicken, lamb, sweetbreads, artichokes, and zucchini dipped in bready egg batter and deep fried in olive oil), and any wild game, especially **cinghiale** (wild boar), which is often cooked *in umido* (stewed with tomatoes), as well as domesticated gamelike **coniglio** (rabbit) and **anatra** (duck). They cook **pollo** (chicken) *arrosto* (roasted), *alla diavola* (with hot spices), or *al mattone* (cooked under the weight of a hot brick), but usually tend to dry it out in doing so. A **lombatina di vitello** is a simple veal chop, prepared in myriad ways.

Tuscans and Umbrians are very fond of the **spiedino** (shish-kebab grill) and seem to like spitting small fowl like the tiny **tordo** (thrush) and hapless **piccione** (pigeon) along with the same mix of meats in a **grigliata mista** with maybe an onion added in. One Tuscan specialty to which Florentines are particularly beholden is **trippa** (tripe, the stomach lining of a cow), most popularly served as **trippa alla fiorentina,** tripe strips or cubes casseroled with vegetables and topped with tomato sauce and *parmigiano*. **Cibrèo** is another local Florentine dish against which you might want to be vigilant—it's a mix of cockscombs and chicken livers mixed with beans and egg yolks and served on toast.

Aside from **fresh fish,** both Tuscans and Umbrians make widespread use of **baccalà,** salt-cured cod they soften in water before cooking and often serve *alla livornese* (cooked with tomatoes and other veggies in white wine and olive oil, occasionally with some tripe thrown in for good measure).

CONTORNI   Tuscans are called the *mangiafagioli* (bean-eaters) by other Italians. And **fagioli** here, the Italian word for beans in general, almost invariably means white cannellini beans (sometimes red kidney beans or green broad beans will show up, increasingly as you get into Umbria). However, a simple plate filled with nothing but *fagioli* or *fagioli in fiasco,* cooked al dente with a liberal supply of olive oil poured on and ground black pepper for taste, is somehow divine within Tuscany's borders. For something zestier, order **fagioli alluccelleto,** in which the beans are stewed with tomatoes and sage.

In Umbria, you can get a plate of **lenticche di Castellúccio,** some of the world's best midget lentil beans. It's a good thing Tuscans and Umbrians cook their beans right, because they tend to boil their other favorite veggies, **spinaci** (spinach) until it's dead dead, and you end up with a pile of green on your plate with very little molecular cohesion left.

Any other vegetable—**melanzane** (eggplant), **pomodoro** (tomato), or **peperone** (bell pepper)—is usually sliced thin, grilled, and served swimming in olive oil. About the only other side dish central Italians turn to is **patate** (potatoes), either *arrosto* (roasted and covered with olive oil and rosemary) or *fritte* (the increasingly popular french fries).

DOLCI   Tuscany's best sweet is the dreamy **gelato,** a dense Italian version of ice cream (see the box "A Big Step Above Ice Cream: Florentine Gelato" in chapter 3 for details), which you should ideally get at a proper *gelateria* and not in a restaurant. The main dish to have after dinner, however, is **cantucci con vin santo.**

Cantucci, or *biscotti di Prato* in that town most famed for them, are the Tuscan variant on the twice-baked hard almond crescent cookies called *biscotti,* usually eaten by dunking them in a small glass of the sweet dessert wine *vin santo.*

Panforte is a very dense fruitcake. (One of Siena's specialties, *pan pepato,* is its medieval predecessor, with more exotic spices added into the sweetness.) A **castagnaccio** is a dense cake made of chestnut flour and topped with pine nuts; **necci** are chestnut-flour crepes; and a **zuccotto** is a concentration of calories in the form of sponge cake filled with *semifreddo* moussed chocolate, cream, candied fruit, and nuts.

Other cookies are **ricciarelli** of honeyed marzipan (a sugar/honey almond paste), **brutti ma buoni** (ugly but good chewy almond-sugar cookies), and **ossi dei morti** (bones of the dead—light, crumble-in-your-mouth matrices of sugar).

CHIANTI, BRUNELLO & OTHER HEADY SPIRITS

Tuscany and Umbria have been wine country for thousands of years, ever since the Etruscans shipped their popular brews south to thirsty Romans and up to the Gauls of France. Since the days they were praised by Pliny the Elder, Tuscan wines have been keenly sought after, and the region is by far the most famous wine zone in Italy, which as a country is the largest producer of wine in the world.

To Italians, wine is the obvious only choice of beverage with dinner, so in most restaurants your only decision will be **rosso o bianco** (red or white). Unless you want to celebrate some special occasion or are in the mood to expand your connoisseurship, the **vino della casa** (house wine) will almost invariably do wonderfully. Sparkling wine, which you'll usually find imported from other Italian zones (the most famous of which is Asti), is called **spumante.** (Those refraining from alcohol for personal or health reasons needn't worry—you won't be met with scowls or discouragement if all you order is a bottle of mineral water; wine consumption is expected at meals but certainly not required.)

To test out a few glasses without the full meal, drop by an **enoteca,** a wine shop or wine bar, where you can often sample before you buy (any regular bar will also pour you a glass of house wine for .50€ to 1€/58¢–$1.15). When tooling around the wine-heavy countryside of Tuscany or Umbria, any sign that touts **vendita diretta** means the owner of those vines will sell to you direct. I've recommended individual producers for the major wines in each relevant chapter, and for a wine-by-wine overview of the best *vini* and their producers, see "The Best Wines & Vineyards" in chapter 1.

CLASSIFICATIONS   In 1963, Italy's wine fell into two classifications, table wine and DOC. **DOC** *(Denominazione di Origine Controllata)* wines are

---

Good Year or Bad?

Because most producers in Tuscany and Umbria are subject to the same basic weather patterns, the generally good and bad years for most labels are, by and large, the same: 1983, 1985, 1988, 1990, and 1993 to 1995 are excellent years. 1997 is what they call a one-year-in-fifty, which means you shouldn't hesitate to scoop up any '97 bottles (if you can still find any) even at what seem inflated prices—it'll be half a century before stuff this good comes around again. And, while it's really too early to tell, it looks as if 1998, 1999, and even 2001 will also be winners. However, steer clear of 1984, 1987, 1989, and 1991 to 1992.

merely those a government board guarantees have come from an official wine-producing area and meet the standard for carrying a certain name on the label. A *vino di tavola* (table wine) classification merely means a bottle doesn't fit the pre-established standards and is no reflection of the wine's quality (see below).

In 1980, a new category was added. **DOCG** (the *G* stands for *Garantita*) is granted to wines with a certain subjective high quality. Traditionally, DOCG labels were merely the highest-profile wines that lobbied for the status (getting DOC or DOCG vastly improves reputations and therefore sales, though the costs of putting up the wine annually for testing are high). In 1992, the laws were rewritten and Italy's original six DOCG wines (three of which were Tuscan) jumped to 15. Six of these are Tuscans (Brunello di Montalcino, Carmignano, Chianti, Chianti Classico, Vino Nobile di Montepulciano, and Vernaccia di San Gimignano) and two are Umbrian (Sagrantino di Montefalco and Torgiano Rosso Riserva).

Though *vino di tavola* usually connotes a quaffable house wine from some indeterminate local producer, in recent years this classification of table wine was the only outlet for estates that wanted to experiment with nontraditional mixtures. Many respectable producers started mixing varietals with French grapes like cabernet and chardonnay to produce wines that, though complex and of high quality, don't fall into the conservative DOC system. Such a wine could, by law, only be called a lowly *vino di tavola.* These highbred wines became known as **Supertuscans** or *super vini di tavola.* There's no guaranteeing the quality of these experimental wines, yet most self-respecting producers won't put on the market a failure or something undrinkable. If you come across a $30 bottle with a fanciful name marked "table wine," it's probably a Supertuscan.

Even the venerable chianti-based wine empire of the Antinori came up with a sangiovese-cabernet mix they call **Tignanello;** they also put out a recommendable full-fledged cabernet sauvignon under the name **Solaia.** Perhaps the highest-profile Supertuscan is **Sassicaia di Bolgheri,** a huge and complex cabernet blend that lives for decades and is priced accordingly. It's produced by a single estate near the coast south of Livorno and, despite the popular status of more well-known wines such as Brunello, is perhaps Italy's finest red wine. The cabernet grapevines used here were transplanted from the Château Lafite in the 1940s.

Wine classification in Italy is changing slowly, as 1992 laws, which also created the **IGT** *(Indicazione Geografica Tipica),* are being applied gradually to regional wine styles.

The practical upshot of all this is: DOC and DOCG wines represent the best of traditional wine formulas. IGT wines are for unique wines from even smaller specific areas or single vintners, and is one of the fastest growing categories amongst the better wines. *Vino da tavola,* while still sometimes slapped on $100 bottles of vineyard one-offs, is increasingly just used for what it was originally intended to mean: simple, hearty, tasty table wines that go well with any meal but probably won't send wine snobs into ecstasies of flowery poetic description.

TUSCAN WINES   Undoubtedly, Italy's most famous wine is the easygoing and versatile **chianti,** traditionally produced all around central Tuscany. The **Chianti Classico** zone of the tall hills between Florence and Siena produces the oldest, most balanced blends; it was the world's first officially established wine area in 1716. In the 19th century, a more exacting formula for chianti was worked out in the hills between Siena and Florence by Baron Ricasoli, with 75% to 90% sangiovese with other local grapes thrown in to mellow it out and make it more drinkable. Only recently were the DOCG laws controlling chianti relaxed to allow fully sangioveto chiantis to be produced, and today, a Chianti Classico can have anywhere from 70% to 100% sangiovese, often rounded out with an imported *cru* like cabernet, merlot, or pinot nero. This has led to a surge in the quality and full-bodiedness of chianti, moving most of it from being a knockabout good table wine to a complex, structured, heavyweight contender in annual wine fairs. Though quality still varies, it's usually thoroughly reliable and is one of the best everyday wines produced anywhere.

Other chianti zones are **Chianti Colli Fiorentini,** Florence's table wine; **Chianti Colli Senesi,** the largest zone, filling in gaps around Siena where yield regulations keep them from growing Brunello, Vino Nobile, or Vernaccia (the chianti can be very good but is unreliable); **Chianti Colli Aretine,** a mellow edition; **Chianti Colli Pisane,** the featherweight contender; **Chianti Montalbano,** the juicy-fruits of the gang; and **Chianti Rúfina**—not to be confused with Ruffino, one of the biggest Chianti Classico houses—which flexes its muscle east of Florence to make chiantis of some complexity and style.

Tuscany's powerhouse red wine—and, depending on whom you ask, the number-one or number-two wine in all Italy—is **Brunello di Montalcino.** It was developed in the 18th century when the Biondi-Santi vineyards were hit with a fungus that left only the dusty slate-blue *sangiovese grosso* grapes alive. It was the first wine to be granted DOCG status. Brunello is 100% *sangiovese grosso,* aged for 4 years (5 for the *riserva* labels), most of it in oak barrels. It's a deep-ruby elixir of remarkable complexity, a full mouth feel, long flavors, and usually a good deal of tannins. It needs steak or game dishes to let it shine; for a lighter-weight adventure try the **Rosso di Montalcino,** a younger, fruitier version.

Vino Nobile di Montepulciano is Tuscany's other long-respected red, a deep-garnet liquid that rolls around the tongue with a lasting flavor of fruits, violets, and damp soil. It's good paired with meats but also with fruit, bread, and cheese on a picnic. Significantly cheaper than Brunello, it's a less complex but more versatile wine.

Two of the oldest wine zones, also founded in 1716, border on Florence, and both have made use of French grapes since the 18th century. The tiny DOC **Pomino** zone to the east of Florence (abutting Chianti Rúfina territory) mixes cabernet, merlot, and sometimes pinot noir into its sangiovese for a pleasant red. DOCG **Carmignano,** near Prato between Florence and Lucca, tosses cabernet into the chianti-like brew to make some of Tuscany's freshest yet still refined and interesting wines. Although they age well and keep forever, these wines can also be drunk practically straight out of the barrel.

Tuscany also produces many fine DOC reds in zones throughout the region, such as the smooth **Rosso delle Colline Lucchesi** around Lucca. One of the best is a Maremma wine, recently terribly trendy in Italy, called **Morellino di Scansano.** Like chianti—to which it's similar but silkier—it's about 80% sangiovese, with some other Tuscan grapes thrown in the mix along with alicante (a Spanish grape known among the French as grenache).

Tuscany's only white wine of note is **Vernaccia di San Gimignano,** a dry wine of variable quality, but it enjoys the status of being one of Italy's few DOCG whites. Few other whites stand out in Tuscany, though the area around **Pitigliano** and the **Valdichiana** both produce drinkable *vino bianco,* and the Chianti zone is making some headway with its lightweight **Galestro.** Perhaps the finest little-known white is the dry **Montecarlo,** from the hills east of Lucca.

UMBRIAN WINES **Torgiano Rosso Riserva** was made DOCG mainly through the efforts of the Lungarotti vineyards and their **Rubesco** label, a blood-red wine making a strong first impression with a musky tannic bite that fades quickly through black fruit flavors. **Sagrantino di Montefalco** is the heavyweight contender DOCG of Umbrian reds, a purple-dark liquid of long flavors with a rounded mouth feel and a strong, lasting tannic hold. Other good local DOC reds are **Colli Altoberini, Colli del Trasimeno,** and **Colli Perugini** (a young zone; also rosé and white)

Umbria's mighty white is the **Orvieto Classico,** an ancient wine that was once an *abboccato* semisweet wine until prevailing tastes led to the mass production of Orvieto Classico *secco,* a dry white that fills wine store shelves across the world. Interestingly, in Orvieto you can still find the old varieties, a straw-colored wine that not only goes well with food, but actually holds its own as a treat to savor. Another good white made in many zones across Umbria is **Grechetto.**

Appendix B:
Useful Terms & Phrases

Tuscan, being the local lingo of Dante, is considered the purest form of Italian. (In Siena they will tell you that, actually, it's Sienese dialect that's perfect; proud Perugians in Umbria disagree, but the academics give the nod to Siena.) That means travel in Tuscany will help you learn the most letter-perfect Italian there is. Here are some key phrases and words to get you started.

1 *Molto Italiano:* A Basic Italian Vocabulary

English	Italian	Pronunciation
Thank you	**Grazie**	*graht*-tzee-yey
Please	**Per favore**	*pehr* fah-*vohr*-eh
Yes	**Sì**	see
No	**No**	noh
Good morning or Good day	**Buongiorno**	bwohn-*djor*-noh
Good evening	**Buona sera**	*Bwohn*-ah *say*-rah
Good night	**Buona notte**	*Bwohn*-ah *noht*-tay
How are you?	**Come sta?**	*koh*-may *stah?*
Very well	**Molto bene**	*mohl*-toh *behn*-ney
Goodbye	**Arrivederci**	ahr-ree-vah-*dehr*-chee
Excuse me (to get attention)	**Scusi**	*skoo*-zee
Excuse me (to get past someone on the bus)	**Permesso**	pehr-*mehs*-soh
Where is . . . ?	**Dovè . . . ?**	doh-*vey?*
the station	**la stazione**	lah stat-tzee-*oh*-neh
a hotel	**un albergo**	oon ahl-*behr*-goh
a restaurant	**un ristorante**	oon reest-ohr-*ahnt*-eh
the bathroom	**il bagno**	eel *bahn*-nyoh
To the right	**A destra**	ah *dehy*-stra
To the left	**A sinistra**	ah see-*nees*-tra
Straight ahead	**Avanti** (or **sempre diritto**)	ahv-vahn-tee (*sehm*-**pray** dee-*reet*-toh)
I would like	**Vorrei**	voh-*ray*
Some (of)	**Un po (di)**	oon poh dee
This/that	**Questo/quello**	*qway*-sto/*qwell*-oh
A glass of	**Un bicchiere di**	oon bee-key-*air*-ay-dee
(mineral) water	**acqua (minerale)**	*ah*-kwah (min-air-*ahl*-lay)
carbonated	**gassata** (or **con gas**)	gahs-*sah*-tah (kohn gahs)
uncarbonated	**senza gas**	*sen*-zah gahs

red wine	**vino rosso**	*vee*-no *roh*-soh
white wine	**vino bianco**	*vee*-no bee-*ahn*-koh
How much is it?	**Quanto costa?**	*kwan*-toh *coh*-sta?
It's too much.	**È troppo.**	ay *tro*-poh
The check, please.	**Il conto, per favore.**	eel kon-toh *pehr* fah-*vohr*-eh
Can I see . . . ?	**Posso vedere . . . ?**	*poh*-soh veh-*dare*-eh?
the church	**la chiesa**	la key-*ay*-zah
the fresco	**l'affresco**	lahf-*fres*-coh
When?	**Quando?**	*kwan*-doh
Is it open?	**È aperto?**	ay ah-*pair*-toe
Is it closed?	**È chiuso?**	ay key-*you*-zoh
Yesterday	**Ieri**	ee-*yehr*-ree
Today	**Oggi**	*oh*-jee
Tomorrow	**Domani**	doh-*mah*-nee
Breakfast	**Prima colazione**	*pree*-mah coh-laht-tzee-*ohn*-ay
Lunch	**Pranzo**	*prahn*-zoh
Dinner	**Cena**	*chay*-nah
What time is it?	**Che ore sono?**	kay *or*-ay *soh*-noh
Monday	**Lunedì**	loo-nay-*dee*
Tuesday	**Martedì**	mart-ay-*dee*
Wednesday	**Mercoledì**	mehr-cohl-ay-*dee*
Thursday	**Giovedì**	joh-vay-*dee*
Friday	**Venerdì**	ven-nehr-*dee*
Saturday	**Sabato**	*sah*-bah-toh
Sunday	**Domenica**	doh-*mehn*-nee-kah

NUMBERS

1	**uno** (*oo*-noh)	30	**trenta** (*trayn*-tah)
2	**due** (*doo*-ay)	40	**quaranta** (kwah-*rahn*-tah)
3	**tre** (tray)	50	**cinquanta** (cheen-*kwan*-tah)
4	**quattro** (*kwah*-troh)	60	**sessanta** (sehs-*sahn*-tah)
5	**cinque** (*cheen*-kway)	70	**settanta** (seht-*tahn*-tah)
6	**sei** (say)	80	**ottanta** (oht-*tahn*-tah)
7	**sette** (*set*-tay)	90	**novanta** (noh-*vahnt*-tah)
8	**otto** (*oh*-toh)	100	**cento** (*chen*-toh)
9	**nove** (*noh*-vay)	1,000	**mille** (*mee*-lay)
10	**dieci** (dee-*ay*-chee)	5,000	**cinque milla** (*cheen*-kway *mee*-lah)
11	**undici** (*oon*-dee-chee)	10,000	**dieci milla** (dee-*ay*-chee *mee*-lah)
20	**venti** (*vehn*-tee)		
21	**ventuno** (vehn-*toon*-oh)		
22	**venti due** (*vehn*-tee *doo*-ay)		

2 From Antipasti to Zuppa Inglese: Italian Menu Terms

FOODS & DISHES

Acciughe or Alici Anchovies.

Acquacotta "Cooked water," a watery vegetable soup thickened with egg and poured over stale bread.

Affettati misti Mix of various salami, prosciutto, and other cured meats; served as an appetizer.

Agnello Lamb.

Agnolotti Semicircular ravioli (often stuffed with meat and cheese together).

Amaretti   Almond-flavored macaroons.

Anatra   Duck.

Anguilla   Eel.

Antipasti   Appetizers.

Aragosta   Lobster.

Arista di maiale   Roast pork loin, usually served in slices, flavored with rosemary, garlic, and cloves.

Baccalà (alla livornese)   Dried salted codfish (cooked in olive oil, white wine, garlic, and tomatoes).

Bistecca alla fiorentina   Florentine-style steak, ideally made with Chianina beef, grilled over wood coals, and then brushed with olive oil and sprinkled with pepper and salt.

Bocconcini   Small veal chunks sautéed in white wine, butter, and herbs. (Also the word for ball-shaped portions of any food, especially mozzarella.)

Bollito misto   Assorted boiled meats.

Braciola   Loin pork chop.

Branzino   Sea bass.

Bresaola   Air-dried, thinly sliced beef filet, dressed with olive oil, lemon, and pepper—usually an appetizer.

Bruschetta   A slab of peasant bread grilled and then rubbed with a garlic clove, drizzled with olive oil, and sprinkled with salt; often served *al pomodoro* (with tomatoes).

Bucatini   Fat, hollow spaghetti. Classically served *allamatriciana* (with a spicy hot tomato sauce studded with pancetta [bacon]).

Cacciucco   Seafood stew of Livrono in a spicy tomato base poured over stale bread.

Cacio or Caciotto   Southern Tuscan name for pecorino cheese.

Calamari   Squid.

Calzone   Pizza dough folded with a number of stuffings, usually cheese and ham, before baking—like a pizza turnover.

Cannellini   White beans, the Tuscan's primary vegetable.

Cannelloni   Pasta tubes filled with meat and baked in a sauce (cream or tomato). The cheese version is usually called **manicotti** (though either name may be used for either stuffing).

Cantucci   Twice-baked hard almond cookies, vaguely crescent-shaped and best made in Prato (where they're known as **biscotti di Prato**). The generic Italian word for them is *biscotti.*

Capocollo   Aged sausage made mainly from pork necks.

Caprese   A salad of sliced mozzarella and tomatoes lightly dressed with olive oil, salt, and pepper.

Capretto   Kid.

Caprino   Soft goat's-milk cheese.

Carciofi   Artichokes.

Carpaccio   Thin slices of raw cured beef, pounded flat and often served topped with arugola and parmigiano shavings.

Casalinga   Home cooking.

Cavolfiore   Cauliflower.

Cavolo   Cabbage.

Ceci   Chickpeas (garbanzo beans).

Cervelli   Brains, often served *fritti* (fried).

Cervo   Venison.

Cibrèo   Stew of chicken livers, cockscombs, and eggs.

Cinghiale   Wild boar.

Cipolla   Onion.

Coniglio   Rabbit.

Cozze   Mussels.

Crespelle alla fiorentina   Thin pancakes wrapped around ricotta and spinach, covered with tomatoes and cheese, and baked in a casserole.

Crostini   Small rounds of bread toasted and covered with various patés, most commonly a tasty liver paste (or in Umbria *milza,* which is spleen).

Dentice   Dentex; a fish similar to perch.

Fagioli   Beans, almost always white cannellini beans.

Faraona   Guinea hen.

Farro   Emmer, a barleylike grain (often in soups).

Fave   Broad fava beans.

Fegato   Liver.

Focaccia   Like pizza dough with nothing on it, this bready snack is laden with olive oil, baked in sheets, sprinkled with coarse salt, and eaten in slices plain or split to stuff as a sandwich. In Florence, it's also popularly called *schiacciato.*

Fontina   Medium-hard cow's-milk cheese.

Formaggio   Cheese.

Frittata   Thick omelet stuffed with meats, cheese, and vegetables; often eaten between slices of bread as a sandwich.

Fritto misto   A deep-fried mix of meats, often paired with fried artichokes or seafood.

Frutti di mare   A selection of shellfish, often boosted with a couple of shrimp and some squid.

Funghi   Mushrooms.

Fusilli   Spiral-shaped pasta; usually long like a telephone cord, not the short macaroni style.

Gamberi (gamberetti)   Prawns (shrimp).

Gelato   Dense version of ice cream (*produzione propria* means homemade).

Gnocchi   Pasta dumplings usually made from potatoes or ricotta and spinach.

Gorgonzola   A soft, creamy blue-veined cheese with a very strong flavor and famously overpowering aroma.

Granchio   Crab.

Granita   Flavored ice; *limone* (lemon) is the classic.

Involtini   Thinly sliced beef or veal rolled with veggies (often celery or artichokes) and simmered in its own juices.

Lampreda   Lamprey (an eel-like fish).

Lenticchie   Lentil beans; Italy's best come from Umbria's eastern Castellúccio plains.

Lepre   Wild hare.

Lombatina di vitello   Loin of veal.

Maiale   Pork.

Manzo   Beef.

Mascarpone   Technically a cheese but more like heavy cream, already slightly sweet and sweetened more to use in desserts like tiramisù.

Melanzana   Eggplant (aubergine).

Merluzzo   Cod.

Minestrone   A little-bit-of-everything vegetable soup, usually flavored with chunks of cured ham.

Mortadella   A very thick mild pork sausage; the original bologna (because the best comes from Bologna).

Mozzarella   A nonfermented cheese, made from the fresh milk of a buffalo (but increasingly these days from a cow), boiled and then kneaded into a rounded ball; served as fresh as possible.

Oca   Goose.

Orata   Sea bream.

Orecchiette   Small, thick pasta disks.

Osso buco   Beef or veal knuckle braised in wine, butter, garlic, lemon, and rosemary; the marrow is a delicacy.

Ostriche   Oysters.

Paglio e fieno   Literally, "hay and straw," yellow (egg) and green (spinach) tagliatelle mixed and served with sauce.

Pancetta   Salt-cured pork belly, rolled into a cylinder and sliced—the Italian bacon.

Panettone   Sweet, yellow cakelike dry bread.

Panforte   Any of a number of huge barlike candies vaguely akin to fruitcake; a dense, flat honey-sweetened mass of nuts, candied fruits, and spices.

Panino   A sandwich.

Panna   Cream (either whipped and sweetened for ice cream or pie; or heavy and unsweetened when included in pasta sauce).

Panzanella   A cold summery salad made of stale bread soaked in water and vinegar mixed with cubed tomatoes, onion, fresh basil, and olive oil.

Pappa al Pomodoro   A bready tomato-pap soup.

Pappardelle alle lepre   Very wide noodles in hare sauce.

Parmigiano   Parmesan, a hard salty cheese usually grated over pastas and soups but also eaten alone; also known as *grana*.

Pecorino   A rich sheep's-milk cheese; in Tuscany it's eaten fresh and soft.

Penne strascicate   Hollow pasta quills in a creamy ragù (meat-and-tomato sauce).

Peperonata   Stewed peppers and onions under oil; usually served cold.

Peperoncini   Hot peppers.

Peperoni   Green, yellow, or red sweet peppers.

Peposo   Beef stew with peppercorns.

Pesce al cartoccio   Fish baked in a parchment envelope.

Pesce spada   Swordfish.

Piccione   Pigeon.

Pici or Pinci   A delicious homemade pasta made with just flour, water, and olive oil, rolled in the hands to produce lumpy, thick, chewy spaghetti to which sauce clings. This local name is used around Siena and to its south.

Pinzimonio   Olive oil with salt and pepper into which you dip raw vegetables. If the oil is flavored with garlic and anchovies, it's called **Bagna cauda.**

Piselli   Peas.

Pizza   Comes in two varieties: *rustica* or *a taglio* (by the slice) and *al frono* in a pizzeria (large, round pizzas for dinner with a thin, crispy crust). Specific varieties include *margherita* (plain pizza of tomatoes, mozzarella, and basil), *napoletana* (tomatoes, oregano, mozzarella, and anchovies), *capricciosa* (a naughty combination of prosciutto, artichokes, olives, and sometimes egg or anchovies), and *quatro stagione* (four seasons of fresh vegetables, sometimes also with ham).

Polenta Cornmeal mush, ranging from soupy to a dense cakelike version related to cornbread; often mixed with mushrooms and other seasonal fillings, served plain alongside game or sometimes sliced and fried.

Pollo Chicken; *alla cacciatore* is huntsman style, with tomatoes and mushrooms cooked in wine; *alla diavola* is spicy hot grilled chicken; *al mattone* is cooked under a hot brick.

Polpette Small veal meatballs.

Polpo Octopus.

Pomodoro Tomato (plural *pomodori*).

Porcini Huge tree mushrooms, best eaten grilled like a steak.

Porri Leeks.

Rape Turnips.

Ribollita A thick, almost stewlike vegetable soup made with black cabbage, olive oil, celery, carrots, and whatever else *Mamma* has left over, all poured over thick slabs of peasant bread.

Ricotta A soft, fluffy, bland cheese made from the watery whey (not curds, as most cheese) and often used to stuff pastas. *Ricotta salata* is a salted, hardened version for nibbling.

Risotto Rice, often arborio, served very watery and sticky.

Rombo Turbot fish.

Salsa verde Green sauce, made from capers, anchovies, lemon juice and/or vinegar, and parsley.

Salsicce Sausage.

Saltimbocca Veal scallop topped with a sage leaf and a slice of prosciutto and simmered in white wine.

Salvia Sage.

Sarde Sardines.

Scaloppine Thin slices of meat, usually veal.

Scamorza An air-dried (sometimes smoked) cheese similar to mozzarella; often sliced and grilled or melted over ham in a casserole, giving it a thin crust and gooey interior.

Schiacciato See "Focaccia."

Scottiglia Stew of veal, chicken, various game, and tomatoes cooked in white wine.

Semifreddo A cousin to *gelato* (ice cream), it's a way of taking nonfrozen desserts (tiramisù, zuppa inglese) and freezing and moussing them.

Seppia Cuttlefish (halfway between a squid and small octopus); its ink is used for flavoring and coloring in certain pastas and risotto dishes.

Sogliola Sole.

Spezzatino Beef or veal stew, often with tomatoes.

Spiedino A shish kebab (skewered bits of meat, onions, and slices of tomato or peppers grilled).

Spigola A fish similar to sea bass or grouper.

Spinaci Spinach (cooked to death).

Stoccafisso Air-dried cod.

Stracciatella Egg-drop soup topped with grated cheese.

Stracotto Overcooked beef, wrapped in bacon and braised with onion and tomato for hours until it's so tender it dissolves in your mouth.

Strangozzi That *a* can be any vowel; this is the name for *pici* (see above) used around Assisi, Spoleto, and southeast Umbria.

Strozzapreti   Ricotta-and-spinach dumplings, usually served in tomato sauce; literally "priest chokers." Also called *strangolaprete.*

Stufato   Beef pot roast in wine, broth, and veggies.

Tacchino   Turkey.

Tagliatelle   Flat noodles.

Tartufo   (1) Truffles; (2) An ice cream ball made with a core of fudge, a layer of vanilla, a coating of chocolate, and a dusting of cocoa; order it *affogato* (drowning), and they'll pour brandy over it.

Tiramisù   Classic Italian dessert, made by layering ladyfingers soaked in espresso (and often liqueur) with sweetened mascarpone cheese and then dusted with cocoa. Its name means "pick me up."

Tonno   Tuna.

Torta   A pie. *Alla nonna* is Grandma's style and usually is a creamy lemony pie; *alle mele* is an apple tart; *al limone* is lemon; *alle fragole* is strawberry; *ai frutti di bosco* is with berries.

Torta al testo   A flat, unleavened bread baked on the hearthstone and often split to be filled with sausage, spinach, or other goodies.

Tortellini   Rings or half-moons of pasta stuffed with ricotta and spinach or chopped meat (chicken and veal). Sometimes also called *tortelli* and *tortelloni.*

Trippa   Tripe (cow's stomach lining). Served *alla fiorentina* means strips or squares of it casseroled with tomatoes and onions, topped with grated parmigiano cheese.

Trota   Trout.

Umbrichelli   Also *ombrichelli,* a slightly thinner version of *pici* (see above) served in Orvieto and southwest Umbria.

Vermicelli   Very thin spaghetti.

Vitello   Veal. A *vitellone* is an older calf about to enter cowhood.

Vongole   Clams.

Zabaglione/zabaione   A custard made of whipped egg yolks, sugar, and Marsala wine.

Zampone   Pig's feet, usually stewed for hours.

Zuccotto   A tall liqueur-soaked sponge cake, stuffed with whipped cream, ice cream, chocolate, and candied fruits.

Zuppa   Soup. Popular varieties are *fagioli e farro* (beans and barley), *porri e patate* (potato-leek), *di pane* (bread and veggies; another name for ribollita), and *pavese* (eggs poached in boiling broth and poured over toasted peasant bread).

Zuppa inglese   An English trifle, layered with liqueur-soaked ladyfingers and chocolate or vanilla cream.

3 Knowing Your Apse from Your Ambone: A Glossary of Architectural & Art Terms

ARCHITECTURE

Ambulatory   Continuation of the side aisles to make a walkway around the chancel space behind the main altar of a church.

Apse   The semicircular space behind the main altar of a church.

Arcade   A series of arches supported by columns, piers, or pilasters.

Architrave   The long vertical element lying directly across the tops of a series of columns (the lowest part of an entablature); or, the molding around a door or window.

Badia   Abbey.

Baldacchino (also **ciborium**)   A stone canopy over a church altar.

Basilica   A form of architecture first used for public halls and law courts in ancient Roman cities. Early Christians adopted the form—a long rectangular room, divided into a central nave with side aisles but no transept—to build their first large churches.

Bay   The space between two columns or piers.

Bifore   Divided vertically into two sections.

Blind Arcade   An arcade of pilasters (the arches are all filled in), a defining architectural feature of the Romanesque style.

Caldarium   The hot tub or steam room of a Roman bath.

Campanile   A bell tower, usually of a church but also those of public buildings; it's often detached or flush against the church rather than sprouting directly from it.

Cantoria   Small church singing gallery, usually set into the wall above the congregation's heads.

Capital   The top of a column. The classical "orders" (types) are **Doric** (plain), **Ionic** (with scrolls, called volutes, at the corners), and **Corinthian** (leafy). There's also **Tuscan** (even simpler than Doric; the column is never fluted or grooved, and usually has no base) and **Composite** (Corinthian superimposed with Ionic). In many Paleo-Christian and Romanesque churches, the capital is carved with primitive animal and human heads or simple biblical scenes.

Cappella   Italian for chapel.

Caryatid   A column carved to resemble a woman (see also *telamon*).

Cattedrale   Cathedral (also *Duomo*).

Cavea   The semicircle of seats in a classical theater.

Cella   The innermost, most sacred room of a Roman pagan temple.

Chancel   Space around the high altar of a church, generally reserved for the clergy and the choir.

Chiesa   Church.

Chiostro   Italian for cloister.

Ciborium   (1) Another word for *baldacchino* (above); (2) Box or tabernacle containing the Host (the symbolic body and blood of Christ taken during communion).

Cloister   A roofed walkway open on one side and supported by columns; usually used in the plural because often four of them faced one another to make interior open-air courtyards, centered around small gardens, found in monasteries and convents.

Collegiata   A collegiate church, having a chapter of canons and a dean or provost to rule over it but lacking the bishop's seat that would make it a cathedral.

Colonnaded   Lined with columns.

Cornice   Protruding section, usually along the very top of a wall, a facade, or an entablature; a pediment is usually framed by a lower cornice and two sloping ones.

Cortile   Courtyard.

Crenellated   Topped by a regular series of protrusions and crevices; these **battlements** often ring medieval buildings or fortresses to aid in defense.

Crypt   An underground burial vault; in churches, usually found below the altar end and in Italy often the remnant of an older version of the church.

Cupola   Dome.

Cyclopian   Adjective describing an unmortered wall built of enormous stones by an unknown central Italian pre-Etruscan people. The sheer size led the ancients to think they were built by the Cyclopses.

Duomo   Cathedral (from *domus*, "house of God"), often used to refer to the main church in town even if it doesn't have a *cathedra*, or bishop's seat—the prerequisite for a cathedral.

Entablature   Section riding above a colonnade, made up of the architrave (bottom), frieze (middle), and cornice (top).

Forum   The main square in a Roman town; a public space used for assemblies, courts, and speeches and on which important temples and civic buildings were located.

Frieze   A decorative horizontal band or series of panels, usually carved in relief and at the center of an entablature.

Frigidarium   Room for cold baths in a Roman bath.

Greek Cross   Building ground plan in the shape of a cross whose arms are of equal length.

Latin Cross   Building ground plan in the shape of a Crucifix-style cross, where one arm is longer than the other three (this is the nave).

Liberty   Italian version of Art Nouveau or Art Deco, popular in the late 19th and early 20th centuries.

Loggia   Roofed porch, balcony, or gallery.

Lozenge   A decorative regularly sided diamond (square on its corner), either marble inlay or as a sunken depression, centered in the arcs of a blind arcade on Romanesque architecture.

Lunette   Semicircular wall space created by various ceiling vaultings or above a door or window; often it's decorated with a painting, mosaic, or relief.

Matroneum   In some Paleo-Christian and early Romanesque churches, the gallery (often on the second floor) reserved for women, who were kept separate from the men during mass.

Narthex   Interior vestibule of a church.

Nave   The longest section of a church, usually leading from the front door to the altar, where the worshipers sit; often divided into aisles.

Palazzo   Traditionally a palace or other important building; in contemporary Italian it refers to any large structure, including office buildings (and has become the common way to refer to a city block, no matter how many separate structures form it).

Paleo-Christian   Early Christian, used generally to describe the era from the 5th to early 11th century.

Pediment   A wide gable at the top of a facade or above a doorway.

Piano Nobile   The primary floor of a palace where the family would live, usually the second (American) but sometimes the third floor. It tends to have higher ceilings and larger rooms and be more highly decorated than the rest of the palazzo. The ground floor was usually for storage or shops and the attic for servants.

Pier   A rectangular vertical support (like a column).

Pietra forte   A dark gray ocher-tinged limestone mined near Florence. Harder than its cousin *pietra serena* (below), it was used more sparingly in Florentine architecture.

Pietra serena   A soft, light-gray limestone mined in the Florentine hills around Fiesole and one of the major building blocks of Florence's architecture—for both the ease with which it could be worked and its color, used to accent door jambs and window frames in houses and columns and chapels in churches.

Pieve   A parish church; in the countryside, often primarily a baptismal site.

Pilaster   Often called pilaster strip, it's a column, either rounded or squared off, set into a wall rather than separate from it.

Porta   Italian for door or city gate.

Portico   A porch.

Refectory   The dining room of a convent or monastery, which, from the Renaissance on, was often painted with a topical Last Supper to aid in religious contemplation at the dinner table.

Sacristy   The room in a church that houses the sacred vestments and vessels.

Sanctuary   Technically the holiest part of a church, the term is used to refer to the area just around or behind the high altar.

Spandrel   Triangular wall space created when two arches in an arcade curve away from each other (or from the end wall).

Spoglio   Architectural recycling; the practice of using pieces of an older building to help raise a new one. (Roman temples were popular mines for both marble and columns to build early churches.)

Sporti   Overhanging second story of a medieval or Renaissance building supported by wooden or stone brackets.

Stele   A headstone.

Stemma   Coat of arms.

Stucco   Plaster composed of sand, powdered marble, water, and lime; often molded into decorative relief, formed into statuary, or applied in a thin layer to the exterior of a building.

Telamon   A column sculpted to look like a man (also see *caryatid*).

Tepidarium   The room for a warm bath in a Roman bath.

Terme   Roman baths, usually divided into the calidarium, tepidarium, and frigidarium.

Torre   Tower.

Transept   The lateral cross-arm of a cruciform church, perpendicular to the nave.

Travertine   A whitish or honey-colored form of porous volcanic tufa mined near Tivoli. The stone from which ancient Rome was built.

Tribune   The raised platform from which an orator speaks; used to describe the raised section of some churches around and behind the altar from which Mass is performed.

Two-light   Of a window, divided vertically into two sections (see also **bifore**). A three-light window is divided vertically into three sections.

Tympanum   The triangular or semicircular space between the cornices of a pediment or between the lintel above a door and the arch above it.

PAINTING, SCULPTURE & CERAMICS

Ambone   Italian for pulpit.

Amphora   A two-handled jar with a tapered neck used by the ancients to keep wine, oil, and other liquids.

Arriccio   The first, rough layer of plaster laid down when applying the art of fresco to a wall. On this layer, the artist makes the rough *sinopia* sketches.

Bottega   The workshop of an artist. (On museum signs, the word means the work was created or carried out by apprentices or assistants in the stated master's workshop.)

Bozzetto   A small model for a larger sculpture (or sketch for a painting); in the later Renaissance and baroque eras, it also came to mean the tiny statuettes turned out for their own sake to satisfy the growing demand among the rich for table art.

Bucchero   Etruscan black earthenware pottery.

Canopic vase   Etruscan funerary vase housing the entrails of the deceased.

Cartoon   In Italian *cartone,* literally "big paper," the full-size preparatory sketch made during the art of fresco.

Chiaroscuro   Using patches of light and dark colors in painting to model figures and create the illusion of three dimensions. (Caravaggio was a master at also using the technique to create mood and tension.)

Cinerary urn   Vase or other vessel containing the ashes of the deceased; Etruscan ones were often carved with a relief on the front and, on the lid, a half-reclining figure representing the deceased at a banquet.

Conatraposto   A twisted pose in a figure, first used by the ancients and revived by Michelangelo; an earmark of the mannerist school.

Diptych   A painting in two sections.

Ex voto   A small plaque, statue, painting, or other memento left by a supplicant, signifying either his or her gratitude to a saint or special Madonna, or imploring the saint's help in some matter; particularly revered icons are often surrounded by them.

Fresco   The multistep art of creating a painting on fresh plaster (*fresco* means "fresh").

Graffiti   Incised decorative designs, usually repetitive, on an outer wall made by painting the surface in two thin layers (one light, the other dark), then scratching away the top layer to leave the designs in contrast.

Grotesques   Carved or painted faces, animals, and designs, often deliberately exaggerated or ugly; used to decorate surfaces and composite sculptures (such as fountains).

Illuminated   Describing a manuscript or book, usually a choir book or bible, that has been decorated with colorful designs, miniatures, figures, scenes, and fancy letters, often produced by anonymous monks.

Intarsia   Inlaid wood, marble, precious stones, or metal.

Majolica   Tin-glazed earthenware pottery usually elaborately painted; a process pioneered and mastered in Italy in the 14th to 17th century.

Pala   Altarpiece.

Pietra dura   The art of inlaying semiprecious stones to form patterns and pictures; often called Florentine mosaic and increasingly popular from the late 15th century on.

Pinacoteca   Painting gallery.

Polyptych   A panel painting having more than one section that's hinged so it can be folded up. Two-paneled ones are called **_diptychs_** (see above), three-paneled one **_triptychs_** (see below). Any more panels use the general term.

Porphyry   Any igneous rock with visible shards of crystals suspended in a matrix of fine particles.

Predella   Small panel or series of panels below the main part of an altarpiece, often used to tell a story of Christ's Passion or a saint's life comic-strip style.

Putti   Cherubs (sing. *putto*); chubby naked toddler boys sculpted or painted, often with wings.

Sarcofagus   A stone coffin or casket.

Schiacciato   Literally "flattened." A sculpture form pioneered by Donatello; figures are carved in extremely low relief so that from straight on they give the illusion of three-dimensionality and great depth, but from the side are oddly squashed.

Sufmato   A painting technique, popularized by Leonardo da Vinci, as important as perspective in achieving the illusion of great depth. The artist cloaks distant objects (usually landscape features like hills) in a filmy haziness; the farther away the object, the blurrier it appears, and the more realistic the distance seems.

Stoup   A holy-water basin.

Tondo   A round painting or sculpture.

Trecento   The 14th century (in Italian, literally 1300s), often used to describe that era of art dominated by the styles of Giotto and the International Gothic (see "Art & Architecture 101" in Appendix A).

Triptych   A painting in three sections.

Index

Speak Italian
like a <u>real</u> native!
(what they never taught you in school)

WILEY'S STREET LANGUAGE SERIES—OVER 200,000 SOLD!

0-471-38438-0
$15.95 US/ $24.95 CAN

0-471-38439-9
$15.95 US/ $24.95 CAN

Available at bookstores everywhere. Or to order now,
call 1-877-762-2974 or visit our Web site at wiley.com

HIT THE ROAD WITH FROMMER'S DRIVING TOURS!

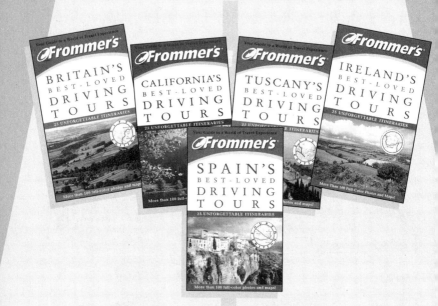

Frommer's Britain's Best-Loved Driving Tours
Frommer's California's Best-Loved Driving Tours
Frommer's Florida's Best-Loved Driving Tours
Frommer's France's Best-Loved Driving Tours
Frommer's Germany's Best-Loved Driving Tours
Frommer's Ireland's Best-Loved Driving Tours
Frommer's Italy's Best-Loved Driving Tours
Frommer's New England's Best-Loved Driving Tours
Frommer's Northern Italy's Best-Loved Driving Tours
Frommer's Scotland's Best-Loved Driving Tours
Frommer's Spain's Best-Loved Driving Tours
Frommer's Tuscany & Umbria's Best-Loved Driving Tours

Available at bookstores everywhere.

FROMMER'S® COMPLETE TRAVEL GUIDES

Alaska
Alaska Cruises & Ports of Call
Amsterdam
Argentina & Chile
Arizona
Atlanta
Australia
Austria
Bahamas
Barcelona, Madrid & Seville
Beijing
Belgium, Holland & Luxembourg
Bermuda
Boston
Brazil
British Columbia & the Canadian
  Rockies
Brussels & Bruges
Budapest & the Best of Hungary
California
Canada
Cancún, Cozumel & the Yucatán
Cape Cod, Nantucket & Martha's
  Vineyard
Caribbean
Caribbean Cruises & Ports of Call
Caribbean Ports of Call
Carolinas & Georgia
Chicago
China
Colorado
Costa Rica
Cuba
Denmark
Denver, Boulder & Colorado Springs
England
Europe
European Cruises & Ports of Call

Florida
France
Germany
Great Britain
Greece
Greek Islands
Hawaii
Hong Kong
Honolulu, Waikiki & Oahu
Ireland
Israel
Italy
Jamaica
Japan
Las Vegas
London
Los Angeles
Maryland & Delaware
Maui
Mexico
Montana & Wyoming
Montréal & Québec City
Munich & the Bavarian Alps
Nashville & Memphis
New England
New Mexico
New Orleans
New York City
New Zealand
Northern Italy
Norway
Nova Scotia, New Brunswick &
  Prince Edward Island
Oregon
Paris
Peru
Philadelphia & the Amish Country
Portugal

Prague & the Best of the Czech
  Republic
Provence & the Riviera
Puerto Rico
Rome
San Antonio & Austin
San Diego
San Francisco
Santa Fe, Taos & Albuquerque
Scandinavia
Scotland
Seattle & Portland
Shanghai
Sicily
Singapore & Malaysia
South Africa
South America
South Florida
South Pacific
Southeast Asia
Spain
Sweden
Switzerland
Texas
Thailand
Tokyo
Toronto
Tuscany & Umbria
USA
Utah
Vancouver & Victoria
Vermont, New Hampshire & Maine
Vienna & the Danube Valley
Virgin Islands
Virginia
Walt Disney World® & Orlando
Washington, D.C.
Washington State

FROMMER'S® DOLLAR-A-DAY GUIDES

Australia from $50 a Day
California from $70 a Day
England from $75 a Day
Europe from $70 a Day
Florida from $70 a Day
Hawaii from $80 a Day

Ireland from $60 a Day
Italy from $70 a Day
London from $85 a Day
New York from $90 a Day
Paris from $80 a Day

San Francisco from $70 a Day
Washington, D.C. from $80 a Day
Portable London from $85 a Day
Portable New York City from $90
  a Day

FROMMER'S® PORTABLE GUIDES

Acapulco, Ixtapa & Zihuatanejo
Amsterdam
Aruba
Australia's Great Barrier Reef
Bahamas
Berlin
Big Island of Hawaii
Boston
California Wine Country
Cancún
Cayman Islands
Charleston
Chicago
Disneyland®
Dublin
Florence

Frankfurt
Hong Kong
Houston
Las Vegas
Las Vegas for Non-Gamblers
London
Los Angeles
Los Cabos & Baja
Maine Coast
Maui
Miami
Nantucket & Martha's Vineyard
New Orleans
New York City
Paris
Phoenix & Scottsdale

Portland
Puerto Rico
Puerto Vallarta, Manzanillo &
  Guadalajara
Rio de Janeiro
San Diego
San Francisco
Savannah
Seattle
Sydney
Tampa & St. Petersburg
Vancouver
Venice
Virgin Islands
Washington, D.C.

FROMMER'S® NATIONAL PARK GUIDES

Banff & Jasper
Family Vacations in the National
  Parks

Grand Canyon
National Parks of the American West
Rocky Mountain

Yellowstone & Grand Teton
Yosemite & Sequoia/Kings Canyon
Zion & Bryce Canyon

Frommer's® Memorable Walks

Chicago
London

New York
Paris

San Francisco

Frommer's® With Kids Guides

Chicago
Las Vegas
New York City

Ottawa
San Francisco
Toronto

Vancouver
Washington, D.C.

Suzy Gershman's Born to Shop Guides

Born to Shop: France
Born to Shop: Hong Kong,
   Shanghai & Beijing

Born to Shop: Italy
Born to Shop: London

Born to Shop: New York
Born to Shop: Paris

Frommer's® Irreverent Guides

Amsterdam
Boston
Chicago
Las Vegas
London

Los Angeles
Manhattan
New Orleans
Paris
Rome

San Francisco
Seattle & Portland
Vancouver
Walt Disney World®
Washington, D.C.

Frommer's® Best-Loved Driving Tours

Britain
California
Florida
France

Germany
Ireland
Italy
New England

Northern Italy
Scotland
Spain
Tuscany & Umbria

Hanging Out™ Guides

Hanging Out in England
Hanging Out in Europe

Hanging Out in France
Hanging Out in Ireland

Hanging Out in Italy
Hanging Out in Spain

The Unofficial Guides®

Bed & Breakfasts and Country
   Inns in:
   California
   Great Lakes States
   Mid-Atlantic
   New England
   Northwest
   Rockies
   Southeast
   Southwest
Best RV & Tent Campgrounds in:
   California & the West
   Florida & the Southeast
   Great Lakes States
   Mid-Atlantic
   Northeast
   Northwest & Central Plains

Southwest & South Central
   Plains
   U.S.A.
Beyond Disney
Branson, Missouri
California with Kids
Central Italy
Chicago
Cruises
Disneyland®
Florida with Kids
Golf Vacations in the Eastern U.S.
Great Smoky & Blue Ridge Region
Inside Disney
Hawaii
Las Vegas
London
Maui

Mexio's Best Beach Resorts
Mid-Atlantic with Kids
Mini Las Vegas
Mini-Mickey
New England & New York with
   Kids
New Orleans
New York City
Paris
San Francisco
Skiing & Snowboarding in the West
Southeast with Kids
Walt Disney World®
Walt Disney World® for
   Grown-ups
Walt Disney World® with Kids
Washington, D.C.
World's Best Diving Vacations

Special-Interest Titles

Frommer's Adventure Guide to Australia &
   New Zealand
Frommer's Adventure Guide to Central America
Frommer's Adventure Guide to India & Pakistan
Frommer's Adventure Guide to South America
Frommer's Adventure Guide to Southeast Asia
Frommer's Adventure Guide to Southern Africa
Frommer's Britain's Best Bed & Breakfasts and
   Country Inns
Frommer's Caribbean Hideaways
Frommer's Exploring America by RV
Frommer's Fly Safe, Fly Smart

Frommer's France's Best Bed & Breakfasts and
   Country Inns
Frommer's Gay & Lesbian Europe
Frommer's Italy's Best Bed & Breakfasts and
   Country Inns
Frommer's Road Atlas Britain
Frommer's Road Atlas Europe
Frommer's Road Atlas France
The New York Times' Guide to Unforgettable
   Weekends
Places Rated Almanac
Retirement Places Rated
Rome Past & Present